Christoph Lymbersky (editor)

Financial Markets Principles

MANAGEMENT
LABORATORY
PRESS

Lymbersky Christoph (editor): **"Financial Markets Principles"**
1st International Edition, 2009

Published by the Management Laboratory Press, a business unit of the Management Laboratory, Christoph Lymbersky, Luetkensallee 41, 22041 Hamburg.

Publication date: January 2009, Hamburg, Germany

Registered with:
Copyclaim: #10000967
U.S. Copyright Clearance Center (CCC)
ISBN-Agentur für die Bundesrepublik Deutschland in der MVB Marketing- und Verlagsservice des Buchhandels GmbH

Bibliografische Information der Deutschen Nationalbibliothek
Die Deutsche Nationalbibliothek verzeichnet diese Publikation in der Deutschen Nationalbibliografie; detaillierte bibliografische Daten sind im Internet über http://dnb.d-nb.de abrufbar.

Front Cover Picture: © Claudia Vogel, www.naecy.de
Interior Pictures: : © Claudia Vogel, www.naecy.de

Text Layout: : © Management Laboratory Press
Graphs: Cortal Consors , if not otherwise specified.

When ordering this title, use ISBN: 978-3941-579-30-9

About the Editor

Christoph Lymbersky has lived, worked and done research in Germany, France, Australia and the United States. He holds a Master of Accounting as well as a MBA from Bond University in Australia and is currently writing his PhD in Turnaround Mangement and distressed investing at the ESC-Lille in France.

He has worked for international companies such as IBM and Wal-Mart, has founded and co-founded different companies like COMODEX Internet, the IT – Management Group and B2B Network. Christoph Lymbersky has written and published a variety of books in International Mangement and Finance. Currently, Mr. Lymbersky serves as the director of the Management Laboratory and is a member of the Council of Economic Advisors of Germany (Wirtschaftsrat) as well as the Strategic Management Society (SMS).

Introduction

We are living in ... I must say ... crazy times. The Stock Market Crash of 2007-2008, but also others, have shown even people that are not interested in finance that the financial market is very volatile, for some investors this has been the first crash of this kind, for others it was nothing new, or even predictable. But after such a crash, what do we learn from it? Well, one thing is sure! We don't know enough about the financial market! How does it really work? Is it predictable? Was Warren Buffet just lucky? Do Graham and Dodds teachings in Security Analysis really work? Is Swing- or Daytrading maybe a better way to earn money? I cannot answer these questions for you, but I can introduce the concepts to you, explain how the financial market works, the risks and benefits and the principals of commodities, bonds, futures, funds, stocks, exchange rates, exchanges, and everything else that is considered to be fundamental in the field of financial markets.

This book is written with an academic background. Some techniques or especially investment strategies, don't have the necessary academic evaluation to be called a verified strategy but they have been around for sometimes more then 100 years and deserve to be mentioned.

However, one thing is for sure ... the next crisis will come, the next bubble will burst and the next undervalued asset is going to bring an immense fortune to some people. The question is if a well educated investor is a better investor that achieves above average returns. I have not found any statistics that I could use to underline my point but I am just taking the liberty that an author has and say, Yes! Education does matter. We can learn out of the past and from the experience of others. In my eyes a well educated investor, analyst or consultant can be better prepared for the up and downs in the financial market.

Nowadays, everybody can call themselves a Financial Analyst, Financial Specialist or Financial Advisor. The market is full of self-proclaimed professionals. However, only a few of them really know the principals of financial markets, how they work, how they are related to each other and how to analyze them. In this textbook I am trying to explain what a financial market is, how it works and how trading can be done. This book is comprehensive enough to serve as a textbook for students that are studying finance and as a reference for professionals who are looking for more background information or that are interested in further educating themselves about different markets, trading styles, technical analysis or investment strategies.

This book is also the textbook for the Certified Financial Markets Professional (CFMP) Certification which is supposed to bring some light into the dark jungle of unqualified investment advisors and analysts.

If you have any comments about the book, questions or additions, please don't hesitate to write me.

Christoph Lymbersky

feedback@management-laboratory.com

Contents

About the Editor ... 5

Introduction ... 7

Contents ... 11

Table of Figures ... 31

Structure of the Book ... 35

General Knowledge ... 37

Securities ... 39

Debt and equity ... 39

The securities market ... 42

Types of Stock ... 45

Preferred Stock ... 45

Common Types of Preferred Stock ... 50

Treasury Stock ... 50

Market sentiment ... 53

Dividends ... 55

Joint Stock Company Dividends ... 55

Disadvantages of Dividents ... 58

Stock Valuation ... 62

Fundamental Criteria (Fair Value) ... 62

Market criteria (potential price) ... 63

Stock Market Prediction ... 65

Prediction Methods ... 65

Validity ... 66

What is a Stock Broker? ... 68

Requirements ... 68

Services Provided ... 68

History ... 69

Explanation of a City Trader's Job ... 71

What is an Investment Bank? ... 73

Organizational Structure of an Investment Bank ... 74

Size of the Industry ... 77

Possible Conflicts of Interest ... 78

Electronic Trading ... 80

The Background of Etrading ... 80

Impact of Electronic Trading ... 81

Technology and Systems ... 82

Value Investing ... 84

History of Value Investing ... 84

Value Investing Performance ... 85

Well known Value Investors ... 86

The Different Types of Orders on the Stock Market ... 88

Market Order ... 88

Limit Order ... 88

Time in Force ... 89

Conditional Orders ... 90

Stop Orders ... 90

Market-if-touched Order ... 91

One Cancels Other Orders ... 91

Tick Sensitive Orders ... 92

Discretionary Order ... 92

Quantity and Display Instructions ... 92

Electronic Markets ... 92

Margins Explained ... 94

Margin Buying ... 94

Margin Requirements ... 95

Minimum Margin Requirement ... 96

Initial and Maintenance Margin Requirements ... 97

Margin Call ... 97

Price of Stock for Margin Calls ... 97

Reduced Margins ... 98

Margin-Equity Ratio ... 98

Return on Margin 98

Random Walk Hypothesis 100

Kondratiev Wave 103

Characteristics of the Cycle 103

Explanation of the Cycleriod. 104

Initial Public Offering 107

Reasons for listing a Company on the Stock Exchange 107

The Procedure of an IPO 108

Business Cycle 109

The Dutch Auction 110

Pricing 110

Quiet Period 111

Secondary Market Offering 112

Behavioral Finance 113

History 113

Methodology 115

Key observations 115

Behavioral finance topics 116

Behavioral Finance Models 117

Criticisms of Behavioral Finance 117

Quantitative Behavioral Finance 118

Financial Basics 119

Investment Theory 120

Efficient-Market Hypothesis 121

Historical Background 121

Theoretical Background 122

Arguments concerning the Validity of the Hypothesis 124

Social Acceptance 127

An alternative Theory: Behavioral Finance 128

Adaptive Market Hypothesis 130

Implications 130

The Cost of Capital **132**

Summary 132

Cost of debt 132

Cost of equity 133

Comments 133

Alpha **136**

Origin of the Concept 137

Relation to Beta 138

Beta **139**

Definition 139

Beta Volatility and Correlation 140

Choice of Benchmark 141

Investing 142

Multiple Beta Model 142

Estimation of Beta 143

Extreme and Interesting Cases 143

Weighted Average Cost of Capital **145**

The formula for a simple case 145

How it works 147

Sources of Information 147

Effect on Valuation 148

Arbitrage Pricing Theory **150**

The APT model 150

Arbitrage and the APT 151

Relationship with the Capital Asset Pricing Model 153

Using the APT 153

The Capital Asset Pricing Model **155**

The Formula 155

Asset pricing 157

Asset-Specific Required Return 157

Risk and Diversification 158

The Efficient Frontier 158

The market portfolio 159

Assumptions of CAPM 159
Shortcomings of CAPM 160

Modern Portfolio Theory **162**

Risk and Return 162
Mathematically 164
The Risk-Free Asset 167
Portfolio Leverage 168
The Market Portfolio 169
Capital Market Line 169
Asset Pricing 169
Applications to Project Portfolios and other "Non-Financial" Assets 172
Applications of Modern Portfolio Theory in other Disciplines 173

Markets 175

Financial Markets **176**

Definition 176
Types of Financial Markets 177
Raising Capital 177

The Capital Market **180**

Primary Market 180
Secondary market 181

The Stock Market **183**

Trading on the Stock Market 183
Market Participants 185
The History of Stock Markets 185
Importance of the Stock Market 186
Stock Market Cycles 190

The Bond Market **194**

Market Structure 194
Types of Bond Markets 194
Bond Market Participants 195
Bond Market Volatility 195

Bond Investments ... 196

Bond Indices ... 196

The Derivatives Market ... **197**

Futures Markets ... 197

Over-the-Counter Markets ... 197

Netting ... 198

The Money Market ... **200**

Common money market instruments ... 201

The Commodities Market ... **202**

History ... 202

The Size of the Commodities Market ... 203

Investment Returns ... 204

Spot Trading ... 204

Forward contracts ... 204

Regulation of Commodity Markets ... 206

Non-conventional Commodities ... 208

The Futures Market ... **211**

History of Futures Exchanges ... 211

Nature of Futures Contracts ... 213

Standardization ... 213

Derivatives Clearing ... 214

Central Counterparty ... 214

Margin and Mark-to-Market ... 214

Regulators ... 215

The Foreign Exchange Market ... **217**

Market Size and Liquidity ... 217

Market Participants ... 218

Trading Characteristics ... 221

Factors affecting Currency Trading ... 223

Algorithmic Trading in Forex ... 225

Financial Instruments ... 226

Speculation ... 227

Options 231

What about Options? **232**

Contract specifications *233*

Types of Options *233*

Valuation Models *234*

Black Scholes Model *235*

Stochastic Volatility Models *235*

Model Implementation *236*

Risks *237*

Trading *239*

Basic Trades of Traded Stock Options (American Style) *239*

Option Strategies *243*

Volatility Index VIX **246**

Bond Options Explained **250**

Types *250*

Embedded option *251*

Credit Default Option **252**

Credit Default Swap **253**

Description *253*

How Credit Default Swaps are used *254*

Terms of a Typical CDS Contract *259*

Settlement *260*

Criticisms *261*

Systemic Risk *262*

LCDS *263*

Call Options **265**

Example of a call option on a stock *265*

Put Options **268**

Example of a put option on a stock *268*

Foreign Exchange Options **270**

Swaption **274**

The first known Swaption *274*

The Swaption Market 275

Swaption Styles 277

Valuation of Swaptions 277

Binary Options **279**

LEAPS **281**

Bonds 283

An Overview over Bonds **284**

Issuing Bonds 284

Features of Bonds 284

Investing in Bonds 287

The Bond Market **290**

Market structure 290

Types of bond markets 290

Bond market participants 291

Bond market volatility 291

The Coupon of a Bond 292

Bond investments 293

Bond indices 293

Corporate Bond **294**

Types 294

Risk Analysis 295

Corporate Bond Indices 295

Government Bond **296**

Risk 296

Municipal Bonds **297**

Purpose of Municipal Bonds 297

Characteristics of Municipal Bonds 298

Risk 299

Disclosures to Investors 300

Comparison to Corporate Bonds 300

High-Yield Debt **302**

Flows and Levels 302

Risk 302

Usage 304

High-Yield Bond Indices 305

Bond Valuation **306**

General Relationship 306

Bond Pricing 308

Futures Contracts 311

What is a Futures Contract? **312**

Futures vs. Forwards **313**

Standardization 315

Margin 315

Settlement 317

Pricing 318

Who trades Futures? 320

Options on Futures 320

Futures Contract Regulations 321

Funds 323

Exchange-Traded Funds **324**

Structure 324

History 326

Investment Uses 327

Types of ETFs 328

Currency ETFs 329

ETFs compared to Mutual Funds 330

Criticism 332

Index Funds **334**

Origins of the Index Fund 334

Economic Theory 335

Indexing Methods 336

Advantages of Index Funds 337

Disadvantages of Index Funds 338

Diversification 339

Stock Market Index **341**

Types of Indices 341

Weighting 342

Mutual Fund **346**

History 346

Usage 347

Net Asset Value 348

Growth vs. Value 352

Index Funds versus Active Management 353

Bond Funds 353

Money Market Funds 354

Funds of Funds 354

Hedge Funds 355

Mutual Funds vs. Other Investments 355

Share Classes 355

Hedge Fund **358**

History 358

Industry Size 359

Hedge Fund Risk 359

Legal Structure 361

Hedge Fund Management Worldwide 363

Regulatory Issues 364

Hedge Fund Indices 369

Debates and Controversies 371

Inverse Exchange-Traded Fund **377**

Strategies for Buy-and-Hold Investors 377

Fees and other Issues 378

Examples 378

Collective Investment Scheme **381**

Generic Information - Advantages 382

Generic Information - Disadvantages 383

Style 384

Types of Risk *386*

Charging Structures and Fees *386*

Internationally Recognised Collective Investments *388*

Closed-End Fund **389**

Availability *389*

Distinguishing Features *390*

Initial Offering *391*

Exchange Traded *391*

Discounts and Premiums *392*

Comparison with Open-Ended Funds *393*

Examples *394*

Traders & Trading Styles 395

What is a Trader? **396**

Stock Trader **397**

Stock Trader versus Stock Investor *397*

Methodology *397*

Expenses, Costs and Risk *398*

Stock Picking *398*

Accumulation / Distribution Method *399*

Over-the-Counter Trading **400**

OTC-Traded Stocks *400*

OTC Contracts *401*

Short Selling **402**

The Concept of Short Selling *403*

Example of Short Selling *404*

History of Short Selling *405*

Mechanism of Short Selling *406*

Fees *408*

Dividend & Short Selling *409*

Markets for Short Selling *409*

Risk *410*

Strategies *412*

Criticism ... 413
The Regulatory Response ... 414

Hedge ... **416**
Origins of Hedging ... 417
Example Hedge ... 417
Types of Hedging ... 419
Categories of Hedgeable Risk ... 419
Hedging Equity and Equity Futures ... 421

Arbitrage ... **423**
Conditions for Arbitrage ... 423
Examples ... 424
Price Convergence ... 426
Risks ... 427
Types of Arbitrage ... 428

Swing Trading ... **433**
The risks involved ... 434

Noise Trader ... **435**

Day Trader ... **436**
Types of Day Traders ... 436

Day Trading ... **438**
Characteristics ... 438
History of Day Trading ... 440
Techniques ... 443
Cost ... 445
Regulations and Restrictions ... 447

Rogue Trader ... **448**

Trading Strategy ... **450**
Development ... 450
Forward Testing ... 450
Executing Strategies ... 451

Trading System ... **452**

Algorithmic Trading **454**

History 454

Communication Standards 456

Strategies 456

Effects 458

Trend Following **459**

Definition 459

Considerations 460

Example 460

Contrarian Investing **462**

Similarity to Value Investing 462

Examples of Contrarian Investing 463

Relationship to Behavioral Finance 464

Scalping (Trading) **465**

Market Manipulation 465

Arbitrage & Scalping 465

Factors affecting Scalping 468

Technical Analysis 471

What is a Technical Analysis? **472**

General Description 472

History 474

Principles 474

Prices Move in Trends 475

History tends to repeat itself 476

Industry 477

Systematic Trading 478

Combination with other Market Forecast Methods 479

Applicability 481

Random Walk Hypothesis 483

Chart Technique **484**

Chart Pattern 484

Candlestick Chart 484

Kagi Chart *488*

Point and Figure Chart *490*

Market Trend **492**

Primary Market Trends *492*

Bull Market *492*

Bear Market *493*

Secondary Market Trends *493*

Secular Market Trends *494*

Stock Market Bottom **497**

Identifying a Market Bottom *498*

Risks of Attempting to invest at a Market Bottom *502*

2008 Market Drop *502*

Concepts **507**

Black–Scholes *507*

Black Model *508*

Dead Cat Bounce *509*

Coppock Curve *510*

Elliott Wave Principle *511*

Momentum *520*

SMA *521*

Hikkake Pattern *522*

Overlays **524**

Support and Resistance *524*

Support *524*

Resistance *524*

Trend Lines *527*

Double Top *529*

Price Channels *530*

Moving Average *530*

Simple Moving Average *531*

Cumulative Moving Average *533*

Weighted Moving Average *534*

Exponential Moving Average *536*

Exponential Smoothing 538

Average True Range 539

Bollinger Bands 541

Head and Shoulders 543

Pivot Point Calculations 545

Price Based Indicators 547

Relative Strength Index 547

MACD 550

Average Directional Index 553

Commodity Channel Index 555

Parabolic SAR 557

Rahul Mohindar Oscillator 559

Stochastic Oscillator 559

Trix 562

Accumulation/Distribution Index 564

Chaikin Oscillator 565

Money Flow 565

Price and Volume Trend 567

On-balance Volume 568

Crashes and troubled Times 571

Financial Crisis 572

Types of Financial Crises 572

Causes and Consequences of a Financial Crises 574

Theories of Financial Crises 578

History 579

Virtuous Circle and Vicious Circle 581

Example in Macroeconomics 581

Recession 584

Attributes of Recessions 584

Predictors of a Recession 584

Responding to a Recession 585

Central Bank Response 585

The Stock Market and Recessions ... 586

Recession and Politics ... 587

History of Recessions ... 588

Possible 2008 Recession in some Countries ... 588

Stock Market Crashes ... **591**

Mathematical Theory of Stock Market crashes ... 591

Wall Street Crash of 1929 ... **593**

Timeline ... 595

Economic Fundamentals ... 596

Impact and Academic Debate ... 597

Black Monday (1987) ... **600**

Timeline ... 602

.Causes ... 603

October 27, 1997 Mini-Crash ... **605**

By the Numbers ... 605

October 28 ... 606

1997 Asian Financial Crisis ... **608**

History ... 609

The Role of the IMF ... 612

Consequences ... 620

1998 Russian Financial Crisis ... **623**

Course of events ... 623

The Crisis and its Effects ... 625

Dot-com Bubble ... **630**

The growth of the Bubble ... 630

Soaring Stocks ... 631

Free Spending ... 631

Thinning the Herd ... 632

Aftermath ... 634

Stock Market Downturn of 2002 ... **636**

Context ... 636

Seeking a Bottom ... *637*

Index Levels ... *637*

Global Financial Crisis of 2008 ... 641

Key Risk Indicators in September 2008 ... *657*

Global Responses ... *658*

2008 Russian Financial Crisis ... 663

Background ... *663*

Timeline ... *664*

Stock Exchanges ... 669

About Stock Exchanges ... 670

History of Stock Exchanges ... *670*

The Role of Stock Exchanges ... *670*

Major Stock Exchanges ... *672*

Listing Requirements ... *674*

Ownership ... *675*

Other Types of Exchanges ... *675*

List of Stock Exchanges ... 678

American Stock Exchange ... 680

History ... *680*

The Market ... *680*

Hours ... *681*

New York Stock Exchange ... 682

Business ... *682*

History ... *684*

Events ... *686*

Australian Securities Exchange ... 688

Market Details ... *688*

History ... *689*

Timeline of significant events ... *689*

Frankfurt Stock Exchange ... 695

History ... *696*

London Stock Exchange ... **698**

History ... 698

Structure ... 701

Tokyo Stock Exchange ... **702**

Structure ... 702

History ... 704

Hours ... 705

Alliances ... 705

Toronto Stock Exchange ... **706**

History ... 706

Trading Hours ... 708

Hong Kong Stock Exchange ... **709**

History ... 709

Differences from US Stock Exchanges ... 710

Trading Hours ... 711

Regulatory Role ... 711

Euronext ... **712**

Background ... 712

Structure and Indices ... 712

Euronext.liffe ... 713

Alternext ... 714

Merger with NYSE ... 714

The World's Major Indeces ... 717

NASDAQ ... **718**

History ... 718

Business ... 720

Dow Jones Industrial Average ... **721**

Calculation ... 721

Criticism ... 722

S&P 500 ... **723**

History ... 724

Selection ... *725*

Weighting ... *726*

Index Maintenance ... *726*

Investing ... *727*

DAX ... **729**

Nikkei 225 ... **730**

Weighting and Modifications ... *730*

Changes to the Components ... *730*

All Ordinaries ... **732**

Hang Seng Index ... **733**

Statistics ... *733*

Hang Seng Industry Classification System ... *734*

General Classification Guidelines: ... *734*

Selection Criteria for the HSI Constituent Stocks ... *734*

Calculation Formula for HSI ... *735*

Appendix ... 739

Capital Gains Tax ... **740**

Tax systems ... *740*

References ... 753

Index ... 761

Financial Markets Certifications ... 811

Certified Financial Markets Professional – Foundation Exam ... **812**

Certified Financial Markets Professional – Practitioner Exam ... **814**

Room for Notes: ... 816

Table of Figures

Picture 1: A rough schematic drawing showing the "World Economy" over time according to the Kondratiev theory 105

Picture 2: Alpha 137

Picture 3: Capital Market Line 162

Picture 4: The Efficient Frontier 167

Picture 5: The Security Market Line 171

Picture 6: Long Call 240

Picture 7: Long Put 241

Picture 8: Short Call 242

Picture 9: Short Put 243

Picture 10: Payoffs from buying a butterfly spread 244

Picture 11:Payoffs from selling a straddle 244

Picture 12: Payoffs from a covered call 245

Picture 13:VIX Index from inception to Oct. 2008 246

Picture 14:Credit default swaps vs. total nominals plus debt 258

Picture 15:Credit default swaps by quality size 258

Picture 16: Uncut coupons on 1822 Mecca Temple construction bond 293

Picture 17: S&P 500, DJIA, NASDAQ 1975 - 2007 341

Picture 18:The values and performance of collective funds are listed in newspapers 381

Picture 19: Diagram of short selling 403

Picture 20: Stock chart showing levels of support (4,5,6, 7, and 8) and resistance (1, 2, and 3); levels of resistance tend to become levels of support and vice versa. 475

Picture 21: AOL stock price 10/2001 to 08/2002 476

Picture 24: Candelsticks Chart 485

Picture 25: Candelsticks 486

Picture 26: Kagi Chart 489

Picture 27: DAX Point and Figure Chart 490

Picture 22: Infineon Stock with MACD 501

Picture 23: DJIA July 2008 - December 2008 506

Picture 28: Coppock Curve 510

Picture 29: From R.N. Elliott's essay, "The Basis of the Wave Principle," October 1940 512

Picture 30:From sakuragi_indofx, "Trading never been so easy eh," December 2007 517

Picture 31: DAX SMA 522

Picture 32: Price Channels 530

Picture 33: Simple Moving Average (grey = SMA; black = price line) 532

Picture 34: Weighted Moving Average with a Period of 20 535

Picture 35: Decreasing weights of the Weighted Moving Average 535

Picture 36: Exponential Moving Average 536

Picture 37: Average True Range 540

Picture 38: Head and Schoulders 544

Picture 39: Head and Schoulders Calculation 545

Picture 40: RSI Wilder 549

Picture 41:RSI Cutler 550

Picture 42: MACD 551

Picture 43: ADX 554

Picture 44: CCI 556

Picture 45: PSAR 557

Picture 46: Stochastic Oscillator Fast & Slow; the Slow O. is smoother with less errors 560

Picture 47: TRIX 563

Picture 48: Triple exponential moving average weightings, N=10 (percentage versus days ago) 564

Picture 49:Vicious Circle 582

Picture 50: Virtuous Circle 583

Picture 52: Crowd gathering on Wall Street after the 1929 crash 594

Picture 53: DJIA (19 July 1987 through 19 January 1988) 601

Picture 54: FTSE 100 Index (19 July 1987 through 19 January 1988) 601

Picture 55: Timeline compiled by the Federal Reserve 602

Picture 51: Countries most affected by the Asian Crisis 609

Picture 56: The technology-heavy NASDAQ Composite index peaked at 5,048 in March 2000, reflecting the high point of the dot-com bubble 634

Picture 57: Dow Jones Industrial Average in 2002 638

Picture 58: Nasdaq 638

Picture 59: The TED spread – an indicator of credit risk – increased dramatically during September 2008 658

Picture 60: Timeline of the Russian Financial Crisis 664

Picture 61: The floor of the New York Stock Exchange in 1908 684

Picture 62: U.S. Secretary of Commerce Donald L. Evans rings the opening bell at the NYSE on April 23, 2003. Former chairman Richard Grasso is also in this picture 685

Picture 64: FSE Main Entrance 695

Picture 65:The trading floor in Frankfurt 696

Picture 66: LSE's current premises are situated in Paternoster Square close to St Paul's Cathedral in the City of London 698

Picture 67: Tokyo Stock Exchange 702

Picture 68: The main trading room of the Tokyo Stock Exchange, where nowadays the trading is done through computers 703

Picture 69: The Toronto Stock Exchange 706

Picture 70: Logo of the Hong Kong Exchange 709

Picture 71: Brussels Bourse/Beurs 713

Picture 63: Linear graph of the S&P 500 from 1950 to March 2007 724

Picture 72: DAX 30 chart in the Frankfurt Stock Exchange 729

Structure of the Book

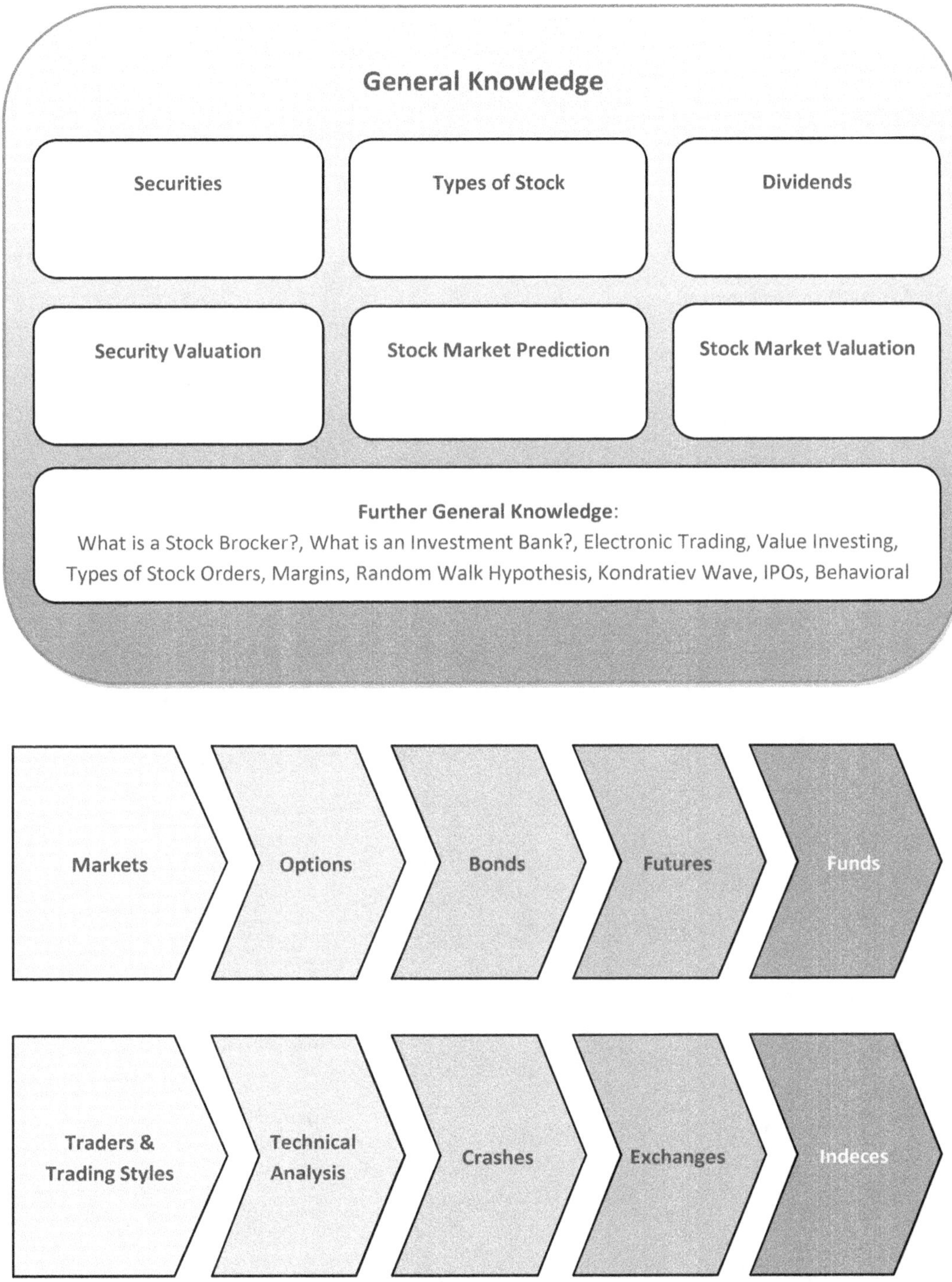

General Knowledge

Securities

A security is a fungible, negotiable instrument representing financial value. Securities are broadly categorized into debt securities (such as banknotes, bonds and debentures), and equity securities, e.g. common stocks. The company or other entity issuing the security is called the issuer. What specifically qualifies as a security is dependent on the regulatory structure in a country. For example private investment pools may have some features of securities, but they may not be registered or regulated as such if they meet various restrictions.

Securities may be represented by a certificate or more typically by an electronic book entry. Certificates may be bearer which means that they entitle the holder to rights under the security merely by holding the security. Certificates can also be registered, meaning they entitle the holder to rights only if he or she appears on a security register. The security register is maintained by the issuer or an intermediary. They include shares of corporate stock or mutual funds, bonds issued by corporations or governmental agencies, stock options or other options, limited partnership units, and various other formal investment instruments that are negotiable and fungible.

Debt and equity

Securities are traditionally divided into debt securities and equities.

Debt

Debt securities may be called debentures, bonds, deposits, notes or commercial paper depending on their maturity and certain other characteristics. The holder of a debt security is typically entitled to the payment of principal and interest, together with other contractual rights under the terms of the issue, such as the right to receive certain information. Debt securities are generally issued for a fixed term and redeemable by the issuer at the end of that term. Debt securities may be protected by collateral or may be unsecured and if they are unsecured, may be contractually "senior" to other unsecured debt meaning their holders would have a priority in a bankruptcy of the issuer. Debt that is not senior is "subordinated".

Corporate bonds represent the debt of commercial or industrial entities. Debentures have a long maturity, typically at least ten years, whereas notes have a shorter maturity .Commercial paper is a simple form of debt security that essentially represents a post-dated check with a maturity of not more than 270 days.

Money market instruments are short term debt instruments that may have characteristics of deposit accounts, such as certificates of deposit, and certain bills of exchange. They are highly liquid and are sometimes referred to as "near cash". Commercial paper is also often highly liquid.

Euro debt securities are securities issued internationally outside their domestic market in a denomination different from that of the issuer's domicile. They include eurobonds and euronotes. Eurobonds are characteristically underwritten, and not secured, and interest is paid gross. A euronote may take the form of euro-commercial paper (ECP) or euro-certificates of deposit.

Government bonds are medium or long term debt securities issued by sovereign governments or their agencies. Typically they carry a lower rate of interest than corporate bonds, and serve as a source of finance for governments. U.S. federal government bonds are called treasuries. Because of their liquidity and perceived low risk, treasuries are used to manage the money supply in the open market operations of non-US central banks.

Sub-sovereign government bonds, known in the U.S. as municipal bonds, represent the debt of state, provincial, territorial, municipal or other governmental units other than sovereign governments.

Supranational bonds represent the debt of international organizations such as the World Bank, the International Monetary Fund, regional multilateral development banks and others.

Equity

An equity security is a share in the capital stock of a company (typically common stock, although preferred equity is also a form of capital stock). The holder of an equity is a shareholder, owning a share or fractional part of the issuer. Unlike debt securities which typically require regular payments (interest) to the holder, equity securities are not entitled to any payment. In bankruptcy, they share only in the residual interest of the issuer after all obligations have been paid out to creditors. However, equity generally entitles the holder to a pro rata portion of control of the company, meaning that a holder of a majority of the equity is usually entitled to control the issuer. Provided that he owns a certain amount of the total shares issued. Equity also enjoys the right to profits and capital gain, whereas holders of debt securities receive only interest and repayment of principal regardless of how well the issuer performs financially. Furthermore, debt securities do not have voting rights outside of bankruptcy. In other words, equity holders are entitled to the "upside" of the business and to control the business.

Hybrid

Hybrid securities combine some of the characteristics of both debt and equity securities.

Preference shares form an intermediate class of security between equities and debt. If the issuer is liquidated, they carry the right to receive interest and/or a return of capital in priority to ordinary shareholders. However, from a legal perspective, they are capital stock and therefore may entitle holders to some degree of control depending on whether they contain voting rights. We will have a closer look at this type of shares later on.

Convertibles are bonds or preferred stock which can be converted, at the election of the holder of the convertibles, into the common stock of the issuing company. The convertibility however, may be forced if the convertible is a callable bond and if the issuer calls the bond. The bondholder has about 1 month to convert it. If he doesn't the company will call the bond by giving the holder the call price, which may be less than the value of the converted stock. This is referred to as a forced conversion.

Equity warrants are options issued by the company that allow the holder of the warrant to purchase a specific number of shares at a specified price within a specified time. They are often issued together with bonds or existing equities, and are, sometimes, detachable from them and separately tradable. When the holder of the warrant exercises it, he pays the money directly to the company, and the company issues new shares to the holder.

Warrants, like other convertible securities, increases the number of shares outstanding, and are always accounted for in financial reports as fully diluted earnings per share, which assumes that all warrants and convertibles will be exercised.

The securities market

Primary and secondary market

The public securities markets can be divided into primary and secondary markets. The distinguishing difference between the two markets is that in the primary market, the money for the securities is received by the issuer of those securities from investors, whereas in the secondary market, the money goes from one investor to the other. When a company issues public stock for the first time, this is called an Initial Public Offering (IPO). A company can later issue more new shares, or issue shares that have been previously registered in a shelf registration. These 'later new' issues are also sold in the primary market, but they are not considered to be an IPO. Issuers usually retain investment banks to assist them in administering the IPO, getting SEC (or other regulatory body) approval, and selling the new issue. When the investment bank buys the entire new issue from the issuer at a discount to resell it at a markup, it is called an underwriting, or firm commitment. However, if the investment bank considers the risk too great for an underwriting, it may only assent to a best effort agreement, where the investment bank will simply do its best to sell the new issue.

In order for the primary market to thrive, there must be a secondary market, or aftermarket, where holders of securities can sell them to other investors for cash, hopefully at a profit. Otherwise, few people would purchase primary issues, and, thus, companies and governments would be unable to raise money for their operations. Organized exchanges constitute the main secondary markets. Many smaller issues and most debt securities trade in the decentralized, dealer-based over-the-counter markets.

In Europe, the principal trade organization for securities dealers is the International Capital Market Association. In the U.S., the principal organization for securities dealers is the Securities Industry and Financial Markets Association, which is the result of the merger of the Securities Industry Association and the Bond Market Association. The Financial Information Services Division of the Software and Information Industry Association (FISD/SIIA) represents a roundtable of market data industry firms, referring to them as Consumers, Exchanges, and Vendors.

Public offer and private placement

In the primary markets, securities may be offered to the public in a public offer. Alternatively, they may be offered privately to a limited number of qualified persons in a private placement. Often a combination of the two is used. The distinction between the two is important to securities regulation and company law. Privately placed securities are often not publicly tradable and may only be bought and sold by sophisticated qualified investors. As a result, the secondary market is not as liquid.

Another category, sovereign debt, is generally sold by auction to a specialized class of dealers.

Listing and OTC dealing

Securities are often listed in a stock exchange, an organized and officially recognized market on which securities can be bought and sold. Issuers may seek listings for their securities in order to attract investors, by ensuring that there is a liquid and regulated market in which investors will be able to buy and sell securities.

Growth in informal electronic trading systems has challenged the traditional business of stock exchanges. Large volumes of securities are also bought and sold "over the counter" (OTC). OTC dealing involves buyers and sellers dealing with each other by telephone or electronically on the basis of prices that are displayed electronically, usually by commercial information vendors such as Reuters and Bloomberg.

There are also eurosecurities, which are securities that are issued outside their domestic market into more than one jurisdiction. They are generally listed on the Luxembourg Stock Exchange or admitted to listing in London. The reasons for listing eurobonds include regulatory and tax considerations, as well as the investment restrictions.

Market

London is the centre of the eurosecurities markets. There was a huge rise in the eurosecurities market in London in the early 1980s. Settlement of trades in eurosecurities is currently effected through two European computerised systems called Euroclear (in Belgium) and Clearstream (formerly Cedelbank) in Luxembourg.

The main market for Eurobonds is the EuroMTS, owned by Borsa Italiana and Euronext.

Types of Stock

Preferred Stock

Preferred stock, also called preferred shares or preference shares, is typically a higher ranking stock than voting shares, and its terms are negotiated between the corporation and the investor.

Preferred stock usually carry no voting rights,but may carry superior priority over common stock in the payment of dividends and upon liquidation. Preferred stock may carry a dividend that is paid out prior to any dividends to common stock holders. This type of stock may have a convertibility feature into common stock. Their holders will be paid out in assets before common stockholders and after debt holders if the firm becomes bankrupt. The exact terms of preferred stock are stated in a "Certificate of Designation".

Rights

Unlike common stock, preferred stock usually has several rights attached to it:

- The core right is that of preference in the payment of dividends and upon liquidation of the company. Before a dividend can be declared on the common shares, any dividend obligation to the preferred shares must be satisfied.
- The dividend rights are often cumulative, such that if the dividend is not paid it accumulates from year to year.
- Preferred stock may or may not have a fixed liquidation value, or par value, associated with it. This represents the amount of capital that was contributed to the corporation when the shares were first issued.
- Preferred stock has a claim on liquidation proceeds of a stock corporation, equivalent to its par or liquidation value unless otherwise negotiated. This claim is senior to that of common stock, which has only a residual claim.
- Almost all preferred shares have a negotiated fixed dividend amount. The dividend is usually specified as a percentage of the par value or as a fixed amount. For example Pacific Gas & Electric 6% Series A preferred. Sometimes, dividends on preferred shares may be negotiated

as floating i.e. may change according to a benchmark interest rate index such as LIBOR.

- Some preferred shares have special voting rights to approve certain extraordinary events (such as the issuance of new shares or the approval of the acquisition of the company) or to elect directors, but most preferred shares provide no voting rights associated with them. Some preferred shares only gain voting rights when the preferred dividends are in arrears for a substantial time.
- Usually preferred shares contain protective provisions which prevent the issuance of new preferred shares with a senior claim. Individual series of preferred shares may have a senior, pari-passu or junior relationship with other series issued by the same corporation.
- Occasionally companies use preferred shares as means of preventing hostile takeovers, creating preferred shares with a poison pill or forced exchange/conversion features that exercise upon a change in control.

The above list, although including several customary rights, is far from comprehensive. Preferred shares, like other legal arrangements. They may specify nearly any right conceivable. Preferred shares in the U.S. normally carry a call provision, enabling the issuing corporation to repurchase the share at its (usually limited) discretion.

Some corporations contain provisions in their charters authorizing the issuance of preferred stock whose terms and conditions may be determined by the board of directors when issued. These "blank check" preferred shares are often used as takeover defense. These shares may be assigned a very high liquidation value that must be redeemed in the event of a change of control or may have enormous super voting powers.

Users

Preferred shares are more common in private or pre-public companies, where it is more useful to distinguish between the control of and the economic interest in the company. Government regulations and the rules of stock exchanges may discourage or encourage the issuance of publicly traded preferred shares. In many countries banks are encouraged to issue preferred stock as a source of Tier 1 capital. On the other hand, the Tel Aviv Stock Exchange prohibits listed companies from having more than one class of capital stock.

A single company may issue several classes of preferred stock. For example, a company may undergo several rounds of financing, with each round receiving separate rights and having a separate class of preferred stock; such a company might have "Series A Preferred", "Series B Preferred", "Series C Preferred" and common stock.

In the United States there are two types of preferred stocks: Straight preferred stocks and convertible preferred stocks. Straight preferred stocks are issued in perpetuity (although some are subject to call by the issuer under certain conditions) and pay the stipulated rate of interest to the holder. Convertible preferred stocks - in addition to the foregoing features of a straight preferred stocks - contain a provision by which the holder may convert the preferred stock into the common stock of the company (or, sometimes, into the common stock of an affiliated company) under certain conditions. Among these conditions may be the specification of a future date when conversion may begin, a certain number of common shares per preferred share, or a certain price per share for the common stock.

There are income tax advantages generally available to corporations that invest in preferred stocks in the United States that are not available to individuals.

Some argue that a straight preferred stock, being a hybrid between a bond and a stock, bears the disadvantages of each of those types of securities without enjoying the advantages of either. Like a bond, a straight preferred stock does not participate in any future earnings and dividend growth of the company and any resulting growth of the price of the common stock. But the bond has greater security than the preferred stock and has a maturity date at which the principal is to be repaid. Like the common stock, the preferred stock has less security protection than the bond. But the potential of increases of market price of the common stock and its dividends paid from future growth of the company is lacking for the preferred stock. One big advantage that the preferred stock provides its issuer is that it gets better equity credit at rating agencies than straight debt, since it is usually perpetual. Also, as pointed out above, certain types of preferred stock qualifies as Tier 1 capital. This allows financial institutions to satisfy regulatory requirements without diluting common stock shareholders. Also through preferred stock, financial institutions are able to put on leverage while getting Tier 1 equity credit.

Example

Suppose that an investor paid par ($100) today for a typical straight preferred stock. Such an investment would give a current yield of just over 6%. Now suppose that in a few years 10-year Treasuries were to yield 13+% to maturity, as they did in 1981; these preferred stocks would yield at least 13%, which would knock their market price down to $46, for a 54% loss. (In all probability, they would yield some 2% more than the Treasuries - or something like 15%, which would take the market price down to $40, for a 60% loss.)

The important difference between straight preferred stocks and Treasuries (or any investment-grade, Federal agency or corporate bond) is that the bonds would move up to par as their maturity date is approached, whereas the straight preferred, having no maturity date, might remain at these $40 levels (or lower) for a very long time.

Advantages of straight preferred stocks posited by some advisers include higher yields and tax advantages (currently yield about 2% more than 10-year Treasuries, rank ahead of common stock in the case of bankruptcy, dividends are taxable at a maximum 15% rather than at ordinary income rates as in the case of bond interest).

Canada

Preferred shares represent a significant portion of Canadian capital markets, with over CAD 5-billion in new preferred shares issued in 2005.

Canadian issuers

Many issuers are financial organizations that may count capital raised in the preferred share market as Tier 1 capital, provided that the shares issued are perpetual. Another class of issuer are "split share corporations".

Canadian investors

Investors in Canadian preferred shares are generally those who wish to hold fixed-income investments in a taxable portfolio. Preferential tax treatment of dividend income, as opposed to interest income, may in many cases result in a greater after-tax return Compared to what might be achieved with bonds.

United Kingdom

United Kingdom issuers

Perpetual non-cumulative preference shares may be included as Tier 1 capital. Perpetual cumulative preferred shares are Upper Tier 2 capital. Dated preferred shares (normally having an original maturity of at least five years) may be included in Lower Tier 2 capital.

United States

In the United States issuance of publicly listed preferred stock is generally limited to financial institutions, REITs and public utilities. Because in the US dividends on preferred stock are not tax deductible (like interest expense), the effective cost of capital raised by preferred stock is 35% greater than issuing the equivalent amount of debt at the same interest rate. This has led to the development of TRuPS (Trust-preferred security) which are essentially debt instruments with the same properties as preferred stock.

However, with a dividend tax of 15% and a top marginal tax rate of 35%, one dollar of dividend income taxed at these rates provides the same after-tax income as approximately $1.30 in interest.

The size of the preferred stock market in the United States has been estimated as USD 200-billion, as of August, 2006, compared to USD 16-trillion for equities and USD 5-trillion for bonds.

France

By a law that dates from June 2004, France allows the creation of preferred shares.

South Africa

Dividends from preference shares are not taxable as income in the hands of individuals.

Czech Republic

In the Czeck Repunlic the amount of a company's preferred stock cannot be more than 50 % of total equity.

Common Types of Preferred Stock

There are various types of preferred stocks that are common to many corporations:

- **Cumulative preferred stock** - If the dividend is not paid, it will accumulate for future payment.
- **Non-cumulative preferred** stock - Dividend for this type of preferred stock will not accumulate if it is unpaid. They are very common in TRuPS and bank preferred stock, since under BIS rules, preferred stock must be non-cumulative if it is to be included in Tier 1 capital.
- **Convertible preferred stock** - This type of preferred stock carries the option to convert into a common stock at a prescribed price.
- **Exchangeable preferred stock** - This type of preferred stock carries the option to be exchanged for some other security upon certain conditions.
- **Monthly income preferred stock** - A combination of preferred stock and subordinated debt.
- **Participating preferred stock** - This type of preferred stock allows the possibility of additional dividend above the stated amount under certain conditions.
- **Perpetual preferred stock** - This type of preferred stock has no fixed date on which invested capital will be returned to the shareholder, although there will always be redemption privileges held by the corporation. Most preferred stock is issued without a set redemption date.
- **Putable preferred stock** - These issues have a "put" privilege whereby the holder may, upon certain conditions, force the issuer to redeem shares.

Treasury Stock

A treasury stock or reacquired stock is stock which is bought back by the issuing company, reducing the amount of outstanding stock on the open market ("open market" including insiders' holdings).

Stock repurchases are often used as a tax-efficient method to put cash into shareholders' hands, rather than pay dividends. Sometimes, companies do this when they feel that their stock is undervalued on the open market. Other times, companies do this to provide a "bonus" to incentive compensation plans for employees. Rather than receive cash, recipients receive an asset that might appreciate in value faster than cash saved in a bank account. Another motive for stock repurchase is to protect the company against a takeover threat.

The United Kingdom equivalent of treasury stock as used in the United States is treasury share. Treasury stocks in the UK refers to government bonds or gilts.

Limitations of Treasury Stock

- Treasury stock does not pay a dividend
- Treasury stock has no voting rights
- The total treasury stock amount cannot exceed the maximum proportion of total capitalization specified by law in the relevant country

When shares are repurchased, they may either be canceled or held for reissue. If not canceled, such shares are referred to as treasury shares. Technically, a repurchased share is a company's own share that has been bought back after having been issued and fully paid.

The possession of treasury shares does not give the company the right to vote, to exercise pre-emptive rights as a shareholder, to receive cash dividends, or to receive assets on company liquidation. Treasury shares are essentially the same as unissued capital and no one advocates classifying unissued share capital as an asset on the balance sheet, as an asset should have probable future economic benefits. Treasury shares simply reduce ordinary share capital.

Buying back Shares

Benefits

In an efficient market, a company buying back its stock should have no effect at all on its stock price. If the market fairly prices a company's shares at $50/share, and the company buys back 100 shares for $5000, it now has $5000 less cash but there are 100 fewer shares outstanding; the net effect should be that the value per share is unchanged. However, buying back shares does improve certain per-share ratios, such as price/earnings (earnings per share is increased due to fewer shares outstanding), but since the market risk increases by the same amount, the share value remains unchanged.

If the market is not efficient, the company's shares may be underpriced. In that case a company can benefit its other shareholders by buying back shares. If a company's shares are overpriced, then a company is actually hurting its remaining shareholders by buying back stock.

Incentives

One other reason for a company to buy back its own stock is to reward holders of stock options. Option holders are hurt by dividend payments, since, typically, they are not eligible to receive them. A share buyback program may increase the value of remaining shares (if the buyback is executed when shares are underpriced); if so, option holders benefit. A dividend payment in the short term always decreases the value of shares after the payment, so, on the day shares go ex-dividend, option holders always lose. Finally, if the sellers into a corporate buyback are actually the option holders themselves, they may directly benefit from temporarily unrealistically favorable pricing.

After the Buyback

The company can either retire the shares (however, retired shares are not listed as treasury stock on the company's financial statements) or hold the shares for later resale. Buying back stock reduces the number of outstanding shares. To see this, note that accompanying the decrease in the number of shares outstanding is a reduction in company assets, in particular cash assets which are used to buy back shares.

Accounting for Treasury Stock

On the balance sheet, treasury stock is listed under shareholder equity as a negative number. The accounts may be called equity reduction or contra-equity.

One way of accounting for treasury stock is with the cost method. Using this method, the paid-in capital account is reduced in the balance sheet when the treasury stock is bought. Once the treasury stock is sold back on the open market, the paid-in capital is either debited or credited if it is sold for more or less than the initial cost respectively.

Another common way for accounting for treasury stock is the par value method. Using the par value method, when the stock is purchased back from the market, the books will reflect the action as a retirement of the shares. Therefore, common stock is debited and treasury stock is credited. However, when the treasury stock is resold back to the market the entry in the books will be the same as the cost method.

In either method, any transaction involving treasury stock cannot increase the amount of retained earnings. If the treasury stock is sold for more than its cost, then the paid-in capital treasury stock is the account that is increased not retained earnings. In auditing financial statements, it is a common practice to check for this error to detect possible attempts to "cook the books".

United States Regulations

In the United States, buybacks are covered by multiple laws.

According to SEC Rule 10b-18:

- **One Broker-dealer per day**: The company repurchasing shares may not use more than one broker or dealer to acquire the shares per each day.
- **Timing of Purchase**: A repurchase may not be the first trade of the day. Repurchases may not be made in the last ten minutes of the trading day. These rules do not apply to over-the-counter securities.
- **Purchase Price**: A repurchase may not be bid at a price higher than the highest independent bid or last price of the last trade.
- **Volume**: Repurchases per day may not exceed 25% of the average daily volume of the previous 4 calendar weeks. Block purchases not effected by a broker-dealer are excluded from this restriction.

United Kingdom Regulations

In the UK, the Companies Act of 1955 disallowed companies from holding their own shares. However, the Companies Act of 1993 later repealed this.

Market sentiment

Market sentiment is the general feeling or mood of the investment community as to the anticipated price movement of the stock market. This feeling or sentiment is the summation of a variety of factors including market data, technical analysis, government reports and/or national and world events. For example, if market sentiment is bullish (bullish is a term for a market that is driven by buyers and therefore the price rises), then most investors would expect upward price movement in the stock market. Likewise if market sentiment is bearish (bearish is a term for a market that is driven by sellers and therefore the price falls), then most investors would expect downward price movement.

There are a variety of technical and statistical methods used to monitor market sentiment such as advancing versus declining stocks and new highs versus new lows comparisons. The importance of market sentiment is discussed by Thomas Dorsey in his book Point and Figure Charting, wherein he states that overall market direction has a "66% influence on the overall movement of an individual stock". This the stock market's demonstration of the expression: all boats float or sink with the tide. In other words, an individual stock is much more likely to go up in price if the overall market is also rising. This principle is aptly summarized in the popular Wall Street phrase "the trend is your friend".

Dividends

Dividends are payments made by a corporation to its shareholder members. When a corporation earns a profit or surplus, that money can be put to two uses:

1. it can either be re-invested in the business (called retained earnings), or
2. it can be paid to the shareholders as a dividend.

Many corporations retain a portion of their earnings and pay the remainder as a dividend.

For a joint stock company, a dividend is allocated as a fixed amount per share. Therefore, a shareholder receives a dividend in proportion to their shareholding. For the joint stock company, paying dividends is not an expense; rather, it is the division of an asset among shareholders. Public companies usually pay dividends on a fixed schedule, but may declare a dividend at any time, sometimes called a special dividend to distinguish it from a regular one.

Cooperatives, on the other hand, allocate dividends according to members' activity, so their dividends are often considered to be a pre-tax expense.

Dividends are usually settled on a cash basis, as a payment from the company to the shareholder. They can take other forms, such as store credits (common among retail consumers' cooperatives) and shares in the company (either newly-created shares or existing shares bought in the market.) Further, many public companies offer dividend reinvestment plans, which automatically use the cash dividend to purchase additional shares for the shareholder.

Joint Stock Company Dividends

Forms of Payment

Cash

Cash dividends are the most common and are those paid out in the form of a cheque. Such dividends are a form of investment income and are usually taxable to the recipient in the year they are paid. This is the most common method of sharing corporate profits with the shareholders of the company.

For each share owned, a declared amount of money is distributed. Thus, if a person owns 100 shares and the cash dividend is $0.50 per share, they will receive $50.00 in total.

Stock

Stock or scrip dividends are those paid out in form of additional stock shares of the issuing corporation, or other corporation (such as its subsidiary corporation). They are usually issued in proportion to shares owned (for example, for every 100 shares of stock owned, 5% stock dividend will yield 5 extra shares). If this payment involves the issue of new shares, this is very similar to a stock splitin that it increases the total number of shares while lowering the price of each share and does not change the market capitalization or the total value of the shares held.

Property

Property dividends or dividends in specie (Latin for "in kind") are those paid out in form of assets from the issuing corporation or another corporation, such as a subsidiary corporation. They are relatively rare and most frequently are securities of other companies owned by the issuer, however they can take other forms, such as products and services.

Other

Dividends can be used in structured finance. Financial assets with a known market value can be distributed as dividends; For example warrants are sometimes distributed in this way.

For large companies with subsidiaries, dividends can take the form of shares in a subsidiary company. A common technique for "spinning off" a company from its parent is to distribute shares in the new company to the old company's shareholders. The new shares can then be traded independently.

Dates

Dividends must be "declared" (approved) by a company's Board of Directors each time they are paid. For public companies, there are four important dates to remember regarding dividends.

Declaration date

The declaration date is the day the Board of Directors announces its intention to pay a dividend. On this day, a liability is created and the company records that liability on its books; it now owes the money to the stockholders. On the declaration date, the Board will also announce a date of record and a payment date.

In-dividend date

This is the last day, which is one trading day before the ex-dividend date, where the stock is said to be cum dividend ('with [including] dividend'). In other words, existing holders of the stock and anyone who buys it on this day will receive the dividend, whereas any holders selling the stock lose their right to the dividend. After this date the stock becomes ex dividend.

Ex-dividend date

The ex-dividend date (typically 2 trading days before the record date for U.S. securities) is the day on which all shares bought and sold no longer come attached with the right to be paid the most recently declared dividend. This is an important date for any company that has many stockholders, including those that trade on exchanges, as it makes reconciliation of who is to be paid the dividend easier. Existing holders of the stock will receive the dividend even if they now sell the stock, whereas anyone who now buys the stock will not receive the dividend.

It is relatively common for a stock's price to decrease on the ex-dividend date by an amount roughly equal to the dividend paid. This reflects the decrease in the company's assets resulting from the declaration of the dividend. The company does not take any explicit action to adjust its stock price; in an efficient market, buyers and sellers will automatically price this in.

Record date

Shareholders who properly registered their ownership on or before the date of record will receive the dividend. Shareholders who are not registered as of this date will not receive the dividend. Registration in most countries is essentially automatic for shares purchased before the ex-dividend date.

Payment date

The payment date is the day when the dividend cheques will actually be mailed to the shareholders of a company or credited to brokerage accounts.

Dividend-reinvestment plans

Some companies have dividend reinvestment plans, or DRIPs. These plans allow shareholders to use dividends to systematically buy small amounts of stock, usually with no commission and sometimes at a slight discount. In some cases the shareholder might not need to pay taxes on these re-invested dividends, but in most cases they do.

Dividend reinvestment plans-in case of mutual funds are a bit special: When the dividend is paid in cash it will attract the dividend distribution tax (DDT) and the same is not taxable in the hands of the person, but in case of a dividend reinvestment plan where the dividend is not paid in cash but distributed as additional units it will not attract the DDT and the same will be taxable in the hands of the person as capital gains when he realizes the gain by selling the units.

Disadvantages of Dividents

- Management and the board may believe that the money is best re-invested into the company's research and development, capital investment, expansion, etc.
- Proponents suggest that a management eager to return profits to shareholders may have run out of good ideas for the future of the company. Some studies have demonstrated that companies that pay dividends have higher earnings growth. Suggesting that dividend payments may be evidence of confidence in earnings growth and sufficient profitability to fund future expansion.
- When dividends are paid, individual shareholders in many countries suffer from double taxation of those dividends. The company pays income tax to the government when it earns any income, and then when the dividend is paid, the individual shareholder pays income tax on the dividend payment. In many countries, the tax rate on dividend income is lower than for other forms of income. This is to compensate for tax paid at the corporate level. Taxation of dividends is often used as justification for retaining earnings, or for performing a stock buyback, in which the company buys back stock, thereby increasing the value of the stock left outstanding.
- In contrast, corporate shareholders often do not pay tax on dividends because the tax regime is designed to tax corporate income (as opposed to individual income) only once. The shareholder will pay a tax on capital gains (which is often taxed at a lower rate than

ordinary income) only when the shareholder chooses to sell the stock.
If a holder of the stock chooses to not participate in the buyback, the price of the holder's shares should rise, but the tax on these gains is delayed until the actual sale of the shares. Certain types of specialized investment companies (such as a REIT in the U.S.) allow the shareholder to partially or fully avoid double taxation of dividends.

- Shareholders in companies which pay little or no cash dividends can reap the benefit of the company's profits when they sell their shareholding, or when a company is wound up and all assets liquidated and distributed amongst the shareholders. This in effect delegates the dividend policy from the board to the individual shareholder.
- Payment of a dividend can increase the borrowing requirement or leverage of a company.

Miscellaneous Specific Types

Franking Credits

In Australia and New Zealand, companies also forward franking credits to shareholders along with dividends. These franking credits represent the tax paid by the company upon its pre-tax profits. One dollar of company tax paid generates one franking credit. Companies can forward any proportion of franking up to a maximum amount that is calculated from the prevailing company tax rate.

For each dollar of dividend paid, the maximum level of franking is the company tax rate divided by (1 - company tax rate). At the current 30% rate, this works out at 0.30 of a credit per 70 cents of dividend, or 42.857 cents per dollar of dividend. The shareholders who are able to use them offset these credits against their income tax bills at a rate of a dollar per credit, thereby effectively eliminating the double taxation of company profits. This system is called dividend imputation.

The UK's taxation system operates along similar lines. when a shareholder receives a dividend. The basic rate of income tax is deemed to already have been paid on that dividend. This ensures that double taxation does not take place, however this creates difficulties for some non-taxpaying entities such as certain trusts, charities and pension funds which are not allowed to reclaim the deemed tax payment and thus are in effect taxed on their income.

Reliability of dividends

There are two metrics which are commonly used to gauge the sustainability of a firm's dividend policy.

The **payout ratio** is calculated by dividing the company's dividend by the earnings per share. A payout ratio of more than 1 means the company is paying out more in dividends for the year than it earned.

The **dividend cover** is calculated by dividing the company's cash flow from operations by the dividend. This ratio is apparently popular with analysts of income trusts in Canada.

Other corporate dividends

Cooperatives

Cooperative businesses may retain their earnings, or distribute part or all of them as dividends to their members. They distribute their dividends in proportion to their members' activity, instead of the value of members' shareholding. Therefore, cooperative business dividends are often treated as pre-tax expenses.

Consumers' cooperatives allocate dividends according to their members' trade with the cooperative business. For example, a credit union will pay a dividend to represent interest on a saver's deposit. A retail co-op store chain may return a percentage of a member's purchases from the co-op, in the form of cash, store credit, or equity. This type of dividend is sometimes known as a patronage dividend or patronage refund, as well as being informally named divi or divvy.

Producer cooperatives, such as worker cooperatives, allocate dividends according to their members' contribution, such as the hours they worked or their salary.

Trusts

In real estate investment trusts and royalty trusts, the distributions paid often will be consistently greater than the company earnings. This can be sustainable because the accounting earnings do not recognize any increasing value of real estate holdings and resource reserves. If there is no economic increase in the value of the company's assets then the excess distribution (or dividend) will be a return of capital and the book value of the company will have shrunk by an equal amount. This may result in capital gains which may be taxed differently than dividends representing distribution of earnings.

Mutuals

The distribution of profits by other forms of mutual organization also varies from that of joint stock companies, though they may not take the form of a dividend.

In the case of mutual insurance, for example in the United States, a distribution of profits to holders of participating life policies is called a dividend. These profits are generated by the investment returns of the insurer's general account, in which premiums are invested and from which claims are paid. The participating dividend may be used to decrease premiums, or to increase the cash value of the policy. Some life policies pay nonparticipating dividends. As a contrasting example, in the United Kingdom, the surrender value of a with-profits policy is increased by a bonus, which also serves the purpose of distributing profits. Life insurance dividends and bonuses, while typical of mutual insurance, are also paid by some joint stock insurers.

Insurance dividend payments are not restricted to life policies. For example, general insurer State Farm Mutual Automobile Insurance Company can distribute dividends to its vehicle insurance policyholders.

Stock Valuation

There are several methods used to value companies and their stocks. They attempt to give an estimate of their fair value, by using fundamental economic criteria. This theoretical valuation has to be perfected with market criteria, as the final purpose is to determine potential market prices.

Fundamental Criteria (Fair Value)

The most theoretically sound stock valuation method, called income valuation or the discounted cash flow (DCF) method, involves discounting of the profits (dividends, earnings, or cash flows) the stock will bring to the stockholder in the foreseeable future, and a final value on disposition. The discounted rate normally includes a risk premium which is commonly based on the capital asset pricing model.

Approximate Valuation Approaches

Average Growth Approximation

Assuming that two stocks have the same earnings growth, the one with a lower P/E is a better value. The P/E method is perhaps the most commonly used valuation method in the stock brokerage industry. By using comparison firms, a target price/earnings (or P/E) ratio is selected for the company, and then the future earnings of the company are estimated. The valuation's fair price is simply estimated earnings times target P/E. This model is essentially the same model as Gordon's model (which will be explained next), if k-g is estimated as the dividend payout ratio (D/E) divided by the target P/E ratio.

Constant growth approximation:

The Gordon model or Gordon's growth model is the best known of a class of discounted dividend models. It assumes that dividends will increase at a constant growth rate (less than the discount rate) forever. The valuation is given by the following formula:

$$P = D \cdot \sum_{i=1}^{\infty} \left(\frac{1+g}{1+k}\right)^{i} = D \cdot \frac{1+g}{k-g}.$$

and the following table defines each symbol:

Symbol	Meaning	Units
P	estimated stock price	\$ or € or £
D	last dividend paid	\$ or € or £
k	discount rate	%
g	the growth rate of the dividends	%

Limited high-growth period approximation:

When a stock has a significantly higher growth rate than its peers, it is sometimes assumed that the earnings growth rate will be sustained for a short time (say, 5 years), and then the growth rate will revert to the mean. This is probably the most rigorous approximation that is practical.

While these DCF models are commonly used, the uncertainty in these values is hardly ever discussed. Note that the models diverge for $k = g$ and hence are extremely sensitive to the difference of dividend growth to discount factor. One might argue that an analyst can justify any value (and that would usually be one close to the current price supporting his call) by fine-tuning the growth/discount assumptions.

Market criteria (potential price)

Some feel that if the stock is listed in a well organized stock market, with a large volume of transactions, the listed price will be close to the estimated fair value. This is called the efficient market hypothesis.

On the other hand, studies made in the field of behavioral finance tend to show that deviations from the fair price are rather common, and sometimes quite large.

Thus, in addition to fundamental economic criteria, market criteria also have to be taken into account a market-based valuation. Valuing a stock is not only to estimate its fair value, but also to determine its potential price range, taking into account market behavior aspects. One of the behavioral valuation tools is the stock image, a coefficient that bridges the theoretical fair value and the market price.

Online Valuation Calculators

At this web address you can find a Discounted Cash Flows Calculator that assumes that a higher growth can be sustained for a limited number of years:

http://www.moneychimp.com/articles/valuation/dcf.htm

A free intrinsic value (or fair value) calculation tool based on the original stock valuation model can be found under this address:

http://www.istockresearch.com/model.html

A free Discounted Cash Flow (DCF) valuation tool for major listed companies:

http://www.valuecruncher.com/

Stock Market Prediction

Stock market prediction is the act of trying to determine the future value of a company stock or other financial instrument traded on a financial exchange. The successful prediction of a stock's future price could yield significant profit. Some believe that stock price movements are governed by the random walk hypothesis and thus are unpredictable. Others disagree and those with this viewpoint possess a myriad of methods and technologies which purportedly allow them to gain future price information. However, a false prediction, bed luck or a "wrong hunch" can also lead to significant losses.

The Random Walk Hypothesis

When applied to a particular financial instrument, the random walk hypothesis states that the price of this instrument is governed by a random walk and hence is unpredictable. If the random walk hypothesis is false then there will be some (potentially non-linear) correlation between the instrument price and some other indicator(s) such as trading volume or the previous day's instrument closing price or any other historical indicator. If this correlation can be determined then a potential profit can be made.

Prediction Methods

Prediction methodologies fall into three broad categories which can (and often do) overlap. They are fundamental analysis, technical analysis (charting) and technological methods.

Fundamental Analysis

Fundamental analysts are concerned with the company that underlies the stock itself. They evaluate a company's past performance as well as the credibility of its accounts. Many performance ratios are created that aid the fundamental analyst with assessing the validity of a stock, such as the P/E ratio. Warren Buffett is perhaps the most famous of all Fundamental Analysts.

Technical Analysis

Technical analysts or chartists are not concerned with any of the company's fundamentals. They seek to determine the future price of a stock based solely on the (potential) trends of the past price (a form of time series analysis). Numerous patterns are employed such as the head and shoulders or cup and saucer. Alongside the patterns, statistical techniques are utilized such as the exponential moving average (EMA).

Technological methods

With the rise of digital computers stock market prediction has moved into the technological realm. The most prominent technique involves the use of artificial neural networks (ANNs). ANNs can be thought of as mathematical function approximators. Their value in stock market prediction is that if a (potentially non-linear) relationship exists then it is possible that it could be found with enough indicators, the correct network structure and a large enough dataset.

The most common form of ANN used for stock market prediction is the feed forward network utilizing the backward propagation of errors algorithm to update the network weights. These networks are commonly referred to as back propagation networks. Since ANNs require training and have a large parameter space, it is useful to modify the network structure for optimal predictive ability. Recently this has involved pairing ANNs with genetic algorithms, a method of finding optima in multi-dimension parameter spaces utilizing the biological concepts of evolution and natural selection. Moreover, some researchers have tried to extract meaningful indicators from news flashes and discussion rooms about a certain stock using data mining techniques. However, different people can have different opinions about the same stock at the same time which still leads to price variations.

Validity

There have been numerous academic studies on the validity of fundamental analysis, technical analysis and Artificial Neural Networks as stock market prediction methods. Some studies report success in all camps, on particular markets and with particular datasets. Others dispute the ability to even predict the stock market at all and adhere to the random walk hypothesis. In fact the theory of pricing financial derivatives relies on the random walk hypothesis (stock prices are usually modeled as random walks in derivative pricing models).

What is a Stock Broker?

A stock broker or stockbroker is a regulated professional who buys and sells shares and other securities through market makers or Agency Only Firms on behalf of investors.

Requirements

In order to become a stockbroker in the United States, a candidate must pass the General Securities Representative Examination (also known as the "Series 7 exam").

In the UK, brokers are required to pass the SII (Securities and Investment Institute link title) Certificate in Securities, this qualification is achieved by passing two exams: Either

- Unit 1: FSA Financial regulations or
- Unit 6 Principles of Financial Regulation for MiFID compliant retail trading,

and either:

- Unit 2: Securities,
- Unit 3: Derivatives or
- Unit 4: for both Securities and Derivatives.

Passing Unit 1 or Unit 6 identifies individuals as having attained FSA Approved Person Status.

Services Provided

A transaction on a stock exchange must be made between two members of the exchange — an ordinary person may not walk into the New York Stock Exchange (for example), and ask to trade stock. Such an exchange must be done through a broker.

There are three types of stock broking service.

- **Execution**-only, which means that the broker will only carry out the client's instructions to buy or sell.
- **Advisory dealing**, where the broker advises the client on which shares to buy and sell, but leaves the final decision to the investor.
- **Discretionary dealing**, where the stockbroker ascertains the client's investment objectives and then makes all dealing decisions on the client's behalf.

In addition to actually trading stocks for their clients, stock brokers may also offer advice to their clients on which stocks, mutual funds, etc. to buy.

History

Philadelphia was the centre of American finance during the first forty years of the new United States. In 1790, the country's first stock exchange was founded there and Chestnut Street was home to the nation's most powerful financial institutions. However, in the 1820s a shift to New York City began and for more than one hundred and fifty years Wall Street has been synonymous with the stock brokerage business. Some sources suggest that historical top-level brokers and a number of other firms rose to prominence over that time, with the top-ranked brokerages in the early 1950s being:

1. Merrill Lynch
2. Paine Webber & Company
3. Morgan Stanley
4. Goldman Sachs
5. Bear Stearns

Since the 1980s stock broking firms have also been allowed to be market makers as long as the appropriate Chinese walls are put in place.

With the advent of automated stock broking systems on the Internet the client often has no personal contact with his/her stock broking firm. The stockbroker's system performs all the stock broking functions: it obtains the best price from the market, executes and settles the trade.

Today, most of the once well-known corporate brand names including midsized firms such as Smith Barney have been swallowed up by global financial conglomerates. Only a few firms remain independent, such as Edward Jones

Investments, Stifel Nicolaus, Oppenheimer & Co, JP Turner & Company and Raymond James. Discount brokers (such as E*TRADE, Scottrade, TD Ameritrade, and Charles Schwab) have taken a large share of the business by offering highly discounted commissions. Discount brokers may offer limited advisory services, but their primary focus tends to be servicing self directed retail accounts.

Similar roles

Roles similar to that of a stockbroker include investment advisor and financial advisor. A stockbroker may or may not be also an investment advisor, and vice versa.

The Certified Financial Planner designation initially offered by the American College in Pennsylvania is considered by many to be the next educational step a stockbroker can take in order to be considered a legitimate and ethical financial consultant. Though not strictly true, it is still vital to assert the authority taken.

Acting as a principal

Stockbrokers also sometimes or exclusively trade on their own behalf, as a principal, speculating that a share or other financial instrument will increase or decline in price. In such cases the term broker makes little sense and the individuals or firms trading in principal capacity sometimes call themselves dealers, stock traders or simply traders. A stock broker is just the main part of being a City Trader. Other types of City Trading include working in the Foreign Exchange.

Transactions by stock brokers in the US and UK

In the US: When acting as an agent, the stock broker typically charges the client a flat fee and/or a percentage-based commission for undertaking the trade. When acting as a principal, the trade could be with another market participant or one of the stockbroker's clients. When trading in a principal capacity with client, the broker informs the client and charges the client a markup or markdown from the prevailing market price.

In the UK: Stock brokers act the same as in the US, except that when trading in a principal capacity with a client, the broker is obliged to inform the client and no commission is charged.

Explanation of a City Trader's Job

Stock broker

A stock broker would deal with shares. Shares and stocks have the same definition; a share is a section of a company that a stock broker can buy and sell if he/she has a suitable amount of money. Specifically, a stock is a piece of money – a share of a company – that a few years ago were represented on a document. Nowadays spreadsheets are often used to keep the record.
For example, a share can be worth 25p, but can be multiplied by 40 to create the total desired value on the document – in this case it would therefore be worth 1000p. The stock broker possesses a number of shares; however he or she can choose how many of these he or she wishes to trade, so that perhaps some can be kept for him or her. Keeping an amount is understandable, because stock-broking is a risky business. This is because the prices that shares are worth are constantly increasing and decreasing, depending on how much money the company you are dealing with is producing.
For example, say a stockbroker buys a share from a dealer, for $1, and then sells it to a client for x sum of money. The next day, the price for that same share value, decreases (the company is not producing as much money), so that it's now worth 50p. The stockbroker had spent $1, however, which was 50p too much. He or she has just lost 50p. That's how stockbrokers lose money. They then continue trading at what they think are suitable times – when it is unlikely for the price of a share to alter (to start with he or she could buy that share back for 50p and sell it again, to another client).

Foreign Exchange Members

These city traders deal with currencies. Their clients are usually called "market makers" (literally makers of markets: shopkeepers are a common example) and are the people they use to earn money. Currencies are traded in the following way:

The stock broker can give his/her client $1, and the client can gives him/her £1 in return, as long as such a deal was discussed and agreed to (as mentioned previously, the person who makes the final decision as to what the deal is going to be depends on the position of the stock broker - in Advisory dealing, for example, the investor makes the concluding decision.) In this case the city trader makes a profit (because he/she gains £1, that is worth more than what he/she gave [$1]), but indeed often the market maker does too (that's how they earn their money).

Bond-Dealers

A bond-dealer is a city trader who lends a sum of money to a stock (section of a company). If a company owns £1,000,000, and this was due to a million bondholders each lending £1 to the stock, than each bondholder lends a bond of £1.

In such ways, city traders trade via market makers, but they are also trading for a group of people - the investors. These are people of a higher status than city traders, for example; chartered accountants. An investor has the right to use money from his brokerage firm if there is a crisis involving him/her losing a sum of money. This doesn't change the fact that they can at the same time be allowing the usual currency/stock deals to take place, enabling them to gain money while providing the investor with money.

You have to bear in mind that these city traders do not have clients at their desk(s) to perform the deal. Keep aware of the various money-exchanges through software on the computer, a particular and more popular one being known as "CREST". Other methods of dealing include using the phone.

There are other occupations within the title of being a "city trader", but these are the main three, in order of which is most common, the most common being the first in the list.

What is an Investment Bank?

Investment banks profit from companies and governments by raising money through issuing and selling securities in the capital markets (both equity and bond), as well as providing advice on transactions such as mergers and acquisitions. To perform these services in the US, an advisor must be a licensed broker-dealer, and is subject to SEC (FINRA) regulation. Until the late 1980s, the United States and Canada maintained a separation between investment banking and commercial banks.

A majority of investment banks offer strategic advisory services for mergers, acquisitions, divestiture or other financial services for clients, such as the trading of derivatives, fixed income, foreign exchange, commodity, and equity securities.

Trading securities for cash or securities (i.e., facilitating transactions, market-making), or the promotion of securities (i.e., underwriting, research, etc.) is referred to as the "sell side."

Dealing with the pension funds, mutual funds, hedge funds, and the investing public who consume the products and services of the sell-side in order to maximize their return on investment constitutes the "buy side". Many firms have buy and sell side components.

The last two major bulge bracket firms on Wall Street were Goldman Sachs and Morgan Stanley until both banks elected to convert to traditional banking institutions on the 22nd of September, 2008, as part of a response to the US financial crisis. Barclays, Citigroup, Credit Suisse, Deutsche Bank, HSBC, JP Morgan Chase, and UBS AG are "universal banks" rather than bulge-bracket investment banks, since they also accept deposits (though not all of them have U.S. branches).

Organizational Structure of an Investment Bank

The Main Activities and Units

On behalf of the bank and its clients, the primary function of the bank is buying and selling products. Banks undertake risk through proprietary trading, done by a special set of traders who do not interface with clients and through "principal risk" which is risk undertaken by a trader after he buys or sells a product to a client and does not hedge his total exposure. Banks seek to maximize profitability for a given amount of risk on their balance sheet. An investment bank is split into the so-called front office, middle office, and back office.

Front Office

Investment banking is the traditional aspect of investment banks which involves helping customers raise funds in the capital markets and advise on mergers and acquisitions. These jobs pay well, bar on the flip side they are frequently extremely stressful and degrading. Investment banking may involve subscribing investors to a security issuance, coordinating with bidders, or negotiating with a merger target. Other terms for the investment banking division include mergers and acquisitions (M&A) and corporate finance. The investment banking division (IBD) is generally divided into industry coverage and product coverage groups. Industry coverage groups focus on a specific industry such as healthcare, industrials or technology, and maintain relationships with corporations within the industry to bring in business for a bank. Product coverage groups focus on financial products, such as mergers and acquisitions, leveraged finance, equity, and high-grade debt.

Investment management is the professional management of various securities (shares, bonds, etc.) and other assets (e.g. real estate), to meet specified investment goals for the benefit of the investors. Investors may be institutions (insurance companies, pension funds, corporations etc.) or private investors (both directly via investment contracts and more commonly via collective investment schemes eg. mutual funds). The investment management division of an investment bank is generally divided into separate groups, often known as Private Wealth Management and Private Client Services. Asset Management deals with institutional investors, while Private Wealth Management manages the funds of high net-worth individuals.

Sales & trading In the process of market making, traders will buy and sell financial products with the goal of making an incremental amount of money on each trade. Sales is the term for the investment banks sales force, whose primary job is to call on institutional and high-net-worth investors to suggest trading ideas (on caveat emptor basis) and take orders. Sales desks then communicate their clients' orders to the appropriate trading desks, who can price and execute trades, or structure new products that fit a specific need.

Structuring has been a relatively recent division as derivatives have come into play, with highly technical and numerate employees working on creating complex structured products which typically offer much greater margins and returns than underlying cash securities. The necessity for numerical ability has created jobs for physics and math Ph.D.s who act as quantitative analysts.

Merchant banking is a private equity activity of investment banks. Examples include Goldman Sachs Capital Partners and JPMorgan One Equity Partners. (Originally, "merchant bank" was the British English term for an investment bank.)

Research is the division which reviews companies and writes reports about their prospects, often with "buy" or "sell" ratings. While the research division generates no revenue, its resources are used to assist traders in trading, the sales force in suggesting ideas to customers and investment bankers by covering their clients. There is a potential conflict of interest between the investment bank and its analysis in that published analysis can affect the profits of the bank. Therefore in recent years the relationship between investment banking and research has become highly regulated requiring a Chinese wall between public and private functions. We will talk about the concept of a Chinese wall in more detail in the next chapters.

Strategy is the division which advises external as well as internal clients on the strategies that can be adopted in various markets. Ranging from derivatives to specific industries, strategists place companies and industries in a quantitative framework with full consideration of the macroeconomic scene. This strategy often affects the way the firm will operate in the market, the direction it would like to take in terms of its proprietary and flow positions, the suggestions salespersons give to clients, as well as the way structurers create new products.

Middle Office

Risk management involves analyzing the market and credit risk that traders are taking onto the balance sheet in conducting their daily trades and setting limits on the amount of capital that they are able to trade in order to prevent 'bad' trades having a detrimental effect to a desk overall. Another key Middle Office role is to ensure that the above mentioned economic risks are captured accurately (as per agreement of commercial terms with the counterparty), correctly (as per standardized booking models in the most appropriate systems) and on time (typically within 30 minutes of trade execution). In recent years the risk of errors has become known as "operational risk" and the assurance Middle Offices provide now includes measures to address this risk. When this assurance is not in place, market and credit risk analysis can be unreliable and open to deliberate manipulation.

Finance areas are responsible for an investment bank's capital management and risk monitoring. By tracking and analyzing the capital flows of the firm, the finance division is the principal adviser to senior management on essential areas such as controlling the firm's global risk exposure and the profitability and structure of the firm's various businesses. In the United States and United Kingdom, a Financial Controller is a senior position, often reporting to the Chief Financial Officer.

Compliance areas are responsible for an investment bank's daily operations' compliance with government regulations and internal regulations. Often also considered a back-office division.

Back Office

Operations involves data-checking trades that have been conducted, ensuring that they are not erroneous, and transacting the required transfers. Many banks have outsourced operations division to other firms. It is however, a critical part of the bank. Due to increased competition in finance related careers college degrees are now mandatory at most Tier 1 investment banks. A finance degree has proved significant in understanding the depth of the deals and transactions that occur across all the divisions of the bank.

Technology refers to the information technology department. Every major investment bank has considerable amounts of in-house software, created by the technology team, who are also responsible for technical support. Technology has changed considerably in the last few years as more sales and trading desks are using electronic trading. Some trades are initiated by complex algorithms, including for hedging purposes.

Chinese Wall

An investment bank can also be split into private and public functions with a Chinese wall which separates the two to prevent information from crossing. The private areas of the bank deal with private insider information that may not be publicly disclosed, while the public areas such as stock analysis deal with public information.

Size of the Industry

Global investment banking revenue increased for the fifth year running in 2007, to $84.3 billion. This was up 21% on the previous year and more than twice the level in 2003. Despite a record year for fee income many investment banks have experienced large losses related to their exposure to U.S. sub-prime securities investments.

The United States was the primary source of investment banking income in 2007, with 53% of the total, a proportion which has fallen somewhat during the past decade. Europe (with Middle East and Africa) generated 32% of the total, slightly up on its 30% share a decade ago. Asian countries generated the remaining 15%. Over the past decade, fee income from the US increased by 80%. This compares with a 217% increase in Europe and 250% increase in Asia during this period. The industry is heavily concentrated in a small number of major financial centers, including New York City, Manila, London and Tokyo.

Investment banking is one of the most global industries and is hence continuously challenged to respond to new developments and innovation in the global financial markets. Throughout the history of investment banking, it is only known that many have theorized that all investment banking products and services would be commoditized. New products with higher margins are constantly invented and manufactured by bankers in hopes of winning over clients and developing trading know-how in new markets. However, since these usually cannot be patented or copyrighted they are very often copied quickly by competing banks pushing down trading margins.

For example, trading bonds and equities for customers is now a commodity business, but structuring and trading derivatives retains higher margins in good times - and the risk of large losses in difficult market conditions, such as the credit crunch that begin in 2007. Each over-the-counter contract has to be uniquely structured and could involve complex pay-off and risk profiles. Listed option contracts are traded through major exchanges, such as the CBOE, and are almost as commoditized as general equity securities.

In addition, while many products have been commoditized, an increasing amount of profit within investment banks has come from proprietary trading, where size creates a positive network benefit (since the more trades an investment bank does the more it knows about the market flow, allowing it to theoretically make better trades and pass on better guidance to clients).

The fastest growing segment of the investment banking industry are private investments into public companies (PIPEs, otherwise known as Regulation D or Regulation S). Such transactions are privately negotiated between companies and accredited investors. These PIPE transactions are non-rule 144A transactions. Large bulge bracket brokerage firms and smaller boutique firms compete in this sector. Special purpose acquisition companies (SPACs) or blank check corporations have been created from this industry.

Vertical integration

In the U.S., the Glass-Steagall Act, initially created in the wake of the Stock Market Crash of 1929, prohibited banks from both accepting deposits and underwriting securities which led to segregation of investment banks from commercial banks. Glass-Steagall was effectively repealed for many large financial institutions by the Gramm-Leach-Bliley Act in 1999.

Another development in recent years has been the vertical integration of debt securitization. Previously, investment banks had assisted lenders in raising more lending funds and having the ability to offer longer term fixed interest rates by converting the lenders' outstanding loans into bonds. For example, a mortgage lender would make a house loan and then use the investment bank to sell bonds to fund the debt The money from the sale of the bonds can be used to make new loans, while the lender accepts loan payments and passes the payments on to the bondholders. This process is called securitization. However, lenders have begun to securitize loans themselves, especially in the areas of mortgage loans. Because of this and because of the fear that this will continue many investment banks have focused on becoming lenders themselves, making loans with the goal of securitizing them. In fact, in the areas of commercial mortgages, many investment banks lend at loss leader interest rates in order to make money securitizing the loans, causing them to be a very popular financing option for commercial property investors and developers. Securitized house loans may have exacerbated the subprime mortgage crisis beginning in 2007, by making risky loans less apparent to investors.

Possible Conflicts of Interest

Potential conflicts of interest may arise between different parts of a bank, creating the potential for financial movements that could be market manipulation. Authorities that regulate investment banking (the FSA in the United Kingdom and the SEC in the United States) require that banks impose a Chinese wall which prohibits communication between investment banking on one side and equity research and trading on the other.

Some of the conflicts of interest that can be found in investment banking are listed here:

Historically, equity research firms were founded and owned by investment banks. One common practice is for equity analysts to initiate coverage on a company in order to develop relationships that lead to highly profitable investment banking business. In the 1990s, many equity researchers allegedly traded positive stock ratings directly for investment banking business. On the flip side of the coin: Companies would threaten to divert investment banking business to competitors unless their stock was rated favorably. Politicians acted to pass laws to criminalize such acts. Increased pressure from regulators and a series of lawsuits, settlements and prosecutions curbed this business to a large extent following the 2001 stock market tumble.

Many investment banks also own retail brokerages. During the 1990s, some retail brokerages sold consumers securities which did not meet their stated risk profile. This behavior may have led to investment banking business or even sales of surplus shares during a public offering to keep public perception of the stock favorable.

Since investment banks engage heavily in trading for their own account, there is always the temptation or possibility that they might engage in some form of front running. Front running is the illegal practice of a stock broker executing orders on a security for their own account before filling orders previously submitted by their customers, thereby benefiting from any changes in prices induced by those orders.

Electronic Trading

Electronic trading, sometimes called etrading, is a method of trading securities (such as stocks, and bonds), foreign currency and exchange traded derivatives electronically. It uses information technology to bring together buyers and sellers through electronic media to create a virtual market place. NASDAQ, NYSE Arca and Globex are examples of electronic market places. Exchanges that facilitate electronic trading in the United States are regulated by the Securities and Exchange Commission and are generally called electronic communications networks or ECNs.

Etrading is widely believed to be more reliable than older methods of trade processing but glitches and cancelled trades do occur.

The Background of Etrading

Historically, stock markets were physical locations where buyers and sellers met and negotiated. With the improvement in communications technology in the late 20th century, the need for a physical location became less important, as traders could transact from remote locations.

Electronic trading makes transactions easier to complete, monitor, clear and settle. NASDAQ, set up in 1971, was the world's first electronic stock market, though it originally operated as an electronic bulletin board, rather than offering straight through processing (STP). By early 2007, organizations like the Chicago Mercantile Exchange were creating electronic trading platforms to support the emerging interest in trading within the foreign exchange market.

Today many investment firms on both the buy side and sell side are increasing their spending on technology for electronic trading. Many floor traders and brokers are being removed from the trading process. Traders are relying on algorithms to analyze market conditions and then execute their orders.

Dates of introduction of electronic trading by leading exchange in 120 countries is provided in a Journal of Finance article published in 2005 "Financial market design and the equity premium: Electronic vs. floor trading,". Leading academic research in this field is conducted by Professor Ian Domowitz and Professor Pankaj Jain.

There are, broadly, two types of trading in the financial markets:

- **Business-to-business** (B2B) trading, often conducted on exchanges, where large investment banks and brokers trade directly with one another, transacting large amounts of securities.
- **Business-to-client** (B2C) trading, where retail (e.g. individuals buying and selling relatively small amounts of stocks and shares) and institutional clients (e.g. hedge funds, fund managers or insurance companies, trading far larger amounts of securities) buy and sell from brokers or "dealers", who act as middle-men between the clients and the B2B markets.

While the majority of retail trading probably now happens over the Internet, retail trading volumes are dwarfed by institutional, inter-dealer and exchange trading.

Before the advent of eTrading, exchange trading would typically happen on the floor of an exchange, where traders in brightly colored jackets (to identify which firm they worked for) would shout and gesticulate at one another - a process known as open outcry or "pit trading" (the exchange floors were often pit-shaped - circular, sloping downwards to the centre, so that the traders could see one another).

For instruments which aren't exchange-traded (e.g. U.S. treasury bonds), the inter-dealer market substitutes for the exchange. This is where dealers trade directly with one another or through inter-dealer brokers (i.e. companies like GFI Group, BGC Partners and Garban, who act as middle-men between dealers such as investment banks). This type of trading traditionally took place over the phone but brokers are beginning to offer eTrading services.

Similarly, B2C trading traditionally happened over the phone and, while much of it still does, more brokers are allowing their clients to place orders using electronic systems. Many retail (or "discount") brokers (e.g. Charles Schwab, E-Trade) went online during the late 1990s and most retail stock-broking probably takes place over the web now.

Impact of Electronic Trading

The increase of eTrading has had some important implications:

- **Reduced cost of transactions** - By automating as much of the process as possible (often referred to as "straight-through processing" or STP) costs are brought down. The goal is to reduce the incremental cost of trades as close to zero as possible, so that increased trading volumes don't lead to significantly increased costs. This has translated to lower costs for investors.
- **Greater liquidity** - electronic systems make it easier to allow different companies to trade with one another no matter where they are located. This leads to greater liquidity (i.e. there are more buyers and sellers) which increases the efficiency of the markets.
- **Greater competition** - While etrading hasn't necessarily lowered the cost of entry to the financial services industry it has removed barriers within the industry and had a globalisation-style competition effect. For example, a trader can trade futures on Eurex, Globex or LIFFE at the click of a button - he or she doesn't need to go through a broker or pass orders to a trader on the exchange floor.
- **Increased transparency** - Etrading has meant that the markets are less opaque. It's easier to find out what the price of securities is when that information is flowing around the world electronically.
- **Tighter spreads** - The "spread" on an instrument is the difference between the best buying and selling prices being quoted. It represents the profit being made by the market makers. The increased liquidity, competition and transparency means that spreads have tightened especially for commoditized exchange-traded instruments.

For retail investors, financial services on the web offer great benefits. The primary benefit is the reduced cost of transactions for all concerned as well as the ease and the convenience. Web-driven financial transactions bypass traditional hurdles such as logistics.

Technology and Systems

Etrading systems are typically proprietary software (etrading platforms), running on COTS hardware and operating systems, often using common underlying protocols such as TCP/IP and ASCII.

Exchanges typically develop their own systems (sometimes referred to as matching engines), although sometimes an exchange will use another exchange's technology (e.g. e-cbot, the Chicago Board of Trade's electronic trading platform uses LIFFE's Connect system) and some newer electronic exchanges use 3rd-party specialist software providers (e.g. the Budapest stock exchange and the Moscow Interbank Currency Exchange use automated trading software originally written and implemented by FMSC an Australian technology company that was acquired by Computershare and whose intellectual property rights are now owned by OMX.

Exchanges and ECNs generally offer two methods of accessing their systems -

- an exchange-provided GUI which the trader runs on his or her desktop and connects directly to the exchange/ECN
- an API which allows dealers to plug their own in-house systems directly into the exchange/ECN's.

From an infrastructure point of view most exchanges will provide "gateways" which sit on a companies' network acting in a manner similar to a proxy connecting back to the exchange's central system.

ECNs will generally forego the gateway/proxy and their GUI or the API will connect directly to a central system across a leased line.

Many brokers develop their own systems although there are some third-party solutions providers specializing in this area. Like ECNs brokers will often offer both a GUI and an API (although it's likely that a slightly smaller proportion of brokers offer an API as compared with ECNs) and connectivity is typically direct to the broker's systems rather than through a gateway.

Investment banks and other dealers have far more complex technology requirements, as they have to interface with multiple exchanges, brokers and multi-dealer platforms, as well as their own pricing, P&L, trade processing and position-keeping systems. Some banks will develop their own etrading systems in-house but this can be costly especially when they need to connect to many exchanges, ECNs and brokers. There are a number of companies who offer solutions in this area.

Larger institutional clients however, will generally place electronic orders via proprietary ECNs such as Bloomberg or TradeWeb (which connect institutional clients to several dealers) or using their brokers' proprietary software.

Value Investing

Value investing is an investment paradigm that derives from the ideas on investment and speculation that Ben Graham & David Dodd began teaching at Columbia Business School in 1928 and subsequently developed in their 1934 text Security Analysis. Although value investing has taken many forms since its inception, it generally involves buying securities whose shares appear underpriced by some form(s) of fundamental analysis. As examples, such securities may be stock in public companies that trade at discounts to book value or tangible book value, have high dividend yields, have low price-to-earning multiples or have low price-to-book ratios.

High profile proponents of value investing, including Berkshire Hathaway chairman Warren Buffett, have argued that the essence of value investing is buying stocks at less than their intrinsic value. The discount of the market price to the intrinsic value is what Benjamin Graham called the "margin of safety". The intrinsic value is the discounted value of all future distributions.

However, the future distributions and the appropriate discount rate can only be assumptions. Warren Buffett has taken the value investing concept even further as his thinking has evolved to where for the last 25 years or so his focus has been on "finding an outstanding company at a sensible price" rather than generic companies at a bargain price.

History of Value Investing

Value investing was established by Benjamin Graham and David Dodd, both professors at Columbia Business School and teachers of many famous investors. In Graham's book The Intelligent Investor, he advocated the important concept of margin of safety — first introduced in Security Analysis, a 1934 book he coauthored with David Dodd — which calls for a cautious approach to investing. In terms of picking stocks, he recommended defensive investment in stocks trading below their tangible book value as a safeguard to adverse future developments often encountered in the stock market.

Further Evolution

However, the concept of value (as well as "book value") has evolved significantly since the 1970s. Book value is most useful in industries where most assets are tangible. Intangible assets such as patents, software, brands or goodwill are difficult to quantify and may not survive the break-up of a company. When an industry is going through fast technological advancements, the value of its assets is not easily estimated. Sometimes, the production power of an asset can be significantly reduced due to competitive disruptive innovation and therefore its value can suffer permanent impairment. One good example of decreasing asset value is a personal computer. An example of where book value does not mean much is the service and retail sectors. One modern model of calculating value is the discounted cash flow model (DCF). The value of an asset is the sum of its future cash flows discounted back to the present.

In his book, "The Four Filters Invention of Warren Buffett and Charlie Munger," Bud Labitan asserts that Buffett and Munger invented an effective Behavioral Finance formula that is underappreciated by the business and academic communities. Made up of 3 qualitative steps and 1 quantitative step for estimating intrinsic value, the four filters appear to have existed in print as early as the 1977 BRK Letter to Shareholders. Warren Buffett mentions the Four Filters this way: "Charlie and I look for companies that have) a business we understand; b) favorable long-term economics; c) able and trustworthy management and d) a sensible price tag." These Four Filters appear to enhance the probability of investment success.

Value Investing Performance

Performance, Value Strategies

Value investing has proven to be a successful investment strategy. There are several ways to evaluate its success. One way is to examine the performance of simple value strategies such as buying low PE ratio stocks, low price-to-cash-flow ratio stocks, or low price-to-book ratio stocks. Numerous academics have published studies investigating the effects of buying value stocks. These studies have consistently found that value stocks outperform growth stocks and the market as a whole.

Performance and Value Investors

Another way to examine the performance of value investing strategies is to examine the investing performance of well-known value investors. Simply examining the performance of the best known value investors would not be instructive because investors do not become well known unless they are successful. This introduces a selection bias. A better way to investigate the performance of a group of value investors was suggested by Warren Buffett, in his May 17, 1984 speech that was published as The Superinvestors of Graham-and-Doddsville. In this speech, Buffett examined the performance of those investors who worked at Graham-Newman Corporation and were thus most influenced by Benjamin Graham. Buffett's conclusion is identical to that of the academic research on simple value investing strategies--value investing is, on average, successful in the long run.

During about a 25-year period (1965-90), published research and articles in leading journals of the value ilk were few. Warren Buffett once commented, "You couldn't advance in a finance department in this country unless you taught that the world was flat."

Well known Value Investors

Benjamin Graham is regarded by many to be the father of value investing. Along with David Dodd he wrote Security Analysis which was first published in 1934. The most lasting contribution of this book to the field of security analysis was to emphasize the quantifiable aspects of security analysis (such as the evaluations of earnings and book value) while minimizing the importance of more qualitative factors such as the quality of a company's management. Graham later wrote The Intelligent Investor, a book that brought value investing to individual investors. Aside from Buffett many of Graham's other students such as William J. Ruane, Irving Kahn and Charles Brandes have gone on to become successful investors in their own right.

Graham's most famous student however, is Warren Buffett who ran successful investing partnerships before closing them in 1969 to focus on running Berkshire Hathaway. Charlie Munger joined Buffett at Berkshire Hathaway in the 1970s and has since worked as Vice Chairman of the company. Buffett has credited Munger with encouraging him to focus on long-term sustainable growth rather than on simply the valuation of current cash flows or assets. Columbia Business School has played a significant role in shaping the principles of the Value Investor, with Professors and students making their mark on history and on each other. Ben Graham's book, The Intelligent Investor was Warren Buffett's bible and he referred to it as "the greatest book on investing ever written." A young Warren Buffett studied under Prof. Ben Graham took his course and worked for his small investment firm, Graham Newman, from 1954 to 1956. Twenty years after Ben Graham, Prof. Roger Murray arrived and taught value investing to a young student named Mario Gabelli. About a decade or so later, Professor Bruce Greenwald arrived and produced his own protégés, including Mr. Paul Sonkin - just as Ben Graham had Mr. Buffett as a protégé and Roger Murray had Mr. Gabelli.

Seth Klarman, the founder and president of The Baupost Group, a Boston-based private investment partnership, authored Margin of Safety, Risk Averse Investing Strategies for the Thoughtful Investor, which since has become a value investing classic. Now out of print, Margin of Safety has sold on Amazon for $1,200 and eBay for $2,000. Another famous value investor is John Templeton. He first achieved investing success by buying shares of a number of companies in the aftermath of the stock market crash of 1929.

Martin J. Whitman is another well-regarded value investor. His approach is called safe-and-cheap which was hitherto referred to as financial-integrity approach. Martin Whitman focuses on acquiring common shares of companies with extremely strong financial position at a price reflecting meaningful discount to the estimated NAV of the company concerned. Martin Whitman believes it is ill-advised for investors to pay much attention to the trend of macro-factors (like employment, movement of interest rate, GDP, etc.) not so much because they are not important as because attempts to predict their movement are almost always futile. Martin Whitman's letters to shareholders of his Third Avenue Value Fund (TAVF) are considered valuable resources "for investors to pirate good ideas" by another famous investor Joel Greenblatt in his book on special-situation investment "You Can Be a Stock Market Genius".

Joel Greenblatt achieved annual returns at the hedge fund Gotham Capital of over 50% per year for 10 years from 1985 to 1995 before closing the fund and returning his investors' money. He is known for investing in special situations such as spin-offs, mergers and divestitures.

The Different Types of Orders on the Stock Market

Market Order

A market order is a buy or sell order to be executed by the broker immediately at current market prices. As long as there are willing sellers and buyers, a market order will be filled.

A market order is the simplest of the order types. Once the order is placed, the customer has no control over the price at which the transaction is executed. The broker is merely supposed to find the best price available at that time. In fast-moving markets, the price paid or received may be quite different from the last price quoted before the order was entered.

A market order for a large number of shares may be split by the broker across multiple participants on the other side of the transaction, resulting in different prices for some of the shares.

Limit Order

A limit order is an order to buy a security at no more (or sell at no less) than a specific price. This gives the customer some control over the price at which the trade is executed, but may prevent the order from being executed ("filled").

A buy limit order can only be executed by the broker at the limit price or lower. For example, if an investor wants to buy a stock but doesn't want to pay more than $20 for the stock, the investor can place a limit order to buy the stock at any price up to $20. By entering a limit order rather than a market order, the investor will not be caught buying the stock at $30 if the price rises sharply.

A sell limit order can only be executed at the limit price or higher.

A limit order to buy may never be executed if the market price surpasses the limit before the order can be filled. Because of the added complexity, some brokerages will charge more for executing a limit order than they would for a market order.

Both buy and sell orders can be additionally constrained. Two of the most common additional constraints are **Fill Or Kill** (FOK) and **All Or None** (AON). FOK orders are either filled (partially or completely) on the first attempt or canceled outright, while AON orders stipulate that the order must be completely filled or not filled at all (but still held on the order book for later execution).

Time in Force

A **day order** (the most common) is good only for one day. It is in force from when it is entered to the end of regular trading on the same day. A day order is assumed unless another type is specified.

A **good-til-cancelled order** requires a specific cancelling order. It can persist indefinitely (although brokers may set some limit, for example, 90 days). This is good for when the investor wishes to sit on the beach for a few weeks or when the investor wants to buy the stock at any price.

Most markets have single-price auctions at the beginning ("open") and the end ("close") of regular trading. An order may be specified on the close or on the open, then it is entered in an auction but has no effect otherwise. There is often some deadline, for example, orders must be in 20 minutes before the auction. They are single-price because all orders, if they transact at all, will transact at the same price, the open price and the close price respectively.

Combined with price instructions, there are market on close (MOC), market on open (MOO), limit on close (LOC), and limit on open (LOO). For example, a market-on-open order is guaranteed to get the open price, whatever that is; a buy limit-on-open order will be filled if the open price is lower and will not be filled if the open price is higher, and may or may not be filled if the open price is the same.

Fill-or-kill orders are usually limit orders that must be executed or cancelled immediately.

Conditional Orders

A conditional order is any order other than a limit order that requires the broker to check whether a specific condition has been met.

Stop Orders

A **stop order** (also stop loss order) is an order to buy (or sell) a security once the price of the security has climbed above (or dropped below) a specified stop price. When the specified stop price is reached, the stop order is entered as a market order (no limit).

With a stop order, the customer does not have to actively monitor how a stock is performing. However, because the order is triggered automatically when the stop price is reached, the stop price could be activated by a short-term fluctuation in a security's price. Once the stop price is reached, the stop order becomes a market order. In a fast-moving market, the price at which the trade is executed may be much different from the stop price. The use of stop orders is much more frequent for stocks, and futures, that trade on an exchange than in the over-the-counter (OTC) market.

A **sell stop order** is an instruction to sell at the best available price after the price goes below the stop price. A sell stop price is always below the current market price. For example, if an investor holds a stock currently valued at $50 and is worried that the value may drop, he/she can place a sell stop order at $40. If the share price drops to $40, the broker will sell the stock at the next available price. This can limit the investor's losses (if the stop price is at or below the purchase price) or lock in some of the investor's profits.

A **buy stop order** is typically used to limit a loss (or to protect an existing profit) on a short sale. A buy stop price is always above the current market price. For example, if an investor sells a stock short hoping the stock price goes down in order to give the borrowed shares back at a lower price (Covering), the investor may use a buy stop order to protect himself against losses if the price goes too high.

A **stop limit order** combines the features of a stop order and a limit order. Once the stop price is reached, the stop-limit order becomes a limit order to buy (or to sell) at no more (or less) than a specified price. As with all limit orders, a stop-limit order will not get filled if the security's price never reaches the specified limit price.

A **trailing stop order** is entered with a stop parameter that creates a moving or trailing activation price, hence the name. This parameter is entered as a percentage change or actual specific amount of rise (or fall) in the security price. Trailing stop sell orders are used to maximize and protect profit as a stock's price rises and limit losses when its price falls. Trailing stop buy orders are used to maximize profit when a stock's price is falling and limit losses when it is rising.

For example, a trader has bought stock ABC at $10.00 and immediately places a trailing stop sell order to sell ABC with a $1.00 trailing stop. This sets the stop price to $9.00. After placing the order, ABC doesn't exceed $10.00 and falls to a low of $9.01. The trailing stop order is not executed because ABC has not fallen $1.00 from $10.00. Later, the stock rises to a high of $15.00 which resets the stop price to $14.00. It then falls to $14.00 ($1.00 from its high of $15.00) and the trailing stop sell order is entered as a market order.

A **trailing stop limit order** is similar to a trailing stop order. Instead of selling at market price when triggered, the order becomes a limit order.

Market-if-touched Order

A **buy market-if-touched order** is an order to buy at the best available price, if the market price goes down to the "if touched" level. As soon as this trigger price is touched the order becomes a market buy order.

A **sell market-if-touched order** is an order to sell at the best available price, if the market price goes up to the "if touched" level. As soon as this trigger price is touched the order becomes a market sell order.

One Cancels Other Orders

One **cancels other orders** (OCO) are used when the trader wishes to capitalize on only one of two or more possible trading possibilities. For instance, the trader may wish to trade stock ABC at $10.00 or XYZ at $20.00. In this case, they would execute an OCO order composed of two parts: A limit order for

ABC at $10.00, and a limit order for XYZ at $20.00. If ABC reaches $10.00, ABC's limit order would be executed, and the XYZ limit order would be canceled.

Tick Sensitive Orders

An uptick is when the last (non-zero) price change is positive, and a downtick is when the last (non-zero) price change is negative. Any tick sensitive instruction can be entered at the trader's option, for example buy on downtick, although these orders are rare.

Discretionary Order

A **discretionary order** is an order that allows the broker to delay the execution at their discretion to try to get a better price. These are sometimes called not held orders.

Quantity and Display Instructions

A broker may be instructed not to display the order to the market. For example an **"All-or-none" buy limit order** is an order to buy at the specified price if another trader is offering to sell the full amount of the order, but otherwise not display the order. A so-called "**iceberg order**" requires the broker to display only a small part of the order, leaving a large undisplayed quantity "below the surface".

Electronic Markets

All of the above orders could be entered into an electronic market, but simple market and limit orders are generally encouraged by order priority rules. Market orders are given greatest priority, followed by limit orders. If a limit order has priority it is the next trade that will be executed at the limit price. Simple limit orders are generally given high priority, based only on a first-come-first-served rule. Conditional orders are generally given priority based on the time the condition is met. "Iceberg orders" and "dark pool orders" (which are not displayed) are given lower priority.

Margins Explained

A margin is collateral that the holder of a position in securities, options, or futures contracts has to deposit to cover the credit risk of his counterparty (most often his broker). This risk can arise if the holder has done any of the following:

- borrowed cash from the counterparty to buy securities or options,
- sold securities or options short, or
- entered into a futures contract.

The collateral can be in the form of cash or securities, and it is deposited in a margin account. On U.S. futures exchanges, "margin" was formally called performance bond.

Margin Buying

Margin buying is buying securities with cash borrowed from a broker, using other securities as collateral. This has the effect of magnifying any profit or loss made on the securities. The securities serve as collateral for the loan. The net value, i.e. the difference between the value of the securities and the loan, is initially equal to the amount of one's own cash used. This difference has to stay above a minimum margin requirement. This is to protect the broker against a fall in value of the securities to the point that they no longer cover the loan.

Some say that in the 1920s, margin requirements were loose. In other words, brokers required investors to put in very little of their own money. When stock markets plummeted, the net value of the positions rapidly fell below the minimum margin requirements, forcing investors to sell their positions. This is cited as a factor contributing to the Stock Market Crash of 1929, which in turn contributed to the Great Depression. However, as reported in Peter Rappoport and Eugene N. White's 1994 paper: “Was the Crash of 1929 Expected”[1], all sources indicate that beginning in either late 1928 or early 1929, "margin requirements began to rise to historic new levels. The typical peak rates on brokers' loans were 40-50 percent. Brokerage houses followed suit and demanded higher margin from investors."

---

[1] http://www.jstor.org/stable/2117982

Example

Jane buys a share in a company for $100, using $20 of her own money, and $80 borrowed from her broker. The net value (share - loan) is $20. The broker wants a minimum margin requirement of $10.

Suppose the share goes down to $85. The net value is now only $5, and Jane will either have to sell the share or repay part of the loan (so that the net value of her position is again above $10).

Margin Requirements

Current Liquidating Margin

The current liquidating margin is the value of a securities position if the position were liquidated now. In other words, if the holder has a short position, this is the money needed to buy back, if he is long it is the money he can raise by selling it.

Variation Margin

The variation margin or maintenance margin is not collateral, but a daily offsetting of profits and losses. Futures are marked-to-market every day, so the current price is compared to the previous day's price. The profit or loss on the day of a position is then paid to or debited from the holder by the futures exchange. This is possible, because the exchange is the central counterparty to all contracts, and the number of long contracts equals the number of short contracts. Certain other exchange traded derivatives, such as options on futures contracts, are marked-to-market in the same way.

Premium Margin

The seller of an option has the obligation to deliver the underlying of the option if it is exercised. To ensure he can fulfill this obligation, he has to deposit collateral. This premium margin is equal to the premium that he would need to pay to buy back the option and close out his position.

Additional Margin

Additional margin is intended to cover a potential fall in the value of the position on the following trading day. This is calculated as the potential loss in a worst-case scenario.

Minimum Margin Requirement

The minimum margin requirement is now the sum of these different types of margin requirements. The margin (collateral) deposited in the margin account has to be at least equal to this minimum. If the investor has many positions with the exchange, these margin requirements can simply be netted.

Example 1

An investor sells a call option, where the buyer has the right to buy 100 shares in Universal Widgets S.A. at 90¢. He receives an option premium of 14¢. The value of the option is 14¢, so this is the premium margin. The exchange has calculated, using historical prices, that the option value won't go above 17¢ the next day, with 99% certainty. Therefore, the additional margin requirement is set at 3¢, and the investor has to post at least 14¢ + 3¢ = 17¢ in his margin account as collateral.

Example 2

Futures contracts on sweet crude oil closed the day at $65. The exchange sets the additional margin requirement at $2, which the holder of a long position pays as collateral in his margin account. A day later, the futures close at $66. The exchange now pays the profit of $1 in the mark-to-market to the holder. The margin account still holds only the $2.

Example 3

An investor is long 50 shares in Universal Widgets Ltd, trading at 120 pence (£1.20) each. The broker sets an additional margin requirement of 20 pence per share, so £10 for the total position. The current liquidating margin is currently £60 in favour of the investor. The minimum margin requirement is now -(!)£60 + £10 = -£50. In other words, the investor can run a deficit of £50 in his margin account and still fulfill his margin obligations. This is the same as saying he can borrow up to £50 from the broker.

Initial and Maintenance Margin Requirements

The initial margin requirement is the amount required to be collateralized in order to open a position. Thereafter, the amount required to be kept in collateral until the position is closed is the maintenance requirement. The maintenance requirement is the minimum amount to be collateralized in order to keep an open position. It is generally lower than the initial requirement. This allows the price to move against the margin without forcing a margin call immediately after the initial transaction. On instruments determined to be especially risky, however, the regulators, the exchange or the broker may set the maintenance requirement higher than normal or equal to the initial requirement to reduce their exposure to the risk accepted by the trader.

Margin Call

When the margin posted in the margin account is below the minimum margin requirement, the broker or exchange issues a margin call. The investor now either has to increase the margin that they have deposited, or they can close out their position. They can do this by selling the securities, options or futures if they are long and by buying them back if they are short. If they don't do any of this the broker can sell his securities to meet the margin call.

Price of Stock for Margin Calls

The minimum margin requirement, sometimes called the maintenance margin requirement, is the ratio set for:

- (Stock Equity - Leveraged Dollars) to Stock Equity

were 60%:

- Stock Equity: $50 * 1000 = $50,000
- Leveraged Dollars or amount borrowed: ($50 * 1000)* (1-60%) = $20,000

So the maintenance margin requirement uses the above variables to form a ratio that investors have to abide by in order to keep the account active.

The point is, let's say the minimum margin requirement is reduced from 60% to 25% - At what price would the investor be getting a margin call? Let P be the price, so 1000P in our case is the Stock Equity.

- (Stock Equity - Leveraged Dollars) divide by Stock Equity = 25%
- (1000P - $20,000)/1000P = 0.25
- (1000P - $20,000) = 250P
- P = $26.67

So if the stock price drops from $50 to $26.67, investors will be called to add additional funds to the account to make up for the loss in stock equity.

Reduced Margins

Margin requirements are reduced for positions that offset each other. For instance spread traders who have offsetting futures contracts do not have to deposit collateral both for their short position and their long position. The exchange calculates the loss in a worst case scenario of the total position.

Margin-Equity Ratio

Margin-equity ratio is a term used by speculators, representing the amount of their trading capital that is being held as margin at any particular time. Traders would rarely (and unadvisedly) hold 100% of their capital as margin. The probability of losing their entire capital at some point would be high. By contrast, if the margin-equity ratio is so low as to make the trader's capital equal to the value of the futures contract itself, then they would not profit from the inherent leverage implicit in futures trading. A conservative trader might hold a margin-equity ratio of 15%, while a more aggressive trader might hold 40%.

Return on Margin

Return on Margin (ROM) is often used to judge performance because it represents the net gain or net loss compared to the exchange's perceived risk as reflected in required margin. ROM may be calculated (realized return) / (initial margin). The annualized ROM is equal to

- $(ROM + 1)^{(year/trade\_duration)} - 1$

For example if a trader earns 10% on margin in two months, that would be about 77% annualized

- $(ROM + 1)^{1/6} - 1 = 0.1$ thus $ROM = 1.1^{6} - 1$

Sometimes, Return on Margin will also take into account peripheral charges such as brokerage fees and interest paid on the sum borrowed.

Random Walk Hypothesis

The random walk hypothesis is a financial theory stating that stock market prices evolve according to a random walk and thus the prices of the stock market cannot be predicted. It has been described as 'jibing' with the efficient market hypothesis. Economists have historically accepted the random walk hypothesis. They have run several tests and continue to believe that stock prices are completely random because of the efficiency of the market.

The term was popularized by the 1973 book, A Random Walk Down Wall Street, by Burton Malkiel, currently a Professor of Economics and Finance at Princeton University, and was used earlier in Eugene Fama's 1965 article Random Walks In Stock Market Prices, which was a less technical version of his Ph.D. thesis. The theory that stock prices move randomly was earlier proposed by Maurice Kendall in his 1953 paper, The Analytics of Economic Time Series.

Testing the Hypothesis

Burton G. Malkiel, an economist professor at Princeton University and writer of A Random Walk Down Wall Street, performed a test where his students were given a hypothetical stock that was initially worth fifty dollars. The closing stock price for each day was determined by a coin flip. If the result was heads, the price would close a half point higher, but if the result was tails, it would close a half point lower. Thus, each time, the price had a fifty-fifty chance of closing higher or lower than the previous day. Cycles or trends were determined from the tests. Malkiel then took the results in a chart and graph form to a chartist, a person who "seeks to predict future movements by seeking to interpret past patterns on the assumption that 'history tends to repeat itself'". The chartist told Malkiel that they needed to immediately buy the stock. When Malkiel told him it was based purely on flipping a coin, the chartist was very unhappy. Malkiel argued that this indicates that the market and stocks could be just as random as flipping a coin.

The random walk hypothesis was also applied to NBA basketball. Psychologists made a detailed study of every shot the Philadelphia 76ers made over one and a half seasons of basketball. The psychologists found no positive correlation between the previous shots and the outcomes of the shots afterwards. Economists and believers in the random walk hypothesis apply this to the stock market. The actual lack of correlation of past and present can be easily seen. If a stock goes up one day, no stock market participant can accurately predict that it will rise again the next. Just as a basketball player with the "hot hand" can miss his or her next shot, the stock that seems to be on the rise can fall at any time, making it completely random.

A Non-Random Walk Hypothesis

There are other economists, professors, and investors who believe that the market is predictable to some degree. These people believe that prices may move in trends and that the study of past prices can be used to forecast future price direction. There have been some economic studies that support this view, and a book has been written by two professors of economics that tries to prove the random walk hypothesis wrong.

Martin Weber, a leading researcher in behavioral finance, has performed many tests and studies on finding trends in the stock market. In one of his key studies, he observed the stock market for ten years. Throughout that period, he looked at the market prices for noticeable trends and found that stocks with high price increases in the first five years tended to become under-performers in the following five years. Weber and other believers in the non-random walk hypothesis cite this as a key contributor and contradictor to the random walk hypothesis.

Another test that Weber ran that contradicts the random walk hypothesis, was finding stocks that have had an upward revision for earnings outperform other stocks in the forthcoming six months. With this knowledge, investors can have an edge in predicting what stocks to pull out of the market and which stocks — the stocks with the upward revision — to leave in. Martin Weber's studies detract from the random walk hypothesis, because according to Weber, there are trends and other tips to predicting the stock market.

Professors Andrew W. Lo and Archie Craig MacKinlay, professors of Finance at the MIT Sloan School of Management and the University of Pennsylvania, respectively, have also tried to prove the random walk theory wrong. They wrote the book A Non-Random Walk Down Wall Street, which goes through a number of tests and studies that try to prove there are trends in the stock market and that they are somewhat predictable.

They prove it with what is called the simple volatility-based specification test, which is an equation that states:

$$X_t = \mu + X_{t-1} + \epsilon_t$$

Where:

X_t is the price of the stock at time t μ is an arbitrary drift parameter ε_t is a random disturbance term.

With this equation, they have been able to put in stock prices over the last number of years, and figure out the trends that have unfolded. They have found small incremental changes in the stocks throughout the years. Through these changes, Lo and MacKinlay believe that the stock market is predictable, thus contradicting the random walk hypothesis. Lo and MacKinlay have authored a paper, the Adaptive Market Hypothesis, which puts forth another way of looking at predictability of price changes.

Kondratiev Wave

Kondratiev waves are also called grand super cycles, surges, long waves or K-waves — are described as regular, sinusoidal cycles in the modern (capitalist) world economy. Averaging fifty and ranging from approximately forty to sixty years in length, the cycles consist of alternating periods between high sectoral growth and periods of slower growth. Most academic economists do not posit the existence of these waves.

The Russian economist Nikolai Kondratiev (1892-1938) was the first to bring these observations international attention in his book The Major Economic Cycles (1925) alongside other works written in the same decade. Two Dutch economists, J. van Gelderen (1891-1940) and Samuel de Wolff, previously argued for the existence of 50- to 60-year cycles in 1913. However, only recently has the work of de Wolff and van Gelderen been translated from Dutch to reach a wider audience.

Later, Joseph Schumpeter suggested in Business Cycles to name the cycle "Kondratieff wave" in honor of the economist who first noticed them. In the 1950s, French economist Francois Simiand proposed to name the ascendant period of the cycle "Phase A" and the downward period "Phase B". Some market commentators divide the Kondratiev wave into four 'seasons', namely, the Kondratiev Spring (improvement - plateau) and Summer (acceleration - prosperity) of the ascendant period and the Kondratiev Fall (recession - plateau) and Winter (acceleration - depression) of the downward characteristics of the cycle

Characteristics of the Cycle

The business cycle is supposedly more visible in international production data than in individual national economies. It affects all the sectors of an economy and concerns output rather than prices (although Kondratieff had made observations about the prices only). According to Kondratieff, the ascendant phase is characterized by an increase in prices and low interest rates, while the other phase consists of a decrease in prices and high interest rates.

Kondratieff identified three phases in the cycle: expansion, stagnation, recession. More common today is the division into four periods with a turning point (collapse) between the first and second two. Writing in the 1920s, Kondratieff proposed to apply the theory to the XIXth century:

- 1790 - 1849 with a turning point in 1815.
- 1850 - 1896 with a turning point in 1873.
- Kondratieff supposed that in 1896, a new cycle had started.

It is tempting to expand the theory to the twentieth and twenty-first centuries. Some economists, such as Schumpeterian, have proposed that the third cycle peaked with World War I and ended with World War II after a turning point in 1929. A fourth cycle may have roughly coincided with the Cold War: beginning in 1949, turning with the economic peak of the mid-1960s and the Vietnam War escalation, hitting a trough in 1982 amidst growing predictions in the United States of worldwide Soviet domination and ending with the fall of the Berlin Wall in 1989. The current cycle most likely peaked in 1999 with a possible winter phase beginning in late 2008. The Austrian-school economists point out that extreme price inflation in the absence of economic growth is a form of capital destruction, allowing either stagflation (as in the 1970s and much of the 2000s during the gold and oil price run-ups) or deflation (as in the 1930s and possibly following the crash in commodity prices beginning in 2008) to represent a recession or depression phase of the Kondratieff theory.

Explanation of the Cycleriod.

Early on, four schools of thought emerged as to why capitalist economies have these long waves. These schools of thought revolved around innovations, capital investment, war and capitalist crisis. According to the innovation theory, these waves arise from the bunching of basic innovations that launch technological revolutions that in turn create leading industrial or commercial sectors. Kondratiev's ideas were taken up by Joseph Schumpeter in the 1930s. The theory hypothesized the existence of very long-run macroeconomic and price cycles, originally estimated to last 50-54 years.

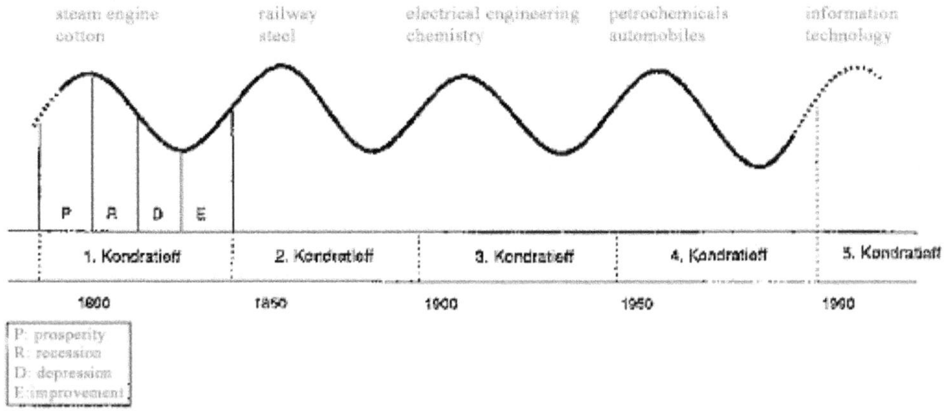

Picture 1: A rough schematic drawing showing the "World Economy" over time according to the Kondratiev theory

Since the inception of the theories, various studies have expanded the range of possible cycles, finding longer or shorter cycles in the data. The Marxist scholar Ernest Mandel revived interest in long wave theory with his 1964 essay predicting the end of the long boom after five years and in his Alfred Marshall lectures in 1979. However, in Mandel's theory, there are no long "cycles", only distinct epochs of faster and slower growth spanning 20-25 years.

Long wave theory is not accepted by most academic economists, but it is one of the bases of innovation-based, development, and evolutionary economics, i.e. the main heterodox stream in economics. Among economists who accept it, there has been no universal agreement about the start and the end years of particular waves. This points to another criticism of the theory which is that it amounts to seeing patterns in a mass of statistics that aren't really there. Moreover, there is a lack of agreement over the cause of this phenomenon.

Most cycle theorists agree, however, with the "Schumpeter-Freeman-Perez" paradigm of five waves so far since the industrial revolution, and the sixth one to come. These five cycles are

- The Industrial Revolution--1771
- The Age of Steam and Railways--1829
- The Age of Steel, Electricity and Heavy Engineering--1875
- The Age of Oil, the Automobile and Mass Production--1908
- The Age of Information and Telecommunications--1971

According to this theory, we are currently at the turning-point of the 5th Kondratiev. Some scholars, particularly Immanuel Wallerstein, argue that cycles of global war are tied to Capitalist Long Waves. Major, highly-destructive wars tend to begin just prior to an output upswing.

Initial Public Offering

Initial public offering (IPO) also referred to simply as a "public offering" is when a company issues common stock or shares to the public for the first time. They are often issued by smaller, younger companies seeking capital to expand but can also be done by large privately-owned companies looking to become publicly traded or by companies that are already on the stock market but want to raise more money. Conery a German solar cells manufacturer raised capital in November 2008 to support their restructuring efforts of the troubled company.

In an IPO, the issuer may obtain the assistance of an underwriting firm which helps it determine what type of security to issue (common or preferred) but also the best offering price and the time to bring it to the market.

IPOs can be a risky investment. For the individual investor, it is tough to predict what the stock or shares will do on its initial day of trading and in the near future since there is often little historical data with which to analyze the company. Also, most IPOs are of companies going through a transitory growth period and they are therefore subject to additional uncertainty regarding their future value.

Reasons for listing a Company on the Stock Exchange

When a company lists its shares on a public exchange it will almost invariably look to issue additional new shares in order to raise extra capital at the same time. The money paid by investors for the newly-issued shares goes directly to the company (in contrast to a later trade of shares on the exchange, where the money passes between investors). An IPO, therefore, allows a company to tap a wide pool of stock market investors to provide it with large volumes of capital for future growth. The company is never required to repay the capital but the new shareholders have a right to future profits distributed by the company and the right to a capital distribution in case of a dissolution.

The existing shareholders will see their shareholdings diluted as a proportion of the company's shares. However, they hope that the capital investment will make their shareholdings more valuable in absolute terms.

In addition, once a company is listed it will be able to issue further shares via a rights issue, thereby again providing itself with capital for expansion without incurring any debt. This regular ability to raise large amounts of capital from the general market, rather than having to seek and negotiate with individual investors, is a key incentive for many companies seeking to list.

The Procedure of an IPO

IPOs generally involve one or more investment banks as "underwriters." The company offering its shares, called the "issuer," enters a contract with a lead underwriter to sell its shares to the public. The underwriter then approaches investors with offers to sell these shares.

The sale (that is, the allocation and pricing) of shares in an IPO may take several forms. Common methods include:

- Dutch auction
- Firm commitment
- Best efforts
- Bought deal
- Self Distribution of Stock

A large IPO is usually underwritten by a "syndicate" of investment banks led by one or more major investment banks (lead underwriter). Upon selling the shares the underwriters keep a commission based on a percentage of the value of the shares sold. Usually, the lead underwriters, i.e. the underwriters selling the largest proportions of the IPO, take the highest commissions—up to 8% in some cases.

Multinational IPOs may have as many as three syndicates to deal with differing legal requirements in both the issuer's domestic market and other regions. For example, an issuer based in the E.U. may be represented by the main selling syndicate in its domestic market, Europe, in addition to separate syndicates or selling groups for US/Canada and for Asia. Usually, the lead underwriter in the main selling group is also the lead bank in the other selling groups.

Because of the wide array of legal requirements, IPOs typically involve one or more law firms with major practices in securities law.

Usually, the offering will include the issuance of new shares, intended to raise new capital, as well the secondary sale of existing shares. However, certain regulatory restrictions and restrictions imposed by the lead underwriter are often placed on the sale of existing shares.

Public offerings are primarily sold to institutional investors but some shares are also allocated to the underwriters' retail investors. A broker selling shares of a public offering to his clients is paid through a sales credit instead of a commission. The client pays no commission to purchase the shares of a public offering The purchase price simply includes the built-in sales credit.

The issuer usually allows the underwriters an option to increase the size of the offering by up to 15% under certain circumstance known as the greenshoe or overallotment option.

Business Cycle

In the United States, during the dot-com bubble of the late 1990s many venture capital driven companies were started and seeking to cash in on the bull market. Hence they quickly offered IPOs. Usually, stock price spiraled upwards as soon as a company went public. Investors sought to get in at the ground-level of the next potential Microsoft and Netscape.

Initial founders could often become overnight millionaires and due to generous stock options employees could make a great deal of money as well. The majority of IPOs could be found on the Nasdaq stock exchange which lists companies related to computer and information technology. However, in spite of the large amounts of financial resources made available to relatively young and untested firms (often in multiple rounds of financing) the vast majority of them rapidly entered a cash crisis. Such a crisis was particularly likely in the case of firms where the founding team liquidated a substantial portion of their stake in the firm at or soon after the IPO (Mudambi and Treichel, 2005).

This phenomenon was not limited to the United States. In Japan, for example, a similar situation occurred. Some companies were operated in a similar way in that their only goal was to have an IPO. Some stock exchanges were set up for those companies such as Nasdaq Japan.

Perhaps the clearest bubbles in the history of hot IPO markets were in 1929 when closed-end fund IPOs sold at enormous premiums to their net asset value and in 1989 when closed-end country fund IPOs sold at enormous premiums to the net asset value. What makes these bubbles so clear is the ability to compare market prices for shares in the closed-end funds to the value of the shares in the funds' portfolios. **When market prices are multiples of the underlying value, bubbles are occurring.**

The Dutch Auction

A venture capitalist named Bill Hambrecht has attempted to devise a method that can reduce the inefficient process of an IPO. He devised a way to issue shares through a Dutch auction as an attempt to minimize the extreme under pricing that underwriters were nurturing. Google is one established company that went public through the use of auction. Google's share price rose 17% in its first day of trading despite the auction method. Perception of IPOs can be controversial. For those who view a successful IPO to be one that raises as much money as possible, the IPO was a total failure. For those who view a successful IPO from the kind of investors that eventually gained from the under pricing, the IPO was a complete success. It's important to note that different sets of investors bid in auctions versus the open market—the more institutions bid, fewer private individuals bid. Google may be a special case however as many individual investors bought the stock based on long-term valuation shortly after it launched its IPO, they drove it beyond institutional valuation.

Pricing

Historically, IPOs both globally and in the US have been underpriced. The effect of initial under pricing an IPO is to generate additional interest in the stock when it first becomes publicly traded. This can lead to significant gains for investors who have been allocated shares of the IPO at the offering price. However, under pricing an IPO results in "money left on the table"—lost capital that could have been raised for the company had the stock been offered at a higher price.

The danger of overpricing is also an important consideration. If a stock is offered to the public at a higher price than the market will pay, the underwriters may have trouble meeting their commitments to sell shares. Even if they sell all of the issued shares, if the stock falls in value on the first day of trading, it may lose its marketability and hence even more of its value.

Investment banks, therefore, take many factors into consideration when pricing an IPO and attempt to reach an offering price that is low enough to stimulate interest in the stock but high enough to raise an adequate amount of capital for the company. The process of determining an optimal price usually involves the underwriters ("syndicate") arranging share purchase commitments from leading institutional investors.

Determining the Issue Price

A company that is planning an IPO appoints lead managers to help it decide on an appropriate price at which the shares should be issued. There are two ways in which the price of an IPO can be determined: Either the company, with the help of its lead managers, fixes a price or the price is arrived at through the process of book building.

Quiet Period

There are two time windows commonly referred to as "quiet periods" during an IPO's history. The first and the one linked above is the period of time following the filing of the company's S-1 but before SEC staff declare the registration statement effective. During this time, issuers, company insiders, analysts and other parties are legally restricted in their ability to discuss or promote the upcoming IPO.

The other "quiet period" refers to a period of 40 calendar days following an IPO's first day of public trading. During this time insiders and any underwriters involved in the IPO are restricted from issuing any earnings forecasts or research reports for the company. Regulatory changes enacted by the SEC as part of the Global Settlement, enlarged the "quiet period" from 25 days to 40 days on July 9, 2002. When the quiet period is over generally the lead underwriters will initiate research coverage on the firm. Additionally, the NASD and NYSE have approved a rule mandating a 10-day quiet period after a Secondary Offering and a 15-day quiet period both before and after expiration of a "lock-up agreement" for a securities offering.

Secondary Market Offering

A follow-on offering (often called secondary public offering or just secondary offering) is an issuance of stock subsequent to the company's initial public offering. A follow-on offering can be either of two types (or a mixture of both): Dilutive and non-dilutive (as rights issue). Furthermore it could be a cash issue or a capital increase in return for stock.

A secondary offering is an offering of securities by a shareholder of the company (as opposed to the company itself, which is a primary offering). For example, Google's initial public offering (IPO) included both a primary offering (issuance of Google stock by Google) and a secondary offering (sale of Google stock held by shareholders including the founders).

In the case of the dilutive offering (seasoned equity offering) the company's board of directors agrees to increase the share float for the purpose of selling more equity in the company. This new inflow of cash might be used to pay off some debt or used for needed company expansion. When new shares are created and then sold by the company the number of shares outstanding increases and this causes dilution of earnings on a per share basis. Usually the gain of cash inflow from the sale is strategic and is considered positive for the longer term goals of the company and its shareholders. Some owners of the stock however may not view the event as favorably over a more short term valuation horizon.

The non-dilutive type of follow-on offering is when privately held shares are offered for sale by company directors or other insiders (such as venture capitalists) who may be looking to diversify their holdings. Because no new shares are created the offering is not dilutive to existing shareholders but the proceeds from the sale do not benefit the company in any way. Usually however, the increase in available shares allows more institutions to take non-trivial positions in the company.

As with an IPO, the investment banks who are serving as underwriters of the follow-on offering will often be offered the use of a greenshoe or over-allotment option by the selling company.

Behavioral Finance

Behavioral economics and behavioral finance are closely related fields which apply scientific research on human, social, cognitive and emotional factors to better understand economic decisions and how they affect market prices, returns and the allocation of resources. The fields are primarily concerned with the bounds of rationality (selfishness, self-control) of economic agents. Behavioral models typically integrate insights from psychology with neo-classical economic theory.

Academics are divided between considering Behavioral Finance as supporting some tools of technical analysis by explaining market trends and considering some aspects of technical analysis as behavioral biases (representativeness heuristic, self fulfilling prophecy).

Behavioral analysts are mostly concerned with the effects of market decisions, but also those of public choice, another source of economic decisions with some similar biases.

History

During the classical period, economics had a close link with psychology. For example Adam Smith wrote The Theory of Moral Sentiments an important text describing psychological principles of individual behavior. Jeremy Bentham wrote extensively on the psychological underpinnings of utility.

Economists began to distance themselves from psychology during the development of neo-classical economics as they sought to reshape the discipline as a natural science with explanations of economic behavior deduced from assumptions about the nature of economic agents. The concept of homo economicus was developed and the psychology of this entity was fundamentally rational. Nevertheless, psychological explanations continued to inform the analysis of many important figures in the development of neo-classical economics such as Francis Edgeworth, Vilfredo Pareto, Irving Fisher and John Maynard Keynes.

Although psychology had nearly disappeared from economic discussions by the mid 20th century, it somehow managed to stage a resurgence. Certain factors were responsible for this resurgence in the continued development of behavioral economics. Expected utility and discounted utility models began to gain wide acceptance, generating testable hypotheses about decision making under uncertainty and intertemporal consumption respectively. Soon a number of observed and repeatable anomalies challenged those hypotheses. Furthermore, during the 1960s cognitive psychology had begun to shed more light on the brain as an information processing device (in contrast to behaviorist models). Psychologists in this field such as Ward Edwards, Amos Tversky and Daniel Kahneman began to compare their cognitive models of decision making under risk and uncertainty to economic models of rational behavior. In Mathematical psychology, there is a longstanding interest in the transitivity of preference and what kind of measurement scale utility constitutes (Luce, 2000).

An important paper in the development of the behavioral finance and economics fields was written by Kahneman and Tversky in 1979. This paper, 'Prospect theory: An Analysis of Decision Under Risk' used cognitive psychological techniques to explain a number of documented divergences of economic decision making from neo-classical theory. Over time many other psychological effects have been incorporated into behavioral finance, such as overconfidence and the effects of limited attention. Further milestones in the development of the field include a special 1997 edition of the Quarterly Journal of Economics ('In Memory of Amos Tversky') devoted to the topic of behavioral economics and the award of the Nobel prize to Daniel Kahneman in 2002 "for having integrated insights from psychological research into economic science, especially concerning human judgment and decision-making under uncertainty".

Prospect theory is an example of generalized expected utility theory. Although not commonly included in discussions of the field of behavioral economics generalized expected utility theory is similarly motivated by concerns about the descriptive inaccuracy of expected utility theory.

Behavioral economics has also been applied to problems of intertemporal choice. The most prominent idea is that of hyperbolic discounting, proposed by George Ainslie (1975), in which a high rate of discount is used between the present and the near future and a lower rate between the near future and the far future. This pattern of discounting is dynamically inconsistent (or time-inconsistent) and therefore inconsistent with some models of rational choice since the rate of discount between time t and t+1 will be low at time t-1, when t is the near future, but high at time t when t is the present and time t+1 the near future. As part of the discussion of hypberbolic discounting has been animal and human work on Melioration theory and Matching Law of Richard Herrnstein. They suggest that behavior is not based on expected utility rather it is based on previous reinforcement experience.

Methodology

At the outset behavioral economics and finance theories had been developed almost exclusively from experimental observations and survey responses, although in more recent times real world data have taken a more prominent position. Functional magnetic resonance imaging fMRI has complemented this effort through its use in determining which areas of the brain are active during various steps of economic decision making. Experiments simulating market situations such as stock market trading and auctions are seen as particularly useful as they can be used to isolate the effect of a particular bias upon behavior. Observed market behavior can typically be explained in a number of ways, carefully designed experiments can help narrow the range of plausible explanations. Experiments are designed to be incentive-compatible, with binding transactions involving real money being the "norm".

Key observations

There are three main themes in behavioral finance and economics:

- **Heuristics**: People often make decisions based on approximate rules of thumb, not strictly rational analysis.
- **Framing**: The way a problem or decision is presented to the decision maker will affect his action.
- **Market inefficiencies**: There are explanations for observed market outcomes that are contrary to rational expectations and market efficiency. These include mis-pricings, non-rational decision making, and return anomalies. Richard Thaler, in particular, has described specific market anomalies from a behavioral perspective.

Recently, Barberis, Shleifer, and Vishny (1998), as well as Daniel, Hirshleifer, and Subrahmanyam (1998) have built models based on extrapolation (seeing patterns in random sequences) and overconfidence to explain security market over- and underreactions, though such models have not been used in the money management industry. These models assume that errors or biases are correlated across agents so that they do not cancel out in aggregate. This would be the case if a large fraction of agents look at the same signal (such as the advice of an analyst) or have a common bias.

More generally, cognitive biases may also have strong anomalous effects in the aggregate if there is a social contamination with a strong emotional content (collective greed or fear), leading to more widespread phenomena such as herding and groupthink. Behavioral finance and economics rests as much on social psychology within large groups as on individual psychology. However, some behavioral models explicitly demonstrate that a small but significant anomalous group can also have market-wide effects (eg. Fehr and Schmidt, 1999).

Behavioral finance topics

Some central issues in behavioral finance include "Why investors and managers (lenders and borrowers as well) make systematic errors". It shows how those errors affect prices and returns (creating market inefficiencies). It also shows what managers of firms, other institutions and financial players might do to take advantage of market inefficiencies (arbitrage behavior).

Behavioral finance highlights certain inefficiencies and among these inefficiencies are underreactions or overreactions to information, as causes of market trends and in extreme cases of bubbles and crashes). Such misreactions have been attributed to limited investor attention, overconfidence / overoptimism, and mimicry (herding instinct) and noise trading.

Other key observations made in behavioral finance literature include the lack of symmetry (disymmetry) between decisions to acquire or keep resources, called colloquially the "bird in the bush" paradox, and the strong loss aversion or regret attached to any decision where some emotionally valued resources (e.g. a home) might be totally lost. Loss aversion appears to manifest itself in investor behavior as an unwillingness to sell shares or other equity, if doing so would force the trader to realise a nominal loss (Genesove & Mayer, 2001). It may also help explain why housing market prices do not adjust downwards to market clearing levels during periods of low demand.

Benartzi and Thaler (1995), applying a version of prospect theory, claim to have solved the equity premium puzzle, something conventional finance models have been unable to do so far.

Some current researchers in experimental finance use the experimental method, e.g. creating an artificial market by some kind of simulation software to study people's decision-making process and behavior in financial markets.

Behavioral Finance Models

Some financial models used in money management and asset valuation use behavioral finance parameters, for example:

- Thaler's model of price reactions to information, with three phases, underreaction-adjustment-overreaction, creating a price trend

  One characteristic of overreaction is that the average return of asset prices following a series of announcements of good news is lower than the average return following a series of bad announcements. In other words overreaction occurs if the market reacts too strongly or for too long (persistent trend) to news that it subsequently needs to be compensated in the opposite direction. As a result, assets that were winners in the past should not be seen as an indication to invest in as their risk adjusted returns in the future are relatively low compared to stocks that were defined as losers in the past.

Criticisms of Behavioral Finance

Critics of behavioral finance, such as Eugene Fama typically support the efficient market theory (though Fama may have reversed his position in recent years). They contend that behavioral finance is more a collection of anomalies than a true branch of finance and that these anomalies will eventually be priced out of the market or explained by appealing to market microstructure arguments. However, a distinction should be noted between individual biases and social biases; the former can be averaged out by the market, while the other can create feedback loops that drive the market further and further from the equilibrium of the "fair price".

A specific example of this criticism is found in some attempted explanations of the equity premium puzzle. It is argued that the puzzle simply arises due to entry barriers (both practical and psychological) which have traditionally impeded entry by individuals into the stock market, and that returns between stocks and bonds should stabilize as electronic resources open up the stock market to a greater number of traders (See Freeman, 2004 for a review). In reply, others contend that most personal investment funds are managed through superannuation funds, so the effect of these putative barriers to entry would be minimal. In addition, professional investors and fund managers seem to hold more bonds than one would expect given return differentials.

Quantitative Behavioral Finance

Quantitative behavioral finance is a new discipline that uses mathematical and statistical methodology to understand behavioral biases in conjunction with valuation. Some of this endeavor has been lead by Gunduz Caginalp (Professor of Mathematics and Editor of Journal of Behavioral Finance during 2001-2004) and collaborators including Vernon Smith (2002 Nobel Laureate in Economics), David Porter, Don Balenovich, Vladimira Ilieva, Ahmet Duran, Huseyin Merdan). Studies by Jeff Madura, Ray Sturm and others have demonstrated significant behavioral effects in stocks and exchange traded funds.

The research can be grouped into the following areas:

1. Empirical studies that demonstrate significant deviations from classical theories
2. Modeling using the concepts of behavioral effects together with the non-classical assumption of the finiteness of assets
3. Forecasting based on these methods
4. Studies of experimental asset markets and use of models to forecast experiments

Financial Basics

Investment Theory

Investment theory encompasses the body of knowledge used to support the decision-making process of choosing investments for various purposes. It includes Portfolio Theory, the Capital Asset Pricing Model, Arbitrage Pricing Theory, and the Efficient Market Hypothesis.

Efficient-Market Hypothesis

The efficient-market hypothesis (EMH) asserts that financial markets are "informationally efficient" or that prices on traded assets e.g., stocks, bonds or property, already reflect all known information. The efficient-market hypothesis states that it is impossible to consistently outperform the market by using any information that the market already knows except through luck. Information or news in the EMH is defined as anything that may affect prices that is unknowable in the present and thus appears randomly in the future.

The EMH was developed by Professor Eugene Fama at the University of Chicago Graduate School of Business as an academic concept of study through his published Ph.D. thesis in the early 1960s at the same school.

Historical Background

The efficient-market hypothesis was first expressed by Louis Bachelier, a French mathematician, in his 1900 dissertation "The Theory of Speculation". His work was largely ignored until the 1950s. However beginning in the 30s scattered, independent work corroborated his thesis. A small number of studies indicated that US stock prices and related financial series followed a random walk model. Also, work by Alfred Cowles in the '30s and '40s showed that professional investors were in general unable to outperform the market.

The efficient-market hypothesis emerged as a prominent theoretic position in the mid-1960s. Paul Samuelson had begun to circulate Bachelier's work among economists. In 1964 Bachelier's dissertation along with the empirical studies mentioned above were published in an anthology edited by Paul Coonter. In 1965 Eugene Fama published his dissertation arguing for the random walk hypothesis and Samuelson published a proof for a version of the efficient-market hypothesis. In 1970 Fama published a review of both the theory and the evidence for the hypothesis. The paper extended and refined the theory and included the definitions for three forms of market efficiency: weak, semi-strong and strong (see below).

Theoretical Background

Beyond the normal utility maximizing agents, the efficient-market hypothesis requires that agents have rational expectations; that on average the population is correct (even if no one person is) and whenever new relevant information appears the agents update their expectations appropriately.

Note that it is not required that the agents be rational (which is different from rational expectations. Rational agents act coldly and achieve what they set out to do). EMH allows that when faced with new information, some investors may overreact and some may underreact. All that is required by the EMH is that investors' reactions be random and follow a normal distribution pattern so that the net effect on market prices cannot be reliably exploited to make an abnormal profit, especially when considering transaction costs (including commissions and spreads). Thus, any one person can be wrong about the market — indeed, everyone can be — but the market as a whole is always right.

A meteorological analogy provides some insight here. For example, all weather reports in a particular geographic area might be wrong about the weather but the weather is right. That is, the measure or benchmark for the meteorologist is the actual weather. The measure or benchmark for investors is the market.

This argument, though perhaps useful in some context is wrought with fallacies. First and foremost it employs a form of tautology, tantamount to "the market is right because it is the market" or "the weather is right because it is the weather." Thus critics of EMH argue that the market is a merely a mutually agreed upon subjective construct (consisting of certain indices, composites, news, etc.) and is neither inherently right or wrong. Despite being based on a logical fallacy of tautology others argue that there is still value in the hypothesis.

There are three common forms in which the efficient-market hypothesis is commonly stated — weak-form efficiency, semi-strong-form efficiency and strong-form efficiency, each of which have different implications for how markets work.

Weak-Form Efficiency

- Excess returns cannot be earned by using investment strategies based on historical share prices.

- Technical analysis techniques will not be able to consistently produce excess returns, though some forms of fundamental analysis may still provide excess returns.
- Share prices exhibit no serial dependencies meaning that there are no "patterns" to asset prices. This implies that future price movements are determined entirely by unexpected information and therefore are random.

Semi-strong-Form Efficiency

- Semi-strong-form efficiency implies that share prices adjust to publicly available new information very rapidly and in an unbiased fashion such that no excess returns can be earned by trading on that information.
- Semi-strong-form efficiency implies that neither fundamental analysis nor technical analysis techniques will be able to reliably produce excess returns.
- To test for semi-strong-form efficiency the adjustments to previously unknown news must be of a reasonable size and must be instantaneous. To test for this, consistent upward or downward adjustments after the initial change must be looked for. If there are any such adjustments it would suggest that investors had interpreted the information in a biased fashion and hence in an inefficient manner.

Strong-Form Efficiency

- Share prices reflect all information, public and private, and no one can earn excess returns.
- If there are legal barriers to private information becoming public, as with insider trading laws, strong-form efficiency is impossible except in the case where the laws are universally ignored.
- To test for strong-form efficiency, a market needs to exist where investors cannot consistently earn excess returns over a long period of time. Even if some money managers are consistently observed to beat the market, no refutation even of strong-form efficiency follows: With hundreds of thousands of fund managers worldwide even a normal distribution of returns (as efficiency predicts) should be expected to produce a few dozen "star" performers.

Arguments concerning the Validity of the Hypothesis

Proponents of Behavioral Finance, Technical, Quantitative and Fundamental Analysis dispute the notion that markets behave consistently with the efficient-market hypothesis, especially in its stronger forms. Some economists, mathematicians and market practitioners cannot believe that man-made markets are strong-form efficient when there are prima facie reasons for inefficiency including the slow diffusion of information, the relatively great power of some market participants (e.g., financial institutions), and the existence of apparently sophisticated professional investors. The way that markets react to surprising news is perhaps the most visible flaw in the efficient-market hypothesis. For example, news events such as surprise interest rate changes from central banks are not instantaneously taken account of in stock prices but rather cause sustained movement of prices over periods from hours to months.

Only a privileged few may have prior knowledge of laws about to be enacted, new pricing controls set by pseudo-government agencies such as the Federal Reserve banks and judicial decisions that affect a wide range of economic parties. The public must treat these as random variables but actors on such inside information can correct the market however this is usually done in a discreet manner to avoid detection.

Another observed discrepancy between the hypothesis and real markets is that at market extremes what fundamentalists might consider irrational behavior is the norm: In the late stages of a bull market, the market is driven by buyers who take little notice of underlying value. Towards the end of a crash, markets go into free fall as participants extricate themselves from positions regardless of the unusually good value that their positions represent. This is indicated by the large differences in the valuation of stocks compared to fundamentals (such as forward P/E ratios) in bull markets compared to bear markets. A theorist might say that rational (and hence, presumably, powerful) participants should always immediately take advantage of the artificially high or artificially low prices caused by the irrational participants by taking opposing positions but this is observably, in general, not enough to prevent bubbles and crashes developing. It may be inferred that many rational participants are aware of the irrationality of the market at extremes and are willing to allow irrational participants to drive the market as far as they will and only take advantage of the prices when they have more than merely fundamental reasons that the market will return towards fair value. Behavioural finance explains that when entering positions market participants are not driven primarily by whether prices are cheap or expensive but by whether they expect them to rise or fall. To ignore this can be hazardous: Alan Greenspan warned of "irrational exuberance" in the markets in 1996 but some traders who sold short new economy stocks that seemed to be greatly overpriced around this time had to accept serious losses as prices reached even more extraordinary levels. As John Maynard Keynes succinctly commented "Markets can remain irrational longer than you can remain solvent."

The efficient-market hypothesis was introduced in the late 1960s. Prior to that, the prevailing view was that markets were inefficient. Inefficiency was commonly believed to exist e.g., in the United States and United Kingdom stock markets. However, earlier work by Kendall (1953) suggested that changes in UK stock market prices were random. Later work by Brealey and Dryden and also by Cunningham found that there were no significant dependences in price changes suggesting that the UK stock market was weak-form efficient.

Further to this evidence that the UK stock market is weak-form efficient, other studies of capital markets have pointed toward them being semi-strong-form efficient. Studies by Firth (1976, 1979, and 1980) in the United Kingdom have compared the share prices existing after a takeover announcement with the bid offer. Firth found that the share prices were fully and instantaneously adjusted to their correct levels, thus concluding that the UK stock market was semi-strong-form efficient. The market's ability to efficiently respond to a short term and widely publicized event such as a takeover announcement, however, cannot necessarily be taken as indicative of a market efficient at pricing regarding more long term and amorphous factors.

Other empirical evidence in support of the EMH comes from studies showing that the return of market averages exceeds the return of actively managed mutual funds. Thus, to the extent that markets are inefficient the benefits realized by seizing upon the inefficiencies are outweighed by the internal fund costs involved in finding them, acting upon them, advertising etc. These findings gave inspiration to the formation of passively managed index funds.

It may be that professional and other market participants who have discovered reliable trading rules or stratagems see no reason to divulge them to academic researchers. It might be that there is an information gap between the academics who study the markets and the professionals who work in them. Some observers point to seemingly inefficient features of the markets that can be exploited e.g. seasonal tendencies and divergent returns to assets with various characteristics. E.g. factor analysis. Studies of returns to different types of investment strategies suggest that some types of stocks may outperform the market long-term (e.g. in the UK, the USA, and Japan).

Skeptics of EMH argue that there exists a small number of investors who have outperformed the market over long periods of time in a way which is difficult to attribute to luck, including Peter Lynch, Warren Buffett, George Soros, and Bill Miller. These investors' strategies are to a large extent based on identifying markets where prices do not accurately reflect the available information, in direct contradiction to the efficient-market hypothesis which explicitly implies that no such opportunities exist. Among the skeptics is Warren Buffett who has argued that the EMH is not correct, on one occasion wryly saying "I'd be a bum on the street with a tin cup if the markets were always efficient" and on another saying "The professors who taught Efficient Market Theory said that someone throwing darts at the stock tables could select stock portfolio having prospects just as good as one selected by the brightest, most hard-working securities analyst. Observing correctly that the market was frequently efficient, they went on to conclude incorrectly that it was always efficient." Adherents to a stronger form of the EMH argue that the hypothesis does not preclude—indeed it predicts—the existence of unusually successful investors or funds occurring through chance. In addition, supporters of the EMH point out that the success of Warren Buffett and George Soros may come as a result of their business management skill rather than their stock picking ability.

It is important to note, however, that the efficient-market hypothesis does not account for the empirical fact that the most successful stock market participants share similar stock picking policies, which would seem to indicate a high positive correlation between stock picking policy and investment success. For example, Warren Buffett, Peter Lynch, and George Soros all made their fortunes exploiting differences between market valuations and underlying economic conditions. This notion is further supported by the fact that all stock market operators who regularly appear in the Forbes 400 list made their fortunes working as full time businesspeople, most of whom received college educations and adhered to a strict stock picking philosophy they developed at a relatively early age. If "throwing darts at the financial pages" were as effective an approach to investment as deliberate financial analysis one would expect to see casual, part time investors appearing in rich lists as frequently as professionals like George Soros and Warren Buffett.

The efficient-market hypothesis also appears to be inconsistent with many events in stock market history. For example, the stock market crash of 1987 saw the S&P 500 drop more than 20% in the Month of October despite the fact that no major news or events occurred prior to the Monday of the crash. The decline seemed to have come from nowhere. This would tend to indicate that rather irrational behavior can sweep stock markets at random.

Burton Malkiel, a well-known proponent of the general validity of EMH, has warned that certain emerging markets such as China are not empirically efficient; that the Shanghai and Shenzhen markets, unlike markets in United States, exhibit considerable serial correlation (price trends), non-random walk, and evidence of manipulation.

Social Acceptance

Despite the best efforts of EMH proponents such as Burton Malkiel, whose book A Random Walk Down Wall Street achieved best-seller status, the EMH has not caught the public's imagination. Popular books and articles promoting various forms of stock-picking such as the books by popular CNBC commentator Jim Cramer and former Fidelity Investments fund manager Peter Lynch, have continued to press the more appealing notion that investors can "beat the market."

EMH is commonly rejected by the general public due to a misconception concerning its meaning. Many believe that EMH says that a security's price is a correct representation of the value of that business, as calculated by what the business's future returns will actually be. In other words, they believe that EMH says a stock's price correctly predicts the underlying company's future results. Since stock prices clearly do not reflect company future results in many cases, many people reject EMH as clearly wrong.

However, the EMH makes no such statement. Rather, it says that a stock's price represents an aggregation of the probabilities of all future outcomes for the company based on the best information available at the time. Whether that information turns out to have been correct is not something required by the EMH. Put another way, the EMH does not require a stock's price to reflect a company's future performance, just the best possible estimate or forecast of future performance that can be made with publicly available information. That estimate may still be grossly wrong without violating the EMH.

Further empirical work has since highlighted the impact transaction costs have on the concept of market efficiency with much evidence suggesting that any anomalies pertaining to market inefficiencies are the result of a cost benefit analysis to those willing to incur the cost of acquiring valuable information in order to trade on it. Tests to return predictability have shown this to be a factor which has been used to make the highlight the existence of an efficient market. Additionally the concept of liquidity is a critical component to capturing "inefficiencies" in tests for abnormal returns. Despite a stronger case being evident for an efficient market, any test of this proposition faces the joint hypothesis problem where it is impossible to ever test for market efficiency, since to do so requires the use of a measuring stick against which abnormal returns are compared. Thus how can one know if the market is efficient if the one does not know if their model correctly stipulates the required rate of return. Consequently, a situation arises where either the asset pricing model is incorrect or the market is inefficient but one cannot know both answers at the same time.

An alternative Theory: Behavioral Finance

Opponents of the EMH sometimes cite examples of market movements that seem inexplicable in terms of conventional theories of stock price determination, for example the stock market crash of October 1987 where most stock exchanges crashed at the same time. It is virtually impossible to explain the scale of those market falls by reference to any news event at the time. The explanation may lie either in the mechanics of the exchanges (e.g. no safety nets to discontinue trading initiated by program sellers) or the peculiarities of human nature.

Behavioural psychology approaches to stock market trading are among some of the more promising alternatives to EMH (and some investment strategies seek to exploit exactly such inefficiencies). A growing field of research called behavioral finance studies (which is explained in more detail above) show how cognitive or emotional biases, which are individual or collective, create anomalies in market prices and returns that may be inexplicable via the EMH alone. However, how and if individual biases manifest inefficiencies in market-wide prices is still an open question. Indeed, the Nobel Laureate co-founder of the programme—Daniel Kahneman—announced his skepticism of resultant inefficiencies: "They're [investors] just not going to do it [beat the market]. It's just not going to happen."

Ironically, the behaviorial finance programme can also be used to tangentially support the EMH—or rather it can explain the skepticism drawn by EMH—in that it helps to explain the human tendency to find and exploit patterns in data even where none exist. Some relevant examples of the Cognitive biases highlighted by the programme are: The Hindsight Bias, the Clustering illusion, the Overconfidence effect, the Observer-expectancy effect, the Gambler's fallacy and the Illusion of control.

The Adaptive Market Hypothesis, as proposed by Dr. Andrew Lo (2004), is a new framework that reconciles theories that imply that the markets are efficient with behavioral alternatives by applying the principles of evolution - competition, adaptation and natural selection - to financial interactions.

Under this approach the traditional models of modern financial economics can coexist alongside behavioral models in an intellectually consistent manner. He argues that much of what behavioralists cite as counterexamples to economic rationality - loss aversion, overconfidence, overreaction and other behavioral biases - are, in fact, consistent with an evolutionary model of individuals adapting to a changing environment using simple heuristics.

Adaptive Market Hypothesis

According to Lo, the Adaptive Markets Hypothesis can be viewed as a new version of the efficient market hypothesis, derived from evolutionary principles. "Prices reflect as much information as dictated by the combination of environmental conditions and the number and nature of "species" in the economy." By species, he means distinct groups of market participants each behaving in a common manner (i.e. pension funds, retail investors, market makers, and hedge-fund managers, etc.). If multiple members of a single group are competing for rather scarce resources within a single market, that market is likely to be highly efficient e.g. the market for 10-Year US Treasury Notes, which reflects most relevant information very quickly indeed. If, on the other hand, a small number of species are competing for rather abundant resources in a given market, that market will be less efficient, e.g. the market for oil paintings from the Italian Renaissance. Market efficiency cannot be evaluated in a vacuum but is highly context-dependent and dynamic. Shortly stated, the degree of market efficiency is related to environmental factors characterizing market ecology such as the number of competitors in the market, the magnitude of profit opportunities available and the adaptability of the market participants.

Implications

The AMH has several implications that differentiate it from the EMH such as:

1. To the extent that a relation between risk and reward exists, it is unlikely to be stable over time.
2. Contrary to the classical EMH, arbitrage opportunities do exist from time to time.
3. Investment strategies will also wax and wane, performing well in certain environments and performing poorly in other environments. This includes quantitatively-, fundamentally- and technically-based methods.
4. Survival is the only objective that matters while profit and utility maximization are secondary relevant aspects
5. Innovation is the key to survival because as risk/reward relation varies through time, the better way of achieving a consistent level of expected returns is to adapt to changing market conditions.

The Cost of Capital

The cost of capital is an expected return that the provider of capital plans to earn on their investment.

Summary

Capital (money) used for funding a business should earn returns for the capital providers who risk their capital. For an investment to be worthwhile, the expected return on capital must be greater than the cost of capital. In other words, the risk-adjusted return on capital (that is, incorporating not just the projected returns, but the probabilities of those projections) must be higher than the cost of capital.

The cost of debt is relatively simple to calculate as it is composed of the rate of interest paid. In practice, the interest-rate paid by the company will include the risk-free rate plus a risk component which itself incorporates a probable rate of default (and an amount of recovery given default). For companies with similar risk or credit ratings, the interest rate is largely exogenous.

Cost of equity is more challenging to calculate as equity does not pay a set return to its investors. Similar to the cost of debt, the cost of equity is broadly defined as the risk-weighted projected return required by investors, where the return is largely unknown. The cost of equity is therefore inferred by comparing the investment to other investments with similar risk profiles to determine the "market" cost of equity.

The cost of capital is often used as the discount rate, the rate at which projected cash flow will be discounted to give a present value or net present value.

Cost of debt

The cost of debt is computed by taking the rate on a non-defaulting bond whose duration matches the term structure of the corporate debt, then adding a default premium. This default premium will rise as the amount of debt increases (since the risk rises as the amount of debt rises). Since in most cases debt expense is a deductible expense, the cost of debt is computed as an after tax cost to make it comparable with the cost of equity (earnings are after-tax as well). Thus, for profitable firms, debt is discounted by the tax rate. But this is basically used for large corporations only.

Cost of equity

Cost of equity = Risk free rate of return + Premium expected for risk

Expected return

The expected return can be calculated as the "dividend capitalization model", which is (dividend per share / price per share) + growth rate of dividends (that is, dividend yield + growth rate of dividends).

Comments

The models states that investors will expect a return that is the risk-free return plus the security's sensitivity to market risk times the market risk premium.

The risk free rate is taken from the lowest yielding bonds in the particular market, such as government bonds.

The risk premium varies over time and place but in some developed countries during the twentieth century it has averaged around 5%. The equity market real capital gain return has been about the same as the annual real GDP growth. The capital gains on the Dow Jones Industrial Average have been 1.6% per year over the period 1910-2005. The dividends have increased the total "real" return on average equity to the double, about 3.2%.

The sensitivity to market risk (β) is unique for each firm and depends on everything from management to its business and capital structure. This value cannot be known "ex ante" (beforehand) but can be estimated from "ex post" (past) returns and past experience with similar firms.

Note that retained earnings are a component of equity and therefore the cost of retained earnings is equal to the cost of equity. Dividends (earnings that are paid to investors and not retained) are a component of the return on capital to equity holders and influence the cost of capital through that mechanism.

Weighted Average Cost of Capital

The Weighted Average Cost of Capital (WACC) is used in finance to measure a firm's cost of capital.

The total capital for a firm is the value of its equity (for a firm without outstanding warrants and options, this is the same as the company's market capitalization) plus the cost of its debt (the cost of debt should be continually updated as the cost of debt changes as a result of interest rate changes). Notice that the "equity" in the debt to equity ratio is the market value of all equity, not the shareholders' equity on the balance sheet.

Calculation of WACC is an iterative procedure which requires estimation of the fair market value of equity capital.

Capital Structure

Because of tax advantages on debt issuance, it will be cheaper to issue debt rather than new equity (this is only true for profitable firms, tax breaks are available only to profitable firms). At some point, however, the cost of issuing new debt will be greater than the cost of issuing new equity. This is because adding debt increases the default risk - and thus the interest rate that the company must pay in order to borrow money. By utilizing too much debt in its capital structure, this increased default risk can also drive up the costs for other sources (such as retained earnings and preferred stock) as well. Management must identify the "optimal mix" of financing – the capital structure where the cost of capital is minimized so that the firm's value can be maximized.

The Thomson Financial league tables show that global debt issuance exceeds equity

Modigliani-Miller Theorem

If there were no tax advantages for issuing debt and equity could be freely issued, Miller and Modigliani showed that under certain assumptions the value of a leveraged firm and the value of an unleveraged firm should be the same. Their paper is foundational in modern corporate finance.

Alpha

Alpha is a risk-adjusted measure of the so-called active return on an investment. It is the return in excess of the compensation for the risk borne and thus commonly used to assess active managers' performances. Often, the return of a benchmark is subtracted in order to consider relative performance which yields Jensen's alpha.

The alpha coefficient (α_i) is a parameter in the capital asset pricing model (CAPM). It is the intercept of the Security Characteristic Line (SCL). Alternatively, it is also the coefficient of the constant in a market model regression.

It can be shown that in an efficient market the expected value of the alpha coefficient equals the return of the risk free asset: $E(\alpha_i) = r_f$.

Therefore the alpha coefficient indicates how an investment has performed after accounting for the risk it involved:

- $\alpha_i < r_f$: the investment has earned too little for its risk (or was too risky for the return)

- $\alpha_i = r_f$: the investment has earned a return adequate for the risk taken

- $\alpha_i > r_f$: the investment has a return in excess of the reward for the assumed risk

For instance, although a return of 20% may appear good, the investment can still have a negative alpha if it involved an excessively risky position.

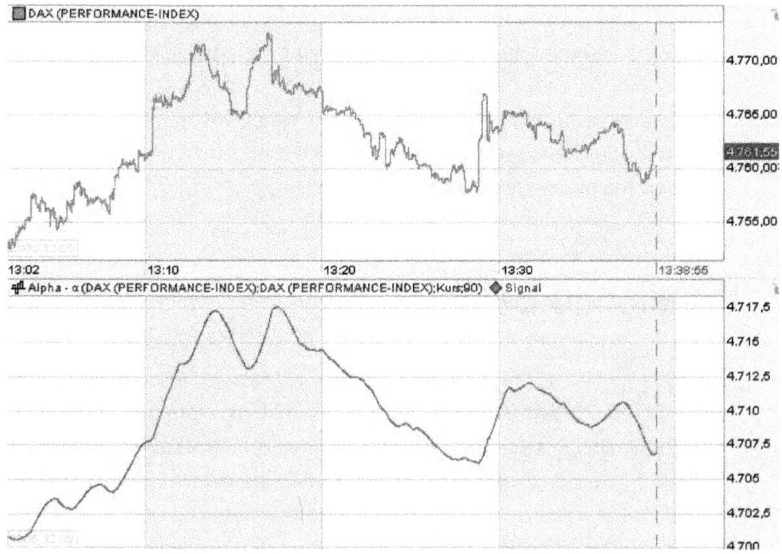

Picture 2: Alpha

Origin of the Concept

The concept and focus on Alpha comes from an observation increasingly made during the middle of the twentieth century that around 75 percent of stock investment managers did not make as much money picking investments as someone who simply invested in every stock in proportion to the weight it occupied in the overall market in terms of market capitalization or indexing. Many academics felt that this was due to the stock market being "efficient" which means that since so many people were paying attention to the stock market all the time, the prices of stocks rapidly moved to the correct price at any one moment and that only random variation beyond the control of the manager made it possible for one manager to achieve better results than another, before fees or taxes were considered. A belief in efficient markets spawned the creation of market capitalization weighted index funds that seek to replicate the performance of investing in an entire market in the weights that each of the equity securities comprises in the overall market. The best examples are the S&P 500 and the Wilshire 5000 which approximately represent the 500 largest equities and the largest 5000 securities respectively, accounting for approximately 80%+ and 99%+ of the total market capitalization of the US market as a whole.

In fact, to many investors, this phenomenon created a new standard of performance that must be matched. An investment manager should not only avoid losing money for the client and should make a certain amount of money but in fact should make more money than the passive strategy of investing in everything equally (since this strategy appeared to be statistically more likely to be successful than the strategy of any one investment manager). The name for the additional return above the expected return of the beta adjusted return of the market is called "Alpha".

Relation to Beta

Besides an investment manager simply making more money than a passive strategy, there is another issue: Although the strategy of investing in every stock appeared to perform better than 75 percent of investment managers, the price of the stock market as a whole fluctuates up and down and could be on a downward decline for many years before returning to its previous price.

The passive strategy appeared to generate the market-beating return over periods of 10 years or more. This strategy may be risky for those who feel they might need to withdraw their money before a 10-year holding period, for example. Thus investment managers who employ a strategy which is less likely to lose money in a particular year are often chosen by those investors who feel that they might need to withdraw their money sooner.

The measure of the correlated volatility of an investment (or an investment manager's track record) relative to the entire market is called beta. Note the "correlated" modifier. An investment can be twice as volatile as the total market but if its correlation with the market is only 0.5, its beta to the market will be 1.

Investors can use both alpha and beta to judge a manager's performance. If the manager has had a high alpha, but also a high beta, investors might not find that acceptable, because of the chance they might have to withdraw their money when the investment is doing poorly.

These concepts not only apply to investment managers, but to any kind of investment.

Beta

The beta coefficient, in terms of finance and investing, describes how the expected return of a stock or portfolio is correlated to the return of the financial market as a whole.

An asset with a **beta of 0** means that its price is not at all correlated with the market; that asset is independent. A **positive beta** means that the asset generally follows the market. A **negative beta** shows that the asset inversely follows the market; the asset generally decreases in value if the market goes up.

Correlations are evident between companies within the same industry or even within the same asset class (such as equities), as was demonstrated in the Wall Street crash of 1929. This correlated risk, measured by Beta, creates almost all of the risk in a diversified portfolio.

The beta coefficient is a key parameter in the capital asset pricing model (CAPM). It measures the part of the asset's statistical variance that cannot be mitigated by the diversification provided by the portfolio of many risky assets, because it is correlated with the return of the other assets that are in the portfolio. Beta can be estimated for individual companies using regression analysis against a stock market index.

Definition

The formula for the Beta of an asset within a portfolio is

$$\beta_a = \frac{\mathrm{Cov}(r_a, r_p)}{\mathrm{Var}(r_p)},$$

where r_a measures the rate of return of the asset, r_p measures the rate of return of the portfolio of which the asset is a part and $\mathrm{Cov}(r_a,r_p)$ is the covariance between the rates of return. In the CAPM formulation, the portfolio is the market portfolio that contains all risky assets and so the r_p terms in the formula are replaced by r_m, the rate of return of the market.

Beta is also referred to as financial elasticity or correlated relative volatility and can be referred to as a measure of the sensitivity of the asset's returns to market returns, its non-diversifiable risk, its systematic risk or market risk. On an individual asset level, measuring beta can give clues to volatility and liquidity in the marketplace. On a portfolio level, measuring beta is thought to separate a manager's skill from his or her willingness to take risk.

The beta movement should be distinguished from the actual returns of the stocks. For example, a sector may be performing well and may have good prospects but the fact that its movement does not correlate well with the broader market index may decrease its beta. However, it should not be taken as a reflection on the overall attractiveness or the loss of it for the sector or stock as the case may be. Beta is a measure of risk and is not to be confused with the attractiveness of the investment.

The beta coefficient was born out of linear regression analysis. It is linked to a regression analysis of the returns of a portfolio (such as a stock index) (x-axis) in a specific period versus the returns of an individual asset (y-axis) in a specific year. The regression line is then called the Security Characteristic Line (SCL).

$$SCL : r_{a,t} = \alpha_a + \beta_a r_{m,t} + \epsilon_{a,t}$$

α_a is called the asset's alpha coefficient and β_a is called the asset's beta coefficient. Both coefficients have an important role in Modern portfolio theory.

For example, in a year where the broad market or benchmark index returns 25% above the risk free rate, suppose two managers gain 50% above the risk free rate. Since this higher return is theoretically possible merely by taking a leveraged position in the broad market to double the beta so it is exactly 2.0, we would expect a skilled portfolio manager to have built the outperforming portfolio with a beta somewhat less than 2, such that the excess return not explained by the beta is positive. If one of the managers' portfolios has an average beta of 3.0, and the other's has a beta of only 1.5, then the CAPM simply states that the extra return of the first manager is not sufficient to compensate us for that manager's risk, whereas the second manager has done more than expected given the risk. Whether investors can expect the second manager to duplicate that performance in future periods is of course a different question.

Beta Volatility and Correlation

$$\beta = (\sigma / \sigma_m) r$$

That is, beta is a combination of volatility and correlation. For example, if one stock has low volatility and high correlation, and the other stock has low correlation and high volatility, beta can decide which one is more "risky".

$$\sigma \geq |\beta| \sigma_m$$

In other words, beta sets a floor on volatility. For example, if market volatility is 10%, any stock (or fund) with a beta of 1 must have a volatility of at least 10%.

Another way of distinguishing between beta and correlation is to think about direction and magnitude. If the market is always up 10% and a stock is always up 20%, the correlation is one (correlation measures direction, not magnitude). However, beta takes into account both direction and magnitude, so in the same example the beta would be 2 (the stock is up twice as much as the market).

Choice of Benchmark

Beta, noted above, can be computed with respect to any portfolio. On the other hand, published betas typically use a stock market index such as S&P 500. This may be because it's a good index, it is well known or just due to laziness. The portfolio for a given investor is what he already owns or at least is considering to own as a result of some analysis. S&P 500 is fine to the extent that it is similar to what the investor owns. Since the S&P 500 is mostly large-cap U.S. stocks, it is good if the investor owns mostly large-cap U.S. stocks and less good if what he owns is not large-cap, not U.S. or not stocks.

For someone who owns UK stocks, it is not great but not terrible, since stocks in the two countries are highly correlated. It's probably not good for Malaysian stocks. For someone who owns mostly government bonds or gold bars, it will, of course, lead to nonsensical results. Stocks may be divided by country but this is not perfect either.

In all cases, what index is being used should be made clear. For example, in the case of a U.S.-based mutual fund that invests in non-U.S. stocks, one source may use S&P 500, while another may use MSCI EAFE. These will, of course, be different. Obviously a number without the index being known is next to useless.

In theoretical discussions, beta with respect to "the market" is investigated. Sometimes the S&P 500 is taken as the market "by definition". Of course this excludes all non-U.S. stocks and a world index such as MSCI World is better. Also the restriction to stocks is somewhat arbitrary. Sometimes the market is defined as "all investable assets". Unfortunately, this includes lots of things for which returns may be hard to measure.

Investing

By definition, the market itself has an underlying beta of 1.0, and individual stocks are ranked according to how much they deviate from the macro market (for simplicity purposes, the S&P 500 is usually used as a proxy for the market as a whole). A stock that swings more than the market (i.e. more volatile) over time has a beta whose absolute value is above 1.0. If a stock moves less than the market, the absolute value of the stock's beta is less than 1.0.

More specifically, a stock that has a beta of 2 follows the market in an overall decline or growth but does so by a factor of 2. This means when the market has an overall decline of 3% a stock with a beta of 2 will fall 6%. Betas can also be negative, meaning the stock moves in the opposite direction of the market. A stock with a beta of -3 would *decline* 9% when the market goes up 3% and conversely would *climb* 9% if the market fell by 3%.

Higher-beta stocks mean greater volatility and are therefore considered to be riskier but are in turn supposed to provide a potential for higher returns. Low-beta stocks pose less risk but also lower returns. In the same way a stock's beta shows its relation to market shifts. It also is used as an indicator for required returns on investment (ROI). If the market with a beta of 1 has an expected return increase of 8%, a stock with a beta of 1.5 should increase return by 12%.

This expected return on equity or equivalently, a firm's cost of equity, can be estimated using the Capital Asset Pricing Model (CAPM). We will have a closer look at the CAPM on the next few pages.

Multiple Beta Model

The arbitrage pricing theory (APT) has multiple betas in its model. In contrast to the CAPM that has only one risk factor, namely the overall market, APT has multiple risk factors. Each risk factor has a corresponding beta indicating the responsiveness of the asset being priced to that risk factor.

Estimation of Beta

To estimate Beta, one needs a list of returns for the asset and returns for the index. These returns can be daily, weekly or any period. Next, a plot should be made with the index returns on the x-axis and the asset returns on the y-axis, in order to check that there are no serious violations of the linear regression model assumptions. The slope of the fitted line from the linear least-squares calculation is the estimated Beta. The y-intercept is the alpha.

- There is an inconsistency between how beta is interpreted and how it is calculated. The usual explanation is that it shows the asset volatility relative to the market volatility. If that were the case it should simply be the ratio of these volatilities. In fact, the standard estimation uses the slope of the least squares regression line - this gives a slope which is less than the volatility ratio. Specifically it gives the volatility ratio multiplied by the correlation of the plotted data. Tofallis, Chris provides a discussion of this topic in their working paper "Investment Volatility: A Critique of Standard Beta Estimation and a Simple Way Forward" together with a real example involving AT&T. The graph showing monthly returns from AT&T is visibly more volatile than the index and yet the standard estimate of beta for this is less than one.

Extreme and Interesting Cases

- Beta has no upper or lower bound and betas as large as 3 or 4 will occur with highly volatile stocks.

- Beta can be zero. Some zero-beta securities are risk-free such as treasury bonds and cash. However, simply because a beta is zero does NOT mean that it is risk free. A beta can be zero simply because the correlation between that item and the market is zero. An example would be betting on horse racing. The correlation with the market will be zero, but it is certainly not a risk free endeavor.

- A negative beta simply means that the stock is inversely correlated with the market. Many gold-related stocks are beta-negative.

- A negative beta might occur even when both the benchmark index and the stock under consideration have positive returns. It is possible that lower positive returns of the index coincide with higher positive returns of the stock or vice versa. The slope of the regression line, i.e. the beta, in such a case will be negative.

- Using beta as a measure of relative risk has its own limitations. Most analysis consider only the magnitude of beta. Beta is a statistical variable and should be considered with its statistical significance (R square value of the regression line). Higher R square value implies higher correlation and a stronger relationship between returns of the asset and the benchmark index.

- Since beta is a result of regression of one stock against the market where it is quoted, betas from different countries are not comparable.

- Staples stocks are thought to be less affected by cycles and usually have lower beta. Procter & Gamble is a classic example. They make soap. Other similar ones are Philip Morris (tobacco) and Anheuser-Busch (alcohol). Utility stocks are thought to be less cyclical and have lower beta as well, for similar reasons.

- Foreign stocks may provide some diversification. World benchmarks such as S&P Global 100 have slightly lower betas than comparable US-only benchmarks such as S&P 100. However, this effect is not as good as it used to be; the various markets are now fairly correlated, especially the US and Western Europe.

Weighted Average Cost of Capital

The weighted average cost of capital (WACC) is the rate that a company is expected to pay to finance its assets. WACC is the minimum return that a company must earn on existing asset base to satisfy its creditors, owners and other providers of capital.

Companies raise money from a number of sources: Common equity, preferred equity, straight debt, convertible debt, exchangeable debt, warrants, options, pension liabilities, executive stock options, governmental subsidies and so on. Different securities are expected to generate different returns. WACC is calculated taking into account the relative weights of each component of the capital structure. Calculation of WACC for a company with a complex capital structure is a laborious exercise.

The formula for a simple case

The weighted average cost of capital is defined by:

$$c = \left(\frac{E}{K}\right) \cdot y + \left(\frac{D}{K}\right) \cdot b(1 - t_C)$$

where

$$K = D + E$$

The following table defines each symbol:

Symbol	Meaning	Units
C	*weighted average cost of capital*	%
y	*required or expected rate of return on equity*, or *cost of equity"*	%
b	*required or expected rate of return on borrowings*, or *cost of debt*	%
t_C	*corporate tax rate*	%
D	*total debt and leases (including current portion of long-term debt and notes payable)*	currency
E	*total market value of equity and equity equivalents*	currency
K	*total capital invested in the going concern*	currency

The equation on the previous page describes only the situation with homogeneous equity and debt. If part of the capital consists, for example, of preferred stock (with different cost of equity *y*), then the formula would include an additional term for each additional source of capital.

or

$$WACC = w_d\ (1\text{-}T)\ r_d + w_e\ r_e$$

w_d = debt portion of value of corporation

T = tax rate

r_d = cost of debt (rate)

w_e = equity portion of value of corporation

r_e = cost of internal equity (rate)

How it works

Since we are measuring expected cost of new capital we should use the market values of the components rather than their book values (which can be significantly different). In addition, other more "exotic" sources of financing such as convertible/callable bonds, convertible preferred stock, etc. would normally be included in the formula if they exist in any significant amounts - since the cost of those financing methods is usually different from the plain vanilla bonds and equity due to their extra features.

WACC is a special way to measure the capital discount of the firms gaining and spending.

Sources of Information

How do we find out the values of the components in the formula for WACC? First let us note that the "weight" of a source of financing is simply the market value of that piece divided by the sum of the values of all the pieces. For example, the weight of common equity in the above formula would be determined as follows:

Market value of common equity / (Market value of common equity + Market value of debt + Market value of preferred equity).

So, let us proceed in finding the market values of each source of financing (namely the debt, preferred stock and common stock).

- The market value for equity for a publicly traded company is simply the price per share multiplied by the number of shares outstanding and tends to be the easiest component to find.
- The market value of the debt is easily found if the company has publicly traded bonds. Frequently, companies also have a significant amount of bank loans, whose market value is not as easily found. However, since the market value of debt tends to be pretty close to the book value (for companies that have not experienced significant

changes in credit rating, at least), the book value of debt is usually used in the WACC formula.

- The market value of preferred stock is again usually easily found on the market and determined by multiplying the cost per share by number of shares outstanding.

Now, let us take care of the costs.

- Preferred equity is equivalent to a perpetuity, where the holder is entitled to fixed payments forever. Thus the cost is determined by dividing the periodic payment by the price of the preferred stock, in percentage terms.
- The cost of common equity is usually determined using the capital asset pricing model.
- The cost of debt is the yield to maturity (YTM) on the publicly traded bonds of the company. The rates of interest charged by the banks on recent loans to the company would also serve as a good cost of debt. Since a corporation normally can write off taxes on the interest it pays on the debt, however, the cost of debt is further reduced by the tax rate that the corporation is subject to. Thus, the cost of debt for a company becomes (YTM on bonds or interest on loans) × (1 – tax rate). In fact, the tax deduction is usually kept in the formula for WACC, rather than being rolled up into cost of debt, as such:

WACC = weight of preferred equity × cost of preferred equity

+ weight of common equity × cost of common equity

+ weight of debt × cost of debt × (1 – tax rate).

Effect on Valuation

Economists Merton Miller and Franco Modigliani showed in the Modigliani-Miller theorem that in an economy with no transaction costs or taxes, financing decisions are irrelevant to the company's value. An all-equity financed company is worth the same as an all-debt financed one. However, many governments allow a tax deduction on interest, thereby creating a bias towards debt financing. However, there is a cost to financial distress (e.g. bankruptcy) which creates a bias towards equity financing. Therefore theoretically, the appropriate level of Debt to Equity in a company will then be the point at which the benefits of the tax shield provided by debt financing are outweighed by the costs of financial distress.

Arbitrage Pricing Theory

Arbitrage pricing theory (APT) is a general theory of asset pricing that has become influential in the pricing of shares. It was initiated by the economist Stephen Ross in 1976.

APT holds that the expected return of a financial asset can be modeled as a linear function of various macro-economic factors or theoretical market indices, where sensitivity to changes in each factor is represented by a factor-specific beta coefficient. The model-derived rate of return will then be used to price the asset correctly - the asset price should equal the expected end of period price discounted at the rate implied by model. If the price diverges, arbitrage should bring it back into line.

The APT model

If APT holds, then a risky asset can be described as satisfying the following relation:

$$E(r_j) = r_f + b_{j1}RP_1 + b_{j2}RP_2 + \cdots + b_{jn}RP_n$$

$$r_j = E(r_j) + b_{j1}F_1 + b_{j2}F_2 + \cdots + b_{jn}F_n + \epsilon_j$$

where

- $E(r_j)$ is the risky asset's expected return,
- RP_k is the risk premium of the factor,
- r_f is the risk-free rate,
- F_k is the macroeconomic factor,
- b_{jk} is the sensitivity of the asset to factor k, also called factor loading,
- and ε_j is the risky asset's idiosyncratic random shock with mean zero.

That is, the uncertain return of an asset *j* is a linear relationship among *n* factors. Additionally, every factor is also considered to be a random variable with mean zero.

Note that there are following assumptions and requirements that have to be fulfilled for the latter to be correct: There must be perfect competition in the market and the total number of factors may never surpass the total number of assets (in order to avoid the problem of matrix singularity),

Arbitrage and the APT

Arbitrage is the practice of taking advantage of a state of imbalance between two (or possibly more) markets and thereby making a risk free profit.

Arbitrage in Expectations

The APT describes the mechanism of arbitrage whereby investors will bring an asset which is mispriced, according to the APT model, back into line with its expected price. Note that under true arbitrage the investor locks-in a guaranteed payoff, whereas under APT arbitrage as described below, the investor locks-in a positive expected payoff. The APT thus assumes "arbitrage in expectations" - i.e. that arbitrage by investors will bring asset prices back into line with the returns expected by the model portfolio theory

Arbitrage Mechanics

In the APT context, arbitrage consists of trading in two assets – with at least one being mispriced. The arbitrageur sells the asset which is relatively too expensive and uses the proceeds to buy one which is relatively too cheap.

Under the APT, an asset is mispriced if its current price diverges from the price predicted by the model. The asset price today should equal the sum of all future cash flows discounted at the APT rate, where the expected return of the asset is a linear function of various factors. The sensitivity to changes in each factor is represented by a factor-specific beta coefficient.

A correctly priced asset here may be in fact a synthetic asset - a portfolio consisting of other correctly priced assets. This portfolio has the same exposure to each of the macroeconomic factors as the mispriced asset. The arbitrageur creates the portfolio by identifying x correctly priced assets (one per factor plus one) and then weighting the assets such that portfolio beta per factor is the same as for the mispriced asset.

Where today's price is too low:

The implication is that at the end of the period the portfolio would have appreciated at the rate implied by the APT, whereas the mispriced asset would have appreciated at more than this rate. The arbitrageur could therefore:

Today:

1. short sell the portfolio
2. buy the mispriced-asset with the proceeds.

At the end of the period:

1. sell the mispriced asset
2. use the proceeds to buy back the portfolio
3. pocket the difference.

Where today's price is too high:

The implication is that at the end of the period the portfolio would have appreciated at the rate implied by the APT, whereas the mispriced asset would have appreciated at less than this rate. The arbitrageur could therefore:

Today:

1. short sell the mispriced-asset
2. buy the portfolio with the proceeds.

At the end of the period:

1. sell the portfolio
2. use the proceeds to buy back the mispriced-asset
3. pocket the difference.

Relationship with the Capital Asset Pricing Model

The APT along with the capital asset pricing model (CAPM) is one of two influential theories on asset pricing. The APT differs from the CAPM in that it is less restrictive in its assumptions. It allows for an explanatory (as opposed to statistical) model of asset returns. It assumes that each investor will hold a unique portfolio with its own particular array of betas, as opposed to the identical "market portfolio". In some ways, the CAPM can be considered a "special case" of the APT in that the securities market line represents a single-factor model of the asset price, where Beta is exposed to changes in value of the market.

Additionally, the APT can be seen as a "supply side" model, since its beta coefficients reflect the sensitivity of the underlying asset to economic factors. Thus, factor shocks would cause structural changes in the asset's expected return, or in the case of stocks, in the firm's profitability.

On the other side, the capital asset pricing model is considered a "demand side" model. Its results, although similar to those in the APT, arise from a maximization problem of each investor's utility function and from the resulting market equilibrium (investors are considered to be the "consumers" of the assets).

Using the APT

Identifying the Factors

As with the CAPM, the factor-specific Betas are found via a linear regression of historical security returns on the factor in question. Unlike the CAPM, the APT, however, does not itself reveal the identity of its priced factors - the number and nature of these factors is likely to change over time and between economies. As a result, this issue is essentially empirical in nature. Several a priori guidelines as to the characteristics required of potential factors are, however, suggested:

1. their impact on asset prices manifests in their unexpected movements
2. they should represent undiversifiable influences (these are, clearly, more likely to be macroeconomic rather than firm-specific in nature)
3. timely and accurate information on these variables is required
4. the relationship should be theoretically justifiable on economic grounds

Chen, Roll and Ross identified the following macro-economic factors as significant in explaining security returns:

- surprises in inflation;
- surprises in GNP as indicted by an industrial production index;
- surprises in investor confidence due to changes in default premium in corporate bonds;
- surprise shifts in the yield curve.

As a practical matter, indices or spot or futures market prices may be used in place of macro-economic factors, which are reported at low frequency (e.g. monthly) and often with significant estimation errors. Market indices are sometimes derived by means of factor analysis. More direct "indices" that might be used are:

- short term interest rates;
- the difference in long-term and short term interest rates;
- a diversified stock index such as the S&P 500 or NYSE Composite Index;
- oil prices
- gold or other precious metal prices
- currency exchange rates

The Capital Asset Pricing Model

The Capital Asset Pricing Model (CAPM) is used to determine a theoretically appropriate required rate of return of an asset, if that asset is to be added to an already well-diversified portfolio, given that asset's non-diversifiable risk. The model takes into account the asset's sensitivity to non-diversifiable risk (also known as systemic risk or market risk), often represented by the quantity beta (β) in the financial industry, as well as the expected return of the market and the expected return of a theoretical risk-free asset.

The model was introduced by Jack Treynor, William Sharpe, John Lintner and Jan Mossin independently, building on the earlier work of Harry Markowitz on diversification and modern portfolio theory. Sharpe received the Nobel Memorial Prize in Economics (jointly with Markowitz and Merton Miller) for this contribution to the field of financial economics.

The Formula

The CAPM is a model for pricing an individual security or a portfolio. For individual securities we made use of the security market line (SML) and its relation to expected return and systemic risk (beta) to show how the market must price individual securities in relation to their security risk class. The SML enables us to calculate the reward-to-risk ratio for any security in relation to that of the overall market. Therefore, when the expected rate of return for any security is deflated by its beta coefficient, the reward-to-risk ratio for any individual security in the market is equal to the market reward-to-risk ratio, thus:

$$\frac{E(R_i) - R_f}{\beta_i} = E(R_m) - R_f$$

The market reward-to-risk ratio is effectively the market risk premium and by rearranging the above equation and solving for E(Ri), we obtain the Capital Asset Pricing Model (CAPM).

$$E(R_i) = R_f + \beta_i(E(R_m) - R_f)$$

Where:

$E(R_i)$ is the expected return on the capital asset

R_f is the risk-free rate of interest such as interest arising from government bonds

β_i (the *beta coefficient*) is the sensitivity of the asset returns to market returns, or also:

$$\beta_i = \frac{\mathrm{Cov}(R_i, R_m)}{\mathrm{Var}(R_m)},$$

$E(R_m)$ is the expected return of the market

$E(R_m) - R_f$ is sometimes known as the market premium or risk premium (the difference between the expected market rate of return and the risk-free rate of return).

Restated, in terms of risk premium, we find that:

$$E(R_i) - R_f = \beta_i(E(R_m) - R_f)$$

which states that the individual risk premium equals the market premium times beta.

Note 1: the expected market rate of return is usually measured by looking at the arithmetic average of the historical returns on a market portfolio (i.e. S&P 500).

Note 2: the risk free rate of return used for determining the risk premium is usually the arithmetic average of historical risk free rates of return and not the current risk free rate of return.

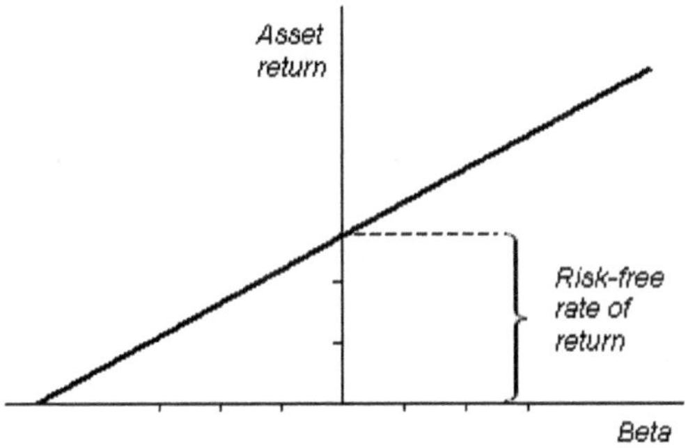

The Security Market Line, seen here in a graph, describes a relation between the beta and the asset's expected rate of return.

Asset pricing

Once the expected return, E(Ri), is calculated using CAPM, the future cash flows of the asset can be discounted to their present value using this rate (E(Ri)), to establish the correct price for the asset.

In theory, therefore, an asset is correctly priced when its observed price is the same as its value calculated using the CAPM derived discount rate. If the observed price is higher than the valuation, then the asset is overvalued (and undervalued when the observed price is below the CAPM valuation).

Alternatively, one can "solve for the discount rate" for the observed price given a particular valuation model and compare that discount rate with the CAPM rate. If the discount rate in the model is lower than the CAPM rate then the asset is overvalued (and undervalued for a too high discount rate).

Asset-Specific Required Return

The CAPM returns the asset-appropriate required return or discount rate - i.e. the rate at which future cash flows produced by the asset should be discounted given that asset's relative riskiness. Betas exceeding one signify more than average "riskiness"; betas below one indicate lower than average. Thus a more risky stock will have a higher beta and will be discounted at a higher rate. Less sensitive stocks will have lower betas and be discounted at a lower rate.

Given the accepted concave utility function, the CAPM is consistent with intuition - investors (should) require a higher return for holding a more risky asset.

Since beta reflects asset-specific sensitivity to non-diversifiable, i.e. market risk, the market as a whole, by definition, has a beta of one. Stock market indices are frequently used as local proxies for the market - and in that case (by definition) have a beta of one. An investor in a large, diversified portfolio (such as a mutual fund) therefore expects performance in line with the market.

Risk and Diversification

The risk of a portfolio comprises systematic risk, also known as undiversifiable risk, and unsystematic risk which is also known as idiosyncratic risk or diversifiable risk. Systematic risk refers to the risk common to all securities - i.e. market risk. Unsystematic risk is the risk associated with individual assets. Unsystematic risk can be diversified away to smaller levels by including a greater number of assets in the portfolio (specific risks "average out"). The same is not possible for systematic risk within one market. Depending on the market, a portfolio of approximately 30-40 securities in developed markets such as UK or US will render the portfolio sufficiently diversified to limit exposure to systemic risk only. In developing markets a larger number is required, due to the higher asset volatilities.

A rational investor should not take on any diversifiable risk, as only non-diversifiable risks are rewarded within the scope of this model. Therefore, the required return on an asset, that is, the return that compensates for risk taken must be linked to its riskiness in a portfolio context - i.e. its contribution to overall portfolio riskiness - as opposed to its "stand alone riskiness." In the CAPM context, portfolio risk is represented by higher variance i.e. less predictability. In other words the beta of the portfolio is the defining factor in rewarding the systematic exposure taken by an investor.

The Efficient Frontier

The CAPM assumes that the risk-return profile of a portfolio can be optimized - an optimal portfolio displays the lowest possible level of risk for its level of return. Additionally, since each additional asset introduced into a portfolio further diversifies the portfolio, the optimal portfolio must comprise every asset, (assuming no trading costs) with each asset value-weighted to achieve the above (assuming that any asset is infinitely divisible). All such optimal portfolios, i.e. one for each level of return, comprise the efficient frontier.

Because the unsystematic risk is diversifiable, the total risk of a portfolio can be viewed as beta.

The market portfolio

An investor might choose to invest a proportion of his or her wealth in a portfolio of risky assets with the remainder in cash - earning interest at the risk free rate (or indeed may borrow money to fund his or her purchase of risky assets in which case there is a negative cash weighting). Here, the ratio of risky assets to risk free asset does not determine overall return - this relationship is clearly linear. It is thus possible to achieve a particular return in one of two ways:

1. By investing all of one's wealth in a risky portfolio,
2. or by investing a proportion in a risky portfolio and the remainder in cash (either borrowed or invested).

For a given level of return, however, only one of these portfolios will be optimal (in the sense of lowest risk). Since the risk free asset is, by definition, uncorrelated with any other asset, option 2 will generally have the lower variance and hence be the more efficient of the two.

This relationship also holds for portfolios along the efficient frontier: A higher return portfolio plus cash is more efficient than a lower return portfolio alone for that lower level of return. For a given risk free rate, there is only one optimal portfolio which can be combined with cash to achieve the lowest level of risk for any possible return. This is the market portfolio.

Assumptions of CAPM

All Investors:

- Aim to maximize economic utility.
- Are rational risk-averse.
- Are price takers i.e., they cannot influence prices.
- Can lend and borrow unlimited under the risk free rate of interest.

- Trade without transaction or taxation costs.
- Deal with securities that are all highly divisible into small parcels.

Shortcomings of CAPM

The model assumes that asset returns are (jointly) normally distributed random variables. It is however frequently observed that returns in equity and other markets are not normally distributed. As a result, large swings (3 to 6 standard deviations from the mean) occur in the market more frequently than the normal distribution assumption would expect.

The model assumes that the variance of returns is an adequate measurement of risk. This might be justified under the assumption of normally distributed returns, but for general return distributions other risk measures (like coherent risk measures) will likely reflect the investors' preferences more adequately.

The model does not appear to adequately explain the variation in stock returns. Empirical studies show that low beta stocks may offer higher returns than the model would predict. Some data to this effect was presented as early as a 1969 conference in Buffalo, New York in a paper by Fischer Black, Michael Jensen, and Myron Scholes. Either that fact is itself rational (which saves the Efficient Market Hypothesis but makes CAPM wrong), or it is irrational (which saves CAPM, but makes the EMH wrong – indeed, this possibility makes volatility arbitrage a strategy for reliably beating the market).

The model assumes that given a certain expected return investors will prefer lower risk (lower variance) to higher risk and conversely given a certain level of risk will prefer higher returns to lower ones. It does not allow for investors who will accept lower returns for higher risk. Casino gamblers clearly pay for risk, and it is possible that some stock traders will pay for risk as well.

The model assumes that all investors have access to the same information and agree about the risk and expected return of all assets (homogeneous expectations assumption).

The model assumes that there are no taxes or transaction costs, although this assumption may be relaxed with more complicated versions of the model.

The market portfolio consists of all assets in all markets, where each asset is weighted by its market capitalization. This assumes no preference between markets and assets for individual investors, and that investors choose assets solely as a function of their risk-return profile. It also assumes that all assets are infinitely divisible as to the amount which may be held or transacted.

The market portfolio should in theory include all types of assets that are held by anyone as an investment (including works of art, real estate, human capital...) In practice, such a market portfolio is unobservable and people usually substitute a stock index as a proxy for the true market portfolio. Unfortunately, it has been shown that this substitution is not innocuous and can lead to false inferences as to the validity of the CAPM, and it has been said that due to the inobservability of the true market portfolio, the CAPM might not be empirically testable. This was presented in greater depth in a paper by Richard Roll in 1977, and is generally referred to as Roll's critique.

Modern Portfolio Theory

Modern portfolio theory (MPT) proposes how rational investors will use diversification to optimize their portfolios and how a risky asset should be priced. The basic concepts of the theory are Markowitz diversification, the efficient frontier, capital asset pricing model, the alpha and beta coefficients, the Capital Market Line and the Securities Market Line.

MPT models an asset's return as a random variable and models a portfolio as a weighted combination of assets so that the return of a portfolio is the weighted combination of the assets' returns. Moreover, a portfolio's return is a random variable and consequently has an expected value and a variance. Risk, in this model, is the standard deviation of return.

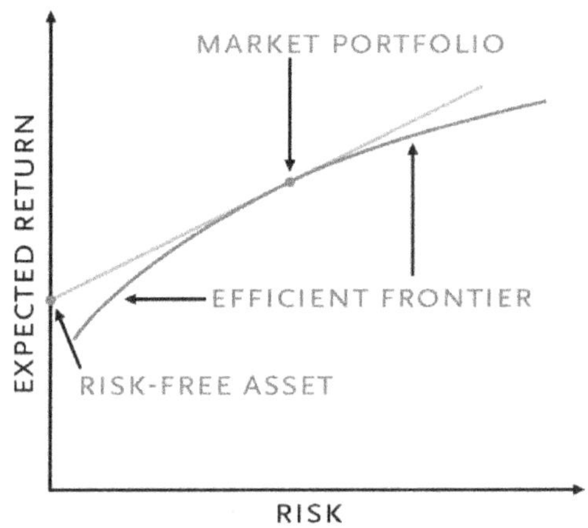

Picture 3: Capital Market Line

Risk and Return

The model assumes that investors are risk averse, meaning that given two assets that offer the same expected return, investors will prefer the less risky one. Thus, an investor will take on increased risk only if compensated by higher expected returns. Conversely, an investor who wants higher returns must accept more risk. The exact trade-off will differ by investor based on individual risk aversion characteristics. The implication is that a rational investor will not invest in a portfolio if a second portfolio exists with a more favorable risk-return profile – i.e., if for that level of risk an alternative portfolio exists which has better expected returns.

Mean and Variance

It is further assumed that an investor's risk / reward preference can be described via a quadratic utility function. The effect of this assumption is that only the expected return and the volatility (i.e., mean return and standard deviation) matter to the investor. The investor is indifferent to other characteristics of the distribution of returns, such as its skew (measures the level of asymmetry in the distribution) or kurtosis (measure of the thickness or so-called "fat tail").

Note that the theory uses a parameter, volatility, as a proxy for risk while return is an expectation on the future. This is in line with the efficient market hypothesis and most of the classical findings in finance such as Black and Scholes European Option Pricing (martingale measure: shortly speaking means that the best forecast for tomorrow is the price of today). Recent innovations in portfolio theory, particularly under the rubric of Post-Modern Portfolio Theory (PMPT), have exposed several flaws in this reliance on variance as the investor's risk proxy:

- The theory uses a historical parameter, volatility, as a proxy for risk, while return is an expectation on the future. (It is noted though that this is in line with the Efficiency Hypothesis and most of the classical findings in finance such as Black and Scholes which make use of the martingale measure, i.e. the assumption that the best forecast for tomorrow is the price of today).
- The statement that "the investor is indifferent to other characteristics" seems not to be true given that skewness risk appears to be priced by the market.

Under the model:

- Portfolio return is the proportion-weighted combination of the constituent assets' returns.
- Portfolio volatility is a function of the correlation ρ of the component assets. The change in volatility is non-linear as the weighting of the component assets changes.

Mathematically

In general:

- Expected return:-

$$\mathrm{E}(R_p) = \sum_i w_i \mathrm{E}(R_i)$$

Where R is return and w_i is the weighting of component asset i.

- Portfolio variance:-

$$\sigma_p^2 = \sum_i w_i^2 \sigma_i^2 + \sum_i \sum_j w_i w_j \sigma_i \sigma_j \rho_{ij}$$

Where i≠j. Alternatively the expression can be written as:

$$\sigma_p^2 = \sum_i \sum_j w_i w_j \sigma_i \sigma_j \rho_{ij}$$

where $\rho_{ij} = 1$ for i=j.

- Portfolio volatility:-

$$\sigma_p = \sqrt{\sigma_p^2}$$

For a Two Asset Portfolio:

- Portfolio return:
$$\mathrm{E}(R_p) = w_A \mathrm{E}(R_A) + (1 - w_A)\mathrm{E}(R_B) = w_A \mathrm{E}(R_A) + w_B \mathrm{E}(R_B)$$

- Portfolio variance:
$$\sigma_p^2 = w_A^2 \sigma_A^2 + w_B^2 \sigma_B^2 + 2 w_A w_B \sigma_A \sigma_B \rho_{AB}$$

matrices are preferred for calculations of the efficient frontier. In matrix form, for a given "risk tolerance" $q \in [0, \infty)$, the efficient front is found by minimizing the following expression:

$$\frac{1}{2} \cdot w^T \Sigma w - q * R^T w$$

where

- *w* is a vector of portfolio weights. Each $w_i \geq 0$ and

  $\sum w_i = 1$

- Σ is the covariance matrix for the assets in the portfolio
- *q* is a "risk tolerance" factor, where 0 results in the portfolio with minimal risk and ∞ results in the portfolio with maximal return
- *R* is a vector of expected returns

The front is calculated by repeating the optimization for various $q \geq 0$.

The optimization can for example be conducted by optimization that is available in many software packages, including Microsoft Excel, Matlab and R.

Diversification

An investor can reduce portfolio risk simply by holding instruments which are not perfectly correlated. In other words, investors can reduce their exposure to individual asset risk by holding a diversified portfolio of assets. Diversification will allow for the same portfolio return with reduced risk.

If all the assets of a portfolio have a correlation of 1, i.e., perfect correlation, the portfolio volatility (standard deviation) will be equal to the weighted sum of the individual asset volatilities. Hence the portfolio variance will be equal to the square of the total weighted sum of the individual asset volatilities.

If all the assets have a correlation of 0 i.e., perfectly uncorrelated, the portfolio variance is the sum of the individual asset weights squared times the individual asset variance (and volatility is the square root of this sum).

If correlation is less than zero i.e. the assets are inversely correlated, the portfolio variance and hence volatility will be less than if the correlation is 0.

Capital Allocation Line

The capital allocation line (CAL) is the line of expected return plotted against risk (standard deviation) that connects all portfolios that can be formed using a risky asset and a riskless asset. It can be proven that it is a straight line and that it has the following equation.

$$\mathrm{CML} : E(r_C) = r_F + \sigma_C \frac{E(r_M) - r_F}{\sigma_M}.$$

In this formula P is the risky portfolio, F is the riskless portfolio, and C is a combination of portfolios P and F.

The Efficient Frontier

Every possible asset combination can be plotted in risk-return space and the collection of all such possible portfolios defines a region in this space. The line along the upper edge of this region is known as the efficient frontier (sometimes "the Markowitz frontier"). Combinations along this line represent portfolios (explicitly excluding the risk-free alternative) for which there is lowest risk for a given level of return. Conversely, for a given amount of risk, the portfolio lying on the efficient frontier represents the combination offering the best possible return. Mathematically the Efficient Frontier is the intersection of the Set of Portfolios with Minimum Variance (MVS) and the Set of Portfolios with Maximum Return.

The efficient frontier is illustrated above with return μp on the y-axis and risk σp on the x-axis. An alternative illustration from the diagram in the CAPM is at below.

The efficient frontier will be convex – this is because the risk-return characteristics of a portfolio change in a non-linear fashion as its component weightings are changed. (As described above, portfolio risk is a function of the correlation of the component assets and thus changes in a non-linear fashion as the weighting of component assets changes.) The efficient frontier is a parabola (hyperbola) when expected return is plotted against variance (standard deviation).

The region above the frontier is unachievable by holding risky assets alone. No portfolios can be constructed corresponding to the points in this region. Points below the frontier are suboptimal. A rational investor will hold a portfolio only on the frontier.

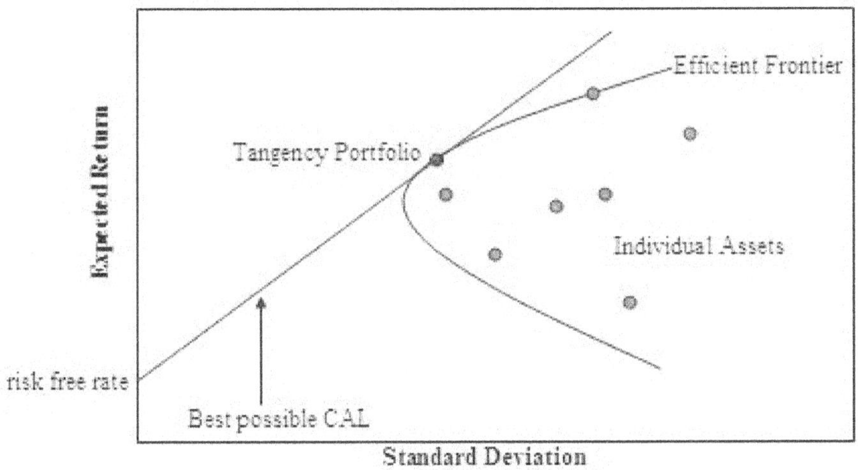

Picture 4: The Efficient Frontier

The Risk-Free Asset

The risk-free asset is the (hypothetical) asset which pays a risk-free rate. It is usually proxied by an investment in short-dated Government securities. The risk-free asset has zero variance in returns (hence is risk-free). It is also uncorrelated with any other asset (by definition: since its variance is zero). As a result, when it is combined with any other asset or portfolio of assets the change in return and also in risk is linear.

Because both risk and return change linearly as the risk-free asset is introduced into a portfolio, this combination will plot a straight line in risk-return space. The line starts at 100% in cash and weight of the risky portfolio = 0 (i.e., intercepting the return axis at the risk-free rate) and goes through the portfolio in question where cash holding = 0 and portfolio weight = 1.

Mathematically

Using the formula for a two asset portfolio as above:

- Return is the weighted average of the risk free asset, ***f***, and the risky portfolio, **p**, and is therefore linear:

Return = $w_f \mathrm{E}(R_f) + w_p \mathrm{E}(R_p)$

- Since the asset is risk free, the portfolio standard deviation is simply a function of the weight of the risky portfolio in the position. This relationship is linear.

Standard deviation = $\sqrt{w_f^2 \sigma_f^2 + w_p^2 \sigma_p^2 + 2 w_f w_p \sigma_{fp}}$

$= \sqrt{w_f^2 \cdot 0 + w_p^2 \sigma_p^2 + 2 w_f w_p \cdot 0}$

$= \sqrt{w_p^2 \sigma_p^2}$

$= w_p \sigma_p$

Portfolio Leverage

An investor adds leverage to the portfolio by borrowing the risk-free asset. The addition of the risk-free asset allows for a position in the region above the efficient frontier. Thus, by combining a risk-free asset with risky assets, it is possible to construct portfolios whose risk-return profiles are superior to those on the efficient frontier.

An investor holding a portfolio of risky assets, with a holding in cash, has a positive risk-free weighting (a de-leveraged portfolio). The return and standard deviation will be lower than the portfolio alone but since the efficient frontier is convex, this combination will sit above the efficient frontier – i.e., offering a higher return for the same risk as the point below it on the frontier.

The investor who borrows money to fund his/her purchase of the risky assets has a negative risk-free weighting – i.e., a leveraged portfolio. Here the return is geared to the risky portfolio. This combination will again offer a return superior to those on the frontier.

The Market Portfolio

The efficient frontier is a collection of portfolios, each one optimal for a given amount of risk. A quantity known as the Sharpe ratio represents a measure of the amount of additional return (above the risk-free rate) a portfolio provides compared to the risk it carries. The portfolio on the efficient frontier with the highest Sharpe Ratio is known as the market portfolio, or sometimes the super-efficient portfolio; it is the tangency-portfolio in the above diagram. This portfolio has the property that any combination of it and the risk-free asset will produce a return that is above the efficient frontier—offering a larger return for a given amount of risk than a portfolio of risky assets on the frontier would.

Capital Market Line

When the market portfolio is combined with the risk-free asset, the result is the Capital Market Line. All points along the CML have superior risk-return profiles to any portfolio on the efficient frontier. Just the special case of the market portfolio with zero cash weighting is on the efficient frontier. Additions of cash or leverage with the risk-free asset in combination with the market portfolio are on the Capital Market Line. All of these portfolios represent the highest possible Sharpe ratio. The CML is illustrated above, with return μp on the y-axis, and risk σp on the x-axis.

One can prove that the CML is the optimal CAL and that its equation is:

$$\mathrm{CML}: E(r_C) = r_F + \sigma_C \frac{E(r_M) - r_F}{\sigma_M}.$$

Asset Pricing

A rational investor would not invest in an asset which does not improve the risk-return characteristics of his existing portfolio. Since a rational investor would hold the market portfolio, the asset in question will be added to the market portfolio. MPT derives the required return for a correctly priced asset in this context.

Systematic Risk and Specific Risk

Specific risk is the risk associated with individual assets - within a portfolio these risks can be reduced through diversification (specific risks "cancel out"). Specific risk is also called diversifiable, unique, unsystematic, or idiosyncratic risk. systematic risk (a.k.a. portfolio risk or market risk) refers to the risk common to all securities - except for selling short as noted below, systematic risk cannot be diversified away (within one market). Within the market portfolio, asset specific risk will be diversified away to the extent possible. Systematic risk is therefore equated with the risk (standard deviation) of the market portfolio.

Since a security will be purchased only if it improves the risk / return characteristics of the market portfolio, the risk of a security will be the risk it adds to the market portfolio. In this context, the volatility of the asset and its correlation with the market portfolio, is historically observed and is therefore a given (there are several approaches to asset pricing that attempt to price assets by modeling the stochastic properties of the moments of assets' returns - these are broadly referred to as conditional asset pricing models). The (maximum) price paid for any particular asset (and hence the return it will generate) should also be determined based on its relationship with the market portfolio.

Systematic risks within one market can be managed through a strategy of using both long and short positions within one portfolio, creating a "market neutral" portfolio.

Security Characteristic Line

The security characteristic line (SCL) represents the relationship between the market return (r_M) and the return r_i of a given asset i at a given time t. In general, it is reasonable to assume that the SCL is a straight line and can be illustrated as a statistical equation:

$$\mathrm{SCL}: r_{i,t} = \alpha_i + \beta r_{M,t} + \epsilon_{i,t}$$

where αi is called the asset's alpha coefficient and βi the asset's beta coefficient.

Securities Market Line

The SML essentially graphs the results from the capital asset pricing model (CAPM) formula. The *x*-axis represents the risk (beta) and the *y*-axis represents the expected return. The market risk premium is determined from the slope of the SML.

The relationship between β and the required return is plotted on the securities market line (SML) which shows expected return as a function of β. The intercept is the nominal risk-free rate available for the market, while the slope is $E(R_m - R_f)$. The securities market line can be regarded as representing a single-factor model of the asset price, where Beta is exposure to changes in value of the Market. The equation of the SML is thus:

$$\mathrm{SML}: E(R_i) - R_f = \beta_i(E(R_M) - R_f).$$

It is a useful tool in determining if an asset being considered for a portfolio offers a reasonable expected return for risk. Individual securities are plotted on the SML graph. If the security's risk versus expected return is plotted above the SML, it is undervalued since the investor can expect a greater return for the inherent risk. And a security plotted below the SML is overvalued since the investor would be accepting less return for the amount of risk assumed.

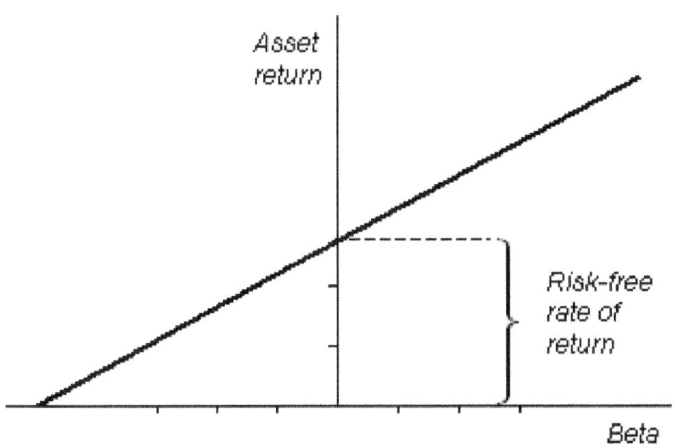

Picture 5: The Security Market Line

Applications to Project Portfolios and other "Non-Financial" Assets

Some experts apply MPT to portfolios of projects and other assets besides financial instruments. When MPT is applied outside of traditional financial portfolios, some differences between the different types of portfolios must be considered.

The assets in financial portfolios are, for practical purposes, continuously divisible while portfolios of projects like new software development are "lumpy". For example, while we can compute that the optimal portfolio position for 3 stocks is, say, 44%, 35%, 21%, the optimal position for an IT portfolio may not allow us to simply change the amount spent on a project. IT projects might be all or nothing or, at least, have logical units that cannot be separated. A portfolio optimization method would have to take the discrete nature of some IT projects into account.

The assets of financial portfolios are liquid, can be assessed or re-assessed at any point in time while opportunities for new projects may be limited and may appear in limited windows of time and projects that have already been initiated cannot be abandoned without the loss of the sunk costs (i.e., there is little or no recovery/salvage value of a half-complete IT project).

Neither of these necessarily eliminate the possibility of using MPT and such portfolios. They simply indicate the need to run the optimization with an additional set of mathematically-expressed constraints that would not normally apply to financial portfolios.

Furthermore, some of the simplest elements of MPT are applicable to virtually any kind of portfolio. The concept of capturing the risk tolerance of an investor by documenting how much risk is acceptable for a given return could be and is applied to a variety of decision analysis problems. MPT, however, uses historical variance as a measure of risk and portfolios of assets like IT projects don't usually have an "historical variance" for a new piece of software. In this case, the MPT investment boundary can be expressed in more general terms like "chance of an ROI less than cost of capital" or "chance of losing more than half of the investment". When risk is put in terms of uncertainty about forecasts and possible losses then the concept is transferable to various types of investment.

Applications of Modern Portfolio Theory in other Disciplines

In the 1970s, concepts from Modern Portfolio Theory found their way into the field of regional science. In a series of seminal works, Michael Conroy modeled the labor force in the economy using portfolio-theoretic methods to examine growth and variability in the labor force. This was followed by a long literature on the relationship between economic growth and volatility.

More recently, modern portfolio theory has been used to model the self-concept in social psychology. When the self attributes comprising the self-concept constitute a well-diversified portfolio then psychological outcomes at the level of the individual such as mood and self-esteem should be more stable than when the self-concept is undiversified. This prediction has been confirmed in studies involving human subjects.

Comparison with arbitrage pricing theory

The SML and CAPM are often contrasted with the arbitrage pricing theory (APT) which holds that the expected return of a financial asset can be modeled as a linear function of various macro-economic factors, where sensitivity to changes in each factor is represented by a factor specific beta coefficient.

The APT is less restrictive in its assumptions. It allows for an explanatory (as opposed to statistical) model of asset returns and assumes that each investor will hold a unique portfolio with its own particular array of betas, as opposed to the identical "market portfolio". Unlike the CAPM, the APT, however, does not itself reveal the identity of its priced factors - the number and nature of these factors is likely to change over time and between economies.

Markets

Financial Markets

A financial market is a mechanism that allows people to easily buy and sell (trade) financial securities (such as stocks and bonds), commodities (such as precious metals or agricultural goods) and other fungible items of value at low transaction costs and at prices that reflect the efficient-market hypothesis.

Financial markets have evolved significantly over several hundred years and are undergoing constant innovation to improve liquidity.

Both general markets (where many commodities are traded) and specialized markets (where only one commodity is traded) exist. Markets work by placing many interested buyers and sellers in one "place", thus making it easier for them to find each other. An economy which relies primarily on interactions between buyers and sellers to allocate resources is known as a market economy in contrast either to a command economy or to a non-market economy such as a gift economy.

Financial markets facilitate: –

- The raising of capital (in the capital markets);
- The transfer of risk (in the derivatives markets);
- International trade (in the currency markets)

– and are used to match those who want capital to those who have it.

Typically a borrower issues a receipt to the lender promising to pay back the capital. These receipts are securities which may be freely bought or sold. In return for lending money to the borrower, the lender will expect some compensation in the form of interest or dividends.

Definition

In economics, typically, the term market means the aggregate of possible buyers and sellers of a thing and the transactions between them.

The term "market" is sometimes used for what are more strictly exchanges, organizations that facilitate the trade in financial securities e.g. a stock exchange or commodity exchange. This may be a physical location (like the NYSE) or an electronic system (like NASDAQ). Much trading of stocks takes place on an exchange. Still, corporate actions (merger, spinoff) are outside an exchange, while any two companies or people, for whatever reason, may agree to sell stock from the one to the other without using an exchange.

Trading of currencies and bonds is largely on a bilateral basis, although some bonds trade on a stock exchange and people are building electronic systems for these as well, similar to stock exchanges.

Financial markets can be domestic or they can be international.

Types of Financial Markets

The financial markets can be divided into different subtypes:

Capital markets which consist of:

- **Stock markets**, which provide financing through the issuance of shares or common stock, and enable the subsequent trading thereof.
    - **Bond markets**, which provide financing through the issuance of bonds, and enable the subsequent trading thereof.
    - **Commodity markets**, which facilitate the trading of commodities.
- **Money markets**, which provide short term debt financing and investment.
- **Derivatives markets**, which provide instruments for the management of financial risk.
    - **Futures markets**, which provide standardized forward contracts for trading products at some future date.
- **Insurance markets**, which facilitate the redistribution of various risks.
- **Foreign exchange markets**, which facilitate the trading of foreign exchange.

The capital markets consist of primary markets and secondary markets. Newly formed (issued) securities are bought or sold in primary markets. Secondary markets allow investors to sell securities that they hold or buy existing securities.

Raising Capital

To understand financial markets let us look at what they are used for i.e. what is their purpose?

Without financial markets borrowers would have difficulty finding lenders themselves. Intermediaries such as banks help in this process. Banks take deposits from those who have money to save. They can then lend money from this pool of deposited money to those who seek to borrow. Banks popularly lend money in the form of loans and mortgages.

More complex transactions than a simple bank deposit require markets where lenders and their agents can meet borrowers and their agents and where existing borrowing or lending commitments can be sold on to other parties. A good example of a financial market is a stock exchange. A company can raise money by selling shares to investors and its existing shares can be bought or sold.

The following table illustrates where financial markets fit in the relationship between lenders and borrowers:

Relationship between lenders and borrowers

Lenders	Financial Intermediaries	Financial Markets	Borrowers
Individuals	Banks	Interbank	Individuals
Companies	Insurance Companies	Stock Exchange	Companies
	Pension Funds	Money Market	Central Government
	Mutual Funds	Bond Market	Municipalities
		Foreign Exchange	Public Corporations

Lenders

Individuals

Many individuals are not aware that they are lenders but almost everybody does lend money in many ways. A person lends money when he or she:

- puts money in a savings account at a bank;
- contributes to a pension plan;
- pays premiums to an insurance company;
- invests in government bonds; or
- invests in company shares.

Companies

Companies tend to be borrowers of capital. When companies have surplus cash that is not needed for a short period of time, they may seek to make money from their cash surplus by lending it via short term markets called money markets.

There are a few companies that have very strong cash flows. These companies tend to be lenders rather than borrowers. Such companies may decide to return cash to lenders (e.g. via a share buyback.) Alternatively, they may seek to make more money on their cash by lending it (e.g. investing in bonds and stocks.)

Borrowers

Individuals borrow money via bankers' loans for short term needs or longer term mortgages to help finance a house purchase.

Companies borrow money to aid short term or long term cash flows. They also borrow to fund modernisation or future business expansion.

Governments often find their spending requirements exceed their tax revenues. To make up this difference, they need to borrow. Governments also borrow on behalf of nationalised industries, municipalities, local authorities and other public sector bodies. In the UK, the total borrowing requirement is often referred to as the Public sector net cash requirement (PSNCR).

Governments borrow by issuing bonds. In the UK, the government also borrows from individuals by offering bank accounts and premium bonds. Government debt seems to be permanent. Indeed the debt seemingly expands rather than being paid off. One strategy used by governments to reduce the value of the debt is to influence inflation.

Municipalities and local authorities may borrow in their own name as well as receiving funding from national governments. In the UK, this would cover an authority like Hampshire County Council.

Public Corporations typically include nationalized industries. These may include the postal services, railway companies and utility companies.

Many borrowers have difficulty raising money locally. They need to borrow internationally with the aid of foreign exchange markets.

The Capital Market

The capital market is the market for securities, where companies and governments can raise longterm funds. The capital market includes the stock market and the bond market. Financial regulators, such as the U.S. Securities and Exchange Commission, oversee the capital markets in their designated countries to ensure that investors are protected against fraud.

The capital markets consist of the primary market and the secondary market. The primary markets is where new stock and bonds issues are sold (underwritten) to investors. The secondary markets are where existing securities are sold and bought from one investor or speculator to another, usually on an exchange (eg.- New York Stock Exchange).

Primary Market

The primary is that part of the capital markets that deals with the issuance of new securities. Companies, governments or public sector institutions can obtain funding through the sale of a new stock or bond issue. This is typically done through a syndicate of securities dealers. The process of selling new issues to investors is called underwriting. In the case of a new stock issue, this sale is an initial public offering (IPO). Dealers earn a commission that is built into the price of the security offering, though it can be found in the prospectus.

Features of primary markets are:

- This is the market for new long term capital. The primary market is the market where the securities are sold for the first time. Therefore it is also called New Issue Market (NIM).
- In a primary issue, the securities are issued by the company directly to investors.
- The company receives the money and issues new security certificates to the investors.
- Primary issues are used by companies for the purpose of setting up new business or for expanding or modernizing the existing business.
- The primary market performs the crucial function of facilitating capital formation in the economy.
- The new issue market does not include certain other sources of new long term external finance such as loans from financial institutions.

Borrowers in the new issue market may be raising capital for converting private capital into public capital; this is known as 'going public'.

Methods of issuing securities in the primary market are:

- Initial public offering,
- Rights issue (for existing companies), and
- Preferential issue.

Secondary market

The secondary market is the financial market for trading of securities that have already been issued in an initial private or public offering. Alternatively, a secondary market can refer to the market for any kind of used goods. The market that exists in a new security just after the new issue, is often referred to as the aftermarket. Once a newly issued stock is listed on a stock exchange investors and speculators can easily trade on the exchange as market makers provide bids and offers in the new stock.

Function

In the secondary market, securities are sold by and transferred from one investor or speculator to another. It is therefore important that the secondary market be highly liquid (originally, the only way to create this liquidity was for investors and speculators to meet at a fixed place regularly.

Secondary marketing is vital to an efficient and modern capital market. Fundamentally, secondary markets mesh the investor's preference for liquidity (i.e., the investor's desire not to tie up his or her money for a long period of time, in case the investor needs it to deal with unforeseen circumstances) with the capital user's preference to be able to use the capital for an extended period of time. For example, a traditional loan allows the borrower to pay back the loan, with interest, over a certain period. For the length of that period of time, the bulk of the lender's investment is inaccessible to the lender, even in cases of emergencies. Likewise, in an emergency, a partner in a traditional partnership is only able to access his or her original investment if he or she finds another investor willing to buy out his or her interest in the partnership. With a securitized loan or equity interest (such as bonds) or tradable stocks, the investor can sell, relatively easily, his or her interest in the investment.

Particularly if the loan or ownership equity has been broken into relatively small parts. This selling and buying of small parts of a larger loan or ownership interest in a venture is called secondary market trading.

Under traditional lending and partnership arrangements, investors may be less likely to put their money into long-term investments and more likely to charge a higher interest rate (or demand a greater share of the profits) if they do. With secondary markets, however, investors know that they can recoup some of their investment quickly, if their own circumstances change.

Related Usage

The term may refer to markets in things of value other than securities. For example, the ability to buy and sell intellectual property such as patents or rights to musical compositions is considered a secondary market because it allows the owner to freely resell property entitlements issued by the government. Similarly, secondary markets can be said to exist in some real estate contexts as well (e.g. ownership shares of time-share vacation homes are bought and sold outside of the official exchange set up by the time-share issuers). These have very similar functions as secondary stock and bond markets in allowing for speculation providing liquidity and financing through securitization.

Private Secondary Markets

Partially as a result of the increased compliance and reporting obligations hoisted on U.S.-listed public companies by the Sarbanes-Oxley Act of 2002 private secondary markets began to emerge. These markets are generally only available to institutional or accredited investors and allow trading of unregistered and private company securities. Goldman Sachs' GS TRuE, Nasdaq's PORTAL, and SecondMarket are all examples of these private secondary markets.

The Stock Market

A stock market or equity market is a private or public market for the trading of company stocks and derivatives of company stock. These derivatives and stocks get traded at an agreed price.

The size of the world stock market was estimated to be about $36.6 trillion US the beginning of October 2008. The world derivatives market has been estimated to be about $480 trillion face or nominal value. That is 12 times the size of the entire world economy. It must be noted though that the value of the derivatives market cannot be directly compared to a stock or a fixed income security. Many such relatively illiquid securities are valued as marked to model rather than an actual market price.

Stocks are listed and traded on stock exchanges. A Stock exchange is an entity, a corporation or a mutual organization specialized in bringing buyers and sellers of company stocks together as well as listing companies in their register. The stock market in the United States includes the trading of all securities listed on the NYSE, the NASDAQ, the Amex as well as on the many regional exchanges, e.g. OTCBB and Pink Sheets. European examples of stock exchanges include the London Stock Exchange, the Deutsche Börse in Germany and the Paris Bourse, now part of Euronext. However, there are many more stock exchanges in the world. Each country usually has many more regional stock exchanges as well. However, this topic will be discussed in more detail later on in the book.

Trading on the Stock Market

Participants in the stock market range from small individual stock investors to large hedge fund traders, who can be based anywhere in the world. Their orders usually go through a stock broker who is directly linked to the stock exchange, and who executes the orders of his clients.

Some exchanges are physical locations where transactions are carried out on a trading floor by a method known as open outcry. This type of auction is used in stock exchanges and commodity exchanges where traders may enter "verbal" bids and offers simultaneously. Another type of stock exchange is a virtual stock exchange. This type is composed of a network of computers where trades are made electronically via traders.

Actual trades are based on an auction market paradigm where a potential buyer bids a specific price for a stock and a potential seller asks a specific price for the stock. (Buying or selling at market means you will accept any ask price or bid price for the stock, respectively.) When the bid and ask prices match and if there are multiple bidders or askers at a given price then a sale takes place on a first come first served basis.

The purpose of a stock exchange is to facilitate the exchange of securities between buyers and sellers, thus providing a marketplace (virtual or real). The exchanges provide real-time trading information on the listed securities, facilitating price discovery.

The New York Stock Exchange is a physical exchange also referred to as a listed exchange — only stocks listed with the exchange may be traded. Orders enter by way of exchange members and flow down to a floor broker who goes to the floor trading post specialist for that stock to trade the order. The specialist's job is to match buy and sell orders using open outcry. If a spread exists, no trade immediately takes place--in this case the specialist should use his/her own resources (money or stock) to close the difference after his/her judged time. Once a trade has been made the details are reported on the "tape" and sent back to the brokerage firm, which then notifies the investor who placed the order. Although there is a significant amount of human contact in this process, computers play an important role, especially for so-called "program trading".

The NASDAQ or XETRA are a virtual listed exchanges, where all of the trading is done over a computer network. The process is similar to the New York Stock Exchange. However, buyers and sellers are electronically matched. One or more NASDAQ market makers will always provide a bid and ask price at which they will always purchase or sell 'their' stock.

The Paris Bourse, now part of Euronext, is an order-driven, electronic stock exchange. It was automated in the late 1980s. Prior to the 1980s, it consisted of an open outcry exchange. Stockbrokers met on the trading floor or the Palais Brongniart. In 1986, the CATS trading system was introduced, and the order matching process was fully automated.

Nowadays securities firms, led by UBS AG, Goldman Sachs Group Inc. and Credit Suisse Group, already steer 12 percent of U.S. security trades away from the exchanges to their internal systems. That share probably will increase to 18 percent by 2010 as more investment banks bypass the NYSE and NASDAQ and pair buyers and sellers of securities themselves, according to data compiled by Boston-based Aite Group LLC, a brokerage-industry consultant.

Now that computers have eliminated the need for trading floors like the Big Board's, the balance of power in equity markets is shifting. By bringing more orders in-house, where clients can move big blocks of stock anonymously and very quickly, brokers pay the stock exchanges less in fees and capture a bigger share of the $11 billion a year that institutional investors pay in trading commissions.

Market Participants

Many years ago, buyers and sellers were individual investors, such as wealthy businessmen, with long family histories (and emotional ties) to particular corporations. Over time, markets have become more "institutionalized". Buyers and sellers are largely institutions (e.g., pension funds, insurance companies, mutual funds, index funds, exchange traded funds, hedge funds, investor groups, banks and various other financial institutions). The rise of the institutional investor has brought with it some improvements in market operations. Thus, the government was responsible for "fixed" (and exorbitant) fees being markedly reduced for the 'small' investor but only after the large institutions had managed to break the brokers' solid front on fees they then went to 'negotiated' fees, but only for large institutions.

However, corporate governance (at least in the western world) has been very much adversely affected by the rise of (largely 'absentee') institutional 'owners'.

The History of Stock Markets

Historian Fernand Braudel suggests that in Cairo in the 11th century, Muslim and Jewish merchants had already set up every form of trade association and had knowledge of many methods of credit and payment, disproving the belief that these were originally invented later by Italians. In 12th century France the courratiers de change were concerned with managing and regulating the debts of agricultural communities on behalf of the banks. Because these men also traded with debts they could be called the first brokers. A common misbelief is that in late 13th century Bruges commodity traders gathered inside the house of a man called Van der Beurze and in 1309 they became the "Brugse Beurse" institutionalizing what had been, until then, an informal meeting. Actually the family Van der Beurze had a building in Antwerp where those gatherings occurred. The idea quickly spread around Flanders and neighboring counties and "Beurzen" soon opened in Ghent and Amsterdam.

In the middle of the 13th century, Venetian bankers began to trade in government securities. In 1351 the Venetian government outlawed spreading rumors intended to lower the price of government funds. Bankers in Pisa, Verona, Genoa and Florence also began trading in government securities during the 14th century. This was only possible because these were independent city states not ruled by a duke but a council of influential citizens. The Dutch later started joint stock companies which let shareholders to invest in business ventures and to get a share of their profits - or losses. In 1602, the Dutch East India Company issued the first shares on the Amsterdam Stock Exchange. It was the first company to issue stocks and bonds.

The Amsterdam Stock Exchange (or Amsterdam Beurs) is also said to have been the first stock exchange to introduce continuous trade in the early 17th century. The Dutch "pioneered short selling, option trading, debt-equity swaps, merchant banking, unit trusts and other speculative instruments, much as we know them today"[2]. There are now stock markets in virtually every developed and most developing economies, with the world's biggest markets being in the United States, Canada, China (Hongkong), India, UK, Germany, France and Japan.

Importance of the Stock Market

The stock market is one of the most important sources for companies to raise money. It allows businesses to be publicly traded or raise additional capital for expansion by selling shares of ownership of the company in a public market. The liquidity that an exchange provides affords investors the ability to quickly and easily sell securities. This is an attractive feature of investing in stocks, compared to other less liquid investments such as real estate.

History has shown that the price of shares and other assets is an important part of the dynamics of economic activity and can influence or be an indicator of social mood. An economy where the stock market is on the rise is considered to be an upcoming economy. In fact, the stock market is often considered the primary indicator of a country's economic strength and development. Rising share prices, for instance, tend to be associated with increased business investment and vice versa. Share prices also affect the wealth of households and their consumption. Therefore, central banks tend to keep an eye on the control and behavior of the stock market and, in general, on the

[2] Murray Sayle, "Japan Goes Dutch", London Review of Books XXIII.7, April 5, 2001

smooth operation of financial system functions. Financial stability is the raison d'être of central banks.

Stock Exchanges also act as the clearinghouse for each transaction, meaning that they collect and deliver the shares and guarantee payment to the seller of a security. This eliminates the risk to an individual buyer or seller that the counterparty could default on the transaction.

Relation of the Stock Market to the Modern Financial System

The financial system in most western countries has undergone a remarkable transformation. One feature of this development is disintermediation. A portion of the funds involved in saving and financing flows directly to the financial markets instead of being routed via the traditional bank lending and deposit operations. The general public's heightened interest in investing in the stock market, either directly or through mutual funds, has been an important component of this process. Statistics show that in recent decades shares have made up an increasingly large proportion of households' financial assets in many countries. In the 1970s, in Sweden, deposit accounts and other very liquid assets with little risk made up almost 60 percent of households' financial wealth, compared to less than 20 percent in the 2000s. The major part of this adjustment in financial portfolios has gone directly to shares but a good deal now takes the form of various kinds of institutional investment for groups of individuals e.g. pension funds, mutual funds, hedge funds, insurance investment of premiums, etc. The trend towards forms of saving with a higher risk has been accentuated by new rules for most funds and insurance permitting a higher proportion of shares to bonds. Similar tendencies are to be found in other industrialized countries. In all developed economic systems such as the European Union, the United States, Japan and other developed nations the trend has been the same. Saving has moved away from traditional (government insured) bank deposits to more risky securities of one sort or another.

The Stock Market, Individual Investors, and Financial Risk

Riskier long-term saving requires that an individual possess the ability to manage the associated increased risks. Stock prices fluctuate widely, in marked contrast to the stability of (government insured) bank deposits or bonds. This is something that could affect not only the individual investor or household but also the economy on a large scale. The following paragraphs deal with some of the risks of the financial sector in general and the stock market in particular. This is certainly more important now that so many newcomers have entered the stock market or have acquired other 'risky' investments (such as 'investment' property, i.e., real estate and collectables).

With each passing year the noise level in the stock market rises. Television commentators, financial writers, analysts and market strategists are all overtaking each other to get investors' attention. At the same time individual investors, immersed in chat rooms and message boards, are exchanging questionable and often misleading tips. Yet, despite all this available information, investors find it increasingly difficult to profit. Stock prices skyrocket with little reason then plummet just as quickly and people who have turned to investing for their children's education and their own retirement become frightened. Sometimes there appears to be no rhyme or reason to the market, only folly.

This is a quote from the preface to a published biography about the long-term value-oriented stock investor Warren Buffett. Buffett began his career with $100 and $105,000 from seven limited partners consisting of Buffett's family and friends. Over the years he has built himself a multi-billion-dollar fortune. The quote illustrates some of what has been happening in the stock market during the end of the 20th century and the beginning of the 21st.

The behavior of the stock market

From experience we know that investors may temporarily pull financial prices away from their long term trend level. Over-reactions may occur—so that excessive optimism (euphoria) may drive prices disproportionately high or excessive pessimism may drive prices unjustifiably low. New theoretical and empirical arguments have been put forward against the notion that financial markets are efficient.

According to the efficient market hypothesis, only changes in fundamental factors such as profits or dividends ought to affect share prices. (But this largely theoretic academic viewpoint also predicts that little or no trading should take place—contrary to fact—since prices are already at or near equilibrium, having priced in all public knowledge.) But the efficient-market hypothesis is sorely tested by such events as the stock market crash in 1987 when the Dow Jones index plummeted 22.6 percent—the largest-ever one-day fall in the United States. This event demonstrated that share prices can fall dramatically even though, to this day, it is impossible to fix a definite cause. A thorough search failed to detect any specific or unexpected development that might account for the crash. It also seems to be the case more generally that many price movements are not occasioned by new information. A study of the fifty largest one-day share price movements in the United States in the post-war period confirms this. Moreover, while the efficient market hypothesis predicts that all price movement (in the absence of change in fundamental information) is random (i.e., non-trending), many studies have shown a marked tendency for the stock market to trend over time periods of weeks or longer.

Various explanations for large price movements have been promulgated. For instance, some research has shown that changes in estimated risk and the use of certain strategies such as stop-loss limits and Value at Risk limits theoretically could cause financial markets to overreact.

Other research has shown that psychological factors may result in exaggerated stock price movements. Psychological research has demonstrated that people are predisposed to 'seeing' patterns and often will perceive a pattern in what is, in fact, just noise. (Something like seeing familiar shapes in clouds or ink blots.) In the present context this means that a succession of good news items about a company may lead investors to overreact positively (unjustifiably driving the price up). A period of good returns also boosts the investor's self-confidence, reducing his (psychological) risk threshold.

Another phenomenon—also from psychology—that works against an objective assessment is group thinking. As social animals, it is not easy to stick to an opinion that differs markedly from that of a majority of the group. An example with which one may be familiar is the reluctance to enter a restaurant that is empty. People generally prefer to have their opinion validated by those of others in the group.

Some researchers draw an analogy with gambling. In normal times the market behaves like a game of roulette. The probabilities are known and largely independent of the investment decisions of the different players. In times of market stress, however, the game becomes more like poker (herding behavior takes over). The players now must give heavy weight to the psychology of other investors and how they are likely to react psychologically.

The stock market, as any other business, is quite unforgiving of amateurs. Inexperienced investors rarely get the assistance and support they need. In the period running up to the recent Nasdaq crash less than 1 percent of the analyst's recommendations had been to sell (and even during the 2000 - 2002 crash the average did not rise above 5%). The media amplified the general euphoria, with reports of rapidly rising share prices and the notion that large sums of money could be quickly earned in the so-called new economy stock market. (And later amplified the gloom which descended during the 2000 -

2002 crash so that by summer of 2002 predictions of a DOW average below 5000 were quite common.)

Irrational Behavior

Sometimes the market tends to react irrationally to economic news even if that news has no real effect on the technical value of securities itself. Therefore, the stock market can be swayed tremendously in either direction by press releases, rumors, euphoria and mass panic.

Over the short-term stocks and other securities can be battered or buoyed by any number of fast market-changing events, making the stock market difficult to predict. Emotions can drive prices up and down. People may not be as rational as they think. Behaviorists argue that investors often behave irrationally when making investment decisions thereby incorrectly pricing securities which causes market inefficiencies which, in turn, are opportunities to make money.

Stock Market Cycles

A cycle or a wave represents a process that tends to repeat itself in time in a more or less regular fashion.

There are many types of business cycles. Some of the most common ones are those that impact the stock market. In his book "The Next Great Bubble Boom" by Harry S. Dent Jr., a Harvard graduate and Fortune 100 consultant, outlines several cycles that have specific relevance to the stock market. Some of these cycles have been quantitatively examined for statistical significance.

Some of the major cycles that have been examined by Mr. Dent and others are:

- The four-year presidential cycle in the USA.
- Annual seasonality, in the USA and other countries.
- "The Halloween indicator" (or "Sell in May and Go Away")
- The "January effect"
- The lunar cycle

Many investors and market traders take recourse to these cycles and the insights they provide when making investment decisions. For example investment advisor Mark Hulbert has tracked the long term performance of Norman Fosback's a Seasonality Timing System that combines month-end and holiday-based buy/sell rules. According to Hulbert this system has been able to outperform the market with significantly less risk. According to him it has the best risk-adjusted performance of any system his newsletter tracks. Other authors and investment advisors contend that there are four stages in any major cycle whether it is an individual stock or a market sector. These four stages are

1. period of consolidation or base building
2. upward advancing stage
3. top area and
4. declining phase.

Causes

Many have theorized as to the possible underlying causes of these statistical cycles. The four year U.S. presidential cycle for example is attributed to politics and its impact on America's economic policies and market sentiment. Either or both of these factors could be the cause for the stock markets statistically improved performance during most of the third and fourth years of a president's four year term. The month-end seasonality on the other hand is generally attributed to the automatic purchases associated with retirement accounts. There other cycles however, for which the explanations are less clear.

Compound Cycles

The presence of multiple cycles of different periods and magnitudes in conjunction with linear trends can give rise to complex patterns that are mathematically generated through Fourier analysis.

In order for an investor to more easily visualize a longer term cycle (or a trend), he sometimes will superimpose a shorter term cycle such as a moving average on top of it.

A common view of a stock market pattern is one that involves a specific time-frame (for example a 6-month chart with daily price intervals). In this kind of a chart one may create and observe any of the following trends or trend relationships:

- A long term trend, which may appear as linear

- Intermediate term trends and their relationship to the long term trend
- Random price movements or consolidation (sometimes referred to as 'noise') and its relationship to one of the above

However, if one looks at a longer time-frame (perhaps a 2-year chart with weekly price intervals) the current trend may appear as a part of a larger cycle (primary trend). Switching to a shorter time-frame (such as a 10-day chart using 15-minute price intervals) may reveal random price movements appearing as high frequency 'noise' in contrast to the primary trend on the chart.

A stock market trader will often use several "screens" on their computer (charts) with different time-frames and price intervals in order to gain valuable information for making profitable buying and selling (trading) decisions.

Some expert traders emphasize the use of multiple time-frames for successful trading. For example, Alexander Elder suggests a Triple Screen Approach. The three screens contain information about:

Longer-term screen: To identify the long term trend and opportunities

Middle screen: To identify the best time (or day) in which to locate a trading opportunity

Finer screen: To identify the optimum intra-day price at which to buy or sell a security

Implications

Several of the stock market 'technical analysis' approaches are based on the underlying assumptions of cyclicity. These include the use of oscillators, moving averages and the Japanese Candlestick style charts. All of these indicators are different methods of analyzing and synthesizing market price and/or volume over time. We will examine each one of these in detail at a later stage, however here are already some broad explanations:

- **Moving Averages:** There are many types of moving average indicators. Some moving average indicators such as the exponential moving average show a slightly different version of the moving average trend by smoothing out the short term fluctuations.

- **Oscillators:** These illustrate the price and volume cycles thereby allowing the investor/trader to identify relevant peaks and valleys within the trend itself.
- **Japanese Candlestick Charts:** This is a specialized type of price chart that provides more information about price activity than the standard "mountain" style chart used by many amateur investors.

The Bond Market

The bond market (also known as the debt, credit, or fixed income market) is a financial market where participants buy and sell debt securities usually in the form of bonds. As of 2006 the size of the international bond market is an estimated $45 trillion of which the size of the outstanding U.S. bond market debt was $25.2 trillion.

Nearly all of the $923 billion average daily trading volume (as of early 2007) in the U.S. bond market takes place between broker-dealers and large institutions in a decentralized over-the-counter (OTC) market. However, a small number of bonds, primarily corporate, are listed on exchanges.

References to the "bond market" usually refer to the government bond market, because of its size, liquidity, lack of credit risk and therefore sensitivity to interest rates. Because of the inverse relationship between bond valuation and interest rates, the bond market is often used to indicate changes in interest rates or the shape of the yield curve.

Market Structure

Bond markets in most countries remain decentralized and lack common exchanges like stock, future and commodity markets. This has occurred, in part, because no two bond issues are exactly alike and the number of different securities outstanding is far larger.

However, the New York Stock Exchange (NYSE) is the largest centralized bond market, representing mostly corporate bonds. The NYSE migrated from the Automated Bond System (ABS) to the NYSE Bonds trading system in April 2007 and expects the number of traded issues to increase from 1000 to 6000.

Types of Bond Markets

The Securities Industry and Financial Markets Association classifies the broader bond market into five specific bond markets.

- Corporate
- Government & agency
- Municipal

- Mortgage backed, asset backed, and collateralized debt obligation
- Funding

Bond Market Participants

Bond market participants are similar to participants in most financial markets and are essentially either buyers (debt issuer) of funds or sellers (institution) of funds and often both.

Participants include:

- Institutional investors
- Governments
- Traders
- Individuals

Because of the specificity of individual bond issues and the lack of liquidity in many smaller issues, the majority of outstanding bonds are held by institutions like pension funds, banks and mutual funds. In the United States approximately 10% of the market is currently held by private individuals.

Bond Market Volatility

For market participants who own a bond, collect the coupon and hold it to maturity, market volatility is irrelevant. Principal and interest are received according to a pre-determined schedule.

But participants who buy and sell bonds before maturity are exposed to many risks most importantly changes in interest rates. When interest rates increase the value of existing bonds falls since new issues pay a higher yield. Likewise, when interest rates decrease the value of existing bonds rise since new issues pay a lower yield. This is the fundamental concept of bond market volatility. Changes in bond prices are inverse to changes in interest rates. Fluctuating interest rates are part of a country's monetary policy and bond market volatility is a response to expected monetary policy and economic changes.

Economists' views of economic indicators versus actual released data contribute to market volatility. A tight consensus is generally reflected in bond prices and there is little price movement in the market after the release of "in-line" data. If the economic release differs from the consensus view the market usually undergoes rapid price movement as participants interpret the data. Uncertainty (as measured by a wide consensus) generally brings more volatility before and after an economic release. Economic releases vary in importance and impact depending on where the economy is in the business cycle.

Bond Investments

Investment companies allow individual investors the ability to participate in the bond markets through bond funds, closed-end funds and unit-investment trusts. In 2006 total bond fund net inflows increased 97% from $30.8 billion in 2005 to $60.8 billion in 2006. Exchange-traded funds (ETFs) are another alternative to trading or investing directly in a bond issue. These securities allow individual investors the ability to overcome large initial and incremental trading sizes.

Bond Indices

A number of bond indices exist for the purposes of managing portfolios and measuring performance similar to the S&P 500 or Russell Indexes for stocks. The most common American benchmarks are the Lehman Aggregate, Citigroup BIG and Merrill Lynch Domestic Master. Most indices are parts of families of broader indices that can be used to measure global bond portfolios, or may be further subdivided by maturity and/or sector for managing specialized portfolios.

The Derivatives Market

The derivatives markets are the financial markets for derivatives. The market can be divided into two, that for exchange traded derivatives and that for over-the-counter derivatives. The legal nature of these products is very different as well as the way they are traded. Many market participants are active in both.

Futures Markets

Futures exchanges, such as Euronext.liffe and the Chicago Mercantile Exchange trade in standardized derivative contracts. These are options contracts and futures contracts on a whole range of underlying products. The members of the exchange hold positions in these contracts with the exchange who acts as central counterparty. When one party goes long (buys) a futures contract another goes short (sells). When a new contract is introduced the total position in the contract is zero. Therefore, the sum of all the long positions must be equal to the sum of all the short positions. In other words, risk is transferred from one party to another. The total notional amount of all the outstanding positions at the end of June 2004 stood at $53 trillion.[3] That figure grew to $81 trillion by the end of March 2008.

Over-the-Counter Markets

Tailor-made derivatives traded on a futures exchange are traded on over-the-counter markets also known as the OTC market. These consist of investment banks who have traders who make markets in these derivatives and clients such as hedge funds, commercial banks, government sponsored enterprises, etc. Products that are always traded over-the-counter are swaps, forward rate agreements, forward contracts, credit derivatives, etc. The total notional amount of all the outstanding positions at the end of June 2004 stood at $220 trillion.[4] By the end of 2007 this figure had risen to $596 trillion.[5]

[3] Bank for International Settlements (BIS)

[4] source: BIS

[5] source: BIS

Netting

The notional outstanding value of OTC derivatives contracts rose by 40% from $298 trillion at end-2005 to $415 trillion at end-2006. The average daily global turnover rose by two thirds from $1,508bn to $2,544bn between April 2004 and April 2007. The UK remains the leading derivatives centre worldwide with its share of turnover stable at 43% in 2007. The US is the only other major location with 24% of trading. Interest rate instruments remain the key driver of trading, accounting for 88% of UK turnover and 70% of global notional value. Derivatives based on foreign exchange contracts account for a further 10% of notional value, with credit, equity-linked and commodity contracts are also important. Energy, metal and freight derivatives have grown rapidly in recent years. The euro's share of interest rate derivatives turnover worldwide has risen to 39% while the US dollar has fallen to 32%. Pound sterling and yen also increased their market share over the past three years. Trading is becoming more concentrated amongst the largest banks while other financial institutions such as hedge funds, mutual funds, insurance companies and smaller banks have become much bigger users of derivatives.

US: Figures below are from 2nd quater, 2008:

- Total derivatives (notional amount): $182.2 trillion (SECOND QUARTER, 2008)
- Interest rate contracts: $145.0 trillion (80%)
- Foreign exchange contracts: $18.2 trillion(10%)
- 2008 Second Quarter, banks reported trading revenues of $1.6 billion
- Total number of commercial banks holding derivatives: 975

Positions in the OTC derivatives market have increased at a rapid pace since the last triennial survey was undertaken in 2004. Notional amounts outstanding of such instruments totaled $516 trillion at the end of June 2007, 135% higher than the level recorded in the 2004 survey. This corresponds to an annualized compound rate of growth of 33%, which is higher than the approximatively 25% average annual rate of increase since positions in OTC derivatives were first surveyed by the BIS in 1995. Notional amounts outstanding provide useful information on the structure of the OTC derivatives market but should not be interpreted as a measure of the riskiness of these positions. Gross market values which represent the cost of replacing all open contracts at the prevailing market prices, have increased by 74% since 2004 to $11 trillion at the end of June 2007.[6]

[6] source: BIS

The Money Market

The money market is the global financial market for short-term borrowing and lending. It provides short-term liquidity funding for the global financial system. The money market is where short-term obligations such as Treasury bills, commercial paper and bankers' acceptances are bought and sold.

The money market consists of financial institutions and dealers in money or credit who wish to either borrow or lend. Participants borrow and lend for short periods of time typically up to thirteen months. Money market trades in short-term financial instruments commonly called "paper." This contrasts with the capital market for longer-term funding which is supplied by bonds and equity.

The core of the money market consists of banks borrowing and lending to each other using commercial paper, repurchase agreements and similar instruments. These instruments are often benchmarked (i.e. priced over and above) to the London Interbank Offered Rate (LIBOR).

Finance companies, such as GMAC, typically fund themselves by issuing large amounts of asset-backed commercial paper (ABCP) which is secured by the pledge of eligible assets into an ABCP conduit. Examples of eligible assets include auto loans, credit card receivables, residential/commercial mortgage loans, mortgage-backed securities and similar financial assets. Certain large corporations with strong credit ratings such as General Electric issue commercial paper on their own credit. Other large corporations arrange for banks to issue commercial paper on their behalf via commercial paper lines.

In the United States, federal, state and local governments all issue paper to meet funding needs. States and local governments issue municipal paper while the US Treasury issues Treasury bills to fund the US public debt.

- Trading companies often purchase bankers' acceptances to be tendered for payment to overseas suppliers.
- Retail and institutional money market funds
- Banks
- Central banks
- Cash management programs
- Arbitrage ABCP conduits which seek to buy higher yielding paper while themselves selling cheaper paper.

Common money market instruments

- **Bankers' acceptance** - A draft issued by a bank that will be accepted for payment, effectively the same as a cashier's check.
- **Certificate of deposit** - A time deposit at a bank with a specific maturity date; large-denomination certificates of deposits can be sold before maturity.
- **Repurchase agreements** - Short-term loans—normally for less than two weeks and frequently for one day—arranged by selling securities to an investor with an agreement to repurchase them at a fixed price on a fixed date.
- **Commercial paper** - Unsecured promissory notes with a fixed maturity of one to 270 days; usually sold at a discount from face value.
- **Eurodollar deposit** - Deposits made in U.S. dollars at a bank or bank branch located outside the United States.
- **Federal Agency Short-Term Securities** - (in the U.S.). Short-term securities issued by government sponsored enterprises such as the Farm Credit System, the Federal Home Loan Banks and the Federal National Mortgage Association.
- **Federal funds** - (in the U.S.). Interest-bearing deposits held by banks and other depository institutions at the Federal Reserve; these are immediately available funds that institutions borrow or lend, usually on an overnight basis. They are lent for the federal funds rate.
- **Municipal notes** - (in the U.S.). Short-term notes issued by municipalities in anticipation of tax receipts or other revenues.
- **Treasury bills** - Short-term debt obligations of a national government that are issued to mature in three to twelve months. For the U.S..
- **Money market mutual funds** - Pooled short maturity, high quality investments which buy money market securities on behalf of retail or institutional investors.
- **Foreign Exchange Swaps** - Exchanging a set of currencies in spot date and the reversal of the exchange of currencies at a predetermined time in the future.

The Commodities Market

Commodity markets are markets where raw or primary products are exchanged. These raw commodities are traded on regulated commodities exchanges in which they are bought and sold in standardized contracts.

This section of the book focuses on the history and current debates regarding global commodity markets. It covers physical product (food, metals, electricity) markets but not the ways that services, including those of governments, nor investment, nor debt can be seen as a commodity. Sections on stock markets, bond markets, option markets and currency markets cover those concerns separately and in more depth. One focus of this section is the relationship between simple commodity money and the more complex instruments offered in the commodity markets.

History

The modern commodity markets have their roots in the trading of agricultural products. While wheat and corn, cattle and pigs were widely traded using standard instruments in the 19th century in the United States, other basic foodstuff such as soybeans were only added quite recently in most markets. For a commodity market to be established there must be very broad consensus on the variations in the product that make it acceptable for one purpose or another.

The economic impact of the development of commodity markets is hard to over-estimate.

The early History of Commodity Markets

Historically, dating from ancient Sumerian use of sheep, goats or other peoples using pigs, rare seashells, or other items as commodity money, people have sought ways to standardize and trade contracts in the delivery of such items, to render trade itself more smooth and predictable.

Commodity money and commodity markets in a crude early form are believed to have originated in Sumer where small baked clay tokens in the shape of sheep or goats were used in trade. Sealed in clay vessels with a certain number of such tokens, with that number written on the outside, they represented a promise to deliver that number. This made them a form of commodity money - more than an "I.O.U." but less than a guarantee by a nation-state or bank.

However, they were also known to contain promises of time and date of delivery - this made them like a modern futures contract. Regardless of the details it was only possible to verify the number of tokens inside by shaking the vessel or by breaking it, at which point the number or terms written on the outside became subject to doubt. Eventually the tokens disappeared but the contracts remained on flat tablets. This represented the first system of commodity accounting.

However, the commodity status of living things is always subject to doubt - it was hard to validate the health or existence of sheep or goats. Excuses for non-delivery were not unknown and there are recovered Sumerian letters that complain of sickly goats, sheep that had already been fleeced, etc.

If a seller's reputation was good, individual "backers" or "bankers" could decide to take the risk of "clearing" a trade. The observation that trust is always required between market participants later led to credit money. But until relatively modern times, communication and credit were primitive.

Classical civilizations built complex global markets trading gold or silver for spices, cloth, wood and weapons, most of which had standards of quality and timeliness. Considering the many hazards of climate, piracy, theft and abuse of military fiat by rulers of kingdoms along the trade routes, it was a major focus of these civilizations to keep markets open and trading in these scarce commodities. Reputation and clearing became central concerns and the states which could handle them most effectively became very powerful empires, trusted by many peoples to manage and mediate trade and commerce.

The Size of the Commodities Market

The trading of commodities consists of direct physical trading and derivatives trading.The commodities markets have seen an upturn in the volume of trading in recent years. In the five years up to 2007, the value of global physical exports of commodities increased by 17% while the notional value outstanding of commodity OTC derivatives increased more than 500% and commodity derivative trading on exchanges more than 200%.

The notional value outstanding of banks' OTC commodities' derivatives contracts increased 27% in 2007 to $9.0 trillion. OTC trading accounts for the majority of trading in gold and silver. Overall, precious metals accounted for 8% of OTC commodities derivatives trading in 2007, down from their 55% share a decade earlier as trading in energy derivatives rose.

Global physical and derivative trading of commodities on exchanges increased more than a third in 2007 to reach 1,684 million contracts. Agricultural contracts trading grew by 32% in 2007, energy 29% and industrial metals by 30%. Precious metals trading grew by 3%, with higher volume in New York being partially offset by declining volume in Tokyo. Over 40% of commodities trading on exchanges was conducted on US exchanges and a quarter in China. Trading on exchanges in China and India has gained in importance in recent years due to their emergence as significant commodities consumers and producers.

Investment Returns

This is a much-debated topic within academia. It is generally agreed that commodities have an expected return of 5% in real terms which is based on the risk premium for 116 different commodities weighted equally since 1888.[7] It is common for investment professionals to mistakenly claim there is no risk premium in commodites.

Spot Trading

Spot trading is any transaction where delivery either takes place immediately or if there is a minimum lag due to technical constraints between the trade and delivery. Commodities constitute the only spot markets which have existed nearly throughout the history of humankind.

Forward contracts

A forward contract is an agreement between two parties to exchange at some fixed future date a given quantity of a commodity for a price defined today. The fixed price today is known as the forward price.

Futures contracts

A futures contract has the same general features as a forward contract but is transacted through a futures exchange.

Commodity and Futures contracts are based on what's termed "Forward" Contracts. Early on these "forward" contracts (agreements to buy now, pay and deliver later) were used as a way of getting products from producer to the

[7] Source Report 219171-Wharton Business School

consumer. These typically were only for food and agricultural Products. Forward contracts have evolved and have been standardized into what we know today as futures contracts. Although more complex today, early "Forward" contracts for example were used for rice in seventeenth century Japan. Modern "forward" or futures agreements began in Chicago in the 1840s with the appearance of the railroads. Chicago, being centrally located, emerged as the hub between Midwestern farmers and producers and the east coast consumer population centers.

Hedging

"Hedging", a common (and sometimes mandatory) practice of farming cooperatives, insures against a poor harvest by purchasing futures contracts in the same commodity. If the cooperative has significantly less of its product to sell due to weather or insects it makes up for that loss with a profit on the markets since the overall supply of the crop is short everywhere that suffered the same conditions.

Whole developing nations may be especially vulnerable and even their currency tends to be tied to the price of those particular commodity items until it manages to be a fully developed nation. For example, one could see the nominally fiat money of Cuba as being tied to sugar prices since a lack of hard currency paying for sugar means less foreign goods per peso in Cuba itself. In effect, Cuba needs a hedge against a drop in sugar prices if it wishes to maintain a stable quality of life for its citizens.

Delivery and Condition Guarantees

In addition, delivery day, method of settlement and delivery point must all be specified. Typically, trading must end two (or more) business days prior to the delivery day so that the routing of the shipment can be finalized via ship or rail and payment can be settled when the contract arrives at any delivery point.

Standardization

U.S. soybean futures, for example, are of standard grade if they are "GMO or a mixture of GMO and Non-GMO No. 2 yellow soybeans of Indiana, Ohio and Michigan origin produced in the U.S.A. (Non-screened, stored in silo) " and of deliverable grade if they are "GMO or a mixture of GMO and Non-GMO No. 2 yellow soybeans of Iowa, Illinois and Wisconsin origin produced in the U.S.A. (Non-screened, stored in silo)." Note the distinction between states and the need to clearly mention their status as "GMO" ("Genetically Modified Organism") which makes them unacceptable to most "organic" food buyers.

Similar specifications apply for cotton, orange juice, cocoa, sugar, wheat, corn, barley, pork bellies, milk, feedstuffs, fruits, vegetables, other grains, other beans, hay, other livestock, meats, poultry, eggs, or any other commodity which is so traded.
The concept of an interchangeable deliverable or guaranteed delivery is always to some degree a fiction. Trade in commodities is like trade in any other physical product or service. No magic of the commodity contract itself makes "units" of the product totally uniform nor gets it to the delivery point safely and on time.

Regulation of Commodity Markets

Cotton, kilowatt-hours of electricity, board feet of wood, long distance minutes, royalty payments due on artists' works and other products and services have been traded on markets of varying scale with varying degrees of success. One issue that presents major difficulty for creators of such instruments is the liability accruing to the purchaser.

Unless the product or service can be guaranteed or insured to be free of liability based on where it came from and how it got to market e.g. kilowatts must come to market free from legitimate claims for smog death from coal burning plants. Wood must be free from claims that it comes from protected forests. Royalty payments must be free of claims of plagiarism or piracy. It becomes impossible for sellers to guarantee a uniform delivery.

Generally, governments must provide a common regulatory or insurance standard and some release of liability or at least a backing of the insurers before a commodity market can begin trading. This is a major source of controversy in for instance the energy market where desirability of different kinds of power generation varies drastically. In some markets, e.g. Toronto, Canada, surveys established that customers would pay 10-15% more for energy that was not from coal or nuclear but strictly from renewable sources such as wind.

In the United States the principal regulator of commodity and futures markets is the Commodity Futures Trading Commission.

Proliferation of Contracts, Terms and Derivatives

However, if there are two or more standards of risk or quality as there seem to be for electricity or soybeans, it is relatively easy to establish two different contracts to trade in the more and less desirable deliverable separately. If the consumer acceptance and liability problems can be solved, the product can be made interchangeable and trading in such units can begin.

Since the detailed concerns of industrial and consumer markets vary widely so do the contracts and "grades" tend to vary significantly from country to country. A proliferation of contract units, terms, and futures contracts have evolved, combined into an extremely sophisticated range of financial instruments.

These are more than one-to-one representations of units of a given type of commodity and represent more than simple futures contracts for future deliveries. These serve a variety of purposes from simple gambling to price insurance.

The underlying of futures contracts are no longer restricted to commodities.

Oil

Building on the infrastructure and credit and settlement networks established for food and precious metals, many such markets have proliferated drastically in the late 20th century. Oil was the first form of energy so widely traded and the fluctuations in the oil markets are of particular political interest.

Some commodity market speculation is directly related to the stability of certain states, e.g. during the Persian Gulf War, speculation on the survival of the regime of Saddam Hussein in Iraq. Similar political stability concerns have from time to time driven the price of oil. Some argue that this is not so much a commodity market but more of an assassination market speculating on the survival (or not) of Saddam or other leaders whose personal decisions may cause oil supply to fluctuate by military action.
The oil market is an exception. Most markets are not so tied to the politics of volatile regions - even natural gas tends to be more stable as it is not traded across oceans by tanker as extensively.

Commodity Markets and Protectionism

Developing countries (democratic or not) have been moved to harden their currencies, accept IMF rules, join the WTO and submit to a broad regime of reforms that amount to a "hedge" against being isolated. China's entry into the WTO signalled the end of truly isolated nations entirely managing their own currency and affairs. The need for stable currency, predictable clearing and rules-based handling of trade disputes has led to a global trade hegemony - many nations "hedging" on a global scale against each other's anticipated "protectionism", were they to fail to join the WTO.

There are signs, however, that this regime is far from perfect. U.S. trade sanctions against Canadian softwood lumber (within NAFTA) and foreign steel (except for NAFTA partners Canada and Mexico) in 2002 signalled a shift in policy towards a tougher regime perhaps more driven by political concerns - jobs, industrial policy, even sustainable forestry and logging practices.

Non-conventional Commodities

Nature's Commodity Outputs

Commodity thinking is undergoing a more direct revival thanks to the theorists of "natural capital" whose products are the only genuine commodities - air, water and calories we consume being mostly interchangeable when they are free of pollution or disease. Whether we wish to think of these things as tradeable commodities rather than birthrights has been a major source of controversy in many nations.

Most types of environmental economics consider the shift to measuring them inevitable, arguing that reframing political economy to consider the flow of these basic commodities first and foremost help to avoid the use of any military fiat except to protect "natural capital" itself and basing credit-worthiness more strictly on commitment to preserving biodiversity aligns the long-term interests of ecoregions, societies and individuals. They seek relatively conservative sustainable development schemes that would be amenable to measuring well-being over long periods of time, typically "seven generations", in line with Native American thought.

Weather Trading

However, this is not the only way in which commodity thinking interacts with ecologists' thinking. Hedging began as a way to escape the consequences of damage done by natural conditions. It has matured not only into a system of interlocking guarantees but also into a system of indirectly trading on the actual damage done by weather using weather derivatives. For a price, this relieves the purchaser of concerns such as whether a freeze will hurt the Brazilian coffee crop, whether there will be a drought in the U.S. Corn Belt and what the chances that we will have a cold winter are, driving natural gas prices higher and creating havoc in Florida orange areas.

Emissions Trading

Weather trading is just one example of "negative commodities", units of which represent harm rather than good.

"Economy is three fifths of ecology" argues Mike Nickerson, one of many economic theorists who holds that nature's productive services and waste disposal services are poorly accounted for. One way to fairly allocate the waste disposal capacity of nature is "cap and trade" market structure that is used to trade toxic emissions rights in the United States e.g. SO_2. This is in effect a "negative commodity", a right to throw something away.

In this market, the atmosphere's capacity to absorb certain amounts of pollutants is measured, divided into units and traded amongst various market players. Those who emit more SO_2 must pay those who emit less. Critics of such schemes argue that unauthorized or unregulated emissions still happen and that "grandfathering" schemes often permit major polluters such as the state governments' own agencies or poorer countries to expand emissions and take jobs while the SO_2 output still floats over the border and causes death.

In practice, political pressure has overcome most such concerns and it is questionable whether this is a capacity that depends on U.S. clout. The Kyoto Protocol established a similar market in global greenhouse gas emissions without U.S. support.

Community as Commodity?

This highlights one of the major issues with global commodity markets of either the positive or negative kind. A community must somehow believe that the commodity instrument is real, enforceable and well worth paying for.

A very substantial part of the anti-globalization movement opposes the commodification of currency, national sovereignty and traditional cultures. The capacity to repay debt, as in the current global credit money regime anchored by the Bank for International Settlements, does not in their view correspond to measurable benefits to human well-being worldwide. They seek a fairer way for societies to compete in the global markets that will not require conversion of natural capital to natural resources, nor human capital to move to developed nations in order to find work.

Some economic systems by green economists would replace the "gold standard" with a "biodiversity standard". It remains to be seen if such plans have any merit other than as political ways to draw attention to the way capitalism itself interacts with life.

Is Human Life a Commodity?

While classical, neoclassical and Marxist approaches to economics tend to treat labor differently they are united in treating nature as a resource.

The green economists and the more conservative environmental economics argue that not only natural ecologies but also the life of the individual human being is treated as a commodity by the global markets. A good example is the IPCC calculations cited by the Global Commons Institute as placing a value on a human life in the developed world "15x higher" than in the developing world based solely on the ability to pay to prevent climate change.

Is Free Time a Commodity?

Accepting this result, one might argue that to put a price on both is the most reasonable way to proceed to optimize and increase that value relative to other goods or services. This has led to efforts in measuring well-being, to assign a commercial "value of life" and to the theory of Natural Capitalism - fusions of green and neoclassical approaches - which focus predictably on energy and material efficiency i.e. using far less of any given commodity input to achieve the same service outputs as a result.

The Futures Market

A futures market is a central financial exchange where people can trade standardized futures contracts. That is, a contract to buy specific quantities of a commodity or financial instrument at a specified price with delivery set at a specified time in the future.

History of Futures Exchanges

The origins of futures trading can supposedly be traced to Ancient Greek or Phoenician times. The first modern organized futures exchange began in 1710 at the Dojima Rice Exchange in Osaka, Japan.

The United States followed in the early 1800s. Chicago is located at the base of the Great Lakes, close to the farmlands and cattle country of the U.S. Midwest, making it a natural center for transportation, distribution and trading of agricultural produce. Gluts and shortages of these products caused chaotic fluctuations in price and this led to the development of a market enabling grain merchants, processors and agriculture companies to trade in "to arrive" or "cash forward" contracts to insulate them from the risk of adverse price change and enable them to hedge.

Forward contracts were standard at the time. However, most forward contracts weren't honored by both the buyer and the seller. For instance, if the buyer of a corn forward contract made an agreement to buy corn and at the time of delivery the price of corn differed dramatically from the original contract price, either the buyer or the seller would back out. Additionally, the forward contracts market was very illiquid and an exchange was needed that would bring together a market to find potential buyers and sellers of a commodity instead of making people bear the burden of finding a buyer or seller.

In 1848, the Chicago Board of Trade (CBOT – the world's first modern futures exchange) was formed. Trading was originally in forward contracts. The first contract (on corn) was written on March 13, 1851. In 1865, standardized futures contracts were introduced.

The Chicago Produce Exchange was established in 1874 and renamed the Chicago Mercantile Exchange (CME) in 1898 and reorganized in 1919. In 1972 the International Monetary Market (IMM), a division of the CME, was formed to offer futures contracts in foreign currencies: British pound, Canadian dollar, German mark, Japanese yen, Mexican peso and Swiss franc.

In 1881, a regional market was founded in Minneapolis, Minnesota and in 1883 introduced futures for the first time. Trading continuously since then, today the Minneapolis Grain Exchange (MGEX) is the only exchange for hard red spring wheat futures and options.

Later in the 1970s saw the development of the financial Futures contracts, which allowed trading in the future value of interest rates. These (in particular the 90-day Eurodollar contract introduced in 1981) had an enormous impact on the development of the interest rate swap market.

Today, the Futures markets have far outgrown their agricultural origins. With the addition of the New York Mercantile Exchange (NYMEX) the trading and hedging of financial products using futures dwarfs the traditional commodity markets and plays a major role in the global financial system, trading over 1.5 trillion U.S. dollars per day in 2005.

The recent history of these exchanges (Aug 2006) finds the Chicago Exchange trading more than 70% of its futures contracts on its "Globex" trading platform and this trend is rising daily. It counts for over 45.5 Billion dollars of nominal trade (over 1 million contracts) every single day in "electronic trading" as opposed to open outcry trading of Futures, Options and Derivatives.

In June 2001, ICE (Intercontinental Exchange) acquired the International Petroleum Exchange (IPE), now ICE Futures, which operated Europe's leading open-outcry energy futures exchange. Since 2003, ICE has partnered with the Chicago Climate Exchange (CCX) to host its electronic marketplace. In April 2005, the entire ICE portfolio of energy futures became fully electronic.

In 2006, the New York Stock Exchange teamed up with the Amsterdam-Brussels-Lisbon-Paris Exchanges "Euronext" electronic exchange to form the first trans-continental Futures and Options Exchange. These two developments as well as the sharp growth of internet Futures trading platforms developed by a number of trading companies clearly points to a race to total internet trading of Futures and Options in the coming years.

In terms of trading volume, the National Stock Exchange of India in Mumbai is the largest stock futures trading exchange in the world, followed by JSE Limited in Sandton, Gauteng, South Africa.

Nature of Futures Contracts

Exchange-traded contracts are standardized by the exchanges where they trade. The contract details what asset is to be bought or sold, and how, when, where and in what quantity it is to be delivered. The terms also specify the currency in which the contract will trade, minimum tick value and the last trading day and expiry or delivery month. Standardized commodity futures contracts may also contain provisions for adjusting the contracted price based on deviations from the "standard" commodity, for example, a contract might specify delivery of heavier USDA Number 1 oats at par value but permit delivery of Number 2 oats for a certain seller's penalty per bushel.

Futures contracts are not issued like other securities but are "created" whenever open interest increases. That is, when one party first buys (goes long) a contract from another party (who goes short). Contracts are also "destroyed" in the opposite manner whenever open interest decreases because traders resell to reduce their long positions or rebuy to reduce their short positions.

Speculators on futures price fluctuations who do not intend to make or take ultimate delivery must take care to "zero their positions" prior to the contract's expiry. After expiry, each contract will be settled either by physical delivery (typically for commodity underlyings) or by a cash settlement (typically for financial underlyings). The contracts ultimately are not between the original buyer and the original seller but between the holders at expiry and the exchange. Because a contract may pass through many hands after it is created by its initial purchase and sale or even be liquidated. The settling parties do not know with whom they have ultimately traded.

Legally, the security represents an obligation of the issuer rather than the buyer and seller. Even if the issuer buys back some securities, they still exist. Only if they are legally cancelled can they disappear.

Standardization

The contracts traded on futures exchanges are always standardized. In principle, the parameters to define a contract are endless. To make sure liquidity is high there is only a limited number of standardized contracts.

Derivatives Clearing

There is usually a division of responsibility between provision of trading facility and settlement of those trades. While derivative exchanges like the CBOE and LIFFE take responsibility for providing efficient, transparent and orderly trading environments, settlement of the resulting trades are usually handled by Clearing Corporations, also known as Clearing Houses. These Clearing Houses serve as central counterparties to trades done in the respective exchanges. For instance, the Options Clearing Corporation and the London Clearing House respectively are the clearing corporations for CBOE and LIFFE. A well known exception to this is the case of Chicago Mercantile Exchange, which clears trades by itself.

Central Counterparty

Derivative contracts are leveraged positions whose value is volatile. They are usually more volatile than their underlying asset. This can lead to situations where one party to a trade loses a big sum of money and is unable to honor its settlement obligation. In a safe trading environment, the parties to a trade need to be assured that their counterparty will honor the trade, no matter how the market has moved. This requirement can lead to messy arrangements like credit assessment, setting of trading limits and so on for each counterparty. It can also take away most of the advantages of a centralised trading facility. To prevent this, Clearing corporations interpose themselves as counterparties to every trade and extend guarantee that the trade will be settled as originally intended. This action is called Novation. As a result, trading firms take no risk on the actual counterparty to the trade but on the clearing corporation. The clearing corporation is able to take on this risk by adopting an efficient margining process.

Margin and Mark-to-Market

Clearing houses charge two types of margins: the Initial Margin and the Mark-To-Market Margin (also referred to as Variation Margin).

The Initial Margin is the sum of money (or collateral) to be deposited by a firm to the clearing corporation to cover possible future loss in the positions (the set of positions held is also called the portfolio) held by a firm. In the simplest case, this is the dollar figure that answers a question of this nature: What is the likely loss that this firm may incur on its portfolio with a 99% confidence and over a period of 2 days? The clause 'with a 99% confidence' and 'over a period 2 days' is to be interpreted as that number such that the actual portfolio loss over 2 days is expected to exceed the number only 1% of the time, although how they know this is unknown. Several popular methods are used to compute initial margins. They include the CME-owned SPAN (a grid simulation method used by the CME and about 70 other exchanges), STANS (a Monte Carlo simulation based methodology used by the OCC), TIMS (earlier used by the OCC and still being used by a few other exchanges like the Bursa Malaysia.

The Mark-to-Market Margin (MTM margin) on the other hand is the margin collected to offset losses (if any) that have already been incurred on the positions held by a firm. This is computed as the difference between the cost of the position held and the current market value of that position. If the resulting amount is a loss, the amount is collected from the firm; else, the amount may be returned to the firm (the case with most clearing houses) or kept in reserve depending on local practice. In either case, the positions are 'marked-to-market' by setting their new cost to the market value used in computing this difference. The positions held by the clients of the exchange are marked-to-market daily and the MTM difference computation for the next day would use the new cost figure in its calculation.

Clients hold a margin account with the exchange and every day the swings in the value of their positions is added to or deducted from their margin account. If the margin account gets too low they have to replenish it. In this way it is highly unlikely that the client will not be able to fulfill his obligations arising from the contracts. As the clearing house is the counterparty to all their trades, they only have to have one margin account. This is in contrast with OTC derivatives where issues such as margin accounts have to be negotiated with all counterparties.

Regulators

Each exchange is normally regulated by a national governmental (or semi-governmental) regulatory agency:

- In Australia, this role is performed by the Australian Securities and Investments Commission.
- In the Chinese mainland, by the China Securities Regulatory Commission.
- In Hong Kong, by the Securities and Futures Commission.
- In India, by the Securities and Exchange Board of India and Forward Markets Commission (FMC)
- In Pakistan, by the Securities and Exchange Commission of Pakistan.

- In Singapore by the Monetary Authority of Singapore.
- In the UK, futures exchanges are regulated by the Financial Services Authority.
- In the USA, by the Commodity Futures Trading Commission.
- In Malaysia, by the Securities Commission.

The Foreign Exchange Market

The foreign exchange (currency, forex or FX) market is where currency trading takes place. FX transactions typically involve one party purchasing a quantity of one currency in exchange for paying a quantity of another. The FX market is one of the largest and most liquid financial markets in the world and includes trading between large banks, central banks, currency speculators, corporations, governments and other institutions. The average daily volume in the global forex and related markets is continuously growing. Traditional turnover was reported to be over US$ 3.2 trillion in April 2007 by the Bank for International Settlement. Since then, the market has continued to grow. According to Euromoney's annual FX Poll, volumes grew a further 41% between 2007 and 2008.

Market Size and Liquidity

The foreign exchange market is unique because of

- its trading volumes,
- the extreme liquidity of the market,
- the large number of, and variety of, traders in the market,
- its geographical dispersion,
- its long trading hours: 24 hours a day except on weekends (from 5pm EST on Sunday until 4pm EST Friday),
- the variety of factors that affect exchange rates.
- the low margins of profit compared with other markets of fixed income (but profits can be high due to very large trading volumes)
- the use of leverage

It has been referred to as the market closest to the ideal perfect competition, notwithstanding market manipulation by central banks. According to the Bank for International Settlements the average daily turnover in global foreign exchange markets is estimated at $3.98 trillion. Trading in the world's main financial markets accounted for $3.21 trillion of this. This approximately $3.21 trillion in main foreign exchange market turnover was broken down as follows:

- $1.005 trillion in spot transactions
- $362 billion in outright forwards
- $1.714 trillion in forex swaps
- $129 billion estimated gaps in reporting

Of the $3.98 trillion daily global turnover, trading in London accounted for around $1.36 trillion or 34.1% of the total, making London by far the global center for foreign exchange. In second and third places respectively, trading in New York accounted for 16.6%, and Tokyo accounted for 6.0%. In addition to "traditional" turnover, $2.1 trillion was traded in derivatives. Exchange-traded forex futures contracts were introduced in 1972 at the Chicago Mercantile Exchange and are actively traded relative to most other futures contracts. Forex futures volume has grown rapidly in recent years, and accounts for about 7% of the total foreign exchange market volume, according to The Wall Street Journal Europe (5/5/06, p. 20).

Foreign exchange trading increased by 38% between April 2005 and April 2006 and has more than doubled since 2001. This is largely due to the growing importance of foreign exchange as an asset class and an increase in fund management assets, particularly of hedge funds and pension funds. The diverse selection of execution venues such as internet trading platforms offered by companies such as First Prudential Markets and Saxo Bank have made it easier for retail traders to trade in the foreign exchange market. Because foreign exchange is an OTC market where brokers/dealers negotiate directly with one another there is no central exchange or clearing house. The biggest geographic trading centre is the UK, primarily London, which according to IFSL estimates has increased its share of global turnover in traditional transactions from 31.3% in April 2004 to 34.1% in April 2007. RPP The ten most active traders account for almost 73% of trading volume, according to The Wall Street Journal Europe (2/9/06 p. 20). These large international banks continually provide the market with both bid (buy) and ask (sell) prices. The bid/ask spread is the difference between the price at which a bank or market maker will sell ("ask" or "offer") and the price at which a market-maker will buy ("bid") from a wholesale customer. This spread is minimal for actively traded pairs of currencies, usually 0–3 pips. For example, the bid/ask quote of EUR/USD might be 1.2200/1.2203 on a retail broker. Minimum trading size for most deals is usually 100,000 units of currency which is a standard "lot". These spreads might not apply to retail customers at banks which will routinely mark up the difference to say 1.2100 / 1.2300 for transfers or say 1.2000 / 1.2400 for banknotes or travelers' checks. Spot prices at market makers vary but on EUR/USD are usually no more than 3 pips wide (i.e. 0.0003). Competition is greatly increased with larger transactions and pip spreads shrink on the major pairs to as little as 1 to 2 pips.

Market Participants

Unlike a stock market, where all participants have access to the same prices, the forex market is divided into levels of access. At the top is the inter-bank market, which is made up of the largest investment banking firms. Within the inter-bank market, spreads, which are the difference between the bid and ask prices, are razor sharp and usually unavailable. They are also not known to players outside the inner circle. The difference between the bid and ask prices widens (from 0-1 pip to 1-2 pips for some currencies such as the EUR). This is due to volume. If a trader can guarantee large numbers of transactions for large amounts they can demand a smaller difference between the bid and ask price which is referred to as a better spread. The levels of access that make up the forex market are determined by the size of the "line" (the amount of money with which they are trading). The top-tier inter-bank market accounts for 53% of all transactions. After that there are usually smaller investment banks followed by large multi-national corporations (which need to hedge risk and pay employees in different countries), large hedge funds and even some of the retail forex-metal market makers. According to Galati and Melvin (2004), "Pension funds, insurance companies, mutual funds, and other institutional investors have played an increasingly important role in financial markets in general and in FX markets in particular, since the early 2000s." In addition, he notes: "Hedge funds have grown markedly over the 2001–2004 period in terms of both number and overall size" central banks also participate in the forex market to align currencies to their economic needs.

Banks

The interbank market caters for both the majority of commercial turnover and large amounts of speculative trading every day. A large bank may trade billions of dollars daily. Some of this trading is undertaken on behalf of customers but much is conducted by proprietary desks, trading for the bank's own account.

Until recently, foreign exchange brokers did large amounts of business, facilitating interbank trading and matching anonymous counterparts for small fees. Today, however, much of this business has moved on to more efficient electronic systems. The broker squawk box lets traders listen in on ongoing interbank trading and is heard in most trading rooms but turnover is noticeably smaller than just a few years ago.

Commercial Companies

An important part of this market comes from the financial activities of companies seeking foreign exchange to pay for goods or services. Commercial companies often trade fairly small amounts compared to those of banks or speculators and their trades often have little short term impact on market rates. Nevertheless, trade flows are an important factor in the long-term direction of a currency's exchange rate. Some multinational companies can have an unpredictable impact when very large positions are covered due to exposures that are not widely known by other market participants.

Central Banks

National central banks play an important role in the foreign exchange markets. They try to control the money supply, inflation and/or interest rates and often have official or unofficial target rates for their currencies. They can use their often substantial foreign exchange reserves to stabilize the market. Milton Friedman argued that the best stabilization strategy would be for central banks to buy when the exchange rate is too low and to sell when the rate is too high — that is, to trade for a profit based on their more precise information. Nevertheless, the effectiveness of a central banks' "stabilizing speculation" is doubtful because central banks do not go bankrupt if they make large losses, like other traders would and there is no convincing evidence that they do make a profit trading.

The mere expectation or rumor of central bank intervention might be enough to stabilize a currency but aggressive intervention might be used several times each year in countries with a dirty float currency regime. Central banks do not always achieve their objectives. The combined resources of the market can easily overwhelm any central bank. Several scenarios of this nature were seen in the 1992–93 ERM collapse and in more recent times in Southeast Asia.

Hedge Funds

Hedge funds have gained a reputation for aggressive currency speculation since 1996. They control billions of dollars of equity and may borrow billions more and thus may overwhelm intervention by central banks to support almost any currency, if the economic fundamentals are in the hedge funds' favor.

Investment Management Firms

Investment management firms (who typically manage large accounts on behalf of customers such as pension funds and endowments) use the foreign exchange market to facilitate transactions in foreign securities. For example, an investment manager bearing an international equity portfolio needs to purchase and sell several pairs of foreign currencies to pay for foreign securities purchases.

Some investment management firms also have more speculative specialist currency overlay operations which manage clients' currency exposures with the aim of generating profits as well as limiting risk. Whilst the number of this type of specialist firms is quite small, many have a large value of assets under management (AUM) and hence can generate large trades.

Retail Forex Brokers

There are two types of retail brokers offering the opportunity for speculative trading. Retail forex brokers or Market makers. Retail traders (individuals) are a small fraction of this market and may only participate indirectly through brokers or banks. Retail forex brokers, while largely controlled and regulated by the CFTC and NFA might be subject to forex scams. At present, the NFA and CFTC are imposing stricter requirements, particularly in relation to the amount of net capitalization required of its members. As a result many of the smaller and perhaps questionable brokers are now gone. It is not widely understood that retail brokers and market makers typically trade against their clients and frequently take the other side of their trades. This can often create a potential conflict of interest and give rise to some of the unpleasant experiences some traders have had. A move toward NDD (No Dealing Desk) and STP (Straight Through Processing) has helped to resolve some of these concerns and restore trader confidence but caution is still advised in ensuring that all is as it is presented.

Other

Non-bank foreign exchange companies offer currency exchange and international payments to private individuals and companies. These are also known as Foreign Exchange Brokers but are distinct from Forex Brokers as they do not offer speculative trading but currency exchange with payments. i.e. there is usually a physical delivery of currency to a bank account.

It is estimated that in the UK, 14% of currency transfers/payments are made via Foreign Exchange Companies. These companies' selling point is usually that they will offer better exchange rates or cheaper payments than the customer's bank. These companies differ from Money Transfer/Remittance Companies in that they generally offer higher-value services.

Money Transfer/Remittance Companies perform high-volume low-value transfers generally by economic migrants back to their home country. In 2007, the Aite Group estimated that there were $369 billion of remittances (an increase of 8% on the previous year). The four largest markets (India, China, Mexico and the Philippines) receive $95 billion. The largest and best known provider is Western Union with 345,000 agents globally.

Trading Characteristics

There is no unified or centrally cleared market for the majority of FX trades and there is very little cross-border regulation. Due to the over-the-counter

(OTC) nature of currency markets, there are rather a number of interconnected marketplaces, where different currencies instruments are traded. This implies that there is not a single exchange rate but rather a number of different rates (prices) depending on what bank or market maker is trading, and where it is. In practice the rates are often very close, otherwise they could be exploited by arbitrageurs instantaneously. Due to London's dominance in the market a particular currency's quoted price is usually the London market price. A joint venture of the Chicago Mercantile Exchange and Reuters, called FxMarketSpace opened in 2007 and aspires to the role of a central market clearing mechanism.

The main trading center is London but New York, Tokyo, Hong Kong and Singapore are all important centers as well. Banks throughout the world participate. Currency trading happens continuously throughout the day; as the Asian trading session ends, the European session begins, followed by the North American session and then back to the Asian session, excluding weekends.

Exchange rate fluctuations are usually caused by actual monetary flows as well as by expectations of changes in monetary flows caused by changes in GDP growth, inflation, interest rates, budget and trade deficits or surpluses, large cross-border M&A deals and other macroeconomic conditions. Major news is released publicly, often on scheduled dates, so many people have access to the same news at the same time. However, the large banks have an important advantage, they can see their customers' order flow.

Currencies are traded against one another. Each pair of currencies thus constitutes an individual product and is traditionally noted XXX/YYY, where YYY is the ISO 4217 international three-letter code of the currency into which the price of one unit of XXX is expressed (called base currency). For instance, EUR/USD is the price of the euro expressed in US dollars, as in 1 euro = 1.5465 dollar. Out of convention, the first currency in the pair, the base currency, was the stronger currency at the creation of the pair. The second currency, counter currency, was the weaker currency at the creation of the pair.

The factors affecting XXX will affect both XXX/YYY and XXX/ZZZ. This causes positive currency correlation between XXX/YYY and XXX/ZZZ.

On the spot market, according to the BIS study, the most heavily traded products were:

- EUR/USD: 27 %
- USD/JPY: 13 %
- GBP/USD (also called sterling or cable): 12 %

and the US currency was involved in 86.3% of transactions, followed by the euro (37.0%), the yen (16.5%) and sterling (15.0%).

Trading in the euro has grown considerably since the currency's creation in January 1990 and how long the foreign exchange market will remain dollar-centered is open to debate. Until recently, trading the euro versus a non-European currency ZZZ would have usually involved two trades: EUR/USD and USD/ZZZ. The exception to this is EUR/JPY, which is an established traded currency pair in the interbank spot market. As the dollar's value has eroded during 2008, interest in using the euro as reference currency for prices in commodities (such as oil) as well as a larger component of foreign reserves by banks has increased dramatically. Transactions in the currencies of commodity-producing countries, such as AUD, NZD, CAD, have also increased.

Factors affecting Currency Trading

Although exchange rates are affected by many factors, in the end, currency prices are a result of supply and demand forces. The world's currency markets can be viewed as a huge melting pot. In a large and ever-changing mix of current events, supply and demand factors are constantly shifting and the price of one currency in relation to another shifts accordingly. No other market encompasses (and distills) as much of what is going on in the world at any given time as foreign exchange.

Supply and demand for any given currency and thus its value, are not influenced by any single element but rather by several. These elements generally fall into three categories: Economic factors, political conditions and market psychology.

Economic Factors

These include economic policy, disseminated by government agencies and central banks, economic conditions, generally revealed through economic reports, and other economic indicators.

Economic policy comprises government fiscal policy (budget/spending practices) and monetary policy (the means by which a government's central bank influences the supply and "cost" of money which is reflected by the level of interest rates).

Economic conditions include:

- **Government budget deficits or surpluses**: The market usually reacts negatively to widening government budget deficits and positively to narrowing budget deficits. The impact is reflected in the value of a country's currency.

- **Balance of trade levels and trends**: The trade flow between countries illustrates the demand for goods and services which in turn indicates demand for a country's currency to conduct trade. Surpluses and deficits in trade of goods and services reflect the competitiveness of a nation's economy. For example, trade deficits may have a negative impact on a nation's currency.
- **Inflation levels and trends**: Typically, a currency will lose value if there is a high level of inflation in the country or if inflation levels are perceived to be rising. This is because inflation erodes purchasing power, thus demand, for that particular currency. However, a currency may sometimes strengthen when inflation rises because of expectations that the central bank will raise short-term interest rates to combat rising inflation.
- **Economic growth and health**: Reports such as gross domestic product (GDP), employment levels, retail sales, capacity utilization and others, detail the levels of a country's economic growth and health. Generally, the more healthy and robust a country's economy, the better its currency will perform and the more demand for it there will be.

Political Conditions

Internal, regional and international political conditions and events can have a profound effect on currency markets.

For instance, political upheaval and instability can have a negative impact on a nation's economy. The rise of a political faction that is perceived to be fiscally responsible can have the opposite effect. Also, events in one country in a region may spur positive or negative interest in a neighboring country and, in the process, affect its currency.

Market Psychology

Market psychology and trader perceptions influence the foreign exchange market in a variety of ways:

- **Flights to quality**: Unsettling international events can lead to a "flight to quality" with investors seeking a "safe haven". There will be a greater demand, thus a higher price, for currencies perceived as stronger over their relatively weaker counterparts. The Swiss franc has been a traditional safe haven during times of political or economic uncertainty.
- **Long-term trends**: Currency markets often move in visible long-term trends. Although currencies do not have an annual growing season like physical commodities, business cycles do make themselves felt.

Cycle analysis looks at longer-term price trends that may rise from economic or political trends.

- "**Buy the rumor, sell the fact**:" This market truism can apply to many currency situations. It is the tendency for the price of a currency to reflect the impact of a particular action before it occurs and, when the anticipated event comes to pass, react in exactly the opposite direction. This may also be referred to as a market being "oversold" or "overbought". To buy the rumor or sell the fact can also be an example of the cognitive bias known as anchoring, when investors focus too much on the relevance of outside events to currency prices.
- **Economic numbers**: While economic numbers can certainly reflect economic policy, some reports and numbers take on a talisman-like effect: The number itself becomes important to market psychology and may have an immediate impact on short-term market moves. "What to watch" can change over time. In recent years, for example, money supply, employment, trade balance figures and inflation numbers have all taken turns in the spotlight.
- **Technical trading considerations**: As in other markets, the accumulated price movements in a currency pair such as EUR/USD can form apparent patterns that traders may attempt to use. Many traders study price charts in order to identify such patterns.

Algorithmic Trading in Forex

In electronic financial markets, algorithmic trading or automated trading, also known as algo trading, black-box trading, or robo trading, is the use of computer programs for entering trading orders with the computer algorithm deciding on certain aspects of the order such as the timing, price or even the final quantity of the order. It is widely used by hedge funds, pension funds, mutual funds and other institutional traders to divide up a large trade into several smaller trades in order to manage market impact, opportunity cost and risk. It is also used by hedge funds and similar traders to make the decision to initiate orders based on information that is received electronically before human traders are even aware of the information.

Algorithmic trading may be used in any investment strategy, including market making, inter-market spreading, arbitrage or pure speculation (including trend following). The investment decision and implementation may be augmented at any stage with algorithmic support or may operate completely automatically.

A third of all EU and US stock trades in 2006 were driven by automatic programs or algorithms, according to Boston-based consulting firm Aite Group LLC. By 2010, that figure will reach 50 percent.

In 2006 at the London Stock Exchange over 40% of all orders were entered by algo traders with 60% predicted for 2007. American markets and equity markets generally have a higher proportion of algo trades than other markets and estimates for 2008 range as high as an 80% proportion in some markets. Foreign exchange markets also have active algo trading (about 25% of orders in 2006). Futures and options markets are considered to be fairly easily integrated into algorithmic trading with about 20% of options volume expected to be computer generated by 2010. Bond markets are moving toward more access to algorithmic traders.

Financial Instruments

Spot

A spot transaction is a two-day delivery transaction (except in the case of the Canadian dollar which settles the next day), as opposed to the futures contracts which are usually three months. This trade represents a "direct exchange" between two currencies, has the shortest time frame, involves cash rather than a contract and interest is not included in the agreed-upon transaction. The data for this study come from the spot market. Spot has the largest share by volume in FX transactions among all instruments.

Forward

One way to deal with the Forex risk is to engage in a forward transaction. In this transaction money does not actually change hands until some agreed upon future date. A buyer and seller agree on an exchange rate for any date in the future and the transaction occurs on that date, regardless of what the market rates are then. The duration of the trade can be a few days, months or years.

Future

Foreign currency futures are forward transactions with standard contract sizes and maturity dates — for example, 500,000 British pounds for next November at an agreed rate. Futures are standardized and are usually traded on an exchange created for this purpose. The average contract length is roughly 3 months. Futures contracts are usually inclusive of any interest amounts.

Swap

The most common type of forward transaction is the currency swap. In a swap two parties exchange currencies for a certain length of time and agree to reverse the transaction at a later date. These are not standardized contracts and are not traded through an exchange.

Option

A foreign exchange option (commonly shortened to just FX option) is a derivative where the owner has the right but not the obligation to exchange money denominated in one currency into another currency at a pre-agreed exchange rate on a specified date. The FX options market is the deepest, largest and most liquid market for options of any kind in the world.

Exchange Traded Fund

Exchange-traded funds (or ETFs) are Open Ended investment companies that can be traded at any time throughout the course of the day. Typically, ETFs try to replicate a stock market index such as the S&P 500 (e.g. SPY) but recently they are now replicating investments in the currency markets with the ETF increasing in value when the US Dollar weakens versus a specific currency such as the Euro. Certain of these funds track the price movements of world currencies versus the US Dollar and increase in value directly counter to the US Dollar, allowing for speculation in the US Dollar for US and US Dollar denominated investors and speculators.

Speculation

Controversy about currency speculators and their effect on currency devaluations and national economies recurs regularly. Nevertheless, economists including Milton Friedman have argued that speculators ultimately are a stabilizing influence on the market and perform the important function of providing a market for hedgers and transferring risk from those people who don't wish to bear it, to those who do. Other economists such as Joseph Stiglitz consider this argument to be based more on politics and a free market philosophy than on economics.

Large hedge funds and other well capitalized "position traders" are the main professional speculators.

Currency speculation is considered a highly suspect activity in many countries. While investment in traditional financial instruments like bonds or stocks often is considered to contribute positively to economic growth by providing capital, currency speculation does not. According to this view, it is simply gambling that often interferes with economic policy. For example, in 1992, currency speculation forced the Central Bank of Sweden to raise interest rates for a few days to 500% per annum and later to devalue the krona. Former Malaysian Prime Minister Mahathir Mohamad is one well known proponent of this view. He blamed the devaluation of the Malaysian ringgit in 1997 on George Soros and other speculators.

Gregory Millman reports on an opposing view, comparing speculators to "vigilantes" who simply help "enforce" international agreements and anticipate the effects of basic economic "laws" in order to profit.

In this view, countries may develop unsustainable financial bubbles or otherwise mishandle their national economies and forex speculators allegedly made the inevitable collapse happen sooner. A relatively quick collapse might even be preferable to continued economic mishandling. Mahathir Mohamad and other critics of speculation are viewed as trying to deflect the blame from themselves for having caused the unsustainable economic conditions. Given that Malaysia recovered quickly after imposing currency controls directly against IMF advice, this view is open to doubt.

Options

What about Options?

An option is a contract written by a seller that conveys to the buyer the right — but not the obligation — to buy (in the case of a call option) or to sell (in the case of a put option) a particular asset, such as a piece of property, shares of stock or some other underlying security. This could be among others a futures contract. In return for granting the option, the seller collects a payment (the premium) from the buyer. What a call and a put option are will be explained later on in this section.

For example, buying a **call option** provides the right to buy a specified quantity of a security at a set strike price at some time on or before expiration, while buying a put **option** provides the right to sell. Upon the option holder's choice to exercise the option, the party who sold, or wrote, the option must fulfill the terms of the contract.

The theoretical value of an option can be evaluated according to several models. These models, which are developed by quantitative analysts, attempt to predict how the value of the option will change in response to changing conditions. Hence, the risks associated with granting, owning, or trading options may be quantified and managed with a greater degree of precision, perhaps, than with some other investments.

Exchange-traded options form an important class of options which have standardized contract features and trade on public exchanges, facilitating trading among independent parties. Over-the-counter options are traded between private parties, often well-capitalized institutions, that have negotiated separate trading and clearing arrangements with each other. Another important class of options, particularly in the U.S., are **employee stock options**, which are awarded by a company to their employees as a form of incentive compensation.

Other types of options exist in many financial contracts, for example **real estate options** are often used to assemble large parcels of land, and **prepayment options** are usually included in mortgage loans. However, many of the valuation and risk management principles apply across all financial options.

Contract specifications

Every financial option is a contract between the two counterparties with the terms of the option specified in a term sheet. Option contracts may be quite complicated; however, at minimum, they usually contain the following specifications:

- whether the option holder has the right to buy (a call option) or the right to sell (a put option)
- the quantity and class of the underlying asset(s) (e.g. 100 shares of XYZ Co. B stock)
- the strike price, also known as the exercise price, which is the price at which the underlying transaction will occur upon exercise
- the expiration date, or expiry, which is the last date the option can be exercised
- the settlement terms, for instance whether the writer must deliver the actual asset on exercise, or may simply tender the equivalent cash amount
- the terms by which the option is quoted in the market to convert the quoted price into the actual premium–the total amount paid by the holder to the writer of the option.

Types of Options

The primary types of financial options are:

- **Exchange traded options** (also called "listed options") are a class of exchange traded derivatives. Exchange traded options have standardized contracts, and are settled through a clearing house with fulfillment guaranteed by the credit of the exchange. Since the contracts are standardized, accurate pricing models are often available. Exchange traded options include:
  1. stock options,
  2. commodity options,
  3. bond options and other interest rate options
  4. index (equity) options, and
  5. options on futures contracts
- **Over-the-counter options** (OTC options, also called "dealer options") are traded between two private parties, and are not listed on an exchange. The terms of an OTC option are unrestricted and may be individually tai-

lored to meet any business need. In general, at least one of the counterparties to an OTC option is a well-capitalized institution. Option types commonly traded over the counter include:

   1. interest rate options
   2. currency cross rate options, and
   3. options on swaps or swaptions.

- **Employee stock options** are issued by a company to its employees as compensation.

Option Styles

Naming conventions are used to help identify properties common to many different types of options. These include:

- **European option** - an option that may only be exercised on expiration.
- **American option** - an option that may be exercised on any trading day on or before expiration.
- **Bermudan option** - an option that may be exercised only on specified dates on or before expiration.
- **Barrier option** - any option with the general characteristic that the underlying security's price must reach some trigger level before the exercise can occur.

Valuation Models

The value of an option can be estimated using a variety of quantitative techniques based on the concept of risk neutral pricing and using stochastic calculus. The most basic model is the Black-Scholes model. More sophisticated models are used to model the volatility smile. These models are implemented using a variety of numerical techniques. In general, standard option valuation models depend on the following factors:

- The current market price of the underlying security,
- the strike price of the option, particularly in relation to the current market price of the underlier (in the money vs. out of the money),
- the cost of holding a position in the underlying security, including interest and dividends,
- the time to expiration together with any restrictions on when exercise may occur, and

- an estimate of the future volatility of the underlying security's price over the life of the option.

More advanced models can require additional factors, such as an estimate of how volatility changes over time and for various underlying price levels, or the dynamics of stochastic interest rates.

The following are some of the principal valuation techniques used in practice to evaluate option contracts.

Black Scholes Model

In the early 1970s, Fischer Black and Myron Scholes made a major breakthrough by deriving a differential equation that must be satisfied by the price of any derivative dependent on a non-dividend-paying stock. By employing the technique of constructing a risk neutral portfolio that replicates the returns of holding an option, Fischer Black and Myron Scholes produced a closed-form solution for a European option's theoretical price. At the same time, the model generates hedge parameters necessary for effective risk management of option holdings. While the ideas behind Black-Scholes were ground-breaking and eventually led to a Nobel Prize in Economics for Myron Scholes and Robert Merton, the application of the model in actual options trading is clumsy because of the assumptions of continuous (or no) dividend payment, constant volatility, and a constant interest rate. Nevertheless, the Black-Scholes model is still one of the most important methods and foundations for the existing financial market in which the result is within the reasonable range.

Stochastic Volatility Models

Since the market crash of 1987, it has been observed that market implied volatility for options of lower strike prices are typically higher than for higher strike prices, suggesting that volatility is stochastic, varying both for time and for the price level of the underlying security. Stochastic volatility models have been developed including one developed by S.L. Heston. One principal advantage of the Heston model is that it can be solved in closed-form, while other stochastic volatility models require complex numerical methods.

Model Implementation

Once a valuation model has been chosen, there are a number of different techniques used to take the mathematical models to implement the models.

Analytic Techniques

In some cases, one can take the mathematical model and using analytic methods to develop closed form solutions. The resulting solutions are useful because they are quick to calculate.

Binomial Tree Pricing Model

Closely following the derivation of Black and Scholes, John Cox, Stephen Ross and Mark Rubinstein developed the original version of the binomial options pricing model. It models the dynamics of the option's theoretical value for discrete time intervals over the option's duration. The model starts with a binomial tree of discrete future possible underlying stock prices. By constructing a riskless portfolio of an option and stock (as in the Black-Scholes model) a simple formula can be used to find the option price at each node in the tree. This value can approximate the theoretical value produced by Black Scholes, to the desired degree of precision. However, the binomial model is considered more accurate than Black-Scholes because it is more flexible, e.g. discrete future dividend payments can be modeled correctly at the proper forward time steps, and American options can be modeled as well as European ones. Binomial models are widely used by professional option traders.

Monte Carlo Models

For many classes of options, traditional valuation techniques are intractable due to the complexity of the instrument. In these cases, a Monte Carlo approach may often be useful. Rather than attempt to solve the differential equations of motion that describe the option's value in relation to the underlying security's price, a Monte Carlo model determines the value of the option for a set of randomly generated economic scenarios. The resulting sample set yields an expectation value for the option.

Finite Difference Models

The equations used to value options can often be expressed in terms of partial differential equations, and once expressed in this form, a finite difference model can be derived.

Other Models

Other numerical implementations which have been used to value options include finite element methods.

Risks

As with all securities, trading options entails the risk of the option's value changing over time. However, unlike traditional securities the return from holding an option varies non-linearly with the value of the underlier and other factors. Therefore, the risks associated with holding options are more complicated to understand and predict.

In general, the change in the value of an option can be derived from Ito's lemma as:

$$dC = \Delta dS + \Gamma \frac{dS^2}{2} + \kappa d\sigma + \theta dt$$

where Δ, Γ, κ and θ are the standard hedge parameters calculated from an option valuation model, such as Black-Scholes.
dS, *dσ* and *dt* are unit changes in the underlier price, the underlier volatility and time, respectively.

Thus, at any point in time, one can estimate the risk inherent in holding an option by calculating its hedge parameters and then estimating the expected change in the model inputs, *dS*, *dσ* and *dt*, provided that the changes in these values are small. This technique can be used effectively to understand and manage the risks associated with standard options. For instance, by offsetting a holding in an option with Δ of shares in the underlier. A trader can form a delta neutral portfolio that is hedged from loss for small changes in the underlier price. The corresponding price sensitivity formula for this portfolio Π is:

$$d\Pi = \Delta dS + \Gamma\frac{dS^2}{2} + \kappa d\sigma + \theta dt = \Gamma\frac{dS^2}{2} + \kappa d\sigma + \theta dt$$

Example

A call option expiring in 99 days on 100 shares of XYZ stock is struck at $50, with XYZ currently trading at $48. With future realized volatility over the life of the option estimated at 25%, the theoretical value of the option is $1.89. The hedge parameters Δ, Γ, κ, θ are (0.439, 0.0631, 9.6, and -0.022), respectively. Assume that on the following day, XYZ stock rises to $48.5 and volatility falls to 23.5%. We can calculate the estimated value of the call option by applying the hedge parameters to the new model inputs as:

$$dC = (0.439 \cdot 0.5) + \left(0.0631 \cdot \frac{0.5^2}{2}\right) + (9.6 \cdot -0.015) + (-0.022 \cdot 1) = 0.0614$$

Under this scenario the value of the option increases by $0.0614 to $1.9514, realizing a profit of $6.14. Note that for a delta neutral portfolio, where by the trader had also sold 44 shares of XYZ stock as a hedge, the net loss under the same scenario would be ($15.81).

Pin Risk

A special situation called pin risk can arise when the underlier closes at or very close to the option's strike value on the last day the option is traded prior to expiration. The option writer (seller) may not know with certainty whether or not the option will actually be exercised or be allowed to expire worthless. Therefore, the option writer may end up with a large, unwanted residual position in the underlier when the markets open on the next trading day after expiration, regardless of their best efforts to avoid such a residual.

Counterparty Risk

A further, often ignored, risk in derivatives such as options is counterparty risk. In an option contract this risk is that the seller won't sell or buy the underlying asset as agreed. The risk can be minimized by using a financially strong intermediary able to make good on the trade, but in a major panic or crash the number of defaults can overwhelm even the strongest intermediaries.

Trading

The most common way to trade options is via standardized options contracts that are listed by various futures and options exchanges. Listings and prices are tracked and can be looked up by ticker symbol. By publishing continuous, live markets for option prices an exchange enables independent parties to engage in price discovery and execute transactions. The benefits the exchange provides to the transaction include:

- fulfillment of the contract is backed by the credit of the exchange, which typically has the highest rating (AAA),
- counterparties remain anonymous,
- enforcement of market regulation to ensure fairness and transparency, and
- maintenance of orderly markets, especially during fast trading conditions.

Over-the-counter options contracts are not traded on exchanges, but instead between two independent parties. Ordinarily, at least one of the counterparties is a well-capitalized institution. By avoiding an exchange, users of OTC options can narrowly tailor the terms of the option contract to suit individual business requirements. In addition, OTC option transactions generally do not need to be advertised to the market and face little or no regulatory requirements. However, OTC counterparties must establish credit lines with each other, and conform to each other's clearing and settlement procedures.

With few exceptions, there are no secondary markets for employee stock options. These must either be exercised by the original grantee or allowed to expire worthless.

Basic Trades of Traded Stock Options (American Style)

These trades are described from the point of view of a speculator. If they are combined with other positions, they can also be used in hedging. An option contract in US markets usually represents 100 shares of the underlying security.

Long Call

A trader who believes that a stock's price will increase might buy the right to purchase the stock (a call option) rather than just buy the stock. He would have no obligation to buy the stock, only the right to do so until the expiration date. If the stock price at expiration is above the exercise price by more than the premium (price) paid, he will profit. If the stock price at expiration is lower than the exercise price, he will let the call contract expire worthless, and only lose the amount of the premium. A trader might buy the option instead of shares, because for the same amount of money, he can obtain a much larger number of options than shares. If the stock rises, he will thus realize a larger gain than if he had purchased shares.

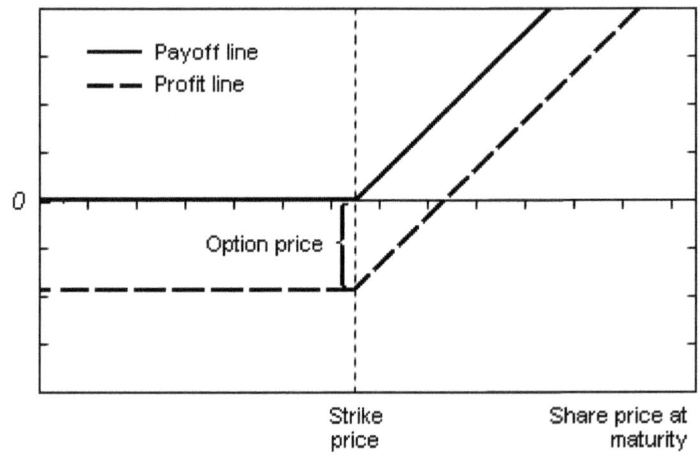

Picture 6: Long Call

Long Put

A trader who believes that a stock's price will decrease can buy the right to sell the stock at a fixed price (a put option). He will be under no obligation to sell the stock, but has the right to do so until the expiration date. If the stock price at expiration is below the exercise price by more than the premium paid, he will profit. If the stock price at expiration is above the exercise price, he will let the put contract expire worthless and only lose the premium paid.

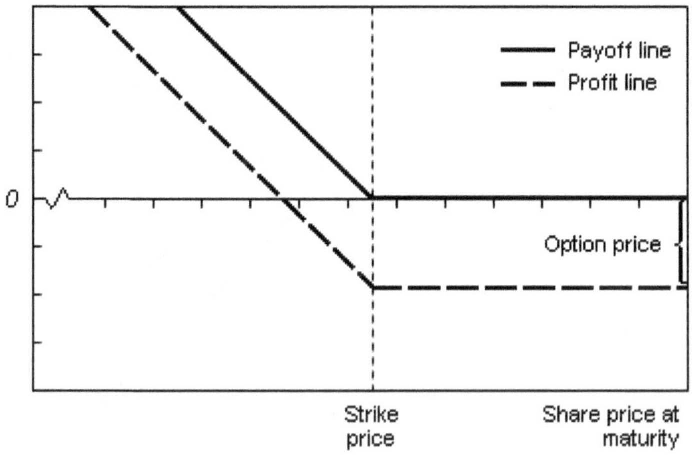

Picture 7: Long Put

Short Call

A trader who believes that a stock price will decrease, can sell the stock short or instead sell, or "write," a call. The trader selling a call has an obligation to sell the stock to the call buyer at the buyer's option. If the stock price decreases, the short call position will make a profit in the amount of the premium. If the stock price increases over the exercise price by more than the amount of the premium, the short will lose money, with the potential loss unlimited.

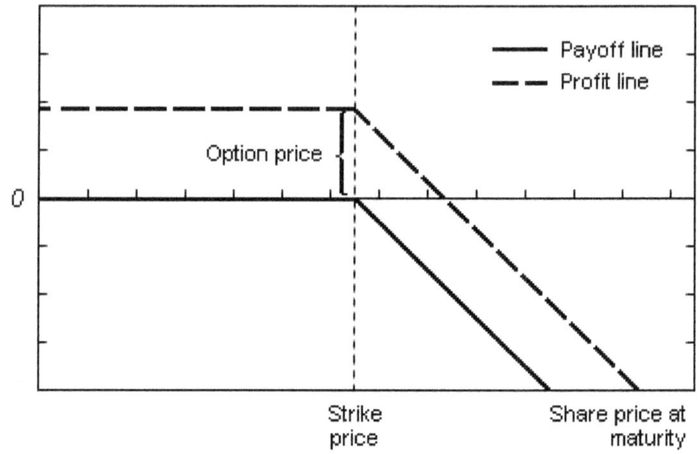

Picture 8: Short Call

Short Put

A trader who believes that a stock price will increase can buy the stock or instead sell a put. The trader selling a put has an obligation to buy the stock from the put buyer at the put buyer's option. If the stock price at expiration is above the exercise price, the short put position will make a profit in the amount of the premium. If the stock price at expiration is below the exercise price by more than the amount of the premium, the trader will lose money, with the potential loss being up to the full value of the stock.

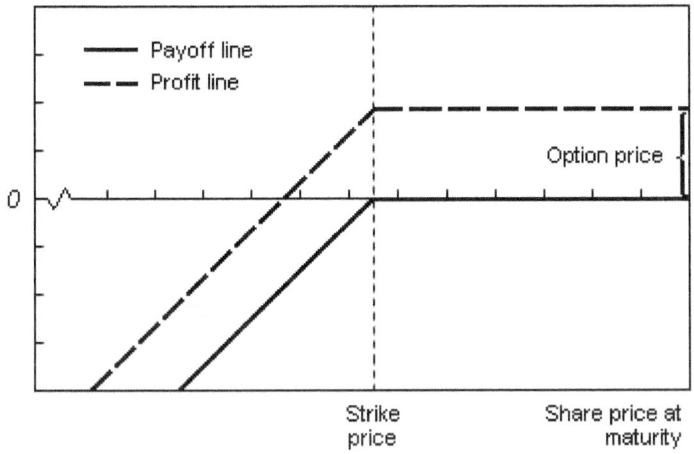

Picture 9: Short Put

Option Strategies

Combining any of the four basic kinds of option trades (possibly with different exercise prices and maturities) and the two basic kinds of stock trades (long and short) allows a variety of options strategies. Simple strategies usually combine only a few trades, while more complicated strategies can combine several trades.

Strategies are often used to engineer a particular risk profile to movements in the underlying security. For example, buying a **butterfly spread** (long one X1 call, short two X2 calls, and long one X3 call) allows a trader to profit if the stock price on the expiration date is near the middle exercise price, X2, and does not expose the trader to a large loss.

An **Iron condor** is a strategy that is similar to a butterfly spread, but with different strikes for the short options - offering a larger likelihood of profit but with a lower net credit compared to the butterfly spread.

Selling a **straddle** (selling both a put and a call at the same exercise price) would give a trader a greater profit than a butterfly if the final stock price is near the exercise price, but might also result in a large loss.

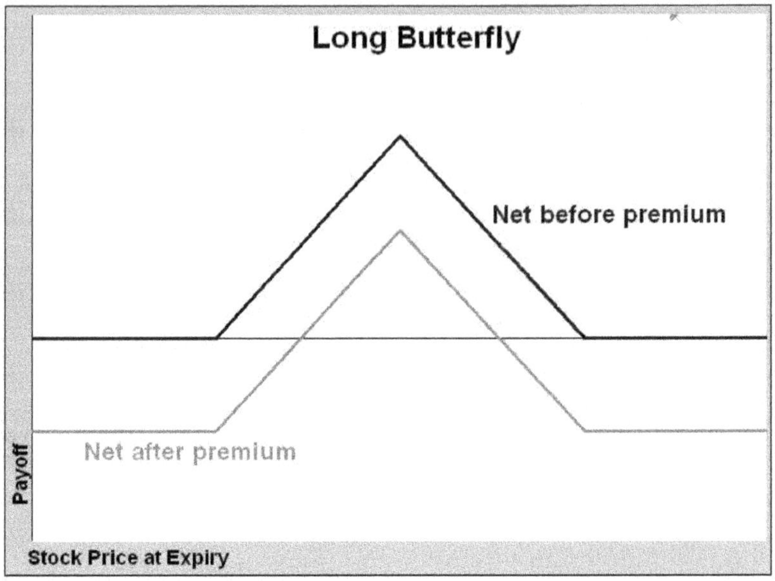

Picture 10: Payoffs from buying a butterfly spread

Similar to the straddle is the **strangle** which is also constructed by a call and a put, but whose strikes are different. They are reducing the net debit of the trade, but also reducing the likelihood of profit in the trade.

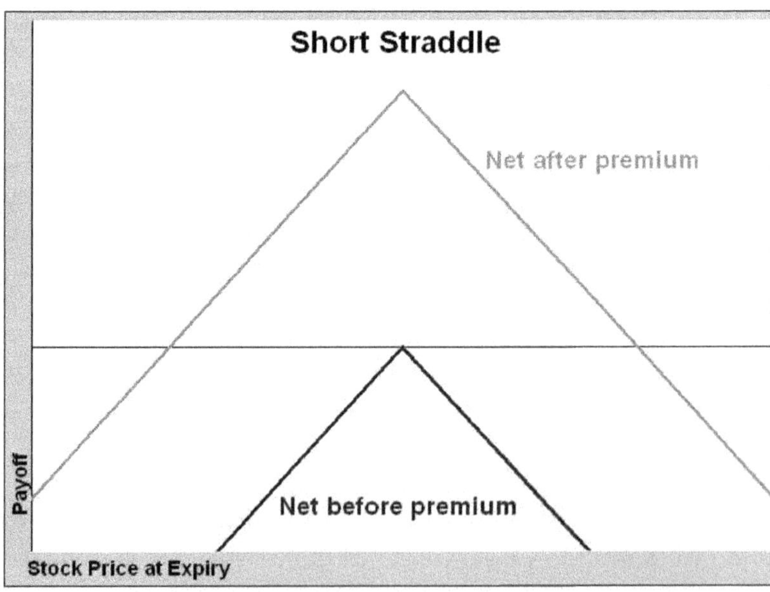

Picture 11:Payoffs from selling a straddle

One well-known strategy is the covered call, in which a trader buys a stock (or holds a previously-purchased long stock position) and sells a call. If the stock price rises above the exercise price the call will be exercised and the trader will get a fixed profit.
If the stock price falls, the trader will lose money on his stock position, but this will be partially offset by the premium received from selling the call. Overall, these payoffs match the payoffs from selling a put.

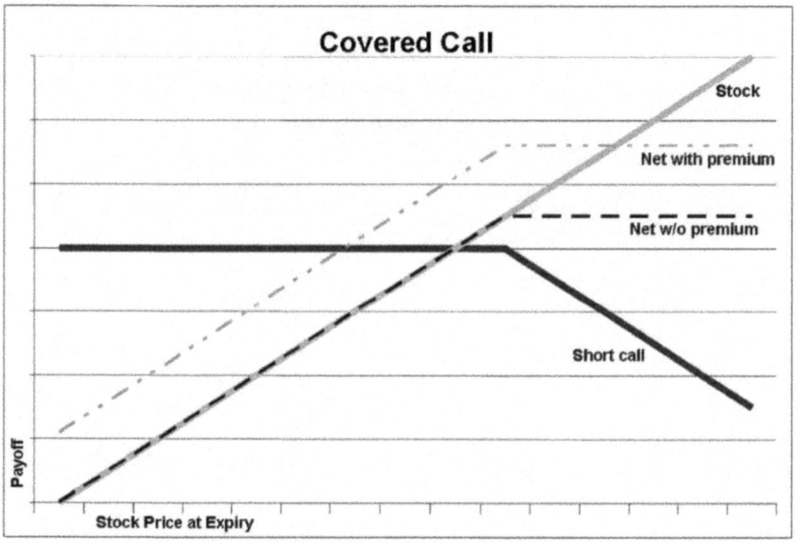

Picture 12: Payoffs from a covered call

Volatility Index VIX

VIX is the ticker symbol for the Chicago Board Options Exchange Volatility Index, a popular measure of the implied volatility of S&P 500 index options. A high value corresponds to a more volatile market and therefore more costly options, which can be used to defray risk from volatility. If investors see high risks of a change in prices, they require a greater premium to insure against such a change by selling options. Often referred to as the fear index, it represents one measure of the market's expectation of volatility over the next 30 day period.

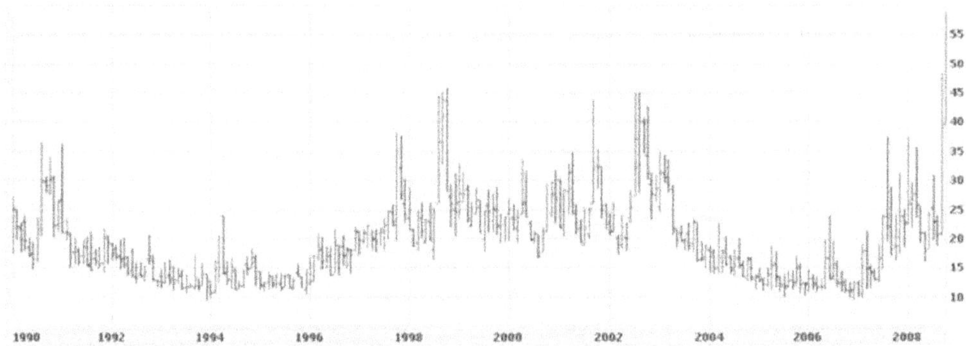

Picture 13:VIX Index from inception to Oct. 2008

Specifications

The VIX is calculated and disseminated in real-time by the Chicago Board Options Exchange. It is a weighted blend of prices for a range of options on the S&P 500 index. The formula uses a kernel-smoothed estimator that takes as inputs the current market prices for all out-of-the-money calls and puts for the front month and second month expirations. The goal is to estimate the implied volatility of the S&P 500 index over the next 30 days.

Interpretation

The VIX is quoted in terms of percentage points and translates roughly to the expected movement in the S&P 500 index over the next 30-day period on an annualized basis.

For example, if the VIX is at 15, this represents an expected annual change of 15%; thus one can infer that the index option markets expect the S&P 500 to move up or down by

$$\frac{15\%}{\sqrt{12}\ months} = 4.33\%$$

over the next 30-day period. Index options are priced with the assumption of a 68% likelihood (one standard deviation) that the magnitude of the S&P 500's 30-day return will be less than 4.33% (up or down).

The price of call options and put options can be used to calculate implied volatility, because volatility is one of the factors used to calculate the value of these options. Higher (or lower) volatility of the underlying security makes an option more (or less) valuable since there is a greater (or smaller) probability that the option will expire in the money (i.e. with a market value above zero). So a higher option price implies greater volatility. Other things being equal.

Investors believe that a high value of VIX translates into a greater degree of market uncertainty, while a low value of VIX is consistent with greater stability.

Note that because the VIX is quoted as a percentage rather than a dollar amount, there are no highly liquid instruments that will realize the VIX's "return" such as ETF can do for regular indices. Nonetheless, VIX-based derivative instruments do exist, including:

- VIX futures contracts, which began trading in 2004, and
- exchange-listed VIX options, which began trading in February 2006.

Similar indices for bonds include MOVE, LBPX indices.

Although the VIX is often called the "fear index" a high VIX is not necessarily bearish for stocks. Instead, the VIX is a measure of fear of volatility in either direction, including to the upside. In practical terms, when investors anticipate large upside volatility they are unwilling to sell upside "call" stock options unless they receive a large premium. Option buyers will be willing to pay such high premiums only if similarly anticipating a large upside move. The resulting aggregate of increases in upside stock option "call" prices raises the VIX. The same happens to the aggregate growth in downside stock "put" option premiums which occurs when option buyers and sellers anticipate a likely sharp move to the downside. When the market is believed as likely to soar as to plummet, writing any option that will cost the writer in the event of a sudden large move in either direction may look equally risky. Hence high VIX readings mean investors see significant risk that the market will move sharply, whether downward or upward. The highest VIX readings occur when investors anticipate that huge moves in either direction are likely. Only when investors perceive neither significant downside risk nor significant upside potential will the VIX be low.

The Black-Scholes formula is a quantification of how an option's value depends on the volatility of the underlying assets.

History

Here is a timeline of some key events in the history of the VIX Index:

- 1993 - The VIX Index was introduced in a paper by Professor Robert E. Whaley of Duke University
- 1993 - The VIX's lowest recorded value (between 1990 and 2008) of 9.48 occurred on Dec 24
- 2003 - Revised, more robust methodology for the VIX Index was introduced. The underlying index is changed from the CBOE S&P 100 Index (OEX) to the CBOE S&P 500 Index (SPX).
- 2004 - On March 26, 2004, the first-ever trading in futures on the VIX Index began on the CBOE Futures Exchange (CFE).
- 2006 - VIX options were launched in February 2006.
- 2008 - On October 24, 2008, the VIX reached an intraday high of 89.53.
- Between 1990 and October 2008, the average value of VIX was 19.04.

In 2004 and 2006, VIX Futures and VIX Options were each named Most Innovative Index Product (respectively) at the Super Bowl of Indexing Conference.

Criticism

Often, when commentators discuss the option markets, the VIX is used to represent overall sentiment for equity options. However, to many practitioners, the relationship of the VIX to individual equity options can be easily overstated. It often appears that different dynamics drive the volatility of index options compared to that of equity options, and the two can often be uncorrelated. In particular, the VIX is limited to a 30-day period, while for most non-index equity options, the most liquidity is usually found in the 2 to 6-month maturities. In addition, volatility is often a function of a market sector. For instance, volatility is usually assumed to be high in technology stocks, and low in utility stocks. Using a single number such as the VIX to represent the volatility for all equity options is usually overly simplistic.

Bond Options Explained

A bond option is an OTC-traded financial instrument that facilitates an option to buy or sell a particular bond at a certain date for a particular price. It is similar to a stock option with the difference that the underlying asset is a bond. Bond options can be valued using the Black Scholes Model.

The present market value for the bond is referred to as the **spot price** while the future value as per the option is referred to as the **strike price**.

Types

- A **European bond option** is an option to buy or sell a bond at a certain date in future for a predetermined price.
- An **American Bond option** is an option to buy or sell a bond on or before a certain date in future for a predetermined price.

Example

Trade Date:	1st March 2003
Maturity Date:	6 March 2006
Option Buyer:	Bank A
Underlying asset:	FNMA Bond.
Spot Price:	$101 ,
Strike Price:	$102

On the Trade Date Bank A enters into an option with Bank B to buy certain FNMA Bonds from Bank B for the Strike Price mentioned. Bank A pays a premium to Bank B which is the premium percentage multiplied by the face value of the bonds.

At the maturity of the option Bank A either exercises the option and buys the bonds from Bank B at the predetermined strike price or chooses not to exercise the option. In either case Bank A has lost the premium to Bank B.

Embedded option

The term "bond option" is also used for option-like features of some bonds. These are an inherent part of the bond rather than a separately traded product. These options are not mutually exclusive so a bond may have lots of options embedded.

- A **callable bond** allows the issuer to buy back the bond at a predetermined price at certain time in future. The holder of such a bond has, in effect, sold a call option to the issuer. Callable bonds cannot be called for the first few years of their life. This period is known as the lock out period.
- A **puttable bond** allows the holder to demand early redemption at a predetermined price at certain time in future. The holder of such a bond has, in effect, purchased a put option on the bond.
- A **convertible bond** allows the holder to demand conversion of bonds into the stock of the issuer at a predetermined price at a certain time period in future.
- An **exchangeable bond** allows the holder to demand conversion of bonds into the stock of a different company, usually a public subsidiary of the issuer, at a predetermined price and at a certain time period in future.

Uses

The major advantage of a bond option is the locking-in price of the underlying bond for the future thereby reducing the credit risk associated with fluctuations in the bond price.

Credit Default Option

In finance, a default option, credit default swaption or credit default option is an option to buy protection (payer option) or sell protection (receiver option) as a credit default swap on a specific reference credit with a specific maturity. The option is usually European, exercisable only at one date in the future at a specific strike price defined as a coupon on the credit default swap.

Credit default options on single credits are extinguished upon default without any cash flows other than the upfront premium paid by the buyer of the option, of course. Therefore buying a payer option is not a good protection against an actual default, only against a rise in the credit spread. However, options on credit indices such as iTraxx and CDX include any defaulted entities in the intrinsic value of the option when exercised.

Credit Default Swap

A credit default swap (CDS) is a credit derivative contract between two counterparties. The buyer makes periodic payments to the seller, and in return receives a payoff if an underlying financial instrument defaults. CDS contracts have been compared to insurance, because the buyer pays a premium, and in return receives a sum of money if a specified event occurs. However, this is a slightly misleading comparison because the buyer of a CDS does not need to own the underlying security; in fact the buyer does not even have to suffer a loss from the default event.

Description

A credit default swap (CDS) is a swap contract in which the buyer of the CDS makes a series of payments to the seller and in exchange receives a payoff if a credit instrument (typically a bond or loan) goes into default or on the occurrence of a specified credit event (for example bankruptcy or restructuring). Credit Default Swaps can be bought by any (relatively sophisticated) investor; it is not necessary for the buyer to own the underlying credit instrument.

Example

Imagine that an investor buys a CDS from ABC Bank where the reference entity is XYZ Corp. The investor will make regular payments to ABC Bank and if XYZ Corp defaults on its debt (i.e., it does not repay it) the investor will receive a one-off payment from ABC Bank and the CDS contract is terminated. If the investor actually owns XYZ Corp debt the CDS can be thought of as hedging. But investors can also buy CDS contracts referencing XYZ Corp debt without actually owning any XYZ Corp debt. This is done for speculative purposes. Betting against the solvency of XYZ Corp in a gamble to make money if it fails.

If the reference entity (XYZ Corp) defaults, one of two things can happen:

- Either the investor delivers a defaulted asset to ABC Bank for a payment of the par value. This is known as physical settlement.
- Or ABC Bank pays the investor the difference between the par value and the market price of a specified debt obligation (even if XYZ Corp defaults, there is usually some recovery; i.e. not all your money will be lost.) This is known as cash settlement.

The price, or spread, of a CDS is the annual amount the protection buyer must pay the protection seller over the length of the contract, expressed as a percentage of the notional amount. For example, if the CDS spread of XYZ Corp is 50 basis points, or 0.5% (1 basis point = 0.01%), then an investor buying $10 million worth of protection from ABC Bank must pay the bank $50,000 per year. These payments continue until either the CDS contract expires or until XYZ Corp defaults.

All things being equal, a company with a higher CDS spread is considered more likely to default by the market since a higher fee is being charged to protect against this happening.

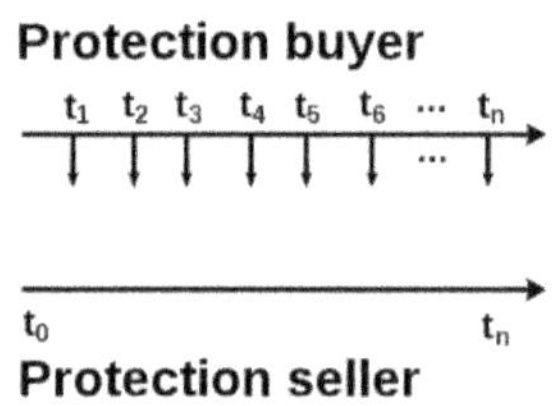

In the case above a Buyer purchased a CDS at time t0 and makes regular premium payments at times t1, t2, t3, and t4. If the associated credit instrument suffers no credit event, then the buyer continues paying premiums at t5, t6 and so on until the end of the contract at time tn.

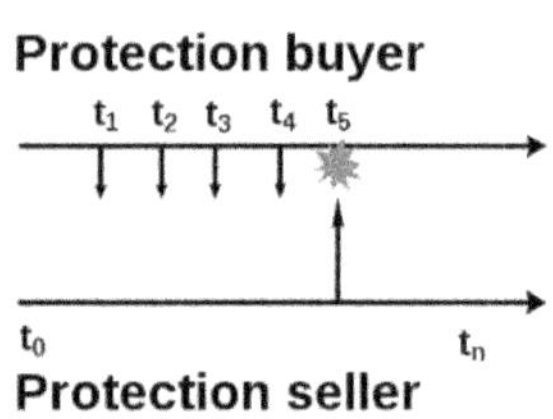

However, if the associated credit instrument suffered a credit event at t5, then the protection seller pays the buyer for the loss and the buyer would cease paying premiums.

How Credit Default Swaps are used

Like most financial derivatives credit default swaps can be used by investors for speculation, hedging and arbitrage.

Speculation

Credit default swaps allow investors to speculate on changes in an entity's credit quality since generally CDS spreads will increase as credit-worthiness declines and decline as credit-worthiness increases. Therefore an investor might buy CDS protection on a company in order to speculate that a company is about to default. Alternatively, an investor might sell protection if they think that a company is not going to default.

Example

A hedge fund believes that XYZ Corp will soon default on its debt. Therefore it buys $10 million worth of CDS protection for 2 years from ABC Bank with XYZ Corp as the reference entity at a spread of 500 basis points (=5%) per annum.

- If XYZ Corp does indeed default after, say, one year, then the hedge fund will have paid $500,000 to ABC Bank but will then receive $10 million (assuming zero recovery rate) thereby making a tidy profit.
- However, if XYZ Corp does not default then the CDS contract will run for 2 years and the hedge fund will have ended up paying $1 million without any return thereby making a loss.

Note that there is a third possibility in the above scenario; the hedge fund could decide to liquidate its position after a certain period of time in an attempt to lock in its gains or losses. For example:

- After 1 year, the market now considers XYZ Corp more likely to default, so its CDS spread has widened from 500 to 1500 basis points. The hedge fund may choose to sell $10 million worth of protection for 1 year to ABC Bank at this higher rate. Therefore over the two years the hedge fund will pay the bank 2*5%*$10 million = $1 million but will receive 1*15%*$10 million = $1.5 million, giving a total profit of $500,000 (so long as XYZ Corp does not default during the second year).
- In another scenario, after one year the market now considers XYZ much less likely to default so its CDS spread has tightened from 500 to 250 basis points. Again, the hedge may choose to sell $10 million worth of protection for 1 year to ABC Bank at this lower spread. Therefore over the two years the hedge fund will pay the bank 2*5%*$10 million = $1 million, but will receive 1*2.5%*$10 million = $0.25 million, giving a total loss of $750,000 (so long as XYZ Corp does not default during the second year). Although this loss is large it

is smaller than the $1 million loss that would have occurred if the second transaction had not been entered into.

Transactions such as these do not even have to be entered into over the long-term. If XYZ Corp's CDS spread had widened by just a couple of basis points of the course of one day the hedge fund could have entered into an offsetting contract immediately and made a small profit over the life of the two CDS contracts.

Hedging

Credit default swaps are often used to manage the credit risk (ie the risk of default) which arises from holding debt. Typically, the holder of for example a corporate bond may hedge their exposure by entering into a CDS contract as the buyer of protection. If the bond goes into default, the proceeds from the CDS contract will cancel out the losses on the underlying bond.

Example

A pension fund owns $10 million of a five-year bond issued by Risky Corp. In order to manage the risk of losing money if Risky Corp defaults on its debt, the pension fund buys a CDS from Derivative Bank in a notional amount of $10 million. The CDS trades at 200 basis points (200 basis points = 2.00 percent). In return for this credit protection, the pension fund pays 2% of 10 million ($200,000) per annum in quarterly installments of $50,000 to Derivative Bank.

If Risky Corporation does not default on its bond payments, the pension fund makes quarterly payments to Derivative Bank for 5 years and receives its $10 million back after 5 years from Risky Corp. Though the protection payments totaling $1 million reduce investment returns for the pension fund and its risk of loss due to Risky Corp defaulting on the bond is eliminated.

If Risky Corporation defaults on its debt 3 years into the CDS contract the pension fund would stop paying the quarterly premium. The Derivative Bank would ensure that the pension fund is refunded for its loss of $10 million (either by physical or cash settlement - see above). The pension fund still loses the $600,000 it has paid over three years but without the CDS contract it would have lost the entire $10 million.

(Note that the pension fund now has counterparty risk with Derivative Bank; if the bank is in financial difficulties it may not be able to refund the full $10 million to the pension fund.)

Arbitrage

Capital Structure Arbitrage is an example of an arbitrage strategy which utilizes CDS transactions. This technique relies on the fact that a company's stock price and its CDS spread should exhibit negative correlation; i.e. if the outlook for a company improves then its share price should go up and its CDS spread should tighten since it is less likely to default on its debt.
However, if its outlook worsens then its CDS spread should widen and its stock price should fall. Techniques reliant on this are known as capital structure arbitrage because they exploit market inefficiencies between different parts of the same company's capital structure; i.e. mis-pricings between a company's debt and equity. An arbitrageur will attempt to exploit the spread between a company's CDS and its equity in certain situations. For example, if a company has announced some bad news and its share price has dropped by 25%, but its CDS spread has remained unchanged, then an investor might expect the CDS spread to increase relative to the share price. Therefore a basic strategy would be to go long the CDS spread (by buying CDS protection) while simultaneously hedging oneself by short-selling the underlying stock. This technique would benefit in the event of the CDS spread widening relative to the equity price, but would lose money if the company's CDS spread tightened relative to its equity.
An interesting situation in which the inverse correlation between a company's stock price and CDS spread breaks down is during a leveraged buyout (LBO). Frequently this will lead to the company's CDS spread widening due to the extra debt that will soon be put on the company's books, but also an increase in its share price, since buyers of a company usually end up paying a premium.

Another common arbitrage strategy aims to exploit the fact that the swap adjusted spread of a CDS should trade closely with that of the underlying cash bond issued by the reference entity. Misalignments in spreads may occur due to technical reasons such as specific settlement differences, shortages in a particular underlying instrument, and the existence of buyers constrained from buying exotic derivatives. The difference between CDS spreads and asset swap spreads is called the **basis** and should theoretically be close to zero. Basis trades can aim to exploit any differences to make risk-free profits.

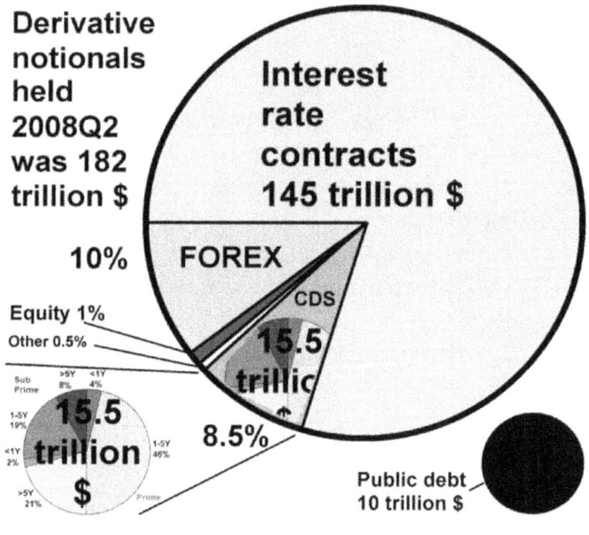

Picture 14:Credit default swaps vs. total nominals plus debt

The above picture shows the proportion of CDSs nominals (lower left) held by United States banks compared to all derivatives, in 2008Q2. The black disc represents the 2008 public debt.

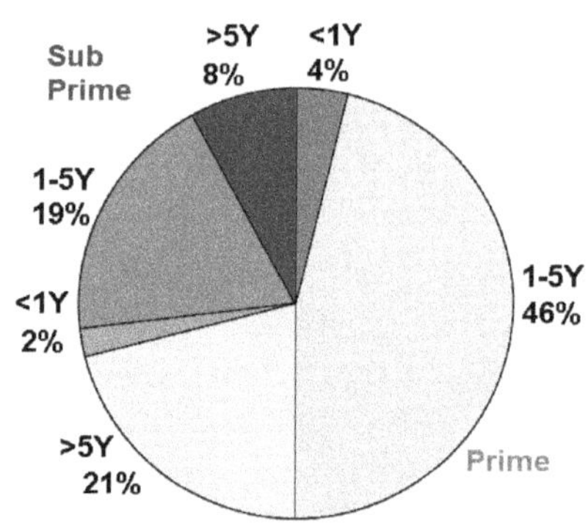

Picture 15:Credit default swaps by quality size

The picture above shows the composition of the United States 15.5 trillion US dollar CDS market at the end of 2008 Q2. Green tints show Prime asset CDSs, reddish tints show sub-prime asset CDSs. Numbers followed by "Y" indicate years until maturity.

Terms of a Typical CDS Contract

A CDS contract is typically documented under a confirmation referencing the credit derivatives definitions as published by the International Swaps and Derivatives Association. The confirmation typically specifies a reference entity, a corporation or sovereign that generally, although not always has debt outstanding and a reference obligation. This usually an unsubordinated corporate bond or government bond. The period over which default protection extends is defined by the contract effective date and scheduled termination date.

The confirmation also specifies a calculation agent who is responsible for making determinations as to successors and substitute reference obligations (for example necessary if the original reference obligation was a loan that is repaid before the expiry of the contract) and for performing various calculation and administrative functions in connection with the transaction. By market convention, in contracts between CDS dealers and end-users the dealer is generally the calculation agent and in contracts between CDS dealers the protection seller is generally the calculation agent. It is not the responsibility of the calculation agent to determine whether or not a credit event has occurred but rather a matter of fact that, pursuant to the terms of typical contracts, must be supported by publicly available information delivered along with a credit event notice. Typical CDS contracts do not provide an internal mechanism for challenging the occurrence or non-occurrence of a credit event and rather leave the matter to the courts if necessary. Though actual instances of specific events being disputed are relatively rare.

CDS confirmations also specify the credit events that will give rise to payment obligations by the protection seller and delivery obligations by the protection buyer. Typical credit events include bankruptcy with respect to the reference entity and failure to pay with respect to its direct or guaranteed bond or loan debt. CDS written on North American investment grade corporate reference entities, European corporate reference entities and sovereigns generally also include restructuring as a credit event whereas trades referencing North American high yield corporate reference entities typically do not. The definition of restructuring is quite technical but is essentially intended to respond to circumstances where a reference entity, as a result of the deterioration of its credit negotiates changes in the terms in its debt with its creditors as an alternative to formal insolvency proceedings (i.e., the debt is restructured). This practice is far more typical in jurisdictions that do not provide protective status to insolvent debtors similar to that provided by Chapter 11 of the United States Bankruptcy Code. In particular, concerns arising out of Conseco's restructuring in 2000 led to the credit event's removal from North American high yield trades.

Finally, standard CDS contracts specify deliverable obligation characteristics that limit the range of obligations that a protection buyer may deliver upon a credit event. Trading conventions for deliverable obligation characteristics vary for different markets and CDS contract types. Typical limitations include that deliverable debt be a bond or loan, that has a maximum maturity of 30 years, that is not subordinated, that is not subject to transfer restrictions (other than Rule 144A), that is of a standard currency and that is not subject to some contingency before becoming due.

Settlement

As described in an earlier section, if a credit event occurs then CDS contracts can either be physically settled or cash settled.

Physical settlement: The protection seller pays the buyer par value and in return takes delivery of a debt obligation of the reference entity.

For example, a hedge fund has bought $5 million worth of protection from a bank on the senior debt of a company. In the event of a default the bank will pay the hedge fund $5 million cash and the hedge fund must deliver $5 million face value of senior debt of the company (typically bonds or loans which will typically be worth very little given that the company is in default).

Cash settlement: The protection seller pays the buyer the difference between par value and the market price of a debt obligation of the reference entity.

For example, a hedge fund has bought $5 million worth of protection from a bank on the senior debt of a company. This company has now defaulted and its senior bonds are now trading at 25 (i.e. 25 cents on the dollar) since the market believes that senior bondholders will receive 25% of the money they are owed once the company is wound up. Therefore, the bank must pay the hedge fund $5 million * (100%-25%) = $3.75 million.

The development and growth of the CDS market has meant that on many companies there is now a much larger outstanding notional value of CDS contracts than the outstanding notional value of its debt obligations. (This is because many parties made CDS contracts for speculative purposes without actually owning any debt for which they wanted to insure against default.)

For example, at the time it filed for bankruptcy on 14 September 2008, Lehman Brothers had approximately $155 billion of outstanding debt but around

$400 billion notional value of CDS contracts had been written which referenced this debt. Clearly not all of these contracts could be physically settled since there was not enough outstanding Lehman Brothers debt to fulfill all of the contracts. This demonstrates the necessity for cash settled CDS trades. The trade confirm produced when a CDS is traded will state whether the contract is to be physically or cash settled.

Criticisms

Critics of the huge credit default swap market have claimed that it has been allowed to become too large without proper regulation, and that because all contracts are privately negotiated that the market has no transparency. Furthermore there have even been claims that CDS's exacerbated the 2008 global financial crisis by hastening the demise of companies such as Lehman Brothers and AIG.

In the case of Lehman Brothers it is claimed that the widening of the bank's CDS spread reduced confidence in the bank and ultimately gave it further problems that it was not able to overcome. However, proponents of the CDS market argue that this confuses cause and effect; CDS spreads simply reflected the reality that the company was in serious trouble. Furthermore they claim that the CDS market allowed investors who had counterparty risk with Lehman Brothers to reduce their exposure in the case of their default.

It was also reported after Lehman's bankruptcy that the $400 billion notional of CDS protection which had been written on the bank could lead to a net payout of $366 billion from protection sellers to buyers (given the cash-settlement auction settled at a final price of 8.625%) and that these large payouts could lead to further bankruptcies of firms without enough cash to settle their contracts. However, industry estimates after the auction suggested that net cash flows would only be in the region of $7 billion. This is because many parties held offsetting positions; for example if a bank writes CDS protection on a company it is likely to then enter an offsetting transaction by buying protection on the same company in order to hedge its risk. Furthermore, CDS deals are marked-to-market frequently. This would have led to margin calls from buyers to sellers as Lehman's CDS spread widened, meaning that the net cash flows on the days after the auction are likely to have been even lower. Senior Bankers have argued that CDS contracts have been acting to distribute risk just as was intended, and that it is not CDSs themselves that need further regulation but the folk who trade them.

Some general criticism of financial derivatives is also relevant to credit derivatives. Warren Buffett famously described derivatives bought speculatively as "financial weapons of mass destruction." In Berkshire Hathaway's annual report to shareholders in 2002, he said, "Unless derivatives contracts are collateralized or guaranteed, their ultimate value also depends on the creditworthiness of the counterparties to them. In the meantime though, before a contract is settled, the counterparties record profits and losses—often huge in amount—in their current earnings statements without so much as a penny changing hands. The range of derivatives contracts is limited only by the imagination of man (or sometimes, so it seems, madmen)." It is true entering in a CDS transaction gives you counterparty risk, but bear in mind that it is also possible to hedge this risk by buying CDS protection on your counterparty! Furthermore, it is not strictly true to say that profit and loss is recorded without any money changing hands since positions are marked-to-market daily and collateral will pass from buyer to seller (or vice versa) to protect both parties against counterparty default.

Systemic Risk

The risk of counterparties defaulting has been amplified during the 2008 financial crisis, particularly because Lehman Brothers and AIG were counterparties in a very large number of CDS transactions. This is an example of systemic risk, risk which threatens an entire market, and a number of commentators have argued that size and deregulation of the CDS market have increased this risk. As an example, imagine a mutual fund bought some Washington Mutual corporate bonds in 2005 and decided to hedge their exposure by buying CDS protection, from Lehman Brothers.

After Lehman's default, this protection was no longer active, and Washington Mutual's sudden default only days later would have led to a massive loss on the bonds; a loss that should have been nullified by the CDS. It was also a worry that after the defaults of Lehman Brothers and AIG, their inability to pay out on CDS contracts could lead to the complex interlinked chain of CDS transactions between financial institutions to completely unravel. So far this does not seem to have happened, although some commentators have noted that because the total CDS exposure of a bank is not public knowledge, the worry that one could face large losses or possibly even default themselves was a contributing factor to the massive decrease in lending liquidity during September/October 2008.

Chains of CDS transactions can arise from a practice known as "netting". Here, company B may buy a CDS from company A with a certain annual "premium", say 2%. If the condition of the reference company worsens, the risk premium will rise. Then company B can sell a CDS to company C with a premium of say, 5%, and pocket the 3% difference. However, if the reference company defaults company B might not have the assets on hand to make good on the contract. It depends on its contract with company A to provide a large payout, which it then passes along to company C. The problem is that if one of the companies in the chain fails, creating a "domino effect" of losses. For example, if company A fails, company B will default on its CDS contract to company C, possibly resulting in bankruptcy and company C will potentially experience a large loss due to the failure to receive compensation for the bad debt it held from the reference company. Even worse, because CDS contracts are private, company C will not know that its fate is tied to company A; since it is only doing business with company B.

As described above the establishment of a central exchange or clearing house for CDS trades would help to solve the "domino effect" problem, since it would mean that all trades faced a central counterparty guaranteed by a consortium of dealers.

Tax Treatment

The U.S federal income tax treatment of credit default swaps is uncertain. Commentators generally believe that, depending on how they are drafted, they are either notional principal contracts or options for tax purposes, but this is not certain. There is a risk of having credit default swaps recharacterized as different types of financial instruments because they resemble put options and credit guarantees. In particular, the degree of risk depends on the type of settlement (physical/cash and binary/FMV) and trigger (default only/any credit event). If a credit default swap is a notional principal contract, periodic and nonperiodic payments on the swap are deductible and included in ordinary income. If a payment is a termination payment, its tax treatment is even more uncertain. In 2004, the Internal Revenue Service announced that it was studying the characterization of credit default swaps in response to taxpayer confusion, but it has not yet issued any guidance on their characterization. A taxpayer must include income from credit default swaps in ordinary income if the swaps are connected with trade or business in the United States.

LCDS

A new type of default swap is the "loan only" credit default swap (LCDS). This is conceptually very similar to a standard CDS, but unlike "vanilla" CDS, the underlying protection is sold on syndicated secured loans of the reference entity rather than the broader category of "Bond or Loan". Also, as of May 22, 2007, for the most widely traded LCDS form, which governs North American single name and index trades, the default settlement method for LCDS shifted to auction settlement rather than physical settlement. The auction method is essentially the same that has been used in the various ISDA cash settlement auction protocols, but does not require parties to take any additional steps following a credit event (i.e., adherence to a protocol) to elect cash settlement. On October 23, 2007, the first ever LCDS auction was held for Movie Gallery.

Because LCDS trades are linked to secured obligations with much higher recovery values than the unsecured bond obligations that are typically assumed to be the cheapest to deliver in respect of vanilla CDS, LCDS spreads are generally much tighter than CDS trades on the same name.

Call Options

This topic has been discussed more broadly at the beginning of this chapter. However we will now have a more closer look at call options and review what we already know. A call option is a financial contract between two parties, the buyer and the seller of this type of option. Often it is simply labeled a "call". As we already said, the buyer of the option has the right, but not the obligation to buy an agreed quantity of a particular commodity or financial instrument (the underlying instrument) from the seller of the option at a certain time (the expiration date) for a certain price (the strike price). The seller (or "writer") is obligated to sell the commodity or financial instrument should the buyer decide so. The buyer pays a fee (called a premium) for this right.

The buyer of a call option wants the price of the underlying instrument to rise in the future; the seller either expects that it will not or is willing to give up some of the upside (profit) from a price rise in return for the premium (paid immediately) and retaining the opportunity to make a gain up to the strike price (see below for examples).

Call options are most profitable for the buyer when the underlying instrument is moving up making the price of the underlying instrument closer to the strike price. When the price of the underlying instrument surpasses the strike price the option is said to be "in the money".

The initial transaction in this context (buying/selling a call option) is not the supplying of a physical or financial asset (the underlying instrument). Rather it is the granting of the right to buy the underlying asset, in exchange for a fee - the option price or premium.

Example of a call option on a stock

```
Buy a call:   The buyer expects that the price may go up.
              The buyer pays a premium that he will never
get back.
              He has the right to exercise the option at the
strike price.

Write a call: The writer receives the premium.
              If the buyer decides to exercise the option,
then
```

the writer has to sell the stock at the strike price.

If the buyer does not exercise the option, then

the writer profits the premium.

'Trader A' (Call Buyer) purchases a Call contract to buy 100 shares of XYZ Corp from 'Trader B' (Call Writer) at $\$50_{/share}$. The current price is $\$45_{/share}$, and 'Trader A' pays a premium of $\$5_{/share}$. If the share price of XYZ stock rises to $\$60_{/share}$ right before expiration, then 'Trader A' can exercise the call by buying 100 shares for $5,000 from 'Trader B' and sell them at $6,000 in the stock market.

Trader A's total earnings (S) can be calculated at $500.

Sale of 100 stock at $60 = $6,000 (P)

Amount paid to 'Trader B' for the 100 stock bought at strike price of $50 = $5,000 (Q)

Call Option premium paid to Trader B for buying the contract of 100 shares @ $\$5_{/share}$, excluding commissions = $500 (R)

S=P-(Q+R)=$6,000-($5,000+$500)=$500'

If however the price of XYZ drops to $\$40_{/share}$ below the strike price then 'Trader A' would not exercise the option. (Why buy a stock from 'Trader B' at 50, the strike price when it can be bought at $40 in the stock market?) Trader A's option would be worthless and the whole investment, the fee (premium) for the option contract, $500 ($5_{/share}$, 100 shares per contract). Trader A's total loss is limited to the cost of the call premium plus the sales commission to buy it.

This example illustrates that a call option has positive monetary value when the underlying instrument has a spot price (S) above the strike price (K). Since the option will not be exercised unless it is "in-the-money", the payoff for a call option is

$$\max[(S-K);0] \quad \text{or formally} \quad (S-K)^+$$

$$\text{where:} \quad (x)^+ = \begin{cases} x \text{ if } x \geq 0 \\ 0 \text{ otherwise} \end{cases}$$

Prior to the exercise, the option value, and therefore the price, varies with the underlying price and with time. The call price must reflect the "likelihood" or chance of the option "finishing in-the-money". The price should thus be higher with more time to expire (except in cases when a significant dividend is present) and with a more volatile underlying instrument. The science of determining this value is the central tenet of financial mathematics. The most common method is to use the Black-Scholes formula. Whatever the formula used, the buyer and seller must agree on the initial value (the premium), otherwise the exchange (buy/sell) of the option will not take place.

Put Options

A put option (sometimes simply called a "put") is a financial contract between two parties, the seller (writer) and the buyer of the option. The put allows its buyer the right but not the obligation to sell a commodity or financial instrument (the underlying instrument) to the writer (seller) of the option at a certain time for a certain price (the strike price). The writer (seller) has the obligation to purchase the underlying asset at that strike price, if the buyer exercises the option.

Note that the writer of the option is agreeing to buy the underlying asset if the buyer exercises the option. In exchange for having this option the buyer pays the writer (seller) a fee (the premium). (Although option writers are frequently referred to as sellers, because they initially sell the option that they create thus taking a long position in the option but they are not the only sellers. An option holder can also sell his short position in the option. However, the difference between the two sellers is that the option writer takes on the legal obligation to buy the underlying asset at the strike price, whereas the option holder is merely selling his long position, and is not contractually obligated by the sold option.)

Exact specifications may differ depending on option style. A European put option allows the holder to exercise the put option for a short period of time right before expiration. An American put option allows exercise at any time during the life of the option.

The most widely-known put option is for stock in a particular company. However, options are traded on many other assets: financial - such as interest rates - and physical, such as gold or crude oil.

Example of a put option on a stock

```
Buy a Put: A Buyer thinks price of a stock will decrease.
           Pay a premium which buyer will never get back,
unless
            it is sold before expiration.
           The buyer has the right to sell the stock
           at strike price.

Write a put: Writer receives a premium.
             If buyer exercises the option,
```

```
writer will buy the stock at strike price.
If buyer does not exercise the option,
writer's profit is premium.
```

'Trader A' (Put Buyer) purchases a put contract to sell 100 shares of XYZ Corp. to 'Trader B' (Put Writer) for $\$50_{/share}$. The current price is $\$55_{/share}$, and 'Trader A' pays a premium of $\$5_{/share}$. If the price of XYZ stock falls to $\$40_{/share}$ right before expiration, then 'Trader A' can exercise the put by buying 100 shares for $4,000 from the stock market, then selling them to 'Trader B' for $5,000.

```
Trader A's total earnings (S) can be calculated at $500.
 Sale of the 100 stock at strike price of $50 to 'Trader B'
= $5,000 (P)
 Purchase of 100 stock at $40 = $4,000 (Q)
 Put Option premium paid to Trader B for buying the contract
of 100
 shares   @ $5/share, excluding commissions = $500 (R)
  S=P-(Q+R)=$5,000-($4,000+$500)=$500
```

If however, the share price never drops below the strike price (in this case, $50), then 'Trader A' would not exercise the option. (Why sell a stock to 'Trader B' at $50, if it would cost 'Trader A' more than that to buy it?). Trader A's option would be worthless and he would have lost the whole investment, the fee (premium) for the option contract, $500 ($5_{/share}$, 100 shares per contract). Trader A's total loss are limited to the cost of the put premium plus the sales commission to buy it.

This example illustrates that the put option has positive monetary value when the underlying instrument has a spot price (S) *below* the strike price (K). Since the option will not be exercised unless it is "in-the-money", the payoff for a put option is

$$\max[(K - S)\,;\,0] \quad \text{or formally,} \quad (K - S)^{+}$$

where:

$$(x)^{+} = \begin{cases} x & \text{if } x \geq 0, \\ 0 & \text{otherwise.} \end{cases}$$

Prior to exercise, the option value, and therefore the price, varies with the underlying price and with time. The put price must reflect the "likelihood" or chance of the option "finishing in-the-money". The price should thus be higher with more time to expiry, and with a more volatile underlying instrument. Determining this value is the central problem of financial mathematics. The most common method is to use the Black-Scholes formula. Whatever the formula used, the buyer and seller must agree on this value initially.

Foreign Exchange Options

A foreign exchange option (commonly shortened to just FX option or currency option) is a derivative financial instrument where the owner has the right but not the obligation to exchange money denominated in one currency into another currency at a pre-agreed exchange rate on a specified date.

The FX options market is the deepest, largest and most liquid market for options of any kind in the world. Most of the FX option volume is traded OTC and is lightly regulated, but a fraction is traded on exchanges like the International Securities Exchange, Philadelphia Stock Exchange, or the Chicago Mercantile Exchange for options on futures contracts. The global market for exchange-traded currency options was notionally valued by the Bank for International Settlements at $158,300 billion in 2005.

Terms

Generally in thinking about options, one assumes that one is buying an asset. For instance, you can have a call option on oil, which allows you to buy oil at a given price. One can consider this situation more symmetrically in FX, where one exchanges: a put on GBPUSD which allows one to exchange GBP for USD: it is at once a put on GBP and a call on USD.

As a vivid example: people usually consider that in a fast food restaurant, one buys hamburgers and pays in dollars, but one can instead say that the restaurant buys dollars and pays in hamburgers.

There are a number of subtleties that follow from this symmetry.

Ratio of notionals

The ratio of the notionals in an FX option is the strike, not the current spot or forward. Notably, when constructing an option strategy from FX options, one must be careful to match the foreign currency notionals not the local currency notionals, otherwise the foreign currencies received and delivered don't offset which would lead to one being left with residual risk.

Non-linear payoff

The payoff for a vanilla option is linear in the underlying, when one denominates the payout in a given numéraire. In the case of an FX option on a rate, one must be careful of which currency is the underlying and which in the numéraire: in the above example, an option on GBPUSD gives a USD value that is linear in GBPUSD (a move from 2.0000 to 1.9000 yields a .10 * $2,000,000 / 2.0000 = $100,000 profit) but has a non-linear GBP value in GBPUSD. Conversely, the GBP value is linear in the USDGBP rate while the USD value is non-linear in the USDGBP rate. This is because inverting a rate has the effect of x -> 1/x, which is non-linear.

Change of numéraire

The implied volatility of an FX option depends on the numéraire of the purchaser because of the non-linearity of x -> 1/x.

Hedging with FX options

Corporations primarily use FX options to hedge uncertain future cash flows in a foreign currency. The general rule is to hedge certain foreign currency cash flows with **forwards**, and uncertain foreign cash flows with **options**.

Example

Suppose a United Kingdom manufacturing firm is expecting to be paid US$100,000 for a piece of engineering equipment to be delivered in 90 days. If the GBP strengthens against the US$ over the next 90 days the UK firm will lose money, as it will receive less GBP when the US$100,000 is converted into GBP. However, if the GBP weakens against the US$, then the UK firm will gain additional money: the firm is exposed to FX risk. Assuming that the cash flow is certain, the firm can enter into a forward contract to deliver the US$100,000 in 90 days time, in exchange for GBP at the current forward rate. This forward contract is free, and, presuming the expected cash arrives, exactly matches the firm's exposure perfectly hedging their FX risk.

If the cash flow is uncertain, the firm will likely want to use options: if the firm enters a forward FX contract and the expected USD cash is not received, then the forward, instead of hedging, exposes the firm to FX risk in the opposite direction.

Using options, the UK firm can purchase a GBP call/USD put option (the right to sell part or all of their expected income for pounds sterling at a predetermined rate), which will:

- protect the GBP value that the firm will receive in 90 day's time (presuming the cash is received)

- cost at most the option premium (unlike a forward, which can have unlimited losses)
- yield a profit if the expected cash is not received but FX rates move in its favor

Valuing FX options: The Garman-Kohlhagen model

As in the Black-Scholes Model for stock options, the value of a European options on an FX rate is typically calculated by assuming that the rate follows a log-normal process.

In 1983 Garman and Kohlhagen extended the Black-Scholes Model to cope with the presence of two interest rates (one for each currency). Suppose that r_d is the risk-free interest rate to expiry of the domestic currency and r_f is the foreign currency risk-free interest rate (where domestic currency is the currency in which we obtain the value of the option; the formula also requires that FX rates - both strike and current spot be quoted in terms of "units of domestic currency per unit of foreign currency"). Then the domestic currency value of a call option into the foreign currency is

$$c = S_0 \exp(-r_f T)\mathbb{N}(d_1) - K \exp(-r_d T)\mathbb{N}(d_2)$$

The value of a put option has value

$$p = K \exp(-r_d T)\mathbb{N}(-d_2) - S_0 \exp(-r_f T)\mathbb{N}(-d_1)$$

where:

$$d_1 = \frac{\ln(S_0/K) + (r_d - r_f + \sigma^2/2)T}{\sigma\sqrt{T}}$$

$$d_2 = d_1 - \sigma\sqrt{T}$$

S_0 is the current spot rate

K is the strike price

N is the cumulative normal distribution function

r_d is domestic risk free simple interest rate

r_f is foreign risk free simple interest rate

T is the time to maturity (calculated according to the appropriate day count convention)

and σ is the volatility of the FX rate.

Risk Management

Garman-Kohlhagen (GK) is the standard model used to calculate the price of an FX option. However, there are a wide range of techniques in use for calculating the options risk exposure, or greeks. Although the price produced by every model will agree, the risk numbers calculated by different models can vary significantly depending on the assumptions used for the properties of the spot price movements, volatility surface and interest rate curves.

After GK, the most common models in use are SABR and local volatility, although when agreeing risk numbers with a counterparty (e.g. for exchanging delta, or calculating the strike on a 25 delta option) the Garman-Kohlhagen numbers are always used.

Swaption

A swaption is an option granting its owner the right but not the obligation to enter into an underlying swap. Although options can be traded on a variety of swaps, the term "swaption" typically refers to options on interest rate swaps.

There are two types of swaption contracts:

- A payer swaption gives the owner of the swaption the right to enter into a swap where they pay the fixed leg and receive the floating leg.
- A receiver swaption gives the owner of the swaption the right to enter into a swap where they will receive the fixed leg, and pay the floating leg.

The buyer and seller of the swaption agree on:

- the premium (price) of the swaption
- the strike rate (equal to the fixed rate of the underlying swap)
- length of the option period (which usually ends two business days prior to the start date of the underlying swap),
- the term of the underlying swap,
- notional amount,
- amortization, if any
- frequency of settlement of payments on the underlying swap

The first known Swaption

The first known swaption was constructed and executed by William Lawton in 1983. Lawton was the Head Trader for Fixed Income Derivatives at First Interstate Bank in Los Angeles at that time. Lawton worked with First Interstate's Treasury Options Desk to manage the concept of an interest rate swaps and an options contracts. The swaption was for a period of one year.

The Swaption Market

The participants in the swaption market are predominantly large corporations, banks, financial institutions and hedge funds. End users such as corporations and banks typically use swaptions to manage interest rate risk arising from their core business or from their financing arrangements. For example, a corporation wanting protection from rising interest rates might buy a payer swaption. A bank which holds a mortgage portfolio might buy a receiver swaption to protect against lower interest rates which might lead to early prepayment of the mortgages. A hedge fund believing interest rates will not rise by more than a certain amount might sell a payer swaption aiming to make money by collecting the premium. Major investment and commercial banks such as JP Morgan Chase, Bank of America Securities and Citigroup make markets in swaptions in the major currencies and these banks trade amongst themselves in the swaption interbank market. The market making banks typically manage large portfolios of swaptions which they have written with various counterparties -- a significant investment in technology and human capital is required to properly monitor the resulting exposure. Swaption markets exist in most of the major currencies in the world, the largest markets being in U.S. Dollars, Euro, Sterling and Japanese Yen.

The swaption market is over-the-counter (OTC) that means it is not traded on any exchange. Legally, a swaption is an agreement between the two counterparties to exchange the required payments. The counterparties are exposed to each others' failure to make scheduled payments on the underlying swap. Although this exposure is typically mitigated through the use of "collateral agreements" whereby margin is posted to cover the anticipated future exposure.

Properties

Unlike ordinary swaps, a swaption not only hedges the buyer against downside risk, it also lets the buyer take advantage of any upside benefits. Like any other option, if the swaption is not exercised by maturity it expires worthless.

- If the strike rate of the swap is more favorable than the prevailing market swap rate then the swaption will be exercised as detailed in the swaption agreement.
- It is designed to give the holder the benefit of the agreed-upon strike rate if the market rates are higher with the flexibility to enter into the current market swap rate if they are lower.

- The converse is true if the holder of the swaption receives the fixed rate under the swap agreement.

Investors can also use swaptions to trade the volatility of the underlying swap rate.

An Example of Illustrating the Use of Swaptions

Joe is in Mexico and he knows there's an election coming up. Joe has some variable rate bonds that are paying very well but would like to hedge against the risk of political upheaval. Dave is in the UK and rates are low and constant. Dave would like some extra money and thinks that political change will not affect the rates too significantly. In this case, Joe would wish to purchase a swaption from Dave.

Joe and Dave engage in a swap; Joe gets fixed cash flows from the UK bond and Dave gets the variable rate bonds. They agree on terms that set the swap as even money (present valued) for both of them. However, they don't do the swap yet because Joe's debt is about to expire and he is going to reinvest and he only wants to do the swap if the variable rates drop below a threshold (at which point his income goes down; he wants to lock in profits). In order to lock in the profits Joe's willing to arrange the option on slightly favorable terms with Dave. Dave wants the higher temporary cash flow and if the variable rates go down (which he doesn't think will happen) and is willing to live with a little risk.

Everyone is happy; the swaption can be exercised and both people may still make a profit depending on the timing and amounts involved. At the very least, both parties either reduced or enhanced their risks/rewards as they desired.

Another Example

Here is another scenario: Doug's Tractor Company needs to engage in a swap for the following reason: They have too much risk. They have a 5 year adjustable rate business loan that they've used to buy machines to make tractors. They've just agreed to sell 10 tractors to Jimbob's Tractor Dealership at the rate of 2 per year for 5 years (they don't sell fast, etc.). The price for the tractors is set in the contract and cannot be renegotiated.

The problem is, if the interest rates go up Doug has to pay lots of money in interest payments, and he loses money on the transaction. He needs to lock in an interest rate even if it's a little above the current rate.

Across town, Stanley's Tire Co. owns a mortgage on their offices that he cannot pay off for tax reasons and due to various legal problems tying up ownership of the property. However, he's locked into a higher long-term rate mortgage loan. He wants to reduce his rates.

Both of them have an opinion about the way short term rates are going to go. Stanley thinks short term rates are going to stay low, and wants to pay less. Doug thinks they're going higher than Stanley's fixed rate. But Doug only needs to do the swap if the rates get that high. Stanley agrees to a swaption. Both are making a bet, and it should help them manage risk better.

Swaption Styles

There are three styles of Swaptions. Each style reflects a different timeframe in which the option can be exercised.

- American swaption, in which the owner is allowed to enter the swap on any day that falls within a range of two dates.
- European swaption, in which the owner is allowed to enter the swap only on the maturity date.
- Bermudan swaption, in which the owner is allowed to enter the swap only certain dates that fall within a range of the start (roll) date and end date.

Valuation of Swaptions

The valuation of swaptions is complicated in that the result depends on several factors:

- the time to expiration,
- the length of underlying swap,
- and the "moneyness" of the swaption.

Here the "at the money" level is the forward swap rate, the forward rate that would apply between the maturity of the option (t) and the tenor of the underlying swap (T) such that the swap, at time t, has an "NPV" of zero. For an at the money swaption, the strike rate equals the forward swap rate, and "moneyness" therefore is determined based on whether the strike rate is higher, lower or at the same level as the forward swap rate.

Given these complications, quantitative analysts attempt to determine relative value between different swaptions, in some cases by constructing complex term structure and short rate models which describe the movement of interest rates over time.

However, a standard practice - particularly amongst traders where speed of calculation is more important - is to value European Swaptions using the Black model, where, for this purpose, the underlier is treated as a forward contract on a swap. Here:

- The forward price is the forward swap rate.
- The volatility is typically "read-off" a two dimensional grid of at-the-money volatilities as observed from prices in the Interbank swaption market. On this grid, one axis is the time to expiration and the other is the length of the underlying swap. Adjustments may then be made for moneyness;

Binary Options

A binary option is a type of option where the payoff is either some fixed amount of some asset or nothing at all. The two main types of binary options are the **cash-or-nothing binary option** and the **asset-or-nothing binary option**. The cash-or-nothing binary option pays some fixed amount of cash if the option expires in-the-money while the asset-or-nothing pays the value of the underlying security. Thus, the options are binary in nature because there are only two possible outcomes. They are also called all-or-nothing options, digital options (more common in forex/interest rate markets), and Fixed Return Options (FROs) (on the American Stock Exchange).

Example

A purchase is made of a binary cash-or-nothing call option on XYZ Corp's stock struck at $100 with a binary payoff of $1000. Then, if at the future maturity date, the stock is trading at or above $100, $1000 is received. If its stock is trading below $100, nothing is received.

In the popular Black-Scholes Model, the value of a digital option can be expressed in terms of the cumulative normal distribution function.

American vs European

Binary options are usually European-style - for a call, the price of the underlying must be above the strike at the expiration date. American binary options exist also, but these automatically exercise whenever the price "touches" the strike price, yielding very different behavior.

Exchange-traded Binary Options

Binary option contracts have long been available Over-the-counter (OTC), i.e. sold directly by the issuer to the buyer. They were generally considered "exotic" instruments and there was no liquid market for trading these instruments between their issuance and expiration. They were often seen embedded in more complex option contracts.

In 2007, the Options Clearing Corporation proposed a rule change to allow binary options, and the Securities and Exchange Commission approved listing cash-or-nothing binary options in 2008. In May 2008, the American Stock

Exchange (Amex) launched exchange-traded European cash-or-nothing binary options, and the Chicago Board Options Exchange (CBOE) followed in June 2008. The standardization of binary options allows them to be exchange-traded with continuous quotations.

Amex offers binary options on some ETFs and a few highly liquid equities such as Citigroup and Google. Amex calls binary options "Fixed Return Options" (FROs); calls are named "Finish High" and puts are named "Finish Low". To reduce the threat of market manipulation of single stocks, Amex FROs use a "settlement index" defined as a volume-weighted average of trades on the expiration day. The American Stock Exchange and Donato A. Montanaro submitted a patent application for exchange-listed binary options using a volume-weighted settlement index in 2005.

CBOE offers binary options on the S&P 500 (SPX) and the CBOE Volatility Index (VIX). The tickers for these are BSZ and BVZ, respectively. CBOE only offers calls, as binary put options are trivial to create synthetically from binary call options. BSZ strikes are at 5-point intervals and BVZ strikes are at 1-point intervals. The actual underlying to BSZ and BVZ are based on the opening prices of index basket members.

Both Amex and CBOE listed options have values between $0 and $1, with a multiplier of 100, and tick size of $0.01, and are cash settled.

In 2008 EZTrader released the first online binary option trading platform.

LEAPS

LEAPS stands for Long Term Equity AnticiPation Security, a financial instrument identical to a regular option except it has a much longer term before expiration. LEAPS are available on approximately 2500 equities and 20 indexes. As with traditional short term options, LEAPS are available in two types, calls and puts.

In this context, "option" refers to the listed option trading on an exchange such as the Chicago Board Options Exchange (CBOE). These differ greatly from the sort of options that employees of major corporations receive though their fundamental purpose is the same.

Options were originally created with expiry cycles of 3, 6, and 9 months, with no option lasting more than a year. These sorts of options still constitute the vast majority of option activity. LEAPS were created relatively recently and typically extend 2 years out. Equity LEAPS always expire in January. For example, if today were November 2005, one could buy a Microsoft January call option that would expire in 2006, 2007, or 2008. (The further out the expiration date, the more expensive the option.) The latter two are LEAPS.

When LEAPS were introduced in 1990, they were instruments solely for equities. However, more recently, equivalent instruments for indices have become available. These are also referred to as LEAPS.

Bonds

An Overview over Bonds

A bond is a debt security in which the authorized issuer owes the holders a debt and is obliged to repay the principal and interest (the coupon) at a later date, termed maturity.

A bond is simply a loan in the form of a security with different terminology: The issuer is equivalent to the borrower, the bond holder to the lender and the coupon to the interest. Bonds enable the issuer to finance long-term investments with external funds. Note that certificates of deposit (CDs) or commercial paper are considered to be money market instruments and not bonds.

Bonds and stocks are both securities, but the major difference between the two is that stock-holders are the owners of the company (i.e., they have an equity stake), whereas bond-holders are lenders to the issuing company. Another difference is that bonds usually have a defined term or maturity, after which the bond is redeemed whereas stocks may be outstanding indefinitely. An exception is a consol bond which is a perpetuity (i.e., bond with no maturity).

Issuing Bonds

Bonds are issued by public authorities, credit institutions, companies and supranational institutions in the primary markets. The most common process of issuing bonds is through underwriting. In underwriting, one or more securities firms or banks, forming a syndicate, buy an entire issue of bonds from an issuer and re-sell them to investors. Government bonds are typically auctioned.

Features of Bonds

The most important features of a bond are:

- **Nominal, principal or face amount**—the amount on which the issuer pays interest, and which has to be repaid at the end.

- **Issue price**—the price at which investors buy the bonds when they are first issued, typically $1,000.00. The net proceeds that the issuer receives are calculated as the issue price, less issuance fees, times the nominal amount.

- **Maturity date**—the date on which the issuer has to repay the nominal amount. As long as all payments have been made, the issuer has no more obligations to the bond holders after the maturity date. The length of time until the maturity date is often referred to as the term or tenure or maturity of a bond. The maturity can be any length of time, although debt securities with a term of less than one year are generally designated money market instruments rather than bonds. Most bonds have a term of up to thirty years. Some bonds have been issued with maturities of up to one hundred years, and some even do not mature at all. In early 2005, a market developed in euros for bonds with a maturity of fifty years. In the market for U.S. Treasury securities, there are three groups of bond maturities:

    - short term (bills): maturities up to one year;
    - medium term (notes): maturities between one and ten years;
    - long term (bonds): maturities greater than ten years.

- **Coupon**—the interest rate that the issuer pays to the bond holders. Usually this rate is fixed throughout the life of the bond. It can also vary with a money market index, such as LIBOR, or it can be even more exotic. The name coupon originates from the fact that in the past, physical bonds were issued which had coupons attached to them. On coupon dates the bond holder would give the coupon to a bank in exchange for the interest payment.

- **Coupon dates**—the dates on which the issuer pays the coupon to the bond holders. In the U.S., most bonds are semi-annual, which means that they pay a coupon every six months. In Europe, most bonds are annual and pay only one coupon a year.

- **Indentures and covenants**—An indenture is a formal debt agreement that establishes the terms of a bond issue, while covenants are the clauses of such an agreement. Covenants specify the rights of bondholders and the duties of issuers, such as actions that the issuer is obligated to perform or is prohibited from performing. In the U.S., federal and state securities and commercial laws apply to the enforcement of these agreements, which are construed by courts as contracts between issuers and bondholders. The terms may be changed only with great difficulty while the bonds are outstanding, with amendments to the governing document generally requiring approval by a majority (or super-majority) vote of the bondholders.

- **Optionality**: A bond may contain an embedded option; that is, it grants option-like features to the holder or the issuer:

    - **Callability**—Some bonds give the issuer the right to repay the bond before the maturity date on the call dates; see call option. These bonds are referred to as callable bonds. Most callable bonds allow the issuer to repay the bond at par. With some bonds, the issuer has to pay a premium, the so called call premium. This is mainly the case for high-yield bonds. These have very strict covenants, restricting the issuer in its operations. To be free from these covenants, the issuer can repay the bonds early, but only at a high cost.

    - **Putability**—Some bonds give the holder the right to force the issuer to repay the bond before the maturity date on the put dates; see put option. (Note: "Putable" denotes an embedded put option; "Puttable" denotes that it may be putted.)

    - **Call dates and put dates**—the dates on which callable and putable bonds can be redeemed early. There are four main categories.

        - A Bermudan callable has several call dates, usually coinciding with coupon dates.

        - A European callable has only one call date. This is a special case of a Bermudan callable.

        - An American callable can be called at any time until the maturity date.

        - A death put is an optional redemption feature on a debt instrument allowing the beneficiary of the estate of the deceased to put (sell) the bond (back to the issuer) in the event of the beneficiary's death or legal incapacitation. Also known as a "survivor's option".

- A sinking fund provision of the corporate bond indenture requires a certain portion of the issue to be retired periodically. The entire bond issue can be liquidated by the maturity date. If that is not the case, then the remainder is called balloon maturity. Issuers may either pay to trustees, which in turn call randomly selected bonds in the issue, or alternatively purchase bonds in open market, then return them to trustees.

- A convertible bond lets a bondholder exchange a bond to a number of shares of the issuer's common stock.

- An exchangeable bond allows for exchange to shares of a corporation other than the issuer.

Investing in Bonds

Bonds are bought and traded mostly by institutions like pension funds, insurance companies and banks. Most individuals who want to own bonds do so through bond funds. Still, in the U.S., nearly ten percent of all bonds outstanding are held directly by households.

As a rule, bond markets rise (while yields fall) when stock markets fall. Thus bonds are generally viewed as safer investments than stocks but this perception is only partially correct. Bonds do suffer from less day-to-day volatility than stocks and bonds' interest payments are higher than dividend payments that the same company would generally choose to pay to its stockholders. Bonds are liquid– it is fairly easy to sell one's bond investments, though not nearly as easy as it is to sell stocks– and the certainty of a fixed interest payment twice per year is attractive. Bondholders also enjoy a measure of legal protection. Under the law of most countries, if a company goes bankrupt, its bondholders will often receive some money back (the recovery amount), whereas the company's stock often ends up valueless. However, bonds can be risky:

- Fixed rate bonds are subject to interest rate risk, meaning that their market prices will decrease in value when the generally prevailing interest rates rise. Since the payments are fixed, a decrease in the market price of the bond means an increase in its yield. When the market's interest rates rise, then the market price for bonds will fall, reflecting investors' improved ability to get a good interest rate for their money elsewhere — perhaps by purchasing a newly issued bond that already features the newly higher interest rate. Note that this drop in the bond's market price does not affect the interest payments to the bondholder at all, so long-term investors need not worry about price swings in their bonds and do not suffer from interest rate risk.

However, price changes in a bond immediately affect mutual funds that hold these bonds. Many institutional investors have to "mark to market" their trading books at the end of every day. If the value of the bonds held in a trading portfolio has fallen over the day, the "mark to market" value of the portfolio may also have fallen. This can be damaging for professional investors such as banks, insurance companies, pension funds and asset managers. If there is any chance a holder of individual bonds may need to sell his bonds and "cash out" for some reason, interest rate risk could become a real problem. (Conversely, the bonds' market prices would increase if the prevailing interest rate were to drop, as it did from 2001 through 2003.) One way to quantify the interest rate risk on a bond is in terms of its duration. Efforts to control this risk are called immunization or hedging.

- Bond prices can become volatile if one of the credit rating agencies like Standard & Poor's or Moody's upgrades or downgrades the credit rating of the issuer. A downgrade can cause the market price of the bond to fall. As with interest rate risk, this risk does not affect the bond's interest payments, but puts at risk the market price which affects mutual funds holding these bonds and holders of individual bonds who may have to sell them.

- A company's bondholders may lose much or all their money if the company goes bankrupt. Under the laws of many countries (including the United States and Canada), bondholders are in line to receive the proceeds of the sale of the assets of a liquidated company ahead of some other creditors. Bank lenders, deposit holders (in the case of a deposit taking institution such as a bank) and trade creditors may take precedence.

There is no guarantee of how much money will remain to repay bondholders. As an example, after an accounting scandal and a Chapter 11 bankruptcy at the giant telecommunications company Worldcom in 2004. Its bondholders ended up being paid 35.7 cents on the dollar. In a bankruptcy involving reorganization or recapitalization, as opposed to liquidation, bondholders may end up having the value of their bonds reduced, often through an exchange for a smaller number of newly issued bonds.

- Some bonds are callable, meaning that even though the company has agreed to make payments plus interest towards the debt for a certain period of time, the company can choose to pay off the bond early. This creates reinvestment risk, meaning the investor is forced to find a new place for his money and the investor might not be able to find as good a deal, especially because this usually happens when interest rates are falling.

The Bond Market

The bond market (also known as the debt, credit, or fixed income market) is a financial market where participants buy and sell debt securities, usually in the form of bonds. As of 2006, the size of the international bond market is an estimated $45 trillion, of which the size of the outstanding U.S. bond market debt was $25.2 trillion.

Nearly all of the $923 billion average daily trading volume (as of early 2007) in the U.S. bond market takes place between broker-dealers and large institutions in a decentralized, over-the-counter (OTC) market. However, a small number of bonds, primarily corporate, are listed on exchanges.

References to the "bond market" usually refer to the government bond market, because of its size, liquidity, lack of credit risk and, therefore, sensitivity to interest rates. Because of the inverse relationship between bond valuation and interest rates, the bond market is often used to indicate changes in interest rates or the shape of the yield curve.

Market structure

Bond markets in most countries remain decentralized and lack common exchanges like stock, future and commodity markets. This has occurred partially because no two bond issues are exactly alike, and the number of different securities outstanding is far larger.

However, the New York Stock Exchange (NYSE) is the largest centralized bond market, representing mostly corporate bonds. The NYSE migrated from the Automated Bond System (ABS) to the NYSE Bonds trading system in April 2007 and expects the number of traded issues to increase from 1000 to 6000.

Types of bond markets

The Securities Industry and Financial Markets Association classifies the broader bond market into five specific bond markets.

- Corporate

- Government & agency
- Municipal
- Mortgage backed, asset backed, and collateralized debt obligation
- Funding

Bond market participants

Bond market participants are similar to participants in most financial markets and are essentially either buyers (debt issuer) of funds or sellers (institution) of funds and often both.

Participants include:

- Institutional investors
- Governments
- Traders
- Individuals

Because of the specificity of individual bond issues, and the lack of liquidity in many smaller issues, the majority of outstanding bonds are held by institutions like pension funds, banks and mutual funds. In the United States, approximately 10% of the market is currently held by private individuals.

Bond market volatility

For market participants who own a bond, collect the coupon and hold it to maturity, market volatility is irrelevant; principal and interest are received according to a pre-determined schedule.

But participants who buy and sell bonds before maturity are exposed to many risks, most importantly changes in interest rates. When interest rates increase, the value of existing bonds fall, since new issues pay a higher yield. Likewise, when interest rates decrease, the value of existing bonds rise, since new issues pay a lower yield. This is the fundamental concept of bond market volatility. Changes in bond prices are inverse to changes in interest rates. Fluctuating interest rates are part of a country's monetary policy and bond market volatility is a response to expected monetary policy and economic changes.

Economists' views of economic indicators versus actual released data contribute to market volatility. A tight consensus is generally reflected in bond prices and there is little price movement in the market after the release of "in-line" data. If the economic release differs from the consensus view the market usually undergoes rapid price movement as participants interpret the data. Uncertainty (as measured by a wide consensus) generally brings more volatility before and after an economic release. Economic releases vary in importance and impact depending on where the economy is in the business cycle.

The Coupon of a Bond

The coupon or coupon rate of a bond is the amount of interest paid per year expressed as a percentage of the face value of the bond.

For example if you hold $10,000 or £10,000 nominal of a bond described as a 4.5% loan stock. You will receive $450 or £450 in interest each year (probably in two installments of $225 or £225 each).

Not all bonds have coupons. Zero coupon bonds are those which do not pay interest, but are sold to investors at a price less than the par value paid out when the bond has matured.

The origin of the expression "coupon" is that bonds were historically issued as bearer certificates, so that possession of the certificate was conclusive proof of ownership. A number of coupons, one for each scheduled interest payment covering a number of years, were printed on the certificate. At the due date the owner would detach the coupon and present it for payment of the interest.

The market price of the bond will be determined by the market, taking into account among other things

- the amount and date of the redemption payment at maturity
- the amounts and dates of the coupons
- the quality of the issuer
- the yield offered by other similar bonds in the market.

Picture 16: Uncut coupons on 1822 Mecca Temple construction bond

Bond investments

Investment companies allow individual investors the ability to participate in the bond markets through bond funds, closed-end funds and unit-investment trusts. In 2006 total bond fund net inflows increased 97% from $30.8 billion in 2005 to $60.8 billion in 2006. Exchange-traded funds (ETFs) are another alternative to trading or investing directly in a bond issue. These securities allow individual investors the ability to overcome large initial and incremental trading sizes.

Bond indices

A number of bond indices exist for the purposes of managing portfolios and measuring performance, similar to the S&P 500 or Russell Indexes for stocks. The most common American benchmarks are the Lehman Aggregate, Citigroup BIG and Merrill Lynch Domestic Master. Most indices are parts of families of broader indices that can be used to measure global bond portfolios, or may be further subdivided by maturity and/or sector for managing specialized portfolios.

Corporate Bond

A Corporate Bond is a bond issued by a corporation. The term is usually applied to longer-term debt instruments, generally with a maturity date falling at least a year after their issue date. (The term "commercial paper" is sometimes used for instruments with a shorter maturity.)

Sometimes, the term "corporate bonds" is used to include all bonds except those issued by governments in their own currencies. Strictly speaking, however, it only applies to those issued by corporations. The bonds of local authorities and supranational organizations do not fit in either category.

Corporate bonds are often listed on major exchanges (bonds there are called "listed" bonds). The coupon (i.e. interest payment) is usually taxable. Sometimes this coupon can be zero with a high redemption value. However, despite being listed on exchanges the vast majority of trading volume in corporate bonds in most developed markets takes place in decentralized, dealer-based, over-the-counter markets.

Some corporate bonds have an embedded call option that allows the issuer to redeem the debt before its maturity date. Other bonds, known as convertible bonds, allow investors to convert the bond into equity.

One can obtain an unfunded synthetic exposure to corporate bonds via credit default swaps.

Types

Corporate debt falls into several broad categories:

secured debt vs. unsecured debt

senior debt vs. subordinated debt

Generally, the higher one's position in the company's capital structure, the stronger one's claims to the company's assets in the event of a default.

Risk Analysis

Compared to government bonds, corporate bonds generally have a higher risk of default. This risk depends, of course, upon the particular corporation issuing the bond, the current market conditions and governments to which the bond issuer is being compared and the rating of the company. Corporate bond holders are compensated for this risk by receiving a higher yield than government bonds.

Consequently, this default risk can be quantified using spread analysis, which seeks to determine the difference in yield between a given corporate bond and a risk-free treasury bond of the same maturity. Common statistics used include Z-spread and option adjusted spread (OAS).

Corporate Bond Indices

Corporate bond indices include the Lehman Brothers Corporate Bond Index and the Dow Jones Corporate Bond Index.

Government Bond

A government bond is a bond issued by a national government denominated in the country's own currency. Bonds issued by national governments in foreign currencies are normally referred to as sovereign bonds. The first ever government bond was issued by the British government in 1693 to raise money to fund a war against France. It was in the form of a tontine.

Risk

Government bonds are usually referred to as risk-free bonds, because the government can raise taxes or simply print more money to redeem the bond at maturity. Some counter examples do exist where a government has defaulted on its domestic currency debt, such as Russia in 1998 (the "ruble crisis"), though this is very rare.

As an example, in the US, Treasury Securities are denominated in US dollars and are the safest US dollar investments. In this instance, the term "risk-free" means free of credit risk. However, other risks still exist, such as currency risk for foreign investors (for example non-US investors of US Treasury Securities would have received lower returns in 2004 because the value of the US dollar declined against most other currencies). Secondly, there is inflation risk, in that the principal repaid at maturity will have less purchasing power than anticipated if the inflation outturn is higher than expected. Many governments issue inflation-indexed bonds, which protect investors against inflation risk.

Municipal Bonds

In the United States, a municipal bond (or muni) is a bond issued by a city or other local government, or their agencies. Potential issuers of municipal bonds include cities, counties, redevelopment agencies, school districts, publicly owned airports and seaports, and any other governmental entity (or group of governments) below the state level. Municipal bonds may be general obligations of the issuer or secured by specified revenues. Interest income received by holders of municipal bonds is often exempt from the federal income tax and from the income tax of the state in which they are issued, although municipal bonds issued for certain purposes may not be tax exempt.

Purpose of Municipal Bonds

Municipal Bond Issuers

Municipal bonds are issued by states, cities, and counties, or their agencies (the municipal issuer) to raise funds. The methods and practices of issuing debt are governed by an extensive system of laws and regulations, which vary by state. Bonds bear interest at either a fixed or variable rate of interest, which can be subject to a cap known as the maximum legal limit. If a bond measure is proposed in a local county election, a Tax Rate Statement may be provided to voters, detailing best estimates of the tax rate required to levy and fund the bond.

The issuer of a municipal bond receives a cash payment at the time of issuance in exchange for a promise to repay the investors who provide the cash payment (the bond holder) over time. Repayment periods can be as short as a few months (although this is rare) to 20, 30, or 40 years, or even longer.

The issuer typically uses proceeds from a bond sale to pay for capital projects or for other purposes it cannot or does not desire to pay for immediately with funds on hand. Tax regulations governing municipal bonds generally require all money raised by a bond sale to be spent on one-time capital projects within three to five years of issuance. Certain exceptions permit the issuance of bonds to fund other items including ongoing operations and maintenance expenses, the purchase of single-family and multi-family mortgages, and the funding of student loans, among many other things.

Because of the special tax-exempt status of most municipal bonds investors usually accept lower interest payments than on other types of borrowing (assuming comparable risk). This makes the issuance of bonds an attractive source of financing to many municipal entities as the borrowing rate available in the open market is frequently lower than what is available through other borrowing channels.

Municipal bonds are one of several ways states, cities and counties can issue debt. Other mechanisms include certificates of participation and lease-buyback agreements. While these methods of borrowing differ in legal structure, they are similar to the municipal bonds described in this paragraph.

Municipal Bond Holders

Municipal bond holders may purchase bonds either directly from the issuer at the time of issuance (on the primary market), or from other bond holders at some time after issuance (on the secondary market). In exchange for an up-front investment of capital, the bond holder receives payments over time composed of interest on the invested principal, and a return of the invested principal itself.

Repayment schedules differ with the type of bond issued. Municipal bonds typically pay interest semi-annually. Shorter term bonds generally pay interest only until maturity. Longer term bonds generally are amortized through annual principal payments. Longer and shorter term bonds are often combined together in a single issue that requires the issuer to make approximately level annual payments of interest and principal. Certain bonds known as zero coupon or capital appreciation bonds, accrue interest until maturity at which time both interest and principal become due.

Characteristics of Municipal Bonds

Taxability

One of the primary reasons municipal bonds are considered separately from other types of bonds is their special ability to provide tax-exempt income. Interest paid by the issuer to bond holders is often exempt from all federal taxes, as well as state or local taxes depending on the state in which the issuer is located, subject to certain restrictions. Bonds issued for certain purposes are subject to the alternative minimum tax.

The type of project or projects that are funded by a bond affects the taxability of income received on the bonds held by bond holders. Interest earnings on bonds that fund projects that are constructed for the public good are generally exempt from federal income tax, while interest earnings on bonds issued to fund projects partly or wholly benefiting only private parties, sometimes referred to as private activity bonds, may be subject to federal income tax.

The laws governing the taxability of municipal bond income are complex. However, bonds are typically certified by a law firm as either tax-exempt (federal and/or state income tax) or taxable before they are offered to the market. Purchasers of municipal bonds should be aware that not all bond are certified.

Risk

The risk ("security") of a municipal bond is a measure of how likely the issuer is to make all payments, on time and in full, as promised in the agreement between the issuer and bond holder (the "bond documents"). Different types of bonds are secured by various types of repayment sources, based on the promises made in the bond documents:

- **General obligation bonds** promise to repay based on the full faith and credit of the issuer. These bonds are typically considered the most secure type of municipal bond, and therefore carry the lowest interest rate.
- **Revenue bonds** promise repayment from a specified stream of future income, such as income generated by a water utility from payments by customers.
- **Assessment bonds** promise repayment based on property tax assessments of properties located within the issuer's boundaries.

In addition, there are several other types of municipal bonds with different promises of security but we only want to focus on the main types above.

The probability of repayment as promised is often determined by an independent reviewer, or "rating agency". The three main rating agencies for municipal bonds in the United States are Standard & Poor's, Moody's, and Fitch. These agencies can be hired by the issuer to assign a bond rating, which is valuable information to potential bond holders that helps sell bonds on the primary market.

Disclosures to Investors

Key information about new issues of municipal bonds includes among other things:

- the security pledged for repayment of the bonds
- the terms of payment of interest
- principal of the bonds
- the tax-exempt status of the bonds
- material financial and operating information about the issuer of the bonds

This information is typically found in the issuer's official statement. Official statements generally are available at no charge from the Electronic Municipal Market Access system (EMMA) at http://emma.msrb.org operated by the Municipal Securities Rulemaking Board (MSRB).

For most municipal bonds issued in recent years, the issuer is also obligated to provide continuing disclosure to the marketplace, including annual financial information and notices of the occurrence of certain material events (including notices of defaults, rating downgrades, events of taxability, etc.).

Comparison to Corporate Bonds

Because municipal bonds are most often tax-exempt, comparing the coupon rates of municipal bonds to corporate or other taxable bonds can be misleading. Taxes reduce the net income on taxable bonds, meaning that a tax-exempt municipal bond has a higher after-tax yield than a corporate bond with the same coupon rate.

This relationship can be demonstrated mathematically, as follows:

$$r_m = r_c(1 - t)$$

where

r_m = interest rate of municipal bond

r_c = interest rate of comparable corporate bond

t = tax rate

For example if: r_c = 10% and t = 38%, then

$$r_m = (10\%)(100\% - 38\%) = 6.2\%$$

A municipal bond that pays 6.2% therefore generates equal interest income after taxes as a corporate bond that pays 10% (assuming all else is equal).

Alternatively, one can calculate the taxable equivalent yield of a municipal bond and compare it to the yield of a corporate bond as follows:

$$r_c = \frac{r_m}{(1-t)}$$

Because longer maturity municipal bonds tend to offer significantly higher after-tax yields than corporate bonds with the same credit rating and maturity, investors in higher tax brackets may be motivated to arbitrage municipal bonds against corporate bonds using a strategy called municipal bond arbitrage.

Some municipal bonds are insured by monoline insurers that take on the credit risk of these bonds for a small fee.

High-Yield Debt

A high yield bond (non-investment grade bond, speculative grade bond or junk bond) is a bond that is rated below investment grade at the time of purchase. These bonds have a higher risk of default or other adverse credit events, but typically pay higher yields than better quality bonds in order to make them attractive to investors.

Flows and Levels

Global issuance of high yield bonds more than doubled in 2003 to nearly $146 billion in securities issued from less than $63 billion in 2002, although this is still less than the record of $150 billion in 1998. Issuance is disproportionately centered in the U.S.A., although issuers in Europe, Asia and South Africa have recently turned to high yield debt in connection with refinancing and acquisitions. In 2006, European companies issued over €31 billion of high yield bonds.

Risk

The holder of any debt is subject to:

- interest rate risk,
- credit risk,
- inflationary risk,
- currency risk,
- duration risk,
- convexity risk,
- repayment of principal risk,
- streaming income risk,
- liquidity risk,
- default risk,
- maturity risk,
- reinvestment risk,
- market risk,
- political risk, and
- taxation adjustment risk.

Interest rate risk refers to the risk of the market value of a bond changing in value due to changes in the structure or level of interest rates or credit spreads or risk premiums.

The credit risk of a high yield bond refers to the probability and probable loss upon a credit event (i.e., the obligor defaults on scheduled payments or files for bankruptcy, or the bond is restructured), or a credit quality change is issued by a rating agency including Fitch, Moody's, or Standard & Poors.

A credit rating agency attempts to describe the risk with a credit rating such as AAA. In North America, the five major agencies are Standard and Poor's, Moody's, Fitch Ratings, Dominion Bond Rating Service and A.M. Best.

Bonds in other countries may be rated by US rating agencies or by local credit rating agencies. Rating scales vary; the most popular scale uses (in order of increasing risk) ratings of AAA, AA, A, BBB, BB, B, CCC, CC, C, with the additional rating D for debt already in arrears. Government bonds and bonds issued by government sponsored enterprises (GSE's) are often considered to be in a zero-risk category above AAA; and categories like AA and A may sometimes be split into finer subdivisions like "AA-" or "AA+".

Bonds rated BBB- and higher are called investment grade bonds. Bonds rated lower than investment grade on their date of issue are called speculative grade bonds, derisively referred to as "junk" bonds.

The lower-rated debt typically offers a higher yield, making speculative bonds attractive investment vehicles for certain types of financial portfolios and strategies. Many pension funds and other investors (banks, insurance companies), however, are prohibited by-law from investing in bonds which have ratings below a particular level. As a result, the lower-rated securities have a different investor base than investment-grade bonds.

The value of speculative bonds is affected to a higher degree than investment grade bonds by the possibility of default. For example, in a recession interest rates may drop, and the drop in interest rates tends to increase the value of investment grade bonds. However, a recession tends to increase the possibility of default in speculative-grade bonds.

Usage

Corporate Debt

The original speculative grade bonds were bonds that once had been investment grade at time of issue, but where the credit rating of the issuer had slipped and the possibility of default increased significantly. These bonds are called "Fallen Angels".

The investment banker Michael Milken realized that fallen angels had regularly been valued less than what they were worth. His time with speculative grade bonds started with his investment in these. Speculative grade bonds became ubiquitous in the 1980s as a financing mechanism in mergers and acquisitions. In a leveraged buyout (LBO) an acquirer would issue speculative grade bonds to help pay for an acquisition and then use the target's cash flow to help pay the debt over time.

In 2005, over 80% of the principal amount of high yield debt issued by U.S. companies went toward corporate purposes rather than acquisitions or buyouts.

Debt Repackaging and Subprime Crisis

High-yield bonds can also be repackaged into collateralized debt obligations (CDO), thereby raising the credit rating of the senior tranches above the rating of the original debt. The senior tranches of high-yield CDOs can thus meet the minimum credit rating requirements of pension funds and other institutional investors despite the significant risk in the original high-yield debt.

When such CDOs are backed by assets of dubious value, such as subprime mortgage loans, and lose market liquidity, the bonds and their derivatives are also referred to as toxic debt. Holding such "toxic" assets has led to the demise of several investment banks and other financial institutions during the subprime mortgage crisis of 2007-08 and led the US Treasury to offer to buy those assets in September 2008 to prevent a systemic crisis.

High-Yield Bond Indices

High-yield bond indices exist for dedicated investors in the market. Indices for the broad high yield market include the CSFB High Yield II Index (CSHY), the Merrill Lynch High Yield Master II (H0A0), and the Bear Stearns High Yield Index (BSIX). Some investors, preferring to dedicate themselves to higher-rated and less-risky investments, use an index that only includes BB-rated and B-rated securities, such as the Merrill Lynch BB/B Index. Other investors focus on the lowest quality debt rated CCC or distressed securities, commonly defined as those yielding 1000 basis points over equivalent government bonds.

Bond Valuation

Bond valuation is the process of determining the fair price of a bond. As with any security or capital investment, the fair value of a bond is the present value of the stream of cash flows it is expected to generate. Hence, the price or value of a bond is determined by discounting the bond's expected cash flows to the present using the appropriate discount rate.

General Relationship

The Present Value Relationship

The fair price of a straight bond (a bond with no embedded option) is determined by discounting the expected cash flows:

- Cash flows:
  - the periodic coupon payments **C**, each of which is made **n** times (n is usually 2) every year
  - the par or face value **F**, which is payable at maturity of the bond after **T** years.(NB final year payments will include the par value plus the coupon payments for the year). In some of the bonds, their Maturity redemption price might be more than par value, in this case the **F** is actually the redemption price.
- Discount rate: the required (annually compounded) yield or rate of return **r**
  - **r** is the market interest rate for bonds with similar terms and risk ratings
  - **m** is the number of coupons to be paid over the remaining lifetime of the bond, ie **n** times **T**. (It is assumed that the previous coupon has just been paid.)

- **u** is (1+r)^(1/n) ie an interest accumulation factor over one coupon period

Bond Price =

$$P_c = \sum_{t=1}^{m} \frac{C}{u^t} + \frac{F}{(1+r)^T}.$$

Because the price is the present value of the cash flows there is an inverse relationship between price and discount rate: The higher the discount rate the lower the value of the bond.

Coupon Yield

The coupon yield is simply the coupon payment (C) as a percentage of the face value (F).

Coupon yield = C / F

Coupon yield is also called nominal yield.

Current Yield

The current yield is simply the coupon payment (C) as a percentage of the bond price (P).

Current yield = C / P_0.

Yield to Maturity

The yield to maturity (YTM) is the discount rate which returns the market price of the bond. It is thus the internal rate of return of an investment in the bond made at the observed price. YTM can also be used to price a bond, where it is used as the required return on the bond.

In other words, it is identical to **r** in the above equation.

To achieve a return equal to YTM, the bond owner must:

- buy the bond at price P_0,
- hold the bond until maturity, and

- redeem the bond at par.

The concept of current yield is closely related to other bond concepts, including yield to maturity, and coupon yield. The relationship between yield to maturity and coupon rate is as follows:

- When a bond sells at a discount, YTM > current yield > coupon yield.
- When a bond sells at a premium, coupon yield > current yield > YTM.
- When a bond sells at par, YTM = current yield = coupon yield amt

Bond Pricing

Relative Price Approach

Here the bond will be priced relative to a benchmark, usually a government security. The yield to maturity on the bond is determined based on the bond's rating relative to a government security with similar maturity or duration. The better the quality of the bond the smaller the spread between its required return and the YTM of the benchmark. This required return is then used to discount the bond cash flows as above to obtain the price.

Arbitrage-Free Pricing Approach

In this approach, the bond price will reflect its arbitrage-free price (arbitrage = practice of taking advantage of a state of imbalance between two or more markets). Here, each cash flow is priced separately and is discounted at the same rate as the corresponding government issue zero coupon bond. (Some multiple of the bond (or the security) will produce an identical cash flow to the government security (or the bond in question).) Since each bond cash flow is known with certainty, the bond price today must be equal to the sum of each of its cash flows discounted at the corresponding risk free rate - i.e. the corresponding government security. Were this not the case, arbitrage would be possible.

Futures Contracts

What is a Futures Contract?

A futures contract is a standardized contract, traded on a futures exchange, to buy or sell a standardized quantity of a specified commodity of standardized quality (which, in many cases, may be such non-traditional "commodities" as foreign currencies, commercial or government paper [e.g., bonds], or "baskets" of corporate equity "stock indices" or other financial instruments) at a certain date in the future, at a price (the futures price) determined by the instantaneous equilibrium between the forces of supply and demand among competing buy and sell orders on the exchange at the time of the purchase or sale of the contract. The future date is called the delivery date or final settlement date. The official price of the futures contract at the end of a day's trading session on the exchange is called the settlement price for that day of business on the exchange.

A futures contract gives the holder the obligation to make or take delivery under the terms of the contract, whereas an option grants the buyer the right, but not the obligation, to establish a position previously held by the seller of the option. In other words, the owner of an options contract may exercise the contract, but both parties of a "futures contract" must fulfill the contract on the settlement date. The seller delivers the underlying asset to the buyer, or, if it is a cash-settled futures contract, then cash is transferred from the futures trader who sustained a loss to the one who made a profit. To exit the commitment prior to the settlement date, the holder of a futures position has to offset his/her position by either selling a long position or buying back (covering) a short position, effectively closing out the futures position and its contract obligations.

Futures contracts, or simply futures, (but not future or future contract) are exchange traded derivatives. The exchange's clearinghouse acts as counterparty on all contracts, sets margin requirements, and crucially also provides a mechanism for settlement.

Futures vs. Forwards

While futures and forward contracts are both contracts to deliver an asset on a future date at a prearranged price, they are different in two main respects:

- Futures are exchange-traded, while forwards are traded over-the-counter.
    - Thus futures are standardized and face an exchange, while forwards are customized and face a non-exchange counterparty.
- Futures are margined, while forwards are not.
    - Thus futures have significantly less credit risk, and have different funding.

Exchange vs. OTC

Futures are always traded on an exchange, whereas forwards always trade over-the-counter, or can simply be a signed contract between two parties.

Thus:

- Futures are highly standardised, being exchange-traded, whereas forwards can be unique, being over-the-counter.
- In the case of physical delivery, the forward contract specifies to whom to make the delivery. The counterparty for delivery on a futures contract is chosen by the clearing house.

Margining

Forwards transact only when purchased and on the settlement date. Futures, on the other hand, are margined daily, every day to the daily spot price of a forward with the same agreed-upon delivery price and underlying asset (based on mark to market).

The result is that forwards have higher credit risk than futures, and that funding is charged differently.

The fact that forwards are not margined daily means that, due to movements in the price of the underlying asset, a large differential can build up between the forward's delivery price and the settlement price.

This means that one party will incur a big loss at the time of delivery (assuming they must transact at the underlying's spot price to facilitate receipt/delivery).

This in turn creates a credit risk for forwards, but not futures. More generally, the risk of a forward contract is that the supplier will be unable to deliver the required asset, or that the buyer will be unable to pay for it on the delivery day.

The margining of futures eliminates much of this credit risk by forcing the holders to update daily to the price of an equivalent forward purchased that day. This means that there will usually be very little additional money due on the final day to settle the futures contract: only the final day's gain or loss, not the lifetime gain or loss.

In addition, the daily futures-settlement failure risk is borne by an exchange, rather than an individual party, limiting credit risk in futures.

Consider a futures contract with a $100 price: Let's say that on day 50, a forward with a $100 delivery price (on the same underlying asset as the future) costs $88. On day 51, that futures contract costs $90. This means that the mark-to-market would require the holder of one side of the future to pay $2 on day 51 to track the changes of the forward price ("post $2 of margin"). This money goes, via margin accounts, to the holder of the other side of the future.

A forward-holder, however, would pay nothing until settlement on the final day, potentially building up a large balance; this may be reflected in the mark by an allowance for credit risk. So, except for tiny effects of convexity bias (due to earning or paying interest on margin), futures and forwards with equal delivery prices result in the same total loss or gain, but holders of futures experience that loss/gain in daily increments which track the forward's daily price changes, while the forward's spot price converges to the settlement price. Thus, while under mark to market accounting, for both assets the gain or loss accrues over the holding period, for a futures this gain or loss is realized daily, while for a forward contract the gain or loss remains unrealized until expiry.

Note that, due to the path dependence of funding, a futures contract is not, strictly speaking, a European derivative: the total gain or loss of the trade depends not only on the value of the underlying asset at expiry, but also on the path of prices on the way. This difference is generally quite small though.

Standardization

Futures contracts ensure their liquidity by being highly standardized, usually by specifying:

- The underlying asset or instrument. This could be anything from a barrel of crude oil to a short term interest rate.
- The type of settlement, either cash settlement or physical settlement.
- The amount and units of the underlying asset per contract. This can be the notional amount of bonds, a fixed number of barrels of oil, units of foreign currency, the notional amount of the deposit over which the short term interest rate is traded, etc.
- The currency in which the futures contract is quoted.
- The grade of the deliverable. In the case of bonds, this specifies which bonds can be delivered. In the case of physical commodities, this specifies not only the quality of the underlying goods but also the manner and location of delivery. For example, the NYMEX Light Sweet Crude Oil contract specifies the acceptable sulphur content and API specific gravity, as well as the pricing point -- the location where delivery must be made.
- The delivery month.
- The last trading date.
- Other details such as the commodity tick, the minimum permissible price fluctuation.

Margin

To minimize credit risk to the exchange, traders must post a margin or a performance bond, typically 5%-15% of the contract's value.

Margin requirements are waived or reduced in some cases for hedgers who have physical ownership of the covered commodity or spread traders who have offsetting contracts balancing the position.

Clearing margin are financial safeguards to ensure that companies or corporations perform on their customers' open futures and options contracts. Clearing margins are distinct from customer margins that individual buyers and sellers of futures and options contracts are required to deposit with brokers.

Customer margin Within the futures industry, financial guarantees required of both buyers and sellers of futures contracts and sellers of options contracts to ensure fulfillment of contract obligations. Futures Commission Merchants are responsible for overseeing customer margin accounts. Margins are determined on the basis of market risk and contract value. Also referred to as performance bond margin.

Initial margin is the money required to open a derivatives position (in futures, forex or CFDs) It is a security deposit to ensure that traders have sufficient funds to meet any potential loss from a trade.

If a position involves an exchange-traded product, the amount or percentage of initial margin is set by the exchange concerned.

In case of loss or if the value of the initial margin is being eroded, the broker will make a margin call in order to restore the amount of initial margin available. Often referred to as "variation margin", margin called for this reason is usually done on a daily basis, however, in times of high volatility a broker can make a margin call or calls intra-day.

Calls for margin are usually expected to be paid and received on the same day. If not, the broker has the right to close sufficient positions to meet the amount called by way of margin. After the position is closed-out the client is liable for any resulting deficit in the client's account.

Some US Exchanges also use the term "maintenance margin", which in effect defines by how much the value of the initial margin can reduce before a margin call is made. However, most non-US brokers only use the term "initial margin" and "variation margin".

The Initial Margin requirement is established by the Futures exchange, in contrast to other securities Initial Margin which is set by the Federal Reserve in the U.S. Markets.

A futures account is marked to market daily. If the margin drops below the margin maintenance requirement established by the exchange listing the futures, a margin call will be issued to bring the account back up to the required level.

Maintenance margin A set minimum margin per outstanding futures contract that a customer must maintain in his margin account.

Margin-equity ratio is a term used by speculators, representing the amount of their trading capital that is being held as margin at any particular time. The low margin requirements of futures results in substantial leverage of the investment. However, the exchanges require a minimum amount that varies depending on the contract and the trader. The broker may set the requirement higher, but may not set it lower. A trader, of course, can set it above that, if he doesn't want to be subject to margin calls.

Performance bond margin The amount of money deposited by both a buyer and seller of a futures contract or an options seller to ensure performance of the term of the contract. Margin in commodities is not a payment of equity or down payment on the commodity itself, but rather it is a security deposit.

Return on margin (ROM) is often used to judge performance because it represents the gain or loss compared to the exchange's perceived risk as reflected in required margin. ROM may be calculated (realized return) / (initial margin). The Annualized ROM is equal to (ROM+1)(year/trade_duration)-1. For example if a trader earns 10% on margin in two months, that would be about 77% annualized.

Settlement

Settlement is the act of consummating the contract, and can be done in one of two ways, as specified per type of futures contract:

- Physical delivery - the amount specified of the underlying asset of the contract is delivered by the seller of the contract to the exchange, and by the exchange to the buyers of the contract. Physical delivery is common with commodities and bonds. In practice, it occurs only on a minority of contracts. Most are cancelled out by purchasing a covering position - that is, buying a contract to cancel out an earlier sale (covering a short), or selling a contract to liquidate an earlier purchase (covering a long). The Nymex crude futures contract uses this method of settlement upon expiration.
- Cash settlement - a cash payment is made based on the underlying reference rate, such as a short term interest rate index such as Euribor, or the closing value of a stock market index. A futures contract

might also opt to settle against an index based on trade in a related spot market. Ice Brent futures use this method.

Expiry (or Expiration in the U.S.) is the time and the day that a particular delivery month of a futures contract stops trading and the final settlement price for that contract month and year obtains. For many equity index and interest rate futures contracts (as well as for most equity options), this happens on the third Friday of certain trading month. On this day the t+1 futures contract becomes the t futures contract. For example, for most CME and CBOT contracts, at the expiration of the December contract, the March futures become the nearest contract. This is an exciting time for arbitrage desks, which try to make quick profits during the short period (perhaps 30 minutes) during which the underlying cash price and the futures price sometimes struggle to converge. At this moment the futures and the underlying assets are extremely liquid and any disparity between an index and an underlying asset is quickly traded by arbitrageurs. At this moment also, the increase in volume is caused by traders rolling over positions to the next contract or, in the case of equity index futures, purchasing underlying components of those indexes to hedge against current index positions. On the expiry date, a European equity arbitrage trading desk in London or Frankfurt will see positions expire in as many as eight major markets almost every half an hour.

Pricing

The situation where the price of a commodity for future delivery is higher than the spot price, or where a far future delivery price is higher than a nearer future delivery, is known as contango. The reverse, where the price of a commodity for future delivery is lower than the spot price, or where a far future delivery price is lower than a nearer future delivery, is known as backwardation.

When the deliverable asset exists in plentiful supply, or may be freely created, then the price of a future is determined via arbitrage arguments. The forward price represents the expected future value of the underlying discounted at the risk free rate—as any deviation from the theoretical price will afford investors a riskless profit opportunity and should be arbitraged away.

Thus, for a simple, non-dividend paying asset, the value of the future/forward, $F(t)$, will be found by compounding the present value $S(t)$ at time t to maturity T by the rate of risk-free return r.

$$F(t) = S(t) \times (1 + r)^{(T-t)}$$

or, with *continuous compounding*

$$F(t) = S(t)e^{r(T-t)}$$

This relationship may be modified for storage costs, dividends, dividend yields, and convenience yields.

In a perfect market the relationship between futures and spot prices depends only on the above variables; in practice there are various market imperfections (transaction costs, differential borrowing and lending rates, restrictions on short selling) that prevent complete arbitrage. Thus, the futures price in fact varies within arbitrage boundaries around the theoretical price.

The above relationship, therefore, is typical for stock index futures, treasury bond futures, and futures on physical commodities when they are in supply (e.g. on corn after the harvest). However, when the deliverable commodity is not in plentiful supply or when it does not yet exist, for example on wheat before the harvest or on Eurodollar Futures or Federal funds rate futures (in which the supposed underlying instrument is to be created upon the delivery date), the futures price cannot be fixed by arbitrage. In this scenario there is only one force setting the price, which is simple supply and demand for the future asset, as expressed by supply and demand for the futures contract.

In a deep and liquid market, this supply and demand would be expected to balance out at a price which represents an unbiased expectation of the future price of the actual asset and so be given by the simple relationship

$$F(t) = E_t \{S(T)\} .$$

In fact, this relationship will hold in a no-arbitrage setting when we take expectations with respect to the risk-neutral probability. In other words: A futures price is martingale with respect to the risk-neutral probability.

With this pricing rule, a speculator is expected to break even when the futures market fairly prices the deliverable commodity.

In a shallow and illiquid market, or in a market in which large quantities of the deliverable asset have been deliberately withheld from market participants (an illegal action known as cornering the market), the market clearing price for the future may still represent the balance between supply and demand but the relationship between this price and the expected future price of the asset can break down.

Who trades Futures?

Futures traders are traditionally placed in one of two groups: Hedgers, who have an interest in the underlying commodity and are seeking to hedge out the risk of price changes; and speculators, who seek to make a profit by predicting market moves and buying a commodity "on paper" for which they have no practical use.

Hedgers typically include producers and consumers of a commodity.

For example, in traditional commodity markets, farmers often sell futures contracts for the crops and livestock they produce to guarantee a certain price, making it easier for them to plan. Similarly, livestock producers often purchase futures to cover their feed costs, so that they can plan on a fixed cost for feed. In modern (financial) markets, "producers" of interest rate swaps or equity derivative products will use financial futures or equity index futures to reduce or remove the risk on the swap.

The social utility of futures markets is considered to be mainly in the transfer of risk, and increase liquidity between traders with different risk and time preferences, from a hedger to a speculator for example.

Options on Futures

In many cases, options are traded on futures. A put is the option to sell a futures contract, and a call is the option to buy a futures contract. For both, the option strike price is the specified futures price at which the future is traded if the option is exercised. See the Black-Scholes model, which is the most popular method for pricing these option contracts.

Futures Contract Regulations

All futures transactions in the United States are regulated by the Commodity Futures Trading Commission (CFTC), an independent agency of the United States Government. The Commission has the right to hand out fines and other punishments for an individual or company who breaks any rules. Although by law the commission regulates all transactions, each exchange can have its own rule, and under contract can fine companies for different things or extend the fine that the CFTC hands out.

The CFTC publishes weekly reports containing details of the open interest of market participants for each market-segment that has more than 20 participants. These reports are released every Friday (including data from the previous Tuesday) and contain data on open interest split by reportable and non-reportable open interest as well as commercial and non-commercial open interest. This type of report is referred to as 'Commitments-Of-Traders'-Report, COT-Report or simply COTR.

Funds

Exchange-Traded Funds

An exchange-traded fund (or ETF) is an investment vehicle traded on stock exchanges, much like stocks. An ETF holds assets such as stocks or bonds and trades at approximately the same price as the net asset value of its underlying assets over the course of the trading day. Most ETFs track an index, such as the Dow Jones Industrial Average or the S&P 500. ETFs may be attractive as investments because of their low costs, tax efficiency, and stock-like features. In a survey of investment professionals conducted in March 2008, 67% called ETFs the most innovative investment vehicle of the last two decades and 60% reported that ETFs have fundamentally changed the way they construct investment portfolios.

An ETF combines the valuation feature of a mutual fund or unit investment trust, which can be purchased or redeemed at the end of each trading day for its net asset value, with the tradability feature of a closed-end fund, which trades throughout the trading day at prices that may be substantially more or less than its net asset value. Closed-end funds are not considered to be exchange-traded funds, even though they are funds and are traded on an exchange. ETFs have been available in the US since 1993 and in Europe since 1999. ETFs traditionally have been index funds, but in 2008 the U.S. Securities and Exchange Commission began to authorize the creation of actively-managed ETFs.

Most investors can buy and sell ETF shares only in market transactions, but institutional investors can redeem large blocks of shares of the ETF (known as "creation units") for a "basket" of the underlying assets or alternatively, exchange the underlying assets for creation units. This creation and redemption of shares enables institutions to engage in arbitrage that causes the value of the ETF to approximate the net asset value of the underlying assets.

Structure

ETFs offer public investors an undivided interest in a pool of securities and other assets and thus are similar in many ways to traditional mutual funds, except that shares in an ETF can be bought and sold throughout the day like stocks on a securities exchange through a broker-dealer. Unlike traditional mutual funds, ETFs do not sell or redeem their individual shares at net asset value or NAV. Instead. Financial institutions purchase and redeem ETF shares directly from the ETF but only in large blocks varying in size by ETF from 25,000 to 200,000 shares called "creation units". Purchases and redemptions of the creation units generally are in kind, with the institutional investor contributing or receiving a basket of securities of the same type and proportion held by the ETF. Some ETFs may require or permit a purchasing or redeeming shareholder to substitute cash for some or all of the securities in the basket of assets.

The ability to purchase and redeem creation units gives ETFs an arbitrage mechanism intended to minimize the potential deviation between the market price and the net asset value of ETF shares. Existing ETFs have transparent portfolios so institutional investors will know exactly what portfolio assets they must assemble if they wish to purchase a creation unit The exchange disseminates the updated net asset value of the shares throughout the trading day typically at 15-second intervals.

In the United States most ETFs are structured as open-end management investment companies (the same structure used by mutual funds and money market funds), although a few ETFs, including some of the largest ones are structured as unit investment trusts. ETFs structured as open-end funds have greater flexibility in constructing a portfolio and are not prohibited from participating in securities lending programs or from using futures and options in achieving their investment objectives. Under existing regulations a new ETF must receive an order from the Securities and Exchange Commission giving it relief from provisions of the Investment Company Act of 1940 that would not otherwise allow the ETF structure. In 2008 however the SEC proposed rules that would allow the creation of ETFs without the need for exemptive orders. Under the SEC proposal, an ETF would be defined as a registered open-end management investment company that:

- Issues (or redeems) creation units in exchange for the deposit (or delivery) of basket assets the current value of which is disseminated on a per share basis by a national securities exchange at regular intervals during the trading day;
- Identifies itself as an ETF in any sales literature;
- Issues shares that are approved for listing and trading on a securities exchange;
- Discloses each business day on its publicly available web site the prior business day's net asset value and closing market price of the fund's shares, and the premium or discount of the closing market price against the net asset value of the fund's shares as a percentage of net asset value;
- Either is an index fund or discloses each business day on its publicly available web site the identities and weighting of the component securities and other assets held by the fund.

The SEC rule proposal would allow ETFs either to be index funds or to be fully transparent actively managed funds. Historically, all ETFs in the United States have been index funds. In 2008, however, the SEC began issuing exemptive orders to fully transparent actively managed ETFs. The first such order was to PowerShares Actively Managed Exchange-Traded Fund Trust and the first actively managed ETF in the United States was the Bear Stearns Current Yield Fund, a short-term income fund that began trading on the American Stock Exchange under the symbol YYY on 25 March 2008. The SEC rule proposal indicates that the SEC is not suggesting that it will not consider future applications for exemptive orders for actively managed ETFs which do not satisfy the proposed rule's transparency requirements.

Some ETFs invest primarily in commodities or commodity-based instruments such as crude oil and precious metals. Although these commodity ETFs are similar in practice to ETFs that invest in securities, they are not "investment companies" under the Investment Company Act of 1940.

Publicly traded grantor trusts, such as Merrill Lynch's HOLDRS securities, are sometimes considered to be ETFs, although they lack many of the characteristics of other ETFs. Investors in a grantor trust have a direct interest in the underlying basket of securities, which does not change except to reflect corporate actions such as stock splits and mergers. Funds of this type are not "investment companies" under the Investment Company Act of 1940.

History

ETFs had their genesis in 1989 with Index Participation Shares, an S&P 500 proxy that traded on the American Stock Exchange and the Philadelphia Stock Exchange. This product, however, was short-lived after a lawsuit by the Chicago Mercantile Exchange was successful in stopping sales in the United States.

A similar product, Toronto Index Participation Shares, started trading on the Toronto Stock Exchange in 1990. The shares, which tracked the TSE 35 and later the TSE 100 stocks, proved to be popular. The popularity of these products led the American Stock Exchange to try to develop something that would satisfy SEC regulation in the United States.

Nathan Most, an executive with the exchange, developed Standard & Poor's Depositary Receipts (AMEX: SPY), which were introduced in January 1993. Known as SPDRs or "Spiders", the fund became the largest ETF in the world. Other U.S. ETFs quickly followed based on other broad market indexes.

Barclays Global Investors, a subsidiary of Barclays plc, entered the fray in 1996 with World Equity Benchmark Shares, or WEBS, subsequently renamed iShares MSCI Index Fund Shares. WEBS were particularly innovative because they gave casual investors easy access to foreign markets. While SPDRs were organized as unit investment trusts, WEBS were set up as a mutual fund, the first of their kind.

In 1998, State Street Global Advisors introduced the "Sector Spiders" which follow the nine sectors of the S&P 500.

Since then ETFs have proliferated, tailored to an increasingly specific array of regions, sectors, commodities, bonds, futures, and other asset classes. As of May 2008, there were 680 ETFs in the U.S., with $610 billion in assets, an increase of $125 billion over the previous twelve months.

Investment Uses

ETFs generally provide the easy diversification, low expense ratios, and tax efficiency of index funds, while still maintaining all the features of ordinary stock, such as limit orders, short selling, and options. Because ETFs can be economically acquired, held, and disposed of, some investors invest in ETF shares as a long-term investment for asset allocation purposes, while other investors trade ETF shares frequently to implement market timing investment strategies. Among the advantages of ETFs are the following:

- Lower costs - ETFs generally have lower costs than other investment products because most ETFs are not actively managed and because ETFs are insulated from the costs of having to buy and sell securities to accommodate shareholder purchases and redemptions. ETFs typically have lower marketing, distribution and accounting expenses Also most ETFs do not have 12b-1 fees.
- Buying and selling flexibility - ETFs can be bought and sold at current market prices at any time during the trading day, unlike mutual funds and unit investment trusts, which can only be traded at the end of the trading day. As publicly traded securities, their shares can be purchased on margin and sold short, enabling the use of hedging strategies, and traded using stop orders and limit orders which allow investors to specify the price points at which they are willing to trade.
- Tax efficiency - ETFs generally generate relatively low capital gains, because they typically have low turnover of their portfolio securities. While this is an advantage they share with other index funds, their

tax efficiency is further enhanced because they do not have to sell securities to meet investor redemptions.

- Market exposure and diversification - ETFs provide an economical way to rebalance portfolio allocations and to "equitize" cash by investing it quickly. An index ETF inherently provides diversification across an entire index. ETFs offer exposure to a diverse variety of markets, including broad-based indexes, broad-based international and country-specific indexes, industry sector-specific indexes, bond indexes, and commodities.
- Transparency - ETFs, whether index funds or actively managed, have transparent portfolios and are priced at frequent intervals throughout the trading day.

Some of these advantages derive from the status of most ETFs as index funds.

Types of ETFs

Index ETFs

Most ETFs are index funds that hold securities and attempt to replicate the performance of a stock market index. An index fund seeks to track the performance of an index by holding in its portfolio either the contents of the index or a representative sample of the securities in the index. Some index ETFs, known as leveraged ETFs or short ETFs, use investments in derivatives to seek a return that corresponds to a multiple of or the inverse (opposite) of the daily performance of the index. As of February 2008 index ETFs in the United States included 415 domestic equity ETFs, with assets of $350 billion; 160 global/international equity ETFs with assets of $169 billion; and 53 bond ETFs with assets of $40 billion.

Some index ETFs invest 100% of their assets proportionately in the securities underlying an index. This manner of investing is called "replication." Other index ETFs use "representative sampling" investing 80% to 95% of their assets in the securities of an underlying index and investing the remaining 5% to 20% of their assets in other holdings such as futures option, swap contracts and securities not in the underlying index. This technique is useful if the fund's adviser believes that it will help the ETF to achieve its investment objective. For index ETFs that invest in indexes with thousands of underlying securities, some index ETFs employ "aggressive sampling" and invest in only a tiny percentage of the underlying securities.

Commodity ETFs

Commodity ETFs invest in commodities, such as precious metals and futures. Among the first commodity ETFs were gold exchange-traded funds which have been offered in a number of countries. Commodity ETFs generally are index funds but track non-securities indexes. Because they do not invest in securities commodity ETFs are not regulated as investment companies under the Investment Company Act of 1940 in the United States. Although their public offering is subject to SEC review and they need an SEC no-action letter under the Securities Exchange Act of 1934. They may however be subject to regulation by the Commodity Futures Trading Commission.

Currency ETFs

In 2005 Rydex Investments launched the first ever currency ETF called the Euro Currency Trust (NYSE: FXE) in New York. Since then Rydex has launched a series of funds tracking all major currencies under their brand CurrencyShares. In 2008 Deutsche Bank's db x-trackers launched Sterling Money Market ETF (LSE: XGBP) and US Dollar Money Market ETF (LSE: XUSD) in London.

Actively Managed ETFs

Actively managed ETFs are quite recent and have been offered only since 25 March 2008 in the United States. The actively managed ETFs approved to date are fully transparent, publishing their current securities portfolios on their web sites daily. However, the SEC has indicated that it is willing to consider allowing actively managed ETFs that are not fully transparent in the future.

The fully transparent nature of existing ETFs means that an actively managed ETF is at risk from arbitrage activities by market participants who might choose to front-run its trades. The initial actively traded equity ETFs have addressed this problem by trading only weekly or monthly. Actively traded debt ETFs which are less susceptible to front-running trade their holdings more frequently.

The initial actively managed ETFs have received a lukewarm response and have been far less successful at gathering assets than were other novel ETFs. Among the reasons suggested for the initial lack of market interest are the steps required to avoid front-running, the time needed to build performance records and the failure of actively managed ETFs to give investors new ways to make hard-to-place bets.

Exchange-Traded Grantor Trusts

An exchange-traded grantor trust share represents a direct interest in a static basket of stocks selected from a particular industry. The leading example is Holding Company Depositary Receipts or HOLDRS, a proprietary Merrill Lynch product. HOLDRS are neither index funds nor actively-managed. Instead the investor has a direct interest in specific underlying stocks. While HOLDRS have some qualities in common with ETFs including low costs, low turnover and tax efficiency many observers consider HOLDRS to be a separate product from ETFs.

Leveraged ETFs

A leveraged exchange-traded fund or simply leveraged ETF are a special type of ETF that attempts to achieve returns that are more sensitive to market movements than a non-leveraged ETF. For instance, a bullish leveraged ETF might attempt to achieve daily returns that are 1.5, 2.0 or 2.5 times more pronounced than the Dow Jones Industrial Average or the S & P 500. Leveraged ETFs require the use of financial engineering techniques, including the use of equity swaps, derivatives and rebalancing to achieve the desired return.

ETFs compared to Mutual Funds

Costs

Since ETFs trade on an exchange each transaction is subject to a brokerage commission. The commissions depend on the broker with various "plans" and different conditions so no simple rule can be given. A "typical" schedule (in the United States) is $10 or $20 increasing slowly or not at all for larger orders. It is clear however that due to the quasi-flat charge, the amount invested has a great bearing. Someone who wishes to invest $100 per month may have 10% of their money vaporized immediately while for someone making a $200K investment the commission may be negligible. Generally, mutual funds obtained directly from the fund company itself do not charge a brokerage fee. Where low or no-cost transactions are available ETFs become very competitive.

Most ETFs have a lower expense ratio than comparable mutual funds. Not only does an ETF have lower shareholder-related expenses but because it does not have to invest cash contributions or fund cash redemptions an ETF does not have to maintain a cash reserve for redemptions. It also saves on brokerage expenses. Mutual funds can charge 1% to 3% or more. Index funds are generally lower while ETFs are almost always in the 0.1% to 1% range. Over the long term these cost differences can compound into a noticeable difference.

Mutual funds may charge for a too short holding period, which is nonexistent with ETFs. In fact, ETFs can be bought and sold in the same day, although it's not obvious that it's a good idea. This has made ETFs subject of some criticism since low fees may cause investors to trade more quickly. In this view traditional mutual funds are doing investors a favor by charging fees such as front loads.

Taxation

ETFs are structured for tax efficiency and can be more attractive than mutual funds. In the U.S. whenever a mutual fund realizes a capital gain that is not balanced by a realized loss the mutual fund must distribute the capital gains to its shareholders. This can happen whenever the mutual fund sells portfolio securities whether to reallocate its investments or to fund shareholder redemptions. These gains are taxable to all shareholders even those who reinvest the gains distributions in more shares of the fund. In contrast, ETFs are not redeemed by holders (instead, holders simply sell their ETF shares on the stock market as they would a stock or effect a non-taxable redemption of a creation unit for portfolio securities) so that investors generally only realize capital gains when they sell their own shares or when the ETF trades to reflect changes in the underlying index. In most cases ETFs are more tax-efficient than conventional mutual funds in the same asset classes or categories.

In the U.K. ETFs can be shielded from capital gains tax by placing them in an Individual Savings Account or self-invested personal pension, in the same manner as many other shares.

Trading

Perhaps the most important benefit of an ETF is the stock-like features offered. Since ETFs trade on the market investors can carry out the same types of trades that they can with a stock. For instance, investors can invest as much or as little money as they wish (there is no minimum investment requirement).

Also, many ETFs have the capability for options (puts and calls) to be written against them. Mutual funds do not offer those features.

For example, an investor in a mutual fund can only purchase or sell at the end of the day at the mutual fund's closing price. This makes stop-loss orders much less useful for mutual funds, and not all brokers even allow them. An ETF is continually priced throughout the day and therefore is not subject to this disadvantage. This allows the user to react to adverse or beneficial market conditions on an intraday basis. This stock-like liquidity allows an investor to trade the ETF for cash throughout regular trading hours and often after-hours on ECNs. ETF liquidity varies according to the trading volume and liquidity of the underlying securities but very liquid ETFs such as SPDRs can be traded pre-market and after-hours with reasonably tight spreads. These characteristics can be important for investors concerned with liquidity risk.

Another advantage is that ETFs, like closed-end funds, are immune from the market timing problems that have plagued open-end mutual funds. In these timing attacks investors trade in and out of a mutual fund quickly exploiting minor variances in price in order to profit at the expense of the long-term shareholders. With an ETF (or closed-end fund) such an operation is not possible—the underlying assets of the fund are not affected by its trading on the market.

Investors can profit from the difference in the share values of the underlying assets of the ETF and the trading price of the ETF's shares. ETF shares will trade at a premium to net asset value when demand is high and at a discount to net asset value when demand is low. In effect, the ETF is providing a system for arbitraging value in the market. As the initial costs are one-off, the ETF vehicle offers some cost advantages over other forms of pooled investment vehicles.

Criticism

John C. Bogle, founder of The Vanguard Group, a leading issuer of index funds (and, since Bogle's retirement, of ETFs) has argued that ETFs represent short-term speculation that their trading expenses decrease returns to investors and that most ETFs provide insufficient diversification. He concedes that a broadly diversified ETF that is held over time can be a good investment.

ETFs are dependent on the efficacy of the arbitrage mechanism in order for their share price to track the net asset value. While the average deviation between the daily closing price and the daily NAV of ETFs that track domestic indexes is generally less than 2%, the deviations may be more significant for ETFs that track certain foreign indexes.

ETFs offer little or no advantage over index funds for tax-deferred long-term retirement investors because such investors typically conduct little if any trading and tax issues are of little concern for them.

In a survey of investment professionals the most frequently cited disadvantage of ETFs was the unknown, untested indexes used by many ETFs followed by the overwhelming number of choices.

Some critics claim that especially commodity ETFs can be used and are used for unhealthy price manipulations.

Major Issuers of ETFs

- Barclays Global Investors issues iShares.
- State Street Global Advisors issues streetTRACKS and SPDRs.
- Vanguard Group issues Vanguard ETFs, formerly known as VIPERs.
- Rydex Investments issues Rydex ETFs.
- ETF Securities issues ETFs or specialised ETCs.
- Merrill Lynch issues HOLDRS.
- PowerShares issues PowerShares ETFs, as well as BLDRS based on American Depositary Receipts.
- Deutsche Bank issues db x-trackers ETFs, as well as managing PowerShares DB commodity- and currency-based ETFs.
- WisdomTree issues fundamentally weighted WisdomTree ETFs.
- Lyxor Asset Management issues Lyxor ETFs.
- ETF Capital Management operates a global fund of ETFs.
- Claymore Securities issues specialty Claymore ETFs.
- ProFunds issues inverse and leveraged ETFs.
- Van Eck Global issues Market Vectors ETFs.
- AdvisorShares proposes to issue actively managed AdvisorShares ETFs.
- RevenueShares issues Revenue-Weighted ETFs.
- SPA ETFs are fundamentally weighted ETFs.
- Jovain Capital has control over BETA-PRO ETFs which are available on the Canadian TSX.
- FocusShares LLC issues specialty ETFs.
- BNP Paribas issues EasyETFs.
- Ameristock issues Ameristock ETFs.
- First Trust Advisors issues specialty First Trust ETFs.

Index Funds

An index fund or index tracker is a collective investment scheme (usually a mutual fund or exchange-traded fund) that aims to replicate the movements of an index of a specific financial market, or a set of rules of ownership that are held constant, regardless of market conditions.

Tracking can be achieved by trying to hold all of the securities that are listed in the index in the same proportions as they are in the index as well. Other methods include statistically sampling the market and holding "representative" securities. Many index funds rely on a computer model with little or no human input in the decision as to which securities are purchased or sold and is therefore a form of passive management.

The lack of active management (stock picking and market timing) usually gives the advantage of lower fees and lower taxes in taxable accounts. However, the fees will generally reduce the return to the investor relative to the index. In addition it is usually impossible to precisely mirror the index as the models for sampling and mirroring, by their nature, cannot be 100% accurate. The difference between the index performance and the fund performance is known as the 'tracking error' or informally 'jitter'.

Index funds are available from many investment managers. Some common indices include the S&P 500, the Wilshire 5000, the FTSE 100 and the FTSE All-Share Index. Less common indexes come from academics like Eugene Fama and Kenneth French, who created "research indexes" in order to develop asset pricing models, such as their Three Factor Model. The Fama French Three Factor model is used by Dimensional Fund Advisors to design their index funds. Robert Arnott and Professor Jeremy Siegel have also created new competing fundamentally based indexes based on such criteria as dividends, earnings, book value, and sales. Companies such as the Dow Jones publish a variety of global indexes as well.

Origins of the Index Fund

In 1973, Burton Malkiel published his book A Random Walk Down Wall Street, which presented academic findings for the lay public. It was becoming well-known in the lay financial press that most mutual funds were not beating the market indices, to which the standard reply was made "of course, you can't buy an index." Malkiel said, "It's time the public can."

John Bogle graduated from Princeton University in 1951 where his senior thesis was titled: "Mutual Funds can make no claims to superiority over the Market Averages." Bogle wrote that his inspiration for starting an index fund came from three sources, all of which confirmed his 1951 research. These sources were Paul Samuelson's 1974 paper, "Challenge to Judgment", Charles Ellis' 1975 study, "The Loser's Game," and Al Ehrbar's 1975 Fortune magazine article on indexing. Bogle founded The Vanguard Group in 1974. It is now the second-largest mutual fund company in the United States as of 2005.

Bogle started the First Index Investment Trust on December 31, 1975. At the time it was heavily derided by competitors as being "un-American" and the fund itself was seen as "Bogle's folly". Fidelity Investments Chairman Edward Johnson was quoted as saying that he "[couldn't] believe that the great mass of investors are going to be satisfied with receiving just average returns". Bogle's fund was later renamed the Vanguard 500 Index Fund, which tracks the Standard and Poor's 500 Index. It started with comparatively meager assets of $11 million but crossed the $100 billion milestone in November 1999; this astonishing increase was funded by the market's increasing willingness to invest in such a product. Bogle predicted in January 1992 that it would very likely surpass the Magellan Fund before 2001, which it did in 2000.

John McQuown and David Booth at Wells Fargo and Rex Sinquefield at American National Bank in Chicago both established the first Standard and Poor's Composite Index Funds in 1973. Both of these funds were established for institutional clients. Individual investors were excluded. Wells Fargo started with $5 million from their own pension fund while Illinois Bell put in $5 million of their pension funds at American National Bank.

In 1981, David Booth and Rex Sinquefield started Dimensional Fund Advisors (DFA), many years later McQuown joined its Board of Directors. DFA further developed indexed based investment strategies and currently has $150 billion under management (as of Oct. 2007).

Wells Fargo sold its indexing operation to Barclay's Bank of London, and it now operates as Barclays Global Investors. It is one of the world's largest money managers with over $1.5 trillion under management as of 2005.

Economic Theory

Economist Eugene Fama said, "I take the market efficiency hypothesis to be the simple statement that security prices fully reflect all available information." A precondition for this strong version of the hypothesis is that information and trading costs, the costs of getting prices to reflect information, are always 0 (Grossman and Stiglitz (1980))." A weaker and economically more sensible version of the efficiency hypothesis says that prices reflect information to the point where the marginal benefits of acting on information (the profits to be made) do not exceed marginal costs (Jensen (1978)). Economists cite the efficient market hypothesis as the fundamental premise that justifies the creation of the index funds. The hypothesis implies that fund managers and stock analysts are constantly looking for securities that may out-perform the market and that this competition is so effective that any new information about the fortune of a company will rapidly be incorporated into stock prices. It is postulated therefore that it is very difficult to tell ahead of time which stocks will out-perform the market. By creating an index fund that mirrors the whole market the inefficiencies of stock selection are avoided.

In particular the EMH says that economic profits cannot be wrung from stock picking. This is not to say that a stock picker cannot achieve a superior return, just that the excess return will not exceed the costs of winning it (including salaries, information costs, and trading costs). The conclusion is that most investors would be better off buying a cheap index fund. Note that return refers to the ex-ante expectation. Ex-post realization of payoffs may make some stock-pickers appear successful.

Indexing Methods

Traditional Indexing

Indexing is traditionally known as the practice of owning a representative collection of securities, in the same ratios as the target index. A Modification of security holdings happens only when companies periodically enter or leave the target index.

Synthetic Indexing

Synthetic indexing is a modern technique of using a combination of equity index futures contracts and investments in low risk bonds to replicate the performance of a similar overall investment in the equities making up the index. Although maintaining the future position has a slightly higher cost structure than traditional passive sampling. Synthetic indexing can result in more favorable tax treatment particularly for international investors who are subject to U.S. dividend withholding taxes. The bond portion can hold higher yielding instruments with a trade-off of corresponding higher risk A technique referred to as enhanced indexing.

Enhanced Indexing

Enhanced indexing is a catch-all term referring to improvements to index fund management that emphasize performance by possibly using active management. Enhanced index funds employ a variety of enhancement techniques including customized indexes (instead of relying on commercial indexes), trading strategies, exclusion rules, and timing strategies. The cost advantage of indexing could be reduced or eliminated by employing active management.

Advantages of Index Funds

Low Costs

Because the composition of a target index is a known quantity it costs less to run an index fund. No highly paid stock pickers or analysts are needed. Typically expense ratios of an index fund ranges from 0.15% for U.S. Large Company Indexes to 0.97% for Emerging Market Indexes. The expense ratio of the average large cap actively managed mutual fund as of 2005 is 1.36%. If a mutual fund produces 10% return before expenses taking account of the expense ratio difference would result in an after expense return of 9.85% for the large cap index fund versus 8.64% for the actively managed large cap fund.

Simplicity

The investment objectives of index funds are easy to understand. Once an investor knows the target index of an index fund, what securities the index fund will hold can be determined directly. Managing one's index fund holdings may be as easy as rebalancing every six months or every year.

Lower Turnovers

Turnover refers to the selling and buying of securities by the fund manager. Selling securities in some jurisdictions may result in capital gains tax charges, which are sometimes passed on to fund investors. Because index funds are passive investments the turnovers are lower than actively managed funds. According to a study conducted by John Bogle over a sixteen-year period, investors get to keep only 47% of the cumulative return of the average actively managed mutual fund, but they keep 87% in a market index fund. This means $10,000 invested in the index fund grew to $90,000 vs. $49,000 in the average actively managed stock mutual fund. That is a 40% gain from the reduction of silent partners.

No Style Drift

Style drift occurs when actively managed mutual funds go outside of their described style (i.e. mid-cap value, large cap income, etc) to increase returns. Such drift hurts portfolios that are built with diversification as a high priority. Drifting into other styles could reduce the overall portfolio's diversity and subsequently increase risk. With an index fund this drift is not possible and accurate diversification of a portfolio is increased.

Disadvantages of Index Funds

Possible Tracking Error from Index

Since index funds aim to match market returns, both under- and over-performance compared to the market is considered a "tracking error". For example, an inefficient index fund may generate a positive tracking error in a falling market by holding too much cash which holds its value compared to the market.

According to The Vanguard Group, a well run S&P 500 index fund should have a tracking error of 5 basis points or less, but a Morningstar survey found an average of 38 basis points across all index funds.

Cannot Outperform the Target Index

By design, an index fund seeks to match rather than outperform the target index. Therefore, a good index fund with low tracking error will not generally outperform the index, but rather produces a rate of return similar to the index minus fund costs.

Not Immune to Market Bubbles

Owning a diversified stock index fund does not make an investor immune to systemic risk (e.g., a stock market bubble). When the U.S. technology sector bubble burst in 2000 the S&P 500 dropped significantly.

Index Composition Changes reduce Return

Whenever an index changes the fund is faced with the prospect of selling all the stock that has been removed from the index and purchasing the stock that was added to the index. The S&P 500 index has a typical turnover between 1% and 9% per year.

In effect, the index, and consequently all funds tracking the index are announcing ahead of time all the trades that they are planning to make. As a result the price of the stock that has been removed from the index tends to be driven down. The price of stock that has been added to the index tends to be driven up. The index fund however, has suffered market impact costs because they had to sell stock whose price was depressed and buy stock whose price was inflated. These losses are small however, relative to an index fund's overall advantage gained by low costs.

Diversification

Diversification refers to the number of different securities in a fund. A fund with more securities is said to be better diversified than a fund with smaller number of securities. Owning many securities reduces volatility by decreasing the impact of large price swings above or below the average return in a single security. A Wilshire 5000 index would be considered diversified, but a bio-tech ETF would not.

Since some indices, such as the S&P 500 and FTSE 100, are dominated by large company stocks, an index fund may have a high percentage of the fund concentrated in a few large companies. This position represents a reduction of diversity and can lead to increased volatility and investment risk for an investor who seeks a diversified fund.

Some advocate adopting a strategy of investing in every security in the world in proportion to its market capitalization, generally by investing in a collection of ETFs in proportion to their home country market capitalization. A global indexing strategy may outperform one based only on home market indexes because there may be less correlation between the returns of companies operating in different markets than between companies operating in the same market.

Asset Allocation and Achieving Balance

Asset allocation is the process of determining the mix of stocks, bonds and other classes of investable assets to match the investor's risk capacity, which includes attitude towards risk, net income, net worth, knowledge about investing concepts, and time horizon. Index funds capture asset classes in a low cost and tax efficient manner and are used to design balanced portfolios.

A combination of various index mutual funds or ETF's could be used to implement a full range of investment policies from low risk to high risk.

Comparison of Index Funds with Index ETFs

Mutual funds are priced at end of day (4:00 pm), while index ETFs have intraday pricing (9:30 am - 4:00 pm).

Some index ETFs have lower expense ratios as compared to regular index funds. Historically, however, ETFs have been subject to high brokerage fees. Recently though, online brokers have begun to reduce or eliminate these fees.

Many investors outside the US are able to purchase US based ETFs, but not US based mutual funds. If mutual funds in their home market are more expensive than US based ETFs then purchasing ETFs may be the cheaper option. This is currently the case for Canadian investors, for example.

U.S. Capital Gains Tax Considerations

U.S. mutual funds are required by law to distribute realized capital gains to their shareholders. If a mutual fund sells a security for a gain, the capital gain is taxable for that year. Similarly a realized capital loss can offset any other realized capital gains.

Example

An investor entered a mutual fund during the middle of the year and experienced an overall loss for the next 6 months. The mutual fund itself sold securities for a gain for the year, therefore must declare a capital gains distribution. The IRS would require the investor to pay tax on the capital gains distribution regardless of the overall loss.

A small investor selling an ETF to another investor does not cause a redemption on ETF itself. Therefore, ETFs are more immune to the effect of forced redemptions causing realized capital gains.

Stock Market Index

A stock market index is a method of measuring a section of the stock market. Many indices are compiled by news or financial services firms and are used to benchmark the performance of portfolios such as mutual funds.

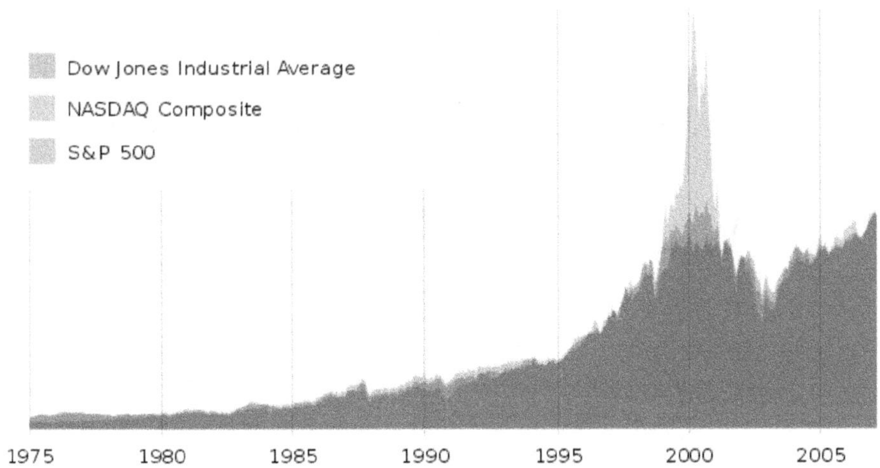

Picture 17: S&P 500, DJIA, NASDAQ 1975 - 2007

The picture above shows a comparison of three major U.S. stock indices: the NASDAQ Composite, Dow Jones Industrial Average, and S&P 500. All three have the same height at March 2007.
Notice the large dot-com spike on the NASDAQ which is a result of the large number of tech companies on that index.

Types of Indices

Stock market indices may be classed in many ways. A broad-base index represents the performance of a whole stock market — and by proxy, reflects investor sentiment on the state of the economy. The most regularly quoted market indexes are broad-base indexes comprised of the stocks of large companies listed on a nation's largest stock exchanges, such as the British FTSE 100, the French CAC 40, the German DAX, the Japanese Nikkei 225, the American Dow Jones Industrial Average and S&P 500 Index, the Indian Sensex, the Australian All Ordinaries and the Hong Kong Hang Seng Index. The major indexes will be discussed later on in this book.

The concept may be extended well beyond an exchange. The Dow Jones Wilshire 5000 Total Stock Market Index, as its name implies, represents the stocks of nearly every publicly traded company in the United States including all U.S. stocks traded on the New York Stock Exchange (but not ADRs) and most traded on the NASDAQ and American Stock Exchange. Russell Investment Group added to the family of indexes by launching the Russell Global Index.

More specialized indices are tracking the performance of specific sectors of the market. The Morgan Stanley Biotech Index, for example, consists of 36 American firms in the biotechnology industry. Other indexes may track companies of a certain size, a certain type of management, or even more specialized criteria — one index published by Linux Weekly News tracks stocks of companies that sell products and services based on the Linux operating environment.

Weighting

An index may also be classified according to the method used to determine its price. In a Price-weighted index such as the Dow Jones Industrial Average and the NYSE ARCA Tech 100 Index, the price of each component stock is the only consideration when determining the value of the index. Thus, price movement of even a single security will heavily influence the value of the index even though the dollar shift is less significant in a relatively highly valued issue and moreover ignoring the relative size of the company as a whole. In contrast, a market-value weighted or capitalization-weighted index such as the Hang Seng Index factors in the size of the company. Thus, a relatively small shift in the price of a large company will heavily influence the value of the index. In a market-share weighted index, price is weighted relative to the number of shares, rather than their total value.

Traditionally, capitalization- or share-weighted indices all had a full weighting i.e. all outstanding shares were included. Recently, many of them have changed to a float-adjusted weighting which helps indexing.

A modified market cap weighted index is a hybrid between equal weighting and capitalization weighting. It is similar to a general market cap with one main difference: The largest stocks are capped to a percent of the weight of the total stock index and the excess weight will be redistributed equally amongst the stocks under that cap. Moreover, in 2005, Standard & Poor's introduced the S&P Pure Growth Style Index and the S&P Pure Value Style Index which was attribute weighted. A stock's weight in the index is decided by the score it gets relative to the value attributes that define the criteria of a specific index. That is the same measure used to select the stocks in the first place. For these two stocks a score is calculated for every stock, be it their growth score or the value score (a stock can't be both) and accordingly they are weighted for the index .

Criticism of Capitalization-Weighting

The use of capitalization-weighted indexes is often justified by the central conclusion of modern portfolio theory that the optimal investment strategy for any investor is to hold the market portfolio, the capitalization-weighted portfolio of all assets. However, empirical tests conclude that market indexes are not efficient. This can be explained by the fact that these indexes do not include all assets or by the fact that the theory does not hold. The practical conclusion is that using capitalization-weighted portfolios is not necessarily the optimal method.

As a consequence, capitalization weighting has been subject to severe criticism (see e.g. Haugen and Baker 1991, Amenc, Goltz, and Le Sourd 2006, or Hsu 2006), pointing out that the mechanics of capitalization weighting lead to trend-following strategies that provide an inefficient risk-return trade-off.

Also, while capitalization weighting is the standard in equity index construction, different weighting schemes exist. First, while most indexes use capitalization weighting, additional criteria are often taken into account, such as sales/revenue and net income (see the "Guide to the Dow Jones Global Titan 50 Index", January 2006). Second, as an answer to the critiques of capitalization-weighting, equity indexes with different weighting schemes have emerged, such as "wealth"-weighted (as in Morris, 1996), "fundamental"-weighted (as in Arnott, Hsu and Moore 2005), "diversity"-weighted (as in Fernholz, Garvy, and Hannon 1998) or equal-weighted indexes.

Indexes and Passive Investment Management

There has been an accelerating trend in recent decades to create passively managed mutual funds that are based on market indices, known as index funds. Advocates claim that index funds routinely beat a large majority of actively managed mutual funds. Over time, the average actively managed fund has returned 1.8% less than the S&P 500 index - a result nearly equal to the average expense ratio of mutual funds (fund expenses are a drag on the funds' return by exactly that ratio). Since index funds attempt to replicate the holdings of an index, they obviate the need for — and thus many costs of — the research entailed in active management and have a lower "churn" rate (the turnover of securities which lose fund managers' favor and are sold with the attendant cost of commissions and capital gains taxes).

Indices are also a common basis for a related type of investment, the exchange-traded fund or ETF. Unlike an index fund, which is priced daily, an ETF is priced continuously, is optionable and can be sold short.

Dr. Emanuele Canegrati of Catholic University of Milan has recently developed the concept of Market Index Leader. Based on the Granger-causality concept, he defined a market index leader one which Granger-causes other indexes and it is not Granger-caused by any other index. Since Granger-causality does not deal with "true" causality, but only with a temporal sequence of events which have a linkage, he discovered that some indexes are first-movers (leaders) and some others follow them. The former Granger-cause the latter.

Ethical Stock Market Indices

A notable specialised index type is those for ethical investing indexes that include only those companies satisfying ecological or social criteria e.g. those of The Calvert Group, KLD, FTSE4Good Index, Dow Jones Sustainability Index and Wilderhill Clean Energy Index.

Another important trend is strict mechanical criteria for inclusion and exclusion to prevent market manipulation e.g. in Canada when Nortel was permitted to rise to over 30% of the TSE 300 index value. Ethical indices have a particular interest in mechanical criteria, seeking to avoid accusations of ideological bias in selection and have pioneered techniques for inclusion and exclusion of stocks based on complex criteria. Another means of mechanical selection is mark-to-future methods that exploit scenarios produced by multiple analysts weighted according to probability, to determine which stocks have become too risky to hold in the index of concern.

Critics of such initiatives argue that many firms satisfy mechanical "ethical criteria" e.g. regarding board composition or hiring practices but fail to perform ethically with respect to shareholders e.g. Enron. Indeed, the seeming "seal of approval" of an ethical index may put investors more at ease, enabling scams. One response to these criticisms is that trust in the corporate management, index criteria, fund or index manager and securities regulator, can never be replaced by mechanical means, so "market transparency" and "disclosure" are the only long-term-effective paths to fair markets.

Environmental Stock Market Indices

An environmental stock market index aims to provide a quantitative measure of the environmental damage caused by the companies in an index. Indices of this nature face much the same criticism as Ethical indices do — that the 'score' given is partially subjective.

However, whereas 'ethical' issues (for example, does a company use a sweat-shop) are largely subjective and difficult to score, an environmental impact is often quantifiable through scientific methods. So it is broadly possible to assign a 'score' to (say) the damage caused by a tonne of mercury dumped into a local river. It is harder to develop a scoring method that can compare different types of pollutant. For example does one hundred tonnes of carbon dioxide emitted to the air cause more or less damage (via climate change) than one tonne of mercury dumped in a river (and poisoning all the fish).

Generally, most environmental economists attempting to create an environmental index would attempt to quantify damage in monetary terms. So one tonne of carbon dioxide might cause $100 worth of damage, whereas one tonne of mercury might cause $50,000 (as it is highly toxic). Companies can therefore be given an 'environmental impact' score, based on the cost they impose on the environment. Quantification of damage in this nature is extremely difficult as pollutants tend to be market externalities and so have no easily measurable cost by definition.

Mutual Fund

A mutual fund is a professionally managed type of collective investment scheme that pools money from many investors and invests it in stocks, bonds, short-term money market instruments and/or other securities. The mutual fund will have a fund manager that trades the pooled money on a regular basis. Currently, the worldwide value of all mutual funds totals more than $26 trillion.

Since 1940, there have been three basic types of investment companies in the United States. Open-end funds, also known in the US as mutual funds, unit investment trusts (UITs) and closed-end funds. Similar funds also operate in Canada. However, in the rest of the world, mutual fund is used as a generic term for various types of collective investment vehicles such as unit trusts, open-ended investment companies (OEICs), unitized insurance funds and undertakings for collective investments in transferable securities (UCITS).

History

Massachusetts Investors Trust (now MFS Investment Management) was founded on March 21, 1924 and after one year, it had 200 shareholders and $392,000 in assets. The entire industry, which included a few closed-end funds represented less than $10 million in 1924.

The stock market crash of 1929 hindered the growth of mutual funds. In response to the stock market crash, Congress passed the Securities Act of 1933 and the Securities Exchange Act of 1934. These laws require that a fund be registered with the Securities and Exchange Commission (SEC) and provide prospective investors with a prospectus that contains required disclosures about the fund, the securities themselves and fund manager. The SEC helped draft the Investment Company Act of 1940, which sets forth the guidelines with which all SEC-registered funds today must comply.

With renewed confidence in the stock market, mutual funds began to blossom. By the end of the 1960s there were approximately 270 funds with $48 billion in assets. The first retail index fund, First Index Investment Trust, was formed in 1976 and headed by John Bogle, who conceptualized many of the key tenets of the industry in his 1951 senior thesis at Princeton University. It is now called the Vanguard 500 Index Fund and is one of the world's largest mutual funds with more than $100 billion in assets.

A key factor in mutual-fund growth was the 1975 change in the Internal Revenue Code allowing individuals to open individual retirement accounts (IRAs). Even people already enrolled in corporate pension plans could contribute a limited amount (at the time up to $2,000 a year). Mutual funds are now popular in employer-sponsored "defined-contribution" retirement plans such as (401(k)s) and 403(b)s as well as IRAs including Roth IRAs.

As of October 2007, there are 8,015 mutual funds that belong to the Investment Company Institute (ICI), a national trade association of investment companies in the United States with combined assets of $12.356 trillion.

Usage

Since the Investment Company Act of 1940 a mutual fund is one of three basic types of investment companies available in the United States.

Mutual funds can invest in many kinds of securities. The most common are cash instruments, stock and bonds but there are hundreds of sub-categories. Stock funds, for instance, can invest primarily in the shares of a particular industry, such as technology or utilities. These are known as sector funds. Bond funds can vary according to risk (e.g., high-yield junk bonds or investment-grade corporate bonds), type of issuers (e.g., government agencies, corporations, or municipalities) or maturity of the bonds (short- or long-term). Both stock and bond funds can invest in primarily U.S. securities (domestic funds), both U.S. and foreign securities (global funds) or primarily foreign securities (international funds).

Most mutual funds' investment portfolios are continually adjusted under the supervision of a professional manager who forecasts cash flows into and out of the fund by investors as well as the future performance of investments appropriate for the fund and chooses those which he or she believes will most closely match the fund's stated investment objective. A mutual fund is administered under an advisory contract with a management company which may hire or fire fund managers.

Mutual funds are subject to a special set of regulatory, accounting and tax rules. In the U.S., unlike most other types of business entities they are not taxed on their income as long as they distribute 90% of it to their shareholders and the funds meet certain diversification requirements in the Internal Revenue Code. Also, the type of income they earn is often unchanged as it passes through to the shareholders. Mutual fund distributions of tax-free municipal bond income are tax-free to the shareholder. Taxable distributions can be either ordinary income or capital gains depending on how the fund earned those distributions. Net losses are not distributed or passed through to fund investors.

Net Asset Value

The net asset value or NAV is the current market value of a fund's holdings less the fund's liabilities, usually expressed as a per-share amount. For most funds the NAV is determined daily after the close of trading on some specified financial exchange but some funds update their NAV multiple times during the trading day. The public offering price or POP is the NAV plus a sales charge. Open-end funds sell shares at the POP and redeem shares at the NAV and so process orders only after the NAV is determined. Closed-end funds (the shares of which are traded by investors) may trade at a higher or lower price than their NAV. This is known as a premium or discount, respectively. If a fund is divided into multiple classes of shares, each class will typically have its own NAV, reflecting differences in fees and expenses paid by the different classes.

Some mutual funds own securities which are not regularly traded on any formal exchange. These may be shares in very small or bankrupt companies. They may be derivatives or they may be private investments in unregistered financial instruments (such as stock in a non-public company). In the absence of a public market for these securities it is the responsibility of the fund manager to form an estimate of their value when computing the NAV. How much of a fund's assets may be invested in such securities is stated in the fund's prospectus.

Average Annual Return

US mutual funds use SEC form N-1A to report the average annual compounded rates of return for 1-year, 5-year and 10-year periods as the "average annual total return" for each fund. The following formula is used:

$$P(1+T)^n = ERV$$

Where:

P = a hypothetical initial payment of $1,000.

T = average annual total return.

n = number of years.

ERV = ending redeemable value of a hypothetical $1,000 payment made at the beginning of the 1-, 5-, or 10-year periods at the end of the 1-, 5-, or 10-year periods (or fractional portion).

Turnover

Turnover is a measure of the fund's securities transactions, usually calculated over a year's time and usually expressed as a percentage of net asset value.

This value is usually calculated as the value of all transactions (buying, selling) divided by 2 divided by the fund's total holdings i.e. the fund counts one security sold and another one bought as one "turnover". Thus turnover measures the replacement of holdings.

In Canada, under NI 81-106 (required disclosure for investment funds) turnover ratio is calculated based on the lesser of purchases or sales divided by the average size of the portfolio (including cash).

Expenses and TER's

Mutual funds bear expenses similar to other companies. The fee structure of a mutual fund can be divided into two or three main components: Management fee, nonmanagement expense and 12b-1/non-12b-1 fees. All expenses are expressed as a percentage of the average daily net assets of the fund.

Management Fees

The management fee for the fund is usually synonymous with the contractual investment advisory fee charged for the management of a fund's investments. However, as many fund companies include administrative fees in the advisory fee component, when attempting to compare the total management expenses of different funds, it is helpful to define management fee as equal to the contractual advisory fee + the contractual administrator fee. This "levels the playing field" when comparing management fee components across multiple funds.

Contractual advisory fees may be structured as "flat-rate" fees i.e. a single fee charged to the fund, regardless of the asset size of the fund. However, many funds have contractual fees which include breakpoints, so that as the value of a fund's assets increases, the advisory fee paid decreases. Another way in which the advisory fees remain competitive is by structuring the fee so that it is based on the value of all of the assets of a group or a complex of funds rather than those of a single fund.

Non-Management Expenses

Apart from the management fee there are certain non-management expenses which most funds must pay. Some of the more significant (in terms of amount) non-management expenses are: Transfer agent expenses (this is usually the person you get on the other end of the phone line when you want to purchase/sell shares of a fund), custodian expense (the fund's assets are kept in custody by a bank which charges a custody fee), legal/audit expense, fund accounting expense, registration expense (the SEC charges a registration fee when funds file registration statements with it), board of directors/trustees expense (the disinterested members of the board who oversee the fund are usually paid a fee for their time spent at meetings) and printing and postage expense (incurred when printing and delivering shareholder reports).

12b-1/Non-12b-1 service fees

12b-1 service fees/shareholder servicing fees are contractual fees which a fund may charge to cover the marketing expenses of the fund. Non-12b-1 service fees are marketing/shareholder servicing fees which do not fall under SEC rule 12b-1. While funds do not have to charge the full contractual 12b-1 fee, they oftdo. When investing in a front-end load or no-load fund the 12b-1 fees for the fund are usually .250% (or 25 basis points). The 12b-1 fees for back-end and level-load share classes are usually between 50 and 75 basis points but may be as much as 100 basis points. While funds are often marketed as "no-load" funds, this does not mean they do not charge a distribution expense through a different mechanism. It is expected that a fund listed on an online brokerage site will be paying for the "shelf-space" in a different manner even if not directly through a 12b-1 fee.

Investor Fees and Expenses

Fees and expenses borne by the investor vary based on the arrangement made with the investor's broker. Sales loads (or contingent deferred sales loads (CDSL)) are not included in the fund's total expense ratio (TER) because they do not pass through the statement of operations for the fund. Additionally, funds may charge early redemption fees to discourage investors from swapping money into and out of the fund quickly, which may force the fund to make bad trades to obtain the necessary liquidity. For example, Fidelity Diversified International Fund (FDIVX) charges a 1 percent fee on money removed from the fund in less than 30 days.

Brokerage Commissions

An additional expense which does not pass through the statement of operations and cannot be controlled by the investor is brokerage commissions. Brokerage commissions are incorporated into the price of the fund and are reported usually 3 months after the fund's annual report in the statement of additional information. Brokerage commissions are directly related to portfolio turnover (portfolio turnover refers to the number of times the fund's assets are bought and sold over the course of a year). Usually the higher the rate of the portfolio turnover, the higher the brokerage commissions. The advisors of mutual fund companies are required to achieve "best execution" through brokerage arrangements so that the commissions charged to the fund will not be excessive.

Types of Mutual Funds

Open-End Fund

The term mutual fund is the common name for what is classified as an open-end investment company by the SEC. Being open-ended means that at the end of every day, the fund issues new shares to investors and buys back shares from investors wishing to leave the fund.

Mutual funds must be structured as corporations or trusts, such as business trusts and any corporation or trust will be classified by the SEC as an investment company if it issues securities and primarily invests in non-government securities. An investment company will be classified by the SEC as an open-end investment company if they do not issue undivided interests in specified securities (the defining characteristic of unit investment trusts or UITs) and if they issue redeemable securities. Registered investment companies that are not UITs or open-end investment companies are closed-end funds. Neither UITs nor closed-end funds are mutual funds (as that term is used in the US).

Exchange-Traded Funds

A relatively recent innovation, the exchange-traded fund or ETF is often structured as an open-end investment company. ETFs combine characteristics of both mutual funds and closed-end funds. ETFs are traded throughout the day on a stock exchange just like closed-end funds but at prices generally approximating the ETF's net asset value. Most ETFs are index funds and track stock market indexes. Shares are issued or redeemed by institutional investors in large blocks (typically of 50,000). Most investors purchase and sell shares through brokers in market transactions. Because the institutional investors normally purchase and redeem in in kind transactions, ETFs are more efficient than traditional mutual funds (which are continuously issuing and redeeming securities and, to effect such transactions, continually buying and selling securities and maintaining liquidity positions) and therefore tend to have lower expenses.

Exchange-traded funds are also valuable for foreign investors who are often able to buy and sell securities traded on a stock market but who, for regulatory reasons, are limited in their ability to participate in traditional U.S. mutual funds.

Equity Funds

Equity funds, which consist mainly of stock investments are the most common type of mutual fund. Equity funds hold 50 percent of all amounts invested in mutual funds in the United States. Often equity funds focus investments on particular strategies and certain types of issuers.

Capitalization

Fund managers and other investment professionals have varying definitions of mid-cap and large-cap ranges. The following ranges are used by Russell Indexes:

- Russell Microcap Index - micro-cap ($54.8 - 539.5 million)
- Russell 2000 Index - small-cap ($182.6 million - 1.8 billion)
- Russell Midcap Index - mid-cap ($1.8 - 13.7 billion)
- Russell 1000 Index - large-cap ($1.8 - 386.9 billion)

Growth vs. Value

Another distinction is made between growth funds which invest in stocks of companies that have the potential for large capital gains and value funds which concentrate on stocks that are undervalued. Value stocks have historically produced higher returns. However, financial theory states this is compensation for their greater risk. Growth funds tend not to pay regular dividends. Income funds tend to be more conservative investments with a focus on stocks that pay dividends. A balanced fund may use a combination of strategies, typically including some level of investment in bonds, to stay more conservative when it comes to risk, yet aim for some growth.

Index Funds versus Active Management

An index fund maintains investments in companies that are part of major stock (or bond) indices such as the S&P 500 while an actively managed fund attempts to outperform a relevant index through superior stock-picking techniques. The assets of an index fund are managed to closely approximate the performance of a particular published index. Since the composition of an index changes infrequently an index fund manager makes fewer trades, on average, than does an active fund manager. For this reason index funds generally have lower trading expenses than actively managed funds and typically incur fewer short-term capital gains which must be passed on to shareholders. Additionally, index funds do not incur expenses to pay for selection of individual stocks (proprietary selection techniques, research, etc.) and deciding when to buy, hold or sell individual holdings. Instead, a fairly simple computer model can identify whatever changes are needed to bring the fund back into agreement with its target index.

Certain empirical evidence seems to illustrate that mutual funds do not beat the market and actively managed mutual funds under-perform other broad-based portfolios with similar characteristics. One study found that nearly 1,500 U.S. mutual funds under-performed the market in approximately half of the years between 1962 and 1992. Moreover, funds that performed well in the past are not able to beat the market again in the future (shown by Jensen, 1968; Grimblatt and Sheridan Titman, 1989).

Bond Funds

Bond funds account for 18% of mutual fund assets. Types of bond funds include term funds which have a fixed set of time (short-, medium-, or long-term) before they mature. Municipal bond funds generally have lower returns but have tax advantages and lower risk. High-yield bond funds invest in corporate bonds, including high-yield or junk bonds. With the potential for high yield, these bonds also come with greater risk.

Money Market Funds

Money market funds hold 26% of mutual fund assets in the United States. Money market funds entail the least risk as well as lower rates of return. Unlike certificates of deposit (CDs) money market shares are liquid and redeemable at any time.

Funds of Funds

Funds of funds (FoF) are mutual funds which invest in other underlying mutual funds (i.e. they are funds comprised of other funds). The funds at the underlying level are typically funds which an investor can invest in individually. A fund of funds will typically charge a management fee which is smaller than that of a normal fund because it is considered a fee charged for asset allocation services. The fees charged at the underlying fund level do not pass through the statement of operations but are usually disclosed in the fund's annual report, prospectus or statement of additional information. The fund should be evaluated on the combination of the fund-level expenses and underlying fund expenses, as these both reduce the return to the investor.

Most FoFs invest in affiliated funds (i.e., mutual funds managed by the same advisor), although some invest in funds managed by other (unaffiliated) advisors. The cost associated with investing in an unaffiliated underlying fund is most often higher than investing in an affiliated underlying because of the investment management research involved in investing in fund advised by a different advisor. Recently, FoFs have been classified into those that are actively managed (in which the investment advisor reallocates frequently among the underlying funds in order to adjust to changing market conditions) and those that are passively managed (the investment advisor allocates assets on the basis of on an allocation model which is rebalanced on a regular basis).

The design of FoFs is structured in such a way as to provide a ready mix of mutual funds for investors who are unable to or unwilling to determine their own asset allocation model. Fund companies such as TIAA-CREF, American Century Investments, Vanguard and Fidelity have also entered this market to provide investors with these options and take the "guess work" out of selecting funds. The allocation mixes usually vary by the time the investor would like to retire: 2020, 2030, 2050, etc. The more distant the target retirement date, the more aggressive the asset mix.

Hedge Funds

Hedge funds in the United States are pooled investment funds with loose SEC regulation and should not be confused with mutual funds. Some hedge fund managers are required to register with SEC as investment advisers under the Investment Advisers Act. The Act does not require an adviser to follow or avoid any particular investment strategies, nor does it require or prohibit specific investments. Hedge funds typically charge a management fee of 1% or more plus a "performance fee" of 20% of the hedge fund's profits. There may be a "lock-up" period, during which an investor cannot cash in shares. A variation of the hedge strategy is the 130-30 fund for individual investors.

Mutual Funds vs. Other Investments

Mutual funds offer several advantages over investing in individual stocks. For example, the transaction costs are divided among all the mutual fund shareholders which allows for cost-effective diversification. Investors may also benefit by having a third party (professional fund managers) apply expertise and dedicate time to manage and research investment options, although there is dispute over whether professional fund managers can, on average, outperform simple index funds that mimic public indexes. Whether actively managed or passively indexed, mutual funds are not immune to risks. They share the same risks associated with the investments made. If the fund invests primarily in stocks, it is usually subject to the same ups and downs and risks as the stock market.

Share Classes

Many mutual funds offer more than one class of shares. For example, you may have seen a fund that offers "Class A" and "Class B" shares. Each class will invest in the same pool (or investment portfolio) of securities and will have the same investment objectives and policies. But each class will have different shareholder services and/or distribution arrangements with different fees and expenses. These differences are supposed to reflect different costs involved in servicing investors in various classes. For example, one class may be sold through brokers with a front-end load and another class may be sold direct to the public with no load but a "12b-1 fee" included in the class's expenses (sometimes referred to as "Class C" shares). Still a third class might have a minimum investment of $10,000,000 and be available only to financial institutions (a so-called "institutional" share class). In some cases, by aggregating regular investments made by many individuals, a retirement plan (such as a 401(k) plan) may qualify to purchase "institutional" shares (and gain the benefit of their typically lower expense ratios) even though no members of the plan would qualify individually. As a result, each class will likely have different performance results.

A multi-class structure offers investors the ability to select a fee and expense structure that is most appropriate for their investment goals (including the length of time that they expect to remain invested in the fund).

Load and Expenses

A front-end load or sales charge is a commission paid to a broker by a mutual fund when shares are purchased, taken as a percentage of funds invested. The value of the investment is reduced by the amount of the load. Some funds have a deferred sales charge or back-end load. In this type of fund an investor pays no sales charge when purchasing shares but will pay a commission out of the proceeds when shares are redeemed depending on how long they are held. Another derivative structure is a level-load fund in which no sales charge is paid when buying the fund but a back-end load may be charged if the shares purchased are sold within a year.

Load funds are sold through financial intermediaries such as brokers, financial planners and other types of registered representatives who charge a commission for their services. Shares of front-end load funds are frequently eligible for breakpoints (i.e., a reduction in the commission paid) based on a number of variables. These include other accounts in the same fund family held by the investor or various family members or committing to buy more of the fund within a set period of time in return for a lower commission "today".

It is possible to buy many mutual funds without paying a sales charge. These are called no-load funds. In addition to being available from the fund company itself, no-load funds may be sold by some discount brokers for a flat transaction fee or even no fee at all. (This does not necessarily mean that the broker is not compensated for the transaction. In such cases, the fund may pay brokers' commissions out of "distribution and marketing" expenses rather than a specific sales charge. The purchaser is therefore paying the fee indirectly through the fund's expenses deducted from profits.)

No-load funds include both index funds and actively managed funds. The largest mutual fund families selling no-load index funds are Vanguard and Fidelity, though there are a number of smaller mutual fund families with no-load funds as well. Expense ratios in some no-load index funds are less than 0.2% per year versus the typical actively managed fund's expense ratio of about 1.5% per year. Load funds usually have even higher expense ratios when the load is considered. The expense ratio is the anticipated annual cost to the investor of holding shares of the fund. For example, on a $100,000 investment an expense ratio of 0.2% means $200 of annual expense while a 1.5% expense ratio would result in $1,500 of annual expense. These expenses are before any sales commissions paid to purchase the mutual fund.

Many fee-only financial advisors strongly suggest no-load funds such as index funds. If the advisor is not of the fee-only type but is instead compensated by commissions, the advisor may have a conflict of interest in selling high-commission load funds.

Hedge Fund

A hedge fund is a private investment fund open to a limited range of investors which is permitted by regulators to undertake a wider range of activities than other investment funds and which pays a performance fee to its investment manager. Although each fund will have its own strategy which determines the type of investments and the methods of investment it undertakes, hedge funds as a class invest in a broad range of investments, from shares, debt and commodities to works of art.

As the name implies, hedge funds often seek to offset potential losses in the principal markets they invest in by hedging their investments using a variety of methods, most notably short selling. However, the term "hedge fund" has come to be applied to many funds that do not actually hedge their investments and in particular to funds using short selling and other "hedging" methods to increase rather than reduce risk, with the expectation of increasing return.

Hedge funds are typically open only to a limited range of professional or wealthy investors. This provides them with an exemption in many jurisdictions from regulations governing short selling, derivative contracts, leverage, fee structures and the liquidity of interests in the fund. A hedge fund will nevertheless commit itself to a particular investment strategy and therefore often particular investment types and leverage levels, via statements in its offering documentation, thereby giving investors some certainty regarding the the nature of the fund.

The net asset value of a hedge fund can run into many billions of dollars and this will usually be multiplied by leverage. Hedge funds dominate certain specialty markets such as trading within derivatives with high-yield ratings and distressed debt.

History

Sociologist, author and financial journalist Alfred W. Jones is credited with the creation of the first hedge fund in 1949. Jones believed that price movements of an individual asset could be seen as having a component due to the overall market and a component due to the performance of the asset itself. In order to neutralise the effect of overall market movement he balanced his portfolio by buying assets whose price he expected to rise and selling short assets he expected to fall. He saw that price movements due to the overall market would be cancelled out because if the overall market rose the loss on shorted assets would be cancelled by the additional gain on assets bought and vice-versa. Because the effect is to 'hedge' that part of the risk due to overall market movements this became known as a hedge fund.

Industry Size

In 2005, Absolute Return magazine found there were 196 hedge funds with $1 billion or more in assets with a combined $743 billion under management - the vast majority of the industry's estimated $1 trillion in assets. However, according to hedge fund advisory group Hennessee, total hedge fund industry assets increased by $215 billion in 2006 to $1.442 trillion up 17.5% on a year earlier, an estimate for 2005 seemingly at odds with Absolute Return.

As large institutional investors have entered the hedge fund industry the total asset levels continue to rise. The 2008 Hedge Fund Asset Flows & Trends Report published by HedgeFund.net and Institutional Investor News estimates total industry assets reached $2.68 trillion in Q3 2007. According to the BarclayHedge Monthly Asset Flow Report, hedge funds received only $15 billion in October, the second-lowest inflow in 2007. Year-to-date hedge funds attracted $278.5 billion, three times year-to-date inflow into equity mutual funds.

Hedge Fund Risk

Investing in certain types of hedge fund can be (but is not necessarily) a riskier proposition than investing in a regulated fund, despite a "hedge" being a means of reducing the risk of a bet or investment. The following are some of the primary reasons for the increased risk in hedge funds as an industry, though by no means all hedge funds have all of these characteristics and some have none:

Leverage

In addition to money invested into the fund by investors, a hedge fund will typically borrow money with certain funds borrowing sums many times greater than the initial investment. If a hedge fund has borrowed $9 for every $1 received from investors, a loss of only 10% of the value of the investments of the hedge fund will wipe out 100% of the value of the investor's stake in the fund, once the creditors have called in their loans. In September 1998, shortly before its collapse, Long Term Capital Management had $125 billion of assets on a base of $4 billion of investors' money, a leverage of over 30 times. It also had off-balance sheet positions with a notional value of approximately $1 trillion.

Short Selling

Due to the nature of short selling the losses that can be incurred on a losing bet are theoretically limitless unless the short position directly hedges a corresponding long position. Therefore, where a hedge fund uses short selling as an investment strategy rather than as a hedging strategy it can suffer very high losses if the market turns against it. Ordinary funds very rarely use short selling in this way.

Appetite for Risk

Hedge funds are culturally more likely than other types of funds to take on underlying investments that carry high degrees of risk, such as high yield bonds, distressed securities and collateralized debt obligations based on subprime mortgages.

Lack of Transparency

Hedge funds are secretive entities with few public disclosure requirements. It can therefore be difficult for an investor to assess trading strategies, diversification of the portfolio and other factors relevant to an investment decision.

Lack of Regulation

Hedge funds are not subject to as much oversight from financial regulators as regulated funds and therefore some may carry undisclosed structural risks.

Investors in hedge funds are, in most countries, required to be sophisticated investors who will be aware of the risk implications of these factors. They are willing to take these risks because of the corresponding rewards. Leverage amplifies profits as well as losses; short selling opens up new investment opportunities. Riskier investments typically provide higher returns. Secrecy helps to prevent imitation by competitors and being unregulated reduces costs and allows the investment manager more freedom to make decisions on a purely commercial basis.

Legal Structure

A hedge fund is a vehicle for holding and investing the funds of its investors. The fund itself is not a genuine business, having no employees and no assets other than its investment portfolio and a small amount of cash while its investors are its clients. The portfolio is managed by the investment manager, which has employees and property and which is the actual business. An investment manager is commonly termed a "hedge fund" (e.g. a person may be said to "work at a hedge fund") but this is not technically correct. An investment manager may have a large number of hedge funds under its management.

Domicile

The specific legal structure of a hedge fund – in particular its domicile and the type of legal entity used – is usually determined by the tax environment of the fund's expected investors. Regulatory considerations will also play a role. Many hedge funds are established in offshore tax havens so that the fund can avoid paying tax on the increase in the value of its portfolio. An investor will still pay tax on any profit it makes when it realizes its investment and the investment manager, usually based in a major financial centre, will pay tax on the fees that it receives for managing the fund.

At end of 2007, 52% of the number of hedge funds were registered offshore. The most popular offshore location was the Cayman Islands (57% of number of offshore funds), followed by British Virgin Islands (16%) and Bermuda (11%). The other offshore centers are the Isle of Man and Mauritius. The US was the most popular onshore location (with funds mostly registered in Delaware) accounting for 65% of the number of onshore funds, followed by Europe with 31%.

The Legal Entity

Limited partnerships are principally used for hedge funds aimed at US-based investors who pay tax, as the investors will receive relatively favorable tax treatment in the US. The general partner of the limited partnership is typically the investment manager (though is sometimes an offshore corporation) and the investors are the limited partners. Offshore corporate funds are used for non-US investors and US entities that do not pay tax (such as pension funds), as such investors do not receive the same tax benefits from investing in a limited partnership. Unit trusts are typically marketed to Japanese investors.

Other than taxation, the type of entity used does not have a significant bearing on the nature of the fund.

Many hedge funds are structured as master/feeder funds. In such a structure the investors will invest into a feeder fund which will in turn invest all of its assets into the master fund. The assets of the master fund will then be managed by the investment manager in the usual way. This allows several feeder funds (e.g. an offshore corporate fund, a US limited partnership and a unit trust) to invest into the same master fund, allowing an investment manager the benefit of managing the assets of a single entity while giving all investors the best possible tax treatment.

The investment manager, which will have organized the establishment of the hedge fund, may retain an interest in the hedge fund, either as the general partner of a limited partnership or as the holder of "founder shares" in a corporate fund. Founder shares typically have no economic rights and voting rights over only a limited range of issues such as selection of the investment manager – most of the fund's decisions are taken by the board of directors of the fund, which is self-appointing and independent but invariably loyal to the investment manager.

Open-Ended Nature

Hedge funds are typically open-ended, in that the fund will periodically issue additional partnership interests or shares directly to new investors, the price of each being the net asset value ("NAV") per interest/share. To realize the investment the investor will redeem the interests or shares at the NAV per interest/share prevailing at that time. Therefore, if the value of the underlying investments has increased (and the NAV per interest/share has therefore also increased) then the investor will receive a larger sum on redemption than it paid on investment. Investors do not typically trade shares among themselves and hedge funds do not typically distribute profits to investors before redemption. This contrasts with a closed-ended fund, which has a limited number of shares which are traded among investor, and which distributes its profits.

Listed Funds

Corporate hedge funds often list their shares on smaller stock exchanges such as the Irish Stock Exchange in the hope that the low level of quasi-regulatory oversight will give comfort to investors and to attract certain funds such as some pension funds that have bars or caps on investing in unlisted shares. Shares in the listed hedge fund are not traded on the exchange but the fund's monthly net asset value and certain other events must be publicly announced there.

A fund listing is distinct from the listing or initial public offering ("IPO") of shares in an investment manager. Although widely reported as a "hedge-fund IPO", the IPO of Fortress Investment Group LLC was for the sale of the investment manager, not of the hedge funds that it managed.

Hedge Fund Management Worldwide

In contrast to the funds themselves, hedge fund managers are primarily located onshore in order to draw on larger pools of financial talent. The US East coast – principally New York City and the Gold Coast area of Connecticut (particularly Stamford and Greenwich) – is the world's leading location for hedge fund managers with approximately double the hedge fund managers of the next largest centre, London. With the bulk of hedge fund investment coming from the US, this distribution is natural. It was estimated there were 7,000 hedge funds in the United States in 2004.

London is Europe's leading centre for the management of hedge funds. At the end of 2007, three-quarters of European hedge fund investments, totaling $400bn (£200bn) were managed from London, having grown from $61bn in 2002. Australia was the most important centre for the management of Asia-Pacific hedge funds, with managers located there accounting for approximately a quarter of the $140bn of hedge fund assets managed in the Asia-Pacific region in 2008.

The Hedge Fund Paradigm Extends to Other Sections of the Industry

The remuneration structure offered by hedge funds makes it very attractive for investment managers to brand their products as "hedge funds", regardless of whether they fit the traditional definition. For example, Cadence Capital Limited is a listed company on the Australian Securities Exchange. Like a traditional hedge fund, Cadence charges a "2+20" fee structure (2% base fee, plus 20% of any benchmark outperformance). Also like a traditional hedge fund, Cadence promises "to ensure it manages money on an absolute return basis". However, Cadence is unlike a traditional hedge fund in several other respects:

- its returns have a correlation of 0.79 with the Australian small cap index;
- its holdings consist mostly of small cap Australian stocks;
- Cadence itself is a company listed on an exchange.

In the Australian market, Cadence would be considered to be just another listed small cap investment fund, except for its "2+20" fee structure and its undertaking to be market neutral.

This specific example illustrates the general point that the hedge fund remuneration structure is very attractive to all sections of the investment management industry. This tends to blur the definition of hedge funds. Indeed, it has been joked that hedge funds are best viewed "... not as a unique asset class or investment strategy, but as a unique "fee structure""

Regulatory Issues

Part of what gives hedge funds their competitive edge and their cachet in the public imagination is that they straddle multiple definitions and categories. Some aspects of their dealings are well-regulated, others are unregulated or at best quasi-regulated.

US Regulation

The typical public investment company in the United States is required to be registered with the U.S. Securities and Exchange Commission (SEC). Mutual funds are the most common type of registered investment companies. Aside from registration and reporting requirements, investment companies are subject to strict limitations on short-selling and the use of leverage. There are other limitations and restrictions placed on public investment company managers, including the prohibition on charging incentive or performance fees.

Although hedge funds fall within the statutory definition of an investment company, the limited-access, private nature of hedge funds permits them to operate pursuant to exemptions from the registration requirements. The two major exemptions are set forth in Sections 3(c)1 and 3(c)7 of the Investment Company Act of 1940. Those exemptions are for funds with 100 or fewer investors (a "3(c) 1 Fund") and funds where the investors are "qualified purchasers" (a "3(c) 7 Fund"). A qualified purchaser is an individual with over US$5,000,000 in investment assets. (Some institutional investors also qualify as accredited investors or qualified purchasers). A 3(c)1 Fund cannot have more than 100 investors, while a 3(c)7 Fund can have an unlimited number of investors. However, a 3(c)7 fund with more than 499 investors must register its securities with the SEC. Both types of funds can charge performance or incentive fees.

In order to comply with 3(c)(1) or 3(c)(7), hedge funds are sold via private placement under the Securities Act of 1933. Thus interests in a hedge fund cannot be offered or advertised to the general public and are normally offered under Regulation D. Although it is possible to have non-accredited investors in a hedge fund, the exemptions under the Investment Company Act, combined with the restrictions contained in Regulation D, effectively require hedge funds to be offered solely to accredited investors. An accredited investor is an individual person with a minimum net worth of US $1,000,000 or, alternatively, a minimum income of US$200,000 in each of the last two years and a reasonable expectation of reaching the same income level in the current year. For banks and corporate entities, the minimum net worth is $5,000,000 in invested assets.

The regulatory landscape for Investment Advisors is changing and there have been attempts to register hedge fund investment managers. There are numerous issues surrounding these proposed requirements. One issue of importance to hedge fund managers is the requirement that a client who is charged an incentive fee must be a "qualified client" under Advisers Act Rule 205-3. To be a qualified client an individual must have US$750,000 in assets invested with the adviser or a net worth in excess of US$1.5 million or be one of certain high-level employees of the investment adviser.

For the funds, the tradeoff of operating under these exemptions is that they have fewer investors to sell to but they have few government-imposed restrictions on their investment strategies. The presumption is that hedge funds are pursuing more risky strategies, which may or may not be true depending on the fund and that the ability to invest in these funds should be restricted to wealthier investors who are presumed to be more sophisticated and who have the financial reserves to absorb a possible loss.

In December 2004, the SEC issued a rule change that required most hedge fund advisers to register with the SEC by February 1, 2006 as investment advisers under the Investment Advisers Act. The requirement, with minor exceptions, applied to firms managing in excess of US$25,000,000 with over 15 investors. The SEC stated that it was adopting a "risk-based approach" to monitoring hedge funds as part of its evolving regulatory regimen for the burgeoning industry. The rule change was challenged in court by a hedge fund manager and in June 2006 the U.S. Court of Appeals for the District of Columbia overturned it and sent it back to the agency to be reviewed. This case is the Goldstein v. SEC case.

Although the SEC is currently examining how it can address the Goldstein decision, commentators have stated that the SEC currently has neither the staff nor expertise to comprehensively monitor the estimated 8,000 U.S. and international hedge funds. One of the Commissioners, Roel Campos, has said that the SEC is forming internal teams that will identify and evaluate irregular trading patterns or other phenomena that may threaten individual investors, the stability of the industry or the financial world. "It's pretty clear that we will not be knocking on doors very often," Campos told several hundred hedge fund managers, industry lawyers and others. And even if it did, "the SEC will never have the degree of knowledge or background that you do."

In February 2007, the President's Working Group on Financial Markets rejected further regulation of hedge funds and said that the industry should instead follow voluntary guidelines.

Comparison to Private Equity Funds

Hedge funds are similar to private equity funds in many respects. Both are lightly regulated, private pools of capital that invest in securities and compensate their managers with a share of the fund's profits. Most hedge funds invest in relatively liquid assets and permit investors to enter or leave the fund, perhaps requiring some months notice. Private equity funds invest primarily in very illiquid assets such as early-stage companies and so investors are "locked in" for the entire term of the fund. Hedge funds often invest in private equity companies' acquisition funds.

Between 2004 and February 2006 some hedge funds adopted 25 month lock-up rules expressly to exempt themselves from the SEC's new registration requirements and cause them to fall under the registration exemption that had been intended to exempt private equity funds

Comparison to U.S. Mutual Funds

Like hedge funds, mutual funds are pools of investment capital (i.e., money people want to invest). However, there are many differences between the two, including:

- Mutual funds are regulated by the SEC, while hedge funds are not

- A hedge fund investor must be an accredited investor with certain exceptions (employees, etc.)
- Mutual funds must price and be liquid on a daily basis

Some hedge funds that are based offshore report their prices to the Financial Times but for most there is no method of ascertaining pricing on a regular basis. Additionally, mutual funds must have a prospectus available to anyone that requests one (either electronically or via US postal mail) and must disclose their asset allocation quarterly, while hedge funds do not have to abide by these terms.

Hedge funds also ordinarily do not have daily liquidity, but rather "lock up" periods of time where the total returns are generated (net of fees) for their investors and then returned when the term ends, through a passthrough requiring CPAs and US Tax W-forms. Hedge fund investors tolerate these policies because hedge funds are expected to generate higher total returns for their investors versus mutual funds.

Recently, however, the mutual fund industry has created products with features that have traditionally only been found in hedge funds.

Mutual funds have appeared which utilize some of the trading strategies noted above. Grizzly Short Fund (GRZZX), for example, is always net short while Arbitrage Fund (ARBFX) specializes in merger arbitrage. Such funds are SEC regulated but they offer hedge fund strategies and protection for mutual fund investors.

Also, a few mutual funds have introduced performance-based fees, where the compensation to the manager is based on the performance of the fund. However, under Section 205(b) of the Investment Advisers Act of 1940, such compensation is limited to so-called "fulcrum fees". Under these arrangements, fees can be performance-based so long as they increase and decrease symmetrically.

For example, the TFS Capital Small Cap Fund (TFSSX) has a management fee that behaves, within limits and symmetrically, similarly to a hedge fund "0 and 50" fee: A 0% management fee coupled with a 50% performance fee if the fund outperforms its benchmark index. However, the 125 bp base fee is reduced (but not below zero) by 50% of underperformance and increased (but not to more than 250 bp) by 50% of outperformance.

Offshore Regulation

Many offshore centers are keen to encourage the establishment of hedge funds. To do this they offer some combination of professional services, a favorable tax environment and business-friendly regulation. Major centers include Cayman Islands, Dublin, Luxembourg, British Virgin Islands and Bermuda. The Cayman Islands have been estimated to be home to about 75% of world's hedge funds with nearly half the industry's estimated $1.225 trillion AUM.

Hedge funds have to file accounts and conduct their business in compliance with the requirements of these offshore centres. Typical rules concern restrictions on the availability of funds to retail investors (Dublin), protection of client confidentiality (Luxembourg) and the requirement for the fund to be independent of the fund manager.

Many offshore hedge funds such as the Soros funds are structured as mutual funds rather than as limited partnerships.

Proposed US Regulation

Hedge funds are exempt from regulation in the United States. Several bills have been introduced in the 110th Congress (2007-08), however, relating to such funds. Among them are:

- S. 681, a bill to restrict the use of offshore tax havens and abusive tax shelters to inappropriately avoid Federal taxation;
- H.R. 3417, which would establish a Commission on the Tax Treatment of Hedge Funds and Private Equity to investigate imposing regulations;
- S. 1402, a bill to amend the Investment Advisors Act of 1940, with respect to the exemption to registration requirements for hedge funds; and
- S. 1624, a bill to amend the Internal Revenue Code of 1986 to provide that the exception from the treatment of publicly traded partnerships as corporations for partnerships with passive-type income shall not apply to partnerships directly or indirectly deriving income from providing investment adviser and related asset management services.
- S. 3268, a bill to amend the Commodity Exchange Act to prevent excessive price speculation with respect to energy commodities. The bill would give the federal regulator of futures markets the resources

to detect, prevent, and punish price manipulation and excessive speculation.

None of the bills has received serious consideration yet.

UK Regulation

Under a proposed regulation announced in July 2008, hedge funds will no longer be able to build secret stakes in companies after the United Kingdom's Financial Services Authority (FSA) announced that it will introduce strict rules on disclosure of derivatives. Large holdings through contracts for difference (CFD), which give investors economic exposure to share price moves but no voting rights, must be disclosed as if they were actual company shares.

Derivatives, particularly CFDs, have become increasingly important as hedge funds attempt to avoid public declarations of their holdings, gain easy access to leverage and, in the UK, avoid stamp duty. Approximately, a third of UK equity trading consists of trading in CFDs.

Hedge Fund Indices

There are a number of indices that track the hedge fund industry. These indices come in two types, Investable and Non-investable, both with substantial problems. There are also new types of tracking product launched by Goldman Sachs and Merrill Lynch, "clone indices" that aim to replicate the returns of hedge fund indices without actually holding hedge funds at all.

Investable indices are created from funds that can be bought and sold and only hedge funds that agree to accept investments on terms acceptable to the constructor of the index are included. Investability is an attractive property for an index because it makes the index more relevant to the choices available to investors in practice and is taken for granted in traditional equity indices such as the S&P500 or FTSE100. However, such indices do not represent the total universe of hedge funds and may under-represent the more successful managers, who may not find the index terms attractive. Fund indexes include Eurekahedge Indices, BarclayHedge, Hedge Fund Research, Credit Suisse Tremont and FTSE Hedge.

The index provider selects funds and develops structured products or derivative instruments that deliver the performance of the index, making investable indices similar in some ways to fund of hedge funds portfolios.

Non-investable benchmarks are indicative in nature and aim to represent the performance of the universe of hedgefunds using some measure such as mean, median or weighted mean from a hedge fund database. There are diverse selection criteria and methods of construction and no single database captures all funds. This leads to significant differences in reported performance between different databases.

Non-investable indices inherit the databases' shortcomings or strengths in terms of scope and quality of data. Funds' participation in a database is voluntary, leading to "self-selection bias" because those funds that choose to report may not be typical of funds as a whole. For example, some do not report because of poor results or because they have already reached their target size and do not wish to raise further money. This tends to lead to a clustering of returns around the mean rather than representing the full diversity existing in the hedge fund universe. Examples of non-investable indices include an equal weighted benchmark series known as the HFN Averages and a revolutionary rules based set known as the Lehman Brothers/HFN Global Index Series which leverages an Enhanced Strategy Classification System.

The short lifetimes of many hedge funds means that there are many new entrants and many departures each year, which raises the problem of "survivorship bias". If we examine only funds that have survived to the present we will overestimate past returns because many of the worst-performing funds have not survived and the observed association between fund youth and fund performance suggests that this bias may be substantial. As the HFR and CISDM databases began in 1994, it is likely that they will be more accurate over the period 1994/2000 than the Credit Suisse database which only began in 2000.

When a fund is added to a database for the first time, all or part of its historical data is recorded ex-post in the database. It is likely that funds only publish their results when they are favorable, so that the average performances displayed by the funds during their incubation period are inflated. This is known as "instant history bias" or "backfill bias".

In traditional equity investment, indices play a central and unambiguous role. They are widely accepted as representative and products such as futures and ETFs provide liquid access to them in most developed markets. However, among hedge funds no index combines these characteristics. Investable indices achieve liquidity at the expense of representativeness. Non-investable indices are representative but their quoted returns may not be available in practice. Neither is wholly satisfactory.

Debates and Controversies

Systemic Risk

Hedge funds came under heightened scrutiny as a result of the failure of Long-Term Capital Management (LTCM) in 1998, which necessitated a bailout coordinated (but not financed) by the U.S. Federal Reserve. Critics have charged that hedge funds pose systemic risks highlighted by the LTCM disaster. The excessive leverage (through derivatives) that can be used by hedge funds to achieve their return is outlined as one of the main factors of the hedge funds' contribution to systemic risk.

The ECB (European Central Bank) issued a warning in June 2006 on hedge fund risk for financial stability and systemic risk: "... the increasingly similar positioning of individual hedge funds within broad hedge fund investment strategies is another major risk for financial stability which warrants close monitoring despite the essential lack of any possible remedies. This risk is further magnified by evidence that broad hedge fund investment strategies have also become increasingly correlated, thereby further increasing the potential adverse effects of disorderly exits from crowded trades."

The Times wrote about this review: "In one of the starkest warnings yet from an official institution over the role of the burgeoning but secretive industry, the ECB sounded a note of alarm over the possible repercussions from any collapse of a hedge fund or group of funds."

However, the ECB statement itself has been criticized by a part of the financial research community. These arguments are developed by the EDHEC Risk and Asset Management Research Centre: The main conclusions of the study are that "the ECB article's conclusion of a risk of 'disorderly exits from crowded trades' is based on mere speculation. While the question of systemic risk is of importance, we do not dispose of enough data to reliably address this question at this stage", "it would be worthwhile for financial regulators to work towards obtaining data on hedge fund leverage and counterparty credit risk. Such data would allow a reliable assessment of the question of systemic risk" and "besides evaluating potential systemic risk, it should be recognized that hedge funds play an important role as 'providers of liquidity and diversification'."

The potential for systemic risk was highlighted by the near-collapse of two Bear Stearns hedge funds in June 2007. The funds invested in mortgage-backed securities. The funds' financial problems necessitated an infusion of cash into one of the funds from Bear Stearns but no outside assistance. It was the largest fund bailout since Long Term Capital Management's collapse in 1998. The U.S. Securities and Exchange commission is investigating.

Transparency

As private, lightly regulated partnerships, hedge funds do not have to disclose their activities to third parties. This is in contrast to a fully regulated mutual fund (or unit trust) which will typically have to meet regulatory requirements for disclosure. An investor in a hedge fund usually has direct access to the investment advisor of the fund and may enjoy more personalized reporting than investors in retail investment funds. This may include detailed discussions of risks assumed and significant positions. However, this high level of disclosure is not available to non-investors, contributing to hedge funds' reputation for secrecy. Several hedge funds are completely "black box", meaning that their returns are uncertain to the investor.

Restrictions on marketing and the lack of regulation means that there are no official hedge fund statistics. An industry consulting group, HFR (hfr.com), reported at the end of the second quarter 2003 that there are 5,660 hedge funds world wide managing $665 billion. For comparison, at the same time the US mutual fund sector held assets of $7.818 trillion (according to the Investment Company Institute).

Some hedge funds, mainly American, do not use third parties either as the custodian of their assets or as their administrator (who will calculate the NAV of the fund). This can lead to conflicts of interest and in extreme cases can assist fraud. In a recent example, Kirk Wright of International Management Associates has been accused of mail fraud and other securities violations which allegedly defrauded clients of close to $180 million.

Market Capacity

Analysis of the rather disappointing hedge fund performance in 2004 and 2005 called into question the alternative investment industry's value proposition. Alpha may have been becoming rarer for two related reasons. First, the increase in traded volume may have been reducing the market anomalies that are a source of hedge fund performance. Second, the remuneration model is attracting more and more managers, which may dilute the talent available in the industry.

However, the market capacity effect has been questioned by the EDHEC Risk and Asset Management Research Centre through a decomposition of hedge fund returns between pure alpha, dynamic betas, and static betas.

While pure alpha is generated by exploiting market opportunities, the dynamic betas depend on the manager's skill in adapting the exposures to different factors, and these authors claim that these two sources of return do not exhibit any erosion. This suggests that the market environment (static betas) explains a large part of the poor performance of hedge funds in 2004 and 2005.

Investigations of illegal Conduct

In the U.S., the SEC is focusing more resources on investigating violations and illegal conduct on the part of hedge funds in the public securities markets. Linda C. Thomsen, enforcement director of the SEC, said in November 2007 that federal regulators were concerned about illegal trading and the potential for harm to hedge fund investors. She said, "These days, the money is in hedge funds, so the potential for abuse, the potential for securities law violations, is there because there is so much money there." Outside firms offering services to the hedge funds such as Prime Brokerage may be held accountable for failing to report illegal conduct on account of their client hedge funds.

Performance Measurement

The issue of performance measurement in the hedge fund industry has led to literature that is both abundant and controversial. Traditional indicators (Sharpe, Treynor, Jensen) work best when returns follow a symmetrical distribution. In that case, risk is represented by the standard deviation. Unfortunately, hedge fund returns are not normally distributed and hedge fund return series are autocorrelated. Consequently, traditional performance measures suffer from theoretical problems when they are applied to hedge funds, making them even less reliable than is suggested by the shortness of the available return series.

Innovative performance measures have been introduced in an attempt to deal with this problem: Modified Sharpe ratio by Gregoriou and Gueyie (2003), Omega by Keating and Shadwick (2002), Alternative Investments Risk Adjusted Performance (AIRAP) by Sharma (2004), and Kappa by Kaplan and Knowles (2004). An overview of these performance measures is available in Géhin, W.,

2006, The Challenge of Hedge Fund Performance Measurement: a Toolbox rather than a Pandora's Box, EDHEC Risk and Asset Management Research Center, Position Paper, December. However, there is no consensus on the most appropriate absolute performance measure, and traditional performance measures are still widely used in the industry.

Relationships with Analysts

In June 2006. the U.S. Senate Judiciary Committee began an investigation into the links between hedge funds and independent analysts and other issues related to the funds. Connecticut Attorney General Richard Blumenthal testified that an appeals court ruling striking down oversight of the funds by federal regulators left investors "in a regulatory void, without any disclosure or accountability." The hearings heard testimony from, among others, Gary Aguirre, a staff attorney who was recently fired by the SEC.

What Role Can Hedge Funds Play in a Mean/Variance Efficient Portfolio?

According to the Modern Portfolio Theory, rational investors will seek to hold portfolios that are mean/variance efficient (that is, portfolios offer the highest level of return per unit of risk and the lowest level of risk per unit of return). One of the unique features of hedge funds (in particular market neutral and similar funds) is that they have a nearly-zero correlation with traditional assets such as equities. This means that hedge funds have a potentially quite valuable role in investment portfolios as diversifiers, reducing overall portfolio risk.

However, there are two reasons why one might not wish to allocate a high proportion of assets into hedge funds. These reasons are:

1. Hedge funds' low correlation with other assets tends to dissipate during stressful market events, making them much less useful for diversification than they initially appear.
2. Hedge fund returns are reduced considerably by the very high fee structures that are typically charged by hedge funds.

One notable study by Mark Krtitzman was reported by the New York Times and by an investment advisory firm. Kritzman performed a mean-variance optimization calculation on an opportunity set that consisted of a stock index fund, a bond index fund and ten hypothetical hedge funds. The optimizer found that a mean-variance effient portfolio would not contain any allocation to hedge funds. This was largely because of the impact of performance fees. To demonstrate this, Kritzman repeated the optimization using an assumption that the hedge funds incurred no performance fees. The result from this second optimization was an allocation of 74% to hedge funds. Kritzman concluded that the "asymmetry effect" of performance fees (where the investor pays fees out of positive returns but bears the full effect of any losses) was critical in making hedge funds unsuitable for a diversified portfolio.

The other factor detracting from the attractiveness of hedge funds in a diversified portfolio is that they tend to under-perform during equity bear markets, which is just when an investor needs part of their portfolio to add value. For example, in January-September 2008, the Credit Suisse/Tremont Hedge Fund Index was down 9.87%. According to the same index series, even "dedicated short bias" funds had a return of -6.08% during September 2008. In other words, even though one would theoretically expect a dedicated short fund to provide a hedge against a decline in equities and commodities, this didn't seem to work in September 2008, which was a particularly turbulent period (including the collapse of Lehman Brothers).

Highest-Earning Hedge Fund Managers

A manager's earnings from a hedge fund are his share of the performance fee plus 100% of the capital gains on his own equity stake in the fund. Exact figures are not made publicly available, meaning that all reported figures are estimations but several publications publish annual lists of top earning hedge fund managers.

Trader Monthly's list of top 10 earners among hedge fund managers in 2007 was:

1. John Paulson, Paulson & Co. - $3 billion+
2. Philip Falcone, Harbinger Capital Partners - $1.5-$2 billion
3. Jim Simons, Renaissance Technologies - $1 billion
4. Steven A. Cohen, SAC Capital Advisors - $1 billion
5. Ken Griffin, Citadel Investment Group - $1–$1.5 billion
6. Chris Hohn, The Children's Investment Fund Management (TCI) - $800–$900 million
7. Noam Gottesman, GLG Partners - $700–$800 million
8. Alan Howard, Brevan Howard Asset Management - $700–$800 million
9. Pierre Lagrange, GLG Partners - $700–$800 million
10. Paul Tudor Jones, Tudor Investment Corp. - $600–$700 million

Largest Hedge Funds by Assets Under Management

single manager funds as of March 5 2008

1. JP Morgan $44.7bn
2. Farallon Capital $36bn
3. Bridgewater Associates $36bn
4. Renaissance Technologies $34bn
5. Och-Ziff Capital Management $33.2bn
6. Goldman Sachs Asset Management $32.5bn
7. DE Shaw $32.2bn
8. Paulson and Company $29bn
9. Barclays Global Investors $18.9bn
10. Man Investments $18.8bn
11. ESL Investments $17.5bn

Inverse Exchange-Traded Fund

An inverse exchange-traded fund is an exchange-traded fund (ETF) traded on a public stock market, which is designed to perform as the inverse of whatever index or benchmark it is designed to track. These funds work by using short selling, trading derivatives such as futures contracts and other leveraged investment techniques.

By providing performance opposite to their benchmark, inverse ETFs give approximately the same results as would short selling the stocks in the index. An inverse S&P 500 ETF, for example, seeks a daily percentage movement opposite that of the S&P. If the S&P 500 rises by 1%, the inverse ETF is designed to fall by 1%; and if the S&P falls by 1%, the inverse ETF should rise by 1%. Because their value rises in a declining market environment, they are popular investments in bear markets.

Short sales have the potential to expose an investor to unlimited losses, whether or not the sale involves a stock or ETF. An inverse ETF, on the other hand, provides many of the same benefits as shorting, yet it exposes an investor only to the loss of the purchase price. Another advantage of inverse ETFs is that they may be held in IRA accounts, while short sales are not permitted in these accounts.

Strategies for Buy-and-Hold Investors

There are a numbers of scenarios where a long-term investor could benefit from short or inverse ETFs. Investors trapped in a long position during a prolonged bear market might want to reduce their losses by using a short or inverse ETF. Another instance might be where a long-term investor has a large paper gain but doesn't want to pay taxes. Rather than watch a market decline eat away at the value of the investor's portfolio, selling short a market-tracking ETF or purchasing an inverse or short ETF would help reduce losses.

Fees and other Issues

Fees

Inverse and leveraged inverse ETFs tend to have higher expense ratios than standard index ETFs, since the funds are by their nature actively managed. These costs can eat away at performance.

Short-Terms vs. Long-Term

Since the market has a long-term upward bias, profit-making opportunities are limited in long time spans. In addition, a flat or rising market means these funds might struggle to make money. Inverse ETFs are designed to be used for relatively short-term investing as part of a market timing strategy.

Compounding Error

A subtle issue with inverse ETFs is that they are not the same as a short position in the underlying (in financial mathematics terms, they are not Delta One products). That is, if one enters into a short position on one day and after some number of days the underlying has changed in value by X%, then one's payoff is -X%, regardless of what has happened in the meantime. However, the payoff of an inverse ETF, being the compound of daily returns, is path dependent and is not the same as a simple short position.

Fundamentally, the reason is that in an inverse ETF (or a leveraged ETF) that tracks daily returns, the quantity of the underlier (the Delta) changes from day to day, while for an ordinary short (or long) position, levered or not, it stays constant.

This discrepancy means that inverse ETFs outperform shorts in slowly trending markets and underperform when markets move back and forth.

Examples

A few examples may illustrate this:

- if one invests \$100 in an inverse ETF position in an asset worth \$100, which over 2 days, moves to \$80 and then \$60, then the position will have made 20% the first day (so worth \$120), then 25% the next day (so a total of \$150, or 50% return), yet a short would have made only \$140, or 40% return. Further, had the stock instead moved \$100, \$100, \$60, the inverse ETF as well would have only been worth \$140.

  Thus inverse ETFs benefit compared to shorts in markets that trend down (but not those that jump down), because the position increases in size over time.

- conversely, if the same asset had moved from \$100 to \$120 to \$150 over 2 days, then a short position would have lost \$50 (\$100 - \$150), but the inverse ETF would have lost 20% the first day (to become worth \$80), and then 25% the next day (to become worth \$60), so only losing 40%.

  Here again the inverse ETF benefits from a trending market, because it progressively decreases in size.

- On the other hand, if the asset moved from \$100 to \$80 to \$100, then the short would show neither a profit nor a loss, but the inverse ETF would show a loss: the first day it gains 20% (\$20/\$100), to be worth \$120 and the second day it loses 25% (\$20/\$80) of this larger position, losing \$30, to be worth \$90, so even though the market has not moved overall, the inverse ETF has lost money.

  Thus if the market moves back and forth – especially, if it is range-bound – inverse ETFs underperform shorts.

Equations

In equations, it may be stated thus: If one invests \$100 in an inverse ETF on a asset that costs \$1 (so one has 100 units of exposure) and the one-day return is r, (say, $r = 5\%$) then the next day one has a position worth $(1 - r)$ in an asset that costs $(1 + r)$, so one has $(1 - r) / (1 + r)$ of one's earlier exposure. In this case one has \$95 of exposure to an asset worth \$1.05, so approximately 90.5 units of exposure, instead of the 100 units one had earlier. With an unlevered long position, by contrast, the quantity does not change, since after one day returns of r, the position is worth $(1 + r)$ times the previous value, and the asset is worth $(1 + r)$ times the previous value, so the new quantity is $(1 + r) / (1 + r) = 1$ times the previous quantity – equal, in other words.

Similar phenomena occur for levered ETFs – a double long levered ETF will see its notional change by (1 + 2r) / (1 + r) each day, while a double short ETF will see its notional change by (1 – 2r) / (1 + r).

To dramatically illustrate the change in quantity, consider a $100 investment in an inverse ETF on an asset worth $100, and the following day the asset moves to $50. Then one has a $150 investment in an asset worth $50, so a quantity of 3, triple what one started (and thus if it moved back to $100, one would lose thrice what one had gained). Conversely, if the asset had moved from $100 to $150, one would have lost $50 and thus have a $50 inverse ETF is an asset worth $150, so a quantity of 1/3 (and if it moved back to $100, one would gain back only one third of what one had lost).

Collective Investment Scheme

A collective investment scheme is a way of investing money with other people to participate in a wider range of investments than those feasible for most individual investors and to share the costs of doing so.

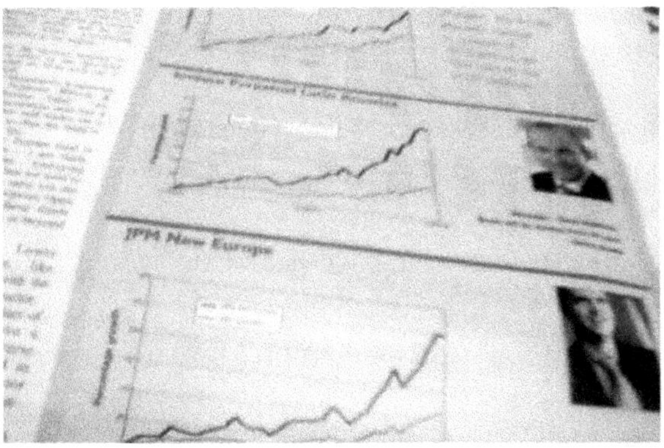

Picture 18:The values and performance of collective funds are listed in newspapers

Terminology varies with country but collective investment schemes are often referred to as investment funds, managed funds, mutual funds or simply funds (note: mutual fund has a specific meaning in the US). Around the world large markets have developed around collective investment and these account for a substantial portion of all trading on major stock exchanges.

Collective investments are promoted with a wide range of investment aims either targeting specific geographic regions (e.g. Emerging Europe) or specified themes (e.g. Technology). Depending on the country there is normally a bias towards the domestic market to reflect national self-interest as perceived by policy makers, familiarity and the lack of currency risk. Funds are often selected on the basis of these specified investment aims, their past investment performance and other factors such as fees.

Generic Information - Advantages

Diversity and Risk

One of the main advantages of collective investment is the reduction in investment risk (capital risk) by diversification. An investment in a single equity may do well, but it may collapse for investment or other reasons (e.g., Marconi, Enron). If your money is invested in such a failed holding you could lose your capital. By investing in a range of equities (or other securities) the capital risk is reduced.

- The more diversified your capital, the lower the capital risk.

This investment principle is often referred to as spreading risk.

Collective investments by their nature tend to invest in a range of individual securities. However, if the securities are all in a similar type of asset class or market sector then there is a systematic risk that all the shares could be affected by adverse market changes. To avoid this systematic risk investment managers may diversify into different non-perfectly-correlated asset classes. For example, investors might hold their assets in equal parts in equities and fixed income securities.

Reduced Dealing Costs

If one investor were to buy a large number of direct investments, the amount they would be able to invest in each holding is likely to be small. Dealing costs are normally based on the number and size of each transaction, therefore the overall dealing costs would take a large chunk out of the capital (affecting future profits). Pooling money with that of other investors gives the advantage of buying in bulk, making dealing costs an insignificant part of the investment.

Generic Information - Disadvantages

Costs

The fund manager managing the investment decisions on behalf of the investors will of course expect remuneration. This is often taken directly from the fund assets as a fixed percentage each year or sometimes a variable (performance based) fee. If the investor managed their own investments, this cost would be avoided.

Often the cost of advice given by a stock broker or financial adviser is built into the scheme. Often referred to as commission or load (in the U.S.) this charge may be applied at the start of the plan or as an ongoing percentage of the fund value each year. While this cost will diminish your returns it could be argued that it reflects a separate payment for an advice service rather than a detrimental feature of collective investment schemes. Indeed it is often possible to purchase units or shares directly from the providers without bearing this cost.

Lack of Choice

Although the investor can choose the type of fund to invest in, they have no control over the choice of individual holdings that make up the fund.

Loss of Owner's Rights

If the investor holds shares directly, they may be entitled to shareholders' perks (for example, discounts on the company's products) and the right to attend the company's annual general meeting and vote on important matters. Investors in a collective investment scheme often have none of the rights connected with individual investments within the fund.

Style

Investment Aims and Benchmarking

Each fund has a defined investment goal to describe the remit of the investment manager and to help investors decide if the fund is right for them. The investment aims will typically fall into the broad categories of Income (value) investment or growth investment. Income or value based investment tends to select stocks with strong income streams, often more established businesses. Growth investment selects stocks that tend to reinvest their income to generate growth. Each strategy has its critics and proponents; some prefer a blend approach using aspects of each.

Funds are often distinguished by asset-based categories such as equity, bonds, property, etc.

Also, perhaps most commonly funds are divided by their geographic markets or themes.

Examples

- The largest markets - U.S., Japan, Europe, UK and Far East are often divided into smaller funds e.g. US large caps, Japanese smaller companies, European Growth, UK mid caps etc.
- Themed funds - Technology, Healthcare, Socially responsible funds

In most instances whatever the investment aim the fund manager will select an appropriate index or combination of indices to measure its performance against; e.g. FTSE 100. This becomes the benchmark to measure success or failure against.

Active or Passive Management

The aim of most funds is to make money by investing in assets to obtain a real return (i.e. better than inflation).

The methods used to make your investment vary and two opposing views exist.

Active management - Active managers believe that by selectively buying within a financial market that it is possible to outperform the market as a whole. Therefore they employ dynamic portfolio strategies buying and selling investments with changing market conditions.

Passive management - Passive managers believe that it is impossible to predict which individual holdings or section of the market will perform better than another therefore their portfolio strategy is determined at outset of the fund and not varied thereafter. Many passive funds are index trackers where the fund tries to mirror the market as a whole. Another example of passive management is the "buy and hold" method used by many traditional Unit Investment Trusts where the portfolio is fixed from outset.

An example of active management success

- In 1998 Richard Branson (head of Virgin) publicly bet Nicola Horlick (head of SG Asset Management) that her SG UK Growth fund would not beat the FTSE 100 index, nor his Virgin Index Tracker fund over three years, nor achieve its stated aim to beat the index by 2% each year. He lost and paid £6,000 to charity.

Alpha, Beta, R-squared and standard deviation

When analysing investment performance, statistical measures are often used to compare 'funds'. These statistical measures are often reduced to a single figure representing an aspect of past performance:

- Alpha represents the fund's return when the benchmark's return is 0. This shows the fund's performance relative to the benchmark and can demonstrate the value added by the fund manager. The higher the 'alpha' the better the manager. Alpha investment strategies tend to favour stock selection methods to achieve growth.
- Beta represents an estimate of how much the fund will move if its benchmark moves by 1 unit. This shows the fund's sensitivity to changes in the market. Beta investment strategies tend to favour asset allocation models to achieve outperformance.
- R-squared is a measure of the association between a fund and its benchmark. Values are between 0 and 1. Perfect correlation is indicated by 1, and 0 indicates no correlation. This measure is useful in determining if the fund manager is adding value in their investment choices or acting as a closet tracker mirroring the market and making

little difference. For example, an index fund will have an R-squared with its benchmark index very close to 1, indicating close to perfect correlation (the index fund's fees and tracking error prevent the correlation from ever equalling 1).

- Standard deviation is a measure of volatility of the fund's performance over a period of time. The higher the figure the greater the variability of the fund's performance. High historical volatility may indicate high future volatility and therefore increased investment risk in a fund.

Types of Risk

Depending on the nature of the investment, the type of 'investment' risk will vary.

A common concern with any investment is that you may lose the money you invest - your capital. This risk is therefore often referred to as capital risk.

If the assets you invest in are held in another currency there is a risk that currency movements alone may affect the value. This is referred to as currency risk.

Many forms of investment may not be readily salable on the open market (e.g. commercial property) or the market has a small capacity and investments may take time to sell. Assets that are easily sold are termed liquid therefore this type of risk is termed liquidity risk.

Note that the investor is indifferent to the type of risk and should not care whether a loss comes from capital risk, currency risk, or liquidity risk - a loss is a loss.

Charging Structures and Fees

Fee Types

There may be an initial charge levied on the purchase of units or shares this covers dealing costs and commissions paid to intermediaries or salespeople. Typically this fee is a percentage of the investment. Some schemes waive the initial charge and apply an exit charge instead. This may be graduated disappearing after a number of years.

The scheme will charge an annual management charge or AMC to cover the cost of administering the scheme and remunerating the investment manager. This may be a flat rate based on the value of the assets or a performance related fee based on a predefined target being achieved.

Different unit/share classes may have different combinations of fees/charges.

Pricing Models

Open-ended schemes are either dual priced or single priced.

Dual priced schemes have a buying (offer) price and selling or (bid) price. The buying price is higher than the selling price, this difference is known as the spread or bid-offer spread. The difference is typically 5% and may be varied by the scheme manger to reflect changes in the market. The amount of variation may be limited by the schemes rules or regulatory rules. The difference between the buying and selling price includes initial charge for entering the fund.

The internal workings of a fund are more complicated that this description suggests. The manager sets a price for creation of units/shares and for cancellation. There is a differential between the cancellation and bid prices and the creation and offer prices. The additional units are created are place in the managers box for future purchasers. When heavy selling occurs units are liquidated from the managers box to protect the existing investors from the increased dealing costs. Adjusting the bid/offer prices closer to the cancellation/creation prices allows the manager to protect the interest of the existing investors in changing market conditions.

Most unit trusts are dual priced.

Single priced schemes notionally have a single price for units/shares and this price is the same if buying or selling. As single prices scheme can't adjust the difference between the buying and selling price to allow for market conditions another mechanism the dilution levy exists. SICAVs, OEICs and U.S. mutual funds are single priced.

A dilution levy can be charged at the discretion of the fund manager to offset the cost of market transactions resulting from large un-matched buy or sell orders. For example if the volume of purchases outweigh the volume of sales in a particular trading period the fund manager will have to go to the market to buy more of the assets underlying the fund, incurring a brokerage fee in the process and having an adverse affect on the fund as a whole ("diluting" the fund). The same is the case with large sell orders. A dilution levy is therefore applied where appropriate and paid for by the investor in order that large single transactions do not reduce the value of the fund as a whole.

Internationally Recognised Collective Investments

- Exchange-traded funds or ETFs - an open-ended fund traded by listed shares on major stock exchanges.
- Real Estate Investment Trusts or REITs - a close-ended fund that invests in real estate.
- Sovereign investment funds

Closed-End Fund

A closed-end fund, or closed-ended fund is a collective investment scheme with a limited number of shares.

New shares are rarely issued after the fund is launched. Shares are not normally redeemable for cash or securities until the fund liquidates. Typically an investor can acquire shares in a closed-end fund by buying shares on a secondary market from a broker, market maker, or other investor as opposed to an open-end fund where all transactions eventually involve the fund company creating new shares on the fly (in exchange for either cash or securities) or redeeming shares (for cash or securities).

The price of a share in a closed-end fund is determined partially by the value of the investments in the fund and partially by the premium (or discount) placed on it by the market. The total value of all the securities in the fund divided by the number of shares in the fund is called the net asset value (NAV) per share. The market price of a fund share is often higher or lower than the per share NAV: When the fund's share price is higher than per share NAV it is said to be selling at a premium. When it is lower, at a discount to the per share NAV.

In the U.S. legally they are called closed-end companies and form one of three SEC recognized types of investment companies along with mutual funds and unit investment trusts. Other examples of closed-ended funds are Investment trusts in the UK and listed investment companies in Australia.

Availability

Closed end funds are typically traded on the major global stock exchanges. In the U.S. the New York Stock Exchange is dominant although the Amex is in competition; in the UK the London Stock Exchange's main market is home to the mainstream funds although AIM supports many small funds especially the Venture Capital Trusts; in Canada, the Toronto Stock Exchange lists many closed-end funds.

Like their better-known open-ended cousins, closed-end funds are usually sponsored by a funds management company which will control how the money is invested. They begin by soliciting money from investors in an initial offering, which may be public or limited. The investors are given shares corresponding to their initial investment. The fund managers pool the money and purchase securities. What exactly the fund manager can invest depends on the fund's charter. Some funds invest in stocks, others in bonds, and some in very specific things (for instance, tax-exempt bonds issued by the state of Florida in the USA).

Distinguishing Features

Some characteristics that distinguish a closed-end fund from an ordinary open-end mutual fund are that:

1. it is closed to new capital after it begins operating, and
2. its shares (typically) trade on stock exchanges rather than being redeemed directly by the fund.
3. its shares can therefore be traded during the market day at any time. An open-end fund can usually be traded only at the closing price at the end of the market day.
4. a CEF usually has a premium or discount. An open-end fund sells at its NAV (except for sales charges).

Another distinguishing feature of a closed-end fund is the common use of leverage or gearing to enhance returns. CEFs can raise additional investment capital by issuing auction rate securities, preferred shares, long-term debt and/or reverse-repurchase agreements, although this is rare in the USA outside of income-focused funds. In doing so, the fund hopes to earn a higher return with this excess invested capital.

When a fund leverages through the issuance of preferred stock, two types of shareholders are created: Preferred stock shareholders and common stock shareholders.

Preferred stock shareholders benefit from expenses based on the total managed assets of the fund. Total managed assets include both the assets attributable to the purchase of stock by common shareholders and those attributable to the purchase of stock by preferred shareholders.

The expenses charged to the common shareholder are based on the common assets of the fund, rather than the total managed assets of the fund. The common shareholder's returns are reduced more significantly than those of the preferred shareholders due to the expenses being spread among a smaller asset base.

For the most part, closed-end fund companies report expenses ratios based on the fund's common assets only. However, the contractual management fees charged to the closed-end funds may be based on the common asset base or the total managed asset base.

The entry into long-term debt arrangements and reverse-repurchase agreements are two additional ways to raise additional capital for the fund. Funds may use a combination of leveraging tactics or each individually. However, it is more common that the fund will use only one leveraging technique.

Since closed-end funds are traded as stock, a customer trading them will pay a brokerage commission similar to one paid when trading stock (as opposed to commissions on open-ended mutual funds where the commission will vary based on the share class chosen and the method of purchasing the fund). In other words, closed-end funds typically do not have sales-based share classes where the commission and annual fees vary between them. The main exception is loan-participation funds.

Initial Offering

Like a company going public, a closed-end fund will have an initial public offering of its shares at which it will sell, say, 10 million shares for $10 each. That will raise $100 million for the fund manager to invest. At that point, however, the fund's 10 million shares will begin to trade on a secondary market, typically the NYSE or the AMEX for American closed-end funds. Any investor who wishes to buy or sell fund shares at that point will have to do so on the secondary market. Excluding exceptional circumstances, closed-end funds do not redeem their own shares. Nor, typically, do they sell more shares after the IPO (although they may issue preferred stock, in essence taking out a loan secured by the portfolio).

Exchange Traded

Closed-end fund shares trade continually at whatever price the market will support. They also qualify for advanced types of orders such as limit orders and stop orders. This is in contrast to open-end funds which are only available for buying and selling at the close of business each day, at the calculated NAV, and for which orders must be placed in advance, before the NAV is known, and can only be simple buy or sell orders. Some funds require that orders be placed hours or days in advance.

Closed-end funds trade on exchanges and in that respect they are like exchange-traded funds (ETFs) but there are important differences between these two kinds of security. The price of a closed-end fund is completely determined by the valuation of the market, and this price often diverges substantially from the NAV of the fund assets. In contrast, the market price of an ETF trades in a narrow range very close to its net asset value, because the structure of ETFs allows major market participants to redeem shares of an ETF for a "basket" of the fund's underlying assets. This feature could lead to potential arbitrage profits if the market price of the ETF were to diverge substantially from its NAV. The market prices of closed-end funds are often ten to twenty percent higher or lower than their NAVs, while the value of an ETF would only very rarely differ from its NAV by more than one-fifth of a percent.

Discounts and Premiums

As a secondary effect of being exchange-traded, the price of CEFs can vary from the NAV. In particular, fund shares often trade at what look to be irrational prices because secondary market prices are often very much out of line with underlying portfolio values. A CEF can also have a premium at some times, and a discount at other times. For example, Morgan Stanley Eastern Europe Fund (RNE) on the NYSE was trading at a premium of 39% in May 2006 and at a discount of 6% in October 2006. These huge swings are difficult to explain.

US closed-end stock funds often have share prices that are typically about 5% less than the Net Asset Value. That is, if a fund has 10 million shares outstanding and if its portfolio is worth $200 million, then each share should be worth $20 and you would expect that the market price of the fund's shares on the secondary market would be around $20. But, very oddly, that's typically not the case. The shares may trade for only $19 or even only $17. In the former case, the fund would be said to be "trading at a 5% discount to NAV." In the latter case, the fund would be said to be "trading at a 15% discount to NAV."

The presence of discounts is also puzzling since if a fund is trading at a discount, theoretically a well-capitalized investor could come along and buy up all the fund's shares at the discounted price in order to gain control of the portfolio and force the fund managers to liquidate it at its (higher) market value (although in reality, liquidity concerns make this impossible since the Bid/offer spread will drastically widen as fewer and fewer shares are available in the market). Benjamin Graham claimed that an investor can hardly go wrong by buying such a fund with a 15% discount. However, the opposing view is that the fund may not liquidate in your timeframe and you may be forced to sell at an even worse discount; but like any investment, these discounts could simply represent the assessment of the marketplace that the investments in the fund may lose value.

Even stranger, funds very often trade at a substantial premium to NAV. Some of these premia are extreme, with premia of several hundred percent having been seen on occasion. Why anyone would pay $30 per share for a fund whose portfolio value per share is only $10 is not well understood, although irrational exuberance has been mentioned. One theory is that if the fund has a strong track record of performance, investors may speculate that the outperformance is due to good investment choices by the fund managers and that the fund managers will continue to make good choices in the future. Thus the premium represents the ability to instantly participate in the fruits of the fund manager's decisions.

A great deal of academic ink has been spent trying to explain why closed-end fund share prices aren't forced by arbitrageurs to be equal to underlying portfolio values. Though there are many strong opinions, the jury is still out. It is easier to understand in cases where the CEF is able to pick and choose assets and arbitrageurs are not able to determine the specific assets until months later, but some funds are forced to replicate a specific index and still trade at a discount.

Comparison with Open-Ended Funds

With open-ended funds, the value is precisely equal to the NAV. So investing $1000 into the fund means buying shares that lay claim to $1000 worth of underlying assets (apart from sales charges). But buying a closed-end fund trading at a premium might mean buying $900 worth of assets for $1000.

Some advantages of closed-end funds over their open-ended cousins are financial. CEFs' fees are usually much lower (since they don't have to deal with the expense of creating and redeeming shares), they tend to keep less cash in their portfolio, and they need not worry about market fluctuations to maintain their "performance record". So if a stock drops irrationally, the closed-end fund may snap up a bargain, while open-ended funds might sell too early.

Also, if there is a market panic, investors may sell en masse. Faced with a wave of sell orders and needing to raise money for redemptions, the manager of an open-ended fund may be forced to sell stocks he'd rather keep and keep stocks he'd rather sell, due to liquidity concerns (selling too much of any one stock causes the price to drop disproportionately). Thus all it may have left are the dud stocks that no one wants to buy. But an investor pulling out of a closed-end fund must sell it on the market to another buyer, so the manager need not sell any of the underlying stock. The CEF's price will likely drop more than the market does (severely punishing those who sell during the panic) but it is more likely to make a recovery when the intrinsically sound stocks rebound.

Because a closed-end fund is on the market, it must obey certain rules, such as filing reports with the listing authority and holding annual stockholder meetings. Thus stockholders can more easily find out about their fund and engage in shareholder activism, such as protest against poor management.

Examples

Among the biggest, long-running CEFs are:

- Adams Express Company (NYSE:ADX)
- Foreign & Colonial Investment Trust plc (LSE:FRCL)
- Witan Investment Trust plc (LSE:WTAN)
- Tri-Continental Corporation (NYSE:TY)
- Gabelli Equity Trust (NYSE:GAB)

Traders & Trading Styles

What is a Trader?

In finance, a trader is someone who buys and sells financial instruments such as stocks, bonds and derivatives.

Traders are either professionals working in a financial institution or a corporation, or individual investors, or day traders, short-term speculators. They buy and sell financial instruments traded in the stock markets, derivatives markets and commodity markets, comprising the stock exchanges, derivatives exchanges and the commodities exchanges.

Several categories and designations for diverse kinds of traders are found in finance, these may include:

- Stock Trader
- Day Trader
- Swing Trager
- Rogue Trader

Stock Trader

A stock trader or a stock investor is an individual or firm who buys and sells stocks or bonds (and possibly other financial assets) in the financial markets.

Stock Trader versus Stock Investor

Individuals or firms trading equity (stock) on the stock markets as their principal capacity are called stock traders. Stock traders usually try to profit from short-term price volatility with trades lasting anywhere from several seconds to several weeks. The stock trader is usually a professional. A person can call themself a full or part-time stock trader/investor while maintaining other professions. When a stock trader/investor has clients, and acts as a money manager or adviser with the intention of adding value to their clients finances, they are also called a financial advisor or manager. In this case, the financial manager could be an independent professional or a large bank corporation employee. This may include managers dealing with investment funds, hedge funds, mutual funds and pension funds, or other professionals in equity investment, fund management and wealth management. Several different types of stock trading exist including day trading, swing trading, market making, scalping (trading), momentum trading, trading the news, and arbitrage.

Stock investors purchase stocks with the intention of holding for an extended period of time, usually several months to years. They rely primarily on fundamental analysis for their investment decisions and fully recognize stock shares as part-ownership in the company. Many investors believe in the buy and hold strategy, which as the name suggests, implies that investors will hold stocks for the very long term, generally measured in years. This strategy was made popular in the equity bull market of the 1980s and 90s where buy-and-hold investors rode out short-term market declines and continued to hold as the market returned to its previous highs and beyond. However, during the 2001-2003 equity bear market, the buy-and-hold strategy lost some followers as broader market indexes like the NASDAQ saw their values decline by over 60%.

Methodology

Stock traders/investors usually need a stock broker such as a bank or a brokerage firm to access the stock market. Since the advent of internet banking, an

Internet connection is commonly used to manage positions. Using the Internet, specialized software and a personal computer, stock traders/investors make use of technical analysis and fundamental analysis to help them in the decision-making process. They may use several information resources. Some of these resources are strictly technical. Using the pivot points calculated from a previous day trading, traders are able to predict the buy and sell points of the current day trading session. This pivot points give a cue to traders as to where price will head for the day; signalling the trader where to enter his trade and where to exit. There is a lot of criticism on the validity of these technical indicators used in technical analysis and many professional stock traders do not even use them.

Expenses, Costs and Risk

Trading activities are not free. They have a considerably high level of risk, uncertainty and complexity, especially for unwise and inexperienced stock traders/investors seeking for an easy way to make money quickly. In addition, stock traders/investors face several costs such as commissions, taxes and fees to be paid for the brokerage and other services, like the buying/selling orders placed at the stock exchange. According to each National or State legislation, a large array of fiscal obligations must be respected and taxes are charged by the State over the transactions, dividends and capital gains. However, these fiscal obligations may vary from jurisdiction to jurisdiction because, among other reasons, it could be assumed that taxation is already incorporated into the stock price through the different taxes companies pay to the state, or that tax free stock market operations are useful to boost economic growth. Beyond these costs, the opportunity costs of money and time, the currency risk, the financial risk and all the Internet Service Provider, data and news agency services and electricity consumption expenses must be added.

Stock Picking

Although many companies offer courses in stock picking and numerous experts report success through technical analysis and fundamental analysis, many economists and academics state that because of the efficient market theory it is unlikely that any amount of analysis can help an investor make any gains above the stock market itself. In a normal distribution of investors, many academics believe that the richest are simply outliers in such a distribution (i.e. in a game of chance, they have flipped heads twenty times in a row).

Accumulation / Distribution Method

Other investors choose a blend of technical, fundamental and environmental factors to influence what they invest in, as well as when they invest. These strategists reject the 'chance' theory of investing, and attribute their higher level of returns to both insight and discipline.

Over-the-Counter Trading

Over-the-counter (OTC) trading is to trade financial instruments such as stocks, bonds, commodities or derivatives directly between two parties. It is contrasted with exchange trading, which occurs via corporate-owned facilities constructed for the purpose of trading (i.e., exchanges), such as futures exchanges or stock exchanges.

OTC-Traded Stocks

In the U.S., over-the-counter trading in stocks is carried out by market makers that make markets in OTCBB and Pink Sheets securities using inter-dealer quotation services such as Pink Quote (operated by Pink OTC Markets) and the OTC Bulletin Board (OTCBB). OTC stocks are not listed or traded on any stock exchange. Although stocks quoted on the OTCBB must comply with SEC reporting requirements, other OTC stocks, such as those stocks categorized as Pink Sheets securities, have no reporting requirements while those stocks categorized as OTCQX have met alternative disclosure guidelines through Pink OTC Markets.

The OTC market presents investment opportunities for informed investors, but also has a high degree of risk. Many OTC issuers are small companies with limited operating histories or are economically distressed. Investments in legitimate OTC companies can often lead to the complete loss of the investment. Investors should avoid the OTC market unless they can afford a complete loss of their investment. Investors should never purchase any security without first evaluating the fundamentals of the company and carefully reviewing the financial statements, management background and other data. Investors who purchase securities based on a "hot tip" or the advice of chat room touts may often be disappointed.

OTC Market Statistics

Data provided by Pink Sheets:

- Securities quoted exclusively on Pink Sheets - 5,019
- Securities dually quoted on Pink Sheets and OTCBB - 3,445
- Securities quoted exclusively on OTCBB - 130
- Total OTC securities - 5,149

OTC Contracts

An over-the-counter contract is a bilateral contract in which two parties agree on how a particular trade or agreement is to be settled in the future. It is usually from an investment bank to its clients directly. Forwards and swaps are prime examples of such contracts. It is mostly done via the computer or the telephone. For derivatives, these agreements are usually governed by an International Swaps and Derivatives Association agreement.

This segment of the OTC market is occasionally referred to as the "Fourth Market."

The NYMEX has created a clearing mechanism for a slate of commonly traded OTC energy derivatives which allows counterparties of many bilateral OTC transactions to mutually agree to transfer the trade to ClearPort, the exchange's clearing house, thus eliminating credit and performance risk of the initial OTC transaction counterparts.

Short Selling

In finance, short selling or "shorting" is the practice of selling a financial instrument that the seller does not own at the time of the sale. Short selling is done with intent of later purchasing the financial instrument at a lower price. Short-sellers attempt to profit from an expected decline in the price of a financial instrument. Short selling or "going short" is contrasted with the more conventional practice of "going long" which occurs when an investment is purchased with the expectation that its price will rise.

Typically, the short-seller will "borrow" or "rent" the securities to be sold and later repurchase identical securities for return to the lender. If the security price falls as expected, the short-seller profits from having sold the borrowed securities for more than he or she later pays for them but if the security price rises, the short seller loses by having to pay more for them than the price at which he or she sold them. The practice is risky in that prices may rise indefinitely, even beyond the net worth of the short seller. The act of repurchasing is known as "closing" a position.

The term "short selling" or "being short" is often also used as a blanket term for strategies that allow an investor to gain from the decline in price of a security. Those strategies include buying options known as puts. A put option consists of the right to sell an asset at a given price. Thus the owner of the option benefits when the market price of the asset falls. Similarly, a short position in a futures contract, or to be short on a futures contract, means the holder of the position has an obligation to sell the underlying asset at a later date, to close out the position.

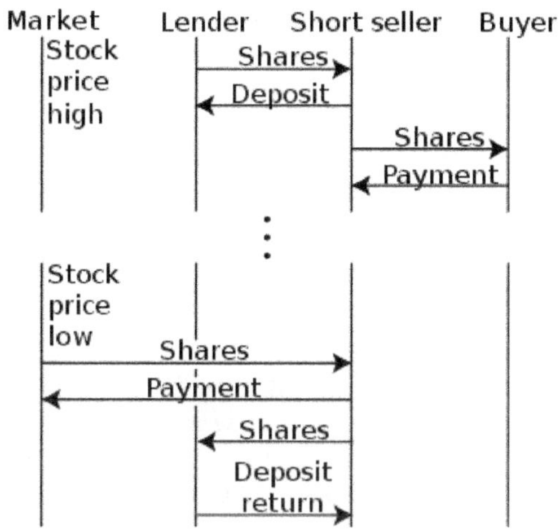

Picture 19: Diagram of short selling

The short seller borrows shares and sells them while the stock price is high. They then wait until the stock price is low and buy back the shares to return to the lender.

The Concept of Short Selling

To profit from a stock price going down, short sellers can borrow a security and sell it, expecting that it will be cheaper to repurchase in the future. When the seller decides that the time is right (or when the lender recalls the shares), the seller buys back the shares in order to return them to the lender. The process generally relies on the fact that securities are fungible, so that the shares returned do not need to be the same shares as were originally borrowed.

The short seller borrows from their broker, who usually in turn has borrowed the shares from some other investor who is holding his shares long. The broker itself seldom actually purchases the shares to lend to the short seller. The lender of the shares does not lose the right to sell the shares.

Short selling is the opposite of "going long." The short seller takes a fundamentally negative, or "bearish" stance, intending to "sell high and buy low," to reverse the conventional adage. The act of buying back the shares which were sold short is called 'covering the short'. Day traders and hedge funds often use short selling to allow them to profit on trading in stocks which they believe are overvalued, just as traditional long investors attempt to profit on stocks which are undervalued by buying those stocks.

In the U.S., in order to sell stocks short, the seller must arrange for a broker-dealer to confirm that it is able to make delivery of the shorted securities. This is referred to as a "locate." Brokers have a variety of means to borrow stocks in order to facilitate locates and make good delivery of the shorted security.

The vast majority of stock borrowed by U.S. brokers come from loans made by the leading custody banks and fund management companies (see list below). Sometimes brokers are able to borrow stocks from their customers who own "long" positions. In these cases, if the customer has fully paid for the long position, the broker cannot borrow the security without the express permission of the customer and the broker must provide the customer with collateral and pay a fee to the customer. In cases where the customer has not fully paid for the long position (meaning the customer borrowed money from the broker in order to finance the purchase of the security), the broker will not need to inform the customer that the long position is being used to effect delivery of another client's short sale.

Most brokers will allow retail customers to borrow shares to short a stock only if one of their own customers has purchased the stock on margin. Brokers will go through the "locate" process outside their own firm to obtain borrowed shares from other brokers only for their large institutional customers.

Stock exchanges such as the NYSE or the NASDAQ typically report the "short interest" of a stock, which gives the number of shares that have been sold short as a percent of the total float. Alternatively, these can also be expressed as the short interest ratio, which is the number of shares sold short as a multiple of the average daily volume. These can be useful tools to spot trends in stock price movements.

Example of Short Selling

For example, assume that shares in XYZ Company currently sell for $10 per share. A short seller would borrow 100 shares of XYZ Company, and then immediately sell those shares for a total of $1000. If the price of XYZ shares later falls to $8 per share, the short seller would then buy 100 shares back for $800, return the shares to their original owner (paying a fee for having borrowed the shares) and make a $200 profit (minus the fee for having borrowed the shares). This practice has the potential for losses as well. For example, if the shares of XYZ that one borrowed and sold in fact went up to $25, the short seller would have to buy back all the shares at $2500, losing $1500. Because a short is the opposite of a long (normal) transaction, everything is the mirror opposite compared to the typical trade: the profit is limited but the loss is unlimited. Since the stock cannot be repurchased at a price lower than zero, the maximum gain is the difference between the current stock price and zero. However, because there is no ceiling on how much the stock price can go up (thereby costing short transactions money in order to buy the stocks back), an investor can theoretically lose an arbitrarily large amount of money if a stock continues to rise. Also, in actual practice, as the price of XYZ Company began to rise, the short seller would eventually receive a margin call from the brokerage, demanding that the short seller either cover his short position or provide additional cash in order to meet the margin requirement for XYZ Company stock.

History of Short Selling

The first case of selling short dates back to 1609 and concerns Dutch trader Isaac Le Maire, a big share holder of the Vereenigde Oostindische Compagnie (VOC). In 1602 he invested about 85,000 guilders in the VOC. By 1609 the VOC still was not paying dividend and Le Maire's ships on the Baltic routes were under constant threats of attack by English ships due to trading conflicts between the British and the VOC. Le Maire decided to sell his shares and sold even more than he had. The notables speak of an outrageous act and this led to the first real stock exchange regulations: A ban on short selling. The ban was revoked a couple of years later.

Short selling has been a target of ire since at least the eighteenth century when England banned it outright. It was perceived as a magnifying effect in the violent downturn in the Dutch tulip market in the seventeenth century.

The term "short" was in use from at least the mid-nineteenth century. It is commonly understood that "short" is used because the short seller is in a deficit position with his brokerage house. Jacob Little was known as The Great Bear of Wall Street who began shorting stocks in the United States in 1822.

Short sellers were blamed for the Wall Street Crash of 1929. Regulations governing short selling were implemented in the United States in 1929 and in 1940. Political fallout from the 1929 crash led Congress to enact a law banning short sellers from selling shares during a downtick; this was known as the uptick rule, and was in effect until 2007. President Herbert Hoover condemned short sellers and even J. Edgar Hoover said he would investigate short sellers for their role in prolonging the Depression. Legislation introduced in 1940 banned mutual funds from short selling (this law was lifted in 1997). A few years later, in 1949, Alfred Winslow Jones founded a fund (that was unregulated) that bought stocks while selling other stocks short, hence hedging some of the market risk and the hedge fund was born.

Some typical examples of mass short-selling activity are during "bubbles", such as the Dot-com bubble. At such periods, short-sellers sell hoping for a market correction. Food and Drug Administration (FDA) announcements approving a drug often cause the market to react irrationally due to media attention. Short sellers use the opportunity to sell into the buying frenzy and wait for the exaggerated reaction to subside before covering their position. Negative news, such as litigation against a company will also entice professional traders to sell the stock short.

During the Dot-com bubble, shorting a start-up company could backfire since it could be taken over at a higher price than what speculators shorted. Short-sellers were forced to cover their positions at acquisition prices, while in many cases the firm often overpaid for the start-up.

In September of 2008 short selling was seen as a contributing factor to undesirable market volatility and subsequently was prohibited by the SEC for 799 financial companies in an effort to stabilize those companies. At the same time the U.K. FSA prohibited short selling for 32 financial companies. On September 22, Australia enacted even more extensive measures with a total ban of short selling. Also on September 22, the Spanish market regulator, CNMV, required investors to notify it of any short positions in financial institutions, if they exceed 0.25% of a company's share capital.

Mechanism of Short Selling

Short selling stock consists of the following:

- An investor borrows shares. If required by law, the investor first ensures that cash or equity is on deposit with his brokerage firm as collateral for the initial short margin requirement. Some short sellers, mainly firms and hedge funds, participate in "naked short" selling (see below), where the shorted shares are not borrowed or delivered.
- In either case the investor sells the shares and the proceeds are credited to his broker's account at the firm upon which the firm can

earn interest. Generally the short seller does not earn interest on the short proceeds.

- The investor may close the position by buying back the shares (called covering). If the price has dropped, he makes a profit. If the stock advanced he takes a loss.
- Finally, the investor may return the shares to the lender or stay short indefinitely.

Securities Lending

When a security is sold, the seller is contractually obliged to deliver it to the buyer. If a seller sells a security short without owning it first, the seller needs to borrow the security from a third party to fulfill its obligation. Otherwise, the seller will "fail to deliver," the transaction will not settle and the seller is subject to a claim from its counterparty. Certain large holders of securities, such as a custodian or investment management firm, often lend out these securities to gain extra income, a process known as securities lending. The lender receives a fee for this service. Similarly, retail investors can sometimes make an extra fee when their broker wants to borrow their securities. This is only possible when the investor has full title of the security, so it cannot be used as collateral for margin buying.

Sources of Short Interest Data

Time delayed short interest data is available in a number of countries, including the US, the UK, Hong Kong and Spain. Some market participants (like Data Explorers Limited) believe that stock lending data provides a good proxy for short interest levels. The amount of stocks being shorted on a global basis has increased in recent years for various structural reasons (e.g. the growth of 130/30 type strategies).

Short selling terms

Days to Cover (DTC) is a numerical term that describes the relationship between the amount of shares in a given equity that have been short sold and the number of days of typical trading that it would require to 'cover' all short positions outstanding. For example, if there are ten million shares of XYZ Inc. that are currently short sold and the average daily volume of XYZ shares traded each day is one million, it would require ten days of trading for all short positions to be covered (10 million / 1 million).

Short Interest is a numerical term that relates the number of shares in a given equity that have been shorted divided by the total shares outstanding for the company, usually expressed as a percent. For example, if there are ten million shares of XYZ Inc. that are currently short sold and the total number of shares issued by the company is one hundred million, the short interest is 10% (10 million / 100 million).

Naked Short Sale

A naked short sale occurs when a security is sold short without first ascertaining that one can borrow the security. In the US, making arrangements to borrow a security before a short sale is called a locate. In 2005, to prevent widespread failure to deliver securities, the U.S. Securities and Exchange Commission (SEC) put in place Regulation SHO, which prevents investors from selling some stocks short before doing a locate. More stringent requirements were put in place in September 2008 after claims that naked short selling was responsible for the failure of Lehman Brothers.

Fees

When a broker facilitates the delivery of a client's short sale, the client is charged a fee for this service, usually a standard commission similar to that of purchasing a similar security.

If the short position begins to move against the holder of the short position (i.e., the price of the security begins to rise), money will be removed from the holder's cash balance and moved to his or her margin balance. If short shares continue to rise in price, and the holder does not have sufficient funds in the cash account to cover the position, the holder will begin to borrow on margin for this purpose, thereby accruing margin interest charges. These are computed and charged just as for any other margin debit.

When a security's ex-dividend date passes, the dividend is deducted from the shortholder's account and paid to the person from whom the stock was borrowed.

For some brokers, the short seller may not earn interest on the proceeds of the short sale or use it to reduce outstanding margin debt. These brokers may not pass this benefit on to the retail client unless the client is very large. This means an individual short-selling $1000 of stock will lose the interest to be earned on the $1000 cash balance in his or her account.

Dividend & Short Selling

If the company distributes the dividend, the short seller is also "short the dividend". This is because he borrowed the stock shares and sold them to another investor. The investor he sold them to expects a dividend. The investor he borrowed the shares from expects a dividend also. This demonstrates that the "borrowing" is not really borrowing in the usual sense because the original shareholder has the use of the stock share, as demonstrated by the fact he still gets the dividend. (If John borrows Jim's shovel, Jim doesn't have use of his shovel anymore). Not so with the type of "borrowing" going on with stocks borrowed in order to short them.

Markets for Short Selling

Futures and Options Contracts

When trading futures contracts, being 'short' means having the legal obligation to deliver something at the expiration of the contract, although the holder of the short position may alternately buy back the contract prior to expiration instead of making delivery. Short futures transactions are often used by producers of a commodity to fix the future price of goods they have not yet produced. Shorting a futures contract is sometimes also used by those holding the underlying asset (i.e. those with a long position) as a temporary hedge against price declines. Shorting futures may also be used for speculative trades in which case the investor is looking to profit from any decline in the price of the futures contract prior to expiration.

An investor can also purchase a put option, giving that investor the right (but not the obligation) to sell the underlying asset (such as shares of stock) at a fixed price. In the event of a market decline, the option holder may exercise these put options, obliging the counterparty to buy the underlying asset at the agreed upon (or "strike") price, which would then be higher than the current quoted spot price of the asset.

Currency

Selling short on the currency markets is different from selling short on the stock markets. Currencies are traded in pairs, each currency being priced in terms of another, so there is no possibility for any single currency to get to zero. In this way selling short on the currency markets is identical to selling long on stocks.

Novice traders or stock traders can be confused by the failure to recognize and understand this point, A contract is always long in terms of one medium and short another.

When the exchange rate has changed the trader buys the first currency again; this time he gets more of it, and pays back the loan. Since he got more money than he had borrowed initially, he makes money. Of course, the reverse can also occur.

An example of this is as follows: Let us say a trader wants to trade with the dollar and the Indian rupee currencies. Assume that the current market rate is $1 to Rs.50 and the trader borrows Rs.100. With this, he buys $2. If the next day, the conversion rate becomes $1 to Rs.51, then the trader sells his $2 and gets Rs.102. He returns Rs.100 and keeps the Rs.2 profit.

One may also take a short position in a currency using futures or options; the preceding method is used to bet on the spot price, which is more directly analogous to selling a stock short.

Risk

Note: this section doesn't apply to currency markets.

It is important to note that buying shares (called "going long") has a very different risk profile from selling short. In the former case, losses are limited (the price can only go down to zero) but gains are unlimited (there is no limit on how high the price can go). In short selling, this is reversed, meaning the possible gains are limited (the stock can only go down to a price of zero), and the seller can lose more than the original value of the share, with no upper limit. For this reason, short selling is usually used as part of a hedge rather than as an investment in its own right.

Many short sellers place a "stop loss order" with their stockbroker after selling a stock short. This is an order to the brokerage to cover the position if the price of the stock should rise to a certain level, in order to limit the loss and avoid the problem of unlimited liability described above. In some cases, if the stock's price skyrockets, the stockbroker may decide to cover the short seller's position immediately and without his consent, in order to guarantee that the short seller will be able to make good on his debt of shares.

The risk of large potential losses through short selling inspired financier Daniel Drew to warn:

"He who sells what isn't his'n, must buy it back or go to pris'n"

Short selling is sometimes referred to as a "negative income investment strategy" because there is no potential for dividend income or interest income. One's return is strictly from capital gains.

Short sellers must be aware of the potential for a short squeeze. When the price of a stock rises significantly, some people who are short the stock will cover their positions to limit their losses (this may occur in an automated way if the short sellers had stop-loss orders in place with their brokers); others may be forced to close their position to meet a margin call. Others may be forced to cover, subject to the terms under which they borrowed the stock, if the person who lent the stock wishes to sell and take a profit. Since covering their positions involves buying shares, the short squeeze causes an ever further rise in the stock's price, which in turn may trigger additional covering. Because of this, most short sellers restrict their activities to heavily traded stocks, and they keep an eye on the "short interest" levels of their short investments. Short interest is defined as the total number of shares that have been sold short, but not yet covered.

On occasion, a short squeeze is deliberately induced. This can happen when a large investor (a company or a wealthy individual) notices significant short positions and buys many shares, with the intent of selling the position at a profit to the short sellers who will be panicked by the initial uptick or who are forced to cover their short positions in order to avoid margin calls.

Short sellers have to deliver the securities to their broker eventually. At that point they will need money to buy them, so there is a credit risk for the broker. To reduce this, the short seller has to keep a margin with the broker.

Short sellers tend to temper overvaluation by selling into exuberance. Likewise, short sellers often provide price support by buying when negative sentiment is exacerbated during a significant price decline. Short selling can have negative implications if it causes a premature or unjustified share price collapse when the fear of cancellation due to bankruptcy becomes contagious.

Finally, short sellers must remember that they are going against the overall upward direction of the market. This, combined with interest costs, can make it unattractive to keep a short position open for a long duration.

Strategies

Speculation

A seller intentionally takes on directional risk in the belief that the value of the shorted asset will fall.

Hedging

Short selling often represents a means of minimizing the risk from a more complex set of transactions. Examples of this are:

- a farmer who has just planted his wheat wants to lock in the price at which he can sell after the harvest. He would take a short position in wheat futures.
- a market maker in corporate bonds is constantly trading bonds when clients want to buy or sell. This can create substantial bond positions. The largest risk is that interest rates overall move. The trader can hedge this risk by selling government bonds short against his long positions in corporate bonds. In this way, the risk that remains is credit risk of the corporate bonds.
- an options trader may short shares in order to remain delta neutral so that he is not exposed to risk from price movements in the stocks that underlie his options

Arbitrage

A short seller may be trying to benefit from market inefficiencies arising from the mispricing of certain products. Examples of this are

- an arbitrageur who buys long futures contracts on a US Treasury security and sells short the underlying US Treasury security.

Against the Box

One variant of selling short involves a long position. "Selling short against the box" is holding a long position on which one enters a short sell order. The term box alludes to the days when a safe deposit box was used to store (long) shares. The purpose of this technique is to lock in paper profits on the long position without having to sell that position (and possibly incur taxes if said position has appreciated). Whether prices increase or decrease, the short position balances the long position and the profits are locked in (less brokerage fees and short financing costs).

U.S. investors considering entering into a "short against the box" transaction should be aware of the tax consequences of this transaction. Unless certain conditions are met, the IRS deems a "short against the box" position to be a "constructive sale" of the long position, which is a taxable event. These conditions include a requirement that the short position be closed out within 30 days of the end of the year and that the investor must hold their long position, without entering into any hedging strategies, for a minimum of 60 days after the short position has been closed.

Criticism

Short sellers are widely regarded with suspicion because, in the views of many people, they are profiting from the misfortune of others. Some businesses campaign against short sellers who target them, sometimes resulting in litigation.

Advocates of short sellers say that the practice is an essential part of the price discovery mechanism. They state that short-seller scrutiny of companies' finances has led to the discovery of instances of fraud which were glossed over or ignored by investors who had held the companies' stock long. Some hedge funds and short sellers claimed that the accounting of Enron and Tyco was suspicious months before their respective financial scandals emerged. Financial researchers at Duke University have provided statistically significant support for the assertion that short interest is an indicator of poor future stock performance and that short sellers exploit market mistakes about firms' fundamentals.

Such noted investors as Seth Klarman and Warren Buffett have said that short sellers help the market. Klarman argued that short sellers are a useful counterweight to the widespread bullishness on Wall Street, while Buffett believes that short sellers are useful in uncovering fraudulent accounting and other problems at companies. In response to the UK and US moves to ban short selling in September 18 and 19 of 2008, UBS stated:

> This can be characterized as a populist reaction of no positive value. Anyone who seriously thinks that the cause of this crisis arises from the actions of evil and manipulative speculators lacks the insight and knowledge to be allowed anywhere near the regulation of financial markets. Short selling may well exacerbate problems, but it was not the cause.
>
> —UBS Investment research's daily roundup

UBS expanded its opinion stating that the banning of short selling is a "policy error" that created problems, referring to the OECD bans of 2008.

The Regulatory Response

In the US, Regulation SHO was the SEC's first update to short selling restrictions since 1938. It established "locate" and "close-out" requirements for broker-dealers, in an effort to curb naked short selling. Compliance with the regulation began on January 3, 2005.

In the US, initial public offerings (IPOs) cannot be sold short for a month after they start trading. This mechanism is in place to ensure a degree of price stability during a company's initial trading period. However, some brokerages that specialize in penny stocks (referred to colloquially as bucket shops) have used the lack of short selling during this month to pump and dump thinly traded IPOs. Canada and other countries do allow selling IPOs (including U.S. IPOs) short.

In the UK, the Financial Services Authority has a moratorium on short selling 29 leading financial stocks, effective from 2300 GMT, 18 September 2008 until 16 January 2009.

In the US, a similar response was made by the Securities and Exchange Commission with a ban on short selling on 799 financial stocks from 19 September 2008 until 2 October 2008. Greater penalties for naked shorting, by mandating delivery of stocks at clearing time, were also introduced. Some state governors have been urging state pension bodies to refrain from lending stock for shorting purposes.

Soon thereafter, between 19 and 21 September 2008, Australia temporarily banned short selling, and later placed an indefinite ban on naked short selling. The ban on short selling was further extended for another 28 days on 21 October 2008.Germany, Ireland, Switzerland and Canada banned short selling leading financial stocks, and France, The Netherlands and Belgium banned naked short selling leading financial stocks.

By contrast, Chinese regulators have responded by allowing short selling, along with a package of other market reforms

Hedge

A hedge is a position established in one market in an attempt to offset exposure to the price risk of an equal but opposite obligation or position in another market — usually, but not always, in the context of one's commercial activity. Hedging is a strategy designed to minimize exposure to such business risks as a sharp contraction in demand for one's inventory, while still allowing the business to profit from producing and maintaining that inventory. A typical hedger might be a farmer with 2000 acres of unharvested wheat in the ground, who would rather tend her crop without the distraction of uncertain prices. She's a farmer, not a speculator, yet her unharvested "inventory" may have lost 35% of its value ($285,000) in the three months she's been planning her planting. She might have decided she could live with a price of only eight or nine dollars a bushel, and to offset her planted position with an approximately equal but opposite position in the market for wheat on the Minneapolis Grain Exchange by selling ten wheat futures contracts for December delivery. This farmer is thereby a hedger indifferent to the movements of the market as a whole, and has reduced her price risk to the difference between the price she will receive from a local buyer at harvest time, and the price at which she will simultaneously liquidate her obligation to the Exchange. Holbrook Working, a pioneer in hedging theory, called this strategy "speculation in the basis," where the basis is the difference between today's market value of (in this example) wheat and today's value of the hedge. If that difference widens, she earns a little more at harvest time. If that difference narrows, she earns a little less. She has mitigated, but not eliminated, the risk of losing the value of her wheat as of the day she established her hedge.

Some form of risk taking is inherent to any business activity. Some risks are considered to be "natural" to specific businesses, such as the risk of oil prices increasing or decreasing is natural to oil drilling and refining firms. Other forms of risk are not wanted, but cannot be avoided without hedging. Someone who has a shop, for example, expects to face natural risks such as the risk of competition, of poor or unpopular products, and so on. The risk of the shopkeeper's inventory being destroyed by fire is unwanted, however, and can be hedged via a fire insurance contract. Not all hedges are financial instruments: a producer that exports to another country, for example, may hedge its currency risk when selling by linking its expenses to the desired currency. Banks and other financial institutions use hedging to control their asset-liability mismatches, such as the maturity matches between long, fixed-rate loans and short-term (implicitly variable-rate) deposits.

A hedger (such as a manufacturing company) is thus distinguished from an arbitrageur or speculator (such as a bank or brokerage firm) in derivative purchase behavior.

Origins of Hedging

The term is derived from the phrase "hedging your bets" used in gambling games such as roulette. The hedges on a roulette table are the lines between numbers or number groups. Placing a hedged bet is one where the chips lie across one or more hedges (i.e. on a line between two numbers or on a corner between three or four numbers). The bet then covers all the numbers involved at an appropriately reduced stake (e.g. 1/2, 1/3, 1/4).

The term gradually moved into common usage within English-speaking cultures and today covers a broad range of risk-reduction activities or conditions.

In the finance lending industry, the term "hedge loan" has come to mean a specific type of financial product based on the melioration of price fluctuation risk in a stock portfolio serving as collateral for a nonrecourse debt structured stock loan.

Example Hedge

A stock trader believes that the stock price of Company A will rise over the next month, due to the company's new and efficient method of producing widgets. He wants to buy Company A shares to profit from their expected price increase. But Company A is part of the highly volatile widget industry. If the trader simply bought the shares based on his belief that the Company A shares were underpriced, the trade would be a speculation.

Since the trader is interested in the company, rather than the industry, he wants to hedge out the industry risk by short selling an equal value (number of shares × price) of the shares of Company A's direct competitor, Company B. If the trader was able to short sell an asset whose price had a mathematically defined relation with Company A's stock price (for example a call option on Company A shares) the trade might be essentially riskless and be called an arbitrage. But since some risk remains in the trade, it is said to be "hedged."

The first day the trader's portfolio is:

- Long 1000 shares of Company A at $1 each
- Short 500 shares of Company B at $2 each

(Notice that the trader has sold short the same value of shares.)

On the second day, a favorable news story about the widgets industry is published and the value of all widgets stock goes up. Company A, however, because it is a stronger company, goes up by 10%, while Company B goes up by just 5%:

- Long 1000 shares of Company A at $1.10 each – $100 gain
- Short 500 shares of Company B at $2.10 each – $50 loss

(In a short position, the investor loses money when the price goes up.)

The trader might regret the hedge on day two, since it reduced the profits on the Company A position. But on the third day, an unfavorable news story is published about the health effects of widgets, and all widgets stocks crash – 50% is wiped off the value of the widgets industry in the course of a few hours. Nevertheless, since Company A is the better company, it suffers less than Company B:

Value of long position (Company A):

- Day 1 – $1000
- Day 2 – $1100
- Day 3 – $550 => $450 loss

Value of short position (Company B):

- Day 1 – -$1000
- Day 2 – -$1050
- Day 3 – -$525

Without the hedge, the trader would have lost $450. But the hedge - the short sale of Company B - gives a profit of $475, for a net profit of $25 during a dramatic market collapse.

Types of Hedging

The example above is a "classic" sort of hedge, known in the industry as a "pairs trade" due to the trading on a pair of related securities. As investors became more sophisticated, along with the mathematical tools used to calculate values, known as models, the types of hedges have increased greatly.

Natural Hedges

Many hedges do not involve exotic financial instruments or derivatives. A natural hedge is an investment that reduces the undesired risk by matching cash flows, i.e. revenues and expenses. For example, an exporter to the United States faces a risk of changes in the value of the U.S. dollar and chooses to open a production facility in that market to match its expected sales revenue to its cost structure. Another example is a company that opens a subsidiary in another country and borrows in the local currency to finance its operations, even though the local interest rate may be more expensive than in its home country. By matching the debt payments to expected revenues in the local currency, the parent company has reduced its foreign currency exposure.

Similarly, an oil producer may expect to receive its revenues in U.S. dollars, but faces costs in a different currency. It would be applying a natural hedge if it agreed to, for example, pay bonuses to employees in U.S. dollars.

One of the oldest means of hedging against risk is the purchase of insurance to protect against financial loss due to accidental property damage or loss, personal injury, or loss of life.

Categories of Hedgeable Risk

For the following categories of the risk, for exporters, that the value of their accounting currency will fall against the value of the importers, also known as volatility risk.

- Interest rate risk – is the risk that the relative value of an interest-bearing asset, such as a loan or a bond, will worsen due to an interest rate increase. Interest rate risks can be hedged using fixed income instruments or interest rate swaps.

- Equity – the risk, or sometimes reward, for those whose assets are equity holdings, that the value of the equity falls
- Securities Lending - Hedged portfolio stock secured loan financing is a form of individual portfolio risk reduction that results typically in a limited recourse loan.

Futures contracts and forward contracts are a means of hedging against the risk of adverse market movements. These originally developed out of commodity markets in the nineteenth century, but over the last fifty years a huge global market developed in products to hedge financial market risk.

Hedging Credit Risk

Credit risk is the risk that money owing will not be paid by an obligor. Since credit risk is the natural business of banks, but an unwanted risk for commercial traders, naturally an early market developed between banks and traders: that involving selling obligations at a discounted rate.

Hedging Currency Risk

Currency hedging (also known as Foreign Exchange Risk hedging) is used both by financial investors to parse out the risks they encounter when investing abroad, as well as by non-financial actors in the global economy for whom multi-currency activities are a necessary evil rather than a desired state of exposure.

For example, labour costs are such that much of the simple commoditized manufacturing in the global economy today goes on in China and South-East Asia (Philippines, Vietnam, Indonesia, etc.). The cost benefit of moving manufacturing to outsource providers outweighs the uncertainties of doing business in foreign countries, so many businesses are moving manufacturing operations overseas. But the benefits of doing this have to be weighted also against currency risk.

If the price of manufacturing goods in another country is fixed in a currency other than the one that the finished goods will be sold for, there is the risk that changes in the values of each currency will reduce profit or produce a loss. Currency hedging is akin to insurance that limits the impact of foreign exchange risk.

Currency hedging is not always available, but is readily found at least in the major currencies of the world economy, the growing list of which qualify as major liquid markets beginning with the "Major Eight" (USD, GBP, EUR, JPY, CHF, HKD, AUD, CAD), which are also called the "Benchmark Currencies", and expands to include several others by virtue of liquidity.

Currency hedging, like many other forms of financial hedging, can be done in two primary ways:

- with standardized contracts, or
- with customized contracts (also known as over-the-counter or OTC).

The financial investor may be a hedge fund that decides to invest in a company in, for example, Brazil, but does not want to necessarily invest in the Brazilian currency. The hedge fund can separate out the credit risk (i.e. the risk of the company defaulting), from the currency risk of the Brazilian Real by "hedging" out the currency risk. In effect, this means that the investment is effectively a USD investment, in Brazil. Hedging allows the investor to transfer the currency risk to someone else, who wants to take up a position in the currency. The hedge fund has to pay this other investor to take on the currency exposure, similar to insuring against other types of events.

As with other types of financial products, hedging may allow economic activity to take place that would otherwise not have been possible (as a loan, for example, may allow an individual to purchase a home that would be "too expensive" if the individual had to pay cash). The increased investment is assumed in this way to raise economic efficiency.

Hedging Equity and Equity Futures

Equity in a portfolio can be hedged by taking an opposite position in futures. To protect your stock picking against systematic market risk, you short futures when you buy equity. Or long futures when you short stock.

There are many ways to hedge and one is the market neutral approach. In this approach, an equivalent dollar amount in the stock trade is taken in futures. Buy 10000 GBP worth of Vodafone and short 10000 worth of FTSE futures.

Another method to hedge is the beta neutral. Beta is the historical correlation between a stock and an index. If the beta of a Vodafone is 2, then for a 10000 GBP long position in Vodafone you will hedge with a 20000 GBP equivalent short position in the FTSE futures (the Index that Vodafone trades in).

Futures Hedging

If you primarily trade in futures, you hedge your futures against synthetic futures. A synthetic in this case is a synthetic future comprising a call and a put position. Long synthetic futures means long call and short put at the same expiry price. So if you are long futures in your trade you can hedge by shorting synthetics, and vice versa.

Contract for Difference

A contract for difference (CFD) is a two way hedge or swap contract that allows the seller and purchaser to fix the price of a volatile commodity. For instance, consider a deal between an electricity producer and an electricity retailer who both trade through an electricity market pool. If the producer and the retailer agree to a strike price of $50 per MWh, for 1 MWh in a trading period and if the actual pool price is $70, then the producer gets $70 from the pool but has to rebate $20 (the "difference" between the strike price and the pool price) to the retailer. Conversely, the retailer pays the difference to the producer if the pool price is lower than the agreed upon contractual strike price.

In effect, the pool volatility is nullified and the parties pay and receive $50 per MWh. However, the party who pays the difference is "out of the money" because without the hedge they would have received the benefit of the pool price.

Arbitrage

"Arbitrage" is a French word and denotes a decision by an arbitrator or arbitration tribunal. In economics and finance, arbitrage is the practice of taking advantage of a price differential between two or more markets. Striking a combination of matching deals that capitalize upon the imbalance, the profit being the difference between the market prices. When used by academics, an arbitrage is a transaction that involves no negative cash flow at any probabilistic or temporal state and a positive cash flow in at least one state; in simple terms, a risk-free profit. A person who engages in arbitrage is called an arbitrageur such as a bank or brokerage firm. The term is mainly applied to trading in financial instruments, such as bonds, stocks, derivatives, commodities and currencies.

If the market prices do not allow for profitable arbitrage, the prices are said to constitute an arbitrage equilibrium or arbitrage-free market. An arbitrage equilibrium is a precondition for a general economic equilibrium. The assumption that there is no arbitrage is used in quantitative finance to calculate a unique risk neutral price for derivatives.

Statistical arbitrage is an imbalance in expected nominal values. A casino has a statistical arbitrage in almost every game of chance that it offers - referred to as the house advantage, house edge, vigorish or house vigorish.

Conditions for Arbitrage

Arbitrage is possible when one of three conditions is met:

1. The same asset does not trade at the same price on all markets ("the law of one price").
2. Two assets with identical cash flows do not trade at the same price.
3. An asset with a known price in the future does not today trade at its future price discounted at the risk-free interest rate (or, the asset does not have negligible costs of storage; as such, for example, this condition holds for grain but not for securities).

Arbitrage is not simply the act of buying a product in one market and selling it in another for a higher price at some later time. The transactions must occur simultaneously to avoid exposure to market risk, or the risk that prices may change on one market before both transactions are complete. In practical terms, this is generally only possible with securities and financial products which can be traded electronically.

In the most simple example, any good sold in one market should sell for the same price in another. Traders may, for example, find that the price of wheat is lower in agricultural regions than in cities, purchase the good and transport it to another region to sell at a higher price. This type of price arbitrage is the most common, but this simple example ignores the cost of transport, storage, risk and other factors. "True" arbitrage requires that there be no market risk involved. Where securities are traded on more than one exchange, arbitrage occurs by simultaneously buying in one and selling on the other.

Mathematically it is defined as follows: $P(V_T \geq 0) = 1$ and $P(V_T \neq 0) > 0$ where V_t means a portfolio at time t.

Examples

- Suppose that the exchange rates (after taking out the fees for making the exchange) in London are £5 = \$10 = ¥1000 and the exchange rates in Tokyo are ¥1000 = \$12 = £6. Converting ¥1000 to \$12 in Tokyo and converting that \$12 into ¥1200 in London, for a profit of ¥200, would be arbitrage. In reality, this "triangle arbitrage" is so simple that it almost never occurs. But more complicated foreign exchange arbitrages, such as the spot-forward arbitrage are much more common.
- A common arbitrage involves borrowing at lower short term rates and investing at higher long term interest rates while pocketing the spread. The risk is that short term loan rates rise higher.
- One example of arbitrage involves the New York Stock Exchange and the Chicago Mercantile Exchange. When the price of a stock on the NYSE and its corresponding futures contract on the CME are out of sync, one can buy the less expensive one and sell it to the more expensive market. Because the differences between the prices are likely to be small (and not to last very long), this can only be done profitably with computers examining a large number of prices and automatically exercising a trade when the prices are far enough out of balance. The activity of other arbitrageurs can make this risky. Those with the fastest computers and the smartest mathematicians take advantage of series of small differentials that would not be profitable if taken individually.
- Economists use the term "global labor arbitrage" to refer to the tendency of manufacturing jobs to flow towards whichever country has the lowest wages per unit output at present and has reached the minimum requisite

level of political and economic development to support industrialization. At present, many such jobs appear to be flowing towards China, though some which require command of English are going to India and the Philippines. In popular terms, this is referred to as offshoring. (Note that "offshoring" is not synonymous with "outsourcing", which means "to subcontract from an outside supplier or source", such as when a business outsources its bookkeeping to an accounting firm. Unlike offshoring, outsourcing always involves subcontracting jobs to a different company, and that company can be in the same country as the outsourcing company.)

- Sports arbitrage - numerous internet bookmakers offer odds on the outcome of the same event. Any given bookmaker will weight their odds so that no one customer can cover all outcomes at a profit against their books. However, in order to remain competitive their margins are usually quite low. Different bookmakers may offer different odds on the same outcome of a given event; by taking the best odds offered by each bookmaker, a customer can under some circumstances cover all possible outcomes of the event and lock a small risk-free profit, known as a Dutch book. This profit would typically be between 1% and 5% but can be much higher. One problem with sports arbitrage is that bookmakers sometimes make mistakes and this can lead to an invocation of the 'palpable error' rule, which most bookmakers invoke when they have made a mistake by offering or posting incorrect odds. As bookmakers become more proficient, the odds of making an 'arb' usually last for less than an hour and typically only a few minutes. Furthermore, huge bets on one side of the market also alert the bookies to correct the market.
- Exchange-traded fund arbitrage - Exchange Traded Funds allow authorized participants to exchange back and forth between shares in underlying securities held by the fund and shares in the fund itself, rather than allowing the buying and selling of shares in the ETF directly with the fund sponsor. ETFs trade in the open market, with prices set by market demand. An ETF may trade at a premium or discount to the value of the underlying assets. When a significant enough premium appears, an arbitrageur will buy the underlying securities, convert them to shares in the ETF, and sell them in the open market. When a discount appears, an arbitrageur will do the reverse. In this way, the arbitrageur makes a low-risk profit, while fulfilling a useful function in the ETF marketplace by keeping ETF prices in line with their underlying value.
- Some types of hedge funds make use of a modified form of arbitrage to profit. Rather than exploiting price differences between identical assets, they will purchase and sell securities, assets and derivatives with similar characteristics, and hedge any significant differences between the two assets. Any difference between the hedged positions represents any remaining risk (such as basis risk) plus profit; the belief is that there remains some difference which, even after hedging most risk, represents pure profit. For example, a fund may see that there is a substantial difference

between U.S. dollar debt and local currency debt of a foreign country, and enter into a series of matching trades (including currency swaps) to arbitrage the difference, while simultaneously entering into credit default swaps to protect against country risk and other types of specific risk.

Price Convergence

Arbitrage has the effect of causing prices in different markets to converge. As a result of arbitrage, the currency exchange rates, the price of commodities and the price of securities in different markets tend to converge to the same prices, in all markets, in each category. The speed at which prices converge is a measure of market efficiency. Arbitrage tends to reduce price discrimination by encouraging people to buy an item where the price is low and resell it where the price is high, as long as the buyers are not prohibited from reselling and the transaction costs of buying, holding and reselling are small relative to the difference in prices in the different markets.

Arbitrage moves different currencies toward purchasing power parity. As an example, assume that a car purchased in the United States is cheaper than the same car in Canada. Canadians would buy their cars across the border to exploit the arbitrage condition. At the same time, Americans would buy US cars, transport them across the border and sell them in Canada. Canadians would have to buy American Dollars to buy the cars and Americans would have to sell the Canadian dollars they received in exchange for the exported cars. Both actions would increase demand for US Dollars, and supply of Canadian Dollars, and as a result, there would be an appreciation of the US Dollar. Eventually, if unchecked, this would make US cars more expensive for all buyers, and Canadian cars cheaper, until there is no longer an incentive to buy cars in the US and sell them in Canada. More generally, international arbitrage opportunities in commodities, goods, securities and currencies, on a grand scale, tend to change exchange rates until the purchasing power is equal.

In reality, of course, one must consider taxes and the costs of travelling back and forth between the US and Canada. Also, the features built into the cars sold in the US are not exactly the same as the features built into the cars for sale in Canada, due, among other things, to the different emissions and other auto regulations in the two countries. In addition, our example assumes that no duties have to be paid on importing or exporting cars from the USA to Canada. Similarly, most assets exhibit (small) differences between countries, transaction costs, taxes, and other costs provide an impediment to this kind of arbitrage.

Similarly, arbitrage affects the difference in interest rates paid on government bonds, issued by the various countries, given the expected depreciations in the currencies, relative to each other.

Risks

Arbitrage transactions in modern securities markets involve fairly low risks. Generally it is impossible to close two or three transactions at the same instant. Therefore, there is the possibility that when one part of the deal is closed, a quick shift in prices makes it impossible to close the other at a profitable price. There is also counter-party risk, that the other party to one of the deals fails to deliver as agreed. Though unlikely, this hazard is serious because of the large quantities one must trade in order to make a profit on small price differences. These risks become magnified when leverage or borrowed money is used.

Another risk occurs if the items being bought and sold are not identical and the arbitrage is conducted under the assumption that the prices of the items are correlated or predictable. In the extreme case this is risk arbitrage, described below. In comparison to the classical quick arbitrage transaction, such an operation can produce disastrous losses.

Competition in the marketplace can also create risks during arbitrage transactions. As an example, if one was trying to profit from a price discrepancy between IBM on the NYSE and IBM on the London Stock Exchange, they may purchase a large number of shares on the NYSE and find that they cannot simultaneously sell on the LSE. This leaves the arbitrageur in an unhedged risk position.

In the 1980s, risk arbitrage was common. In this form of speculation, one trades a security that is clearly undervalued or overvalued, when it is seen that the wrong valuation is about to be corrected by events. The standard example is the stock of a company, undervalued in the stock market, which is about to be the object of a takeover bid. The price of the takeover will more truly reflect the value of the company, giving a large profit to those who bought at the current price—if the merger goes through as predicted. Traditionally, arbitrage transactions in the securities markets involve high speed and low risk. At some moment a price difference exists, and the problem is to execute two or three balancing transactions while the difference persists (that is, before the other arbitrageurs act). When the transaction involves a delay of weeks or months, as above, it may entail considerable risk if borrowed money is used to magnify the reward through leverage. One way of reducing the risk is through the illegal use of inside information, and in fact risk arbitrage with regard to leveraged buyouts was associated with some of the famous financial scandals of the 1980s such as those involving Michael Milken and Ivan Boesky.

Types of Arbitrage

Merger Arbitrage

Also called risk arbitrage, merger arbitrage generally consists of buying the stock of a company that is the target of a takeover while shorting the stock of the acquiring company.

Usually the market price of the target company is less than the price offered by the acquiring company. The spread between these two prices depends mainly on the probability and the timing of the takeover being completed as well as the prevailing level of interest rates.

The bet in a merger arbitrage is that such a spread will eventually be zero, if and when the takeover is completed. The risk is that the deal "breaks" and the spread massively widens.

Municipal Bond Arbitrage

Also called municipal bond relative value arbitrage, municipal arbitrage, or just muni arb, this hedge fund strategy involves one of two approaches.

Generally, managers seek relative value opportunities by being both long and short municipal bonds with a duration-neutral book. The relative value trades may be between different issuers, different bonds issued by the same entity, or capital structure trades referencing the same asset (in the case of revenue bonds). Managers aim to capture the inefficiencies arising from the heavy participation of non-economic investors (i.e., high income "buy and hold" investors seeking tax-exempt income) as well as the "crossover buying" arising from corporations' or individuals' changing income tax situations (i.e., insurers switching their munis for corporates after a large loss as they can capture a higher after-tax yield by offsetting the taxable corporate income with underwriting losses). There are additional inefficiencies arising from the highly fragmented nature of the municipal bond market which has two million outstanding issues and 50,000 issuers in contrast to the Treasury market which has 400 issues and a single issuer.

Second, managers construct leveraged portfolios of AAA- or AA-rated tax-exempt municipal bonds with the duration risk hedged by shorting the appropriate ratio of taxable corporate bonds. These corporate equivalents are typically interest rate swaps referencing Libor or SIFMA(Security Industry and Financial Markets Association) (merged with and preceded by BMA (short for Bond Market Association])). The arbitrage manifests itself in the form of a relatively cheap longer maturity municipal bond, which is a municipal bond that yields significantly more than 65% of a corresponding taxable corporate bond. The steeper slope of the municipal yield curve allows participants to collect more after-tax income from the municipal bond portfolio than is spent on the interest rate swap; the carry is greater than the hedge expense. Positive, tax-free carry from muni arb can reach into the double digits. The bet in this municipal bond arbitrage is that, over a longer period of time, two similar instruments--municipal bonds and interest rate swaps--will correlate with each other; they are both very high quality credits, have the same maturity and are denominated in U.S. dollars. Credit risk and duration risk are largely eliminated in this strategy. However, basis risk arises from use of an imperfect hedge, which results in significant, but range-bound principal volatility. The end goal is to limit this principal volatility, eliminating its relevance over time as the high, consistent, tax-free cash flow accumulates. Since the inefficiency is related to government tax policy and hence is structural in nature, it has not been arbitraged away.

Convertible Bond Arbitrage

A convertible bond is a bond that an investor can return to the issuing company in exchange for a predetermined number of shares in the company.

A convertible bond can be thought of as a corporate bond with a stock call option attached to it.

The price of a convertible bond is sensitive to three major factors:

- interest rate. When rates move higher, the bond part of a convertible bond tends to move lower, but the call option part of a convertible bond moves higher (and the aggregate tends to move lower).
- stock price. When the price of the stock the bond is convertible into moves higher, the price of the bond tends to rise.
- credit spread. If the creditworthiness of the issuer deteriorates (e.g. rating downgrade) and its credit spread widens, the bond price tends

to move lower, but, in many cases, the call option part of the convertible bond moves higher (since credit spread correlates with volatility).

Given the complexity of the calculations involved and the convoluted structure that a convertible bond can have, an arbitrageur often relies on sophisticated quantitative models in order to identify bonds that are trading cheap versus their theoretical value.

Convertible arbitrage consists of buying a convertible bond and hedging two of the three factors in order to gain exposure to the third factor at a very attractive price.

For instance an arbitrageur would first buy a convertible bond, then sell fixed income securities or interest rate futures (to hedge the interest rate exposure) and buy some credit protection (to hedge the risk of credit deterioration). Eventually what he'd be left with is something similar to a call option on the underlying stock, acquired at a very low price. He could then make money either selling some of the more expensive options that are openly traded in the market or delta hedging his exposure to the underlying shares.

Depository Receipts

A depository receipt is a security that is offered as a "tracking stock" on another foreign market. For instance a Chinese company wishing to raise more money may issue a depository receipt on the New York Stock Exchange, as the amount of capital on the local exchanges is limited. These securities, known as ADRs (American Depositary Receipt) or GDRs (Global Depositary Receipt) depending on where they are issued, are typically considered "foreign" and therefore trade at a lower value when first released. However, they are exchangeable into the original security (known as fungibility) and actually have the same value. In this case there is a spread between the perceived value and real value, which can be extracted. Since the ADR is trading at a value lower than what it is worth, one can purchase the ADR and expect to make money as its value converges on the original. However there is a chance that the original stock will fall in value too, so by shorting it you can hedge that risk.

Dual-Listed Companies

A dual-listed company (DLC) structure involves two companies incorporated in different countries contractually agreeing to operate their businesses as if they were a single enterprise, while retaining their separate legal identity and existing stock exchange listings. In integrated and efficient financial markets, stock prices of the twin pair should move in lockstep. In practice, DLC share prices exhibit large deviations from theoretical parity. Arbitrage positions in DLCs can be set-up by obtaining a long position in the relatively underpriced part of the DLC and a short position in the relatively overpriced part. Such arbitrage strategies start paying off as soon as the relative prices of the two DLC stocks converge toward theoretical parity. However, since there is no identifiable date at which DLC prices will converge, arbitrage positions sometimes have to be kept open for considerable periods of time. In the meantime, the price gap might widen. In these situations, arbitrageurs may receive margin calls, after which they would most likely be forced to liquidate part of the position at a highly unfavorable moment and suffer a loss. Arbitrage in DLCs may be profitable, but is also very risky.

A good illustration of the risk of DLC arbitrage is the position in Royal Dutch Shell - which had a DLC structure until 2005 - by the hedge fund Long-Term Capital Management (LTCM, see also the discussion below). Lowenstein (2000) describes that LTCM established an arbitrage position in Royal Dutch Shell in the summer of 1997, when Royal Dutch traded at an 8 to 10 percent premium. In total $2.3 billion was invested, half of which long in Shell and the other half short in Royal Dutch (Lowenstein). In the autumn of 1998 large defaults on Russian debt created significant losses for the hedge fund and LTCM had to unwind several positions. Lowenstein reports that the premium of Royal Dutch had increased to about 22 percent and LTCM had to close the position and incur a loss. According to Lowenstein, LTCM lost $286 million in equity pairs trading and more than half of this loss is accounted for by the Royal Dutch Shell trade.

Regulatory arbitrage

Regulatory arbitrage is where a regulated institution takes advantage of the difference between its real (or economic) risk and the regulatory position. For example, if a bank, operating under the Basel I accord, has to hold 8% capital against default risk, but the real risk of default is lower, it is profitable to securitize the loan, removing the low risk loan from its portfolio. On the other hand, if the real risk is higher than the regulatory risk then it is profitable to make that loan and hold on to it, provided it is priced appropriately.

This process can increase the overall riskiness of institutions under a risk insensitive regulatory regime, as described by Alan Greenspan in his October 1998 speech on The Role of Capital in Optimal Banking Supervision and Regulation.

In economics, regulatory arbitrage (sometimes, tax arbitrage) may be used to refer to situations when a company can choose a nominal place of business with a regulatory, legal or tax regime with lower costs. For example, an insurance company may choose to locate in Bermuda due to preferential tax rates and policies for insurance companies. This can occur particularly where the business transaction has no obvious physical location. In the case of many financial products, it may be unclear "where" the transaction occurs.

Telecom Arbitrage

Telecom arbitrage companies allow mobile phone users to make international calls for free through certain access numbers. The telecommunication arbitrage companies get paid an interconnect charge by the UK mobile networks and then buy international routes at a lower cost. The calls are seen as free by the UK contract mobile phone customers since they are using up their allocated monthly minutes rather than paying for additional calls. The end effect is telecom arbitrage. This is usually marketed as "free international calls". The profit margins are usually very small. However, with enough volume, enough money is made from the cost difference to turn a profit.

Swing Trading

Swing trading sits in the middle of the continuum between day trading and trend following. Swing traders hold a particular stock for a period of time, generally between a few days and two or three weeks, and trade the stock on the basis of its intra-week or intra-month oscillations between optimism and pessimism.

It should be noted that in either of the two market extremes, the bear-market environment or bull market, swing trading proves to be a rather different challenge than in a market that is between these two extremes. In these extremes, even the most active stocks will not exhibit the same up-and-down oscillations that they would when indices are relatively stable for a few weeks or months. In a bear market or a bull market, momentum will generally carry stocks for a long period of time in one direction only, thereby ensuring that the best strategy will be to trade on the basis of the longer-term directional trend.

The swing trader, therefore, is best positioned when markets are going nowhere—when indices rise for a couple of days and then decline for the next few days, only to repeat the same general pattern again and again. A couple of months might pass with major stocks and indices roughly the same as their original levels, but the swing trader has had many opportunities to catch the short terms movements up and down (sometimes within a channel).

Of course, the problem with both swing trading and long-term trend following is that success is based on correctly identifying what type of market is currently being experienced. Looking back over the past few years, trend following would have been the ideal strategy for the raging bull market of the last half of the 1990s, while swing trading probably would have been best for 2000 and 2001. With the 2002 bear market, the best strategy would have been to follow the trend and short everything in sight. As economists and traders would agree, the most accurate insight into trends is viewed in retrospect.

Much research on historical data has proven that in a market conducive to swing trading, liquid stocks tend to trade above and below a baseline value, which is portrayed on a chart with an exponential moving average (EMA). In his book "Come Into My Trading Room: A Complete Guide to Trading" Alexander Elder uses his understanding of a stock's behavior above and below the baseline to describe the swing trader's strategy of "buying normalcy and selling mania" or "shorting normalcy and covering depression." Once the swing trader has used the EMA to identify the typical baseline on the stock chart, he or she goes long at the baseline when the stock is heading up and short at the baseline when the stock is on its way down.

So, swing traders are not looking to hit the home run with a single trade—they are not concerned about perfect timing to buy a stock exactly at its bottom and sell exactly at its top (or vice versa). In a perfect trading environment, they wait for the stock to hit its baseline and confirm its direction before they make their moves. The story gets more complicated when a stronger up-trend or down-trend is at play. The trader may paradoxically go long when the stock jumps below its EMA and wait for the stock to go back up in an uptrend, or he or she may short a stock that has stabbed above the EMA and wait for it to drop if the longer trend is down.

When it comes time to take profits, the swing trader will want to exit the trade as close as possible to the upper or lower channel line without being overly precise, which may cause the risk of missing the best opportunity. In a strong market, when a stock is exhibiting a strong directional trend, traders can wait for the channel line to be reached before taking their profit, but in a weaker market they may take their profits before the line is hit (in the event that the direction changes and the line does not get hit on that particular swing).

Swing trading, while a good trading style for beginning traders, still offers significant profit potential for intermediate and advanced traders. Swing traders can realize sufficient rewards on their trades after a couple of days, which keep them motivated, but their long and short positions of several days are of ideal duration so as to not lead to distraction. By contrast, trend following offers greater profit potential if a trader is able to catch a major market trend of weeks or months, but there are few traders with sufficient discipline to hold a position for that period of time without getting distracted. On the other hand, trading dozens of stocks per day (day trading) may just prove too great a white-knuckle ride for some, making swing trading the perfect medium between the extremes.

The risks involved

There is a risk that prices will break the channel and that swing traders buy or sell at the worst time

Noise Trader

A noise trader is a stock trader that does not have any specific information of the security. If the efficient market hypothesis holds, NTs add liquidity to a market while not distorting valuations. The concept of noise traders is one of the central aspects Behavioral Finance is based on.

In fact, a market without noise traders will tend to break down, because prices in such a market will become fully revealing. Informed traders will not enter a market without noises, because it is impossible to profit from trading in a completely efficient market. Informed traders need the existence of noise traders to "hide" their trades and by trading on their private information, informed traders make profits. Through trading, informed traders gradually release relevant information to the market prices and together with the noise traders, they help bring the market back to equilibrium.

Some Behavioral Finance articles point out that the risk generated by noise traders can lead to limited arbitrage. Thus, the presence of noise traders undermines the classical no-arbitrage reasoning. However, whether noise traders can survive in the long run and if they can, how much of a pricing distortion they create, are still open questions.

Day Trader

A day trader is a trader who buys and sells financial instruments (e.g. stocks, options, futures, derivatives, currencies) within the same trading day such that all positions will usually be closed before the market close of the trading day. This trading style is called day trading. Depending on one's trading strategy, it may range from several to hundreds of orders a day.

Types of Day Traders

There are 2 major types of day traders: institutional and retail.

An **institutional day trader** is a trader who works for financial institution. This type of trader has certain advantages over retail traders as he/she generally has access to more resources, tools, equipment, large amounts of capital and leverage, large availability of fresh fund inflows to trade continuously on the markets, dedicated and direct lines to data centers and exchanges, expensive and high-end trading and analytical software, support teams to help and more. All these advantages give them certain edges over retail day traders.

A **retail day trader** is a trader who works for himself, or in partnership with a few other traders. A retail trader generally trades with his own capital, though he may also trade with other people's money. Law has restricted the amount of other people's money a retail trader can manage. In the United States, day traders may not advertise as advisors or financial managers. Although not required, nearly all retail day traders use direct access brokers as they offer the fastest order entry and to the exchanges, as well as superior software trading platforms.

In the past, most day traders were institutional traders due to the huge advantages they had over retail traders. However, since the technology boom in the second half of the 1990s, advances in personal computing and communications technology, realized in the accessibility of powerful personal computers and the Internet, have brought fast online trading and powerful market analytical tools to the mainstream. Low, affordable commissions from discount brokers as well as regulation improvements in favor of retail traders have also helped level the trading playing field, making success as a retail trader a possibility for many and a reality for some.

Day Trading

Day trading refers to the practice of buying and selling financial instruments within the same trading day such that all positions are usually closed before the market close of the trading day. Traders that participate in day trading are called day traders.

Some of the more commonly day-traded financial instruments are stocks, stock options, currencies, and a host of futures contracts such as equity index futures, interest rate futures, and commodity futures.

Day trading used to be the preserve of financial firms and professional investors and speculators. Many day traders are bank or investment firm employees working as specialists in equity investment and fund management. However, with the advent of electronic trading and margin trading, day trading has become increasingly popular among casual, at home traders.

Characteristics

Trade Frequency

Although collectively called day trading, there are many sub-trading styles within day trading. A day trader is actively searching for potential trading setups (that is, any stock or other financial instruments that, in the judgment of the day trader, is in a tension state, ready to move in price, that when traded well has a potential for a profit). Depending on one's trading system (game), strategy, the number of trades the trader can make a day may vary from none to dozens.

Some day traders focus on very short-term trading within the trading day, in which a trade may last just a few minutes. Day traders may buy and sell many times in a trading day and may receive trading fee discounts from their broker for trading volume.

Some day traders focus only on price momentum, others on technical patterns and still others on an unlimited number of strategies they feel can be profitable.

Day traders exit positions before the market closes to avoid any and all unmanageable risks --- negative price gaps (differences between the previous day's close and the next day's open price) at the open --- overnight price movements against the position held. Day traders, like all traders, have their rules.

Other traders believe they should let the profits run, so it is acceptable to stay with a position after the market closes.

Day traders sometimes borrow money to trade. This is called margin trading. Since margin interests are typically only charged on overnight balances, there is no cost to the day trader for the margin benefit.

Profit and Risks

Because of the nature of financial leverage and the rapid returns that are possible, day trading can be either extremely profitable or extremely unprofitable and high-risk profile traders can generate either huge percentage returns or huge percentage losses. Some day traders manage to earn millions per year solely by day trading.

Because of the high profits (and losses) that day trading makes possible, these traders are sometimes portrayed as "bandits" or "gamblers" by other investors. Some individuals, however, make a consistent living from day trading.

Nevertheless day trading can be very risky, especially if any of the following is present while trading:

- trading a loser's game/system rather than a game that's at least winnable,
- trading with poor discipline (ignoring your own day trading strategy, tactics, rules),
- inadequate risk capital with the accompanying excess stress of having to "survive",
- incompetent money management (i.e. executing trades poorly).

The common use of buying on margin (using borrowed funds) amplifies gains and losses, such that substantial losses or gains can occur in a very short period of time. In addition, brokers usually allow bigger margins for day traders. Where overnight margins required to hold a stock position are normally 50% of the stock's value, many brokers allow pattern day trader accounts to use levels as low as 25% for intraday purchases. This means a day trader with the legal minimum $25,000 in his or her account can buy $100,000 worth of stock during the day, as long as half of those positions are exited before the market close. Because of the high risk of margin use and of other day trading practices, a day trader will often have to exit a losing position very quickly, in order to prevent a greater, unacceptable loss, or even a disastrous loss, much larger than his or her original investment, or even larger than his or her total assets.

History of Day Trading

Originally, the most important U.S. stocks were traded on the New York Stock Exchange. A trader would contact a stockbroker, who would relay the order to a specialist on the floor of the NYSE. These specialists would each make markets in only a handful of stocks. The specialist would match the purchaser with another broker's seller; write up physical tickets that, once processed, would effectively transfer the stock; and relay the information back to both brokers. Brokerage commissions were fixed at 1% of the amount of the trade, i.e. to purchase $10,000 worth of stock cost the buyer $100 in commissions.

One of the first steps to make day trading of shares potentially profitable was the change in the commission scheme. In 1975, the United States Securities and Exchange Commission (SEC) made fixed commission rates illegal, giving rise to discount brokers offering much reduced commission rates.

Financial Settlement

Financial settlement periods used to be much longer: Before the early 1990s at the London Stock Exchange, for example, stock could be paid for up to 10 working days after it was bought, allowing traders to buy (or sell) shares at the beginning of a settlement period only to sell (or buy) them before the end of the period hoping for a rise (or fall) in price. This activity was identical to modern day trading, but for the longer duration of the settlement period. But today, to reduce market risk, the settlement period is typically three working days. Reducing the settlement period reduces the likelihood of default, but was impossible before the advent of electronic ownership transfer.

Electronic Communication Networks

The systems by which stocks are traded have also evolved, the second half of the twentieth century having seen the advent of Electronic Communication Networks (ECNs). These are essentially large proprietary computer networks on which brokers could list a certain amount of securities to sell at a certain price (the asking price or "ask") or offer to buy a certain amount of securities at a certain price (the "bid").

ECNs and exchanges are usually known to traders by a three- or four-letter designators, which identify the ECN or exchange on Level II stock screens. The first of these was Instinet (or "inet"), which was founded in 1969 as a way for major institutions to bypass the increasingly cumbersome and expensive NYSE, also allowing them to trade during hours when the exchanges were closed. Early ECNs such as Instinet were very unfriendly to small investors, because they tended to give large institutions better prices than were available to the public. This resulted in a fragmented and sometimes illiquid market.

The next important step in facilitating day trading was the founding in 1971 of NASDAQ --- a virtual stock exchange on which orders were transmitted electronically. Moving from paper share certificates and written share registers to "dematerialized" shares, computerized trading and registration required not only extensive changes to legislation but also the development of the necessary technology: online and real time systems rather than batch. Electronic communications rather than the postal service, telex or the physical shipment of computer tapes and the development of secure cryptographic algorithms.

These developments heralded the appearance of "market makers": the NASDAQ equivalent of a NYSE specialist. A market maker has an inventory of stocks to buy and sell, and simultaneously offers to buy and sell the same stock. Obviously, it will offer to sell stock at a higher price than the price at which it offers to buy. This difference is known as the "spread". It is of no importance to the market-maker whether the price of a stock goes up or down, as it has enough stock and capital to constantly buy for less than it sells. Today there are about 500 firms who participate as market-makers on ECNs, each generally making a market in four to forty different stocks. Without any legal obligations, market-makers were free to offer smaller spreads on ECNs than on the NASDAQ. A small investor might have to pay a $0.25 spread (e.g. he might have to pay $10.50 to buy a share of stock but could only get $10.25 for selling it), while an institution would only pay a $0.05 spread (buying at $10.40 and selling at $10.35).

Technology Bubble (1997–2000)

In 1997, the SEC adopted "Order Handling Rules" which required market-makers to publish their best bid and ask on the NASDAQ. Another reform made during this period was the "Small Order Execution System", or "SOES", which required market makers to buy or sell, immediately, small orders (up to 1000 shares) at the MM's listed bid or ask. A defect in the system gave rise to arbitrage by a small group of traders known as the "SOES bandits", who made fortunes buying and selling small orders to market makers.

The existing ECNs began to offer their services to small investors. New brokerage firms which specialized in serving online traders who wanted to trade on the ECNs emerged. New ECNs also arose, most importantly Archipelago ("arca") and Island ("isld"). Archipelago eventually became a stock exchange and in 2005 was purchased by the NYSE. (At this time, the NYSE has proposed merging Archipelago with itself, although some resistance has arisen from NYSE members.) Commissions plummeted. To give an extreme example (trading 1000 shares of Google), an online trader in 2005 might have bought $300,000 of stock at a commission of about $10, compared to the $3,000 commission the trader would have paid in 1974. Moreover, the trader was able in 2005 to buy the stock almost instantly and got it at a cheaper price.

ECNs are in constant flux. New ones are formed, while existing ones are bought or merged. As of the end of 2006, the most important ECNs to the individual trader were:

- Instinet (which bought Island in 2005),
- Archipelago (although technically it is now an exchange rather than an ECN),
- the Brass Utility ("brut"), and
- the SuperDot electronic system now used by the NYSE.

This combination of factors has made day trading in stocks and stock derivatives (such as ETFs) possible. The low commission rates allow an individual or small firm to make a large number of trades during a single day. The liquidity and small spreads provided by ECNs allow an individual to make near-instantaneous trades and to get favorable pricing. High-volume issues such as Intel or Microsoft generally have a spread of only $0.01, so the price only needs to move a few pennies for the trader to cover his commission costs and show a profit.

The ability for individuals to day trade coincided with the extreme bull market in technological issues from 1997 to early 2000, known as the Dot-com bubble. From 1997 to 2000, the NASDAQ rose from 1200 to 5000. Many naive investors with little market experience made huge profits buying these stocks in the morning and selling them in the afternoon, at 400% margin rates.

Adding to the day-trading frenzy were the enormous profits made by the "SOES bandits" who, unlike the new day traders, were highly-experienced professional traders able to exploit the arbitrage opportunity created by SOES.)

In March, 2000, this bubble burst and a large number of less-experienced day traders began to lose money as fast, or faster, than they had made during the buying frenzy. The NASDAQ crashed from 5000 back to 1200; many of the less-experienced traders went broke, although a small minority of traders made fortunes shorting the market all the way down.

Techniques

The following are several basic strategies by which day traders attempt to make profits. Besides these, some day traders also use contrarian (reverse) strategies (more commonly seen in algorithmic trading) to trade specifically against irrational behavior from day traders using these approaches.

Some of these approaches require shorting stocks instead of buying them normally: In this case the trader borrows stock from his broker and sells the borrowed stock, hoping that the price will fall and he will be able to purchase the shares at a lower price. There are several technical problems with short sales --- the broker may not have shares to lend in a specific issue, some short sales can only be made if the stock price or bid has just risen (known as an "uptick"), and the broker can call for the return of its shares at any time. Some of these restrictions (in particular the uptick rule) don't apply to trades of stocks that are actually shares of an exchange-traded fund (ETF).

The Securities and Exchange Commission removed the uptick requirement for short sales on July 6, 2007.

Trend Following

Trend following, a strategy used in all trading time-frames, assumes that financial instruments which have been rising steadily will continue to rise, and vice versa with falling. The trend follower buys an instrument which has been rising, or short-sells a falling one, in the expectation that the trend will continue.

Contrarian Investing

Contrarian investing is a market timing strategy used in all trading time-frames. It assumes that financial instruments which have been rising steadily will reverse and start to fall, and vice versa with falling. The contrarian trader buys an instrument which has been falling, or short-sells a rising one, in the expectation that the trend will change.

Range Trading

Range trading is a trading style in which stocks are watched that have either been rising off a support price or falling off a resistance price. That is, every time the stock hits a high, it falls back to the low and vice versa. Such a stock is said to be "trading in a range", which is the opposite of trending. The range trader therefore buys the stock at or near the low price and sells (and possibly short sells) at the high. A related approach to range trading is looking for moves outside of an established range, called a breakout (price moves up) or a breakdown (price moves down) and assume that once the range has been broken prices will continue in that direction for some time.

Scalping

Scalping originally referred to spread trading. Scalping is a trading style where small price gaps created by the bid-ask spread are exploited. It normally involves establishing and liquidating a position quickly, usually within minutes or even seconds.

Scalping highly liquid instruments for off the floor day traders involves taking quick profits while minimizing risk (loss exposure). It applies technical analysis concepts such as over/under-bought, support and resistance zones as well as trendline, trading channel to enter the market at key points and take quick profits from small moves. The basic idea of scalping is to exploit the inefficiency of the market when volatility increases and the trading range expands.

Rebate Trading

Rebate Trading is an equity trading style that uses ECN rebates as a primary source of profit and revenue, considering the payment structure of ECN paying per share. Traders maximize their returns by trading low priced, high volume stocks. This enables them to trade more shares and have more liquidity with a set amount of capital.

News Playing

News playing is primarily the realm of the day trader. The basic strategy is to buy a stock which has just announced good news, or short sell on bad news. Such events provide enormous volatility in a stock and therefore the greatest chance for quick profits (or losses). Determining whether news is "good" or "bad" must be determined by the price action of the stock, because the market reaction may not match the tone of the news itself. The most common cause for this is when rumors or estimates of the event (like those issued by market and industry analysts) were already circulated before the official release, and prices have already moved in anticipation---the news is already priced in the stock.

Cost

Trading Equipment

Some day trading strategies (including scalping and arbitrage) require relatively sophisticated trading systems and software. This software can cost up to $45,000 or more. Many day traders use multiple monitors or even multiple computers to execute their orders. Some use real time filtering software which is programmed to send stock symbols to a screen which meet specific criteria during the day, such as displaying stocks that are turning from positive to negative.

A fast Internet connection, such as broadband, is essential for day trading.

Brokerage

Day traders do not use retail brokers because they are slower to execute trades and charge higher commissions than direct access brokers, who allow the trader to send their orders directly to the ECNs. Direct access trading offers substantial improvements in transaction speed and will usually result in better trade execution prices (reducing the costs of trading).

Commission

Commissions for direct-access brokers are calculated based on volume. The more you trade, the cheaper the commission is. While a retail broker might charge $10 or more per trade regardless of the trade size, a typical direct-access broker may charge as little as $0.004 per share traded, or $0.25 per futures contract. A scalper can cover such costs with even a minimal gain.

As for the calculation method, some use pro-rata to calculate commissions and charges, where each tier of volumes charge different commissions. Other brokers use a flat-rate, where all commissions charges are based on which volume threshold one reaches.

Spread

The numerical difference between the bid and ask prices is referred to as the bid-ask spread. Most worldwide markets operate on a bid-ask-based system.

The ask prices are immediate execution (market) prices for quick buyers (ask takers) while bid prices are for quick sellers (bid takers). If a trade is executed at quoted prices, closing the trade immediately without queuing would not cause a loss because the bid price is always less than the ask price at any point in time.

The bid-ask spread is two sides of the same coin. The spread can be viewed as trading bonuses or costs according to different parties and different strategies. On one hand, traders who do NOT wish to queue their order, instead paying the market price, pay the spreads (costs). On the other hand, traders who wish to queue and wait for execution receive the spreads (bonuses). Some day trading strategies attempt to capture the spread as additional, or even the only, profits for successful trades.

Market Data

Market data is necessary for day traders, rather than using the delayed (by anything from 10 to 60 minutes, per exchange rules) market data that is available for free. A real-time data feed requires paying fees to the respective stock exchanges, usually combined with the broker's charges. These fees are usually very low compared to the other costs of trading. The fees may be waived for promotional purposes or for customers meeting a minimum monthly volume of trades. Even a moderately active day trader can expect to meet these requirements, making the basic data feed essentially "free."

In addition to the raw market data, some traders purchase more advanced data feeds that include historical data and features such as scanning large numbers of stocks in the live market for unusual activity. Complicated analysis and charting software are other popular additions. These types of systems can cost from tens to hundreds of dollars per month to access.

Regulations and Restrictions

Day trading is considered a risky trading style, and regulations require brokerage firms to ask whether the clients understand the risks of day trading and whether they have prior trading experience before entering the market.

Pattern Day Trader

In addition, NASD and SEC further restrict the entry by means of "pattern day trader" amendments. Pattern day trader is a term defined by the SEC to describe any trader who buys and sells a particular security in the same trading day (day trades), and does this four or more times in any five consecutive business day period. A pattern day trader is subject to special rules, the main rule being that in order to engage in pattern day trading the trader must maintain an equity balance of at least $25,000 in a margin account.

Rogue Trader

A rogue trader is an authorized employee making unauthorized trades on behalf of their employer. It is most often applicable to financial trading, and as such is a term used to describe persons - professional traders - making unapproved financial transactions.

This activity is in the grey area between civil and criminal illegality for the reason that the perpetrator is a legitimate employee of a company or institution, yet enters into transactions on behalf of their employer without permission.

One famous rogue trader is Nick Leeson, whose losses were sufficient to bankrupt Barings Bank in 1995 following his ill-advised and unauthorized investments in index futures. Through a combination of poor judgment on his part, lack of oversight by management, a naive regulatory environment and unfortunate outside events like the Kobe earthquake, Leeson incurred a $1.3 billion loss that bankrupted the centuries-old financial institution.

Table of largest Rogue Trader Losses

Name	Loss	Institution	Market Activity	Sentence
Nick Leeson, 1995	£827 m..	**Barings Bank**	Nikkei index futures	6.5 years jail
Toshihide Iguchi, 1995	£557 m.	**Resona Holdings**	US Treasury bonds	4 years jail
Yasuo Hamanaka, 1996	$2.6 b.	**Sumitomo Corporation**	Copper	8 years jail
John Rusnak, 2002	£350 m.	**Allied Irish Banks**	FX options	7.5 years jail
Luke Duffy, Oct 03 - Jan 04	AU$360 m.	**National Australia Bank**	FX options	16 months jail
Chen Jiulin, 2005	$550 m.	**China Aviation Oil**	jet fuel future	51 months jail
Jérôme Kerviel, 2006 - 2008	$7.2 b.	**Société Générale**	European stock index futures	investigation in progress
Boris Picano-Nacci, Oct 2008	€751 m.	**Caisse d'Epargne**	-	investigation in progress

Trading Strategy

Traders, investment firms and fund managers use a trading strategy to help make wiser investment decisions and help eliminate the emotional aspect of trading. A trading strategy is governed by a set of rules that do not deviate. Emotional bias is eliminated because the systems operate within the parameters known by the trader. The parameters can be trusted based on historical analysis (backtesting) and real world market studies (forward testing), so that the trader can have confidence in the strategy and its operating characteristics.

Development

When developing a trading strategy, many things must be considered:

- Return
- Risk
- Volatility
- Timeframe
- Style
- Correlation with the markets
- Methods, etc.

After developing a strategy, it can be backtested using computer programs. Although backtesting is no guarantee of future performance, it gives the trader confidence that the strategy has worked in the past. If the strategy is not over-optimized, data-mined, or based on random coincidences, it might have a good chance of working in the future.

Forward Testing

Forward testing a strategy give the trader a much better picture of how it will work in the future. Forward testing, or out-of-sample results, are the best way to measure its quality.

Executing Strategies

A trading strategy can be executed by a trader (manually) or automated (by computer). Manual trading requires a great deal of skill and discipline. It is tempting for the trader to deviate from the strategy, which usually reduces its performance.

An automated trading strategy wraps trading formulas into automated order and execution systems. Advanced computer modeling techniques, combined with electronic access to world market data and information, enable traders using a trading strategy to have a unique market vantage point. A trading strategy can automate all or part of your investment portfolio. Computer trading models can be adjusted for either conservative or aggressive trading styles.

Trading System

In electronic financial markets, trading system, also known as algorithmic trading (which will be explained in on the following couple pages), is the use of computer programs for entering trading orders with the computer algorithm deciding on certain aspects of the order such as the timing, price, quantity of order. It is widely used by hedge funds, pension funds, mutual funds, and other institutional traders to divide up a large trade into several smaller trades in order to manage market impact, opportunity cost and risk. It is also used by hedge funds and similar traders to make the decision to initiate orders based on information that is received electronically, before human traders are even aware of the information.

Computerization of the order flow in financial markets began in the early 1970s with some landmarks being the introduction of the New York Stock Exchange's "designated order turnaround" system.

Recent years have seen a surge in the growth of automated trading. The global electronic markets continue to attract more volume, as firms worldwide utilize trading automation at an increasing rate.

This allows traders to deploy complex strategies that would be impossible to execute manually.

Market data rates are skyrocketing as a result of automated electronic trading. In the last 10 years, market data has grown by roughly two orders of magnitude, requiring ongoing upgrades of data networks and computing systems.

And this growth is continuing, so today's data infrastructures will require persistent improvement and expansion to keep up with constantly increasing market data volume.

Technologies devised for automated trading are making markets more interdependent. As bigger data pipes and faster computers are increasingly deployed by trading firms to monitor real-time prices across multiple markets, the window of time required to capture inter-market arbitrage opportunities is diminishing.

Today, using information and trading platforms has become a de facto requirement for successful trading in the financial markets. Their advantages as compared to conventional trading schemes include, for example, an unprecedented speed of processing and delivery of information to end users, the level of integration with data providers, and a wide array of built-in technical analysis instruments.

At the same time, an investor opening an account with a brokerage firm simply cannot simultaneously manage the real-time analysis and trade in more than 4-6 financial instruments in several markets 24 hours 7 days a week. This brings about the need to employ automatic trading systems in the form of runtime environment with client and server parts and the programs to control these systems (scripts).

Various software components embrace the entire target sector of the market from analytics and forecasting to complex trade and administration. The components of a trading platform provide its clients—brokers, dealers, traders, financial analysts and advisors—just the service they need at the very moment they need it, from immediate round-the-clock access to information of concern by means of mobile devices, to multi-move trading operations in the major client terminal.

Algorithmic Trading

Algorithmic trading or automated trading, also known as algo trading, black-box trading, or robo trading, is the use of computer programs for entering trading orders with the computer algorithm deciding on certain aspects of the order such as the timing, price, or even the final quantity of the order. It is widely used by hedge funds, pension funds, mutual funds and other institutional traders to divide up a large trade into several smaller trades in order to manage market impact, opportunity cost, and risk. It is also used by hedge funds and similar traders to make the decision to initiate orders based on information that is received electronically, before human traders are even aware of the information.

Algorithmic trading may be used in any investment strategy, including market making, inter-market spreading, arbitrage or pure speculation (including trend following). The investment decision and implementation may be augmented at any stage with algorithmic support or may operate completely automatically.

A third of all EU and US stock trades in 2006 were driven by automatic programs, or algorithms, according to Boston-based consulting firm Aite Group LLC. By 2010, that figure will reach 50 percent, according to Aite.

In 2006 at the London Stock Exchange, over 40% of all orders were entered by algo traders, with 60% predicted for 2007. American markets and equity markets generally have a higher proportion of algo trades than other markets, and estimates for 2008 range as high as an 80% proportion in some markets. Foreign exchange markets also have active algo trading (about 25% of orders in 2006). Futures and options markets are considered to be fairly easily integrated into algorithmic trading, with about 20% of options volume expected to be computer generated by 2010. Bond markets are moving toward more access to algorithmic traders.

History

Computerization of the order flow in financial markets began in the early 1970s with some landmarks being the introduction of the New York Stock Exchange's "designated order turnaround" system (DOT and later SuperDOT) which routed orders electronically to the proper trading post to be executed manually and the "opening automated reporting system" (OARS) which aided the specialist in determining the market clearing opening price.

Program trading is defined by the New York Stock Exchange as an order to buy or sell 15 or more stocks valued at over $1 million total. In practice this means that all program trades are entered with the aid of a computer. In the 1980s program trading became widely used in trading between equity and futures markets.

In stock index arbitrage a trader would buy (sell) a stock index futures contract such as the S&P 500 futures and sell (buy) a portfolio of up to 500 stocks at the NYSE matched against the futures trade. The program trade at the NYSE would be pre-programmed into a computer to enter the order automatically into the NYSE's electronic order routing system at a time when the futures price and the stock index were far enough apart to make a profit.

At about the same time portfolio insurance was designed to create a synthetic put option on a stock portfolio by dynamically trading stock index futures according to a computer model based on the Black-Scholes option pricing model.

Both strategies, often simply lumped together as "program trading," were blamed by many people (for example by the Brady report) for exacerbating or even starting the 1987 stock market crash.

Financial markets with fully electronic execution and similar electronic communication networks developed in the late 1980s and 1990s. In the U.S., decimalization, which changed the minimum tick size from 1/16th of a dollar ($0.0625) to $0.01 per share, may have encouraged algorithmic trading as it changed the market microstructure by permitting smaller differences between the bid and offer prices, decreasing the market-makers' trading advantage, thus decreasing market liquidity.

This decreased market liquidity led to institutional traders splitting up orders according to computer algorithms in order to execute their orders at a better average price. These average price benchmarks are measured and calculated by computers by applying the time weighted (i.e unweighted) average price TWAP or more usually by the volume weighted average price VWAP.

As more electronic markets opened, other algorithmic trading strategies became possible including arbitrage, statistical arbitrage, trend following, mean reversion. These strategies are more easily implemented by computers because machines can react more rapidly to temporary mispricing and examine prices from several markets simultaneously.

Communication Standards

Algorithmic trades require communicating considerably more parameters than traditional market and limit orders. A trader on one end (the "buy side") must enable their trading system (often called an "Order Management System" or "Execution Management System") to understand a constantly proliferating flow of new algorithmic order types. The R&D and other costs to construct complex new algorithmic orders types, along with the execution infrastructure and marketing costs to distribute them, are fairly substantial. What was needed was a way that marketers (the "sell side") could express algo orders electronically such that buy-side traders could just drop the new order types into their system and be ready to trade them without constant coding custom new order entry screens each time.

FIX Protocol LTD http://www.fixprotocol.org is a trade association that publishes free, open standards in the securities trading area. Members include virtually all large and many midsize and smaller broker dealers, money center banks, institutional investors, mutual funds, etc. This institution dominates standard setting in the pretrade and trade areas of security transactions. In 2006-2007 several members got together and published a draft XML standard for expressing algorithmic order types. The standard is called FIX Algorithmic Trading Definition Language (FIXatdl). Currently targeting 2009 for final release, FIXatdl is now in broad beta testing with the following firms participating: Barclays, Bloomberg Tradebook, Cheuvreux, Citigroup, Credit Suisse, Fidelity Investments, Goldman Sachs, ITG, JPMorgan Chase, Merrill Lynch, Morgan Stanley, NeoNet, Pragma@Weeden, and UBS AG.

Strategies

Many different algorithms have been developed to implement different trading strategies. These algorithms or techniques are commonly given names such as "iceberging", "Dagger", "Guerrilla", "benchmarking", "Sniper" and "Snif-fer".

Transaction Cost Reduction

Large orders are broken down into several smaller orders and entered into the market over time. This basic strategy is called "iceberging". The success of this strategy may be measured by the average purchase price against the VWAP for the market over that time period. One algorithm designed to find hidden orders or icebergs is called "Guerrilla".

Arbitrage

A classical arbitrage strategy might involve three or four securities such as covered interest rate parity in the foreign exchange market which gives a relation between the prices of a domestic bond, a bond denominated in a foreign currency, the spot price of the currency and the price of a forward contract on the currency. If the market prices are sufficiently different from those implied in the model to cover transactions cost then four transactions can be made to guarantee a risk-free profit. Algorithmic trading allows similar arbitrages using models of greater complexity involving many more than 4 securities.

Market Making

Market making involves placing a limit order to sell (or offer) above the current market price or a buy limit order (or bid) below the current price in order to benefit from the bid-ask spread. Automated Trading Desk, which was bought by Citigroup in July 2007, has been an active market maker, accounting for about 6% of total volume on both NASDAQ and the New York Stock Exchange.

More Complicated Strategies

A "benchmarking" algorithm is used by traders attempting to mimic an index's return. An algorithm designed to discover which markets are most volatile or unstable is called "Snif-fer".

Any type of algo trading which depends on the programming skills of other algo traders is called gaming. Dark pools are alternative electronic stock exchanges where trading takes place anonymously, with most orders hidden or "iceburged." Gamers or "sharks" sniff out large orders by "pinging" small market orders to buy and sell. When several small orders are filled the sharks may have discovered the presence of a large iceburged order. They then front run the order.

"They look for big, dumb elephants leaving big footprints," said Joe Saluzzi, head of equity trading at Themis Trading.... "If you're getting tapped by odd lots, if it happens 40 times...you're being gamed." Any sort of pattern recognition or predictive model can be used to initiate algo trading. Neural networks and genetic programming have been used to create these models.

"Now it's an arms race," said Andrew Lo, director of the Massachusetts Institute of Technology's Laboratory for Financial Engineering. "Everyone is building more sophisticated algorithms and the more competition exists, the smaller the profits."

Effects

Though its development may have been prompted by decreasing trade sizes caused by decimalization, algorithmic trading has reduced trade sizes further. Jobs once done by human traders are being switched to computers. The speeds of computer connections, measured in milliseconds, have become very important.

More fully automated markets such as NASDAQ have gained market share from less automated markets such as the NYSE. Economies of scale in electronic trading have contributed to lowering commissions and trade processing fees, and contributed to international mergers and consolidation of financial exchanges.

Competition is developing among exchanges for the fastest processing times for completing trades. For example the London Stock Exchange, in June 2007, started a new system called TradElect, which promises an average 10 millisecond turnaround time from placing an order to final confirmation, and can process 3,000 orders per second.

Spending on computers and software in the financial industry increased to $26.4 billion in 2005.

Brokers have found it more difficult to monitor the risk of their clients' positions, especially for clients such as hedge funds.

Trend Following

Trend following is an investment strategy that tries to take advantage of long-term moves that seem to play out in various markets. The system aims to work on the market trend mechanism and take benefit from both sides of the market enjoying the profits from the ups and downs of the stock market.

Traders who use this approach can use current market price calculation, moving averages and channel breakouts to determine the general direction of the market and to generate trade signals. Traders who subscribe to a trend following strategy do not aim to forecast or predict markets or price levels; they simply jump on the trend and ride it.

Definition

This trading method involves a risk management component that uses three elements. The current market price, equity level in an account and current market volatility. An initial risk rule determines position size at time of entry. Exactly how much to buy or sell is based on the size of the trading account. Changes in price may lead to a gradual reduction or increase of the initial trade. On the other hand, adverse price movements may lead to an exit for the entire trade.

These systems traders normally enter in the market after the trend properly establishes itself and for this reason, they miss the initial turning point.

If there is a turn contrary to the trend, these systems signal a pre-programmed exit or wait until the turn establishes itself as a trend in the opposite direction. In case the system signals an exit, the trader re-enters when the trend re-establishes.

With the words of Van K. Tharp, in the book Trade Your Way to Financial Freedom

" Let's break down the term Trend Following into its components. The first part is "trend". Every trader needs a trend to make money. If you think about it, no matter what the technique, if there is not a trend after you buy, then you will not be able to sell at higher prices..."Following" is the next part of the term.

We use this word because trend followers always wait for the trend to shift first, then "follow" it."

Considerations

Price: One of the first rules of trend following is that price is the main concern. Traders may use other indicators showing where price will go next or what it should but as a general rule these should be disregarded. A trader need only be worried about what the market is doing, not what the market might do. The current price and only the price tells you what the market is doing.

Money Management: Another decisive factor of trend following is not the timing of the trade or the indicator, but rather the decision of how much to trade over the course of the trend.

Risk Control: Cut losses is the rule. This means that during periods of higher market volatility, the trading size is reduced. During losing periods, positions are reduced and trade size is cut back. The main objective is to preserve capital until more positive price trends reappear.

Rules: Trend following should be systematic. Price and time are pivotal at all times. This technique is not based on an analysis of fundamental supply or demand factors.

Trend Following answers the questions:

How and when to enter the market.

- How many contracts or shares to trade at any time.
- How much money to risk on each trade.
- How to exit the trade if it becomes unprofitable.
- How to exit the trade if it becomes profitable.

Example

A trader would identify a security to trade (curriencies/commodities/financials) and would come up with a preliminary strategy, such as:

- Commodity: soyabean oil
- Trading approach: long and short alternatively.
- Entrance: When the 50 period Simple moving average(SMA) crosses over the 100 period SMA, go long when the market opens. The crossover suggests that the trend has recently turned up.
- Exit: Exit long and go short the next day when 100 period SMA crosses over 50 period SMA. The crossover suggests that the trend has turned down.
- Stop loss: Set a stop loss based on maximum loss acceptable. For example if the recent, say 10 day, Average True Range is 0.5%, stop loss could be set at 4x0.5% = 2%.

The trader would then backtest the strategy using actual data using a software system such as Wealth-Lab Pro, StrategyDesk or Trade2Win and would evaluate the strategy. The simulator would generate estimated number of trades, the fraction of winning/losing trades, average profit/loss, average holding time, maximum drawdown and the overall profit/loss. The trader can then experiment and refine the strategy.

It is possible that a large fraction (perhaps majority) of the trades may be unprofitable, but by "cutting the losses" and "letting profits run", the overall strategy may be profitable.

Trend Followers

Trend following systems have enjoyed popularity over the years - well-known trend followers include Bill Dunn, Ed Seykota, John W. Henry, Richard Dennis, and Richard Donchian.

Many traders like original Turtles Paul Rabar and Jerry Parker say that following a market trend is their winning trading strategy.

Dennis and Donchian are the fathers of the trend following. During the 1980s Richard made a bet with partner William Eckhardt that he could train non-traders this technique. He won the bet and these people rank in the top 10 Commodity Trading Advisors rankings, they became known as the turtles.

Contrarian Investing

A contrarian is one who attempts to profit by investing in a manner that differs from the conventional wisdom, when the consensus opinion appears to be wrong.

A contrarian believes that certain crowd behavior among investors can lead to exploitable mispricing in securities markets. For example, widespread pessimism about a stock can drive a price so low that it overstates the company's risks and understates its prospects for returning to profitability. Identifying and purchasing such distressed stocks and selling them after the company recovers, can lead to above-average gains. Conversely, widespread optimism can result in unjustifiably high valuations that will eventually lead to drops, when those high expectations don't pan out. Avoiding investments in over-hyped investments reduces the risk of such drops. These general principles can apply whether the investment in question is an individual stock, an industry sector, or an entire market or any other asset class.

Some contrarians have a permanent bear market view, while the majority of investors bet on the market going up. However, a contrarian does not necessarily have a negative view of the overall stock market, nor does he have to believe that it is always overvalued, or that the conventional wisdom is always wrong. Rather, a contrarian seeks opportunities to buy or sell specific investments when the majority of investors appear to be doing the opposite, to the point where that investment has become mispriced. While more "buy" candidates are likely to be identified during market declines (and vice versa), these opportunities can occur during periods when the overall market is generally rising or falling.

Similarity to Value Investing

Contrarian investing is related to value investing in that the contrarian is also looking for mispriced investments and buying those that appear to be undervalued by the market. Some well-known value investors such as John Neff have questioned whether there is a such thing as a "contrarian", seeing it as essentially synonymous with value investing. One possible distinction is that a value stock, in finance theory, can be identified by financial metrics such as the book value or P/E ratio. A contrarian investor may look at those metrics, but is also interested in measures of "sentiment" regarding the stock among other investors, such as sell-side analyst coverage and earnings forecasts, trading volume and media commentary about the company and its business prospects.

In the example of a stock that has dropped because of excessive pessimism, one can see similarities to the "margin of safety" that value investor Benjamin Graham sought when purchasing stocks -- essentially, being able to buy shares at a discount to their intrinsic value. Arguably that margin of safety is more likely to exist when a stock has fallen a great deal and that type of drop is usually accompanied by negative news and general pessimism.

Notable Contrarian Investors

Warren Buffet is a famous contrarian, who believes that best time to invest in a stock is when shortsightedness of the market has beaten down the price.

David Dreman is a money manager often associated with contrarian investing. He has authored several books on the topic and writes the "Contrarian" column in Forbes magazine.

John Neff, who managed the Vanguard Windsor fund for many years, is also considered a contrarian, though he has described himself as a value investor (and questioned the distinction).

Examples of Contrarian Investing

Commonly used contrarian indicators for investor sentiment are volatility indexes (informally also referred to as "Fear indexes"), like VIX, which by tracking the prices of financial options, gives a numeric measure of how pessimistic or optimistic market actors at large are. A low number in this index indicates a prevailing optimistic or confident investor outlook for the future, while a high number indicates a pessimistic outlook. By comparing the VIX to the major stock-indexes over longer periods of time, it is evident that peaks in this index generally present good buying opportunities.

Another example of a simple contrarian strategy is Dogs of the Dow. When purchasing the stocks in the Dow Jones Industrial Average that have the highest relative dividend yield, an investor is often buying many of the "distressed" companies among those 30 stocks. These "Dogs" have high yields not because dividends were raised, but rather because their share prices fell. The company is experiencing difficulties, or simply is at a low point in their business cycle. By repeatedly buying such stocks, and selling them when they no longer meet the criteria, the "Dogs" investor is systematically buying the least-loved of the Dow 30, and selling them when they become loved again.

When the Dot com bubble started to deflate, an investor would have profited by avoiding the technology stocks that were the subject of most investors' attention. Asset classes such as value stocks and real estate investment trusts were largely ignored by the financial press at the time, despite their historically low valuations and many mutual funds in those categories lost assets. These investments experienced strong gains amidst the large drops in the overall US stock market when the bubble unwound.

Relationship to Behavioral Finance

Contrarians are attempting to exploit some of the principles of behavioral finance and there is significant overlap between these fields. For example, studies in behavioral finance have demonstrated that investors as a group tend to overweight recent trends when predicting the future. A poorly-performing stock will remain bad and a strong performer will remain strong. This lends credence to the contrarian's belief that investments may drop "too low" during periods of negative news, due to incorrect assumptions by other investors regarding the long-term prospects for the company.

Scalping (Trading)

Scalping, when used in reference to trading in securities, commodities and foreign exchange, may refer to

1. a fraudulent form of market manipulation or
2. a legitimate method of arbitrage of small price gaps created by the bid-ask spread.

Market Manipulation

Scalping in this sense is the practice of purchasing a security for one's own account shortly before recommending that security for long-term investment and then immediately selling the security at a profit upon the rise in the market price following the recommendation. The Supreme Court of the United States has ruled that scalping by an investment adviser operates as a fraud or deceit upon any client or prospective client and is a violation of the Investment Advisers Act of 1940. The prohibition on scalping has been applied against persons who are not registered investment advisers, and it has been ruled that scalping is also a violation of Rule 10b-5 under the Securities Exchange Act of 1934 if the scalper has a relationship of trust and confidence with the persons to whom the recommendation is made. The Securities and Exchange Commission has stated that it is committed to stamping out scalping schemes. Scalping differs from pumping and dumping in that a pump and dump does not involve a relationship of trust and confidence between the fraudster and his victims.

Arbitrage & Scalping

How Scalping Works

Playing the Spread

Scalpers attempt to act like traditional market makers or specialists. To make the spread means to buy at the Bid price and sell at the Ask price, to gain the bid/ask difference. This procedure allows for profit even when the bid and ask don't move at all, as long as there are traders who are willing to take market prices. It normally involves establishing and liquidating a position quickly, usually within minutes or even seconds.

Role

The role of a scalper is actually the role of market makers or specialists who are to maintain the liquidity and order flow of a product of a market.

A market maker is basically a specialized scalper. The volume he trades are many times more than the average individual scalpers. He has a sophisticated trading system to monitor trading activity. However, he is bound by strict exchange rules while the individual trader is not. For instance, NASDAQ requires each market maker to post at least one bid and one ask at some price level, so as to maintain a two-sided market for each stock he represents.

Due to role overlapping, a scalper is always competing with the market maker for profits. Unfortunately, the low-end scalper is almost always at a disadvantage due to the following market maker's advantages:

1. superior execution speed as an insider
2. a greater knowledge of trading and the actual market situation due to its information gathering capacity
3. huge amount of capital to backup and support market makers
4. the ability to provide false impression to the market by placing a larger/smaller bid or ask to bluff the trader

Principles

Spreads are Bonuses as well as Costs

Most worldwide markets operate on a bid and ask based system. The numerical difference between the bid and ask prices is referred to as the spread between them.

The ask prices are immediate execution (market) prices for quick buyers (ask takers). Bid prices for quick sellers (bid takers). If a trade is executed at market prices, closing that trade immediately without queuing would not get you back the amount paid because of the bid/ask difference.

The spread can be viewed as trading bonuses or costs according to different parties and different strategies. On one hand, traders who do NOT wish to queue their order, instead paying the market price, pay the spreads (costs). On the other hand, traders who wish to queue and wait for execution receive the spreads (bonuses). Some day trading strategies attempt to capture the spread as additional, or even the only, profits for successful trades.

Lower Exposure, Lower Risks

Scalpers are only exposed in a relatively short period. They do not hold overnights. As the period one holds decreases, the chances of running into extreme adverse movements, causing huge losses, decreases.

Smaller Moves, easier to obtain

A change in price results from imbalance of buying and selling powers. Most of the time within a day, prices stay stable, moving within a small range. This means neither buying nor selling power control the situation. There are only a few times which price moves towards one direction, ie. either buying or selling power controls the situation. It requires bigger imbalances for bigger price changes.

It is what scalpers look for - capturing smaller moves which happen most of the time, as opposed to larger ones.

Large Volume, adding Profits up

Since the profit obtained per share or contract is very small due to its target of spread, they need to trade large in order to add up the profits. Scalping is not suitable for small-capital traders.

Different Parties and Spreads

Who pays the Spreads (Costs)

The following traders pay the spreads:

- **Momentum traders on technicals** - They look for fast movements hinted from quotes, prices and volumes, charts. When a real breakout occurs, price becomes volatile. A sudden rise or fall may occur within any second. They need to get in quick before the price moves out of the base.
- **Momentum traders on news** - When news break out, the price becomes very volatile as many people watching the news will react at more or less the same time. One needs to take the market prices immediately or the golden opportunities which may vanish after a second or so.

- **Cut losses on market prices** - The spread becomes a cost if the price moves against the expected direction and the trader wishes to cut losses immediately on market price.

Who receives the Spreads (Bonuses)

The following traders receive the spreads:

- **Individual scalpers** - obviously they trade for spreads and can benefit from larger spreads.
- **Market makers and specialists** - people who provide liquidity place their orders on their market books. Over the course of a single day, a market maker may fill orders for hundreds of thousands or millions of shares.
- **Spot Forex (exchanges of foreign currencies) brokers** - they do not charge any commissions because they make profits from the bid/ask spread quotes. On July 10 2006, the exchange rate between Euro and United States dollar is 1.2733 at 15:45. The internal (inter-bank dealers) bid/ask price is 1.2732-5/1.2733-5. However the forex brokers or middlemen will not offer the same competitive prices to their clients. Instead they provide their own version of bid and ask quotes, say 1.2731/1.2734, of which their commissions are already "hidden" in it. More competitive brokers do not charge more than 2 pips spread on a currency where the interbank market has a 1 pip spread and some offer better than this by quoting prices in fractional pips.

Factors affecting Scalping

Liquidity

Liquidity of a market affects the performance of scalping. Each product within the market receives different spread, due to popularity differentials. The more liquid the markets and the products are, the tighter the spreads are. Scalpers like to trade in a more liquid market since they can make thousands of trades a day to add up their small profits offered on each trade.

If they are to trade in less liquid markets, they will try to cover their risks by widening their bid and ask prices.

Volatility

Unlike momentum traders, scalpers like stable or silent products. Imagine if its price does not move all day, scalpers can profit all day simply by placing their orders on the same bid and ask, making hundreds or thousands of trades. They do not need to worry about sudden price changes which kill them unprepared.

Time Frame

Scalpers operate on a very short time frame, looking to profit from market waves that are sometimes too small to be seen even on the one minute chart. This maximizes the number of moves during the day that the scalper can use to make a profit.

Risk Management

Rather than looking for one big trade, the way a swing trader might, the scalper looks for hundreds of small profits throughout the day. In this process the scalper might also take hundreds of small losses during the same time period. For this reason a scalper must have very strict risk management never allowing a loss to accumulate against him.

Technical Analysis

What is a Technical Analysis?

Technical analysis is a financial markets technique that claims the ability to forecast the future direction of security prices through the study of past market data, primarily price and volume. In its purest form, technical analysis considers only the actual price and volume behavior of the market or instrument, on the assumption that price and volume are the two most relevant factors in determining the future direction and behavior of a particular stock or market. Technical analysts may employ models and trading rules based, for example, on price and volume transformations, such as the relative strength index, moving averages, regressions, inter-market and intra-market price correlations, cycles or, classically, through recognition of chart patterns.

Technical analysis is widely used among traders and financial professionals, but is considered in academia to be pseudoscience. Academics such as Eugene Fama say the evidence for technical analysis is sparse and is inconsistent with the weak form of the generally-accepted efficient market hypothesis. Economist Burton Malkiel argues, "Technical analysis is an anathema to the academic world." He further argues that under the weak form of the efficient market hypothesis, "...you cannot predict future stock prices from past stock prices."

However, there are also many stock traders who proclaim technical analysis not as a science for predicting the future but instead as a valuable tool to identify favorable trading opportunities and trends. The assumption is that all of the fundamental information and current market opinions are already reflected in the current price and when viewed in conjunction with past prices often reveals recurring price and volume patterns that provide clues to potential future price movement.

In the foreign exchange markets, its use may be more widespread than fundamental analysis. While some isolated studies have indicated that technical trading rules might lead to consistent returns in the period prior to 1987, most academic work has focused on the nature of the anomalous position of the foreign exchange market. It is speculated that this anomaly is due to central bank intervention.

General Description

Technical analysts (or technicians) seek to identify price patterns and trends in financial markets and attempt to exploit those patterns. While technicians use various methods and tools, the study of price charts is primary. Technicians especially search for archetypal patterns, such as the well-known head and shoulders reversal pattern, and also study such indicators as price, volume, and moving averages of the price. Many technical analysts also follow indicators of investor psychology (market sentiment).

Critics argue that these 'patterns' are simply random effects on which humans impose causation. They state that humans see patterns that aren't there and then ascribe value to them.

Technical analysts also extensively use indicators, which are typically mathematical transformations of price or volume. These indicators are used to help determine whether an asset is trending, and if it is, its price direction. Technicians also look for relationships between price, volume and, in the case of futures, open interest. Examples include the relative strength index and MACD. Other avenues of study include correlations between changes in options (implied volatility) and put/call ratios with price.

Essentially, technical analysis examines two areas of investing: the analysis of market "psych" (or sentiment) and the analysis of supply/demand (whether investors have the funds to support their hopes and fears). A bullish investor without funds cannot take the market higher.

Technicians seek to forecast price movements such that large gains from successful trades exceed more numerous but smaller losing trades, producing positive returns in the long run through proper risk control and money management.

There are several schools of technical analysis. Adherents of different schools (for example, candlestick charting, Dow Theory, and Elliott wave theory) may ignore the other approaches, yet many traders combine elements from more than one school. Technical analysts use judgment gained from experience to decide which pattern a particular instrument reflects at a given time and what the interpretation of that pattern should be.

Technical analysis is frequently contrasted with fundamental analysis, the study of economic factors that some analysts say can influence prices in financial markets. Technical analysis holds that prices already reflect all such influences before investors are aware of them, hence the study of price action alone. Some traders use technical or fundamental analysis exclusively, while others use both types to make trading decisions.

History

The principles of technical analysis derive from the observation of financial markets over hundreds of years. The oldest known example of technical analysis was a method developed by Homma Munehisa during early 18th century which evolved into the use of candlestick techniques and is today a main charting tool.

Dow Theory is based on the collected writings of Dow Jones co-founder and editor Charles Dow and inspired the use and development of modern technical analysis from the end of the 19th century. Other pioneers of analysis techniques include Ralph Nelson Elliott and William Delbert Gann who developed their respective techniques in the early 20th century.

Many more technical tools and theories have been developed and enhanced in recent decades, with an increasing emphasis on computer-assisted techniques.

Principles

Technicians say that a market's price reflects all relevant information, so their analysis looks more at "internals" than at "externals" such as news events. Price action also tends to repeat itself because investors collectively tend toward patterned behavior – hence technicians' focus on identifiable trends and conditions.

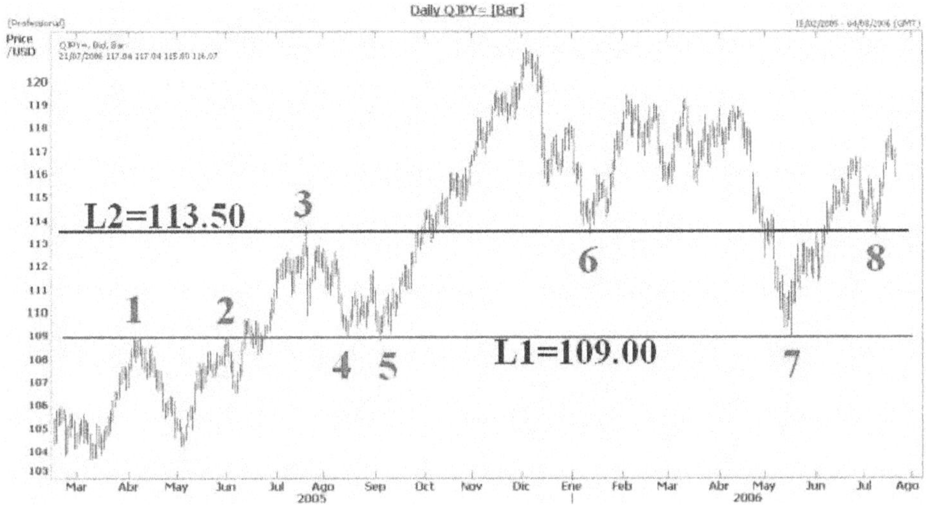

Picture 20: Stock chart showing levels of support (4,5,6, 7, and 8) and resistance (1, 2, and 3); levels of resistance tend to become levels of support and vice versa.

Market Action discounts Everything

Based on the premise that all relevant information is already reflected by prices, pure technical analysts believe it is redundant to do fundamental analysis – they say news and news events do not significantly influence price, and cite supporting research such as the study by Cutler, Poterba, and Summers titled "What Moves Stock Prices?"

On most of the sizable return days [large market moves]...the information that the press cites as the cause of the market move is not particularly important. Press reports on adjacent days also fail to reveal any convincing accounts of why future profits or discount rates might have changed. Our inability to identify the fundamental shocks that accounted for these significant market moves is difficult to reconcile with the view that such shocks account for most of the variation in stock returns.

Prices Move in Trends

Technical analysts believe that prices trend. Technicians say that markets trend up, down, or sideways (flat). This basic definition of price trends is the one put forward by Dow Theory.

An example of a security that had an apparent trend is AOL from November 2001 through August 2002. A technical analyst or trend follower recognizing this trend would look for opportunities to sell this security. AOL consistently moves downward in price. Each time the stock rose, sellers would enter the market and sell the stock. Hence the "zig-zag" movement in the price. The series of "lower highs" and "lower lows" is a tell tale sign of a stock in a down trend. In other words, each time the stock edged lower, it fell below its previous relative low price. Each time the stock moved higher, it could not reach the level of its previous relative high price.

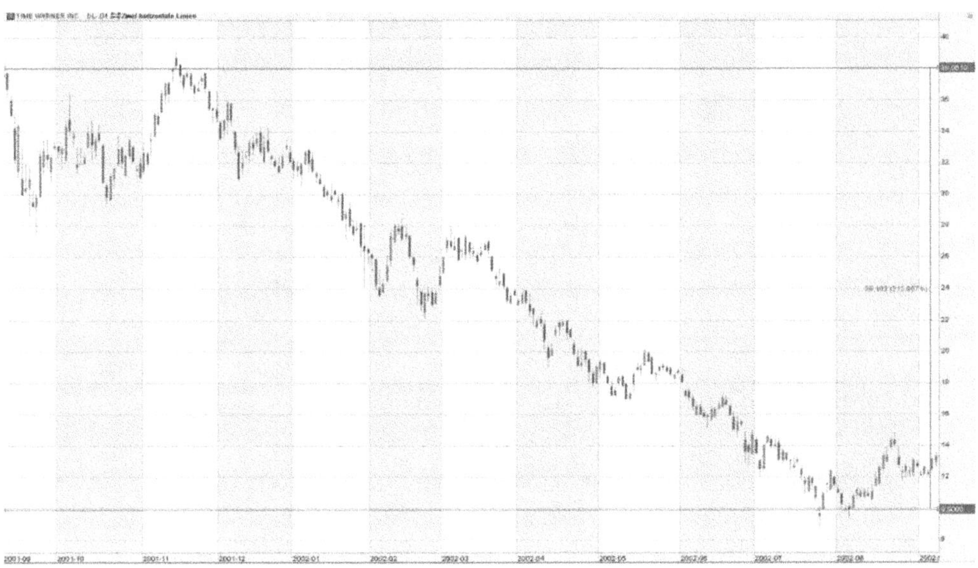

Picture 21: AOL stock price 10/2001 to 08/2002

Note that the sequence of lower lows and lower highs did not begin until August. Then AOL makes a low price that doesn't pierce the relative low set earlier in the month. Later in the same month, the stock makes a relative high equal to the most recent relative high. In this a technician sees strong indications that the down trend is at least pausing and possibly ending and would likely stop actively selling the stock at that point.

History tends to repeat itself

Technical analysts believe that investors collectively repeat the behavior of the investors that preceded them. "Everyone wants in on the next Microsoft," "If this stock ever gets to $50 again, I will buy it," "This company's technology will revolutionize its industry, therefore this stock will skyrocket" – these are all examples of investor sentiment repeating itself. To a technician, the emotions in the market may be irrational, but they exist. Because investor behavior repeats itself so often, technicians believe that recognizable (and predictable) price patterns will develop on a chart.

Technical analysis is not limited to charting, but it always considers price trends. For example, many technicians monitor surveys of investor sentiment. These surveys gauge the attitude of market participants, specifically whether they are bearish or bullish. Technicians use these surveys to help determine whether a trend will continue or if a reversal could develop; they are most likely to anticipate a change when the surveys report extreme investor sentiment. Surveys that show overwhelming bullishness, for example, are evidence that an uptrend may reverse – the premise being that if most investors are bullish they have already bought the market (anticipating higher prices). And because most investors are bullish and invested, one assumes that few buyers remain. This leaves more potential sellers than buyers, despite the bullish sentiment. This suggests that prices will trend down, and is an example of contrarian trading.

Empirical Studies and Theoretical Problems

The Wall Street Journal Europe states "Whether technical analysis is really useful ... is a matter of some dispute on Wall Street. Some investors believe that it is impossible to forecast the market's ups and downs. Academic studies have shown that when most people, professionals and amateurs alike, try to move money in and out of stocks to beat market fluctuations, they tend to wind up with losses." The same article shows how several technical analysts can simultaneously make contradictory predictions when exposed to the same data.

Industry

Globally, the industry is represented by The International Federation of Technical Analysts (IFTA). In the United States the industry is represented by two national organizations: The Market Technicians Association (MTA), and the American Association of Professional Technical Analysts (AAPTA). In Canada the industry is represented by the Canadian Society of Technical Analysts.

Use

Many traders say that trading in the direction of the trend is the most effective means to be profitable in financial or commodities markets. John W. Henry, Larry Hite, Ed Seykota, Richard Dennis, William Eckhardt, Victor Sperandeo, Michael Marcus and Paul Tudor Jones (some of the so-called Market Wizards in the popular book of the same name by Jack D. Schwager) have each amassed massive fortunes via the use of technical analysis and its concepts. George Lane, a technical analyst, coined one of the most popular phrases on Wall Street, "The trend is your friend!"

Many non-arbitrage algorithmic trading systems rely on the idea of trend-following, as do many hedge funds. A relatively recent trend, both in research and industrial practice, has been the development of increasingly sophisticated automated trading strategies. These often rely on underlying technical analysis principles (see the algorithmic trading section of this book for an overview).

Systematic Trading

Neural Networks

Since the early 1990s when the first practically usable types emerged, artificial neural networks (ANNs) have rapidly grown in popularity. They are artificial intelligence adaptive software systems that have been inspired by how biological neural networks work. They are used because they can learn to detect complex patterns in data. In mathematical terms, they are universal function approximators, meaning that given the right data and configured correctly, they can capture and model any input-output relationships. This not only removes the need for human interpretation of charts or the series of rules for generating entry/exit signals, but also provides a bridge to fundamental analysis, as the variables used in fundamental analysis can be used as input.

As ANNs are essentially non-linear statistical models, their accuracy and prediction capabilities can be both mathematically and empirically tested. In various studies, authors have claimed that neural networks used for generating trading signals given various technical and fundamental inputs have significantly outperformed buy-hold strategies as well as traditional linear technical analysis methods when combined with rule-based expert systems.

While the advanced mathematical nature of such adaptive systems has kept neural networks for financial analysis mostly within academic research circles, in recent years more user friendly neural network software has made the technology more accessible to traders. However, large-scale application is problematic because of the problem of matching the correct neural topology to the market being studied.

Rule-Based Trading

Rule-based trading is an approach intended to create trading plans using strict and clear-cut rules. Unlike some other technical methods and the approach of fundamental analysis, it defines a set of rules that determine all trades, leaving minimal discretion. The theory behind this approach is that by following a distinct set of trading rules you will reduce the number of poor decisions, which are often emotion based.

For instance, a trader might make a set of rules stating that he will take a long position whenever the price of a particular instrument closes above its 50-day moving average, and shorting it whenever it drops below.

Combination with other Market Forecast Methods

John Murphy says that the principal sources of information available to technicians are price, volume and open interest. Other data, such as indicators and sentiment analysis, are considered secondary.

However, many technical analysts reach outside pure technical analysis, combining other market forecast methods with their technical work. One such approach, fusion analysis, overlays fundamental analysis with technical, in an attempt to improve portfolio manager performance. Another advocate for this approach is John Bollinger, who coined the term rational analysis for the intersection of technical analysis and fundamental analysis.

Technical analysis is also often combined with quantitative analysis and economics. For example, neural networks may be used to help identify intermarket relationships. A few market forecasters combine financial astrology with technical analysis. Chris Carolan's article "Autumn Panics and Calendar Phenomenon", which won the Market Technicians Association Dow Award for best technical analysis paper in 1998, demonstrates how technical analysis and lunar cycles can be combined. It is worth to note, however, that some of the calendar related phenomena, such as the January effect in the stock market, have been associated with tax and accounting related reasons.

Investor and newsletter polls, and magazine cover sentiment indicators, are also used by technical analysts.

Charting Terms and Indicators

Concepts

- Average true range - averaged daily trading range
- Coppock - Edwin Coppock developed the Coppock Indicator with one sole purpose: to identify the commencement of bull markets
- Dead cat bounce - generically refers to what turns out to be a significant but temporary price rise during a sustained decline, typically for what are thought to be technical reasons
- Elliott wave principle and the golden ratio to calculate successive price movements and retracements
- Hikkake Pattern - pattern for identifying reversals and continuations
- Momentum - the rate of price change
- Point and figure charts - charts based on price without time
- BPV Rating - pattern for identifying reversals using both volume and price

Overlays

Overlays are generally superimposed over the main price chart.

- Resistance - an area that brings on increased selling
- Support - an area that brings on increased buying
- Breakout - when a price passes through and stays above an area of support or resistance
- Trend line - a sloping line of support or resistance
- Channel - a pair of parallel trend lines
- Moving average - lags behind the price action but filters out short term movements
- Bollinger bands - a range of price volatility

- Pivot point - derived by calculating the numerical average of a particular currency's or stock's high, low and closing prices

Price-Based Indicators

These indicators are generally shown below or above the main price chart.

- Accumulation/distribution index—based on the close within the day's range
- Average Directional Index — a widely used indicator of trend strength
- Commodity Channel Index - identifies cyclical trends
- MACD - moving average convergence/divergence
- Parabolic SAR - Wilder's trailing stop based on prices tending to stay within a parabolic curve during a strong trend
- Relative Strength Index (RSI) - oscillator showing price strength
- Rahul Mohindar Oscillator - a trend indentifying indicator
- Stochastic oscillator, close position within recent trading range
- Trix - an oscillator showing the slope of a triple-smoothed exponential moving average, developed in the 1980s by Jack Hutson

Volume Based Indicators

- Money Flow - the amount of stock traded on days the price went up
- On-balance volume - the momentum of buying and selling stocks
- PAC charts - two-dimensional method for charting volume by price level

Applicability

Lack of Evidence

Critics of technical analysis include well known fundamental analysts. For example, Peter Lynch once commented, "Charts are great for predicting the past." Warren Buffett has said, "I realized technical analysis didn't work when I turned the charts upside down and didn't get a different answer" and "If past history was all there was to the game, the richest people would be librarians."

Most academic studies say technical analysis has little predictive power, but some studies say it may produce excess returns. For example, measurable forms of technical analysis, such as non-linear prediction using neural networks, have been shown to occasionally produce statistically significant prediction results. A Federal Reserve working paper regarding support and resistance levels in short-term foreign exchange rates "offers strong evidence that the levels help to predict intraday trend interruptions," although the "predictive power" of those levels was "found to vary across the exchange rates and firms examined."

Cheol-Ho Park and Scott H. Irwin reviewed 95 modern studies on the profitability of technical analysis and said 56 of them find positive results, 20 obtain negative results, and 19 indicate mixed results: "Despite the positive evidence...most empirical studies are subject to various problems in their testing procedures, e.g., data snooping, ex post selection of trading rules or search technologies, and difficulties in estimation of risk and transaction costs. Future research must address these deficiencies in testing in order to provide conclusive evidence on the profitability of technical trading strategies."

The influential 1992 study by Brock et al. which appeared to find support for technical trading rules was tested for data snooping and other problems in 1999; while the sample covered by Brock et al was robust to data snooping, "..the superior performance of the best trading rule is not repeated in the out-of-sample experiment covering the period 1987-1996". Indeed, "there is scant evidence that technical trading rules were of any economic value during the period 1987-1996."

Subsequently, a comprehensive study of the question by Amsterdam economist Gerwin Griffioen concludes that: "for the U.S., Japanese and most Western European stock market indices the recursive out-of-sample forecasting procedure does not show to be profitable, after implementing little transaction costs. Moreover, for sufficiently high transaction costs it is found, by estimating CAPMs, that technical trading shows no statistically significant risk-corrected out-of-sample forecasting power for almost all of the stock market indices."

These are particularly applicable to "momentum strategies". A comprehensive 1996 review of the data and studies concluded that even small transaction costs would lead to an inability to capture any excess from such strategies.

MIT finance professor Andrew Lo argues that "several academic studies suggest that...technical analysis may well be an effective means for extracting useful information from market prices."

In 2008 Dr. Emanuele Canegrati, in his unpublished paper "A Non-random Walk Down Canary Wharf" conducted the biggest econometric study ever made to demostrate the validity of technical analysis for the first biggest companies listed on the FTSE. By analysing more than 70 technical indicators, some of them almost unknown until then, the study demonstrated how market returns can be predicted, at least to a certain degree, by some technical indicators.

Random Walk Hypothesis

The random walk hypothesis may be derived from the weak-form efficient markets hypothesis, which is based on the assumption that market participants take full account of any information contained in past price movements (but not necessarily other public information). In his book A Random Walk Down Wall Street, Princeton economist Burton Malkiel said that technical forecasting tools such as pattern analysis must ultimately be self-defeating: "The problem is that once such a regularity is known to market participants, people will act in such a way that prevents it from happening in the future." In a 1999 response to Malkiel, Andrew Lo and Craig McKinlay collected empirical papers that questioned the hypothesis' applicability that suggested a non-random and possibly predictive component to stock price movement, though they were careful to point out that rejecting random walk does not necessarily invalidate EMH.

Technicians say the EMH and random walk theories both ignore the realities of markets, in that participants are not completely rational (they can be greedy, overly risky, etc.) and that current price moves are not independent of previous moves. Critics reply that one can find virtually any chart pattern after the fact, but that this does not prove that such patterns are predictable. Technicians maintain that both theories would also invalidate numerous other trading strategies such as index arbitrage, statistical arbitrage and many other trading systems.

Chart Technique

Chart Pattern

A chart pattern is a pattern that is formed within a chart when prices are graphed. In stock and commodity markets trading, chart pattern studies play a large role during technical analysis. When data is plotted there is usually a pattern which naturally occurs and repeats over a period of time. Chart patterns are used as either reversal or continuation signals.

Some people claim that by recognizing chart patterns they are able to predict future stock prices and profit by this prediction; other people respond by quoting "past performance is no guarantee of future results" and argue that chart patterns are merely illusions created by people's subconscious. Certain theories of economics hold that if there were a way to predict future stock prices and profit by it then when enough people used these techniques they would become ineffective and cease to be profitable. On the other hand, if you can predict what other people will predict the market to do then that would be valuable information.

Candlestick Chart

A candlestick chart is a style of bar-chart used primarily to describe price movements of an equity over time.

It is a combination of a line-chart and a bar-chart, in that each bar represents the range of price movement over a given time interval. It is most often used in technical analysis of equity and currency price patterns. They appear superficially similar to error bars, but are unrelated.

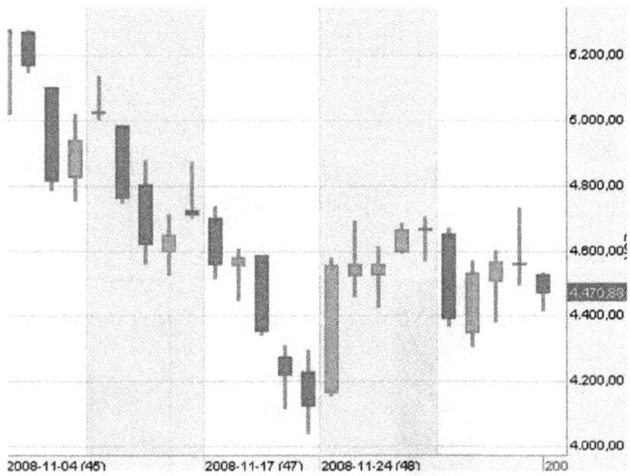

Picture 22: Candelsticks Chart

History

Candlestick charts are said to have been developed in the 18th century by legendary Japanese rice trader Homma Munehisa. The charts gave Homma and others an overview of open, high, low, and close market prices over a certain period. This style of charting is very popular due to the level of ease in reading and understanding the graphs. Since the 17th century, there has been a lot of effort to relate chart patterns to the likely future behavior of a market. This method of charting prices proved to be particularly interesting, due to the ability to display five data points instead of one. The Japanese rice traders also found that the resulting charts would provide a fairly reliable tool to predict future demand.

The method was picked up by Charles Dow around 1900 and remains in common use by today's traders of financial instruments.

Candlestick Chart Topics

Candlesticks are usually composed of the body (black or white, or red and green), an upper and a lower shadow (wick). The wick illustrates the highest and lowest traded prices of a stock during the time interval represented. The body illustrates the opening and closing trades. If the stock closed higher than it opened, the body is white, with the opening price at the bottom of the body and the closing price at the top. If the stock closed lower than it opened, the body is black, with the opening price at the top and the closing price at the bottom. A candlestick need not have either a body or a wick.

Candlestick Simple Patterns

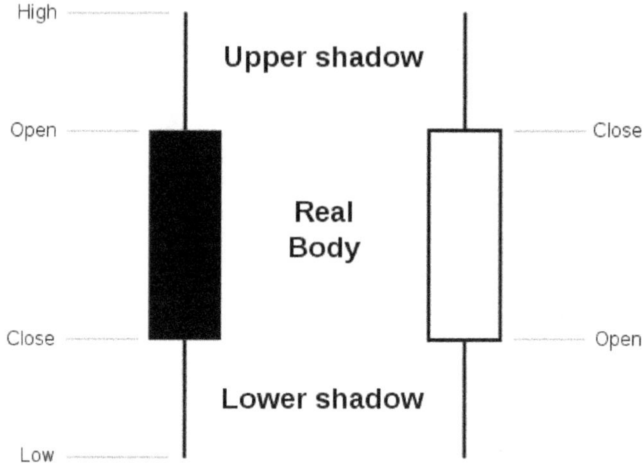

Picture 23: Candelsticks

There are multiple forms of candlestick chart patterns, with the simplest depicted at right. Here is a quick overview of their names:

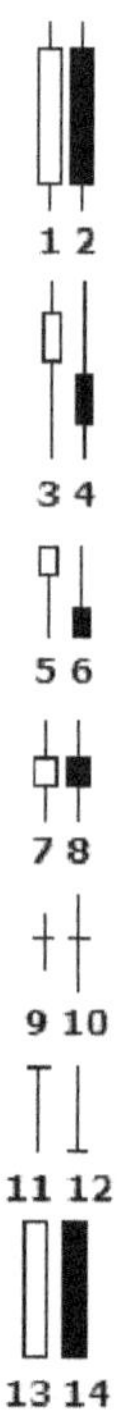

1. White (green) candlestick - signals uptrend movement (those occur in different lengths; the longer the body, the more significant the price increase)
2. Black (red) candlestick - signals downtrend movement (those occur in different lengths; the longer the body, the more significant the price decrease)
3. Long lower shadow - bullish signal (the lower wick must be at least the body's size; the longer the lower wick, the more reliable the signal)
4. Long upper shadow - bearish signal (the upper wick must be at least the body's size; the longer the upper wick, the more reliable the signal)
5. Hammer - a bullish pattern during a downtrend (long lower wick and small or no body); Shaven head - a bullish pattern during a downtrend & a bearish pattern during an uptrend (no upper wick); Hanging man - bearish pattern during an uptrend (long lower wick, small or no body; wick has the multiple length of the body.
6. Inverted hammer - signals bottom reversal, however confirmation must be obtained from next trade (may be either a white or black body); Shaven bottom - signaling bottom reversal, however confirmation must be obtained from next trade (no lower wick); Shooting

star - a bearish pattern during an uptrend (small body, long upper wick, small or no lower wick)

7. Spinning top white - neutral pattern, meaningful in combination with other candlestick patterns
8. Spinning top black - neutral pattern, meaningful in combination with other candlestick patterns
9. Doji - neutral pattern, meaningful in combination with other candlestick patterns
10. Long legged doji - signals a top reversal
11. Dragonfly doji - signals trend reversal (no upper wick, long lower wick)
12. Gravestone doji - signals trend reversal (no lower wick, long upper wick)
13. Marubozu white - dominant bullish trades, continued bullish trend (no upper, no lower wick)
14. Marubozu black - dominant bearish trades, continued bearish trend (no upper, no lower wick)

Complex Patterns

Despite those rather simple patterns depicted in the section above, there are more complex and difficult patterns, which have been identified since the charting method's inception.

Candlestick charts also convey more information than other forms of charts, such as bar charts. Just as with bar charts, they display the absolute values of the open, high, low, and closing price for a given period. But, they also show

how those prices are relative to the prior periods' prices, so one can tell by looking at one bar if the price action is higher or lower than the prior one. That and they are visually easier to look at, and can be colorized for even better definition.

Use of Candlestick Charts

Candlestick charts are a visual aid for decision making in stock, forex, commodity, and options trading. For example, when the bar is white and high relative to other time periods, it means buyers are very bullish. The opposite is true for a black bar.

Kagi Chart

The Kagi chart is a chart used for tracking price movements and to make decisions on purchasing stock. It differs from traditional stock charts, such as the Candlestick chart by being mostly independent of time. This feature aids in producing a chart that reduces random noise.

Due to its effectiveness in showing a clear path of price movements, the Kagi chart is one of the various charts that investors use to make better decision on the stocks. The most important benefit of this chart is that it is independent of time and change of direction occurs only when a specific amount is reached.

The Kagi chart was originally developed in Japan during the 1870s when the Japanese stock market started trading.

It was used for tracking the price movement of rice and found use in determining the general levels of supply and demand for certain assets.

Construction

Kagi charts look similar to swing charts and do not have a time axis. A Kagi chart is created with a series of vertical lines connected by short horizontal lines. The thickness and direction of the lines is based on the price of the underlying stock or asset, as follows:

The thickness of the line changes when the price reaches the high or low of the previous vertical line.

The direction of the line changes when the price reaches a preset reversal amount, which is usually set at 4%. When a direction change occurs, a short horizontal line is drawn between the lines of opposite direction.

Alternatively, thin and thick lines can be replaced with lines of different colors, such as the green/red example in the figure.

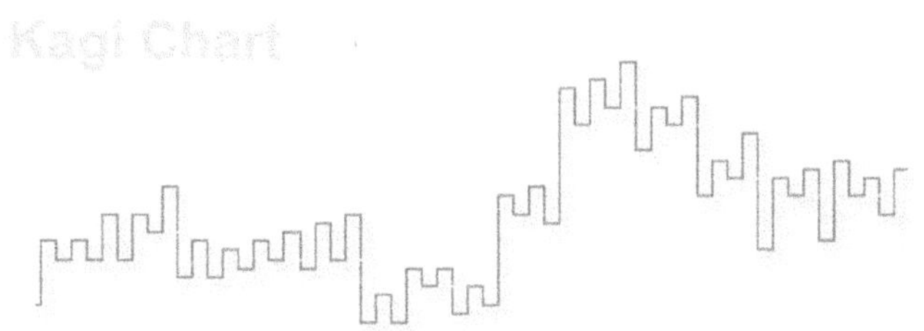

Picture 24: Kagi Chart

Changes in line thickness are used to generate transaction signals. Buy signals are generated when the Kagi line goes from thin to thick and sell signals are generated when the line turns from thick to thin.

How to plot a Kagi Chart

Find the starting point. The starting point is generally considered the first closing price. From this point forward, you compare each day's closing price with the starting price.

1. Draw a thin vertical line from the starting price to each day's closing price, while the trend does not reverse.
2. If a day's closing price moves in the opposite direction to the trend by more than the reversal amount, draw a short horizontal line and a new vertical line, beginning from the horizontal line to the new closing price.
3. If the price on a day is greater than or equal to the previous high, change to a thick line and continue the vertical line. If the price on that day is less than or equal to the previous low, then change to a thin line.

Point and Figure Chart

A point and figure chart is used for technical analysis of securities. Unlike most other investment charts, point and figure charts do not present a linear representation of time. Instead, they show trends in price.

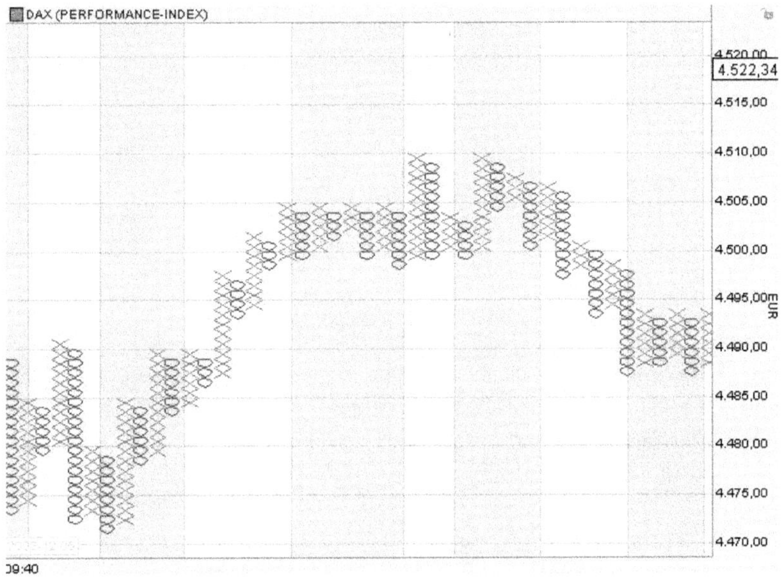

Picture 25: DAX Point and Figure Chart

The aim of point and figure charting is to filter out the "noise" (unimportant price movement) and focus on the main direction of the price trend.

Point and figure charting is said to have had its origins in the US during the early 1900s and with the first book appearing to by deVilliers, V. (1933), The point & figure method of anticipating stock price movements showed that these charting technique was already known by insiders and stock traders. Point and figure charts where already there in the trading rooms for the purpose to record daily tick movements of stocks when Charles Dow was beginning to create his famous index. Several books have been written during the 20th century.

There are two typical ways to plot point and figure charts - using closing prices, or with high/low prices. The most common method is high/low prices of a specific timeframe normally daily prices. The close (EOD) method was used until 1947 when A.W. Cohen invented a different system to work with point and figure charts using high/low prices.

Since point and figure charting in the last part of the 19th century and the first part of the 20th century was used to record price movement of tick charts the close only price would be one tick to be specific our last tick for the trading day.

In the 1980's Jeremy du Plessis was one of the first to print point and figure charts with the computer and with this help is was much easier to track many stocks at the same time thus helping to speed up the analytical process dramatically.

Market Trend

A Market Trend is the direction in which a financial market is going. Market trends can be classified as primary trends, secondary trends (short-term), and secular trends (long-term). This belief is closely related to the idea that market cycles would occur with regularity and persistence.

This belief is considered generally consistent with the practice of technical analysis and broadly inconsistent with the standard academic view of financial markets, the efficient market hypothesis. Another popular viewpoint is that market prices follow a random walk model and that any apparent past 'trends' are purely an accumulation of random variations and do not serve as a predictor for future performance. Random walk theory suggests that it is therefore not possible to outperform the general market using traditional evaluations of its "fundamentals" or by using technical analysis.

However, the assumption that market prices move in trends is one of the major components of technical analysis, and consideration of market trends is common to most Wall Street investors. Market trends are described as sustained movements in market prices over a period of time. The terms bull market and bear market describe upward and downward movements respectively: This can relate either to the market as a whole or to specific sectors and securities (stocks). The expressions "bullish" and "bearish" can also mean optimistic and pessimistic respectively ("bullish on technology stocks," or "bearish on gold", etc).

Primary Market Trends

A primary trend has broad support throughout the entire market or market sector and lasts for a year or more.

Bull Market

A bull market tends to be associated with increasing investor confidence, motivating investors to buy in anticipation of future price increases and future capital gains. In describing financial market behavior, the largest group of market participants is often referred to, metaphorically, as a herd. This is especially relevant to participants in bull markets since bulls are herding animals. A bull market is also sometimes described as a bull run. Dow Theory attempts to describe the character of these market movements.

India's BSE Index SENSEX was in a bull run for almost one year from January 2007 to January 2008 as it increased from 14,000 points to 21,000 points. Another notable and recent bull market was in the 1990s when the U.S. and many other global financial markets rose rapidly.

Bear Market

A bear market is described as being accompanied by widespread pessimism. Investors anticipating further losses are often motivated to sell, with negative sentiment feeding on itself in a vicious circle. The most famous bear market in history was preceded by the Wall Street Crash of 1929 and lasted from 1930 to 1932, marking the start of the Great Depression. A milder, low-level, long-term bear market occurred from about 1973 to 1982, encompassing the stagflation of U.S. economy, the 1970s energy crisis, and the high unemployment of the early 1980s. The financial crisis of 2007–2008 has all the traits of the start of new global bear market.

Prices fluctuate constantly on the open market. To take the example of a bear stock market, it is not a simple decline, but a substantial drop in the prices of the majority of stocks over a defined period of time. According to The Vanguard Group, "While there's no agreed-upon definition of a bear market, one generally accepted measure is a price decline of 20% or more over at least a two-month period."

Secondary Market Trends

Secondary trends are short-term changes in price direction against a primary trend. They usually last between a few weeks and a few months. Whether a trend is a secondary trend, or the beginning of a primary trend, can only be known once it has either ended or has exceeded the extent of a secondary trend.

A decline in prices during a primary trend bull market is called a market correction. A correction is usually a decline of 10% to 20%, but some experts say it can be a third or more. It differs from a bear market mostly in that it has a smaller magnitude and duration.

An increase in prices during a primary trend bear market is called a bear market rally. A bear market rally is sometimes defined as an increase of 10% to 20%. Bear market rallies typically begin suddenly and are often short-lived. Notable bear market rallies occurred in the Dow Jones index after the 1929 stock market crash leading down to the market bottom in 1932, and throughout the late 1960s and early 1970s. The Japanese Nikkei stock average has been typified by a number of bear market rallies since the late 1980s while experiencing an overall long-term downward trend.

Secular Market Trends

A secular market trend is a long-term trend that usually lasts 5 to 25 years (but whose distribution is more or less bell shaped around 17 years, in the stock market), and consists of sequential 'primary' trends. In a secular bull market the 'primary' bear markets have in the past almost always been shorter and less punishing than the 'primary' bull markets were rewarding. Each bear market has rarely (if ever) wiped out the real (inflation adjusted) gains of the previous bull markets, and the succeeding bull markets have usually made up for the real losses of any previous bear markets. This is one of the reasons why a secular market trend may be said to encompass the primary trends within it. The United States was described as being in a secular bull market from about 1983 to late 2007, with brief upsets including the crash of 1987 and the dot-com bust of 2000–2002.

In a secular bear market, the 'primary' bull markets are sometimes shorter than the 'primary' bear markets and rarely compensate for the real losses of the 'primary' bear markets occurring during this extended cycle. For example, in the 1966–82 secular bear market in stocks, there was hardly any nominal loss. But in real terms the loss was devastating. (In the past most 'housing recessions' were of a slow nature, thereby allowing inflation to keep housing prices steady.) Another example of a secular bear market was seen in gold during the period between January 1980 to June 1999. During this period the nominal gold price fell from a high of $850/oz ($30/g) to a low of $253/oz ($9/g), and became part of the Great Commodities Depression. The S&P 500 experienced a secular bull market over a similar time period (~1982–2000).

Market Events

An exaggerated bear market, that tends to be associated with falling investor confidence and panic selling, can lead to a market crash associated with a recession. An exaggerated bull market, on the other hand, fueled by overconfidence and/or speculation can lead to a market bubble — characterized by an extreme inflation of the price/earnings P/E ratios of the stocks in that market.

Cause of Market Events

Market movements may respond to new information becoming available to the market, but may also be influenced by investors' cognitive biases and emotional biases. Expectations play a large part in financial markets. Often there will be significant price reaction to financial data, information or news. Unexpected news or information that is perceived as positive for the economy or for a particular market sector or company will of course increase stock prices and vice versa.

Etymology

The precise origin of the phrases "bull market" and "bear market" are obscure. The Oxford English Dictionary cites an 1891 use of the term "bull market".

The most common etymology points to London bearskin "jobbers" (market makers), who would sell bearskins before the bears had actually been caught in contradiction of the proverb ne vendez pas la peau de l'ours avant de l'avoir tué ("don't sell the bearskin before you've killed the bear")—an admonition against over-optimism. By the time of the South Sea Bubble of 1721, the bear was also associated with short selling. Jobbers would sell bearskins they did not own in anticipation of falling prices, which would enable them to buy them later for an additional profit.

Another plausible origin is from the word "bulla" which means bill, or contract. When a market is rising, holders of contracts for future delivery of a commodity see the value of their contract increase. However in a falling market, the counterparties—the "bearers" of the commodity to be delivered, win because they have locked in a future delivery price that is higher than the current price.

Some analogies that have been used as mnemonic devices:

- Bull is short for 'bully', in its now mostly obsolete meaning of 'excellent'.

- It relates to the common use of these animals in blood sport, i.e bear-baiting and bull-baiting.
- It refers to the way that the animals attack: a bull attacks upwards with its horns, while a bear swipes downwards with its paws.
- It relates to the speed of the animals: bulls usually charge at very high speed whereas bears normally are lazy and cautious movers.
- They were originally used in reference to two old merchant banking families, the Barings and the Bulstrodes.
- Bears hibernate, while bulls do not.
- The word "bull" plays off the market's returns being "full" whereas "bear" alludes to the market's returns being "bare".

Stock Market Bottom

A stock market bottom is a trend reversal that marks the end of a market downturn and the beginning of an upward moving trend. A "bottom" may occur because of the presence of a cycle, or because of panic selling as a reaction to an adverse financial development.

It is easy to identify a bottom in hindsight but very difficult to identify a bottom (referred to by investors as "bottom picking") while it is occurring. This is because the upturn following a decline is often shortlived and may result in a continued price decline and hence a loss of capital for the investor who purchased stock(s) during a misperceived or "fake" market bottom.

Some of the more notable market bottoms, in terms of the closing values of the Dow Jones Industrial Average (DJIA) include:

- Black Monday: The DJIA hit a bottom at 1738.74 on 10/19/1987, as a result of the decline from 2722.41 on 8/25/1987.
- The bursting of the Dot-com bubble: A bottom of 7286.27 was reached on the DJIA on 10/9/2002 as a result of the decline from 11722.98 on 1/14/2000. This included an intermediate bottom of 8235.81 on 9/21/2001 which led to an intermediate top of 10635.25 on 3/19/2002.
- A decline associated with the Subprime mortgage crisis starting at 14164.41 on 10/9/2007 (DJIA) and caused a short term bottom of 11740.15 on 3/10/2008. After a rallying to a temporary top on 5/2/2008 at 13058.20 the primary trend of the declining, "bear" market, resumed.

Baron Rothschild is said to have advised that the best time to buy is when there is "blood in the streets", i.e. when the markets have fallen drastically and investor sentiment is extremely negative. At that time adherants of the trend following approach have already exited the market, however those who view the stock markets as a cyclical process and feel they have clearly "picked a bottom", might become interested in buying because this is when profit potential is at its peak.

An investor who enters the market at a perceived bottom has concluded:

- The market has fallen to such a degree that the current price is far below normal expected values.

- The market is not likely to fall further.
- A valid uptrend is about to begin.

Identifying a Market Bottom

Market valuation (Long term indicator): A proper market valuation is accomplished by considering both earnings and earnings growth using a formal Discounted Cash Flow Model. Some of the organizations who perform proper market valuations are:

- Morningstar uses a market valuation graph giving the ratio of price to fair value for the median stock in each coverage universe over time. A ratio below 1.00 indicates that the stock's price is lower than the estimate of its fair value.

- Valueline's VLMAP (market appreciation potential) attempts to project a stock's appreciation over the next 3-5 years. Its use has been studied by Peter Bernstein and Dan Seiver, who uses it in his PAD system report. When the Valueline indicator rises above 100, it is taken to be a buy signal. This method of measurement gave buy signals during the bottoms of October 2002 and March 2003, and the panic low immediately following the 9/11 terrorist attacks. However its record as a sell indicator (at a market top) is thought by many to be questionable.

- A common but less accurate method of market valuation is to utilize the company's profit and earnings P/E ratio. It does not take potential growth into account.

Investor sentiment (Long term indicator): When an extremely large percentage of investors and financial advisors express a bearish (negative) sentiment, it is a strong signal that a market bottom may be near. However the predictive capabilities of this kind of investor sentiment are thought to be highest when investor sentiment reaches extreme values. Indicators that measure investor sentiment may include:

- Investor Intelligence Sentiment Index: If the Bull-Bear spread (% of Bulls - % of Bears) is close to a historical low, it may signal a bottom.

On July 22, 2008 it stood at -20.20%, a remarkably low value for past three year period.

- American Association of Individual Investors (AAII) sentiment indicator: Many feel that the majority of the decline has already occurred once this indicator gives a reading of minus 15% or below.

- Mark Hulbert's Stock Newsletter Sentiment Index (HSNSI): During the March 2008 bottom this indicator gave a reading of minus 29.4%. As of June 30, 2008, it stood at minus 35.9, which was its lowest value in a decade.

- Other sentiment indicators include the Nova-Ursa ratio and Short Interest/Total Market Float

Market Oversold Indicators:

- Relative strength index (RSI)is a momentum indicator that compares recent gains to recent losses. It is measured in values between 0 and 100. When the RSI is below 30, the market or stock is considered to be significantly oversold and therefore undervalued. For example here is an RSI chart for the NASDAQ Composite.

- Greatly Undervalued securities: Prices that are below several multiples (2 to 4) of the standard deviation from the 50-day moving average. (See also Bollinger Bands.) For example here is the chart for NASDAQ Composite MA with 2% deviation.

- 'Standard and Poor's (S&P) oscillator': This is a proprietary tool offerred by Standard and Poor's, a renowned investiment research company and one can access the S&P oscillator through a paid subscription with S&P. Standard and Poor's, This oscillator is thought to be based on a formula originally proposed by George Angell. For a given bar, it is given by ((High - Open) + (Close - Low)) / (100*2 * (High - Low)) minus 50%; market lows are supposed to be marked by minus 4% to minus 9% (i.e. 4 to 9% below average).

Market capitulation: In a severe down trending market there may be a certain threshold after which large numbers of investors can no longer tolerate the financial losses incurred as a result of the current downturn. This majority group of investors then capitulates (gives up) and sells in panic or finds that their pre-set sell stops have been triggered thereby automatically liquidating their shares of a given stock. This dramatic increase in the number of sellers causes a further increase in the speed and severity of the stock's price decline. Margin calls and mutual fund and hedge fund redemptions significantly contribute to capitualtions. In other words market capitulation occurs when there is a sudden steep decline in price caused by high volume selling, for example note the high volume selling in this chart of the NASDAQ composite index (QQQQ) when it experienced a bottom(s). The peak in volume may precede an actual bottom.

Other Signs of a Market Bottom

- Decline in the number of new price lows. Chart for Nasdaq & NYSE Composite New Lows

- Moving average convergance divergence (MACD) is used to assess longer term trends and the MACD histogram is used for shorter term trends. When the MACD line crosses over to a positive range (top half of the chart) it is a sign that the uptrend has resumed. For example the MACD of the QQQQ at a market bottom might look something like this chart.

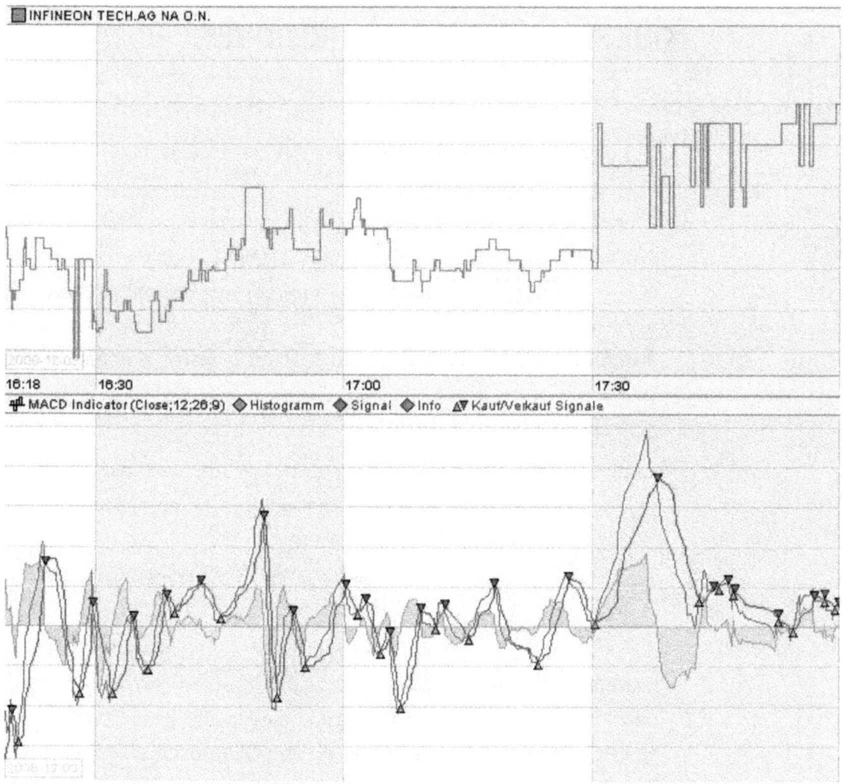

Picture 26: Infineon Stock with MACD

- Very high volatility as measured by the volatility index VIX or VXO. A VXO reading above 30 that creates a sharp one or two day peak on a chart is often indicative of a market bottom.

Chart patterns: A bottom is often seen as a long term price pattern within a chart. Some of the more common chart patterns used to evaluate a potential bottom reversal of a stock or the stock market in general are:

- Inverted head and shoulders, double bottom (a W-shaped formation), triple bottom, or cup and handle patterns.

- Japanese candlestick patterns: Abandoned baby bull, Morning star bull or Morning Doji star pattern

Risks of Attempting to invest at a Market Bottom

It is very difficult to identify the exact day(s) during which a market bottom is reached. Investing at the time of a perceived bottom can be quite risky, and is often compared to catching a falling knife. In this kind of a situation many investment advisors recommend that an investor proceed with extreme caution and:

- Carefully assess the current and future outlook of the market.
- Invest only when the market and its component stocks are grossly undervalued.
- Make an investment/purchase in three sections (over time), instead of one single purchase.

Examples of investors who incorrectly guessed a market bottom during the period of Oct. 30, 1929-Oct 31, 1931 (see Wall Street Crash of 1929). The average P/E (price to earnings) ratio of S&P Composite stocks was 32.6 in September 1929 clearly above historical norms.

When the recovery is only a short one, it is termed a dead cat bounce.

When a recovery represents only a short term rise within a generally declining market, it is referred to as a bear-market rally.

2008 Market Drop

The sharp stock market decline of early October 2008 resulted in considerable discussion about the placement of a stock market bottom. The Chicago Board Options Exchange volatility index (VIX) reached levels never seen before, and a large number of new lows had also been observed. However as of October 9th the massive volume that generally accompanies a capitulation had not yet been observed.

The volume peaked on Oct 10, 2008, which was followed by a surge in the index the next trading day on Oct 13, 2008. VIX continued to rise and reached an intraday high of 89.53 on Oct 24, 2008. The S&P 500 index reached an intraday low of 839.80 on Oct. 10, 2008. The bottom was retested on Oct 28, 2008, when the intraday low of 845.27 was reached.

Oct 2008 S&P 500 Drop			
Date	Index Change	Volume	VIX
24-Oct-08	-3.6%	6,550,050,000	79.13
23-Oct-08	+1.3%	7,184,180,000	67.80
22-Oct-08	-6.1%	6,147,980,000	69.65
21-Oct-08	-3.1%	5,121,830,000	53.11
20-Oct-08	+4.8%	5,175,640,000	52.97
17-Oct-08	-0.6%	6,581,780,000	70.33
16-Oct-08	+4.3%	7,984,500,000	67.61
15-Oct-08	-9.0%	6,542,330,000	69.25
14-Oct-08	-0.5%	8,161,990,400	55.13
13-Oct-08	+11.6%	7,263,369,600	54.99
10-Oct-08	-1.2%	11,456,230,400	69.95

9-Oct-08	-7.6%	6,819,000,000	63.92
8-Oct-08	-1.1%	8,716,329,600	57.53
7-Oct-08	-5.7%	7,069,209,600	53.68
6-Oct-08	-3.9%	7,956,020,000	52.05
3-Oct-08	-1.4%	6,716,120,000	45.14
2-Oct-08	-4.0%	6,285,640,000	45.26
1-Oct-08	-0.3%	5,782,130,000	39.81
30-Sep-08	+5.3%	4,937,680,000	39.39
29-Sep-08	-8.8%	7,305,060,000	46.72

Jim Cramer, founder and owner of TheStreet.com and host of the CNBC show Mad Money, expressed his view on October 7, 2008 that "we are nowhere near a bottom". He said that "three things that need to happen before a bottom in tech can occur. First, the earnings estimates for these companies need to be cut repeatedly until the companies can beat them. Second, companies with bulging inventories need to work through those inventories. And finally, the economy needs to turn around."

Ed Yardeni, of Yardeni Research stated on October 7, 2008 "I'm not sure, but that sure seemed like capitulation yesterday ... stocks are cheap, with the S&P 500 trading at a mere 10.8-times estimated earnings".

The technical analyst Jeff de Graaf stated "we're only in about the 5th inning of the downturn." He said "The total number of new companies making 52-

week lows has reached 57% .. usually when the number crosses 50% it signals a wash-out... Right now we're 250 days into the bear market. Typically a bear market runs about 600 days."

Mark Hulbert on Oct. 7, 2008 pointed out that the Hulbert Stock Newsletter Sentiment Index (HSNSI), as of Monday evening, stood at minus 33.5%. As of immediate past Friday's close, in contrast, the HSNSI stood at minus 36.1%. This slight rise suggests that capitulation has not yet occurred.

Vanguard Group founder John Bogle stated on Oct. 8 2008, that "the stock market bloodbath is probably more than halfway over".

In an interview at night on Oct. 9 2008, Jeremy Siegel expressed the view that if libor rate goes down to 2%-1.5%, it will result in a huge rally. He suggested a turnaround in the afternoon of 10 Oct 2008 is possible, although one can never be certain.

Blackrock Vice Chairman Robert Doll said on early morning of 10 Oct 2008 "Often you see double, triple normal volume and we've just not seen that kind of capitulation yet". However later on 10 Oct 2008 high volume was reported. "Nearly 1.1 billion shares trading hands by midday, close to half of what most experts consider enough for capitulation."

On Oct 17, in a New York Times article, Warren Buffett announced he is starting to buying stocks for his personal account. He gave a rule: Be fearful when others are greedy, and be greedy when others are fearful." On Oct 20, Forsyth noted a thaw in the credit market.

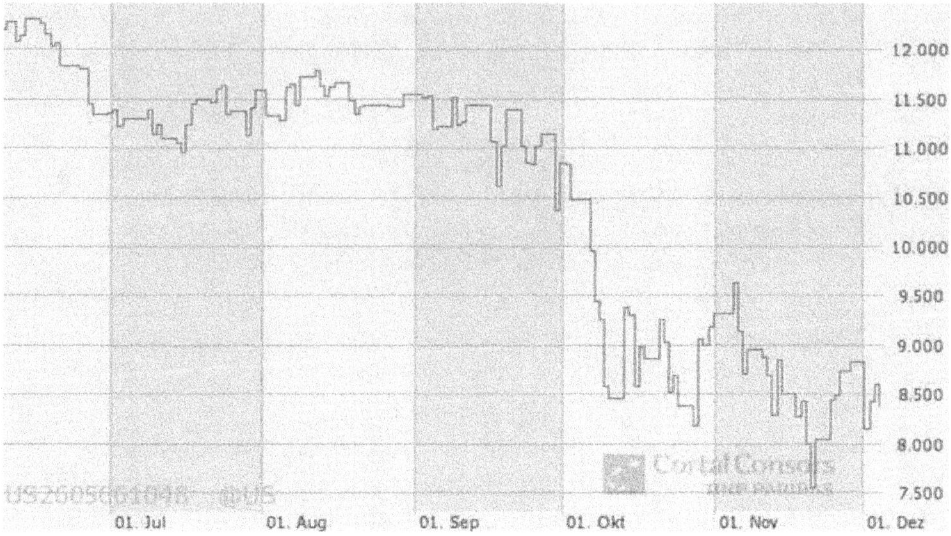

Picture 27: DJIA July 2008 - December 2008

Concepts

Black–Scholes

The term Black–Scholes refers to three closely related concepts:

- The Black–Scholes model is a mathematical model of the market for an equity, in which the equity's price is a stochastic process.
- The Black–Scholes PDE is a partial differential equation which (in the model) must be satisfied by the price of a derivative on the equity.
- The Black–Scholes formula is the result obtained by solving the Black-Scholes PDE for European put and call options.

Robert C. Merton was the first to publish a paper expanding the mathematical understanding of the options pricing model and coined the term "Black-Scholes" options pricing model, by enhancing work that was published by Fischer Black and Myron Scholes. The paper was first published in 1973. The foundation for their research relied on work developed by scholars such as Louis Bachelier, A. James Boness, Sheen T. Kassouf, Edward O. Thorp, and Paul Samuelson. The fundamental insight of Black-Scholes is that the option is implicitly priced if the stock is traded.

Merton and Scholes received the 1997 Nobel Prize in Economics for this and related work. Though ineligible for the prize because of his death in 1995, Black was mentioned as a contributor by the Swedish academy.

The Model

The Black-Scholes model of the market for an equity makes the following assumptions:

- The price of the underlying instrument St follows a geometric Brownian motion defined by $dS_t = \mu S_t\,dt + \sigma S_t\,dW_t$ where Wt is a Wiener process with constant drift μ and volatility σ.
- It is possible to short sell the underlying stock.
- There are no arbitrage opportunities.
- Trading in the stock is continuous.
- There are no transaction costs or taxes.

- All securities are perfectly divisible (i.e. it is possible to buy any fraction of a share).
- It is possible to borrow and lend cash at a constant risk-free interest rate.
- The stock does not pay a dividend.

Black Model

The Black model (sometimes known as the Black-76 model) is a variant of the Black-Scholes option pricing model. Its primary applications are for pricing bond options, interest rate caps / floors, and swaptions. It was first presented in a paper written by Fischer Black in 1976.

Black's model can be generalized into a class of models known as log-normal forward models, also referred to as LIBOR Market Model.

The Black formula

The Black formula is similar to the Black-Scholes formula for valuing stock options except that the spot price of the underlying is replaced by the forward price F.

The Black formula for a call option on an underlying strike at K, expiring T years in the future is

$$c = e^{-rT} * [FN(d_1) - KN(d_2)]$$

The put price is

$$p = e^{-rT} * [KN(-d_2) - FN(-d_1)]$$

where

$$d_1 = \frac{\ln(F/K) + (\sigma^2/2)T}{\sigma\sqrt{T}}$$

$$d_2 = \frac{\ln(F/K) - (\sigma^2/2)T}{\sigma\sqrt{T}} = d_1 - \sigma\sqrt{T}.$$

Derivation and Assumptions

The derivation of the pricing formulas in the model follows that of the Black-Scholes model almost exactly. The assumption that the spot price follows a log-normal process is replaced by the assumption that the forward price at maturity of the option is log-normally distributed. From there the derivation is identical and so the final formula is the same except that the spot price is replaced by the forward - the forward price represents the undiscounted expected future value.

Dead Cat Bounce

A dead cat bounce is a figurative term used by traders in the finance industry to describe a pattern wherein a spectacular decline in the price of a stock is immediately followed by a moderate and temporary rise before resuming its downward movement, with the connotation that the rise was not an indication of improving circumstances in the fundamentals of the stock. It is derived from the notion that "even a dead cat will bounce if it falls from a great height".

The phrase has been used on the trading floors for many years. However the earliest recorded use of the phrase dates from 1985 when the Singaporean and Malaysian stock markets bounced back after a hard fall during the recession of that year. Journalist Christopher Sherwell of the Financial Times reported a stock broker as saying the market rise was a "dead cat bounce". It has also been used in reference to political polling numbers.

The reasons for such a bounce can be technical, as investors may have standing orders to buy shorted stocks if they fall below a certain level or to cover certain option positions. Once those limits are reached, the buy orders are activated and the sudden rise in demand causes the price of the stock to rise as well. The bounce may also be the result of speculation. Since bounces often occur, traders buy into what they hope is the bottom of the market, expecting a bounce and thereby reaping a quick profit. Thus, the very act of anticipating a bounce can create and magnify it.

A market rise after a sharp fall can only really be seen to be a "dead cat bounce" with the benefit of hindsight. If the stock starts to fall again in the following days and weeks, then it was a true dead cat bounce. If the market starts to climb again after the first short bounce, then the continued rise in price action would be considered a trend reversal and not a dead cat bounce.

Since this distinction only becomes obvious in hindsight, the evaluation may vary depending upon the initial and final points of reference.

Coppock Curve

The Coppock curve or Coppock indicator is a technical analysis indicator created by Edwin Coppock, first published in Barron's Magazine in 1962.

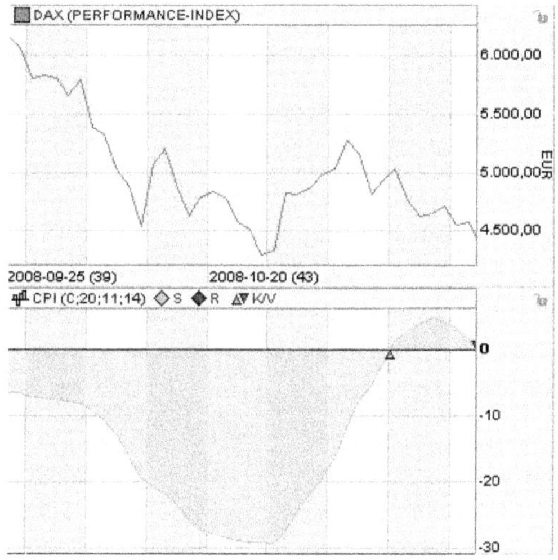

Picture 28: Coppock Curve

The indicator is designed for use on a monthly time scale. It's the sum of a 14-month rate of change and 11-month rate of change, smoothed by a 10-period weighted moving average.

$$Coppock = WMA[10] \ of \ (ROC[14] + ROC[11]).$$

Coppock was an economist and he had been asked by the Episcopal Church to identify buying opportunities for long-term investors. He thought market downturns were like bereavements and required a period of mourning. He asked the church bishops how long that normally took for people, their answer was 11 to 14 months and so he used those periods in his calculation.

A buy signal is generated when the indicator is below zero and turns upwards from a trough. No sell signals are generated (that not being its design). The indicator is trend-following, and based on averages, so by its nature it doesn't pick a market bottom, but rather shows when a rally has become established.

Coppock designed the indicator for the S&P 500 index, and it's been applied to similar stock indexes like the Dow Jones Industrial Average. It's not regarded as well-suited to commodity markets, since bottoms there are more rounded than the spike lows found in stocks.

Although designed for monthly use, a daily calculation over the same period can be made, converting the periods to 294 day and 231 day rate of changes, and a 210 day weighted moving average.

A slightly different version of the indicator is still used by the Investors Chronicle, a British investment magazine. The main difference is that the Investors Chronicle version does include the sell signals, although it stresses that they are to be treated with caution. This is because such signals could merely be a dip in a continuing bull market

Elliott Wave Principle

The Elliott wave principle is a form of technical analysis that attempts to forecast trends in the financial markets and other collective activities. It is named after Ralph Nelson Elliott (1871–1948), an accountant who developed the concept in the 1930s: he proposed that market prices unfold in specific patterns, which practitioners today call Elliott waves. Elliott published his views of market behavior in the book The Wave Principle (1938), in a series of articles in Financial World magazine in 1939, and most fully in his final major work, Nature's Laws – The Secret of the Universe (1946). Elliott argued that because humans are themselves rhythmical, their activities and decisions could be predicted in rhythms, too. Critics argue that the Elliott wave principle is pseudoscientific and contradicts the efficient market hypothesis.

Overall Design

The wave principle posits that collective investor psychology (or crowd psychology) moves from optimism to pessimism and back again. These swings create patterns, as evidenced in the price movements of a market at every degree of trend.

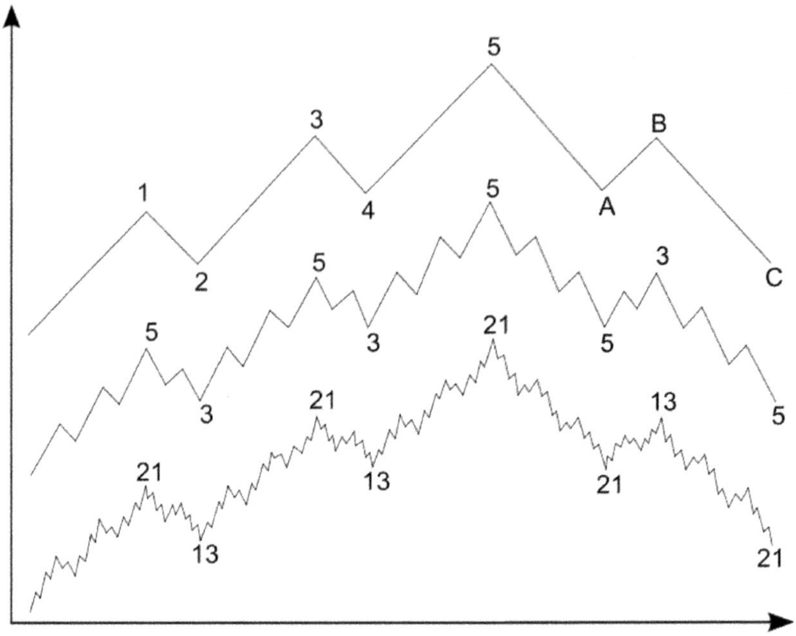

Picture 29: From R.N. Elliott's essay, "The Basis of the Wave Principle," October 1940

From R.N. Elliott's essay, "The Basis of the Wave Principle," October 1940.Practically all developments which result from (human) socialeconomic processes follow a law that causes them to repeat themselves in similar and constantly recurring series of waves of definite number and pattern. R. N. Elliott's model, in Nature's Law: The Secret of the Universe says that market prices alternate between five waves and three waves at all degrees within a trend, as the illustration shows. As these waves develop, the larger price patterns unfold in a self-similar fractal geometry. Within the dominant trend, waves 1, 3, and 5 are "motive" waves, and each motive wave itself subdivides in five waves. Waves 2 and 4 are "corrective" waves, and subdivide in three waves. In a bear market the dominant trend is downward, so the pattern is reversed—five waves down and three up. Motive waves always move with the trend, while corrective waves move opposite it.

Degree

The patterns link to form five and three-wave structures which themselves underlie self-similar wave structures of increasing size or higher "degree." Note the lower most of the three idealized cycles. In the first small five-wave sequence, waves 1, 3 and 5 are motive, while waves 2 and 4 are corrective. This signals that the movement of the wave one degree higher is upward. It also signals the start of the first small three-wave corrective sequence. After the initial five waves up and three waves down, the sequence begins again and the self-similar fractal geometry begins to unfold according the five and three-wave structure which it underlies one degree higher. The completed motive pattern includes 89 waves, followed by a completed corrective pattern of 55 waves.

Each degree of a pattern in a financial market has a name. Practitioners use symbols for each wave to indicate both function and degree—numbers for motive waves, letters for corrective waves (shown in the highest of the three idealized series of wave structures or degrees). Degrees are relative; they are defined by form, not by absolute size or duration. Waves of the same degree may be of very different size and/or duration.

The classification of a wave at any particular degree can vary, though practitioners generally agree on the standard order of degrees (approximate durations given):

Grand supercycle: multi-decade to multi-century

- Supercycle: a few years to a few decades
    - Cycle: one year to a few years
        - Primary: a few months to a couple of years
            - Intermediate: weeks to months
                - Minor: weeks
                    - Minute: days
                        - Minuette: hours
                            - Subminuette: minutes

Behavioral Characteristics and Wave "Signature"

Elliott Wave analysts (or "Elliotticians") hold that it is not necessary to look at a price chart to judge where a market is in its wave pattern. Each wave has its own "signature" which often reflects the psychology of the moment. Understanding how and why the waves develop is key to the application of the Wave Principle; that understanding includes recognizing the characteristics described below.

These wave characteristics assume a bull market in equities. The characteristics apply in reverse in bear markets.

Five Wave Pattern (dominant trend)

Wave 1:

Wave one is rarely obvious at its inception. When the first wave of a new bull market begins, the fundamental news is almost universally negative. The previous trend is considered still strongly in force. Fundamental analysts continue to revise their earnings estimates lower; the economy probably does not look strong. Sentiment surveys are decidedly bearish, put options are in vogue, and implied volatility in the options market is high. Volume might increase a bit as prices rise, but not by enough to alert many technical analysts.

Wave 2:

Wave two corrects wave one, but can never extend beyond the starting point of wave one. Typically, the news is still bad. As prices retest the prior low, bearish sentiment quickly builds, and "the crowd" haughtily reminds all that the bear market is still deeply ensconced. Still, some positive signs appear for those who are looking: volume should be lower during wave two than during wave one, prices usually do not retrace more than 61.8% of the wave one gains, and prices should fall in a three wave pattern.

Wave 3:

Wave three is usually the largest and most powerful wave in a trend (although some research suggests that in commodity markets, wave five is the largest). The news is now positive and fundamental analysts start to raise earnings estimates. Prices rise quickly, corrections are short-lived and shallow. Anyone looking to "get in on a pullback" will likely miss the boat. As wave three starts, the news is probably still bearish, and most market players remain negative; but by wave three's midpoint, "the crowd" will often join the new bullish trend. Wave three often extends wave one by a ratio of 1.618:1.

Wave 4:

Wave four is typically clearly corrective. Prices may meander sideways for an extended period, and wave four typically retraces less than 38.2% of wave three. Volume is well below than that of wave three. This is a good place to buy a pull back if you understand the potential ahead for wave 5. Still, the most distinguishing feature of fourth waves is that they often prove very difficult to count.

Wave 5:

Wave five is the final leg in the direction of the dominant trend. The news is almost universally positive and everyone is bullish. Unfortunately, this is when many average investors finally buy in, right before the top. Volume is lower in wave five than in wave three, and many momentum indicators start to show divergences (prices reach a new high, the indicator does not reach a new peak). At the end of a major bull market, bears may very well be ridiculed.

Three Wave Pattern (corrective trend)

Wave A:

Corrections are typically harder to identify than impulse moves. In wave A of a bear market, the fundamental news is usually still positive. Most analysts see the drop as a correction in a still-active bull market. Some technical indicators that accompany wave A include increased volume, rising implied volatility in the options markets and possibly a turn higher in open interest in related futures markets.

Wave B:

Prices reverse higher, which many see as a resumption of the now long-gone bull market. Those familiar with classical technical analysis may see the peak as the right shoulder of a head and shoulders reversal pattern. The volume during wave B should be lower than in wave A. By this point, fundamentals are probably no longer improving, but they most likely have not yet turned negative.

Wave C:

Prices move impulsively lower in five waves. Volume picks up, and by the third leg of wave C, almost everyone realizes that a bear market is firmly entrenched. Wave C is typically at least as large as wave A and often extends to 1.618 times wave A or beyond.

Pattern Recognition and Fractals

Elliott's market model relies heavily on looking at price charts. Practitioners study developing price moves to distinguish the waves and wave structures, and discern what prices may do next. Thus the application of the wave principle is a form of pattern recognition.

The structures Elliott described also meet the common definition of a fractal (self-similar patterns appearing at every degree of trend). Elliott wave practitioners say that just as naturally-occurring fractals often expand and grow more complex over time, the model shows that collective human psychology develops in natural patterns, via buying and selling decisions reflected in market prices: "It's as though we are somehow programmed by mathematics. Seashell, galaxy, snowflake or human: we're all bound by the same order."

Fibonacci Relationships

R. N. Elliott's analysis of the mathematical properties of waves and patterns eventually led him to conclude that "The Fibonacci Summation Series is the basis of The Wave Principle." Numbers from the Fibonacci sequence surface repeatedly in Elliott wave structures, including motive waves (1, 3, 5), a single full cycle (5 up, 3 down = 8 waves), and the completed motive (89 waves) and corrective (55 waves) patterns. Elliott developed his market model before he realized that it reflects the Fibonacci sequence. "When I discovered The Wave Principle action of market trends, I had never heard of either the Fibonacci Series or the Pythagorean Diagram."

The Fibonacci sequence is also closely connected to the Golden ratio (ca 1.618). Practitioners commonly use this ratio and related ratios to establish support and resistance levels for market waves, namely the price points which help define the parameters of a trend.

Finance professor Roy Batchelor and researcher Richard Ramyar, a former Director of the United Kingdom Society of Technical Analysts and Head of UK Asset Management Research at Reuters Lipper, studied whether Fibonacci ratios appear non-randomly in the stock market, as Elliott's model predicts. The researchers said the "idea that prices retrace to a Fibonacci ratio or round fraction of the previous trend clearly lacks any scientific rationale." They also said "there is no significant difference between the frequencies with which price and time ratios occur in cycles in the Dow Jones Industrial Average, and frequencies which we would expect to occur at random in such a time series."

Robert Prechter replied to the Batchelor-Ramyar study, saying that it "does not challenge the validity of any aspect of the Wave Principle...it supports wave theorists' observations," and that because the authors had examined ratios between prices achieved in filtered trends rather than Elliott waves, "their method does not address actual claims by wave theorists." The Socionomics Institute also reviewed data in the Batchelor-Ramyar study, and said this data shows "Fibonacci ratios do occur more often in the stock market than would be expected in a random environment."'

Example of The Elliott Wave Principle and The Fibonacci Relationship

The GBP/JPY currency chart gives an example of a fourth wave retracement apparently halting between the 38.2% and 50.0% Fibonacci retracements of a completed third wave. The chart also highlights how the Elliott Wave Principle works well with other technical analysis tendencies as prior support (the bottom of wave-1) acts as resistance to wave-4. The wave count depicted in the chart would be invalidated if GBP/JPY moves above the wave-1 low.

Picture 30:From sakuragi_indofx, "Trading never been so easy eh," December 2007

After Elliott

Following Elliott's death in 1948, other market technicians and financial professionals continued to use the wave principle and provide forecasts to investors. Charles Collins, who had published Elliott's "Wave Principle" and helped introduce Elliott's theory to Wall Street, ranked Elliott's contributions to technical analysis on a level with Charles Dow. Hamilton Bolton, founder of The Bank Credit Analyst, provided wave analysis to a wide readership in the 1950s and 1960s. Bolton introduced Elliott's wave principle to A.J. Frost, who provided weekly financial commentary on the Financial News Network in the 1980s. Frost co-authored Elliott Wave Principle with Robert Prechter in 1979.

Rediscovery and current use

Robert Prechter came across Elliott's works while working as a market technician at Merrill Lynch. His fame as a forecaster during the bull market of the 1980s brought the greatest exposure to date to Elliott's theory, and today Prechter remains the most widely known Elliott analyst.

Among market technicians, wave analysis is widely accepted as a component of their trade. Elliott Wave Theory is among the methods included on the exam that analysts must pass to earn the Chartered Market Technician (CMT) designation, the professional accreditation developed by the Market Technicians Association (MTA).

Robin Wilkin, Global Head of FX and Commodity Technical Strategy at JPMorgan Chase, says "the Elliott Wave principle... provides a probability framework as to when to enter a particular market and where to get out, whether for a profit or a loss."

Jordan Kotick, Global Head of Technical Strategy at Barclays Capital and past President of the Market Technicians Association, has said that R. N. Elliott's "discovery was well ahead of its time. In fact, over the last decade or two, many prominent academics have embraced Elliott's idea and have been aggressively advocating the existence of financial market fractals."

One such academic is the physicist Didier Sornette, visiting professor at the Department of Earth and Space Science and the Institute of Geophysics and Planetary Physics at UCLA. A paper he co-authored in 1996 ("Stock Market Crashes, Precursors and Replicas") said,

> "It is intriguing that the log-periodic structures documented here bear some similarity with the 'Elliott waves' of technical analysis .... A lot of effort has been developed in finance both by academic and trading institutions and more recently by physicists (using some of their statistical tools developed to deal with complex times series) to analyze past data to get information on the future. The 'Elliott wave' technique is probably the most famous in this field. We speculate

> that the 'Elliott waves', so strongly rooted in the financial analysts' folklore, could be a signature of an underlying critical structure of the stock market."

Paul Tudor Jones, the billionaire commodity trader, calls Prechter and Frost's standard text on Elliott "a classic," and one of "the four Bibles of the business" --

> "[McGee and Edwards'] Technical Analysis of Stock Trends and The Elliott Wave Theorist both give very specific and systematic ways to approach developing great reward/risk ratios for entering into a business contract with the marketplace, which is what every trade should be if properly and thoughtfully executed."

Pauline Novak-Reich in her provocatively entitled book, "The Bell Does Ring; Timing the Australian Stock Market with Gann and Elliott Strategies" counters the claims of the Efficient Market Hypothesis of Eugene Fama in an exposition that integrates Elliott Wave Theory with the Gann approach.

Criticism

The premise that markets unfold in recognizable patterns contradicts the efficient market hypothesis, which says that prices cannot be predicted from market data such as moving averages and volume. By this reasoning, if successful market forecasts were possible, investors would buy (or sell) when the method predicted a price increase (or decrease), to the point that prices would rise (or fall) immediately, thus destroying the profitability and predictive power of the method. In efficient markets, knowledge of the Elliott wave principle among investors would lead to the disappearance of the very patterns they tried to anticipate, rendering the method, and all forms of technical analysis, useless.

Benoit Mandelbrot has questioned whether Elliott waves can predict financial markets:

> "But Wave prediction is a very uncertain business. It is an art to which the subjective judgement of the chartists matters more than the objective, replicable verdict of the numbers. The record of this, as of most technical analysis, is at best mixed."

Robert Prechter had previously said that ideas in an article by Mandelbrot "originated with Ralph Nelson Elliott, who put them forth more comprehensively and more accurately with respect to real-world markets in his 1938 book The Wave Principle."

Critics also say the wave principle is too vague to be useful, since it cannot consistently identify when a wave begins or ends, and that Elliott wave forecasts are prone to subjective revision. Some who advocate technical analysis of markets have questioned the value of Elliott wave analysis. Technical analyst David Aronson wrote:

> The Elliott Wave Principle, as popularly practiced, is not a legitimate theory, but a story, and a compelling one that is eloquently told by Robert Prechter. The account is especially persuasive because EWP has the seemingly remarkable ability to fit any segment of market history down to its most minute fluctuations. I contend this is made possible by the method's loosely defined rules and the ability to postulate a large number of nested waves of varying magnitude. This gives the Elliott analyst the same freedom and flexibility that allowed pre-Copernican astronomers to explain all observed planet movements even though their underlying theory of an Earth-centered universe was wrong.

However, Robert R. Prechter Jr. set an all time record in the United States Trading Championship by returning 444.4% in a monitored real-money options account in the four month contest period. During the contest, he traded using the Elliott Wave Principle. In December 1989, Financial News Network named him "Guru of the Decade".

Momentum

Momentum and rate of change (ROC) are simple technical analysis indicators showing the difference between today's closing price and the close N days ago. Momentum is the absolute difference:

$$momentum = close_{today} - close_{N\ days\ ago}$$

Rate of change scales by the old close, so as to represent the increase as a fraction,

$$rate\ of\ change = \frac{close_{today} - close_{N\ days\ ago}}{close_{N\ days\ ago}}$$

"Momentum" in general refers to prices continuing to trend. The momentum and ROC indicators show trend by remaining positive while an uptrend is sustained, or negative while a downtrend is sustained.

A crossing up through zero may be used as a signal to buy, or a crossing down through zero as a signal to sell. How high (or how low when negative) the indicators get shows how strong the trend is.

The way momentum shows an absolute change means it shows for instance a $3 rise over 20 days, whereas ROC might show that as 0.25 for a 25% rise over the same period. One can choose between looking at a move in dollar terms or proportional terms. The zero crossings are the same in each, of course, but the highs or lows showing strength are on the respective different bases.

SMA

Momentum is the change in an N-day simple moving average (SMA) between yesterday and today, with a scale factor N, ie.

$$\frac{momentum}{N} = SMA_{today} - SMA_{yesterday}$$

This is the slope or steepness of the SMA line, like a derivative. This relationship is not much discussed generally, but it's of interest in understanding the signals from the indicator.

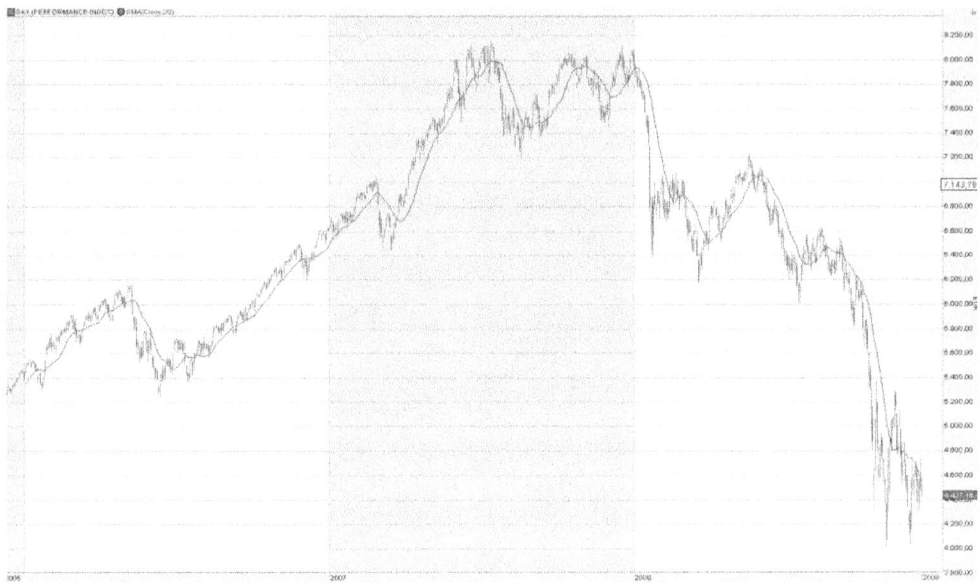

Picture 31: DAX SMA

When momentum crosses up through zero it corresponds to a trough in the SMA, and when it crosses down through zero it's a peak. How high (or low) momentum gets represents how steeply the SMA is rising (or falling).

The TRIX indicator is similarly based on changes in a moving average (a triple exponential in that case).

Hikkake Pattern

The Hikkake Pattern (or Hikkake), is a technical analysis pattern used for determining market turning-points and continuations. It is a simple pattern that can be observed in market price data, using traditional bar charts, or Japanese candlestick charts.

The phrase "Hikkake" is a Japanese verb which means to "trick" or "ensnare." The pattern is comprised of a measurable period of rest and volatility contraction in the market, followed by a relatively brief price move that encourages unsuspecting traders and investors to adopt a false assumption regarding the likely future direction of price. Some technical analysts may also refer to the hikkake pattern as an "inside day false breakout," however this term has never been formally adopted. The pattern, once formed, yields its own set of trading parameters for the time and price of market entry, the dollar risk amount (i.e., where to place protective stops), and the expected profit target. The pattern is not meant as a standalone "system" for market speculation, but rather as an ancillary technique to traditional technical and fundamental market analysis methods.

Due to its popularity among institutional traders, the hikkake pattern has been adopted for use by INTSTREAM, a Nordic power trading software company, in their E2 Energy Market Analysis Platform.

Growing interest in the hikkake pattern among traders and investors has also spawned attention from various book authors. See: "Technical Analysis: The Complete Resource for Financial Market Technicians" by Charles D. Kirkpatrick and Julie R. Dahlquist, and "Long/Short Market Dynamics: Trading Strategies for Today's Markets" by Clive M. Corcoran.

The hikkake pattern was first discovered and introduced to the financial community through a series of published articles written by technical analyst Daniel L. Chesler.

Overlays

Support and Resistance

Support and resistance is a concept in technical analysis that the movement of the price of a security will tend to stop and reverse at certain predetermined price levels.

Support

A support level is a price level where the price tends to find support as it is going down. This means the price is more likely to "bounce" off this level rather than break through it. However, once the price has passed this level, even by a small amount, it is likely to continue dropping until it finds another support level.

Resistance

A resistance level is the opposite of a support level. It is where the price tends to find resistance as it is going up. This means the price is more likely to "bounce" off this level rather than break through it. However, once the price has passed this level, even by a small amount, it is likely that it will continue rising until it finds another resistance level.

Identifying Support and Resistance Levels

Support and resistance levels can be identified by trend lines. Some traders believe in using pivot point calculations.

The more often a support/resistance level is "tested" (touched and bounced off by price), the more significance given to that specific level.

If a price breaks past a support level, that support level often becomes a new resistance level. The opposite is true as well, if price breaks a resistance level, it will often find support at that level in the future.

Using Support and Resistance Levels

This is an example of support switching roles with resistance, and vice versa:

If a stock price is moving between support and resistance levels, then a basic investment strategy commonly used by traders, is to buy a stock at support and sell at resistance, then short at resistance and cover the short at support as per the following example:

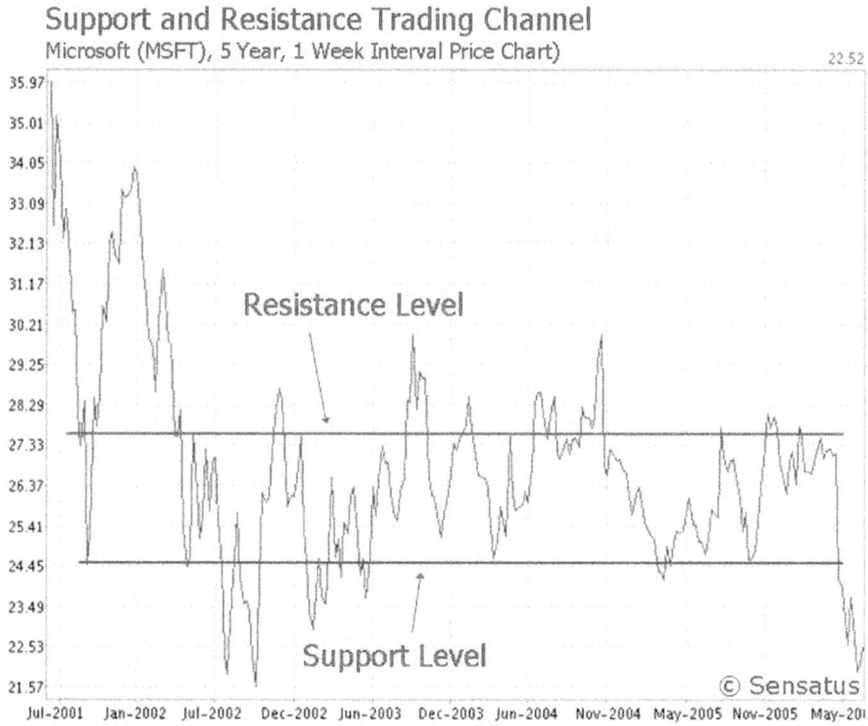

When judging entry and exit investment timing using support or resistance levels it is important to choose a chart based on a price interval period that aligns with your trading strategy timeframe. Short term traders tend to use charts based on interval periods, such as 1 minute (i.e. the price of the security is plotted on the chart every 1 minute), with longer term traders using price charts based on hourly, daily, weekly or monthly interval periods. Typically traders use shorter term interval charts when making a final decisions on when to invest, such as the following example based on 1 week of historical data with price plotted every 15 minutes. In this example the early signs that the stock was coming out of a downtrend was when it started to form support at $30.48 and then started to form higher highs and higher lows signalling a change from negative to positive trending.

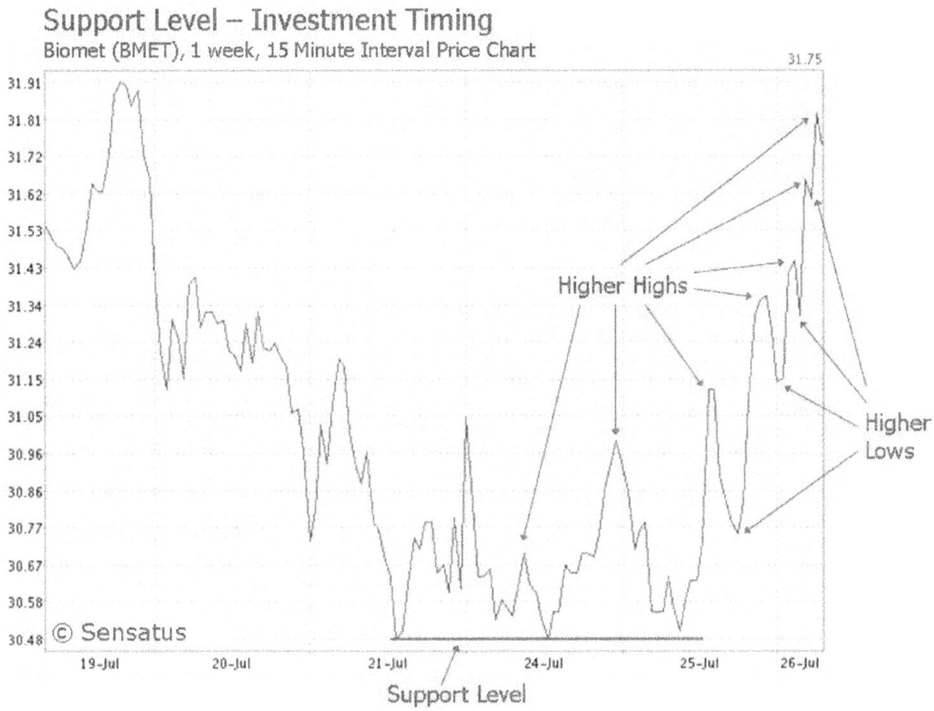

Trend Lines

A trend line is formed when you can draw a diagonal line between two or more price pivot points. They are commonly used to judge entry and exit investment timing when trading securities.

A trend line is a bounding line for the price movement of a security. A support trend line is formed when a securities price decreases and then rebounds at a pivot point that aligns with at least two previous support pivot points. Similarly a resistance trend line is formed when a securities price increases and then rebounds at a pivot point that aligns with at least two previous resistance pivot points. The following chart provides an example of support and resistance trend lines:

Trend lines are a simple and widely used technical analysis approach to judging entry and exit investment timing. To establish a trend line historical data, typically presented in the format of a chart such as the above price chart, is required. Historically, trend lines have been drawn by hand on paper charts, but it is now more common to use charting software that enables trend lines to be drawn on computer based charts. There are some charting software that will automatically generate trend lines, however most traders prefer to draw their own trendlines.

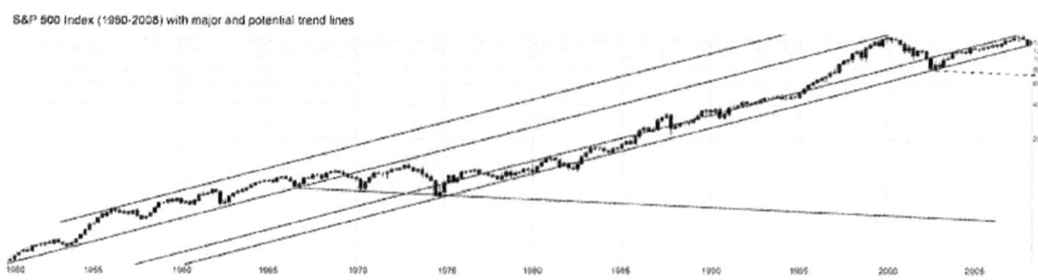

When establishing trend lines it is important to choose a chart based on a price interval period that aligns with your trading strategy. Short term traders tend to use charts based on interval periods, such as 1 minute (i.e. the price of the security is plotted on the chart every 1 minute), with longer term traders using price charts based on hourly, daily, weekly and monthly interval periods.

However, time periods can also be viewed in terms of years. For example, below is a chart of the S&P 500 since the earliest data point until April 2008. Please note that while the Oracle example above uses a linear scale of price changes, long term data is more often viewed as logarithmic: e.g. the changes are really an attempt to approxiamate percentage changes than pure numerical value. If we were to view this same chart linearly, we would not be able to see any detail from 1950 to about 1990 simply because all the data would be compressed to the bottom.

Trend lines are typically used with price charts, however they can also be used with a range of technical analysis charts such as MACD and RSI. Trend lines can be used to identify positive and negative trending charts, whereby a positive trending chart forms an upsloping line when the support and the resistance pivots points are aligned, and a negative trending chart froms a downsloping line when the support and resistance pivot points are aligned.

Trend lines are used in many ways by traders. If a stock price is moving between support and resistance trendlines, then a basic investment strategy commonly used by traders, is to buy a stock at support and sell at resistance, then short at resistance and cover the short at support. The logic behind this, is that when the price returns to an existing principal trendline it may be an opportunity to open new positions in the direction of the trend, in the belief that the trendline will hold and the trend will continue further. A second way is that when price action breaks through the principal trendline of an existing trend, it is evidence that the trend may be going to fail, and a trader may consider trading in the opposite direction to the existing trend, or exiting positions in the direction of the trend.

Double Top

A double top is a reversal chart pattern which is defined by a chart where a financial instrument makes a run up to a particular level, then drops back from that level, then makes a second run at that level, and then finally drops back off again.

Significance for Traders

The double top pattern shows demand outpacing supply (buyers predominate) up to the first top, causing prices to rise. The supply/demand situation then reverses; supply outpaces demand (sellers predominate), causing prices to fall. After a price "valley", buyers again predominate and prices rise. If traders see that prices are not pushing past their level at the first top, sellers may again prevail, lowering prices and causing a double top to form. It is generally regarded as a bearish sign if prices drop below their level at the earlier valley between the two tops.

Price Channels

A price channel is a pair of parallel trend lines that form a chart pattern for a stock or commodity. Channels may be horizontal, ascending or descending. When prices pass through and stay through a trendline representing support or resistance the trend is said to be broken and there is a "breakout".

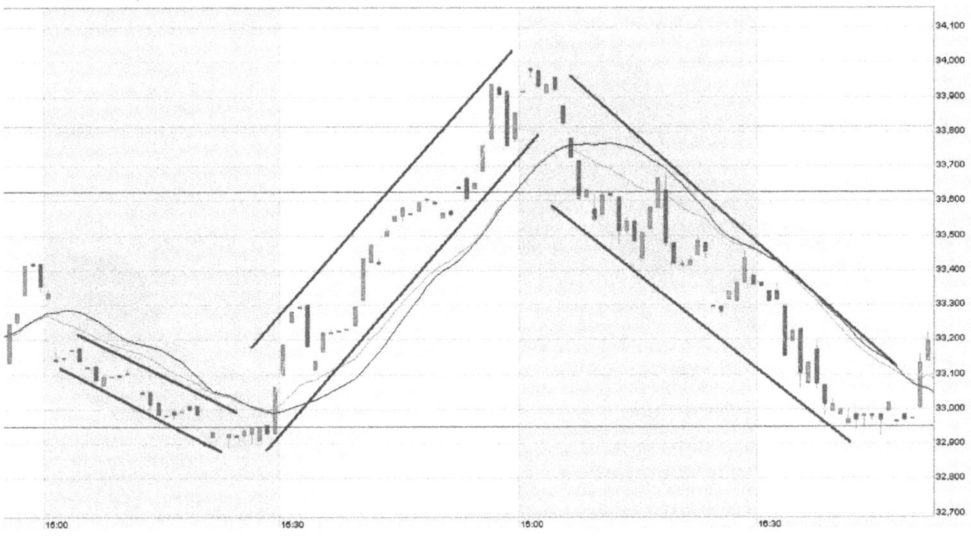

Picture 32: Price Channels

Moving Average

In statistics, a moving average, also called a rolling average and sometimes a running average, refers to a statistical technique used to analyze a set of data points by creating an average of one subset of the full data set at a time. So a moving average is not a single number, but it is a set of numbers, each of which is the average of the corresponding subset of a larger set of data points. A simple example is if you had a data set with 100 data points, the first value of the moving average might be the arithmetic mean (one simple type of average) of data points 1 through 25. The next value would be this simple average of data points 2 through 26, and so forth, until the final value, which would be the same simple average of data points 76 through 100.

The size of the subset being averaged is often constant, as in the previous example, but need not be. In particular, a cumulative average is a type of moving average where each value is the average of all previous data points in the full data set. So the size of the subset being averaged grows by one as each new value of the moving average is calculated. A moving average could also use a weighted average instead of a simple average, perhaps in order to place more emphasis on more recent data points than on other data points longer ago in time.

A moving average can be applied to any data set, but is perhaps most commonly used with time series data to smooth out short-term fluctuations and highlight longer-term trends or cycles. The threshold between short-term and long-term depends on the application, and the parameters of the moving average will be set accordingly. For example, it is often used in technical analysis of financial data, like stock prices, returns or trading volumes. It is also used in economics to examine gross domestic product, employment or other macroeconomic time series. Mathematically, a moving average is a type of convolution and so it is also similar to the low-pass filter used in signal processing. When used with non-time series data, a moving average simply acts as a generic smoothing operation without any specific connection to time, although typically some kind of ordering is implied.

Simple Moving Average

Prior Moving Average

A simple moving average (SMA) is the unweighted mean of the previous n data points. For example, a 10-day simple moving average of closing price is the mean of the previous 10 days' closing prices. If those prices are then the formula is

$$SMA = \frac{p_M + p_{M-1} + \cdots + p_{M-9}}{10}$$

When calculating successive values, a new value comes into the sum and an old value drops out, meaning a full summation each time is unnecessary,

$$SMA_{\text{today}} = SMA_{\text{yesterday}} - \frac{p_{M-n+1}}{n} + \frac{p_{M+1}}{n}$$

In technical analysis there are various popular values for n, like 10 days, 40 days, or 200 days. The period selected depends on the kind of movement one is concentrating on, such as short, intermediate, or long term. In any case moving average levels are interpreted as support in a rising market, or resistance in a falling market.

In all cases a moving average lags behind the latest data point, simply from the nature of its smoothing. An SMA can lag to an undesirable extent, and can be disproportionately influenced by old data points dropping out of the average. This is addressed by giving extra weight to more recent data points, as in the weighted and exponential moving averages.

One characteristic of the SMA is that if the data have a periodic fluctuation, then applying an SMA of that period will eliminate that variation (the average always containing one complete cycle). But a perfectly regular cycle is rarely encountered in economics or finance.

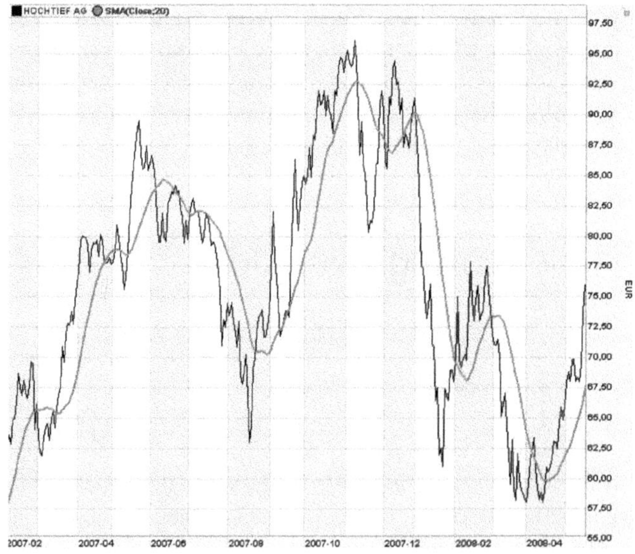

Picture 33: Simple Moving Average (grey = SMA; black = price line)

Central Moving Average

For a number of applications it is advantageous to avoid the shifting induced by using only 'past' data. Hence a central moving average can be computed, using both 'past' and 'future' data. The 'future' data in this case are not predictions, but merely data obtained after the time at which the average is to be computed.

Weighted and exponential moving averages (see below) can also be computed centrally.

Cumulative Moving Average

The cumulative moving average is also frequently called a running average or a long running average although the term running average is also used as synonym for a moving average. This section uses the term cumulative moving average or simply cumulative average since this term is more descriptive and unambiguous.

In some data acquisition systems, the data arrives in an ordered data stream and the statistician would like to get the average of all of the data up until the current data point. For example, an investor may want the average price of all of the stock transactions for a particular stock up until the current time. As each new transaction occurs, the average price at the time of the transaction can be calculated for all of the transactions up to that point using the cumulative average. This is the cumulative average, which is typically an unweighted average of the sequence of i values x1, ..., xi up to the current time:

$$CA_i = \frac{x_1 + \cdots + x_i}{i}.$$

The brute force method to calculate this would be to store all of the data and calculate the sum and divide by the number of data points every time a new data point arrived. However, it is possible to simply update cumulative average as a new value xi+1 becomes available, using the formula:

$$CA_{i+1} = CA_i + \frac{x_{i+1} - CA_i}{i+1},$$

where CA_0 can be taken to be equal to 0.

Thus the current cumulative average for a new data point is equal to the previous cumulative average plus the difference between the latest data point and the previous average divided by the number of points received so far.

When all of the data points arrive (i = N), the cumulative average will equal the final average.

The derivation of the cumulative average formula is straightforward. Using

$$x_1 + \cdots + x_i = iCA_i\,,$$

and similarly for i + 1, it is seen that

$$x_{i+1} = (x_1 + \cdots + x_{i+1}) - (x_1 + \cdots + x_i) = (i+1)CA_{i+1} - iCA_i\,.$$

Solving this equation for CA_{i+1} results in:

$$CA_{i+1} = \frac{(x_{i+1} + iCA_i)}{i+1} = CA_i + \frac{x_{i+1} - CA_i}{i+1}\,.$$

Weighted Moving Average

A weighted average is any average that has multiplying factors to give different weights to different data points. Mathematically, the moving average is the convolution of the data points with a moving average function; in technical analysis, a weighted moving average (WMA) has the specific meaning of weights which decrease arithmetically.

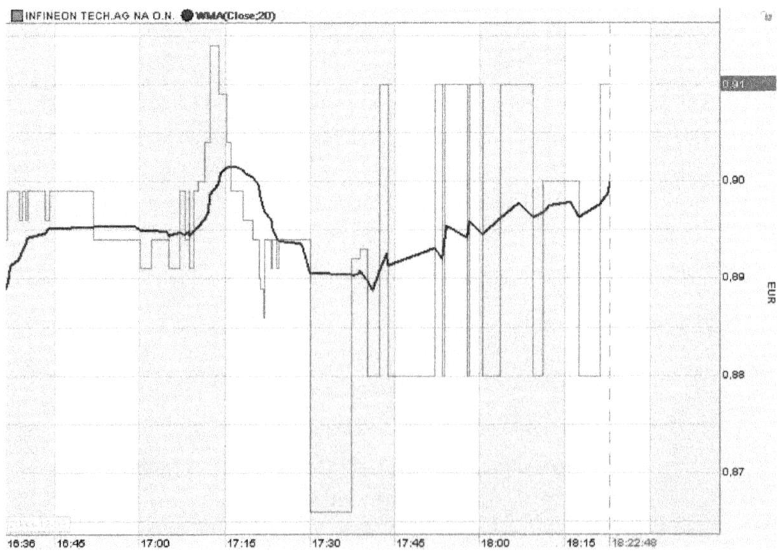

Picture 34: Weighted Moving Average with a Period of 20

In an n-day WMA the latest day has weight n, the second latest n - 1, etc, down to zero.

$$WMA_M = \frac{np_M + (n-1)p_{M-1} + \cdots + 2p_{M-n+2} + p_{M-n+1}}{n + (n-1) + \cdots + 2 + 1}$$

The denominator is a triangle number, and can be easily computed as

$$\frac{n(n+1)}{2}.$$

When calculating the WMA across successive values, it can be noted the difference between the numerators of WMA_{M+1} and WMAM is $np_{M+1} - p_M - \ldots - p_{M-n+1}$. If we denote the sum $p_M + \ldots + p_{M-n+1}$ by $Total_M$, then

$$Total_{M+1} = Total_M + p_{M+1} - p_{M-n+1}$$

$$Numerator_{M+1} = Numerator_M + np_{M+1} - Total_M$$

$$WMA_{M+1} = \frac{Numerator_{M+1}}{n + (n-1) + \cdots + 2 + 1}$$

The graph at the below shows how the weights decrease, from highest weight for the most recent data points, down to zero. It can be compared to the weights in the exponential moving average which follows.

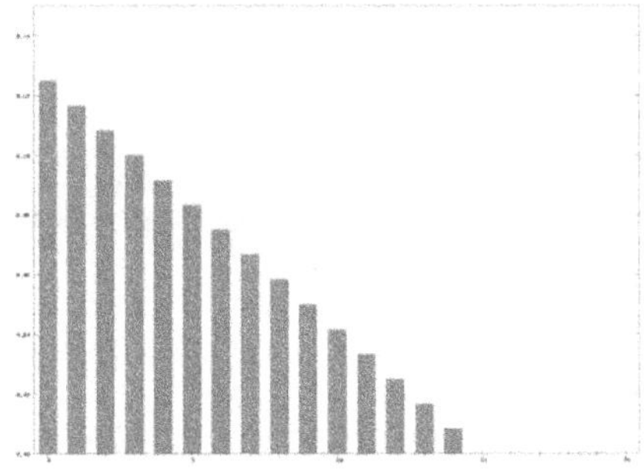

Picture 35: Decreasing weights of the Weighted Moving Average

Exponential Moving Average

An exponential moving average (EMA), sometimes also called an exponentially weighted moving average (EWMA), applies weighting factors which decrease exponentially. The weighting for each older data point decreases exponentially, giving much more importance to recent observations while still not discarding older observations entirely. The graph at below shows an example of the exponential moving average.

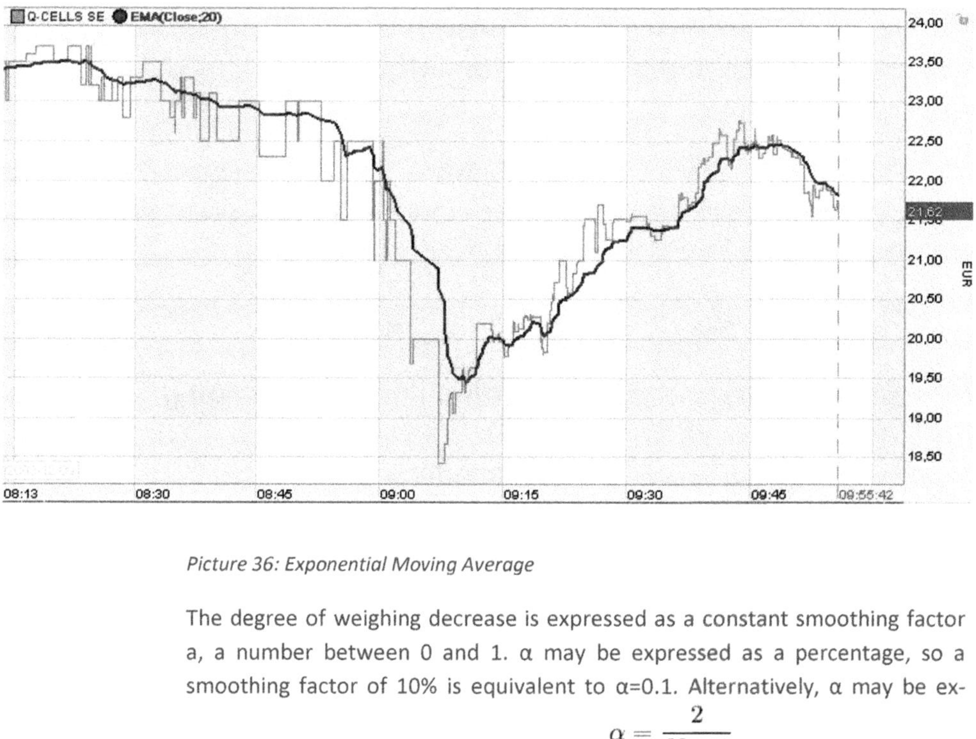

Picture 36: Exponential Moving Average

The degree of weighing decrease is expressed as a constant smoothing factor a, a number between 0 and 1. α may be expressed as a percentage, so a smoothing factor of 10% is equivalent to α=0.1. Alternatively, α may be expressed in terms of N time periods, where $\alpha = \frac{2}{N+1}$.

For example, N=19 is equivalent to α=0.1. The half-life of the weights (the interval over which the weights decrease by a factor of two) is approximately $\frac{N}{2.8854}$ (within 1% if N>5).

The observation at a time period t is designated Y_t, and the value of the EMA at any time period t is designated S_t. S_1 is undefined. S_2 may be initialized in a number of different ways, most commonly by setting S_2 to Y_1, though other techniques exist, such as setting S_2 to an average of the first 4 or 5 observations. The prominence of the S_2 initialization's effect on the resultant moving average depends on α; smaller α values make the choice of S_2 relatively more important than larger α values, since a higher α discounts older observations faster.

The formula for calculating the EMA at time periods t=2 is:

$$S_t = \alpha \times Y_{t-1} + (1-\alpha) \times S_{t-1}$$

This formulation is according to Hunter (1986) an alternate approach. Roberts (1959) uses Y_t in place of Y_{t-1}:

$$S_{t,alternate} = \alpha \times Y_t + (1-\alpha) \times S_{t-1}$$

This formula can also be expressed in technical analysis terms as follows, showing how the EMA steps towards the latest data point, but only by a proportion of the difference (each time):

$$EMA_{\text{today}} = EMA_{\text{yesterday}} + \alpha \times (price - EMA_{\text{yesterday}})$$

Expanding out $EMA_{yesterday}$ each time results in the following power series, showing how the weighting factor on each data point p_1, p_2, etc, decrease exponentially:

$$EMA = \frac{p_1 + (1-\alpha)p_2 + (1-\alpha)^2 p_3 + (1-\alpha)^3 p_4 + \cdots}{1 + (1-\alpha) + (1-\alpha)^2 + (1-\alpha)^3 + \cdots}$$

In theory this is an infinite sum, but because 1-α is less than 1, the terms become smaller and smaller, and can be ignored once small enough. The denominator approaches 1/α, and that value can be used instead of adding up the powers, provided one is using enough terms that the omitted portion is negligible.

The *N* periods in an *N*-day EMA only specify the α factor. *N* is not a stopping point for the calculation in the way it is in an SMA or WMA. The first *N* data points in an EMA represent about 86% of the total weight in the calculation.

The power formula above gives a starting value for a particular day, after which the successive days formula shown first can be applied.

The question of how far back to go for an initial value depends, in the worst case, on the data. If there are huge *p* price values in old data then they'll have an effect on the total even if their weighting is very small. If one assumes prices don't vary too wildly then just the weighting can be considered. The weight omitted by stopping after *k* terms is

$$(1-\alpha)^k + (1-\alpha)^{k+1} + \cdots,$$

which is

$$(1-\alpha)^k \times (1 + (1-\alpha) + (1-\alpha)^2 \cdots),$$

i.e. a fraction

$$\frac{(1-\alpha)^k}{\alpha}$$

out of the total weight.

For example, to have 99.9% of the weight,

$$k = \frac{\log(0.001 \times \alpha)}{\log(1-\alpha)}$$

terms should be used. Since $\log(1-\alpha)$ approaches $\frac{-2}{N+1}$

as N increases, this simplifies to approximately

$$k = 3.45 \times (N+1)$$

for this example (99.9% weight).

Exponential Smoothing

In statistics, exponential smoothing refers to a particular type of moving average technique applied to time series data, either to produce smoothed data for presentation, or to make forecasts. The time series data themselves are a sequence of observations. The observed phenomenon may be an essentially random process, or it may be an orderly, but noisy, process.

Exponential smoothing is commonly applied to financial market and economic data, but it can be used with any discrete set of repeated measurements. The raw data sequence is often represented by $\{x_t\}$, and the output of the exponential smoothing algorithm is commonly written as $\{s_t\}$ which may be regarded as our best estimate of what the next value of x will be. When the sequence of observations begins at time $t = 0$, the simplest form of exponential smoothing is given by the formulas

$$s_0 = x_0$$
$$s_t = \alpha x_t + (1 - \alpha)s_{t-1}$$

where α is the smoothing factor, and $0 < \alpha < 1$.

Average True Range

Average True Range (ATR) is a technical analysis indicator developed by J. Welles Wilder, based on trading ranges smoothed by an N-day exponential moving average.

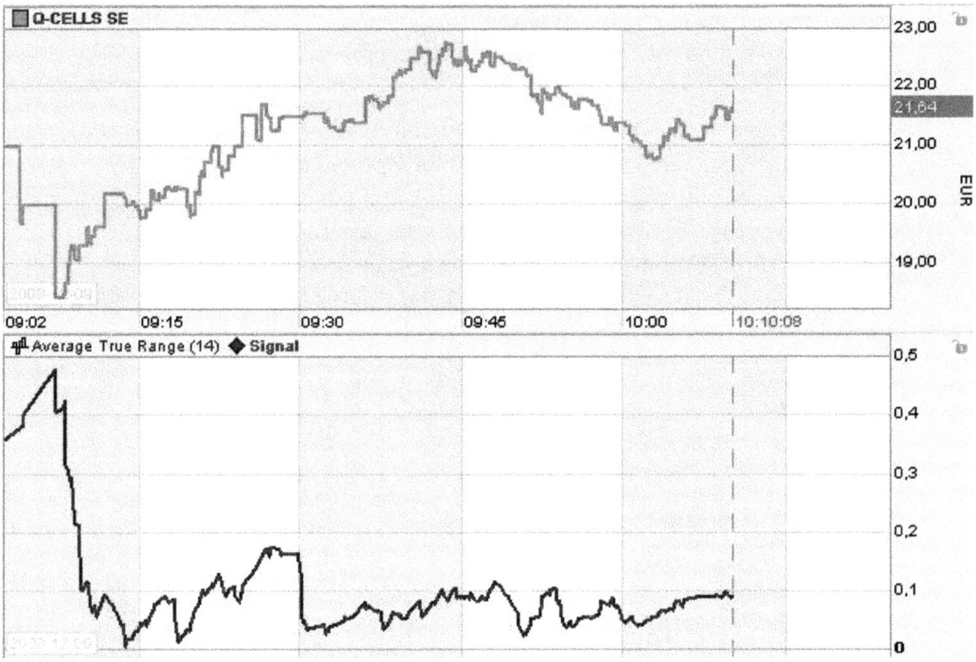

Picture 37: Average True Range

The range of a day's trading is simply high – low. The true range extends it to yesterday's closing price if it was outside of today's range:

$$\text{true range} = \max(\text{high}, \text{close}_{\text{prev}}) - \min(\text{low}, \text{close}_{\text{prev}})$$

The average true range is then an N-day exponential moving average of the true range values. Wilder recommended a 14-period smoothing. Note this is by his reckoning of EMA periods (see the EMA section on that), meaning an $\alpha=1/14$.

The idea of ranges is that they show the commitment or enthusiasm of traders. Large or increasing ranges suggest traders prepared to continue to bid up or sell down a stock through the course of the day. Decreasing range suggests waning interest.

Bollinger Bands

Bollinger Bands are a technical analysis tool invented by John Bollinger in the 1980s. Having evolved from the concept of trading bands, Bollinger Bands can be used to measure the highness or lowness of the price relative to previous trades.

Bollinger Bands consist of:

- a middle band being an N-period simple moving average
- an upper band at K times an N-period standard deviation above the middle band
- a lower band at K times an N-period standard deviation below the middle band

Typical values for N and K are 20 and 2, respectively. The default choice for the average is a simple moving average, but other types of averages can be employed as needed. Exponential moving averages are a common second choice. Usually the same average is used for both the middle band and the calculation of standard deviation.

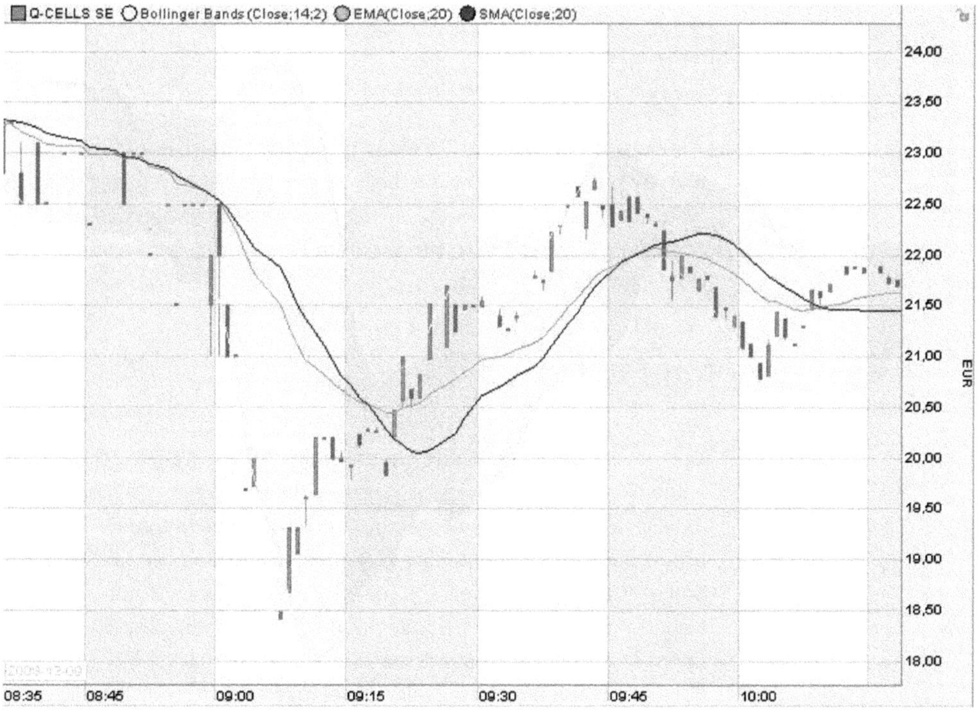

Indicators Derived from Bollinger Bands

There are two indicators derived from Bollinger Bands, %b and BandWidth.

%b, pronounced 'percent b', is derived from the formula for stochastics and tells you where you are in relation to the bands. %b equals 1 at the upper band and 0 at the lower band.

%b = (last - lowerBB) / (upperBB - lowerBB)

BandWidth tells you how wide the Bollinger Bands are on a normalized basis.

BandWidth = (upperBB - lowerBB) / middleBB

Using the default parameters of a 20-period look back and plus/minus two standard deviations, BandWidth is equal to four times the 20-period coefficient of variation.

Uses for %b include system building and pattern recognition. Uses for BandWidth include identification of opportunities arising from relative extremes in volatility and trend identification.

Purpose

The purpose of Bollinger Bands is to provide a relative definition of high and low. By definition, prices are high at the upper band and low at the lower band. This definition can aid in rigorous pattern recognition and is useful in comparing price action to the action of indicators to arrive at systematic trading decisions.

Interpretation

The use of Bollinger Bands varies wildly among traders. Some traders buy when price touches the lower Bollinger Band and exit when price touches the moving average in the center of the bands. Other traders buy when price breaks above the upper Bollinger Band or sell when price falls below the lower Bollinger Band. Moreover, the use of Bollinger Bands is not confined to stock traders, options traders, most notably implied volatility traders, often sell options when Bollinger Bands are historically far apart or buy options when the Bollinger Bands are historically close together, in both instances, expecting volatility to revert back towards the average historical volatility level for the stock.

When the bands lie close together a period of low volatility in stock price is indicated. When they are far apart a period of high volatility in price is indicated. When the bands have only a slight slope and lie approximately parallel for an extended time the price of a stock will be found to oscillate up and down between the bands as though in a channel.

Effectiveness

Bollinger Band trading strategies may be effective in the Chinese marketplace as concluded by a recent study that states, "Finally, we find significant positive returns on buy trades generated by the contrarian version of the moving average crossover rule, the channel breakout rule, and the Bollinger band trading rule, after accounting for transaction costs of 0.50 percent."

Statistical Properties

Security prices have no known statistical distribution, Normal or otherwise. They are known to have fat tails, compared to the Normal. The sample size typically used, 20, is too small for conclusions derived from statistical techniques like the Central Limit Theorem to be reliable. Such techniques usually require the sample to be independent and identically distributed which is not the case for a time series like security prices.

For these three primary reasons, it is incorrect to assume that the percentage of the data outside the Bollinger Bands will always be limited to a certain amount. So, instead of finding about 95% of the data inside the bands, as would be the expectation with the default parameters if the data were normally distributed, one will typically find less; how much less is a function of the security's volatility.

Head and Shoulders

The head and shoulders pattern is a commonly found pattern in the price charts of financially traded assets (stocks, bonds, futures, etc). The pattern derives its name from the fact that its structure is visually similar to that of a head with two shoulders.

The Structure of a Head and Shoulders Pattern

Head and shoulders patterns have four elements: a left shoulder, which is essentially a relative peak; a head, which is a peak above both shoulders; a right shoulder, which is a peak that is approximately parallel to the left shoulder; and a neckline, which serves as a support, or bottom, of price activity within the range of the head and shoulders pattern. The chart below illustrates.

Picture 38: Head and Schoulders

Interpretation

Traders often look to enter a position on the break of the neckline, interpreting the neckline as a support level. Upon a break of the neckline, traders will frequently set a target profit equal to the distance between the neckline and the head of the chart. A stop loss order is frequently set at where the right shoulder is. As a result, the head and shoulders pattern can be used by traders not only to identify entry points, but also to manage the risk of the trade as well.

The image below illustrates how a head and shoulders pattern can help traders identify entry points, stop-loss levels, and target profit levels.

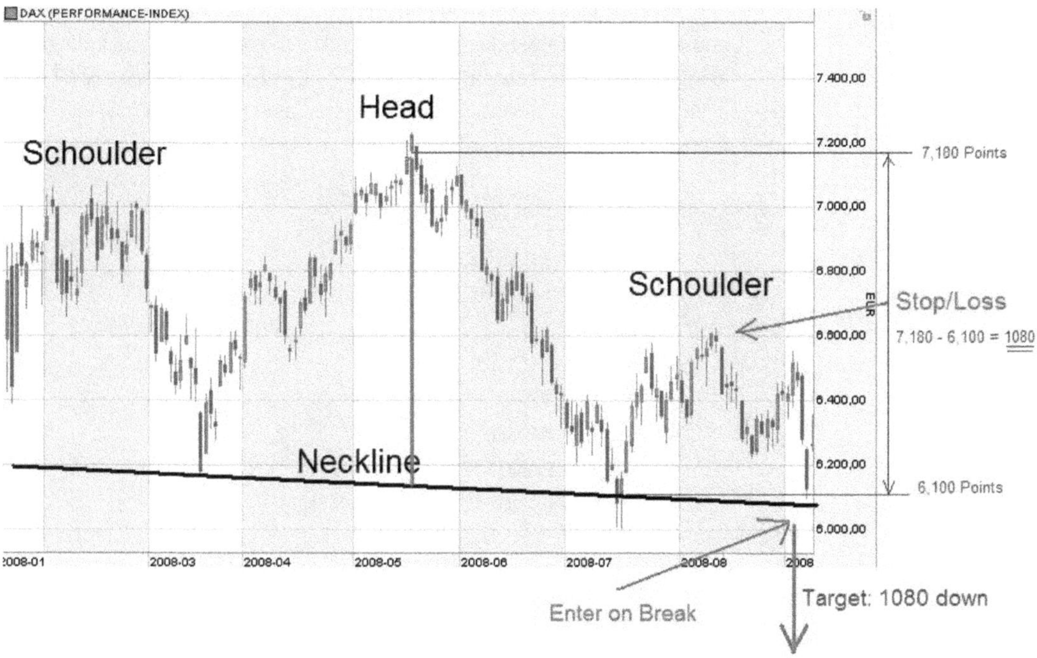

Picture 39: Head and Schoulders Calculation

Pivot Point Calculations

Pivot point calculations are used by security traders to attempt to predict support and resistance levels. They are commonly used in the forex and commodity futures markets. Pivot point analysis is a subset of technical analysis, although it is not as popular or well known as other technical methods.

Pivot points are frequently used by foreign exchange traders as a means to calculate resistance and support levels which are, in turn, used as visual cues to execute trades. Pivot point calculations provide traders with objective visual bench marks which some use to predict price changes, although the validity of these levels is still subject to debate.

Calculating Points

The popular pivot points include PP, and various "support" and "resistance" points based on PP. There are various ways to calculate PP, including the averaging of the High, Low, and Close (H, L, C) of the previous day's trading, or including the Open trading price in the average. Some popular examples follow:

- R4 = PP + RANGE*3
- R3 = PP + RANGE*2
- R2 = PP + RANGE
- R1 = 2 * PP - L
- PP = (H+L+C) / 3
- S1 = 2 * PP - H
- S2: PP - RANGE
- S3: PP - RANGE*2
- S4: PP - RANGE*3

Price Based Indicators

Relative Strength Index

The Relative Strength Index (RSI) is a financial technical analysis oscillator showing price strength by comparing upward and downward close-to-close movements.

The RSI is popular because it is relatively easy to interpret. It was developed by J. Welles Wilder and published in Commodities magazine (now called Futures magazine) in June 1978, and in his New Concepts in Technical Trading Systems the same year.

Note that the term relative strength also refers to the strength of a security in relation to its sector or the overall market. For instance, XYZ might rise 2% when S&P 500 rises 1%. This is sometimes called comparative relative strength to avoid confusion. It's unrelated to the Relative Strength Index described here.

Calculation

For each day an upward change U or downward change D amount is calculated. On an up day, ie. today's close higher than yesterday's,

$$U = closetoday - closeyesterday$$

$$D = 0$$

Or conversely on a down day (notice D is a positive number),

$$U = 0$$

$$D = closeyesterday - closetoday$$

If today's close is the same as yesterday's, both U and D are zero. An average for U is calculated with an exponential moving average using a given N-days smoothing factor, and likewise for D. The ratio of those averages is the Relative Strength,

$$RS = \frac{EMA[N]\ of\ U}{EMA[N]\ of\ D}$$

This is converted to a Relative Strength Index between 0 and 100,

$$RSI = 100 - 100 \times \frac{1}{1 + RS}$$

This can be rewritten as follows to emphasize the way RSI expresses the up as a proportion of the total up and down (averages in each case),

$$RSI = 100 \times \frac{EMA[N]\ of\ U}{(EMA[N]\ of\ U) + (EMA[N]\ of\ D)}$$

The EMA in theory uses an infinite amount of past data (as discussed in the EMA section). It's necessary either to go back far enough, or alternately at the start of data begin with a simple average of N days instead,

$$AvgU_{initial} = \frac{U_1 + U_2 + \cdots + U_N}{N}$$

and then continue from there with the usual EMA formula,

$$AvgU_{today} = \alpha \times U_{today} + (1 - \alpha) \times AvgU_{yesterday}$$

(Similarly with D.)

Interpretation

Wilder recommended a smoothing period of 14. This is by his reckoning of EMA smoothing, ie. α=1/14 or N=27.

Wilder considered a security overbought if it reached the 70 level, meaning that the speculator should consider selling. Or conversely oversold at the 30 level. The principle is that when there's a high proportion of daily movement in one direction it suggests an extreme, and prices are likely to reverse. Levels 80 and 20 are also used, or may be varied according to market conditions (eg. a bull market may have an upward bias).

Large surges and drops in securities will affect RSI, but it could just be a false buy or sell. The RSI is best used as a complement with other technical analysis indicators.

The RSI should confirm price movement. Therefore, if the stock price is moving up, the RSI should be moving up as well.

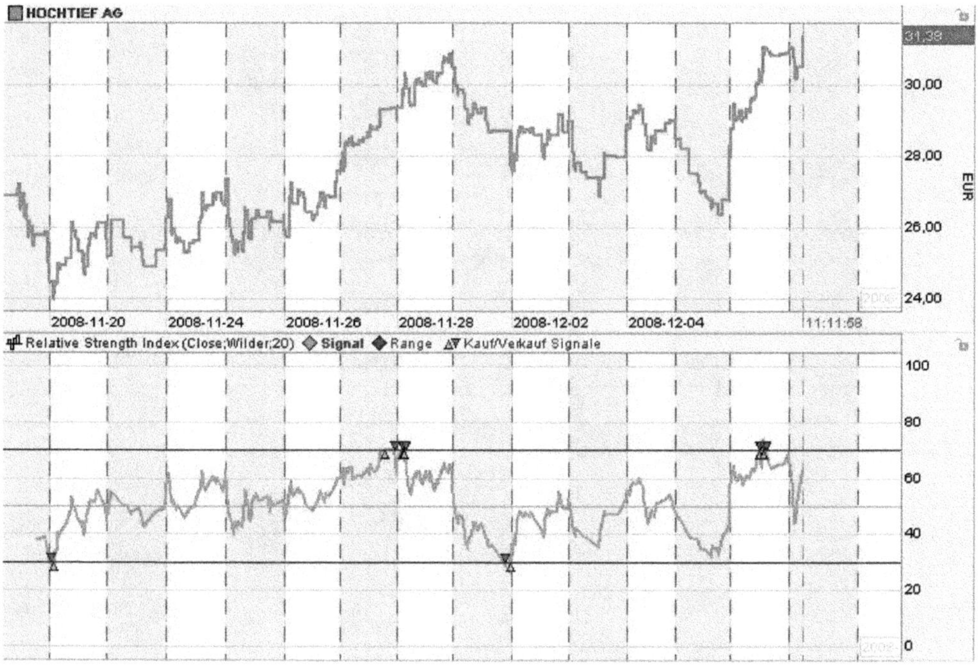

Picture 40: RSI Wilder

Cutler's RSI

A variation called Cutler's RSI is based on a simple moving average of U and D, instead of the exponential average above.

$$RS = \frac{SMA[N]\ of\ U}{SMA[N]\ of\ D}$$

This is like the initial data point calculation shown above, but used on every day, not just the first. The divisor N in the SMAs in the numerator and denominator cancel out, so one needn't do those divisions, instead just a sum of U and a sum of D over the past N days can be made.

Cutler's RSI generally comes out slightly different from the normal Wilder RSI, but the two are similar, since SMA and EMA are similar.

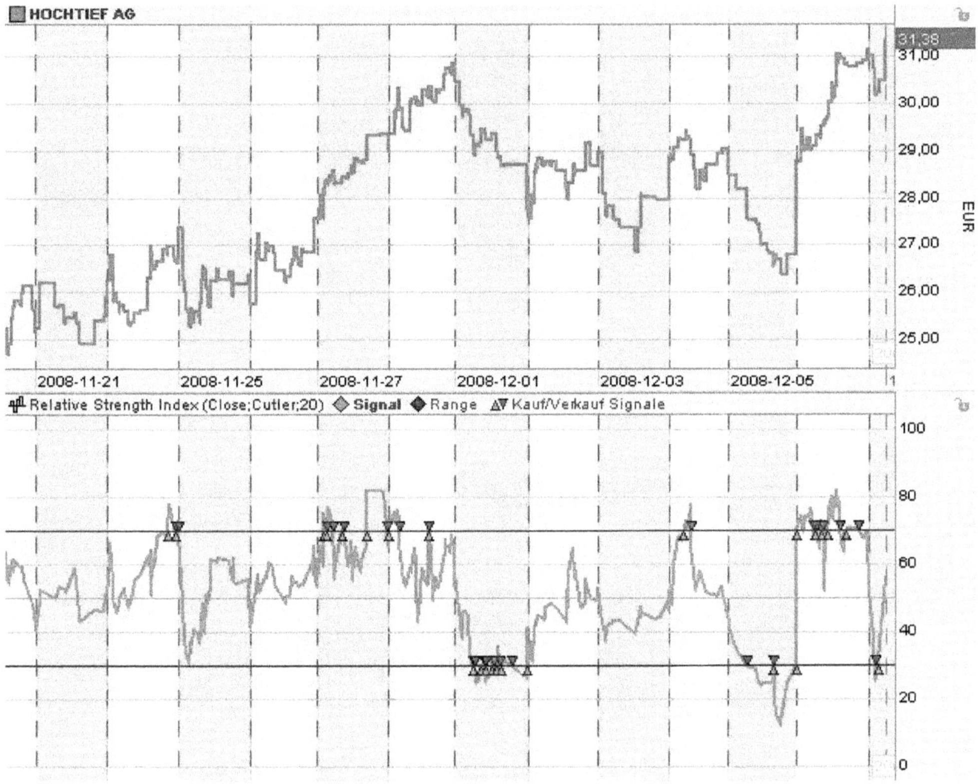

Picture 41:RSI Cutler

MACD

MACD, which stands for Moving Average Convergence / Divergence, is a technical analysis indicator created by Gerald Appel in the 1960s. It shows the difference between a fast and slow exponential moving average (EMA) of closing prices. During the 1980s MACD proved to be a valuable tool for any trader. The standard periods recommended back in the 1960s by Gerald Appel are 12 and 26 days:

$$MACD = EMA[12]\, of\, price - EMA[26]\, of\, price$$

A signal line (or trigger line) is then formed by smoothing this with a further EMA. The standard period for this is 9 days,

$$signal = EMA[9]\,of\,MACD$$

The difference between the MACD and the signal line is often calculated and shown not as a line, but a solid block histogram style. This construction was made by Thomas Aspray in 1986. The calculation is simply

$$histogram = MACD - signal$$

The example graph below shows all three of these together. The upper graph is the prices. The lower graph has the MACD line in blue and the signal line in red. The solid white histogram style is the difference between them.

The set of periods for the averages, often written as say 12,26,9, can be varied. Appel and others have experimented with various combinations.

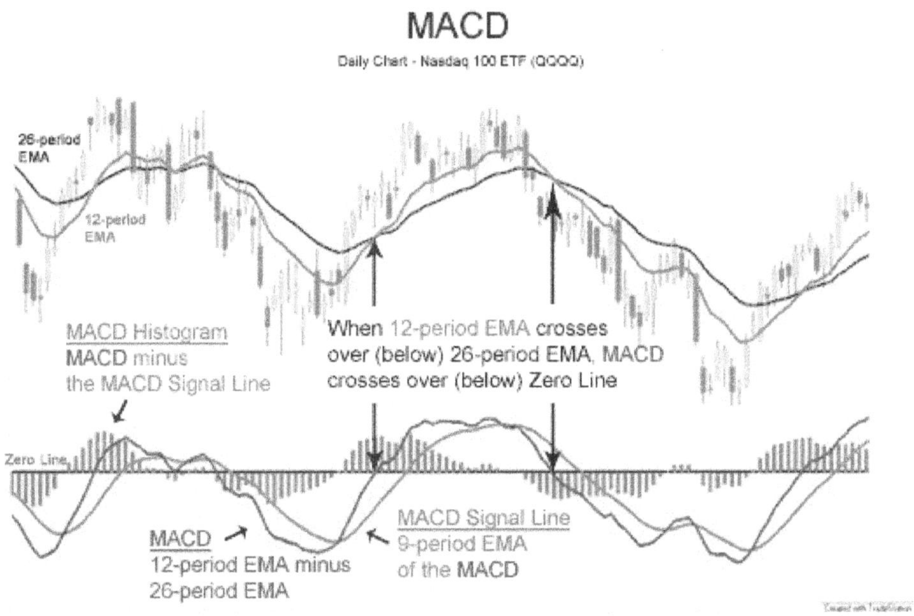

Picture 42: MACD

Interpretation

MACD is a trend following indicator, and is designed to identify trend changes. It's generally not recommended for use in ranging market conditions. Three types of trading signals are generated,

- MACD line crossing itself.
- MACD line crossing 10.
- Divergence between price and 10.

The signal line crossing is the usual trading rule. This is to buy when the MACD crosses up through the signal line, or sell when it crosses down through the signal line. These crossings may occur too frequently, and other tests may have to be applied.

The histogram shows when a crossing occurs. When the MACD line crosses through zero on the histogram it is said that the MACD line has crossed the signal line. The histogram can also help visualizing when the two lines are coming together. Both may still be rising, but coming together, so a falling histogram suggests a crossover may be approaching.

A crossing of the MACD line up through zero is interpreted as bullish, or down through zero as bearish. These crossings are of course simply the original EMA(12) line crossing up or down through the slower EMA(26) line.

Positive divergence between MACD and price arises when price makes a new selloff low, but the MACD doesn't make a new low (i.e. it remains above where it fell to on that previous price low). This is interpreted as bullish, suggesting the downtrend may be nearly over. Negative divergence is the same thing when rising (i.e. price makes a new rally high, but MACD doesn't rise as high as before), this is interpreted as bearish.

Divergence may be similarly interpreted on the price versus the histogram, where the new price levels are not confirmed by new histogram levels. Longer and sharper divergences (distinct peaks or troughs) are regarded as more significant than small shallow patterns in this case.

It is recommended to look at a MACD on a weekly scale before looking at a daily scale to avoid making short term trades against the direction of the intermediate trend.

Sometimes it is prudent to apply a price filter to the Bullish Moving Average Crossover to ensure that it will hold. An example of a price filter would be to buy if MACD breaks above the 9-day EMA and remains above for three days. The buy signal would then commence at the end of the third day.

Signal Processing

The MACD is a filtered measure of the velocity. The velocity has been passed through two first order linear low pass filters. The "signal line" is that resulting velocity, filtered again. The difference between those two, the histogram, is a measure of the acceleration, with all three filters applied. The "MACD crossing the signal line" suggests that the direction of the acceleration is changing. "MACD line crossing zero" suggests that the average velocity is changing direction.

Criticism

With the emergence of computerized analysis, it has become highly unreliable in the modern era, and standard MACD based trade execution now produces a greater distribution of losing trades. Some additions have been made to MACD over the years but even with the addition of the MACD histogram, it remains a lagging indicator. It has often been criticized for failing to respond in mild/volatile market conditions. Since the crash of the market in 2000, most strategies no longer recommend using MACD as the primary method of analysis, but instead believe it should be used as a monitoring tool only. It is prone to whipsaw, and if a trader is not careful it is possible that they might suffer substantial loss, especially if they are leveraged or trading options.

Average Directional Index

The Average Directional Index (ADX) was developed in 1978 by J. Welles Wilder as an indicator of trend strength in a series of prices of a financial instrument. ADX has become a widely-used indicator for technical analysts, and is provided as a standard in collections of indicators offered by various trading platforms.

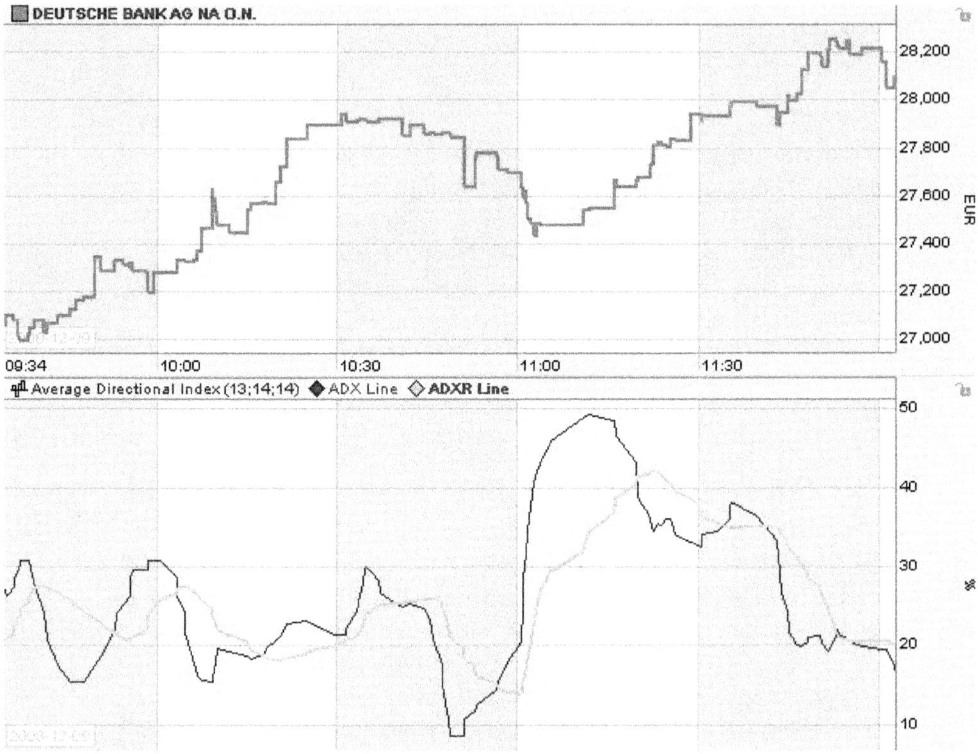

Picture 43: ADX

Calculation

The ADX is a combination of two other indicators developed by Wilder, the positive directional indicator (abbreviated +DI) and negative directional indicator (-DI). The ADX combines them and smooths the result with an exponential moving average.

To calculate +DI and -DI, one needs price data consisting of high, low, and closing prices each period (typically each day). One first calculates the Directional Movement (+DM and -DM):

- UpMove = Today's High – Yesterday's High
- DownMove = Yesterday's Low – Today's Low
- if UpMove > DownMove and UpMove > 0, then +DM = UpMove, else +DM = 0
- if DownMove > UpMove and DownMove > 0, then -DM = DownMove, else -DM = 0

After selecting the number of periods (Wilder used 14 days originally), +DI and -DI are:

- +DI = exponential moving average of +DM divided by Average True Range
- -DI = exponential moving average of -DM divided by Average True Range

The exponential moving average is calculated over the number of periods selected, and the average true range is an exponential average of the true ranges. Then:

- ADX = 100 times the exponential moving average of the Absolute value of (+DI – -DI) divided by (+DI + -DI)

Variations of this calculation typically involve using different types of moving averages, such as a weighted moving average or an adaptive moving average.

Interpretation

The ADX does not indicate trend direction, only trend strength. It is a lagging indicator; that is, a trend must have established itself before the ADX will generate a signal that a trend is underway. ADX will range between 0 and 100. Generally, ADX readings below 20 indicate trend weakness, and readings above 40 indicate trend strength.

Commodity Channel Index

The Commodity Channel Index (CCI) is an oscillator originally introduced by Donald Lambert in an article published in the October 1980 issue of Commodities magazine (now known as Futures magazine).

Since its introduction, the indicator has grown in popularity and is now a very common tool for traders in identifying cyclical trends not only in commodities, but also equities and currencies. The CCI can be adjusted to the timeframe of the market traded on by changing the averaging period.

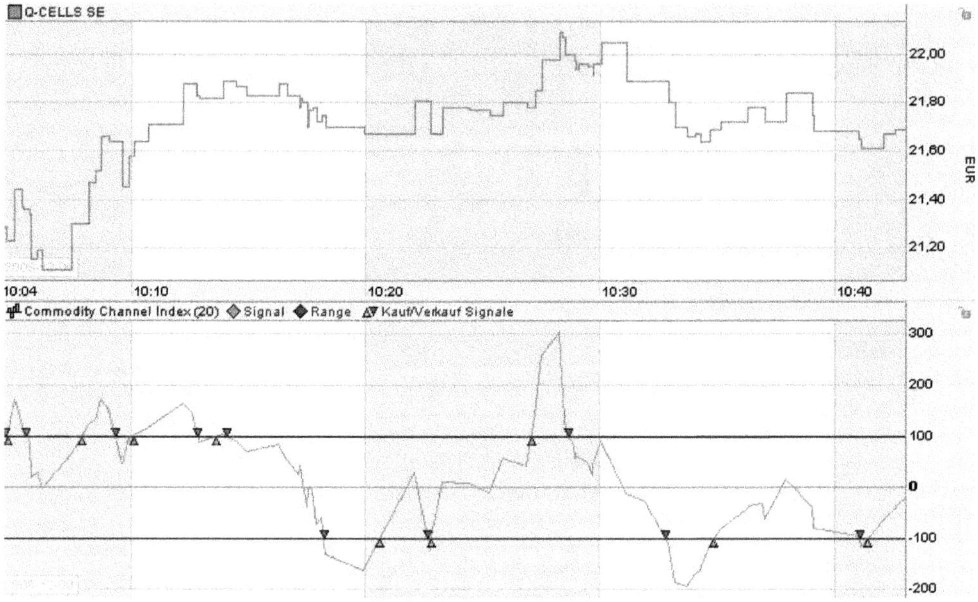

Picture 44: CCI

Calculation

The CCI is calculated as the difference between the typical price of a commodity and its simple moving average, divided by the mean deviation of the typical price. The index is usually scaled by a factor of 1/0.015 to provide more readable numbers:

$$CCI = \frac{1}{0.015} \frac{p_t - SMA(p_t)}{\sigma(p_t)}$$

where the pt is the typical price (average of the high, low, and closing prices), SMA is the simple moving average, and σ is the mean deviation.

Interpretation

The Commodity Channel Index is often used for detecting divergences from price trends as an overbought/oversold indicator, and to draw patterns on it and trade according to those patterns. In this respect, it is similar to bollinger bands, but is presented as an indicator rather than as overbought/oversold levels.

The CCI typically oscillates above and below a zero line. Normal oscillations will occur within the range of +100 and -100. Readings above +100 imply an overbought condition, while readings below -100 imply an oversold condition. As with other overbought/oversold indicators, this means that there is a large probability that the price will correct to more representative levels.

Parabolic SAR

In the field of technical analysis, Parabolic SAR (SAR - stop and reverse) is a method devised by J. Welles Wilder, Jr. to find trends in market prices or securities. It may be used as a trailing stop loss based on prices tending to stay within a parabolic curve during a strong trend.

The concept draws on the idea that time is an enemy, and unless a security can continue to generate more profits over time, it should be liquidated. The indicator generally works well in trending markets, but provides "whipsaws" during non-trending, sideways phases. A parabola below the price is generally bullish, while a parabola above is generally bearish.

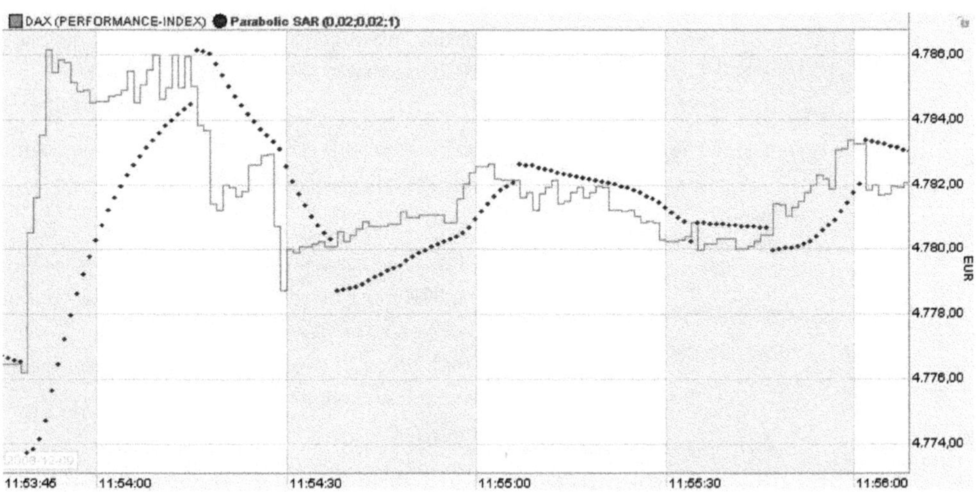

Picture 45: PSAR

Construction

The Parabolic SAR is calculated almost independently for each **trend** in the price. When the price is in an uptrend, the SAR appears below the price and converges upwards towards it. Similarly, on a downtrend, the SAR appears above the price and converges downwards.

At each step within a trend, the SAR is calculated ahead of time. That is, tomorrow's SAR value is built using data available today. The general formula used for this is:

$$SAR_{n+1} = SAR_n + \alpha(EP - SAR_n)$$

Where SAR_n and SAR_{n+1} represent today's and tomorrow's SAR values, respectively.

The extreme point, *EP*, is a record kept during each trend that represents the highest value reached by the price during the current uptrend — or lowest value during a downtrend. On each period, if a new maximum (or minimum) is observed, the EP is updated with that value.

The α value represents the acceleration factor. Usually, this is set to a value of 0.02 initially. This factor is increased by 0.02 each time a new EP is recorded. In other words, each time a new EP is observed, it will increase the acceleration factor. This will then quicken the rate at which the SAR converges towards the price. To keep it from getting too large, a maximum value for the acceleration factor is normally set at 0.20, so that it never goes beyond that.

The SAR is recursively calculated in this manner for each new period. There are, however, two special cases that will modify the SAR value:

- If tomorrow's SAR value lies within (or beyond) today's or yesterday's price range, the SAR must be set to the closest price bound. For example, if in an uptrend, the new SAR value is calculated and it results to be greater than today's or yesterday's lowest price, the SAR must be set equal to that lower boundary.

- If tomorrow's SAR value lies within (or beyond) tomorrow's price range, a new trend direction is then signaled, and the SAR must "switch sides."

Upon a trend switch, several things happen. The first SAR value for this new trend is set to the last EP recorded on the previous trend. The EP is then reset accordingly to this period's maximum. The acceleration factor is reset to its initial value of 0.02.

Rahul Mohindar Oscillator

The Rahul Mohindar Oscillator (RMO) is a type of technical analysis developed by Rahul Mohindar of Viratech India. It detects trends in financial markets, and is designed to work on Open-High-Low-Close charts for a wide variety of securities including stocks, commodities and FX.

Stochastic Oscillator

The stochastic oscillator is a momentum indicator used in technical analysis, introduced by George Lane in the 1950s, to compare the closing price of a commodity to its price range over a given time span.

This indicator is usually calculated as:

$$STS = 100\frac{\text{closing price} - \text{price low}}{\text{price high} - \text{price low}}$$

and can be manipulated by changing the period considered for highs and lows.

Interpretation

The idea behind this indicator is that prices tend to close near their past highs in bull markets, and near their lows in bear markets. Transaction signals can be spotted when the stochastic oscillator crosses its **moving average**.

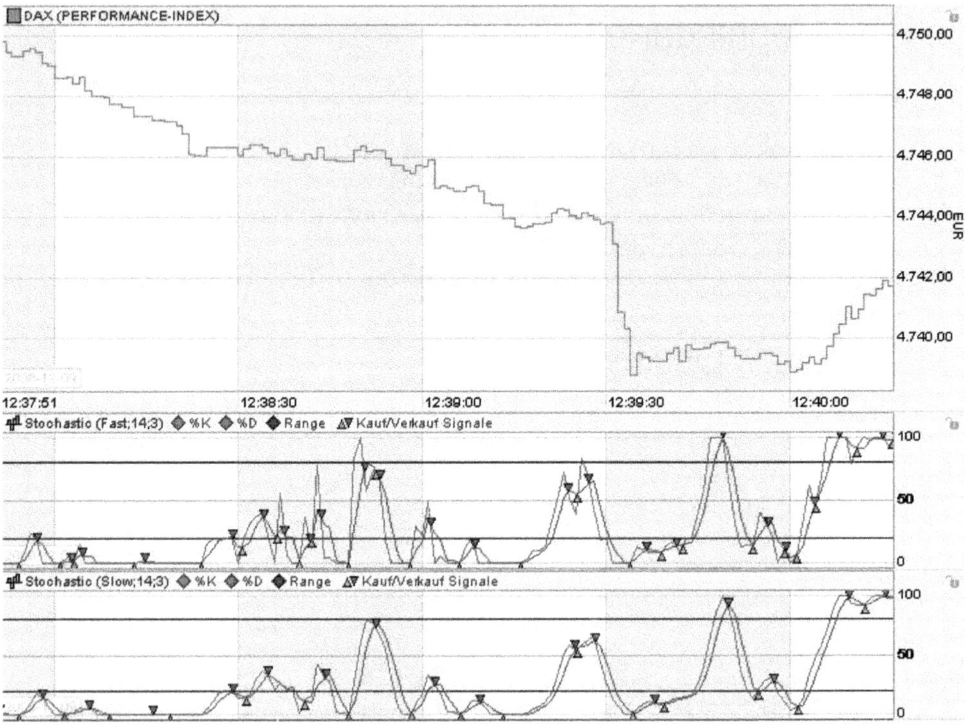

Picture 46: Stochastic Oscillator Fast & Slow; the Slow O. is smoother with less errors

Two stochastic oscillator indicators are typically calculated to assess future variations in prices, a fast (%K) and slow (%D). Comparisons of these statistics are a good indicator of speed at which prices are changing or the Impulse of Price. %K is the same as Williams %R, though on a scale 0 to 100 instead of -100 to 0, but the terminology for the two are kept separate.

The fast stochastic oscillator or Stoch %K calculates the ratio of two closing price statistics: the difference between the latest closing price and the lowest price in the last N days over the difference between the highest and lowest prices in the last N days:

$$\%K = \frac{CP_{today's} - LOW_{lowestNDays}}{HIGH_{highestNdays} - LOW_{lowestNDays}} \times 100$$

Where:

CP is closing price

LOW is low price

HIGH is high price

The usual "N" is 14 days but this can be varied. When the current closing price is the low for the last N-days, the %K value is 0, when the current closing price is a high for the last N-days, %K=100.

The slow stochastic oscillator or Stoch %D calculates the **simple moving average** of the Stoch %K statistic across s periods . Usually s=3:

$$\%D = SMA_3 \; of \; \%K$$

or more generally:

$$\%D_n = \sum_{k=0}^{s} \frac{\%K_{n-k}}{s}.$$

The %K and %D oscillators range from 0 to 100 and are often visualized using a line plot. Levels near the extremes 100 and 0, for either %K or %D, indicate strength or weakness (respectively) because prices have made or are near new N-day highs or lows.

There are two well known methods for using the %K and %D indicators to make decisions about when to buy or sell stocks. The first involves crossing of %K and %D signals, the second involves basing buy and sell decisions on the assumption that %K and %D oscillate.

In the first case, %D acts as a trigger or signal line for %K. A buy signal is given when %K crosses up through %D, or a sell signal when it crosses down through %D. Such crossovers can occur too often, and to avoid repeated whipsaws one can wait for crossovers occurring together with an overbought/oversold pullback, or only after a peak or trough in the %D line. If price volatility is high, a simple moving average of the Stoch %D indicator may be taken. This statistic smooths out rapid fluctuations in price.

In the second case, some analysts argue that %K or %D levels above 80 and below 20 can be interpreted as overbought or oversold. On the theory that the prices oscillate, many analysts including George Lane, recommend that buying and selling be timed to the return from these thresholds. In other words, one should buy or sell after a bit of a reversal. Practically, this means that once the price exceeds one of these thresholds, the investor should wait for prices to return through those thresholds (e.g. if the oscillator were to go above 80, the investor waits until it falls below 80 to sell).

George Lane, a financial analyst from the 1950s is one of the first to publish on the use of stochastic oscillators to forecast prices. According to Lane you use the stochastics indicator with a good knowledge of "Elliot Wave Theory". A Center piece of his teaching is the divergence and convergence of trend lines drawn on stochastics as diverging/ converging to trend lines drawn on price cycles. Stochastics has the power to predict tops and bottoms.

It should be noted that the existence of price oscillations is hypothetical and statistical at best--stock price movements are a consequence of the actions of human decision-makers and past behavior of market variables does not necessarily predict future behavior.

Trix

Trix (or TRIX) is a technical analysis oscillator developed in the 1980s by Jack Hutson, editor of Technical Analysis of Stocks and Commodities magazine. It shows the slope (ie. derivative) of a triple-smoothed exponential moving average. The name Trix is from "triple exponential."

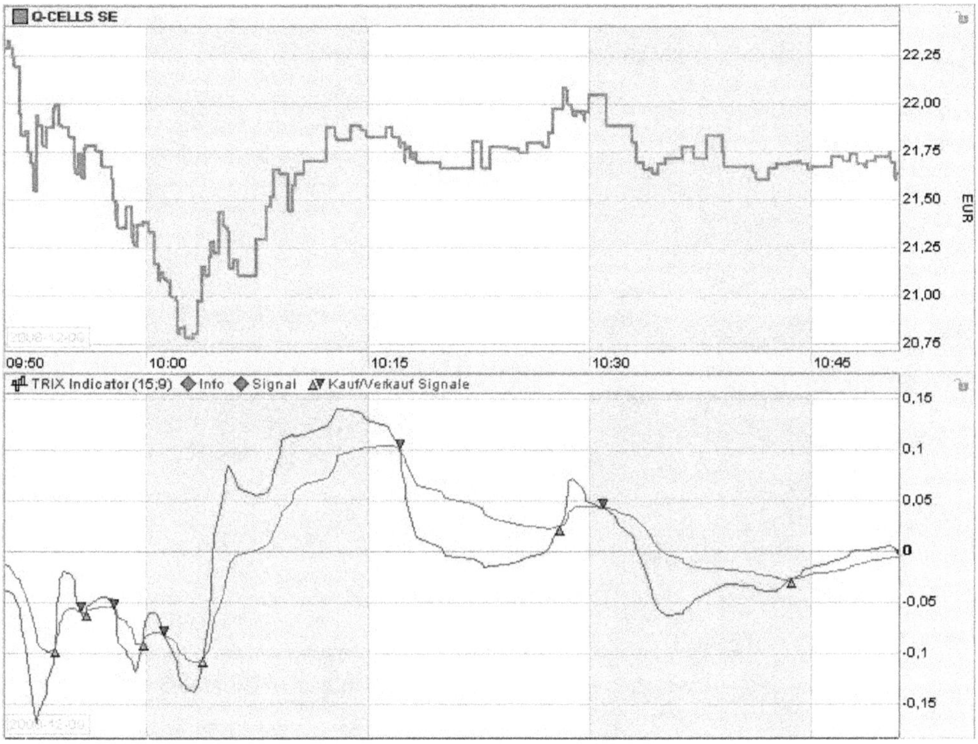

Picture 47: TRIX

Trix is calculated with a given N-day period as follows:

- Smooth prices (often closing prices) using an N-day exponential moving average (EMA).
- Smooth that series using another N-day EMA.
- Smooth a third time, using a further N-day EMA.
- Calculate the percentage difference between today's and yesterday's value in that final smoothed series.

Like any moving average, the triple EMA is just a smoothing of price data and therefore is trend-following. A rising or falling line is an uptrend or downtrend and Trix shows the slope of that line, so it's positive for a steady uptrend, negative for a downtrend, and a crossing through zero is a trend-change, ie. a peak or trough in the underlying average.

The triple-smoothed EMA is very different from a plain EMA. In a plain EMA the latest few days dominate and the EMA follows recent prices quite closely; however, applying it three times results in weightings spread much more broadly, and the weights for the latest few days are in fact smaller than those of days further past. The following graph shows the weightings for an N=10 triple EMA (most recent days at the left):

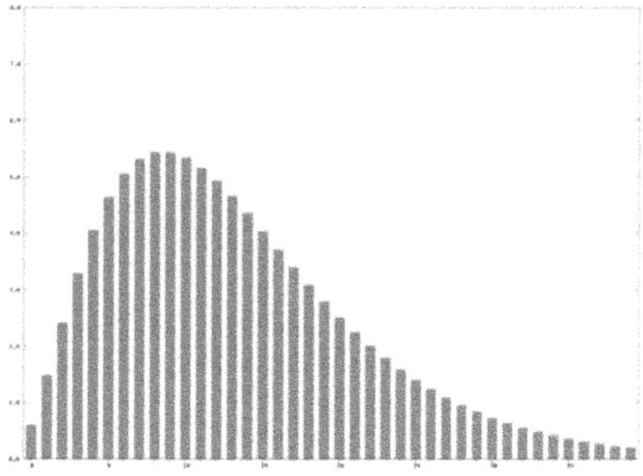

Picture 48: Triple exponential moving average weightings, N=10 (percentage versus days ago)

The easiest way to calculate the triple EMA based on successive values is just to apply the EMA three times, creating single-, then double-, then triple-smoothed series. The triple EMA can also be expressed directly in terms of the prices as below, with p_0 today's close, p_1 yesterday's, etc, and with $f = 1 - \frac{2}{N+1}$ (as for a plain EMA):

$$TripleEMA_0 = (1-f)^3(p_0 + 3fp_1 + 6f^2p_2 + 10f^3p_3 + \ldots)$$

The coefficients are the triangle numbers, *n(n+1)/2*. In theory, the sum is infinite, using all past data, but as *f* is less than 1 the powers f^n become smaller as the series progresses, and they decrease faster than the coefficients increase, so beyond a certain point the terms are negligible.

Accumulation/Distribution Index

Accumulation/Distribution index is a cumulative total volume technical analysis indicator created by Marc Chaikin, which adds or subtracts each day's volume in proportion to where the close is between the day's high and low.

First a close location value is formed,

$$CLV = \frac{(close - low) - (high - close)}{high - low}$$

This ranges from -1 when the close is the low of the day, to +1 when it's the high. For instance if the close is 3/4 the way up the range then CLV is +0.5. The accumulation/distribution index adds up volume multiplied by the CLV factor, ie.

$$accdist = accdist_{prev} + volume \times CLV$$

The starting point for the acc/dist total, ie. the zero point, is arbitrary, only the shape of the resulting indicator is used, not the actual level of the total.

The name accumulation/distribution comes from the idea that during accumulation buyers are in control and the price will be bid up through the day, or will make a recovery if sold down, in either case more often finishing near the day's high than the low. The opposite applies during distribution.

The accumulation/distribution index is similar to on balance volume, but acc/dist is based on the close within the day's range, instead of the close-to-close up or down that the latter uses.

Chaikin Oscillator

A Chaikin oscillator is formed by subtracting a 10-day exponential moving average from a 3-day moving average of the accumulation/distribution index. Being an indicator of an indicator, it can give various sell or buy signals, depending on the context and other indicators.

Money Flow

Money flow in technical analysis is typical price multiplied by volume, a kind of approximation to the dollar value of a day's trading.

Money flow index (MFI) is an oscillator calculated over an N-day period, ranging from 0 to 100, showing money flow on up days as a percentage of the total of up and down days.

The calculations are as follows. The typical price for each day is the average of high, low and close,

$$typical\ price = \frac{high + low + close}{3}$$

Money flow is the product of typical price and the volume on that day.

$$money\ flow = typical\ price \times volume$$

Totals of the money flow amounts over the given N days are then formed. Positive money flow is the total for those days where the typical price is higher than the previous day's typical price, and negative money flow where below. (If typical price is unchanged then that day is discarded.) A money ratio is then formed

$$money\ ratio = \frac{positive\ money\ flow}{negative\ money\ flow}$$

From which a money flow index ranging from 0 to 100 is formed,

$$MFI = 100 - \frac{100}{1 + money\ ratio}$$

This can be expressed equivalently as follows. This form makes it clearer how the MFI is a percentage,

$$MFI = 100 \times \frac{positive\ money\ flow}{positive\ moneyflow + negative\ money\ flow}$$

MFI is used as an oscillator. A value of 80 is generally considered overbought, or a value of 20 oversold. Divergences between MFI and price action are also considered significant, for instance if price makes a new rally high but the MFI high is less than its previous high then that may indicate a weak advance, likely to reverse.

It will be noted the MFI is constructed in a similar fashion to the relative strength index. Both look at up days against total up plus down days, but the scale, ie. what is accumulated on those days, is volume (or dollar volume approximation rather) for the MFI, as opposed to price change amounts for the RSI.

It's important to be clear about what "money flow" means. It refers to dollar volume, ie. the total value of shares traded. Sometimes finance commentators speak of money "flowing into" a stock, but that expression only refers to the enthusiasm of buyers (obviously there's never any net money in or out, because for every buyer there's a seller of the same amount).

For the purposes of the MFI, "money flow", ie. dollar volume, on an up day is taken to represent the enthusiasism of buyers, and on a down day to represent the enthusiasm of sellers. An excessive proportion in one direction or the other is interpreted as an extreme, likely to result in a price reversal.

Price and Volume Trend

Price and Volume Trend (PVT) is a technical analysis indicator intended to relate price and volume in the stock market. PVT is based on a running total volume, with volume added according to the percentage change in closing price over the previous close.

The formula is:

$$PVT = PVT_{prev} + volume \times \frac{close_{today} - close_{prev}}{close_{prev}}$$

The starting point for the PVT total, ie. the zero point, is arbitrary. Only the shape of the resulting indicator is used, not the actual level of the total.

PVT is similar to On-balance Volume (OBV), but where OBV takes volume just according to whether the close was higher or lower, PVT includes how much higher or lower it was.

PVT is interpreted in similar ways to OBV. Generally the idea is that volume is higher on days with a price move in the dominant direction, for example in a strong uptrend more volume on up days than down days. So when prices are going up, PVT should be going up too, and when prices make a new rally high, PVT should too. If PVT fails to go past its previous rally high then this is a negative divergence, suggesting a weak move.

On-balance Volume

On-balance Volume (OBV) is a technical analysis indicator intended to relate price and volume in the stock market. OBV is based on a cumulative total volume. Volume on an up day (close higher than previous close) is added and volume on a down day is subtracted.

The formula is

$$OBV = OBV_{prev} + \begin{cases} volume & \text{if } close > close_{prev} \\ 0 & \text{if } close = close_{prev} \\ -volume & \text{if } close < close_{prev} \end{cases}$$

The starting point for an OBV total, ie. the zero point, is arbitrary. Only the shape of the resulting indicator is used, not the actual level of the total.

The technique was investigated in the 1940s by Woods and Vignolia and presented in a course by them in 1946. They called it "cumulative volume". Joseph Granville gave it the name "on-balance volume" and popularized the technique in his 1963 book Granville's New Key to Stock Market Profits. It can be applied to stocks individually based upon their daily up or down close, or the market as a whole using breadth of market data, i.e. the advance/decline ratio.

OBV is generally used to confirm price moves. The idea is that volume is higher on days where the price move is in the dominant direction, for example in a strong uptrend more volume on up days than down days.

So when prices are going up, OBV should be going up too, and when prices make a new rally high, OBV should too. If OBV fails to go past its previous rally high then this is a negative divergence, suggesting a weak move.

Crashes and troubled Times

Financial Crisis

The term financial crisis is applied broadly to a variety of situations in which some financial institutions or assets suddenly lose a large part of their value. In the 19th and early 20th centuries, many financial crises were associated with banking panics, and many recessions coincided with these panics. Other situations that are often called financial crises include stock market crashes and the bursting of other financial bubbles, currency crises, and sovereign defaults.

Many economists have offered theories about how financial crises develop and how they could be prevented. There is little consensus, however, and financial crises are still a regular occurrence around the world.

Types of Financial Crises

Banking Crises

When a commercial bank suffers a sudden rush of withdrawals by depositors, this is called a bank run. Since banks lend out most of the cash they receive in deposits, it is difficult for them to quickly pay back all deposits if these are suddenly demanded, so a run may leave the bank in bankruptcy, causing many depositors to lose their savings unless they are covered by deposit insurance. A situation in which bank runs are widespread is called a systemic banking crisis or just a banking panic. A situation without widespread bank runs, but in which banks are reluctant to lend, because they worry that they have insufficient funds available, is often called a credit crunch.

Examples of bank runs include the run on the Bank of the United States in 1931 and the run on Northern Rock in 2007. The collapse of Bear Stearns in 2008 is also sometimes called a bank run, even though Bear Stearns was an investment bank rather than a commercial bank. The U.S. savings and loan crisis of the 1980s led to a credit crunch which is seen as a major factor in the U.S. recession of 1990-1991.

Speculative Bubbles and Crashes

Economists say that a financial asset (stock, for example) exhibits a bubble when its price exceeds the value of the future income (such as interest or dividends) that would be received by owning it to maturity. If most market participants buy the asset primarily in hopes of selling it later at a higher price, instead of buying it for the income it will generate, this could be evidence that a bubble is present. If there is a bubble, there is also a risk of a crash in asset prices: market participants will go on buying only as long as they expect others to buy, and when many decide to sell the price will fall. However, it is difficult to tell in practice whether an asset's price actually equals its fundamental value, so it is hard to detect bubbles reliably. Some economists insist that bubbles never or almost never occur.

Well-known examples of bubbles (or purported bubbles) and crashes in stock prices and other asset prices include the Dutch tulip mania, the Wall Street Crash of 1929, the Japanese property bubble of the 1980s, the crash of the dot-com bubble in 2000-2001, and the now-deflating United States housing bubble.

International Financial Crises

When a country that maintains a fixed exchange rate is suddenly forced to devalue its currency because of a speculative attack, this is called a currency crisis or balance of payments crisis. When a country fails to pay back its sovereign debt, this is called a sovereign default. While devaluation and default could both be voluntary decisions of the government, they are often perceived to be the involuntary results of a change in investor sentiment that leads to a sudden stop in capital inflows or a sudden increase in capital flight.

Several currencies that formed part of the European Exchange Rate Mechanism suffered crises in 1992-93 and were forced to devalue or withdraw from the mechanism. Another round of currency crises took place in Asia in 1997-98. Many Latin American countries defaulted on their debt in the early 1980s. The 1998 Russian financial crisis resulted in a devaluation of the ruble and default on Russian government debt.

Wider Economic Crises

A downturn in economic growth lasting several quarters or more is usually called a recession. An especially prolonged recession may be called a depression, while a long period of slow but not necessarily negative growth is sometimes called economic stagnation. Since these phenomena affect much more than the financial system, they are not usually considered financial crises per se. But some economists have argued that many recessions have been caused in large part by financial crises. One important example is the Great Depression, which was preceded in many countries by bank runs and stock market crashes. The subprime mortgage crisis and the bursting of other real estate bubbles around the world is widely expected to lead to recession in the U.S. and a number of other countries in 2008.

Nonetheless, some economists argue that financial crises are caused by recessions instead of the other way around. Also, even if a financial crisis is the initial shock that sets off a recession, other factors may be more important in prolonging the recession. In particular, Milton Friedman and Anna Schwartz argued that the initial economic decline associated with the crash of 1929 and the bank panics of the 1930s would not have turned into a prolonged depression if it had not been reinforced by monetary policy mistakes on the part of the Federal Reserve, and Ben Bernanke has acknowledged that he agrees.

Causes and Consequences of a Financial Crises

Strategic Complementarities in Financial Markets

It is often observed that successful investment requires each investor in a financial market to guess what other investors will do. George Soros has called this need to guess the intentions of others 'reflexivity'. Similarly, John Maynard Keynes compared financial markets to a beauty contest game in which each participant tries to predict which model other participants will consider most beautiful.

Furthermore, in many cases investors have incentives to coordinate their choices. For example, someone who thinks other investors want to buy lots of Japanese yen may expect the yen to rise in value, and therefore has an incentive to buy yen too. Likewise, a depositor in IndyMac Bank who expects other depositors to withdraw their funds may expect the bank to fail, and therefore has an incentive to withdraw too. Economists call an incentive to mimic the strategies of others strategic complementarity.

It has been argued that if people or firms have a sufficiently strong incentive to do the same thing they expect others to do, then self-fulfilling prophecies may occur. For example, if investors expect the value of the yen to rise, this may cause its value to rise; if depositors expect a bank to fail this may cause it to fail. Therefore, financial crises are sometimes viewed as a vicious circle in which investors shun some institution or asset because they expect others to do so.

Leverage

Leverage, which means borrowing to finance investments, is frequently cited as a contributor to financial crises. When a financial institution (or an individual) invests its own money, it can, in the very worst case, lose its own money. But when it borrows in order to invest more, it can potentially earn more from its investment, but it can also lose more than all it has. Therefore leverage magnifies the potential returns from investment, but also creates a risk of bankruptcy. Since bankruptcy means that a firm fails to honor all its promised payments to other firms, it may spread financial troubles from one firm to another (see 'Contagion' below).

The average degree of leverage in the economy often rises prior to a financial crisis. For example, borrowing to finance investment in the stock market ("margin buying") became increasingly common prior to the Wall Street Crash of 1929.

Asset-liability Mismatch

Another factor believed to contribute to financial crises is asset-liability mismatch, a situation in which the risks associated with an institution's debts and assets are not appropriately aligned. For example, commercial banks offer deposit accounts which can be withdrawn at any time and they use the proceeds to make long-term loans to businesses and homeowners. The mismatch between the banks' short-term liabilities (its deposits) and its long-term assets (its loans) is seen as one of the reason bank runs occur (when depositors panic and decide to withdraw their funds more quickly than the bank can get back the proceeds of its loans). Likewise, Bear Stearns failed in 2007-08 because it was unable to renew the short-term debt it used to finance long-term investments in mortgage securities.

In an international context, many emerging market governments are unable to sell bonds denominated in their own currencies, and therefore sell bonds denominated in US dollars instead. This generates a mismatch between the currency denomination of their liabilities (their bonds) and their assets (their local tax revenues), so that they run a risk of sovereign default due to fluctuations in exchange rates.

Regulatory Failures

Governments have attempted to eliminate or mitigate financial crises by regulating the financial sector. One major goal of regulation is transparency: Making institutions' financial situation publicly known by requiring regular reporting under standardized accounting procedures. Another goal of regulation is making sure institutions have sufficient assets to meet their contractual obligations, through reserve requirements, capital requirements, and other limits on leverage.

Some financial crises have been blamed on insufficient regulation, and have led to changes in regulation in order to avoid a repeat. For example, the Managing Director of the IMF, Dominique Strauss-Kahn, has blamed the financial crisis of 2008 on 'regulatory failure to guard against excessive risk-taking in the financial system, especially in the US'. Likewise, the New York Times singled out the deregulation of credit default swaps as a cause of the crisis.

However, excessive regulation has also been cited as a possible cause of financial crises. In particular, the Basel II Accord has been criticized for requiring banks to increase their capital when risks rise, which might cause them to decrease lending precisely when capital is scarce, potentially aggravating a financial crisis.

Fraud

Fraud has played a role in the collapse of some financial institutions, when companies have attracted depositors with misleading claims about their investment strategies, or have embezzled the resulting income. Examples include Charles Ponzi's scam in early 20th century Boston, the collapse of the MMM investment fund in Russia in 1994, and the scams that led to the Albanian Lottery Uprising of 1997.

Many rogue traders that have caused large losses at financial institutions have been accused of acting fraudulently in order to hide their trades. Fraud in mortgage financing has also been cited as one possible cause of the 2008 subprime mortgage crisis; government officials stated on Sept. 23, 2008 that the FBI was looking into possible fraud by mortgage financing companies Fannie Mae and Freddie Mac, Lehman Brothers, and insurer American International Group.

Œcopathy

Swedish psychologist Torbjorn K A Eliazon have proposed a new psychological concept of œcopathy, when economic smartness or greed crosses the borders to an extreme blinding speed and computational proposal unit. Œcopathy is an economic understanding without moral values, where the word "more" has become a central existential position and have no ulterior border in the same manner as that of drug abusers or people denying humanity and mortality. Œcopathy can be both existing in an individual subject (as a personality disorder) and been developed as a structurally built-in-operative - an esprit de corps - within organizations.

Contagion

Contagion refers to the idea that financial crises may spread from one institution to another, as when a bank run spreads from a few banks to many others, or from one country to another, as when currency crises, sovereign defaults, or stock market crashes spread across countries. When the failure of one particular financial institution threatens the stability of many other institutions, this is called systemic risk.

One widely-cited example of contagion was the spread of the Thai crisis in 1997 to other countries like South Korea. However, economists often debate whether observing crises in many countries around the same time is truly caused by contagion from one market to another, or whether it is instead caused by similar underlying problems that would have affected each country individually even in the absence of international linkages.

Recessionary Effects

Some financial crises have little effect outside of the financial sector, like the Wall Street crash of 1987, but other crises are believed to have played a role in decreasing growth in the rest of the economy. There are many theories why a financial crisis could have a recessionary effect on the rest of the economy. These theoretical ideas include the 'financial accelerator', 'flight to quality' and 'flight to liquidity', and the Kiyotaki-Moore model. Some 'third generation' models of currency crises explore how currency crises and banking crises together can cause recessions.

Theories of Financial Crises

World Systems Theory

Recurrent major depressions in the world economy at the pace of 20 and 50 years have been the subject of empirical and econometric research especially in the world systems theory and in the debate about Nikolai Kondratiev and the so-called 50-years Kondratiev waves. Major figures of world systems theory, like Andre Gunder Frank and Immanuel Wallerstein, consistently warned about the crash that the world economy is now facing. World systems scholars and Kondratiev cycle researchers always implied that Washington Consensus oriented economists never understood the dangers and perils, which leading industrial nations will be facing and are now facing at the end of the long economic cycle which began after the oil crisis of 1973.

Minsky's Theory

Hyman Minsky has proposed a simplified explanation that is most applicable to a closed economy. He theorized that financial fragility is a typical feature of any capitalist economy. High fragility leads to a higher risk of a financial crisis. To facilitate his analysis, Minsky defines three types of financing firms choose according to their tolerance of risk. They are hedge finance, speculative finance, and Ponzi finance. Ponzi finance leads to the most fragility.

Financial fragility levels move together with the business cycle. After a recession, firms have lost much financing and choose only hedge, the safest. As the economy grows and expected profits rise, firms tend to believe that they can allow themselves to take on speculative financing. In this case, they know that profits will not cover all the interest all the time. Firms, however, believe that profits will rise and the loans will eventually be repaid without much trouble. More loans lead to more investment, and the economy grows further. Then lenders also start believing that they will get back all the money they lend. Therefore, they are ready to lend to firms without full guarantees of success. Lenders know that such firms will have problems repaying. Still, they believe these firms will refinance from elsewhere as their expected profits rise. This is Ponzi financing. In this way, the economy has taken on much risky credit. Now it is only a question of time before some big firm actually defaults. Lenders understand the actual risks in the economy and stop giving credit so easily. Refinancing becomes impossible for many, and more firms default. If no new money comes into the economy to allow the refinancing process, a real economic crisis begins. During the recession, firms start to hedge again, and the cycle is closed.

Coordination Games

Mathematical approaches to modeling financial crises have emphasized that there is often positive feedback between market participants' decisions. Positive feedback implies that there may be dramatic changes in asset values in response to small changes in economic fundamentals. For example, some models of currency crises (including that of Paul Krugman) imply that a fixed exchange rate may be stable for a long period of time, but will collapse suddenly in an avalanche of currency sales in response to a sufficient deterioration of government finances or underlying economic conditions.

According to some theories, positive feedback implies that the economy can have more than one equilibrium. There may be an equilibrium in which market participants invest heavily in asset markets because they expect assets to be valuable, but there may be another equilibrium where participants flee asset markets because they expect others to flee too. This is the type of argument underlying Diamond and Dybvig's model of bank runs, in which savers withdraw their assets from the bank because they expect others to withdraw too. Likewise, in Obstfeld's model of currency crises, when economic conditions are neither too bad nor too good, there are two possible outcomes: speculators may or may not decide to attack the currency depending on what they expect other speculators to do.

History

A short list of some major financial crises since 1980

- 1980s: Latin American debt crisis, beginning in Mexico
- 1989-91: United States Savings & Loan crisis
- 1990s: Collapse of the Japanese asset price bubble
- 1992-3: Speculative attacks on currencies in the European Exchange Rate Mechanism
- 1994-5: 1994 economic crisis in Mexico: speculative attack and default on Mexican debt
- 1997-8: Asian Financial Crisis: devaluations and banking crises across Asia
- 1998: 1998 Russian financial crisis: devaluation of the ruble and default on Russian debt

- 2001-2: Argentine economic crisis (1999-2002): breakdown of banking system
- 2008: Global financial crisis and USA, Europe: spread of the U.S. subprime mortgage crisis

Virtuous Circle and Vicious Circle

A virtuous circle or a vicious circle is a complex of events that reinforces itself through a feedback loop toward greater instability. A virtuous circle (or virtuous cycle) has favorable results, and a vicious circle (or vicious cycle) has deleterious results. A virtuous circle can transform into a vicious circle if eventual negative feedback is ignored.

Both circles are complexes of events with no tendency towards equilibrium (at least in the short run). Both systems of events have feedback loops in which each iteration of the cycle reinforces the first (positive feedback). These cycles will continue in the direction of their momentum until an exogenous factor intervenes and stops the cycle. The prefix "hyper" is sometimes used to describe these cycles. The most well known vicious circle is hyperinflation.

Example in Macroeconomics

Vicious Circle

Hyperinflation is a spiral of inflation which causes even higher inflation. The initial exogenous event might be a sudden large increase in international interest rates or a massive increase in government debt due to excessive spending. Whatever the cause, the government could pay down some of its debt by printing more money (called monetizing the debt). This increase in the money supply could increase the level of inflation. In an inflationary environment, people tend to spend their money quickly because they expect its value to decrease further in the future. They convert their financial assets into physical assets while their money still has some purchasing power. Often they will purchase on credit. Because of this, the level of savings in the country is very low and the government could have problems refinancing its debt. Its solution could be to print still more money starting another iteration of the vicious cycle.

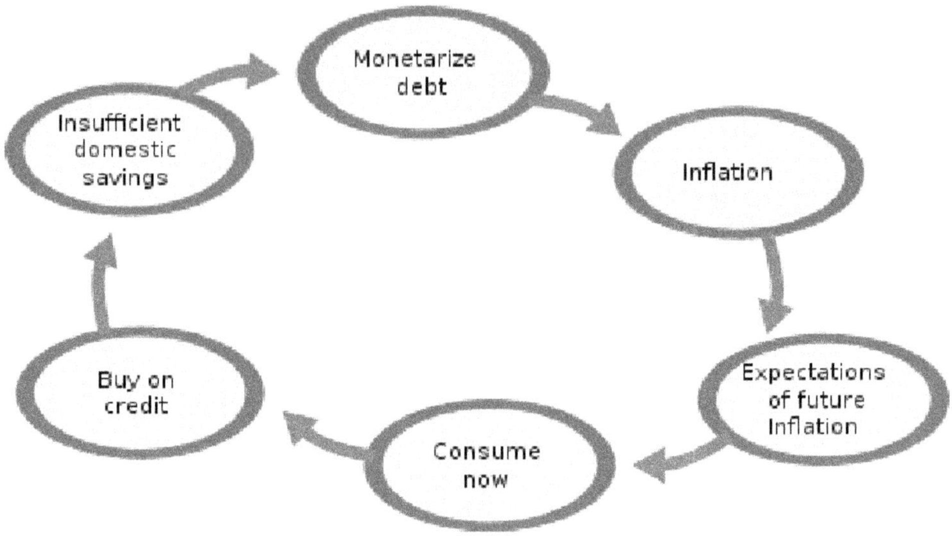

Picture 49:Vicious Circle

Virtuous Circle

Economic growth can be seen as a virtuous circle. It might start with an exogenous factor like technological innovation. As people get familiar with the new technology, there could be learning curve effects and economies of scale. This could lead to reduced costs and improved production efficiencies. In a competitive market structure, this will likely result in lower average prices. As prices decrease, consumption could increase and aggregate output also. Increased levels of output leads to more learning and scale effects and a new cycle starts.

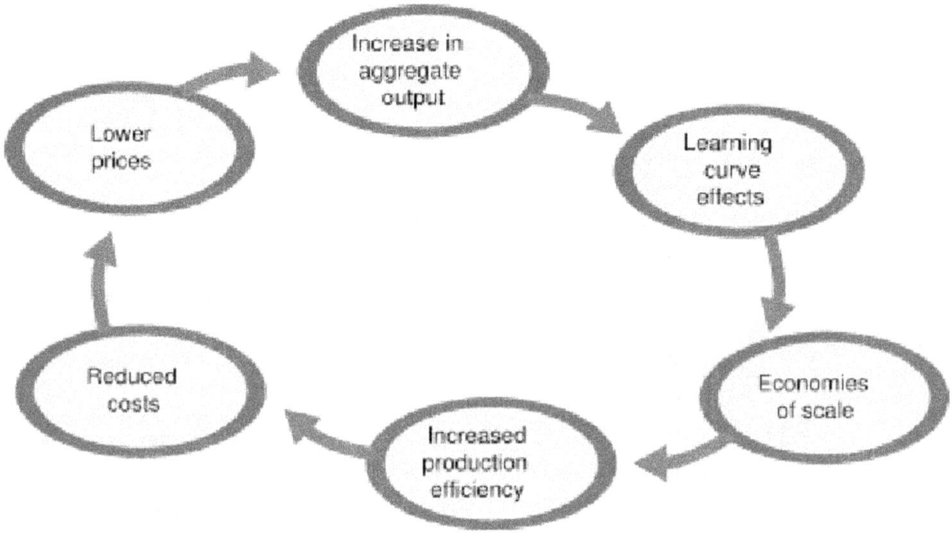

Picture 50: Virtuous Circle

Recession

A recession is a contraction phase of the business cycle, or "a period of reduced economic activity." The U.S. based National Bureau of Economic Research (NBER) defines a recession more broadly as "a significant decline in economic activity spread across the economy, lasting more than a few months, normally visible in real GDP growth, real personal income, employment (non-farm payrolls), industrial production, and wholesale-retail sales." A sustained recession may become a depression.

Some business & investment glossaries add to the general definition a rule of thumb that recessions are often indicated by two consecutive quarters of negative growth (or contraction) of gross domestic product (GDP). Newspapers often quote this rule of thumb, however the measure fails to register several official (NBER defined) US recessions.

Attributes of Recessions

A recession has many attributes that can occur simultaneously and can include declines in coincident measures of overall economic activity such as employment, investment, and corporate profits. Recessions are the result of falling demand and may be associated with falling prices (deflation), or sharply rising prices (inflation) or a combination of rising prices and stagnant economic growth (stagflation). A severe or prolonged recession is referred to as an economic depression. Although the distinction between a recession and a depression is not clearly defined, it is often said that a decline in GDP of more than 10% constitutes a depression. A devastating breakdown of an economy (essentially, a severe depression, or hyperinflation, depending on the circumstances) is called economic collapse.

Predictors of a Recession

There are no completely reliable predictors. These are regarded to be possible predictors.

- In the U.S. a significant stock market drop has often preceded the beginning of a recession. However about half of the declines of 10%

or more since 1946 have not been followed by recessions. In about 50% of the cases a significant stock market decline came only after the recessions had already begun.

- Inverted yield curve, the model developed by Fed economist Jonathan Wright, uses yields on 10-year and three-month Treasury securities as well as the Fed's overnight funds rate. Another model developed by Federal Reserve Bank of New York economists uses only the 10-year/three-month spread. It is, however, not a definite indicator; it is sometimes followed by a recession 6 to 18 months later.
- The three-month change in the unemployment rate and initial jobless claims.
- Index of Leading (Economic) Indicators (includes some of the above indicators).

Responding to a Recession

Strategies for moving an economy out of a recession vary depending on which economic school the policymakers follow. While Keynesian economists may advocate deficit spending by the government to spark economic growth, supply-side economists may suggest tax cuts to promote business capital investment. Laissez-faire economists may simply recommend the government remain "hands off" and not interfere with natural market forces. Populist economists may suggest that benefits for consumers, in the form of subsidies or lower-bracket tax reductions are more effective, and serve a double purpose including relieving the suffering caused by a recession.

Both government and business have responses to recessions. In the Philadelphia Business Journal, Strategic Business adviser Carter Schelling has discussed precautions businesses take to prepare for looming recession, likening it to fire drill. First, he suggests that business owners gauge customers' ability to resist recession and redesign customer offerings accordingly. He goes on to suggest they use lean principles, replace unhappy workers with those more motivated, eager and highly competitive. Also over-communicate. "Companies," he says, "get better at what they do during bad times." He calls his program the "Recession Drill."

Central Bank Response

Usually, central banks respond to recessions by easing monetary conditions, e.g. lowering interest rates. In the United States, the Federal Reserve has responded to potential slowdowns by lowering the target Federal funds rate during recessions and other periods of lower growth. In fact, the Federal Reserve's lowering has even predated recent recessions. The charts below show the impact on the S&P500 and short and long term interest rates.

- July 13, 1990 - September 4, 1992: 8.00% to 3.00% (Includes 1990-1991 recession)
- February 1, 1995 - November 17, 1998: 6.00% to 4.75%
- May 16, 2000 - June 25, 2003: 6.50% to 1.00% (Includes 2001 recession)
- June 29, 2006 - (October 8, 2008): 5.25% to 1.50%

Siegel points out that cuts in the Federal funds rate are now widely anticipated. Thus, cuts are no longer followed by a longer-term rise in stock market indexes.

The declining frequency of recessions in the past two decades and the reduction in declines in GDP suggest that the Federal Reserve has been successful in moderating contractions. However some critics argue that reducing the Federal funds rate has had the effect of adding too much liquidity to the financial markets and excess debt accumulation by consumers. Empirical research by the staff of European Central Bank showed a correlation between excessive money growth and the depth of post-boom recessions.

The Stock Market and Recessions

Some recessions have been anticipated by stock market declines. In Stocks for the long run, Siegel mentions that since 1948, ten recessions were preceded by a stock market decline, by a lead time of 0 to 13 months (average 5.7 months). It should be noted that ten stock market declines of greater than 10% in the DJIA were not followed by a recession.

The real-estate market also usually weakens before a recession. However real-estate declines can last much longer than recessions.

Since the business cycle is very hard to predict, Siegel argues that it is not possible to take advantage of economic cycles for timing investments. Even the National Bureau of Economic Research (NBER) takes a few months to determine if a peak or trough has occurred in the US.

During an economic decline, high yield stocks such as financial services, pharmaceuticals, and tobacco tend to hold up better. However when the economy starts to recover and the bottom of the market has passed (sometimes identified on charts as a MACD), growth stocks tend to recover faster. There is significant disagreement about how health care and utilities tend to recover. Diversifying one's portfolio into international stocks may provide some safety; however, economies that are closely correlated with that of the U.S.A. may also be affected by a recession in the U.S.A.

Recession and Politics

Generally an administration gets credit or blame for the state of economy during its time. This has caused disagreements about when a recession actually started. In an economic cycle, a downturn can be considered a consequence of an expansion reaching an unsustainable state, and is corrected by a brief decline. Thus it is not easy to isolate the causes of specific phases of the cycle.

The 1981 recession is thought to have been caused by the tight-money policy adopted by Paul Volcker, chairman of the Federal Reserve Board, before Ronald Reagan took office. Reagan supported that policy. Economist Walter Heller, chairman of the Council of Economic Advisers in the 1960s, said that "I call it a Reagan-Volcker-Carter recession. The resulting taming of inflation did, however, set the stage for a robust growth period during Reagan's administration.

It is generally assumed that government activity has some influence over the presence or degree of a recession. Economists usually teach that to some degree recession is unavoidable, and its causes are not well understood. Consequently, modern government administrations attempt to take steps, also not agreed upon, to soften a recession. They are often unsuccessful, at least at preventing a recession, and it is difficult to establish whether they actually made it less severe or longer lasting.

Understanding of the word "recession" differs between economists, newspapers, and the general public. Generally speaking, a recession is present when graphs are sloping down in respect to production and employment. Consequently, a politician can truthfully say "the recession is over," even though little has improved. This may imply to the public that the economy is in recovery, suggesting the graphs are sloping upward, though there may actually exist a period of stagnation, when numbers remain low even though they are no longer dropping.

History of Recessions

Global Recessions

There is no commonly accepted definition of a global recession. The IMF estimates that global recessions seem to occur over a cycle lasting between 8 and 10 years. During what the IMF terms the past three global recessions of the last three decades, global per capita output growth was zero or negative.

Economists at the International Monetary Fund (IMF) state that a global recession would take a slowdown in global growth to three percent or less. By this measure, three periods since 1985 qualify: 1990-1993, 1998 and 2001-2002.

United States Recessions

According to economists, since 1854, the U.S.A. has encountered 32 cycles of expansions and contractions, with an average of 17 months of contraction and 38 months of expansion. However, since 1980 there have been only eight periods of negative economic growth over one fiscal quarter or more, and three periods considered recessions:

- January-July 1980 and July 1981-November 1982: 2 years total
- July 1990-March 1991: 8 months
- November 2001-November 2002: 12 months

From 1991 to 2000, the U.S. experienced 37 quarters of economic expansion, the longest period of expansion on record.

For the past three recessions, the NBER decision has approximately conformed with the definition involving two consecutive quarters of decline. However the 2001 recession did not involve two consecutive quarters of decline, it was preceded by two quarters of alternating decline and weak growth.

Possible 2008 Recession in some Countries

Since 2007, there had been speculation of a possible recession starting in late 2007 or early 2008 in some countries.

In January 2008, the IMF predicted that 2008 global growth would fall from 4.9 percent to 4.0 percent (as measured in terms of purchasing power parity), however 2 months later it was announced that this projection was not low enough.

There was significant speculation about a possible U.S. recession in 2008. If such a recession happened, it was expected to have a global impact. The U.S. represents about 21 percent of the global economy, and impact of a U.S. recession could spread through the following:

- Less spending by American consumers and companies reduce demand for imports.
- The crisis of the U.S. subprime-mortgage market has pushed up credit costs worldwide and forced European and Asian banks to write down billions of dollars in holdings.
- Dropping U.S. stock prices drag down markets elsewhere.

United States

The United States housing market correction (a consequence of United States housing bubble) and subprime mortgage crisis had significantly contributed to anticipation of a possible recession.

U.S. employers shed 63,000 jobs in February 2008, the most in five years. Former Federal Reserve chairman Alan Greenspan said on April 6, 2008 that "There is more than a 50 percent chance the United States could go into recession.". On October 1st, the Bureau of Economic Analysis reported that an additional 156,000 jobs had been lost in September. On April 29, 2008, nine US states were declared by Moody's to be in a recession.

Although the US Economy grew in the first quarter by 1%, by June 2008 some analysts stated that due to a protracted credit crisis and "rampant inflation in commodities such as oil, food and steel", the country was nonetheless in a recession. The third quarter of 2008 brought on a GDP retraction of .3% the biggest decline since 2001. The 6.4% decline in spending during Q3 on non-durable goods, like clothing and food, was the largest since 1950.

Other Countries

A few other countries have seen the rate of growth of GDP decrease, generally attributed to reduced liquidity, sector price inflation in food and energy, and the US slowdown. These include the United Kingdom, Japan, China, India, New Zealand and the euro zone.

Stock Market Crashes

A stock market crash is a sudden dramatic decline of stock prices across a significant cross-section of a stock market. Crashes are driven by panic as much as by underlying economic factors. They often follow speculative stock market bubbles.

Stock market crashes are in fact social phenomena where external economic events combine with crowd behavior and psychology in a positive feedback loop where selling by some market participants drives more market participants to sell. Generally speaking, crashes usually occur under the following conditions: a prolonged period of rising stock prices and excessive economic optimism, a market where Price to Earnings ratios exceed long-term averages, and extensive use of margin debt and leverage by market participants.

There is no numerically specific definition of a crash but the term commonly applies to steep double-digit percentage losses in a stock market index over a period of several days. Crashes are often distinguished from bear markets by panic selling and abrupt, dramatic price declines. Bear markets are periods of declining stock market prices that are measured in months or years. While crashes are often associated with bear markets, they do not necessarily go hand in hand. The crash of 1987 for example did not lead to a bear market. Likewise, the Japanese Nikkei bear market of the 1990s occurred over several years without any notable crashes.

Mathematical Theory of Stock Market crashes

The mathematical characterisation of stock market movements has been a subject of intense interest. The conventional assumption that stock markets behave according to a random Gaussian or normal distribution is incorrect. Large movements in prices (i.e. crashes) are much more common than would be predicted in a normal distribution. Research at the Massachusetts Institute of Technology shows that there is evidence that the frequency of stock market crashes follow an inverse cubic power law. This and other studies suggest that stock market crashes are a sign of self-organized criticality in financial markets. In 1963, Benoît Mandelbrot proposed that instead of following a strict random walk, stock price variations executed a Lévy flight. A Lévy flight is a random walk which is occasionally disrupted by large movements. In 1995, Rosario Mantegna and Gene Stanley analyzed a million records of the S&P 500 market index, calculating the returns over a five year period. Their conclusion was that stock market returns are more volatile than a Gaussian distribution but less volatile than a Lévy flight.

Researchers continue to study this theory, particularly using computer simulation of crowd behaviour, and the applicability of models to reproduce crash-like phenomena.

Wall Street Crash of 1929

The Wall Street Crash of 1929, also known as the '29 Crash, the Crash of 1929, or simply the Great Crash, was the most devastating stock market crash in the history of the United States, taking into consideration the full extent and longevity of its fallout.

Three phrases - Black Thursday, Black Monday, and Black Tuesday - are used to describe this collapse of stock values. All three are appropriate, for the crash was not a one-day affair. The initial crash occurred on Black Thursday (October 24, 1929), but it was the catastrophic downturn of Black Monday and Tuesday (October 28 and October 29, 1929) that precipitated widespread panic and the onset of unprecedented and long-lasting consequences for the United States. The collapse continued for a month.

Economists and historians disagree as to what role the crash played in subsequent economic, social, and political events. The Economist writes, "Briefly, the Depression did not start with the stockmarket crash." On November 23, 1929, The Economist asked: "Can a very serious Stock Exchange collapse produce a serious setback to industry when industrial production is for the most part in a healthy and balanced condition? ... Experts are agreed that there must be some setback, but there is not yet sufficient evidence to prove that it will be long or that it need go to the length of producing a general industrial depression." But The Economist cautioned: "Some bank failures, no doubt, are also to be expected. In the circumstances will the banks have any margin left for financing commercial and industrial enterprises or will they not? The position of the banks is without doubt the key to the situation, and what this is going to be cannot be properly assessed until the dust has cleared away."

Picture 51: Crowd gathering on Wall Street after the 1929 crash

The October 1929 crash came during a period of declining real estate values in America (which peaked in 1925) near the beginning of a chain of events that led to the Great Depression, a period of economic decline in the industrialized nations. This led to the institution of landmark financial reforms and new trading regulations.

At the time of the crash, New York City had grown to be a major metropolis, and its Wall Street district was one of the world's leading financial centers.The New York Stock Exchange (NYSE) was the largest stock market in the world.

The Roaring Twenties, which was a precursor to the Crash, was a time of prosperity and excess in the city, and despite warnings against speculation, many believed that the market could sustain high price levels. Shortly before the crash, Irving Fisher famously proclaimed, "Stock prices have reached what looks like a permanently high plateau." The euphoria and financial gains of the great bull market were shattered on Black Thursday, when share prices on the NYSE collapsed. Stock prices fell on that day and they continued to fall, at an unprecedented rate, for a full month.

In the days leading up to Black Tuesday, the market was severely unstable. Periods of selling and high volumes of trading were interspersed with brief periods of rising prices and recovery. Economist and author Jude Wanniski later correlated these swings with the prospects for passage of the Smoot-Hawley Tariff Act, which was then being debated in Congress. After the crash, the Dow Jones Industrial Average (DJIA) recovered early in 1930, only to reverse and crash again, reaching a low point of the great bear market in 1932. The Dow did not return to pre-1929 levels until late 1954, and was lower at its July 8, 1932 level than it had been since the 1800s.

" Anyone who bought stocks in mid-1929 and held onto them saw most of his or her adult life pass by before getting back to even. "

—Richard M. Salsman

Timeline

After a five-year run when the world saw the Dow Jones Industrial Average increase in value fivefold, prices peaked at 381.17 on September 3, 1929. The market then fell sharply for a month, losing 17% of its value on the initial leg down. Prices then recovered more than half of the losses over the next week, only to turn back down immediately afterwards. The decline then accelerated into the so-called "Black Thursday", October 24, 1929. A record number of 12.9 million shares were traded on that day. At 1 p.m. on Friday, October 25, several leading Wall Street bankers met to find a solution to the panic and chaos on the trading floor. The meeting included Thomas W. Lamont, acting head of Morgan Bank; Albert Wiggin, head of the Chase National Bank; and Charles E. Mitchell, president of the National City Bank. They chose Richard Whitney, vice president of the Exchange, to act on their behalf. With the bankers' financial resources behind him, Whitney placed a bid to purchase a large block of shares in U.S. Steel at a price well above the current market. As amazed traders watched, Whitney then placed similar bids on other "blue chip" stocks. This tactic was similar to a tactic that ended the Panic of 1907, and succeeded in halting the slide that day. In this case, however, the respite was only temporary.

Over the weekend, the events were covered by the newspapers across the United States. On Monday, October 28, the first "Black Monday", more investors decided to get out of the market, and the slide continued with a record loss in the Dow for the day of 13%. The next day, "Black Tuesday", October 29, 1929, about 16 million shares were traded. The volume on stocks traded on October 29, 1929 was "...a record that was not broken for nearly 40 years, in 1968." Author Richard M. Salsman wrote that on October 29—amid rumors that U.S. President Herbert Hoover would not veto the pending Hawley-Smoot Tariff bill—stock prices crashed even further." William C. Durant joined with members of the Rockefeller family and other financial giants to buy large quantities of stocks in order to demonstrate to the public their confidence in the market, but their efforts failed to stop the slide. The DJIA lost another 12% that day. The ticker did not stop running until about 7:45 that evening. The market lost $14 billion in value that day, bringing the loss for the week to $30 billion, ten times more than the annual budget of the federal government, far more than the U.S. had spent in all of World War I.

Dow Jones Industrial Average for 10/28/1929 and 10/29/1929

date	**change**	**% change**	**close**
October 28, 1929	-38.33	-12.82	260.64
October 29, 1929	-30.57	-11.73	230.07

An interim bottom occurred on November 13, with the Dow closing at 198.6 that day. The market recovered for several months from that point, with the Dow reaching a secondary peak (ie, dead cat bounce) at 294.0 in April 1930. The market embarked on a steady slide in April 1931 that did not end until 1932 when the Dow closed at 41.22 on July 8, concluding a shattering 89% decline from the peak. This was the lowest the stock market had been since the 19th century.

Economic Fundamentals

The crash followed a speculative boom that had taken hold in the late 1920s, which had led hundreds of thousands of Americans to invest heavily in the stock market, a significant number even borrowing money to buy more stock. By August 1929, brokers were routinely lending small investors more than 2/3 of the face value of the stocks they were buying. Over $8.5 billion was out on loan, more than the entire amount of currency circulating in the U.S. The rising share prices encouraged more people to invest; people hoped the share prices would rise further. Speculation thus fueled further rises and created an economic bubble. The average P/E (price to earnings) ratio of S&P Composite stocks was 32.6 in September 1929, clearly above historical norms. Most economists view this event as the most dramatic in modern economic history. On October 24, 1929 (with the Dow just past its September 3 peak of 381.17), the market finally turned down, and panic selling started. 12,894,650 shares were traded in a single day as people desperately tried to mitigate the situation. This mass sale is often considered a major contributing factor to the

Great Depression. Some hold that political over-reactions to the crash, such as the passage of the Smoot-Hawley Tariff Act through the U.S. Congress, caused more harm than the crash itself. According to Thomas K. McCraw, a professor at the Harvard Business School, the Smoot-Hawley Tariff Act "...exacerbated the problem by preventing Europeans from selling enough goods in the United States to earn enough dollars to pay off their debts from World War I.

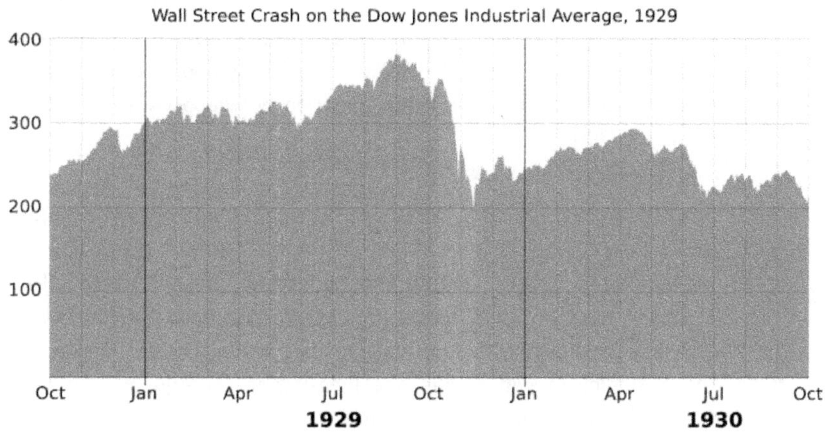

Official Investigation of the Crash

In 1931, the Pecora Commission was established by the U.S. Senate to study the causes of the crash. The U.S. Congress passed the Glass-Steagall Act in 1933, which mandated a separation between commercial banks, which take deposits and extend loans, and investment banks, which underwrite, issue, and distribute stocks, bonds, and other securities.

After the experience of the 1929 crash, stock markets around the world instituted measures to temporarily suspend trading in the event of rapid declines, claiming that they would prevent such panic sales. The one-day crash of Black Monday, October 19, 1987, however, was even more severe than the crash of 1929, when the Dow Jones Industrial Average fell a full 22.6%. (The markets quickly recovered, posting the largest one-day increase since 1933 only two days later.)

Impact and Academic Debate

Together, the 1929 stock market crash and the Great Depression "...was the biggest financial crisis of the" 20th century. "The panic of that October day has come to serve as a symbol of the economic contraction that gripped the world during the next decade." "The crash of 1929 caused 'fear mixed with a vertiginous disorientation', but 'shock was quickly cauterized with denial, both official and mass-delusional'.", "The falls in share prices on October 24 and 29, 1929 ... were practically instantaneous in all financial markets, except Japan." The Wall Street Crash had a major impact on the U.S. and world economy, and it has been the source of intense academic debate—historical, economic and political—from its aftermath until the present day. "Some people believed that abuses by utility holding companies contributed to the Wall Street Crash of 1929 and the Depression that followed.", "Many people blamed the crash on commercial banks that were too eager to put deposits at risk on the stock market. "

The "1929 crash brought the Roaring Twenties shuddering to a halt." As "tentatively expressed" by "economic historian Charles Kindleberger", in 1929 there was no "...lender of last resort effectively present", which, if it had existed and were "properly exercised", would have been "key in shortening the business slowdown(s) that normally follows financial crises." The crash marked the beginning of widespread and long-lasting consequences for the United States. The main question is: Did the "'29 Crash spark The Depression?", or did it merely coincide with the bursting of a credit-inspired economic bubble? The decline in stock prices caused bankruptcies and severe macroeconomic difficulties including business closures, firing of workers and other economic repression measures. The resultant rise of mass unemployment and the depression is seen as a direct result of the crash, though it is by no means the sole event that contributed to the depression; it is usually seen as having the greatest impact on the events that followed. Therefore the Wall Street Crash is widely regarded as signaling the downward economic slide that initiated the Great Depression.

True or not, the consequences were dire for almost everybody. "Most academic experts agree on one aspect of the crash: It wiped out billions of dollars of wealth in one day, and this immediately depressed consumer buying." The failure set off a worldwide run on US gold deposits (i.e., the dollar), and forced the Federal Reserve to raise interest rates into the slump. Some 4,000 lenders were ultimately driven to the wall. Also, the uptick rule, which "...allowed short selling only when the last tick in a stock's price was positive," "...was implemented after the 1929 market crash to prevent short sellers from driving the price of a stock down in a bear run."

Many academics see the Wall Street Crash of 1929 as part of a historical process that was a part of the new theories of boom and bust. According to economists such as Joseph Schumpeter and Nikolai Kondratieff the crash was merely a historical event in the continuing process known as economic cycles.

The impact of the crash was merely to increase the speed at which the cycle proceeded to its next level.

Milton Friedman's monumental A Monetary History of the United States, co-written with Anna Schwartz, makes the now standard interpretation of what made the "great contraction" so severe. It was not the downturn in the business cycle, trade protectionism or the 1929 stock market crash that plunged the country into deep depression. It was the collapse of the banking system during three waves of panics over the 1930-33 period."

Black Monday (1987)

In financial markets, Black Monday refers to Monday, October 19, 1987, when stock markets around the world crashed, shedding a huge value in a very short period. The crash began in Hong Kong, spread west through international time zones to Europe, hitting the United States after other markets had already declined by a significant margin. The Dow Jones Industrial Average (DJIA) dropped by 508 points to 1739 (22.6%). By the end of October, stock markets in Hong Kong had fallen 45.8%, Australia 41.8%, Spain 31%, the United Kingdom 26.4%, the United States 22.68%, and Canada 22.5%. New Zealand's market was hit especially hard, falling about 60% from its 1987 peak, and taking several years to recover. (The terms Black Monday and Black Tuesday are also applied to October 28 and 29, 1929, which occurred after Black Thursday on October 24, which started the Stock Market Crash of 1929. In Australia and New Zealand the 1987 crash is also referred to as Black Tuesday because of the timezone difference.)

The Black Monday decline was the largest one-day percentage decline in stock market history. Other large declines have occurred after periods of market closure, such as on Monday, September 17, 2001, the first day that the market was open following the September 11, 2001 attacks. (Saturday, December 12, 1914, is sometimes erroneously cited as the largest one-day percentage decline of the DJIA. In reality, the ostensible decline of 24.39% was created retroactively by a redefinition of the DJIA in 1916.)

Interestingly, the DJIA was positive for the 1987 calendar year. It opened on January 2, 1987, at 1,897 points and would close on December 31, 1987, at 1,939 points. The DJIA would not regain its August 25, 1987 closing high of 2,722 points until almost two years later.

A degree of mystery is associated with the 1987 crash, and it has been labeled as a black swan event. Important assumptions concerning human rationality, the efficient market hypothesis, and economic equilibrium were brought into question by the event. Debate as to the cause of the crash still continues many years after the event, with no firm conclusions reached.

In the wake of the crash, markets around the world were put on restricted trading primarily because sorting out the orders that had come in was beyond the computer technology of the time. This also gave the Federal Reserve and other central banks time to pump liquidity into the system to prevent a further downdraft. While pessimism reigned, the DJIA bottomed on October 20.

Following the stock market crash, a group of 33 eminent economists from various nations met in Washington, D.C. in December 1987, and collectively predicted that "the next few years could be the most troubled since the 1930s."

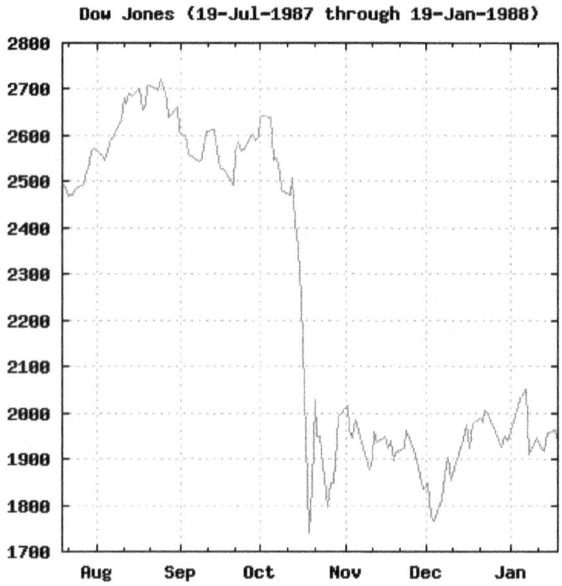

Picture 52: DJIA (19 July 1987 through 19 January 1988)

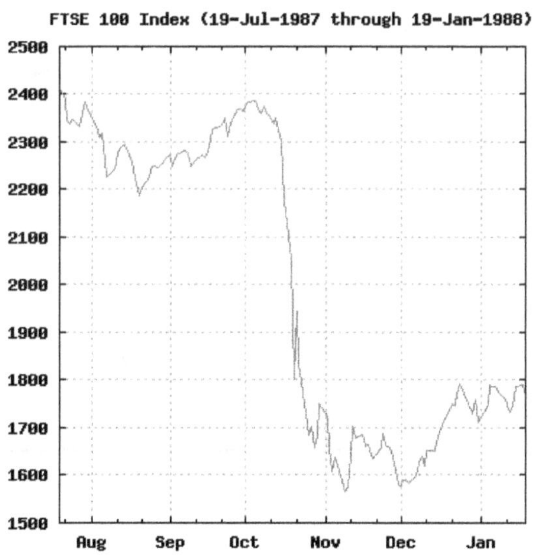

Picture 53: FTSE 100 Index (19 July 1987 through 19 January 1988)

Timeline

In 1986, the United States economy began shifting from a rapidly growing recovery to a slower growing expansion, which resulted in a "soft landing" as the economy slowed and inflation dropped. The stock market advanced significantly, with the Dow peaking in August 1987 at 2722 points, or 44% over the previous year's closing of 1895 points.

On October 14, the DJIA dropped 95.46 points (a then record) to 2412.70, and fell another 58 points the next day, down over 12% from the August 25 all-time high. On Friday, October 16, the DJIA closed down another 108.35 points to close at 2246.74 on record volume. Treasury Secretary James Baker stated concerns about the falling prices. That weekend many investors worried over their stock investments.

The crash began in Far Eastern markets the morning of October 19. Later that morning, two U.S. warships shelled an Iranian oil platform in the Persian Gulf in response to Iran's Silkworm missile attack on the U.S. flagged ship MV Sea Isle City.

S&P 500 index around the time of the crash

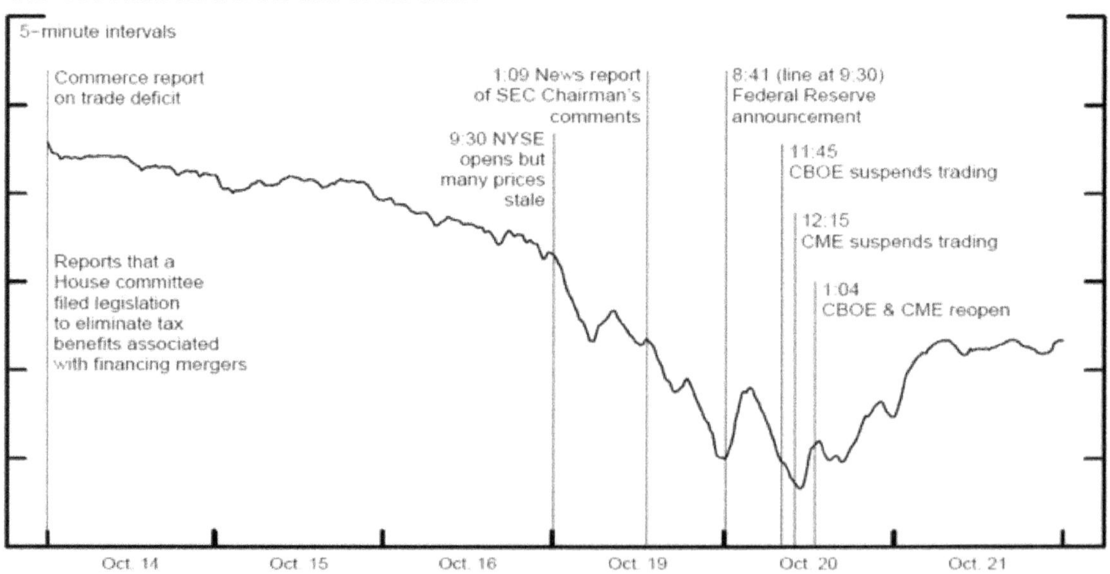

Source: Market data.

Picture 54: Timeline compiled by the Federal Reserve

.Causes

Potential causes for the decline include program trading, overvaluation, illiquidity, and market psychology.

The most popular explanation for the 1987 crash was selling by program traders. U.S. Congressman Edward J. Markey, who had been warning about the possibility of a crash, stated that "Program trading was the principal cause." In program trading, computers perform rapid stock executions based on external inputs, such as the price of related securities. Common strategies implemented by program trading involve an attempt to engage in arbitrage and portfolio insurance strategies. The trader Paul Tudor Jones predicted and profited from the crash, attributing it to portfolio insurance derivatives which were "an accident waiting to happen" and that the "crash was something that was imminently forecastable". Once the market started going down, the writers of the derivatives were "forced to sell on every down-tick" so the "selling would actually cascade instead of dry up."

As computer technology became more available, the use of program trading grew dramatically within Wall Street firms. After the crash, many blamed program trading strategies for blindly selling stocks as markets fell, exacerbating the decline. Some economists theorized the speculative boom leading up to October was caused by program trading, while others argued that the crash was a return to normalcy. Either way, program trading ended up taking the majority of the blame in the public eye for the 1987 stock market crash.

New York University's Richard Sylla divides the causes into macroeconomic and internal reasons. Macroeconomic causes included international disputes about foreign exchange and interest rates, and fears about inflation.

> "The internal reasons included innovations with index futures and portfolio insurance. I've seen accounts that maybe roughly half the trading on that day was a small number of institutions with portfolio insurance. Big guys were dumping their stock. Also, the futures market in Chicago was even lower than the stock market, and people tried to arbitrage that. The proper strategy was to buy futures in Chicago and sell in the New York cash market. It made it hard -- the portfolio insurance people were also trying to sell their stock at the same time."

Economist Richard Roll believes the international nature of the stock market decline contradicts the argument that program trading was to blame. Program trading strategies were used primarily in the United States, Roll writes. Markets where program trading was not prevalent, such as Australia and Hong Kong, would not have declined as well, if program trading was the cause. These markets might have been reacting to excessive program trading in the United States, but Roll indicates otherwise. The crash began on October 19 in Hong Kong, spread west to Europe, and hit the United States only after Hong Kong and other markets had already declined by a significant margin.

Another common theory states that the crash was a result of a dispute in monetary policy between the G7 industrialized nations, in which the United States, wanting to prop up the dollar and restrict inflation, tightened policy faster than the Europeans. The crash, in this view, was caused when the dollar-backed Hong Kong stock exchange collapsed, and this caused a crisis in confidence.

October 27, 1997 Mini-Crash

The October 27, 1997 mini-crash is the name of a global stock market crash that was caused by an economic crisis in Asia (a.k.a "Asian flu"). The points loss that the Dow Jones Industrial Average suffered on this day still ranks as the sixth biggest points loss in its 112-year existence. The crash halted trading of stocks on the New York Stock Exchange for the first time ever. This crash is considered a "mini-crash" because the percentage loss was relatively small compared to some other notaSynopsis.

The crash started overnight in Asia as Hong Kong's Hang Seng Index plummeted 6%. However, the most widely watched Asian market, Japan's Nikkei 225, only fell 2% on the day. The losses spread to the European markets where London's FTSE 100 Index fell 98.90 points, or just about 2%, to 4,871.30. Frankfurt's DAX index fell sharply as well. The U.S. markets were widely expected to open lower for the day. The Dow, NASDAQ, and S&P 500 all sank, never going to positive territory. At 2:36 P.M., the Dow smashed through its first trading curb halt when it fell 350 points. Trading was halted for 30 minutes. When trading started again at 3:06 P.M., stocks continued their immense slide eventually pushing the Dow through the NYSE's second trading curb at 550 points and ending trading for the day at 3:35 P.M. The second halt in trading is usually an hour timeout, but since there was only 25 minutes left in trading for the session the New York Stock Exchange had no choice but to take the controversial action of closing the Exchange early. Nasdaq trading went on until 4:00 P.M as usual.

By the Numbers

Controversial Halts

The reason why this action was so controversial is because when the Dow went through its first trading curb at 350 points, the loss in the Dow only equated to 4.54%, not nearly enough to justify halting trading. One must also consider the fact that the Dow has fallen more than 4.5% on eleven different occasions between 1945 and 1997. Currently, the New York Stock Exchange sets the curbs at 10, 20, and 30%, and determines how much 10, 20, and 30% exactly is in point terms by where the Dow finishes at the end of the quarter.

Closing Time

By the end of the day, the Dow Jones Industrial Average plummeted 554.26 points, or 7.18%, to 7,161.15. This was the 12th biggest percentage loss and 3rd biggest points loss on record. The NASDAQ Composite fell 7%, or 115.41 to 1,535.51. The S&P 500 fell 64.63, or 6.86%, to 877.01. Several stock market analysts saw this crash as a "correction" to the overheated markets, which had doubled in value in 30 months. Even though this crash put the Dow down 12% from its all-time high of 8,259 on August 6, it still remained up from 1997's start level of 6,448.27. Volume also hit a record high. New York Stock Exchange volume topped 695 million shares, outstripping the previous record of 684 million shares traded on January 23, 1997. In 2006 terms, this would be considered extremely light volume. $663 billion in market capitalization was wiped out.

October 28

U.S. stock markets were widely expected to open lower for October 28 due to the Asian markets falling even more than they did on the 27th. Hong Kong's Hang Seng Index declined a staggering 14%. The Nikkei fell 4.26%. The U.S. stock markets initially continued their drop from the 27th, but abruptly ended, and began to climb. The Dow was down as much as 186 points by 10:06 A.M., and soon thereafter a rally started. By 10:20 A.M. The Dow was down only 25 points. Five minutes later, the Dow roared back into positive territory and was up 50 points. Nine minutes later at 10:34 A.M., the Dow rallied to a triple-digit advance up 137.27 points. Stock prices continued to soar in choppy trading throughout the rest of the day. At the close of trading at 4:00 P.M., the Dow finished with a record 337.17 point gain (recovering 61% of the previous day's loss) to close at 7,498.32. The market restored $384 billion of the $663 billion in market capitalization lost the previous day. One billion shares were traded on the New York Stock Exchange for the first time ever, with a volume of 1.21 billion shares. In 2006 terms, this amount is considered very light. The NASDAQ Composite also made a record gain on record volume, gaining 67.93 to 1,603.02. The NASDAQ also saw its first-ever one-billion share day with 1.23 billion shares changing hands.

1997 Asian Financial Crisis

The Asian Financial Crisis was a period of financial crisis that gripped much of Asia beginning in July 1997, and raised fears of a worldwide economic meltdown (financial contagion). It is also commonly referred to as the IMF crisis.

The crisis started in Thailand with the financial collapse of the Thai baht caused by the decision of the Thai government to float the baht, cutting its peg to the USD, after exhaustive efforts to support it in the face of a severe financial overextension that was in part real estate driven. At the time, Thailand had acquired a burden of foreign debt that made the country effectively bankrupt even before the collapse of its currency. As the crisis spread, most of Southeast Asia and Japan saw slumping currencies, devalued stock markets and other asset prices, and a precipitous rise in private debt.

Though there has been general agreement on the existence of a crisis and its consequences, what is less clear were the causes of the crisis, as well as its scope and resolution. Indonesia, South Korea and Thailand were the country's most affected by the crisis. Hong Kong, Malaysia, Laos and the Philippines were also hurt by the slump. The People's Republic of China, India, Taiwan, Singapore, Brunei and Vietnam were less affected, although all suffered from a loss of demand and confidence throughout the region.

Foreign debt-to-GDP ratios rose from 100% to 167% in the four large ASEAN economies in 1993-96, then shot up beyond 180% during the worst of the crisis. In Korea, the ratios rose from 13-21% and then as high as 40%, while the other Northern NICs (Newly Industrialized Countries) fared much better. Only in Thailand and Korea did debt service-to-exports ratios rise.

Although most of the governments of Asia had seemingly sound fiscal policies, the International Monetary Fund (IMF) stepped in to initiate a $40 billion program to stabilize the currencies of South Korea, Thailand, and Indonesia, economies particularly hard hit by the crisis. The efforts to stem a global economic crisis did little to stabilize the domestic situation in Indonesia, however. After 30 years in power, President Suharto was forced to step down in May 1998 in the wake of widespread rioting that followed sharp price increases caused by a drastic devaluation of the rupiah. The effects of the crisis lingered through 1998. In the Philippines growth dropped to virtually zero in 1998. Only Singapore and Taiwan proved relatively insulated from the shock, but both suffered serious hits in passing, the former more so due to its size and geographical location between Malaysia and Indonesia. By 1999, however, analysts saw signs that the economies of Asia were beginning to recover.

Picture 55: Countries most affected by the Asian Crisis

History

Until 1997, Asia attracted almost half of the total capital inflow from developing countries. The economies of Southeast Asia in particular maintained high interest rates attractive to foreign investors looking for a high rate of return. As a result the region's economies received a large inflow of money and experienced a dramatic run-up in asset prices. At the same time, the regional economies of Thailand, Malaysia, Indonesia, Singapore, and South Korea experienced high growth rates, 8-12% GDP, in the late 1980s and early 1990s. This achievement was widely acclaimed by financial institutions including the IMF and World Bank, and was known as part of the "Asian economic miracle".

In 1994, noted economist Paul Krugman published an article attacking the idea of an "Asian economic miracle". He argued that East Asia's economic growth had historically been the result of capital investment, leading to growth in productivity. However, total factor productivity had increased only marginally or not at all. Krugman argued that only growth in total factor productivity, and not capital investment, could lead to long-term prosperity. Krugman's views would be seen by many as prescient after the financial crisis had become full-blown[neutrality disputed], though he himself stated that he had not predicted the crisis nor foreseen its depth.

The causes of the debacle are many and disputed. Thailand's economy developed into a bubble fueled by "hot money". More and more was required as the size of the bubble grew. The same type of situation happened in Malaysia, although Malaysia had better political leadership, and Indonesia, which had the added complication of what was called "crony capitalism". The short-term capital flow was expensive and often highly conditioned for quick profit. Development money went in a largely uncontrolled manner to certain people only, not particularly the best suited or most efficient, but those closest to the centers of power.

At the time of the mid-1990s, Thailand, Indonesia and South Korea had large private current account deficits and the maintenance of fixed exchange rates encouraged external borrowing and led to excessive exposure to foreign exchange risk in both the financial and corporate sectors. In the mid-1990s, two factors began to change their economic environment. As the U.S. economy recovered from a recession in the early 1990s, the U.S. Federal Reserve Bank under Alan Greenspan began to raise U.S. interest rates to head off inflation. This made the U.S. a more attractive investment destination relative to Southeast Asia, which had attracted hot money flows through high short-term interest rates, and raised the value of the U.S. dollar, to which many Southeast Asian nations' currencies were pegged, thus making their exports less competitive. At the same time, Southeast Asia's export growth slowed dramatically in the spring of 1996, deteriorating their current account position.

Some economists have advanced the impact of China on the real economy as a contributing factor to ASEAN nations' export growth slowdown, though these economists maintain the main cause of the crises was excessive real estate speculation. China had begun to compete effectively with other Asian exporters particularly in the 1990s after the implementation of a number of export-oriented reforms. Most importantly, the Thai and Indonesian currencies were closely tied to the dollar, which was appreciating in the 1990s. Western importers sought cheaper manufacturers and found them, indeed, in China whose currency was depreciated relative to the dollar. Other economists dispute this claim noting that both ASEAN and China experienced simultaneous rapid export growth in the early 1990s.

Many economists believe that the Asian crisis was created not by market psychology or technology, but by policies that distorted incentives within the lender-borrower relationship. The resulting large quantities of credit that became available generated a highly-leveraged economic climate, and pushed up asset prices to an unsustainable level. These asset prices eventually began to collapse, causing individuals and companies to default on debt obligations. The resulting panic among lenders led to a large withdrawal of credit from the crisis countries, causing a credit crunch and further bankruptcies. In addition, as investors attempted to withdraw their money, the exchange market was flooded with the currencies of the crisis countries, putting depreciative pressure on their exchange rates. In order to prevent a collapse of the currency values, these countries' governments were forced to raise domestic interest rates to exceedingly high levels (to help diminish the flight of capital by making lending to that country relatively more attractive to investors) and to intervene in the exchange market, buying up any excess domestic currency at the fixed exchange rate with foreign reserves. Neither of these policy responses could be sustained for long. Very high interest rates, which can be extremely damaging to an economy that is relatively healthy, wreaked further havoc on economies in an already fragile state, while the central banks were hemorrhaging foreign reserves, of which they had finite amounts. When it became clear that the tide of capital fleeing these countries was not to be stopped, the authorities ceased defending their fixed exchange rates and allowed their currencies to float. The resulting depreciated value of those currencies meant that foreign currency-denominated liabilities grew substantially in domestic currency terms, causing more bankruptcies and further deepening the crisis.

Other economists, including Joseph Stiglitz and Jeffrey Sachs, have downplayed the role of the real economy in the crisis compared to the financial markets due to the speed of the crisis. The rapidity with which the crisis happened has prompted Sachs and others to compare it to a classic bank run prompted by a sudden risk shock. Sachs pointed to strict monetary and contractory fiscal policies implemented by the governments on the advice of the IMF in the wake of the crisis, while Frederic Mishkin points to the role of asymmetric information in the financial markets that led to a "herd mentality" among investors that magnified a relatively small risk in the real economy. The crisis had thus attracted interest from behavioral economists interested in market psychology. Another possible cause of the sudden risk shock may also be attributable to the handover of Hong Kong sovereignty on July 1, 1997. During the 1990s, hot money flew into the Southeast Asia region but investors were often ignorant of the actual fundamentals or risk profiles of the respective economies. The uncertainty regarding the future of Hong Kong led investors to shrink even further away from Asia, exacerbating economic conditions in the area (subsequently leading to the devaluation of the Thai baht on July 2, 1997).

The foreign ministers of the 10 ASEAN countries believed that the well co-ordinated manipulation of currencies was a deliberate attempt to destabilize the ASEAN economies. Former Malaysian Prime Minister Mahathir Mohamad accused George Soros of ruining Malaysia's economy with "massive currency speculation." (Soros appeared to have had his bets in against the Asian currency devaluations, incurring a loss when the crisis hit.) At the 30th ASEAN Ministerial Meeting held in Subang Jaya, Malaysia, they issued a joint declaration on 25 July 1997 expressing serious concern and called for further intensification of ASEAN's cooperation to safeguard and promote ASEAN's interest in this regard. Coincidentally, on that same day, the central bankers of most of the affected countries were at the EMEAP (Executive Meeting of East Asia Pacific) meeting in Shanghai, and they failed to make the 'New Arrangement to Borrow' operational. A year earlier, the finance ministers of these same countries had attended the 3rd APEC finance ministers meeting in Kyoto, Japan on 17 March 1996, and according to that joint declaration, they had been unable to double the amounts available under the 'General Agreement to Borrow' and the 'Emergency Finance Mechanism'. As such, the crisis could be seen as the failure to adequately build capacity in time to prevent currency manipulation. This hypothesis enjoyed little support among economists, however, who argue that no single investor could have had enough impact on the market to successfully manipulate the currencies' values. In addition, the level of organization necessary to coordinate a massive exodus of investors from Southeast Asian currencies in order to manipulate their values rendered this possibility remote.

The Role of the IMF

Such was the scope and the severity of the collapses involved that outside intervention, considered by many as a new kind of colonialism, became urgently needed. Since the countries melting down were among not only the richest in their region, but in the world, and since hundreds of billions of dollars were at stake, any response to the crisis had to be cooperative and international, in this case through the International Monetary Fund (IMF). The IMF created a series of bailouts ("rescue") packages for the most affected economies to enable affected nations to avoid default, tying the packages to reforms that were intended to make the restored Asian currency, banking, and financial systems as much like those of the United States and Europe as possible. In other words, the IMF's support was conditional on a series of drastic economic reforms influenced by neoliberal economic principles called a "structural adjustment package" (SAP). The SAPs called on crisis-struck nations to cut back on government spending to reduce deficits, allow insolvent banks and financial institutions to fail, and aggressively raise interest rates. The reasoning was that these steps would restore confidence in the nations' fiscal solvency, penalize insolvent companies, and protect currency values. Above all, it was stipulated that IMF-funded capital had to be administered rationally in the future, with no favored parties receiving funds by preference. There were to be adequate government controls set up to supervise all financial activities, ones that were to be independent, in theory, of private interest. Insolvent institutions had to be closed, and insolvency itself had to be clearly defined. In short, exactly the same kinds of financial institutions found in the United States and Europe had to be created in Asia, as a condition for IMF support. In addition, financial systems had to become "transparent", that is, provide the kind of reliable financial information used in the West to make sound financial decisions.

However, the greatest criticism of the IMF's role in the crisis was targeted towards its response. As country after country fell into crisis, many local businesses and governments that had taken out loans in US dollars, which suddenly became much more expensive relative to the local currency which formed their earned income, found themselves unable to pay their creditors. The dynamics of the situation were closely similar to that of the Latin American debt crisis. The effects of the SAPs were mixed and their impact controversial. Critics, however, noted the contractionary nature of these policies, arguing that in a recession, the traditional Keynesian response was to increase government spending, prop up major companies, and lower interest rates. The reasoning was that by stimulating the economy and staving off recession, governments could restore confidence while preventing economic pain. They pointed out that the U.S. government had pursued expansionary policies, such as lowering interest rates, increasing government spending, and cutting taxes, when the United States itself entered a recession in 2001.

Although such reforms were, in most cases, long needed, the countries most involved ended up undergoing an almost complete political and financial restructuring. They suffered permanent currency devaluations, massive numbers of bankruptcies, collapses of whole sectors of once-booming economies, real estate busts, high unemployment, and social unrest. For most of the countries involved, IMF intervention has been roundly criticized. The role of the International Monetary Fund was so controversial during the crisis that many locals called the financial crisis the "IMF crisis". To begin with, many commentators in retrospect criticized the IMF for encouraging the developing economies of Asia down the path of "fast track capitalism", meaning liberalization of the financial sector (elimination of restrictions on capital flows); maintenance of high domestic interest rates in order to suck in portfolio investment and bank capital; and pegging of the national currency to the dollar to reassure foreign investors against currency risk. In other words, that the IMF itself was the cause.

Thailand

From 1985 to 1996, Thailand's economy grew at an average of over 9% per year, the highest economic growth rate of any country at the time. In 1996, an American hedge fund sold US$400 million of the Thai currency. From 1978 until 2 July 1997, the baht was pegged at 25 to the dollar.

On 14 May and 15 May 1997, the Thai baht was hit by massive speculative attacks. On 30 June 1997, Prime Minister Chavalit Yongchaiyudh said that he would not devalue the baht. This was the spark that ignited the Asian financial crisis as the Thai government failed to defend the baht, which was pegged to the U.S. dollar, against international speculators. Thailand's booming economy came to a halt amid massive layoffs in finance, real estate, and construction that resulted in huge numbers of workers returning to their villages in the countryside and 600'000 foreign workers being sent back to their home countries. The baht devalued swiftly and lost more than half of its value. The baht reached its lowest point of 56 units to the US dollar in January 1998. The Thai stock market dropped 75%. Finance One, the largest Thai finance company until then, collapsed.

The Thai government was eventually forced to float the Baht, on 2 July 1997. On 11 August 1997, the IMF unveiled a rescue package for Thailand with more than $17 billion, subject to conditions such as passing laws relating to bankruptcy (reorganizing and restructuring) procedures and establishing strong regulation frameworks for banks and other financial institutions. The IMF approved on 20 August, 1997, another bailout package of $3.9 billion.

Thai opposition parties claimed that former Prime Minister Thaksin Shinawatra had profited from the devaluation, although subsequently the opposition parties did not investigate the issue.

By 2001, Thailand's economy had recovered. The increasing tax revenues allowed the country to balance its budget and repay its debts to the IMF in 2003, four years ahead of schedule. The Thai baht continued to appreciate to 34 Baht to the Dollar in July 2008.

Indonesia

In June 1997, Indonesia seemed far from crisis. Unlike Thailand, Indonesia had low inflation, a trade surplus of more than $900 million, huge foreign exchange reserves of more than $20 billion, and a good banking sector. But a large number of Indonesian corporations had been borrowing in U.S. dollars. During the preceding years, as the rupiah had strengthened respective to the dollar, this practice had worked well for these corporations; their effective levels of debt and financing costs had decreased as the local currency's value rose.

In July 1997, when Thailand floated the baht, Indonesia's monetary authorities widened the rupiah trading band from 8% to 12%. The rupiah suddenly came under severe attack in August. On 14 August 1997, the managed floating exchange regime was replaced by a free-floating exchange rate arrangement.

The rupiah dropped further. The IMF came forward with a rescue package of $23 billion, but the rupiah was sinking further amid fears over corporate debts, massive selling of rupiah, and strong demand for dollars. The rupiah and the Jakarta Stock Exchange touched a historic low in September. Moody's eventually downgraded Indonesia's long-term debt to 'junk bond'.

Although the rupiah crisis began in July and August 1997, it intensified in November when the effects of that summer devaluation showed up on corporate balance sheets. Companies that had borrowed in dollars had to face the higher costs imposed upon them by the rupiah's decline, and many reacted by buying dollars through selling rupiah, undermining the value of the latter further. The inflation of the rupiah and the resulting steep hikes in the prices of food staples led to rioting throughout the country in which more than 500 people died in Jakarta alone. In February 1998, President Suharto sacked the governor of Bank Indonesia, but this had proved insufficient. Suharto was forced to resign in mid-1998 and B. J. Habibie became President. Before the crisis, the exchange rate between the rupiah and the dollar was roughly 2000 rupiah to 1 USD. The rate had plunged to over 18000 rupiah to 1 USD at various points during the crisis. Indonesia lost 13.5% of its GDP that year.

South Korea

Macroeconomic fundamentals in South Korea were good but the banking sector was burdened with non-performing loans as its large corporations were funding aggressive expansions. During that time, there was a haste to build great conglomerates to compete on the world stage. Many businesses ultimately failed to ensure returns and profitability. The Korean conglomerates, more or less completely controlled by the government, simply absorbed more and more capital investment. Eventually, excess debt led to major failures and takeovers. For example, in July 1997, South Korea's third-largest car maker, Kia Motors, asked for emergency loans. In the wake of the Asian market downturn, Moody's lowered the credit rating of South Korea from A1 to A3, on November 28, 1997, and downgraded again to B2 on December 11. That contributed to a further decline in Korean shares since stock markets were already bearish in November. The Seoul stock exchange fell by 4% on 7 November 1997. On November 8, it plunged by 7%, its biggest one-day drop to that date. And on November 24, stocks fell a further 7.2% on fears that the IMF would demand tough reforms. In 1998, Hyundai Motor took over Kia Motors. Samsung Motors' $5 billion dollar venture was dissolved due to the crisis, and eventually Daewoo Motors was sold to the American company General Motors (GM).

The Korean won, meanwhile, weakened to more than 1,700 per dollar from around 800. Despite an initial sharp economic slowdown and numerous corporate bankruptcies, Korea has managed to triple its per capita GDP in dollar terms since 1997. Indeed, it resumed its role as the world's fastest-growing economy -- since 1960, per capita GDP has grown from $80 in nominal terms to more than $21,000 as of 2007. However, like the chaebol, South Korea's government did not escape unscathed. Its national debt-to-GDP ratio more than doubled (app. 13% to 30%) as a result of the crisis.

Philippines

The Philippine Central Bank raised interest rates by 1.75 percentage points in May 1997 and again by 2 points on 19 June. Thailand triggered the crisis on 2 July and on 3 July, the Philippine Central Bank was forced to intervene heavily to defend the peso, raising the overnight rate from 15% to 24%. The peso fell significantly, from 26 pesos per dollar at the start of the crisis, to 38 pesos in 2000, and to 40 pesos by the end of the crisis.

The Philippine economy recovered from a contraction of 0.6% in GDP during the worst part of the crisis to GDP growth of some 3% by 2001, despite scandals of the administration of Joseph Estrada in 2001, most notably the "jueteng" scandal, causing the PSE Composite Index, the main index of the Philippine Stock Exchange, to fall to some 1000 points from a high of some 3000 points in 1997. The peso fell even further, trading at levels of about 55 pesos to the US dollar. Later that year, Estrada was on the verge of impeachment but his allies in the senate voted against the proceedings to continue further. This led to popular protests culminating in the "EDSA II Revolution", which finally forced his resignation and elevated Gloria Macapagal-Arroyo to the presidency. Arroyo managed to lessen the crisis in the country, which led to the recovery of the Philippine peso to about 50 pesos by the year's end and is now trading at around 41 pesos to a dollar by end 2007. The stock market also reached an all time high in 2007 and the economy is growing by at least more than 7 percent, its highest in nearly 2 decades.

Hong Kong

Although the two events were unrelated, the collapse of the Thai baht on July 2, 1997, came only 24 hours after the United Kingdom handed over sovereignty of Hong Kong to the People's Republic of China. In October 1997, the Hong Kong dollar, which had been pegged at 7.8 to the U.S. dollar since 1983, came under speculative pressure because Hong Kong's inflation rate had been significantly higher than the U.S.'s for years. Monetary authorities spent more than US$1 billion to defend the local currency. Since Hong Kong had more than US$80 billion in foreign reserves, which is equivalent to 700% of its M1 money supply and 45% of its M3 money supply, the Hong Kong Monetary Authority (effectively the city's central bank) managed to maintain the peg.

Stock markets became more and more volatile; between 20 October and 23 October the Hang Seng Index dropped 23%. The Hong Kong Monetary Authority then promised to protect the currency. On 15 August 1998, it raised overnight interest rates from 8% to 23%, and at one point to 500%. The HKMA had recognized that speculators were taking advantage of the city's unique currency-board system, in which overnight rates automatically increase in proportion to large net sales of the local currency. The rate hike, however, increased downward pressure on the stock market, allowing speculators to profit by short selling shares. The HKMA started buying component shares of the Hang Seng Index in mid-August.

The HKMA and Donald Tsang, then the Financial Secretary, declared war on speculators. The Government ended up buying approximately HK$120 billion (US$15 billion) worth of shares in various companies, and became the largest shareholder of some of those companies (e.g. the government owned 10% of HSBC) at the end of August, when hostilities ended with the closing of the August Hang Seng Index futures contract. The Government started selling those shares in 2001, making a profit of about HK$30 billion (US$4 billion).

Malaysia

Before the crisis, Malaysia had a large current account deficit of 5% of its GDP. At the time, Malaysia was a popular investment destination, and this was reflected in KLSE activity which was regularly the most active stock exchange in the world (with turnover exceeding even markets with far higher capitalization like the NYSE). Expectations at the time were that the growth rate would continue, propelling Malaysia to developed status by 2020, a government policy articulated in Wawasan 2020. At the start of 1997, the KLSE Composite index was above 1,200, the ringgit was trading above 2.50 to the dollar, and the overnight rate was below 7%.

In July 1997, within days of the Thai baht devaluation, the Malaysian ringgit was "attacked" by speculators. The overnight rate jumped from under 8% to over 40%. This led to rating downgrades and a general sell off on the stock and currency markets. By end of 1997, ratings had fallen many notches from investment grade to junk, the KLSE had lost more than 50% from above 1,200 to under 600, and the ringgit had lost 50% of its value, falling from above 2.50 to under 3.80 to the dollar.

In 1998, the output of the real economy declined plunging the country into its first recession for many years. The construction sector contracted 23.5%, manufacturing shrunk 9% and the agriculture sector 5.9%. Overall, the country's gross domestic product plunged 6.2% in 1998. During that year, the ringgit plunged below 4.7 and the KLSE fell below 270 points. In September that year, various defensive measures were announced in order to overcome the crisis. The principal measure taken were to move the ringgit from a free float to a fixed exchange rate regime. Bank Negara fixed the ringgit at 3.8 to the dollar. Capital controls were imposed while aid offered from the IMF was refused. Various task force agencies were formed. The Corporate Debt Restructuring Committee dealt with corporate loans. Danaharta discounted and bought bad loans from banks to facilitate orderly asset realization. Danamodal recapitalized banks.

Growth then settled at a slower but more sustainable pace. The massive current account deficit became a fairly substantial surplus. Banks were better capitalized and NPLs were realised in an orderly way. Small banks were bought out by strong ones. (Unfortunately, this was an excuse for the government-linked banks, which were actually in a weak financial position to force the smaller banks out of the market. Ironically, it was the smaller banks, managed in a sound financial manner, that were dissolved, instead of the larger politically-favored banks.) A large number of PLCs were unable to regulate their financial affairs and were delisted. Compared to the 1997 current account, by 2005, Malaysia was estimated to have a US$14.06 billion surplus. Asset values however, have not returned to their pre-crisis highs. In 2005 the last of the crisis measures were removed as the ringgit was taken off the fixed exchange system. But unlike the pre-crisis days, it did not appear to be a free float, but a managed float, like the Singapore dollar.

Singapore

As the financial crisis spread the economy of Singapore dipped into a short recession. The relatively short duration and milder effect on its economy was credited to the active management by the government. For example, the Monetary Authority of Singapore allowed for a gradual 20% depreciation of the Singapore dollar to cushion and guide the economy to a soft landing. The timing of government programs such as the Interim Upgrading Program and other construction related projects were brought forward. Instead of allowing the labor markets to work, the National Wage Council pre-emptively agreed to Central Provident Fund cuts to lower labor costs, with limited impact on disposable income and local demand. Unlike in Hong Kong, no attempt was made to directly intervene in the capital markets and the Straits Times Index was allowed to drop 60%. In less than a year, the Singaporean economy fully recovered and continued on its growth trajectory.

China

The Chinese currency, the renminbi (RMB), had been pegged to the US dollar at a ratio of 8.3 RMB to the dollar, in 1994. Having largely kept itself above the fray throughout 1997-1998 there was heavy speculation in the Western press that China would soon be forced to devalue its currency to protect the competitiveness of its exports vis-a-vis those of the ASEAN nations, whose exports became cheaper relative to China's. However, the RMB's non-convertibility protected its value from currency speculators, and the decision was made to maintain the peg of the currency, thereby improving the country's standing within Asia. The currency peg was partly scrapped in July 2005 rising 2.3% against the dollar, reflecting pressure from the United States.

Unlike investments of many of the Southeast Asian nations, almost all of China's foreign investment took the form of factories on the ground rather than securities, which insulated the country from rapid capital flight. While China was relatively unaffected by the crisis compared to Southeast Asia and South Korea, GDP growth slowed sharply in 1998 and 1999, calling attention to structural problems within its economy. In particular, the Asian financial crisis convinced the Chinese government of the need to resolve the issues of its enormous financial weaknesses, such as having too many non-performing loans within its primitive and inefficient banking system, and relying heavily on trade with the United States.

United States and Japan

Further information: Economy of the United States and Economy of Japan

The "Asian flu" had also put pressure on the United States and Japan. Their markets did not collapse, but they were severely hit. On 27 October 1997, the Dow Jones industrial plunged 554 points or 7.2%, amid ongoing worries about the Asian economies. The New York Stock Exchange briefly suspended trading. The crisis led to a drop in consumer and spending confidence (see October 27, 1997 mini-crash). Japan was affected because its economy is prominent in the region. Asian countries usually run a trade deficit with Japan because the latter's economy was more than twice the size of the rest of Asia together; about 40% of Japan's exports go to Asia. The Japanese yen fell to 147 as mass selling began, but Japan was the world's largest holder of currency reserves at the time, so it was easily defended, and quickly bounced back. GDP real growth rate slowed dramatically in 1997, from 5% to 1.6% and even sank into recession in 1998, due to intense competition from cheapened rivals. The Asian financial crisis also led to more bankruptcies in Japan. In addition, with

South Korea's devalued currency, and China's steady gains, many companies complained outright that they could not compete.

Another longer-term result was the changing relationship between the U.S. and Japan, with the U.S. no longer openly supporting the highly artificial trade environment and exchange rates that governed economic relations between the two countries for almost five decades after World War II.

Consequences

Asia

The crisis had significant macro-level effects, including sharp reductions in values of currencies, stock markets, and other asset prices of several Asian countries. The nominal US dollar GDP of ASEAN fell by US$9.2 billion in 1997 and $218.2 billion (31.7%) in 1998. In Korea, the $170.9 billion fall in 1998 was equal to 33.1% of the 1997 GDP. Many businesses collapsed, and as a consequence, millions of people fell below the poverty line in 1997-1998. Indonesia, South Korea and Thailand were the countries most affected by the crisis.

The economic crisis also led to political upheaval, most notably culminating in the resignations of President Suharto in Indonesia and Prime Minister General Chavalit Yongchaiyudh in Thailand. There was a general rise in anti-Western sentiment, with George Soros and the IMF in particular singled out as targets of criticisms. Heavy U.S. investment in Thailand ended, replaced by mostly European investment, though Japanese investment was sustained. Islamic and other separatist movements intensified in Southeast Asia as central authorities weakened.

More long-term consequences included reversal of the relative gains made in the boom years just preceding the crisis. Nominal US dollar GDP per capital fell 42.3% in Indonesia in 1997, 21.2% in Thailand, 19% in Malaysia, 18.5% in Korea and 12.5% in the Philippines. The CIA World Factbook reported that the per capita income (measured by purchasing power parity) in Thailand declined from $8,800 to $8,300 between 1997 and 2005; in Indonesia it declined from $4,600 to $3,700; in Malaysia it declined from $11,100 to $10,400. Over the same period, world per capita income rose from $6,500 to $9,300. Indeed, the CIA's analysis asserted that the economy of Indonesia was still smaller in 2005 than it had been in 1997, suggesting an impact on that country similar to that of the Great Depression. Within East Asia, the bulk of investment and a significant amount of economic weight shifted from Japan and ASEAN to China and India.

The crisis has been intensively analyzed by economists for its breadth, speed, and dynamism; it affected dozens of countries, had a direct impact on the livelihood of millions, happened within the course of a mere few months, and at each stage of the crisis leading economists, in particular the international institutions, seemed a step behind. Perhaps more interesting to economists was the speed with which it ended, leaving most of the developed economies unharmed. These curiosities have prompted an explosion of literature about financial economics and a litany of explanations why the crisis occurred. A number of critiques have been leveled against the conduct of the IMF in the crisis, including one by former World Bank economist Joseph Stiglitz. Politically there were some benefits. In several countries, particularly South Korea and Indonesia, there was renewed push for improved corporate governance. Rampaging inflation weakened the authority of the Suharto regime and led to its toppling in 1998, as well as accelerating East Timor's independence.

Outside Asia

After the Asian crisis, international investors were reluctant to lend to developing countries, leading to economic slowdowns in developing countries in many parts of the world. The powerful negative shock also sharply reduced the price of oil, which reached a low of $8 per barrel towards the end of 1998, causing a financial pinch in OPEC nations and other oil exporters. This reduction in oil revenue contributed to the 1998 Russian financial crisis, which in turn caused Long-Term Capital Management in the United States to collapse after losing $4.6 billion in 4 months. A wider collapse in the financial markets was avoided when Alan Greenspan and the Federal Reserve Bank of New York organized a $3.625 billion bail-out. Major emerging economies Brazil and Argentina also fell into crisis in the late 1990s.

The crisis in general was part of a global backlash against the Washington Consensus and institutions such as the IMF and World Bank, which simultaneously became unpopular in developed countries following the rise of the anti-globalization movement in 1999. Four major rounds of world trade talks since the crisis, in Seattle, Doha, Cancún, and Hong Kong, have failed to produce a significant agreement as developing countries have become more assertive, and nations are increasingly turning toward regional or bilateral FTAs (Free Trade Agreements) as an alternative to global institutions. Many nations learned from this, and quickly built up foreign exchange reserves as a hedge against attacks, including Japan, China, South Korea. Pan Asian currency swaps were introduced in the event of another crisis. However, interestingly enough, such nations as Brazil, Russia, and India as well as most of East Asia began copying the Japanese model of weakening their currencies, restructuring their economies so as to create a current account surplus to build large foreign currency reserves. This has led to an ever increasing funding for US treasury bonds, allowing or aiding housing (in 2001-2005) and stock asset bubbles (in 1996-2000) to develop in the United States.

1998 Russian Financial Crisis

Inkombank was one of the most high-profile casualties of the events of August 1998. Once one of Russia's largest banks, whose billboards proudly announced its motto "We are for real, we are here to stay", it closed its doors almost overnight. Their Nizhny Novgorod building, which was one of the city's symbols of the new Russian capitalism, is now owned by a printing press, but above its name in blue one can still see (2006) brown glue patches suggesting the shape of the removed Inkombank logo.The Russian financial crisis (also called "Ruble crisis") hit Russia on 17 August 1998. It was exacerbated by the Asian financial crisis, which started in July 1997. Given the ensuing decline in world commodity prices, countries heavily dependent on the export of raw materials, such as oil, were among those most severely hit. (Petroleum, natural gas, metals, and timber accounted for more than 80% of Russian exports, leaving the country vulnerable to swings in world prices. Oil was also a major source of government tax revenue.) The sharp decline in the price of oil had severe consequences for Russia. However, the primary cause of the Russian Financial Crisis was not the fall of oil prices directly, but the result of non-payment of taxes by the energy and manufacturing industries.

Course of events

Prior to the culmination of the economic crisis, the GKO bonds issuance policy was described as similar to a pyramid scheme or Ponzi scheme (Hyman Minsky 1992), with the interest on matured obligations being paid off using the proceeds of newly issued obligations. Note however this scheme is used in the issuance of currency through a central bank but is limited by Fractional-reserve banking practices.

Declining productivity, an artificially high fixed exchange rate between the ruble and foreign currencies to avoid public turmoil, and a chronic fiscal deficit were the background to the meltdown. The economic cost of the first war in Chechnya that is estimated at $5.5 billion (not including the rebuilding of the ruined Chechen economy) was also a cause of the crisis. In the first half of 1997, the Russian economy showed some signs of improvement. However, soon after this, the problems began to gradually intensify. Two external shocks, the Asian financial crisis that had begun in 1997 and the following declines in demand for (and thus price of) crude oil and nonferrous metals, also impacted Russian foreign exchange reserves. A political crisis came to a head in March when Russian president Boris Yeltsin suddenly dismissed Prime

Minister Viktor Chernomyrdin and his entire cabinet on March 23. Yeltsin named Energy Minister Sergei Kiriyenko, aged 35, as acting prime minister. On May 29, Yeltsin appointed Boris Fyodorov Head of the State Tax Service. The growth of internal loans could only be provided at the expense of the inflow of foreign speculative capital, which was attracted by very high interest rates: In an effort to prop up the currency and stem the flight of capital, in June Kiriyenko hiked GKO interest rates to 150%. The situation was worsened by irregular internal debt payments. Despite government efforts, the debts on wages continued to grow, especially in the remote regions. By the end of 1997, the situation with the tax receipts was very tense, and it had a negative effect on the financing of the major budget items (pensions, communal utilities, transportation etc).

A $22.6 billion International Monetary Fund and World Bank financial package was approved on July 13 to support reforms and stabilize the Russian market by swapping out an enormous volume of the quickly maturing GKO short-term bills into long-term Eurobonds. This had started to be implemented with some success by July 24, yet the Russian government decided to keep the exchange rate of the ruble within a narrow band, although many economists, including Andrei Illarionov and George Soros, urged the government to abandon its support of the ruble. On May 12, 1998 Coal miners went on strike over unpaid wages, blocking the Trans-Siberian Railway. By August 1, 1998 there were approximately $12.5 billion in unpaid wages owed to Russian workers. On August 14 the exchange rate of the Russian ruble to the US dollar was still 6.29. Despite the bailout, July monthly interest payments on Russia's debt rose to a figure 40 percent greater than its monthly tax collections. Additionally, on July 15 the State Duma dominated by left-wing parties refused to adopt most of government anti-crisis plan so that the government was forced to rely on presidential decrees. On July 29 Yeltsin interrupted his vacation in Valdai Lake region and flew to Moscow, prompting fears of a Cabinet reshuffle, but he only replaced Federal Security Service Chief Nikolai Kovalyov with Vladimir Putin.

At the time, Russia employed a "floating peg" policy toward the ruble, meaning that the Central Bank at any given time committed that the ruble-to-dollar (or RUR/USD) exchange rate would stay within a particular range. If the ruble threatened to devalue outside of that range (or "band"), the Central Bank would intervene by spending foreign reserves to buy rubles. For instance, during approximately the one year prior to the Crisis, the Central Bank committed to maintain a band of 5.3 to 7.1 RUR/USD meaning that it would buy rubles if the market exchange rate threatened to exceed 7.1 rubles per dollar.

The manifest inability of the Russian government to implement a coherent set of economic reforms led to a severe erosion in investor confidence and a chain-reaction that can be likened to a run on the Central Bank. Investors fled the market by selling rubles and Russian assets (such as securities), which also put downward pressure on the ruble. This forced the Central Bank to spend its foreign reserves to defend the ruble, which in turn further eroded investor confidence and undermined the ruble. It is estimated that between October 1, 1997 and August 17, 1998, the Central Bank expended approximately $27 billion of its U.S. dollar reserves to maintain the floating peg.

It was later revealed that about $5 billion of the international loans provided by the World Bank and International Monetary Fund were stolen upon the funds' arrival in Russia on the eve of the meltdown.

On August 13, 1998, the Russian stock, bond, and currency markets collapsed as a result of investor fears that the government would devalue the ruble, default on domestic debt, or both. Annual yields on ruble denominated bonds were more than 200 percent. The stock market had to be closed for 35 minutes as prices plummeted. When the market closed, it was down 65 percent with a small number of shares actually traded. From January to August the stock market had lost more than 75 percent of its value, 39 percent in the month of May alone.

The Crisis and its Effects

On August 17, 1998, the Russian government and the Central Bank of Russia issued a "Joint Statement" announcing, in substance, that:

- the ruble/dollar trading band would be widened from 5.3-7.1 RUR/USD to 6.0-9.5 RUR/USD;
- Russia's ruble-denominated debt would be restructured in a manner to be announced at a later date; and, to prevent mass Russian bank default,
- a temporary 90-day moratorium would be imposed on the payment of some bank obligations, including certain debts and forward currency contracts. At the same time, in addition to widening the currency band, the authorities also announced that they intended to allow the RUR/USD rate to move more freely within the wider band.

At the time, the Moscow Interbank Currency Exchange (or "MICEX") set a daily "official" exchange rate through a series of iterative auctions based on written bids submitted by buyers and sellers. When the buy and sell prices matched this "fixed" or "settled" the official MICEX exchange rate, which would then be published by Reuters. The MICEX rate was (and is) commonly used by banks and currency dealers worldwide as the reference exchange rate for transactions involving the Russian ruble and foreign currencies.

From August 17 to August 25, the ruble steadily depreciated on the MICEX, moving from 6.43 to 7.86 RUR/USD. On August 26, the Central Bank terminated ruble-dollar trading on the MICEX, and the MICEX did not fix a ruble-dollar rate that day.

On September 2 the Central Bank of the Russian Federation decided to abandon the "floating peg" policy and float the ruble freely. By September 21 the exchange rate had reached 21 rubles to the US dollar--meaning it had, stupendously, lost two thirds of its value of less than a month earlier.

On September 28 Boris Fyodorov was fired from the position of the Head of the State Tax Service.

The moratorium imposed by the Joint Statement expired on November 15, 1998, and the Russian government and Central Bank did not renew it.

Russian inflation in 1998 reached 84 percent and welfare costs grew considerably. Many banks, including Inkombank, Oneximbank and Tokobank, were closed down as a result of the crisis. The salaries of miners alone were to consume $919 million, more than 1 percent of the federal budget. By August of that year, the government had paid $4 billion to settle miners' strikes. Prices for almost all Russian food items have gone up by almost 100%, while imports have quadrupled in price. Many citizens were stocking up for bad times and throughout the country shop shelves were being emptied, leaving a shortage of even the most basic items, such as vegetable oil, sugar or washing powder. The crisis has reduced demand for food and lowered food consumption, because substantial depreciation of the ruble significantly raises domestic prices for food stuffs. The crisis also increased social tension; The middle class that was already forming by that time, and had some hope for stability, ceased to exist as millions of people lost their bank savings. On October 7 that year, demonstrations were held in many cities: around 100,000 took to the streets in Moscow, In Vladivostok 4,000, in Krasnoyarsk 3,000 and in Yekaterinburg 6,000. Defence Minister Igor Sergeyev cancelled his scheduled visit to Greece in the first week of October, in order to be at hand should matters get out of control. Similarly select military units were placed in a state of readiness. On 20 October, President Boris Yeltsin also signed a presidential decree barring "mass protests" in Moscow between the hours of 10 p.m. and 7 a.m.and limiting them to a maximum of five days.

As the crisis deepened, regional governors had been introducing emergency measures: In Krasnoyarsk Krai in Siberia, governor Aleksandr Lebed, had signed a resolution to hold down prices "using administrative methods", a television report said. The authorities in the far eastern city of Vladivostok had banned deliveries of food to areas beyond the port city, and there had been talks of introducing rationing there. In Russia's Kaliningrad enclave on the Baltic, the governor announced a suspension of tax payments to the federal authorities.

The regional budgets also suffered from the 1998 crisis. The spending of the regions declined from 18.2% of the GDP in 1997 to 14.8% of the GDP. Spending on the economy (by 1.5% of the GDP) and social expenditures (by 1.6% of the GDP) were especially heavily reduced. The expenditures continued to decline in the following period. They dropped another 1% of the GDP in 1999 to 13.8% of the GDP, and to 10.8% of the GDP in the first quarter of 2000. One of the main factors in the reduction was the decline in subsidies for housing and municipal services, from 3.5% to 2.7% of the GDP.

Political Fallout

The financial collapse resulted in a political crisis as Yeltsin, with his domestic support evaporating, had to contend with an emboldened opposition in the parliament. A week later, on August 23, Yeltsin fired Kiriyenko and declared his intention of returning Chernomyrdin to office as the country slipped deeper into economic turmoil. Powerful business interests, fearing another round of reforms that might cause leading concerns to fail, welcomed Kiriyenko's fall, as did the Communists.

Yeltsin, who began to lose his hold on power as his health deteriorated, wanted Chernomyrdin back; In a televised address to the nation, Yeltsin said that “heavyweights” such as Chernomyrdin, who was ousted as prime minister in March 1998 for failing to vigorously promote economic reforms, were needed to stem the nation's financial collapse. Yeltsin also suggested that Chernomyrdin would be named his successor as president when Yeltsin's term expires in 2000. But the legislature refused to give its approval. After the Duma rejected Chernomyrdin's candidacy twice, Yeltsin, his power clearly on the wane, backed down. Instead, he nominated Foreign Minister Yevgeny Primakov, who on September 11 was overwhelmingly approved by the Duma.

Primakov's appointment restored political stability, because he was seen as a compromise candidate able to heal the rifts between Russia's quarreling interest groups. There was popular enthusiasm for Primakov as well. Primakov promised to make the payment of wage and pension arrears his government's first priority, and invited members of the leading parliamentary factions into his Cabinet. Communists and the Federation of Independent Trade Unions of Russia staged a nationwide strike on October 7 and called on President Yeltsin to resign. On October 9, Russia, which was also suffering from a bad harvest, appealed for international humanitarian aid, including food.

Recovery

Russia bounced back from the August 1998 financial crash with surprising speed. Much of the reason for the recovery is that world oil prices rapidly rose during 1999–2000 (just as falling energy prices on the world market helped to deepen Russia's financial troubles), so that Russia ran a large trade surplus in 1999 and 2000. Another reason is that domestic industries, such as food processing, had benefited from the devaluation, which caused a steep increase in the prices of imported goods. Also, since Russia's economy was operating to such a large extent on barter and other non-monetary instruments of exchange, the financial collapse had far less of an impact on many producers than it would had the economy been dependent on a banking system. Finally, the economy has been helped by an infusion of cash; as enterprises were able to pay off arrears in back wages and taxes, it in turn allowed consumer demand for the goods and services of Russian industry to rise. For the first time in many years, unemployment in 2000 fell as enterprises added workers. Since the 1998 crisis, the Russian government has managed to keep social and political pressures under control, and this has played a vital role in bringing about the current recovery.

Effects on other Countries

Baltic States

The Russian crisis affected Baltic countries more than was expected. Estonia, Latvia and Lithuania sank into recession. The figures for 1999 showed a heavy decline in Baltic's exports to Russia and a significant decline in the growth rates of these economies. Food and beverage as well as processing industries as a whole have suffered the most.

Belarus

Overall, economic activity slowed down substantially in the immediate aftermath of the Russian crisis, with output growth falling from about 8.5 percent in 1998 to 3.4 percent in 1999. Both exports and imports contracted substantially, resulting in a drop in the current account deficit from 6.1 percent of GDP in 1998 to 2.2 percent of GDP in 1999. Externally, exports to Russia, which accounted for more than 60 percent of total exports, fell during the second half of 1998 by 10 percent. Demand for Belarusian products was weak through 1999, showing signs of recovery only during the final quarter, with the revival of economic activity in Russia. Also, in the first quarter of 1999 as compared with 1998, except for investments, all the budget expenditures were smaller. The biggest cuts were done in national security (1.9 percent of GDP compared with 2.5 percent of GDP in the first quarter of 1998) and social policy (1.5 and 2.4 percent of GDP, respectively) where the expenditures were lowered almost by one third.

Kazakhstan

The Russian crisis was a hard hitting blow to the Kazakh economy. Kazakhstan lost its price competitiveness and its exports were in shambles. On the other hand, cheap Russian goods were flowing into the economy that was killing the domestic industries. There was huge downward pressure on the tenge and their balance of payments had worsened. However the NBK was still holding on to the tenge. In fact, they had spent close to a billion dollars to maintain the level of tenge. Their foreign exchange reserves halved.

Moldova

Moldova received an IMF special mission advising the government on how to cope with the effects of the Russian crisis. Russia bought at that time 85% of Moldova's wine and brandy and most of its canned goods and tobacco. After the rouble crashed, most Russian importers put deals with Moldova on hold. The Moldovan president Petru Luchinski was quoted as saying that the Russian crisis had cost Moldova as much as five per cent of its GDP. The country's parliament was discussing a programme aimed at reducing imports and searching for new markets outside Russia.

Ukraine

The crisis cost a lot for Ukraine: the Hryvnia devaluated by 60%, domestic prices increased by 20%, the National Bank of Ukraine lost 40% of its gross reserves.

Uzbekistan

In the central Asian state, the government banned the free unlicensed sales of food, most of which is imported from Russia, as a preventative measure against price rises and panic.

Dot-com Bubble

The "dot-com bubble" (or sometimes the "I.T. bubble") was a speculative bubble covering roughly 1995–2001 (with a climax on March 10, 2000 with the NASDAQ peaking at 5132.52) during which stock markets in Western nations saw their value increase rapidly from growth in the new Internet sector and related fields. The period was marked by the founding (and, in many cases, spectacular failure) of a group of new Internet-based companies commonly referred to as dot-coms. A combination of rapidly increasing stock prices, individual speculation in stocks, and widely available venture capital created an exuberant environment in which many of these businesses dismissed standard business models, focusing on increasing market share at the expense of the bottom line.

The growth of the Bubble

The venture capitalists saw record-setting rises in stock valuations of dot-com companies, and therefore moved faster and with less caution than usual, choosing to mitigate the risk by starting many contenders and letting the market decide which would succeed. The low interest rates in 1998–99 helped increase the start-up capital amounts. Although a number of these new entrepreneurs had realistic plans and administrative ability, most of them lacked these characteristics but were able to sell their ideas to investors because of the novelty of the dot-com concept.

A canonical "dot-com" company's business model relied on harnessing network effects by operating at a sustained net loss to build market share (or mind share). These companies expected that they could build enough brand awareness to charge profitable rates for their services later. The motto "get big fast" reflected this strategy. During the loss period the companies relied on venture capital and especially initial public offerings of stock to pay their expenses. The novelty of these stocks, combined with the difficulty of valuing the companies, sent many stocks to dizzying heights and made the initial controllers of the company wildly rich on paper.

Historically, the dot-com boom can be seen as similar to a number of other technology-inspired booms of the past including railroads in the 1840s, automobiles and radio in the 1920s, transistor electronics in the 1950s, computer time-sharing in the 1960s, and home computers and biotechnology in the early 1980s.

Soaring Stocks

In financial markets a stock market bubble is a self-perpetuating rise or boom in the share prices of stocks of a particular industry. The term may be used with certainty only in retrospect when share prices have since crashed. A bubble occurs when speculators note the fast increase in value and decide to buy in anticipation of further rises, rather than because the shares are undervalued. Typically many companies thus become grossly overvalued. When the bubble "bursts," the share prices fall dramatically, and many companies go out of business.

The dot-com model was inherently flawed. A vast number of companies all had the same business plan of monopolizing their respective sectors through network effects, and it was clear that even if the plan was sound, there could only be at most one network-effects winner in each sector, and therefore that most companies with this business plan would fail. In fact, many sectors could not support even one company powered entirely by network effects.

In spite of this, however, a few company founders made vast fortunes when their companies were bought out at an early stage in the dot-com stock market bubble. These early successes made the bubble even more buoyant. An unprecedented amount of personal investing occurred during the boom, and the press reported the phenomenon of people quitting their jobs to become full-time day traders.

Free Spending

According to dot-com theory, an Internet company's survival depended on expanding its customer base as rapidly as possible, even if it produced large annual losses. The phrase "Get large or get lost" was the wisdom of the day. At the height of the boom, it was possible for a promising dot-com to make an initial public offering (IPO) of its stock and raise a substantial amount of money even though it had never made a profit — or, in some cases, earned any revenue whatsoever. In such a situation, a company's lifespan was measured by its burn rate: That is, the rate at which a non-profitable company lacking a viable business model ran through its capital served as the measuring stick.

Public awareness campaigns were one way that dot-coms sought to grow their customer base. These included television ads, print ads, and targeting of professional sporting events. Many dot-coms named themselves with onomatopoeic nonsense words that they hoped would be memorable and not easily confused with a competitor. Super Bowl XXXIV in January 2000 featured seventeen dot-com companies that each paid over two million dollars for a thirty-second spot. By contrast, in January 2001, just three dot-coms bought advertising spots during Super Bowl XXXV. In a similar vein, CBS-backed iWon.com gave away ten million dollars to a lucky contestant on an April 15, 2000, half-hour primetime special that was broadcast on CBS.

Not surprisingly, the "growth over profits" mentality and the aura of "new economy" invincibility led some companies to engage in lavish internal spending, such as elaborate business facilities and luxury vacations for employees. Executives and employees who were paid with stock options in lieu of cash became instant millionaires when the company made its initial public offering; many invested their new wealth into yet more dot-coms.

Cities all over the United States sought to become the "next Silicon Valley" by building network-enabled office space to attract Internet entrepreneurs. Communication providers, convinced that the future economy would require ubiquitous broadband access, went deeply into debt to improve their networks with high-speed equipment and fiber optic cables. Companies that produced network equipment, such as Cisco Systems, profited greatly from these projects.

Similarly, in Europe the vast amounts of cash the mobile operators spent on 3G licences in Germany, Italy, and the United Kingdom, for example, led them into deep debt. The investments were far out of proportion to both their current and projected cash flow, but this was not publicly acknowledged until as late as 2001 and 2002. Due to the highly networked nature of the IT (information-technology) industry, this quickly led to problems for small companies dependent on contracts from operators.

Thinning the Herd

Over 1999 and early 2000, the Federal Reserve had increased interest rates six times, and the runaway economy was beginning to lose speed. The dot-com bubble burst, numerically, on March 10, 2000, when the technology heavy NASDAQ Composite index peaked at 5,048.62 (intra-day peak 5,132.52), more than double its value just a year before. The NASDAQ fell slightly after that, but this was attributed to correction by most market analysts; the actual reversal and subsequent bear market may have been triggered by the adverse findings of fact in the United States v. Microsoft case which was being heard in federal court. The findings, which declared Microsoft a monopoly, were widely expected in the weeks before their release on April 3.

One possible cause for the collapse of the NASDAQ (and all dotcoms) was massive, multi-billion dollar sell orders for major bellwether high tech stocks (Cisco, IBM, Dell, etc.) that happened by chance to be processed simultaneously on the Monday morning following the March 10 weekend. This selling resulted in the NASDAQ opening roughly four percentage points lower on Monday March 13 from 5,038 to 4,879—the greatest percentage 'pre-market' selloff for the entire year.

The massive initial batch of sell orders processed on Monday, March 13 triggered a chain reaction of selling that fed on itself as investors, funds, and institutions liquidated positions. In just six days the NASDAQ had lost nearly nine percent, falling from roughly 5,050 on March 10 to 4,580 on March 15.

Another reason may have been accelerated business spending in preparation for the Y2K switchover. Once New Year had passed without incident, businesses found themselves with all the equipment they needed for some time, and business spending quickly declined. This correlates quite closely to the peak of U.S. stock markets. The Dow Jones peaked on January 14, 2000 (closed at 11,722.98, with an intra-day peak of 11,750.28 and theoretical peak of 11,908.50) and the broader S&P 500 on March 24, 2000 (closed at 1,527.46, with an intra-day peak of 1,553.11); while, even more dramatically the UK's FTSE 100 Index peaked at 6,950.60 on the last day of trading in 1999 (December 30). Hiring freezes, layoffs, and consolidations followed in several industries, especially in the dot-com sector.

The bursting of the bubble may also have been related to the poor results of Internet retailers following the 1999 Christmas season. This was the first unequivocal and public evidence that the "Get Big Fast" Internet strategy was flawed for most companies. These retailers' results were made public in March when annual and quarterly reports of public firms were released.

By 2001 the bubble was deflating at full speed. A majority of the dot-coms ceased trading after burning through their venture capital, many having never made a net profit. Investors often jokingly referred to these failed dot-coms as either "dot-bombs" or "dot-compost".

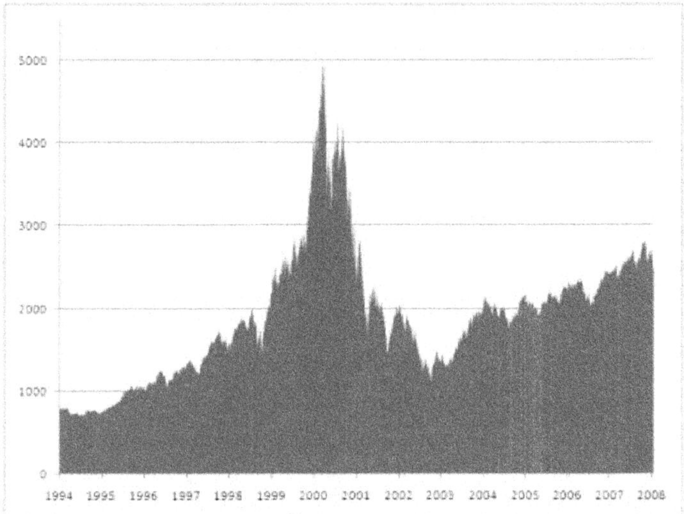

Picture 56: The technology-heavy NASDAQ Composite index peaked at 5,048 in March 2000, reflecting the high point of the dot-com bubble

Aftermath

On January 11, 2000, America Online, a favorite of dot-com investors and pioneer of dial-up Internet access, acquired Time Warner, the world's largest media company. Within two years, boardroom disagreements drove out both of the CEOs who made the deal, and in October 2003 AOL Time Warner dropped "AOL" from its name, a symbol of the dominance of old industry during periods of technological growth.

Several communication companies, burdened with unredeemable debts from their expansion projects, sold their assets for cash or filed for bankruptcy. WorldCom, the largest of these, was found to have used illegal accounting practices to overstate its profits by billions of dollars. The company's stock crashed when these irregularities were revealed, and within days it filed the largest corporate bankruptcy in U.S. history. Other examples include NorthPoint Communications, Global Crossing, JDS Uniphase, XO Communications, and Covad Communications. Demand for the new high-speed infrastructure never materialized, and it became dark fiber.

Many dot-coms ran out of capital and were acquired or liquidated; the domain names were picked up by old-economy competitors or domain name investors. Several companies and their executives were accused or convicted of fraud for misusing shareholders' money, and the U.S. Securities and Exchange Commission fined top investment firms like Citigroup and Merrill Lynch millions of dollars for misleading investors. Various supporting industries, such as advertising and shipping, scaled back their operations as demand for their services fell. A few large dot-com companies, such as Amazon.com and eBay, survived the turmoil and appear assured of long-term survival.

The Dot-com bubble crash wiped out $5 trillion in market value of technology companies from March 2000 to October 2002.

Recent research suggests, however, that as many as 50% of the dot-coms survived through 2004, reflecting two facts: the destruction of public market wealth did not necessarily correspond to firm closings, and second, that most of the dot-coms were small players who were able to weather the financial markets storm.

Nevertheless, laid-off technology experts, such as computer programmers, found a glutted job market. In the U.S., International outsourcing and the recently allowed increase of skilled visa "guest workers" (e.g., those participating in the U.S. H-1B visa program) exacerbated the situation. University degree programs for computer-related careers saw a noticeable drop in new students. Anecdotes of unemployed programmers going back to school to become accountants or lawyers were common.

Some believe the crash of the dot-com bubble contributed to the housing bubble in the U.S. Yale economist Robert Shiller said in 2005, "Once stocks fell, real estate became the primary outlet for the speculative frenzy that the stock market had unleashed. Where else could plungers apply their newly acquired trading talents? The materialistic display of the big house also has become a salve to bruised egos of disappointed stock investors. These days, the only thing that comes close to real estate as a national obsession is poker.

Stock Market Downturn of 2002

The stock market downturn of 2002 (some say "stock market crash" or "the Internet bubble bursting") is the sharp drop in stock prices during 2002 in stock exchanges across the United States, Canada, Asia, and Europe. After recovering from lows reached following the September 11, 2001 attacks, indices slid steadily starting in March 2002, with dramatic declines in July and September leading to lows last reached in 1997 and 1998. The dollar declined steadily against the euro, reaching a 1-to-1 valuation not seen since the euro's introduction.

Context

This downturn can be viewed as part of a larger bear market or correction, after a decade-long bull market had led to unusually high stock valuations. In fact, some Internet companies (Webvan, Exodus Communications, and Pets.com) went bankrupt. Others (Amazon.com, eBay, and Yahoo!) went down dramatically in value, but remain in business to this day and have generally good long term growth prospects. An outbreak of accounting scandals (Enron, Arthur Andersen, Adelphia, and WorldCom) was also a factor in the speed of the fall, as numerous large corporations were forced to restate earnings (or lack thereof) and investor confidence suffered. The September 11 attacks also contributed heavily to the stock market downturn, as investors became unsure about the prospect of terrorism affecting the United States economy.

The International Monetary Fund had expressed concern about instability in United States stock markets in the months leading up to the sharp downturn. The technology-heavy NASDAQ stock market peaked on March 10, 2000, hitting an intra-day high of 5,132.52 and closing at 5,048.62. The Dow Jones Industrial Average, a price-weighted average (adjusted for splits and dividends) of 30 large companies on the New York Stock Exchange, peaked on January 14, 2000 with an intra-day high of 11,750.28 and a closing price of 11,722.98. In 2001, the DJIA was largely unchanged overall but had reached a secondary peak of 11,337.92 (11,350.05 intra-day) on May 21.

The downturn may be viewed as a reversion to average stock market performance in a longer-term context. From 1987 to 1995, the Dow rose each year by about 10%, but from 1995 to 2000, the Dow rose 15% a year. While the bear market began in 2000, by July and August 2002, the index had only dropped to the same level it would have achieved if the 10% annual growth rate followed during 1987-1995 had continued up to 2002.

Seeking a Bottom

After falling for 11 of 12 consecutive days closing below Dow 8000 on July 23, 2002, the market rallied. The Dow rose 13% over the next four trading days, but then fell sharply again in early August. On August 5, the NASDAQ fell below its July 23 low. However, the markets rose sharply over the rest of the week, and eventually surpassed Dow 9000 during several trading sessions in late August. After that, the Dow dropped to a four-year low on September 24, 2002, while the NASDAQ reached a 6-year low. The markets continued their declines, breaking the September low to five-year lows on October 7 and reaching a nadir (below Dow 7200 and just above 1100 on the NASDAQ) on October 9. Stocks recovered slightly from their October lows to year-end, with the Dow remaining in the mid-8000s from November 2002 to mid-January 2003. The markets reached a final low below Dow 7500 in mid-March 2003.

Scale

As of September 24, 2002, the Dow Jones Industrial Average had lost 27% of the value it held on January 1, 2001: a total loss of 5 trillion dollars. It should be noted that the Dow Jones had already lost 9% of its peak value at the start of 2001, while the Nasdaq had lost 44%. At the March 2000 top, the sum in valuation of all NYSE-listed companies stood at $12.9 trillion, and the valuation sum of all NASDAQ-listed companies stood at $5.4 trillion, for a total market value of $18.3 trillion. The NASDAQ subsequently lost nearly 80% and the S&P 500 lost 50% to reach the October 2002 lows. The total market value of NYSE (7.2) and NASDAQ (1.8) companies at that time was only $9 trillion, for an overall market loss of $9.3 trillion.

Index Levels

To put the downturn of 2002 in perspective, here is a look at annual U.S. stock market declines in 2000, 2001, and 2002:

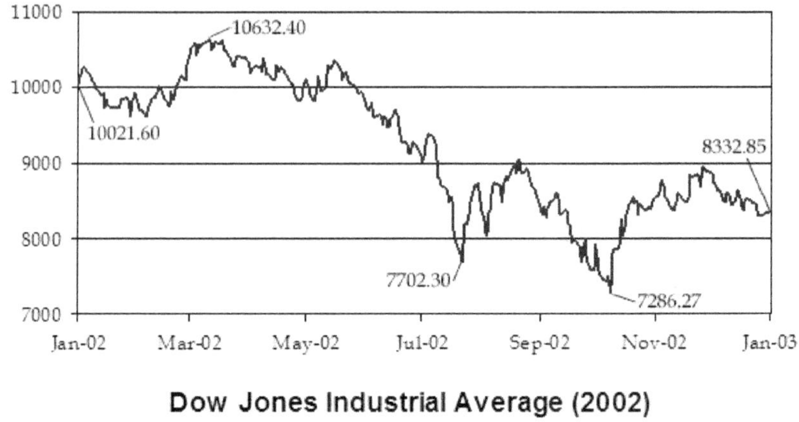

Picture 57: Dow Jones Industrial Average in 2002

- In 2000, the Dow lost 6.17% of its value (11,497.10 to 10,788.00)
- In 2001, the Dow lost 5.35% of its value (10,788.00 to 10,021.60)
- In 2002, the Dow lost 16.76% of its value (10,021.60 to 8,341.63)

Picture 58: Nasdaq

- In 2000, the Nasdaq lost 39.28% of its value (4,069.31 to 2,470.52).
- In 2001, the Nasdaq lost 21.05% of its value (2,470.52 to 1,950.40).
- In 2002, the Nasdaq lost 31.53% of its value (1,950.40 to 1,335.51).

Here is a historical view of the stock market downturn of 2002 including figures from the stock market bubble of the late 1990s:

Date	Nasdaq	% Chng.§	Dow Jones	% Chng.§	Notes
January 1, 1997	1,291.03	—	6,448.30	—	
January 1, 1998	1,570.35	+21.63%	7,908.30	+22.64%	
January 1, 1999	2,192.69	+39.63%	9,181.40	+16.10%	
January 1, 2000	4,069.31	+85.58%	11,497.10	+25.22%	
January 14, 2000	4,064.27	-0.12%	11,723.00	+1.97%	The day the DJIA peaked.
March 10, 2000	5,048.62	+24.22%	9,928.80	-15.31%	The day the Nasdaq peaked.
January 1, 2001	2,470.52	-51.07%	10,788.00	+8.65%	
January 20, 2001	2,770.38	+12.14%	10,587.60	-1.86%	President Bush takes office.
September 10, 2001	1,695.38	-38.80%	9,605.50	-9.28%	Levels before September 11, 2001 attacks.
September 21, 2001	1,423.19	-16.05%	8,235.80	-14.26%	Lows after markets reopened.
January 1, 2002	1,950.40	+37.04%	10,021.60	+21.68%	
October 9, 2002	1,114.11	-42.88%	7,286.27	-27.29%	2002 lows.
January 1, 2003	1,335.51	+19.87%	8,341.63	+14.48%	

January 1, 2004	2,003.37	+50.01%	10,453.92	+25.32%

§Values represent percent change from previous date listed in table.

Global Financial Crisis of 2008

The global financial crisis of 2008 is a major ongoing financial crisis, the worst of its kind since the Great Depression. It became prominently visible in September, 2008 with the failure, merger or conservatorship of several large United States-based financial firms. The underlying causes leading to the crisis had been reported in business journals for many months before September, with commentary about the financial stability of leading U.S. and European investment banks, insurance firms and mortgage banks consequent to the subprime mortgage crisis.

Beginning with failures of large financial institutions in the United States, it rapidly evolved into a global crisis resulting in a number of European bank failures and declines in various stock indexes, and significant reductions in the market-value of equities (stock) and commodities worldwide. The crisis has led to a liquidity problem and the de-leveraging of financial institutions especially in the United States and Europe, which further accelerated the liqudity crisis. World political leaders and national ministers of finance and central bank directors have coordinated their efforts to reduce fears but the crisis is ongoing and continues to change, evolving at the close of October into a currency crisis with investors transferring vast capital resources into stronger currencies such as the yen, the dollar and the Swiss franc, leading many emergent economies to seek aid from the International Monetary Fund. The crisis has roots in the subprime mortgage crisis and is an acute phase of the Financial crisis of 2007-2008.

Week of September 7, 2008

The United States director of the Federal Housing Finance Agency (FHFA), James B. Lockhart III, on September 7, 2008 announced his decision to place two United States Government sponsored enterprises (GSEs), Fannie Mae (Federal National Mortgage Association) and Freddie Mac (Federal Home Loan Mortgage Corporation), into conservatorship run by FHFA. United States Treasury Secretary Henry Paulson, at the same press conference stated that placing the two GSEs into conservatorship was a decision he fully supported, and said that he advised "that conservatorship was the only form in which I would commit taxpayer money to the GSEs." He further said that "I attribute the need for today's action primarily to the inherent conflict and flawed business model embedded in the GSE structure, and to the ongoing housing correction." The same day, Federal Reserve Bank Chairman Ben Bernanke stated in support: "I strongly endorse both the decision by FHFA Director Lockhart to place Fannie Mae and Freddie Mac into conservatorship and the actions taken by

Treasury Secretary Paulson to ensure the financial soundness of those two companies."

Week of September 14, 2008

Major Financial Firm Crisis

On Sunday, September 14, it was announced that Lehman Brothers would file for bankruptcy after the Federal Reserve Bank declined to participate in creating a financial support facility for Lehman Brothers. The significance of the Lehman Brothers bankruptcy is disputed with some assigning it a pivotal role in the unfolding of subsequent events. The principals involved, Ben Bernanke and Henry Paulson, dispute this view, citing a volume of toxic assets at Lehman which made a rescue impossible. Immediately following the bankruptcy, J.P. Morgan provided the broker dealer unit of Lehman Brothers with $138 billion to "settle securities transactions with customers of Lehman and its clearance parties" according to a statement made in a New York City Bankruptcy court filing.

The same day, the sale of Merrill Lynch to Bank of America was announced. The beginning of the week was marked by extreme instability in global stock markets, with dramatic drops in market values on Monday, September 15, and Wednesday, September 17. On September 16, the large insurer American International Group (AIG), a significant participant in the credit default swaps markets suffered a liquidity crisis following the downgrade of its credit rating. The Federal Reserve, at AIG's request, and after AIG has shown that it could not find lenders willing to save it from insolvency, created a credit facility for up to US$85 billion in exchange for an 79.9% equity interest, and the right to suspend dividends to previously issued common and preferred stock.

Money Market Funds Insurance and Short Sales Prohibitions

On September 16, the Reserve Primary Fund, a large money market mutual fund, lowered its share price below $1 because of exposure to Lehman debt securities. This resulted in demands from investors to return their funds as the financial crisis mounted. By the morning of September 18, money market sell orders from institutional investors totalled $0.5 trillion, out of a total market capitalization of $4 trillion, but a $105 billion liquidity injection from the Federal Reserve averted an immediate collapse. On September 19 the U.S. Treasury offered temporary insurance (akin to FDIC insurance of bank accounts) to money market funds. Toward the end of the week, short selling of financial stocks was suspended by the Financial Services Authority in the United Kingdom and by the Securities and Exchange Commission in the United States. Similar measures were taken by authorities in other countries. Some restoration of market confidence occurred with the publicity surrounding efforts of the Treasury and the Securities Exchange Commission.

Troubled Asset Relief Program

On September 19, 2008, a plan intended to ameliorate the difficulties caused by the subprime mortgage crisis was proposed by the Secretary of the Treasury, Henry Paulson. He proposed a Troubled Asset Relief Program, later incorporated into the Emergency Economic Stabilization Act of 2008, which would permit for the United States government to purchase illiquid assets, also termed toxic assets, from financial institutions. The value of the securities is extremely difficult to determine.

Consultations between the Secretary of the Treasury, the Chairman of the Federal Reserve, and the Chairman of the U.S. Securities and Exchange Commission, Congressional leaders and the President of the United States moved forward plans to advance a comprehensive solution to the problems created by illiquid mortgage-backed securities. At the close of the week the Secretary of the Treasury and President Bush announced a proposal for the federal government to buy up to US$700 billion of illiquid mortgage backed securities with the intent to increase the liquidity of the secondary mortgage markets and reduce potential losses encountered by financial institutions owning the securities. The draft proposal of the plan was received favorably by investors in the stock market. Details of the bailout remained to be acted upon by Congress.

Week of September 21, 2008

On Sunday, September 21, the two remaining investment banks, Goldman Sachs and Morgan Stanley, with the approval of the Federal Reserve, converted to bank holding companies, a status subject to more regulation, but with readier access to capital. On September 21, Treasury Secretary Henry Paulson announced that the original proposal, which would have excluded foreign banks, had been widened to include foreign financial institutions with a presence in the US. The US administration was pressuring other countries to set up similar bailout plans.

On Monday and Tuesday during the week of September 22, appearances were made by the Secretary of the Treasury and the Chairman of the Board of Governors of the Federal Reserve before Congressional committees and on Wednesday a prime time presidential address was delivered by the President of the United States on television. Behind the scenes, negotiations were held refining the proposal which had grown to 42 pages from its original 3 and was reported to include both an oversight structure and limitations on executive salaries, with other provisions under consideration.

On September 25, agreement was reported by congressional leaders on the basics of the package; however, general and vocal opposition to the proposal was voiced by the public. On Thursday afternoon at a White House meeting attended by congressional leaders and the presidential candidates, John McCain and Barack Obama, it became clear that there was no congressional consensus, with Republican representatives and the ranking member of the Senate Banking Committee, Richard C. Shelby, strongly opposing the proposal. The alternative advanced by conservative House Republicans was to create a system of mortgage insurance funded by fees on those holding mortgages; as the working week ended, negotiations continued on the plan, which had grown to 102 pages and included mortgage insurance as an option. On Thursday evening Washington Mutual, the nation's largest savings and loan, was seized by the Federal Deposit Insurance Corporation and most of its assets transferred to JPMorgan Chase. Wachovia, one of the largest US banks, was reported to be in negotiations with Citigroup and other financial institutions.

Week of September 28, 2008

Early into Sunday morning an announcement was made by the United States Secretary of the Treasury and congressional leaders that agreement had been reached on all major issues: The total amount of $700 billion remained with provision for the option of creating a scheme of mortgage insurance.

It was reported on Sunday, September 28, that a rescue plan had been crafted for the British mortgage lender Bradford & Bingley. Grupo Santander, the largest bank in Spain, was slated to take over the offices and savings accounts while the mortgage and loans business would be nationalized.

Fortis, a huge Benelux banking and finance company was partially nationalized on September 28, 2008, with Belgium, the Netherlands and Luxembourg investing a total of €11.2 billion (US$16.3 billion) in the bank. Belgium will purchase 49% of Fortis's Belgian division, with the Netherlands doing the same for the Dutch division. Luxembourg has agreed to a loan convertible into a 49% share of Fortis's Luxembourg division.

It was reported on Monday morning, September 29, that Wachovia, the 4th largest bank in the United States, would be acquired by Citigroup.

On Monday the German finance minister announced a rescue of Hypo Real Estate, a Munich-based holding company comprised of a number of real estate financing banks, but the deal collapsed on Saturday, 4 October.

The same day the government of Iceland nationalized Glitnir, Iceland's third largest lender.

Stocks fell dramatically Monday in Europe and the US despite infusion of funds into the market for short term credit. In the US the Dow dropped 777 points (6.98%), the largest one-day point-drop in history (but only the 17th largest percentage drop).

The U.S. bailout plan, now named the Emergency Economic Stabilization Act of 2008 and expanded to 110 pages was slated for consideration in the House of Representatives on Monday, September 29 as HR 3997 and in the Senate later in the week. The plan failed after the vote being held open for 40 minutes in the House of Representatives, 205 for the plan, 228 against. Meanwhile US stock markets suffered steep declines, the Dow losing 300 points in a matter of minutes, ending down 777.68, the Nasdaq losing 199.61, falling below the 2000 point mark, and the S.&P. 500 off 8.77% for the day. By the end of the day, the Dow suffered the largest drop in the history of the index. The S&P 500 Banking Index fell 14% on September 29 with drops in the stock value of a number of US banks generally considered sound, including Bank of New York Mellon, State Street and Northern Trust; three Ohio banks, National City, Fifth Third, and KeyBank were down dramatically.

On Tuesday, September 30, stocks rebounded but credit markets remained tight with the London Interbank Offered Rate (overnight dollar Libor) rising 4.7% to 6.88%.

On Tuesday, September 30, 9 billion was made available by the French, Belgian and Luxembourg governments to the French-Belgian bank Dexia.

After Irish banks came under pressure on Monday, September 29, the Irish government undertook a two year "guarantee arrangement to safeguard all deposits (retail, commercial, institutional and inter-bank), covered bonds, senior debt and dated subordinated debt (lower tier II)" of 6 Irish banks: Allied Irish Banks, Bank of Ireland, Anglo Irish Bank, Irish Life and Permanent, Irish Nationwide and the EBS Building Society. The potential liability involved is about 400 billion dollars.

The United States Senate's version of the $700 billion bailout plan, HR1424, modified to expand bank deposit guarantees to $250,000 and to include $100 billion in tax breaks for businesses and alternative energy, passed with bipartisan support 74-25 on October 1st. Reaction in the House was mixed, but in a vote on Friday the House of Representatives passed the Emergency Economic Stabilization Act of 2008, as refashioned by the Senate, 263-171 in a bipartisan vote.

Discussions were ongoing in Europe regarding possible remedies for financial instability in Europe leading up to a conference Saturday afternoon in Paris hosted by Nicolas Sarkozy, president of France. UniCredit of Italy was reported to be the latest bank to come under pressure. During the night of October 2 Greece followed Ireland's lead and guaranteed all bank deposits.

On October 3 it was reported that Wachovia had rejected the previous offer from Citigroup in favor of acquisition by Wells Fargo, resulting in a legal dispute with Citigroup.

In Britain, the Financial Services Authority announced on October 3 that effective Tuesday, October 7, the amount of the guarantee of bank deposits would be raised to £50,000 from £35,000. On Friday, October 3, the government of the Netherlands took over the Dutch operations of Fortis, replacing the bailout plan of September 28.

Week of October 5

Over the weekend and on Monday a major banking and financial crisis emerged in Iceland with its currency the krona, dropping 30% against the euro. At a meeting on Monday night emergency legislation was passed granting broad powers to the government to seize and regulate banks. The Landsbanki and Glitnir were seized, while Kaupthing was subjected to a rescue plan.

On October 6, the Icelandic Financial Supervisory Authority decided temporarily to suspend from trading on regulated markets all financial instruments issued by Glitnir banki hf., Kaupþing banki hf., Landsbanki Íslands hf., Straumur-Burðarás fjárfestingarbanki hf., Spron hf., and Exista hf..

Before the opening of the business day, October 6. BNP Paribas, the French bank, assumed control of the remaining assets of Fortis following Dutch nationalization of the operations of the bank in The Netherlands. Denmark, Austria, and possibly Germany, joined Ireland and Greece in guaranteeing bank deposits on Monday, October 6. Following this, the FTSE100 index of leading British shares took its worst one-day hit in history. A banking Bill easing rescues is slated for introduction in the British Parliament on Tuesday, October 7. On 6 October German chancellor Angela Merkel pledged that the government would guarantee all German private bank savings. The government also announced a revised bailout plan for German mortgage lender Hypo Real Estate (HRE). On Monday, October 6, the Dow Jones Industrial Average closed below 10,000, a drop of 30% from its high above 14,000 a year earlier on October 9, 2007. In Brazil and Russia trading was suspended on Monday following dramatic drops in their markets.

On October 7, the Icelandic Financial Supervisory Authority took control of Landsbank. On the same day, the Central Bank of Iceland announced that Russia had agreed to provide a €4 billion loan, however this was soon denied by Russian authorities, and the Icelandic Finance Minister had to correct the earlier announcement and now stated that discussions had been initiated with Russia on providing a loan to Iceland. This was also denied by Russian Deputy Finance Minister Dmitry Pankin. Late in the evening, however, Russia's Finance Minister Alexei Kudrin did concede that a request had been received, to which Russia was positive, and that discussions on financial matters would be conducted later in the week when an Icelandic delegation was expected to arrive in Moscow. Standard & Poor's also cut Iceland's foreign-currency sovereign credit rating from A-/A-2 to BBB/A-3 and local-currency sovereign credit rating from A+/A-1 to BBB+/A-2. S&P also lowered Iceland's banking industry country risk assessment from group 5 to group 8, worrying that "In a severe recession scenario, the cumulative amount of nonperforming and restructured loans could reach 35% to 50% of total outstanding loans in Iceland.

On October 7 the Federal reserve announced formation of a Commercial Paper Funding Facilty (CPFF) which will serve as a funding backstop to facilitate the issuance of term commercial paper by eligible issuers. Several countries announced new or increased deposit guarantees: Taiwan outlined plans to double the guarantee to NT$3 million ($92,000) and the European Union agreed to increase guarantees across the EU to at least €50,000 per saver. Several EU states then announced increases on top of this minimum: Netherlands, Spain, Belgium, and Greece each announced they would guarantee up to €100,000.

The government of Britain announced on the morning of Wednesday, October 8 that it would make £25 billion available as "Tier 1 capital" (preference share capital or "PIBS" (Permanent Interest-Bearing Securities)) to the following financial institutions: Abbey, Barclays, HBOS, HSBC Bank plc, Lloyds TSB, Nationwide Building Society, Royal Bank of Scotland, and Standard Chartered as part of a bank rescue package. An additional £25 billion was scheduled to be made available to other financial institutions, including British subsidiaries of foreign banks. "In reviewing these applications the Government will give due regard to an institution's role in the UK banking system and the overall economy". The plan included increased ability to borrow from the government, offered assistance in raising equity, and a statement of support for international efforts. The plan has been characterized as partial nationalization.

On Wednesday, October 8, the European Central Bank, Bank of England, Federal Reserve, Bank of Canada, Swedish Riksbank and Swiss National Bank all announced simultaneous cuts of 0.5% to their base rates at 11:00 UTC. Shortly afterwards, the Central Bank of the People's Republic of China also cut interest rates. On October 8 there were sharp losses on stock markets worldwide with a loss of over 9% in Japan. Trading was suspended in Russia and Indonesia after steep morning losses. In the United States, following the funds cut by the Federal Reserve, stocks were volatile, finishing down. On October 8 the Federal Reserve loaned AIG $37.8 billion, in addition to the previous loan of $85 billion.

On Wednesday night, October 8, the Central Bank of Iceland abandoned its attempt to peg the Icelandic króna at 131 króna to the euro after trying to set this peg on Monday, October 6. By Thursday October 9, the Icelandic króna was trading at 340 to the euro when the government suspended all trade in the currency.

On Thursday, October 9, the Icelandic Financial Supervisory Authority took control of the country's biggest bank Kaupthing Banki hf. This occurred when the Kaupthing Board resigned and asked the national authorities to take control. This came about when "Britain transferred control of the business of Kaupthing Edge, its Internet bank, to ING Direct and put Kaupthing's UK operations into administration" placing Kaupthing in technical default according to loan agreements. This marked an escalating row between Iceland and the United Kingdom over the growing crisis. All trade was also suspended on the Iceland Stock Exchange until Monday October 13.

On Thursday, October 9, the one-year anniversary of the Dow's peak, the cost of short term credit rose while there were heavy losses in the United States stock market; the Dow dropped below 8600, reaching a five year low. It was the first time since August 2003 that the Dow closed below 9000; losses were moderate in Europe. The following day, Friday, October 10, there were large losses in Asian and European markets Yamato Life filed for bankruptcy. Beset by falling commodities prices, Russia's stock markets remained closed on October 10. The Russian Parliament passed a plan authorizing lending of $36 billion gained from global oil sales to banks which met creditworthiness requirements. Special attention is being paid to shoring up Rosselkhozbank, the bank which provides credit to the reviving agricultural sector. The amount of funds available is limited due to falling oil prices. The government of the United States, as authorized by the Emergency Economic Stabilization Act, announced plans to infuse funds into banks by purchasing equity interests in them, in effect, partial nationalization, as done in Britain. The Treasury secretary Henry M. Paulson Jr. met Friday in Washington with world financial leaders. A meeting of international financial leaders hosted by President Bush at the White House in Washington is planned on Saturday to attempt to coordinate global response to the financial crisis. The annual meetings of both the International Monetary Fund and World Bank was scheduled to be held in Washington over that weekend.

On Friday, October 10th, stock markets crashed across Europe and Asia. London, Paris and Frankfurt dropped 10% within an hour of trading and again when Wall Street opened for trading. Global markets have experienced their worst weeks since 1987 and some indices, S&P 500, since the Wall Street Crash of 1929.

On October 10th, within the first five minutes of the trading session on Wall Street, the Dow Jones Industrial Average plunged 697 points, falling below 7900 to its lowest level since March 17, 2003. Later in the afternoon, the Dow made violent swings back and forth across the breakeven line, toppling as much as 600 points and rising 322 points. The Dow ended the day losing only 128 points, or 1.49%. Trading on New York Stock Exchange closed for the week with the Dow at 8,451, down 1,874 points, or 18% for the week, and after 8 days of losses, 40% down from its record high October 9, 2007. Trading on Friday was marked by extreme volatility with a steep loss in the first few minutes followed by a rise into positive territory, closing down at the end of the day. In S&P100 some financial corporate showing signals upwards also. President George W. Bush reassured investors that the government will solve the financial crisis gripping world economies.

The bonds of the bankrupt Lehman Brothers were auctioned on Friday, October 10. They sold for a little over 8 cents on the dollar. Many of the bonds of Lehman Brothers were insured with credit default swaps. Apprehension that payments to the holders of Lehman bonds might severely damage the firms or hedge funds which issued the swaps proved unfounded, despite anticipated claims estimated to be several hundred billion dollars, as countervailing claims canceled each other out resulting in only 5.2 billion dollars changing hands.

As meetings proceeded with global financial leaders in Washington on Saturday, October 11, the United States government announced a change in emphasis in its rescue efforts from buying illiquid assets to recapitalizing banks, including strong banks, in exchange for preferred equity; and purchase of mortgages by Fannie Mae and Freddie Mac. These remedies can be put into effect quicker than the prior plan which was estimated to take a month to set into operation.

Week of October 12

On Sunday the British government was in negotiations with Royal Bank of Scotland, HBOS, Lloyds TSB and Barclays, major British banks, regarding recapitalization which would give the British government a substantial equity interest. An investment of more than 37 billion pounds is contemplated. Some purchases would be common stock with existing shareholders given a right of first refusal (the government would only purchase the shares if existing shareholders did not). Previously announced recapitalization plans contemplated only purchases of preferred equity without government participation in governance of the banks, however, as the financial emergency has rapidly developed, more aggressive measures are being advanced. On Sunday, October 12, European leaders, meeting in Paris, led by France and Germany, announced recapitalization plans for Europe's banks. Plans were announced to guarantee bank deposits for five years. European countries would finance their own rescue plans and tailor them to local conditions. Mechanisms are also planned to increase the availability of short term credit. The total rescue plan totaled €1 trillion. Australia and New Zealand also announced bank guarantee plans. On Monday, October 13, the markets were closed in Japan and the bond market was closed in the United States.

On Sunday, in Norway, which is not in the euro zone, the Norwegian cabinet in a hastily called press conference announced a US$57.4 billion (350 billion Norwegian kroner) plan of offering Norwegian banks new government bonds. This came three days ahead of Wednesday's hastened interest rate meeting at Norges Bank to decide whether or not to announce rate cuts similar to the coordinated cuts of October 8. Central bank Governor Svein Gjedrem also made critical comments about some of the measures that had been implemented already by other countries, among them the concerted rate cuts which he said "was a strong card, which had a two-hour impact". He further commented that "It's important to be careful with measures – so that one addresses the problems one really faces," and he also emphasized that acting at the right time was important saying "there are unusually many examples that show one can do too much too early." He cited the Icelandic government's takeover of banks as an example of quick action with no guarantee that the problems would be solved.

The G7 nations, at their meeting in Washington over the weekend pledged to "support systemically important financial institutions and prevent their failure". This decision is based on analysis of the consequences of the bankruptcy of Lehman Brothers which resulted in the loss of funds by other financial institutions. It is thought that those losses may have triggered a tightening of the credit crunch as banks ceased to lend to one another. No enforceable mechanism was created to support the pledge, but it is believed to extend to major firms such as Morgan Stanley and Goldman Sachs.

On October 13 stock markets worldwide rose with the Dow Jones industrial average showing a 400 point leap at the start of trading. At the close of trading the average was up 936 points, a record climb, up 11%, closing above 9,000 at 9,387. After announcement in France of a 320 billion euro rescue and guarantee plan, French CAC40 rose by 11.18% within the day. Germany announced a €400 billion plan. On Monday the International Monetary Fund offered possible technical and financial aid to Hungary which has suffered during the crisis due to the flight of investors to euro, Swiss franc, and dollar denominated investments. As in the rest of the world, on Monday stock prices rose on the Hungarian exchange and pressure on the national currency, the forint eased. The forint has dropped 30% against the dollar since July. The prime minister of Spain, Jose Luis Rodriguez Zapatero, announced that Spain would provide up to €100 billion of guarantees for new debt issued by commercial banks in 2008. This plan followed a meeting at the euro zone summit over the weekend to try to develop a coordinated effort to combat the credit crisis. The UK government started the nationalization process by injecting £37 billion in the nation's three largest banks. The UK government would end up owning a majority share in the Royal Bank of Scotland (RBS) and over a 40% share in Lloyds and HBOS. In return for the bailout, the banks agreed to cancel dividend payments until the loans are repaid, have board members appointed by the Treasury, and limit executive pay. The European Central Bank attempted to revive credit market by weekly injections of unlimited euro funds at an interest rate of 3.75%. The ECB president, Jean-Claude Trichet, was also contemplating relaxing the collateral standards to make the funds more accessible to banks. Following its European partners, Italy pledged to intervene as necessary to prevent any bank failures in its country. Finance minister, Giulio Tremonti, said Italy would guarantee new bank bonds of up to 5 years until the end of 2009 and the Bank of Italy would provide €40 billion in treasury bills to banks to refinance inferior assets that cannot be currently used as collateral. In coordination with other euro zone countries, the Dutch government announced that it would guarantee interbank lending up to €200 billion. This followed the set up of a €20 billion Dutch fund to help recapitalize banks and insurers.

On Tuesday the United States announced a plan to take an equity interest of $250 billion in US banks with 25 billion going to each of the four largest banks. The 9 largest banks in the US: Goldman Sachs, Morgan Stanley, J.P. Morgan, Bank of America, Merrill Lynch, Citigroup, Wells Fargo, Bank of New York Mellon and State Street were called in to a meeting on Monday morning and pressured to sign; all eventually agreed. The plan will be open to any bank for 30 days. The equity interests purchased by the government are preferred shares that pay 5% but rise to 9% after 5 years; it is expected that the companies will repurchase this interest when they can raise private capital to do so. The plan also includes an option allowing the government to purchase common stock according to a formula which could return substantial profit to the taxpayers should the stock price of the companies substantially appreciate. The total liability assumed is \$2.25 trillion including a \$1.5 trillion guarantee of new senior debt issued by banks and a \$500 billion guarantee of deposits in noninterest-bearing accounts (business accounts used to pay current obligations such as payroll). The theory is that with additional capitalization and the guarantees, banks will be willing to resume a normal lending pattern with each other and borrowers.

Also on that day, United Arab Emirates' (UAE) ministry of finance added a \$19 billion liquidity injection to domestic banks bringing the total dollars injected to \$32.7 billion. The UAE central bank offered 13.6 billion in liquidity to help domestic banks in September. To protect local deposits, the UAE government guaranteed all deposits and interbank lending. Japan announced a plan that will help steady the Japanese market and avoid the worse of the credit crisis. Among the measures included are lifting restrictions on companies buying back their shares, strengthening disclosure on short selling, and the temporary suspension of the sale of government-owned stocks. The Australian government unveiled a \$10.4 billion stimulus package. The Economic Security Strategy is designed to help pensioners, low and middle income families, and first time home buyers withstand the credit crisis and global economic slowdown. This followed the Australian government announcing that it would guarantee all bank deposits for three years, guarantee all term wholesaling funding by Australian banks in international markets and double its planned purchase of residential mortgage backed securities. The Icelandic stock exchange began trading again after a three day shutdown. The opening did not include Iceland's three largest banks which were nationalized last week.

On Wednesday, October 15, the London stock exchange FTSE 100 fell substantially, surrendering over 314 points to slip down 7.16 percent. The losses precipitated more losses in the U.S., as the Dow Jones Industrial Average suffered its largest drop in terms of percentage since 1987, falling over 733 points. The NASDAQ plunged almost eight and a half percent, and the Standard & Poor collapsed down over nine percent.

On October 16, a rescue plan was announced for the Swiss banks UBS and Credit Suisse. Recapitalization involved Swiss government funds, private investors, and the sovereign wealth fund of Qatar. A Swiss agency was set up to purchase and workout toxic funds. UBS had suffered substantial withdrawals by domestic Swiss depositors but still reported profits; Credit Suisse has reported losses. Most large banks in the United States continued to report large losses.

Week of October 19

Following a conference at Camp David over the weekend of October 18th and 19th attended by President Nicolas Sarkozy of France and José Manuel Barroso, President of the European Commission, President George W. Bush announced on Wednesday, October 22 that he would host an international conference of financial leaders on November 15 in Washington, D.C. Participants would be drawn from both the developed world and the developing world, including participants from the G20 industrial nations such as India, Brazil and China.

On Sunday, October 19 the government of the Netherlands bailed out ING, the Dutch bank, with a €10 billion capital rescue plan. On Monday the government of Belgium rescued the insurance company Ethias with a €1.5 billion capital injection. In Germany BayernLB has decided to apply for funds from the German €500 billion rescue program. Sweden announced formation of a 1.5 trillion kronor fund to support inter-bank lending and a 15 billion kronor capital injection plan. Swedish banks were reported to be increasingly affected by the financial crisis. An IMF rescue plan for Iceland was reported to be near finalization while Ukraine was reported to be in discussions with the IMF. Iceland was reported to have also received assistance from Denmark and Norway while Britain has offered a loan to support compensation of British depositors in failed Icelandic bank Landsbanki. On Monday France announced a €10.5 billion rescue plan for six of its largest banks, including Crédit Agricole, BNP and Société Générale.

Despite some improvement in the availability of credit, stock markets and weak currencies such as the British pound and the euro continued to decline worldwide during the week of October 19. Markets across Asia suffered particularly heavy losses while European markets experienced substantial losses too, but to a lesser extend compared to those in Asia. The Dow Industrials Index, on the other hand, experienced a week of extreme volatility with violent swings both upwards and downwards, eventually ending lower. The yen and the dollar showed particular strength with the yen rising with respect to the dollar. This "flight to quality" had baleful effects on the economies of all nations including the United States and Japan. On Wednesday, Pakistan joined Iceland, Hungary, Serbia and Ukraine and requested aid from the International Monetary Fund in dealing with severe balance of payments difficulties. Hungary, Russia, Ukraine, Pakistan, Turkey, South Africa, Argentina, Iceland, Estonia, Latvia, Lithuania, Romania and Bulgaria are all experiencing financial difficulties with others threatened. These countries did not hold securities based on subprime mortgages, but are affected by inability to borrow money, the credit crisis. Plans are under discussion to increase credit available to the IMF, perhaps to a trillion dollars.

On Friday, October 24, stock markets plummeted worldwide amidst growing fears among investors that a deep global recession is imminent if not already settled in. The panic was partly fueled by remarks made by Alan Greenspan that the crisis is "a one in a century credit tsunami" and by comments made by Gordon Brown during a speech, admitting essentially that Great Britain is already in recession mode. Following the trend, the US stock markets also fell sharply on opening and ended with the Dow Industrial Index down 312 points. Friday and Saturday (October 24 and 25) the 7th Asia-Europe Meeting was held in Beijing with the European Union meeting Asian states in an attempt to discuss a common approach ahead of the Emergency International Meeting that is scheduled to take place in Washington on November 15. No specific recommendations to solve the crisis were developed.

Week of October 26

On Sunday, October 26, Hungary and Ukraine made tentative arrangements with the International Monetary Fund for emergency aid packages. In Poland the value of stocks has fallen 50% for the year and the zloty, the Polish currency, has fallen against both the dollar and the euro. The crisis has affected South Africa, Brazil and Turkey. South Africa was particularly affected by a dramatic drop in the price of platinum, a commodity used in automobile manufacturing. In addition to Iceland, Ukraine and Hungary, Belarus and Pakistan are also engaged in emergency discussions with the IMF. Pakistan has what is described as a "growing balance of payments crisis". In the Gulf states, impacted by the falling price of oil and a drop in equities prices of 40% for the year, the Gulf Cooperation Council met in Riyadh on Saturday to discuss a coordinated response to the crisis.

On Monday, October 27, Hong Kong stocks crashed, losing more than 12% of their value while in Japan, the Nikkei 225 Index plummeted by 6.4% to its lowest level since 1982. European stock markets showed mixed results. After suffering an initial drop, the Dow Jones Industrial Average was in slightly positive territory for much of the trading day but eventually closed down 203 points. Oil futures continued to decline and the yen continued to rise against all other currencies. There was consideration given by both the G7 and the Japanese government to take measures to support other currencies as against the yen.

In a second round of recapitalization, the U.S. Treasury has funded 22 banks with 38 billion dollars. The list of banks aided was confidential, but some banks including BB&T, Capital One, SunTrust Banks, City National Bank, Comerica, First Niagara Bank, Huntington Bancshares, Northern Trust, State Street Corporation, UCBH Holdings, First Horizon National Corporation, PNC Financial Services (buyer of the National City Corporation), Regions Financial Corporation,

Valley National Bancorp KeyBank, and Washington Federal Savings said they would receive government money. Fifth Third Bank announced that they would apply. Criteria for funding was based on the strength of the bank with stronger banks with higher CAMELS ratings having a greater chance of being offered aid. The American Bankers Association stated that due to restrictions on salaries and payment of dividends that some U.S. banks may not participate. Another concern was that acceptance of the recapitalization plan might give a false signal that a bank was troubled.

On Tuesday, October 28, stocks rose dramatically worldwide in anticipation of rate cuts by central banks. In the U.S. the Dow Industrial Average rose 10.8%, closing at over 9000. On Wednesday, October 29, markets in the U.S. closed down slightly despite announcement by the Federal Open Market Committee of a reduction in the federal funds rate 50 points to 1 percent. Markets in the U.S. were up Thursday and Friday, closing up for the week, cutting losses to the Dow Industrial Average during October to 17%, down 30% for the year.

In Russia the $50 billion rescue program administered by the state development bank Vnesheconombank (VEB) is assisting Russian firms controlled by Russian oligarchs who gave ownership of portions of their companies as security for loans from Western financial institutions. Recipients include Oleg Deripaska of Rusal owner of Norilsk Nickel and Mikhail Fridman of Alfa Group whose assets VimpelCom and TNK-BP were threatened. Stock markets in Russian have crashed, down 70% and there is lack of faith in its currency the ruble. Despite significant foreign reserves from the sale of oil, Russia is now faced with sharply reduced commodities prices.

In Asia Japan announced its second economic stimulus plan of $51 billion on Thursday, October 30. Hong Kong and Taiwan cut interest rates while an interest cut to .3% was announced by the Bank of Japan on Friday. Also on Thursday the Federal Reserve established a $30 billion currency swap line with South Korea and Singapore as well as Brazil and Mexico.

JPMorgan Chase, the largest bank in the United States, announced that it would work with homeowners who demonstrate a willingness to pay their mortgages by reducing interest payments or principal. Counseling centers are planned for troubled areas. Washington Mutual, and EMC Mortgage Corporation, a loan servicing company, acquired by JPMorgan, will be included. Bank of America has announced a similar program, as has Countrywide Financial as the result of a court settlement.

Week of November 2

Reports of Economic Activity

October sales of car and light trucks in the United States fell precipitously in October with General Motors falling 45%, Ford falling 30%, Chrysler falling 35%, Toyota falling 23%, Honda falling 25%, and Nissan falling 33%. Much of the falloff in sales was attributable to customers being unable to arrange financing. In the UK, car sales fell by 23% in October, following a 21% decline in September.(Except for Wal-Mart, which posted a slight gain, retail sales were off during October), 2008 as compared with October, 2007 in the United states with some moderate priced stores reporting double digit decreases.

Employment reports released by the Labor Department on Friday, November 7, showed that about 500,000 jobs were lost in the United States during September and October, 2008 with unemployment rising to 6.5% at the end of October. The September figure was revised to 284,000 from the initial 159,000 reported. The initial October figure was 240,000. This is a substantial acceleration from the average 75,000 jobs lost each month since the beginning of 2008. It is anticipated by experts that unemployment will rise to 8% by the middle of 2009.

Events

Amid predictions of a "deep recession" in the UK and the Eurozone, on Thursday, November 6, the Bank of England, citing a reduced danger of inflation due to falling commodities prices, lowered its base rate by 1.5%, from 4.5% to 3%.This was accompanied by a 50 basis point drop in the base rate to 3.25% by the European Central Bank (ECB).

On November 6, the IMF at Washington. D.C., predicted for 2009 a wordwide -0.3% decrease of the BIP for the developed economies (-0.7% for the USA and -0.8% for Germany).

Week of November 8

On Sunday, November 8, the People's Republic of China announced a 586 billion dollar domestic stimulus package for the remainder of 2008, 2009, and 2010. Economic growth has slowed in China with sharp drops in property and stock values. The money from the stimulus package will be spent on upgrading infrastructure, particularly roads, railways, airports and the power grids throughout the country and raise rural incomes via land reform. Also spending will be made on social welfare projects such as affordable housing and environmental protection.

Key Risk Indicators in September 2008

The TED spread – an indicator of credit risk – increased dramatically during September 2008.Key risk indicators became highly volatile during September 2008, a factor leading the U.S. government to pass the Emergency Economic Stabilization Act of 2008. The "TED spread" is a measure of credit risk for interbank lending. It is the difference between: 1) the risk-free three-month U.S. treasury bill rate; and 2) the three-month London InterBank Offered Rate (LIBOR), which represents the rate at which banks typically lend to each other. A higher spread indicates banks perceive each other as riskier counterparties. The t-bill is considered "risk-free" because the full faith and credit of the U.S. government is behind it. Theoretically, the government could just print money so that the principal is fully repaid at maturity. The TED spread reached record levels in late September 2008. The diagram indicates that the Treasury yield movement was a more significant driver than the changes in LIBOR. A three month t-bill yield so close to zero means that people are willing to forgo interest just to keep their money (principal) safe for three months – a very high level of risk aversion and indicative of tight lending conditions. Driving this change were investors shifting funds from money market funds (generally considered nearly risk free but paying a slightly higher rate of return than t-bills) and other investment types to t-bills. These issues are consistent with the September 2008 aspects of the subprime mortgage crisis which prompted the Emergency Economic Stabilization Act of 2008 signed into law by the U.S. President on October 2, 2008.

In addition, an increase in LIBOR means that financial instruments with variable interest terms are increasingly expensive. For example, car loans and credit card interest rates are often tied to LIBOR; some estimate as much as $150 trillion in loans and derivatives are tied to LIBOR. Higher interest rates place additional downward pressure on consumption, increasing the risk of recession.

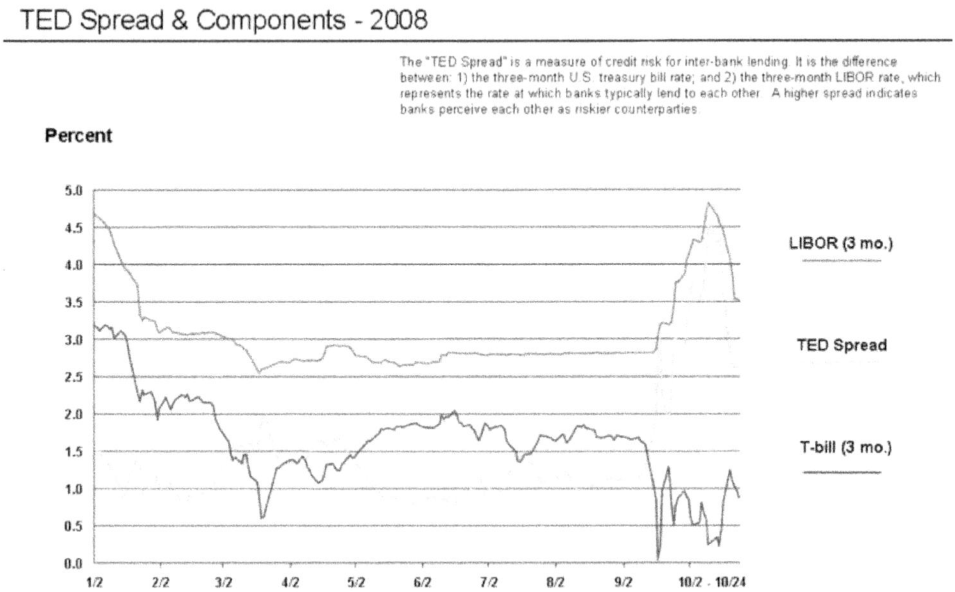

Picture 59: The TED spread – an indicator of credit risk – increased dramatically during September 2008

Global Responses

Responses by the UK and US in proportion to their GDPs on September 15, 2008 China cut its interest rate for the first time since 2002. Indonesia reduced its overnight repo rate, at which commercial banks can borrow overnight funds from the central bank, by two percentage points to 10.25 percent. The Reserve Bank of Australia injected nearly $1.5 billion into the banking system, nearly three times as much as the market's estimated requirement. The Reserve Bank of India added almost $1.32 billion, through a refinance operation, its biggest in at least a month.

In Taiwan, the central bank on September 16, 2008 said it would cut its required reserve ratios for the first time in eight years. The central bank added $3.59 billion into the foreign-currency interbank market the same day. Bank of Japan pumped $29.3 billion into the financial system on September 17, 2008 and the Reserve Bank of Australia added $3.45 billion the same day. The European Central Bank injected $99.8 billion in a one-day money-market auction. The Bank of England pumped in $36 billion. Altogether, central banks throughout the world added more than $200 billion from the beginning of the week to September 17.

On September 29, 2008 the Belgian, Luxembourg and Dutch authorities partially nationalized Fortis. The German government bailed out Hypo Real Estate.

U.S. Responses

The Federal Reserve, Treasury, and Securities and Exchange Commission took several steps on September 19 to intervene in the crisis. To stop the potential run on money market mutual funds, the Treasury also announced on September 19 a new $50 billion program to insure the investments, similar to the Federal Deposit Insurance Corporation (FDIC) program. Part of the announcements included temporary exceptions to section 23A and 23B (Regulation W), allowing financial groups to more easily share funds within their group. The exceptions would expire on January 30, 2009, unless extended by the Federal Reserve Board. The Securities and Exchange Commission announced termination of short-selling of 799 financial stocks, as well as action against naked short selling, as part of its reaction to the mortgage crisis.

Loans to Banks for Asset-backed Commercial Paper

During the week ending September 19, 2008, money market mutual funds had begun to experience significant withdrawals of funds by investors. This created a significant risk because money market funds are integral to the ongoing financing of corporations of all types. Individual investors lend money to money market funds, which then provide the funds to corporations in exchange for corporate short-term securities called asset-backed commercial paper (ABCP). However, a potential bank run had begun on certain money market funds. If this situation had worsened, the ability of major corporations to secure needed short-term financing through ABCP issuance would have been significantly affected. To assist with liquidity throughout the system, the Treasury and Federal Reserve Bank announced that banks could obtain funds via the Federal Reserve's Discount Window using ABCP as collateral.

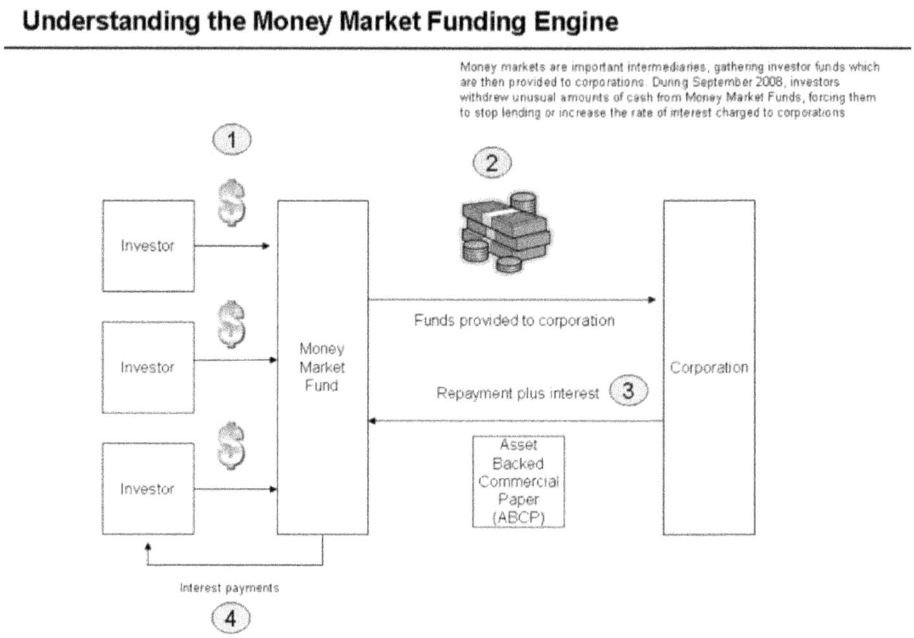

Federal Reserve Actions to lower Interest Rates and stimulate the Economy

Federal reserve rates changes (Just data after January 1, 2008)					
Date	**Discount rate**	**Discount rate**	**Discount rate**	**Fed funds**	**Fed funds rate**
		Primary	**Secondary**		
	rate change	**new interest rate**	**new interest rate**	**rate change**	**new interest rate**
Oct 8, 2008*	-.50%	1.75%	2.25%	-.50%	1.50%

Apr 30, 2008	-.25%	2.25%	2.75%	-.25%	2.00%
Mar 18, 2008	-.75%	2.50%	3.00%	-.75%	2.25%
Mar 16, 2008	-.25%	3.25%	3.75%		
Jan 30, 2008	-.50%	3.50%	4.00%	-.50%	3.00%
Jan 22, 2008	-.75%	4.00%	4.50%	-.75%	3.50%

* Part of a coordinated global rate cut of 50 basis point by main central banks.

Legislation

The Secretary of the United States Treasury, Henry Paulson and President George W. Bush proposed legislation for the government to purchase up to US$700 billion of "troubled mortgage-related assets" from financial firms in hopes of improving confidence in the mortgage-backed securities markets and the financial firms participating in it. Discussion, hearings and meetings among legislative leaders and the administration later made clear that the the proposal would undergo significant change before it could be approved by Congress. On October 1, a revised compromise version was approved by the Senate with a 74-25 vote, the sole Senator not to vote was cancer-stricken Ted Kennedy of Massachusetts. The bill, HR1424 was passed by the House on October 3, 2008 and signed into law.

Fed Response

In an effort to increase available funds for commercial banks and lower the fed funds rate, on September 29 the U.S. Federal Reserve announced plans to double its Term Auction Facility to $300 billion. Because there appeared to be a shortage of U.S. dollars in Europe at that time, the Federal Reserve also announced it would increase its swap facilities with foreign central banks from $290 billion to $620 billion.

UK Responses

On the October 8, 2008 the British Government announced a bank rescue package of around £500 billion ($850 billion). The plan comprises three parts: Firstly £200 billion will be made available to the banks in the Bank of England's Special Liquidity scheme. Secondly the Government will increase the banks' market capitalization, through the Bank Recapitalization Fund, with an initial £25 billion and another £25 billion to be provided if needed. Thirdly the Government will temporarily underwrite any eligible lending between British banks up to around £250 billion.

2008 Russian Financial Crisis

The 2008 Russian financial crisis is an ongoing crisis on Russian markets, as nervousness over the global banking crisis has been compounded by political fears after the war with Georgia, as well as renewed concern about state intervention in corporations of strategic interest. Russia's economy is also heavily dependent on energy prices, especially oil which has lost more than half of its value since its record peak of USD 147 on 11 July 2008.

Background

Russia is a major exporter of commodities such as oil and metals, its equity market has been hit hard by the decline in the price of many commodities. In addition, investors have pulled billions of dollars out of Russia on concerns over escalating geopolitical tensions with the West following the military conflict between Georgia and Russia, as well as concerns about state interference in the economy. Those concerns were underscored in July by Prime Minister Vladimir Putin's criticism of steel company Mechel which wiped out billions of dollars of its market capitalization. By September 2008, the RTS stock index plunged almost 54%, making it one of the worst performing markets in the world. Compounding the volatile situation in Russia's financial system has been also involvement in the US subprime mortgage crisis with the Russian Central Bank owning US$100 Billion of mortgage-backed securities in the two American mortgage giants Fannie Mae and Freddie Mac that were taken over by the US government that most likely will have to be written off.

Members of the government of Russia, including President Dmitry Medvedev, Prime Minister Vladimir Putin and Finance Minister Alexey Kudrin, fully attribute the decline in the Russian stock market to the impact of the liquidity crisis in the United States and contend that the crisis in Russia has little if anything to do with internal problems in its economy and the government policies. However, many analysts, including Andrei Illarionov, former economic policy adviser to then-President Vladimir Putin, claim that in Russia the crisis in the stock market was deepened dramatically by internal factors, including concerns over state interference in the economy fueled in June by Putin's criticism of Mechel and the conflict over TNK-BP, lack of transparency in banking and political risks associated with escalating geopolitical tensions following the 2008 South Ossetia war in August. Swedish Foreign minister Carl Bildt said on 17 September that the current Russian financial crisis is "obviously more worrying" than the ongoing subprime mortgage crisis in view of the political development in Russia.

According to the Wall Street Journal, as the Russian market declined in September, conspiracy theories circulated in Russia among the leadership that the U.S. government allegedly incited American investors to withdraw their capitals from Russia, punishing Moscow for the recent war in Georgia.

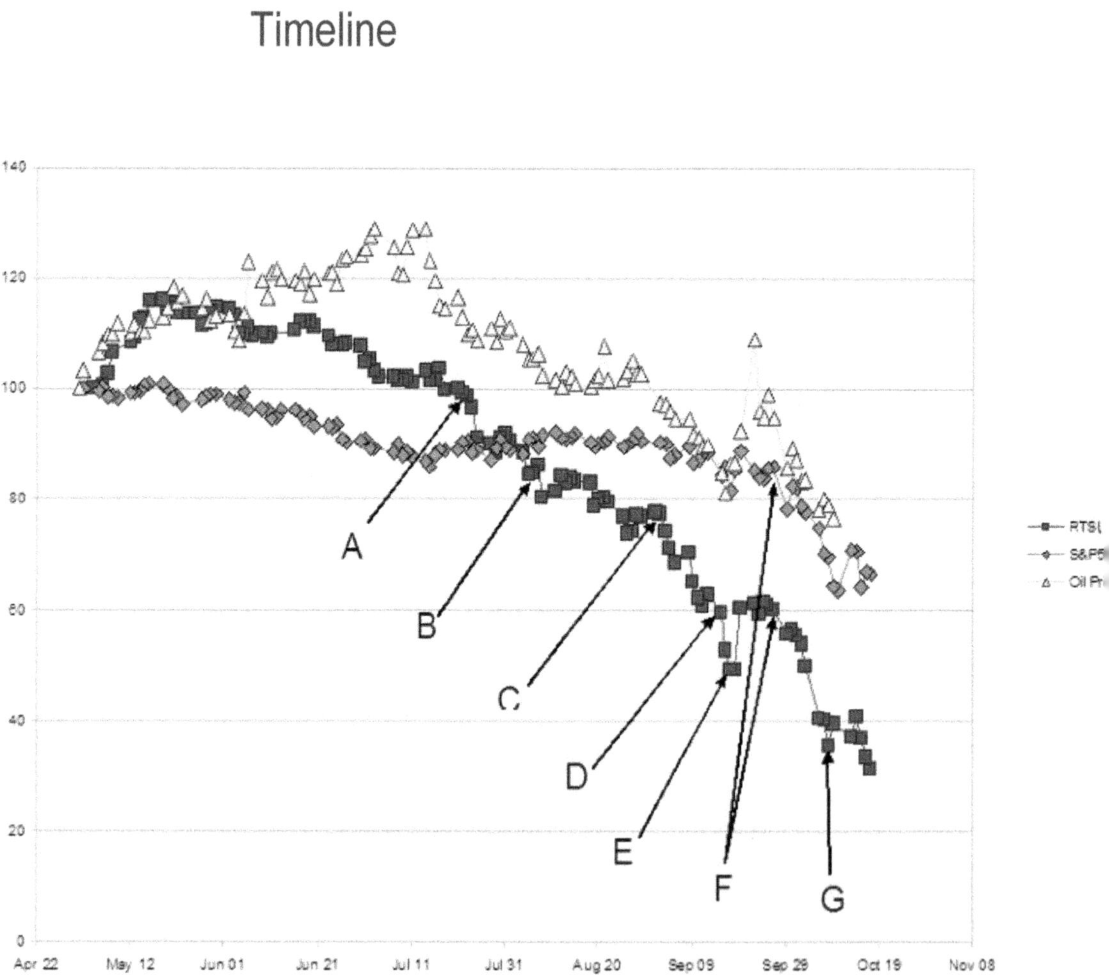

Picture 60: Timeline of the Russian Financial Crisis

Major Russian stock market RTS Index with S&P 500 and Oil Spot Prices. All data are in percentages to 1 May 2008 values.

- A - Vladmir Putin criticises Mechel;
- B - 2008 South Ossetia war starts;
- C - Recognition of Abkhazia and South Ossetia by Russia;
- D - Alexei Kudrin "no systematic crisis" speech;
- E - measures to save major banks are adopted by the Russian government;
- F - Global financial crisis of September–October 2008;
- G - President Dmitri Medvedev announced additional bailout financing.

24 July

Mechel's stock plunged by almost 38 percent on 24 July 2008 after Russia's Prime Minister Vladimir Putin criticized its CEO Igor Zyuzin, and accused the company of selling resources to Russia at higher prices than those charged to foreign countries. The comments, which raised fears of another attack similar to that made on Yukos in 2004, contrasted sharply with previous efforts by President Dmitry Medvedev to improve Russia's reputation as an investor-friendly country.

25 July

On the following day, Mechel issued a contrite statement promising full cooperation with federal authorities, while share values rebounded by nearly 15 percent.

28 July

On 28 July presidential aide Arkady Dvorkovich then sought to restore calm, declaring that all parties would "act in a civilized way," and confirming that Mechel was cooperating with antitrust authorities. Just hours later, however, Putin announced that Mechel had been avoiding taxes, by using foreign subsidiaries to sell its products internationally. His renewed attack caused share prices to tumble once more—this time by almost 33 percent.

16 September

Russia's most liquid stock exchange MICEX and the dollar-denominated RTS were suspended trade for one hour after the worst one-day fall in 10 years as Finance Minister Alexei Kudrin reassured markets there was no "systemic" crisis.

On 15 September-16 the KIT Finance brokerage failed to pay off its debt, signalling problems in Russia's financial sector. On 8 October the Russian Railways and Alrosa agreed to acquire a 90% stake in KIT Finance.

17 September

Trading was suspended for the second day in succession on Russia's two main stock exchanges (MICEX and RTS) after shares fell dramatically, forcing the Federal Financial Markets Service to intervene.

Russia's government lent the country's three biggest banks, Sberbank, VTB Bank and Gazprombank, as much as 1.13 trillion rubles ($44 billion) for at least three months to boost liquidity.

On 17 September the Central Bank of the Russian Federation decided to lower the reserve requirement ratio to improve liquidity supply. The decision came into effect on 18 September.

On 17 September Finance Minister Alexey Kudrin sought assurances from U.S. Treasury Secretary Henry Paulson that the U.S. didn't play politics with Russia in the crisis.

18 September

Trading is suspended for the third day in succession on Russia's two main stock exchanges amidst fear of financial collapse. News agencies are quoting Russia's finance minister Alexei Kudrin as saying trading on Russian exchanges won't resume until 19 September 2008.

Officials at MICEX stock exchange describe conditions in the Russian markets as "extraordinary"

Russia is facing its worst stock market decline in a decade mainly because of a confidence crisis rather than liquidity problems, Deputy Finance Minister Pyotr Kazakevich says.

Russian President Dmitry Medvedev orders ministers to inject another 500 billion roubles of funds from the state budget into the markets and pledges that the financial system would receive "all necessary support".

29 September

On 29 September Vladimir Putin announced several new measures that would be taken to mitigate the crisis. In order to pay off its debt to foreign creditors under the loans raised before 25 September, any Russian bank or company is now entitled to obtain a loan through Vneshekonombank, an institution which is used by the Russian government to support and develop the Russian economy and to manage Russian state debts. Vneshekonombank will for that purpose be provided with up to $50 billion by the Central Bank. The Central Bank is also recommended to grant unsecured stabilization loans to certain banks during the current crisis.

6 October

On 6 October the MICEX and RTS crashed by 18.6% and 19.1% respectively. The losses forced the Federal Financial Markets Service to suspend the stocks three times. The decreases in other world markets on that day were considerable, but less dramatic than in Russia.

7 October

The MICEX and RTS trading is suspended. Russian companies have augmented in price at London LSE.

President Medvedev announces an additional $36 billion for banks on top of the $150 billion approved in September.

Meanwhile, Russian ambassador to Iceland, Victor I. Tatarintsev, announces that Iceland will receive a €4 billion loan from Russia to mitigate the 2008 Icelandic financial crisis. The loan will be given across three or four years, and the interest rates will be 30 to 50 points above LIBOR. Prime minister Geir Haarde had been investigating the possibility of a loan provided by Russia since the mid-summer. Iceland's Central bank Governor Davíð Oddsson later clarified that the loan was still being negotiated.

8 October

The MICEX and RTS plunged 14.4% and 11.3% respectively, trading on the markets was halted until 10 October, respectively.

9 October

The MICEX trading is resumed ahead of schedule, and the stock market rises 14.7%.

10 October

Due to decreases in American and Asian markets, the Federal Financial Markets Service decided not to open trading on Friday.

23 October

Standard & Poor's changes the long-term outlook on the sovereign credit ratings of Russia from stable to negative, warning of the costs of bailing out troubled banks and a rising risk of a budget deficit in 2009. It also lowered Russia's Transfer and Convertibility (T&C) assessment to BBB+ from A-. At the same time, the 'BBB+' long-term foreign currency, the 'A-' long-term local currency ratings and the short-term ratings of A-2 were affirmed.

Stock Exchanges

About Stock Exchanges

A stock exchange, securities exchange or (in Europe) bourse is a corporation or mutual organization which provides "trading" facilities for stock brokers and traders, to trade stocks and other securities. Stock exchanges also provide facilities for the issue and redemption of securities as well as other financial instruments and capital events including the payment of income and dividends. The securities traded on a stock exchange include: Shares issued by companies, unit trusts and other pooled investment products and bonds. To be able to trade a security on a certain stock exchange, it has to be listed there. Usually there is a central location at least for recordkeeping, but trade is less and less linked to such a physical place, as modern markets are electronic networks, which gives them advantages of speed and cost of transactions. Trade on an exchange is by members only. The initial offering of stocks and bonds to investors is by definition done in the primary market and subsequent trading is done in the secondary market. A stock exchange is often the most important component of a stock market. Supply and demand in stock markets is driven by various factors which, as in all free markets, affect the price of stocks.

There is usually no compulsion to issue stock via the stock exchange itself, nor must stock be subsequently traded on the exchange. Such trading is said to be off exchange or over-the-counter. This is the usual way that bonds are traded. Increasingly, stock exchanges are part of a global market for securities.

History of Stock Exchanges

In 11th century France the courtiers de change were concerned with managing and regulating the debts of agricultural communities on behalf of the banks. As these men also traded in debts, they could be called the first brokers. For a more detailed history and the development of stock exchanges see Markets Section.

The Role of Stock Exchanges

Stock exchanges have multiple roles in the economy, this may include the following:

1. Raising capital for businesses:
   The Stock Exchange provides companies with the facility to raise capital for expansion through selling shares to the investing public.

2. Mobilizing savings for investment:
   When people draw their savings and invest in shares, it leads to a more rational allocation of resources because funds, which could have been consumed, or kept in idle deposits with banks, are mobilized and redirected to promote business activity with benefits for several economic sectors such as agriculture, commerce and industry, resulting in a stronger economic growth and higher productivity levels and firms.

3. Facilitating company growth:
   Companies view acquisitions as an opportunity to expand product lines, increase distribution channels, hedge against volatility, increase its market share, or acquire other necessary business assets. A takeover bid or a merger agreement through the stock market is one of the simplest and most common ways for a company to grow by acquisition or fusion.

4. Redistribution of wealth:
   Stocks exchanges do not exist to redistribute wealth. However, both casual and professional stock investors, through dividends and stock price increases that may result in capital gains, will share in the wealth of profitable businesses.

5. Corporate governance:
   By having a wide and varied scope of owners, companies generally tend to improve on their management standards and efficiency in order to satisfy the demands of these shareholders and the more stringent rules for public corporations imposed by public stock exchanges and the government. Consequently, it is alleged that public companies (companies that are owned by shareholders who are members of the general public and trade shares on public exchanges) tend to have better management records than privately-held companies (those companies where shares are not publicly traded, often owned by the company founders and/or their families and heirs, or otherwise by a small group of investors). However, some well-documented cases are known where it is alleged that there has been considerable slippage in corporate governance on the part of some public companies. The dot-com bubble in the early 2000s, and the subprime mortgage crisis in 2007-08, are classical examples of corporate mismanagement. Companies like Pets.com (2000), Enron Corporation (2001), One.Tel (2001), Sunbeam (2001),

Webvan (2001), Adelphia (2002), MCI WorldCom (2002), Parmalat (2003), Fannie Mae (2008), Freddie Mac (2008), Lehman Brothers (2008), were among the most widely scrutinized by the media.

6. Creating investment opportunities for small investors:
   As opposed to other businesses that require huge capital outlay, investing in shares is open to both the large and small stock investors because a person buys the number of shares they can afford. Therefore the Stock Exchange provides the opportunity for small investors to own shares of the same companies as large investors.

7. Government capital-raising for development projects:
   Governments at various levels may decide to borrow money in order to finance infrastructure projects such as sewage and water treatment works or housing estates by selling another category of securities known as bonds. These bonds can be raised through the Stock Exchange whereby members of the public buy them, thus loaning money to the government. The issuance of such bonds can obviate the need to directly tax the citizens in order to finance development, although by securing such bonds with the full faith and credit of the government instead of with collateral, the result is that the government must tax the citizens or otherwise raise additional funds to make any regular coupon payments and refund the principal when the bonds mature.

8. Barometer of the economy:
   At the stock exchange, share prices rise and fall depending, largely, on market forces. Share prices tend to rise or remain stable when companies and the economy in general show signs of stability and growth. An economic recession, depression, or financial crisis could eventually lead to a stock market crash. Therefore the movement of share prices and in general of the stock indexes can be an indicator of the general trend in the economy.

Major Stock Exchanges

Twenty Major Stock Exchanges In The World: Market Capitalization & Year-to-date Turnover at the end of October 2007:

Region	Stock Exchange	Market Value	Total Turnover	Share

		(trillions of US dollars)	(trillions of US dollars)
Africa	JSE Securities Exchange	$0.940	$0.349
Americas	NASDAQ	$4.39	$12.4
Americas	São Paulo Stock Exchange	$1.40	$0.476
Americas	Toronto Stock Exchange	$2.29	$1.36
Americas/Europe	NYSE Euronext	$20.7	$28.7
Asia-Pacific	Australian Securities Exchange	$1.45	$1.00
South Asia	Bombay Stock Exchange	$1.61	$0.263
Asia-Pacific	Hong Kong Stock Exchange	$2.97	$1.70
Asia-Pacific	Korea Exchange	$1.26	$1.66
South Asia	National Stock Exchange of India	$1.46	$0.564
Asia-Pacific	Shanghai Stock Exchange	$3.02	$3.56
Asia-Pacific	Shenzhen Stock Exchange	$0.741	$1.86
Asia-Pacific	Tokyo Stock Exchange	$4.63	$5.45
Europe	Frankfurt Stock Exchange (Deutsche Börse)	$2.12	$3.64

Europe	London Stock Exchange	\$4.21	\$9.14
Europe	Madrid Stock Exchange (Bolsas y Mercados Españoles)	\$1.83	\$2.49
Europe	Milan Stock Exchange (Borsa Italiana)	\$1.13	\$1.98
Europe	Moscow Interbank Currency Exchange (MICEX)	\$0.965	\$0.488
Europe	Nordic Stock Exchange Group OMX	\$1.38	\$1.60
Europe	Swiss Exchange	\$1.33	\$1.58

Sources: World Federation of Exchanges - Statistics/Monthly
Remarks: There are 2 pending major mergers: NASDAQ with OMX; and London Stock Exchange with Milan Stock Exchange

Listing Requirements

Listing requirements are the set of conditions imposed by a given stock exchange upon companies that want to be listed on that exchange. Such conditions sometimes include minimum number of shares outstanding, minimum market capitalization, and minimum annual income.

Requirements by Stock Exchange

Companies have to meet the requirements of the exchange in order to have their stocks and shares listed and traded there, but requirements vary by stock exchange:

- London Stock Exchange: The main market of the London Stock Exchange has requirements for a minimum market capitalization (£700,000), three years of audited financial statements, minimum public float (25 per cent) and sufficient working capital for at least 12 months from the date of listing.

- NASDAQ Stock Exchange: To be listed on the NASDAQ a company must have issued at least 1.25 million shares of stock worth at least $70 million and must have earned more than $11 million over the last three years.
- New York Stock Exchange: To be listed on the New York Stock Exchange (NYSE), for example, a company must have issued at least a million shares of stock worth $100 million and must have earned more than $10 million over the last three years.
- Bombay Stock Exchange: Bombay Stock Exchange (BSE) has requirements for a minimum market capitalization of Rs.250 Million and minimum public float equivalent to Rs.100 Million.

Ownership

Stock exchanges originated as mutual organizations, owned by its member stock brokers. There has been a recent trend for stock exchanges to demutualize, where the members sell their shares in an initial public offering. In this way the mutual organization becomes a corporation, with shares that are listed on a stock exchange. Examples are Australian Securities Exchange (1998), Euronext (merged with New York Stock Exchange), NASDAQ (2002), the New York Stock Exchange (2005), Bolsas y Mercados Españoles, and the São Paulo Stock Exchange (2007). The Shenzhen and Shanghai stock exchanges can been characterized as quasi-state institutions insofar as they were created by government bodies in China and their leading personnel are directly appointed by the China Securities Regulatory Commission.

Other Types of Exchanges

In the 19th century, exchanges were opened to trade forward contracts on commodities. Exchange traded forward contracts are called futures contracts. These commodity exchanges later started offering future contracts on other products, such as interest rates and shares, as well as options contracts. They are now generally known as futures exchanges.

The Future of Stock Exchanges

The future of stock trading appears to be electronic, as competition is continually growing between the remaining traditional New York Stock Exchange specialist system against the relatively new, all Electronic Communications Networks, or ECNs. ECNs point to their speedy execution of large block trades, while specialist system proponents cite the role of specialists in maintaining orderly markets, especially under extraordinary conditions or for special types of orders.

The ECNs contend that an array of special interests profit at the expense of investors in even the most mundane exchange-directed trades. Machine-based systems, they argue, are much more efficient, because they speed up the execution mechanism and eliminate the need to deal with an intermediary.

Historically, the 'market' (which, as noted, encompasses the totality of stock trading on all exchanges) has been slow to respond to technological innovation, thus allowing growing pure speculation to continue. Conversion to all-electronic trading could erode/eliminate the trading profits of floor specialists and the NYSE's "upstairs traders", who, like in September and October 2008, earned billions of dollars selling shares they did not have, and days later buying the same amount of shares, but maybe 15 % cheaper, so these shares could be handed to their buyers, therebuy making the market fall deeply.

William Lupien, founder of the Instinet trading system and the OptiMark system, has been quoted as saying "I'd definitely say the ECNs are winning... Things happen awfully fast once you reach the tipping point. We're now at the tipping point."

One example of improved efficiency of ECNs is the prevention of front running, by which manual Wall Street traders use knowledge of a customer's incoming order to place their own orders so as to benefit from the perceived change to market direction that the introduction of a large order will cause. By executing large trades at lightning speed without manual intervention, ECNs make impossible this illegal practice, for which several NYSE floor brokers were investigated and severely fined in recent years. Under the specialist system, when the market sees a large trade in a name, other buyers are immediately able to look to see how big the trader is in the name, and make inferences about why s/he is selling or buying. All traders who are quick enough are able to use that information to anticipate price movements.

ECNs have changed ordinary stock transaction processing (like brokerage services before them) into a commodity-type business. ECNs could regulate the fairness of initial public offerings (IPOs), oversee Hambrecht's OpenIPO process, or measure the effectiveness of securities research and use transaction fees to subsidize small- and mid-cap research efforts.

Some, however, believe the answer will be some combination of the best of technology and "upstairs trading" — in other words, a hybrid model.

Trading 25,000 shares of General Electric stock (2007 quote: $34.76; recent volume: 44,760,300) would be a relatively simple e-commerce transaction; trading 100 shares of Berkshire Hathaway Class A stock (recent quote: $139,700.00; recent volume: 850) may never be. The choice of system should be clear (but always that of the trader), based on the characteristics of the security to be traded.

Even with ECNs forming an important part of a national market system, opportunities presumably remain to profit from the spread between the bid and offer price. That is especially true for investment managers that direct huge trading volume, and own a stake in an ECN or specialist firm. For example, in its individual stock-brokerage accounts, "Fidelity Investments runs 29% of its undesignated orders in NYSE-listed stocks, and 37% of its undesignated market orders through the Boston Stock Exchange, where an affiliate controls a specialist post."

List of Stock Exchanges

This is an active list of stock exchanges. Those futures exchanges that also offer trading in securities besides trading in futures contracts are listed both here and the list of futures exchanges.

The following table shows the twenty major stock exchanges in the world: Market Capitalization & Year-to-date Turnover at the end of October 2007

Region	**Stock Exchange**	**Market Value (trillions of US dollars)**	**Total Share Turnover (trillions of US dollars)**
Africa	JSE Securities Exchange	\$0.940	\$0.349
Americas	NASDAQ	\$4.39	\$12.4
Americas	São Paulo Stock Exchange	\$1.40	\$0.476
Americas	Toronto Stock Exchange	\$2.29	\$1.36
Americas/Europe	NYSE Euronext	\$20.7	\$28.7
Asia-Pacific	Australian Securities Exchange	\$1.45[3]	\$1.00[3]
South Asia	Bombay Stock Exchange	\$1.61	\$0.263
Asia-Pacific	Hong Kong Stock Exchange	\$2.97	\$1.70
Asia-Pacific	Korea Exchange	\$1.26	\$1.66

South Asia	National Stock Exchange of India	\$1.46	\$0.564
Asia-Pacific	Shanghai Stock Exchange	\$3.02	\$3.56
Asia-Pacific	Shenzhen Stock Exchange	\$0.741	\$1.86
Asia-Pacific	Tokyo Stock Exchange	\$4.63	\$5.45
Europe	Frankfurt Stock Exchange (Deutsche Börse)	\$2.12	\$3.64
Europe	London Stock Exchange	\$4.21	\$9.14
Europe	Madrid Stock Exchange (Bolsas y Mercados Españoles)	\$1.83	\$2.49
Europe	Milan Stock Exchange (Borsa Italiana)	\$1.13	\$1.98
Europe	Moscow Interbank Currency Exchange (MICEX)	\$0.965[2]	\$0.488[2]
Europe	Nordic Stock Exchange Group OMX[1]	\$1.38	\$1.60
Europe	Swiss Exchange	\$1.33	\$1.58

Note 1: includes the Copenhagen, Helsinki, Iceland, Stockholm, Tallinn, Riga and Vilnius Stock Exchanges
Note 2: latest data available is at the end of June 2007
Note 3: latest data available is at the end of September 2007
Sources: World Federation of Exchanges - Statistics/Monthly
Remarks: There are 2 pending major mergers: NASDAQ with OMX; and London Stock Exchange with Milan Stock Exchange

American Stock Exchange

The American Stock Exchange (AMEX) is an American stock exchange situated in New York. AMEX was a mutual organization, owned by its members. Until 1953 it was known as the New York Curb Exchange. On January 17, 2008 NYSE Euronext announced it would acquire the American Stock Exchange for $260 million in stock. On October 1, 2008, NYSE Euronext completed acquisition of the American Stock Exchange. Before the closing of the acquisition, NYSE Euronext announced that the Exchange will be integrated with Alternext European small-cap exchange and renamed NYSE Alternext U.S..

History

The Exchange traces its roots back to colonial times, when stock brokers created outdoor markets in New York City to trade new government-issued securities. The AMEX started out in 1842 as such a market at the curbstone on Broad Street near Exchange Place. The curb brokers gathered around the lamp posts and mail boxes, resisting wind and weather, putting up lists of stocks for sale. As trading activity increased so did the volume of the transactions; the shouting reached such a high level that stock hand signals had to be introduced so that the brokers could continue trading over the din. In 1921 the market was moved indoors into the building at 86 Trinity Place, Manhattan, where it still resides. The hand signals remained in place for decades even after the move, as a means of covenient communication. The building was declared a National Historic Landmark in 1978.

The Market

AMEX's core business has shifted over the years from stocks to options and Exchange-traded funds, although it continues to trade small to mid-size stocks. An effort in the mid-1990s to initiate an Emerging Company Marketplace ended in failure, as the reduced listing standards (beyond the existing lenient AMEX standards) caused penny stock promoters to move their scams to a national exchange. In the mid 1990s the exchange was dogged by allegations of trading scandals, which were highlighted by BusinessWeek in 1999. In 1998, the American Stock Exchange merged with the National Association of Securities Dealers (operators of NASDAQ) to create "The Nasdaq-Amex Market Group" where AMEX is an independent entity of the NASD parent company.

After tension between the NASD and AMEX members, the latter group bought out the NASD and acquired control of the AMEX in 2004.

Out of the three major American stock exchanges, the AMEX is known to have the most liberal policies concerning company listing, as most of its companies are generally smaller compared to the NYSE and NASDAQ. The Amex also specialises in the trading of ETFs, and hybrid/structured securities. The majority of US listed ETF's are traded at the AMEX including the SPDR and most Powershares.

In 2006, the AMEX attempted to popularize an American implementation of the Canadian income trust model. Listed Equity Income Hybrid Securities, (more commonly known as Income Deposit Securities) listed on the AMEX are B & G Foods Holding Corp. (BGF), Centerplate, Inc. (CVP), Coinmach Service Corp. (DRY), and Otelco Inc. (OTT). Recently Coinmach Service Corp, has been attempting to restructure itself away from being an income trust.

The AMEX also produces stock market indices; perhaps the most notable of these is an index of stocks of internet companies now known as the Inter@ctive Week Internet Index. Recently, the AMEX has also developed a unique set of indices known as Intellidexes, which attempt to gain alpha by creating indices weighted on fundamental factors. The AMEX Composite, a value-weighted index of all stocks listed on the exchange, established a record monthly close of 2,069.16 points on November 30, 2006.

Located near the former World Trade Center, the operation of the AMEX was temporarily affected by the September 11 attacks. The Exchange's operations were temporarily shifted to the Philadelphia Stock Exchange.

Hours

The exchange's normal trading sessions are from 9:30am to 4:00pm on all days of the week except Saturdays, Sundays and holidays declared by the Exchange in advance.

New York Stock Exchange

The New York Stock Exchange (NYSE) is a stock exchange based in New York City, New York. It is the largest stock exchange in the world by dollar volume and has 2,764+ listed securities. It ranks fourth in the world in terms of company listings with 3,200 companies, behind the Bombay Stock Exchange, London Stock Exchange, and NASDAQ. As of December 31, 2006, the combined capitalization of all New York Stock Exchange listed companies was $25 trillion.

The NYSE is operated by NYSE Euronext, which was formed by the NYSE's merger with the fully electronic stock exchange Euronext. Its trading floor is located at 11 Wall Street and is composed of four rooms used for the facilitation of trading. A fifth trading room, located at 30 Broad Street, was closed in February 2007. The main building, located at 18 Broad Street between the corners of Wall Street and Exchange Place, was designated a National Historic Landmark in 1978.

Business

The New York Stock Exchange (sometimes referred to as "the Big Board") gives an efficient method for buyers and sellers to trade shares of stock in companies registered for public trading. The exchange provides price discovery via an auction environment designed to produce the fairest price for both parties. Since September 30, 1985, the NYSE trading hours have been 9:30–16:00 ET on all days of the week except Saturdays, Sundays and holidays declared by the Exchange in advance.

As of January 24, 2007, all NYSE stocks can be traded via its electronic Hybrid Market (except for a small group of very high-priced stocks). Customers can now send orders for immediate electronic execution, or route orders to the floor for trade in the auction market. In excess of 50% of all order flow is now delivered to the floor electronically.

On the trading floor, the NYSE trades in a continuous auction format. Here, the human interaction and expert judgment as to order execution differentiates the NYSE from fully electronic markets. There is one specific location on the trading floor where each listed stock trades. Exchange members interested in buying and selling a particular stock on behalf of investors gather around the appropriate post where a specialist broker, who is employed by an NYSE member firm (that is, he/she is not an employee of the New York Stock Exchange), acts as an auctioneer in an open outcry auction market environment to bring buyers and sellers together and to manage the actual auction. They do on occasion (approximately 10% of the time) facilitate the trades by committing their own capital and as a matter of course disseminate information to the crowd that helps to bring buyers and sellers together. The frenzied commotion of men and women in colored smocks has been captured in several movies, including Wall Street.

In the mid-1960s, the NYSE Composite Index (NYSE: NYA) was created, with a base value of 50 points equal to the 1965 yearly close, to reflect the value of all stocks trading at the exchange instead of just the 30 stocks included in the Dow Jones Industrial Average. To raise the profile of the composite index, in 2003 the NYSE set its new base value of 5,000 points equal to the 2002 yearly close. (Previously, the index had stood just below 500 points, with lifetime highs and lows of 670 points and 33 points, respectively.)

The right to directly trade shares on the exchange is conferred upon owners of the 1366 "seats". The term comes from the fact that up until the 1870s NYSE members sat in chairs to trade; this system was eliminated long ago. In 1868, the number of seats was fixed at 533, and this number was increased several times over the years. In 1953, the exchange stopped at 1366 seats. These seats are a sought-after commodity as they confer the ability to directly trade stock on the NYSE. Seat prices have varied widely over the years, generally falling during recessions and rising during economic expansions. The most expensive inflation-adjusted seat was sold in 1929 for $625,000, which, today, would be over six million dollars. In recent times, seats have sold for as high as $4 million in the late 1990s and $1 million in 2001. In 2005, seat prices shot up to $3.25 million as the exchange was set to merge with Archipelago and become a for-profit, publicly traded company. Seat owners received $500,000 cash per seat and 77,000 shares of the newly formed corporation. The NYSE now sells one-year licenses to trade directly on the exchange.

History

The origin of the NYSE can be traced to May 17, 1792, when the Buttonwood Agreement was signed by 24 stock brokers outside of 68 Wall Street in New York under a buttonwood tree on Wall Street which earlier was the site of a stockade fence. On March 8, 1817, the organization drafted a constitution and renamed itself the "New York Stock & Exchange Board". (This name was shortened to its current form in 1863.) Anthony Stockholm was elected the Exchange's first president.

Picture 61: The floor of the New York Stock Exchange in 1908

The first central location of the NYSE was a room rented for $200 a month in 1817 located at 40 Wall Street. The NYSE was destroyed in the Great Fire of New York (1835). It moved to a temporary headquarters. In 1863 it changed its name to the New York Stock Exchange (NYSE). In 1865 it moved to 10-12 Broad Street. The Dow Jones Industrial Average (DJIA) was created by Dow Jones & Company, a financial news publisher, in 1896.

The volume of stocks traded increased sixfold in the years between 1896 and 1901 and a larger space was required to conduct business in the expanding marketplace. Eight New York City architects were invited to participate in a design competition for a new building and the Exchange selected the neoclassic design from architect George B. Post. Demolition of the existing building at 10 Broad Street and the adjacent lots started on May 10, 1901.

Picture 62: U.S. Secretary of Commerce Donald L. Evans rings the opening bell at the NYSE on April 23, 2003. Former chairman Richard Grasso is also in this picture

The New York Stock Exchange building opened at 18 Broad Street on April 22, 1903 at a cost of $4 million. The trading floor was one of the largest volumes of space in the city at the time at 109 x 140 feet (33 x 42.5 m) with a skylight set into a 72-foot (22 m) high ceiling. The main façade of the building features marble sculpture by John Quincy Adams Ward in the pediment, above six tall Corinthian capitals, called “Integrity Protecting the Works of Man”. The building was listed as a National Historic Landmark and added to the National Register of Historic Places on June 2, 1978.

In 1922, a building designed by Trowbridge & Livingston was added at 11 Broad Street for offices, and a new trading floor called "the garage". Additional trading floor space was added in 1969 and 1988 (the "blue room") with the latest technology for information display and communication. Another trading floor was opened at 30 Broad Street in 2000. With the arrival of the Hybrid Market, a greater proportion of trading was executed electronically and the NYSE decided to close the 30 Broad Street trading room in early 2006. In late

2007 the exchange closed the rooms created by the 1969 and 1988 expansions due to the declining number of traders and employees on the floor, a result of increased electronic trading.

Events

The exchange was closed shortly after the beginning of World War I (July 31, 1914), but it partially re-opened on November 28 of that year in order to help the war effort by trading bonds, and completely reopened for stock trading in mid-December.

On September 16, 1920, a bomb exploded on Wall Street outside the NYSE building, killing 33 people and injuring more than 400. The perpetrators were never found. The NYSE building and some buildings nearby, such as the JP Morgan building, still have marks on their facades caused by the bombing.

The Black Thursday crash of the Exchange on October 24, 1929, and the sell-off panic which started on Black Tuesday, October 29, are often blamed for precipitating the Great Depression of 1929. In an effort to try to restore investor confidence, the Exchange unveiled a fifteen-point program aimed to upgrade protection for the investing public on October 31, 1938.

On October 1, 1934, the exchange was registered as a national securities exchange with the U.S. Securities and Exchange Commission, with a president and a thirty-three member board. On February 18, 1971 the non-profit corporation was formed, and the number of board members was reduced to twenty-five.

One of Abbie Hoffman's well-known protests took place on August 24, 1967, when he led members of the movement to the gallery of the New York Stock Exchange (NYSE). The protesters threw fistfuls of dollars (most of the bills were fake) down to the traders below, some of whom booed, while others began to scramble frantically to grab the money as fast as they could. Hoffman claimed to be pointing out that, metaphorically, that's what NYSE traders "were already doing." "We didn't call the press," wrote Hoffman, "at that time we really had no notion of anything called a media event." The press was quick to respond and by evening the event was reported around the world. Since that incident, the stock exchange has spent $20,000 to enclose the gallery with bulletproof glass.

On October 19, 1987, the Dow Jones Industrial Average (DJIA) dropped 508 points, a 22.6% loss in a single day, the second-biggest one-day drop the exchange had experienced, prompting officials at the exchange to invoke for the first time the "circuit breaker" rule to halt all trading. This was a very controversial move and led to a quick change in the rule; trading now halts for an hour, two hours, or the rest of the day when the DJIA drops 10, 20, or 30 percent, respectively. In the afternoon, the 10% and 20% drops will halt trading for a shorter period of time, but a 30% drop will always close the exchange for the day. The rationale behind the trading halt was to give investors a chance to cool off and reevaluate their positions. Black Monday was followed by Terrible Tuesday, a day in which the Exchange's systems did not perform well and some people had difficulty completing their trades.

There was a panic similar to many with a fall of 7.2% in value (554.26 points) on October 27, 1997 prompted by falls in Asian markets, from which the NYSE recovered quickly.

On January 26, 2000, an altercation during filming of the music video for Sleep Now in the Fire, which was directed by Michael Moore, caused the doors of the exchange to be closed and the band, Rage Against the Machine, to be escorted from the site by security, after band members attempted to gain entry into the exchange. Trading on the exchange floor, however, continued uninterrupted.

The NYSE was closed from September 11 until September 17, 2001 as a result of the September 11, 2001 attacks.

On September 17, 2003, NYSE chairman and chief executive Richard Grasso stepped down as a result of controversy concerning the size of his deferred compensation package. He was replaced as CEO by John S. Reed, the former Chairman of Citigroup.

The NYSE announced its plans to acquire Archipelago on April 21, 2005, in a deal intended to reorganize the NYSE as a publicly traded company. NYSE's governing board voted to acquire rival Archipelago on December 6, 2005, and become a for-profit, public company. It began trading under the name NYSE Group on March 8, 2006. A little over one year later, on April 4, 2007, the NYSE Group completed its merger with Euronext, the European combined stock market, thus forming the NYSE Euronext, the first transatlantic stock exchange.

Presently, Marsh Carter is Chairman of the New York Stock Exchange, having succeeded John S. Reed and the CEO is Duncan Niederauer, having succeeded John Thain.

Australian Securities Exchange

The Australian Securities Exchange (ASX) is the primary stock exchange in Australia. The ASX began as separate state-based exchanges established as early as 1861. Today trading is all-electronic and the exchange is a public company, listed on the exchange itself.

The Australian Securities Exchange as it is now known resulted from the merger of the Australian Stock Exchange and the Sydney Futures Exchange in December 2006.

The biggest stocks traded on the ASX, in terms of their market capitalisation, include BHP Billiton, Commonwealth Bank of Australia, Telstra Corporation, Rio Tinto, National Australia Bank and Australia and New Zealand Banking Group. As at 31-Dec-2006 the three largest sectors by market cap were financial services (34%), commodities (20%) and listed property trusts (10%).

The major market index is the S&P/ASX 200, an index made up of the top 200 shares in the ASX. This supplanted the previously significant All Ordinaries index, which still runs parallel to the S&P ASX 200. Both are commonly quoted together. Other indices for the bigger stocks are the S&P/ASX 100 and S&P/ASX 50.

The ASX is a public company, and its own shares are traded on the ASX. However, the corporation's charter restricts maximum individual holdings to a small fraction of the company.

While the ASX regulates other listed companies listed on the ASX, it cannot regulate itself, and is regulated by the Australian Securities and Investments Commission (ASIC).

The current managing director Robert Elstone was appointed in July 2006. Prior to the merger of ASX with the Sydney Futures Exchange (SFE), Robert Elstone was the CEO of the SFE.

Market Details

ASX has a pre-market session from 07:00am to 10:00am AEST and a normal trading session from 10:00am to 04:00pm AEST.

The market opens alphabetically in single price auctions, phased over the first ten minutes, with a small random time built in to prevent exact prediction of the first trades. There is also a single-price auction between 4:10pm and 4:12pm to set the daily closing prices. As of 30 March 2007, 2014 stocks were listed on the ASX with a total market capitalisation of A$1.39 trillion (US$1.098 trillion). At the end of 2004 it was the 8th largest world equity market (on free float basis), comprising around 2.2% of the MSCI World index. The market turnover during 2004 was $A779bn.

Brokers that dominate market share in Australia (in decreasing order) include Macquarie Bank, Goldman Sachs JBWere, UBS, Citigroup, Merrill Lynch, CSFB, Deutsche Bank, ABN AMRO, CommSec and Morgan Stanley. Retail investors account for around 20% of market turnover. Market ownership is broken down as 30% institutional, 40% foreign, 30% retail.

History

The exchange began as six separate exchanges established in the state capitals Melbourne (1861), Sydney (1871), Hobart (1882), Brisbane (1884), Adelaide (1887) and Perth (1889). An exchange in Launceston merged into the Hobart exchange too.

The first interstate conference was held in 1903 at Melbourne Cup time. The exchanges then met on an informal basis until 1937 when the Australian Associated Stock Exchanges (AASE) was established, with representatives from each exchange. Over time the AASE established uniform listing rules, broker rules, and commission rates.

Trading was conducted by a call system, where an exchange employee called the names of each company and brokers bid or offered on each. In the 1960s this changed to a post system. Exchange employees called "chalkies" wrote bids and offers in chalk on blackboards continuously, and recorded transactions made.

Timeline of significant events

- In 1969 there was a mining boom, triggered by Poseidon NL discovering nickel in Western Australia.

- In 1976 the Australian Options Market was established, trading call options.
- In 1980 the separate Melbourne and Sydney stock exchange indices were replaced by Australian Stock Exchange indices.
- In 1984 broker's commission rates were deregulated. Commissions have gradually fallen ever since, with today rates as low as 0.12% or 0.1% from discount internet-based brokers.
- In 1987, following work begun in 1985, the separate exchanges merged to form the ASX. Also in 1987 the all-electronic SEATS trading system (below) was introduced. It started on just a limited range of stocks, progressively all stocks were moved to it and the trading floors were closed in 1990.
- In 1990 the warrants market (below) was established.
- In 1993 fixed interest securities were added (see interest rate market below). Also in 1993 the FAST system of accelerated settlement was established, and the following year the CHESS system (see settlement below) was introduced, superseding FAST.
- In 1994 the Sydney Futures Exchange announced futures over individual ASX stocks. The ASX responded with low exercise price options (see below). The SFE went to court, claiming LEPOs were futures (certainly their effect is like futures) and therefore the ASX could not offer them. But the court held they were options and so LEPOs were introduced in 1995.
- In 1995 stamp duty on share transactions was halved from 0.3% to 0.15%. The ASX had agreed with the Queensland State Government to locate staff in Brisbane in exchange for the stamp duty reduction there, and the other states followed suit so as not to lose brokerage business to Queensland. In 2000 stamp duty was abolished in all states as part of the introduction of the GST.
- In 1996 the exchange members (brokers etc) voted to demutualise. The exchange was incorporated as ASX Limited and in 1998 the company was listed on the ASX itself. The ASX arranged with the Australian Securities and Investments Commission to have it enforce listing rules for ASX Limited.
- In 1997 a phased transition to the electronic CLICK system for derivatives began.
- In 2006 the ASX announced a merger with the Sydney Futures Exchange, the primary derivatives exchange in Australia.

Settlement

Investors hold shares in one of two forms. Both operate with bank-account style holding statements rather than share certificates.

- Issuer sponsored: The company's share register administers the investor's holding and issues them with a Shareholder Registration Number (SRN) which may be quoted when selling.
- Broker sponsored: The investors sharebroker sponsors the client into CHESS, the Clearing House Electronic Subregister System. The investor is given a Holder Identification Number (HIN) and monthly statements are sent to the investor from the CHESS system.

Holdings may be moved from issuer sponsored to broker sponsored or between different brokers on request.

Short Selling

Short selling of shares is permitted on the ASX, but only among designated stocks and with certain conditions,

- The sell order must be at a price not lower than the last trade.
- No more than a total 10% of the shares on issue may be sold short. (Brokers report net short positions to the ASX daily.)
- Margin cover of 20% of the current share price must be posted.

Many brokers don't offer short selling to small private investors. LEPOs (below) can serve as an equivalent. Contracts for difference offered by third party providers are another alternative. Some CFD providers enter orders directly into the SEATS system (instead of making a synthetic market), giving investors the equivalent of exchange trading.

Options

Options over leading shares are traded on the ASX, with standardised sets of strike prices and expiry dates. Liquidity is provided by market makers who are required to provide quotes. Each market maker is assigned two or more stocks. A stock can have more than one market maker, and they compete with one another. A market maker may choose one or both of,

- Make a market continuously, on a set of 18 options.
- Make a market in response to a quote request, in any option up to 9 months out.

In both cases there's a minimum quantity (5 or 10 contracts depending on the shares) and a maximum spread permitted.

Due to the higher risks in options, brokers must check clients suitability before allowing them to trade options. Clients may both take (ie. buy) and write (ie. sell) options. For written positions the client must put up margin.

Exchange Traded CFDs - ASX CFDs

ASX CFDs are a new form of contract for difference that will be traded through an exchange based mechanism. Current CFD providers focus on either the direct market access or market maker models. This new development is set to be launched in November 2007 on the ASX and will be offered by Australia's leading online brokers and over-the-counter (OTC) CFD providers including First Prudential Markets (FPM) and Commsec.[8]

ASX CFDs will enjoy the traditional benefits of leverage enjoyed by over the counter contracts for difference but with reduced transaction costs from the central counter clearing model negating the financing charges traditionally imposed by third party cfd providers.

Only accredited brokers will offer ASX CFDs and multiple market makers have been appointed to facilitate liquidity. Additional information about ASX CFDs, including market developments is available here.

ASX has also launched (24 September 2007) an ASX CFD Trading Simulator. The simulator allow a user to learn the basics of the ASX CFD market as well as explore trading strategies in a life-like environment... without risk to their capital.

Warrants

Warrants on the ASX are options over a company's shares issued by a third party. Issuers are usually investment banks or large stockbrokers. The issuer decides terms for an issue based on what it thinks market participants might be interested in buying. On exercise the warrant holder transacts directly with the issuer (there's no separate clearing house for that). Warrants come in the following types, suitable either as trading vehicles like options above, or as longer term investments.

- Trading warrants: Calls or puts with various exercise style, expiry date, and contract size (ie. how many warrants correspond to one

---

[8] Source: ASX website www.asx.com.au

share). Issuers assess market demand to decide what sets of terms they will offer.

- Knockout warrants: Like trading warrants, but starting in-the-money and terminating (ie. knocked-out) if the share price touches the strike (falls to the strike for a call, rises to it for a put).
- Installment warrants: Call options with a final additional payment to be made on exercise. The final payment is in effect a loan by the issuer. The warrant holder receives dividends and has voting rights in the underlying shares.
- Endowment warrants: Call options with long-dated expiry and varying exercise price. The exercise price represents an outstanding amount to pay. It's reduced by dividends and increased by ongoing interest fees. The idea is the warrant holder pays say half the share price up front (as the premium), and the dividends then pay off the rest over say 10 years. If the dividends pay off the balance sooner then the warrant holder receives fully paid shares at that time.
- Perth mint gold: Call warrants of low exercise price over spot gold, issued by the Perth Mint. These work like an unleveraged long position in gold.

Warrants are traded on the SEATS system (see above) the same as shares. The issuer makes a market in their warrants by providing at least a bid for the life of the warrant. Due to the leverage, brokers must get a separate client agreement before the client can trade warrants.

Low Exercise Price Options

A low exercise price option (LEPO) is a European style call option with a low exercise price of $0.01 and a contract size of 1000 shares to be delivered on exercise. LEPOs are traded on margin, and a trader may take a long or short position. Market makers ensure continuous price quotations.

LEPOs work like a futures contract. Being European style means they cannot be exercised until expiry, the premium is practically the whole share price, and a trader only posts margin, not the full price.

LEPOs were introduced in 1994, in response to the Sydney Futures Exchange offering futures over individual ASX shares. Regulations at the time prevented the ASX offering futures contracts, hence the LEPO form. Presently LEPOs are available on 47 leading stocks.

Interest Rate Market

The interest rate market on the ASX is the set of corporate bonds, floating rate notes, and bond-like preference shares listed on the exchange. Those securities are all traded and settled the same as ordinary shares, but the ASX provides information such as their maturity, effective interest rate, etc, to aid comparison.

Futures

The ASX trades futures over the ASX 50, ASX 200 and ASX property indexes, and over grain, electricity and wool. Options over grain futures are also traded.

Futures are traded on DTP, the Derivatives Trading Platform (also known as CLICK).

Market Indices

The ASX maintains stock indexes concerning stocks traded on the exchange in conjunction with Standard & Poors. There is a hierarchy of index groups called the S&P/ASX 20, S&P/ASX 50, S&P/ASX 100, S&P/ASX 200 and S&P/ASX 300, notionally containing the 20, 50, 100, 200 and 300 largest companies listed on the exchange, subject to some qualifications. Details of the index components are at the ASX website.

Frankfurt Stock Exchange

The Frankfurt Stock Exchange (German: FWB Frankfurter Wertpapierbörse) is a stock exchange located in Frankfurt, Germany.

Picture 63: FSE Main Entrance

The Frankfurt Stock Exchange is one of the biggest and most efficient exchange places in the world. It is owned and operated by Deutsche Börse, which also owns the European futures exchange Eurex and clearing company Clearstream.

The Frankfurt Stock Exchange has over 90 percent of turnover in the German market and a big share in the European market. Here the Frankfurt Stock Exchange floor trading loses, but in fast developing and expanding electronic trading (Xetra trading system) the FSE gains in European and international trade: Partner-exchanges adopted the Xetra (trading system) (as the Vienna Stock Exchange in 1999, the Irish Stock Exchange in 2000 and the Budapest Stock Exchange in 2003); consolidation continues.

Picture 64:The trading floor in Frankfurt

Mainly through Xetra, the German stock market was opened to foreign investors and market participants. About 47% of the 300 market participants in Frankfurt come from abroad.

The trading indices in Frankfurt are DAX, DAXplus, CDAX, DivDAX, LDAX, MDAX, SDAX, TecDAX, VDAX and EuroStoxx 50.

Trading runs from 09:00 to 17:30 with closing auction from 17:30-17:35. In November 2003, Late DAX was introduced running from 17:45 to 20:00 and in 2006 X-DAX was introduced running from 17:45-22:00 (in line with US trading hours).

History

The origins of the Frankfurt Stock Exchange go back to the 9th century and a free letter by Emperor Louis the German to hold free trade fairs. By the 16th century Frankfurt developed into a wealthy and busy city with an economy based on trade and financial services.

Frankfurt Stock Exchange floorIn 1585 a bourse was established to set up fixed currency exchange rates. During the following centuries Frankfurt developed into one of the world's first stock exchanges - next to London and Paris. Bankers like Mayer Amschel Rothschild and Max Warburg had substantial influence on Frankfurt's financial trade.

It was only in 1949 after World War II that the Frankfurt Stock Exchange finally established as the leading stock exchange in Germany with consequently incoming national and international investments.

During the 1990s the Frankfurt Stock Exchange was also bourse for the Neuer Markt (German for New Market) as part of the world wide dot-com boom.

In 1993 the Frankfurter Wertpapierbörse (Frankfurt Stock Exchange) became Deutsche Börse AG, operating businesses for the exchange.

From the early 1960s onwards the Frankfurt Stock Exchange took advantage of the close by Bundesbank which effectively decided on financial policies in Europe until the introduction of the euro in 2002. Since then the exchange profits from the presence of the European Central Bank in Frankfurt am Main.

In 2002 and 2004 Deutsche Börse was in advanced negotiations to take over London Stock Exchange, which were broken off twice.

Today, with a total turnover of €5.2 trillion per year the Frankfurt Stock Exchange strengthens its position as the world's 3rd largest trade-place for stocks and the world's 6th largest by market capitalization.

London Stock Exchange

The London Stock Exchange or LSE is a stock exchange located in London, England. Founded in 1801, it is one of the largest stock exchanges in the world, with many overseas listings as well as British companies. The LSE is part of the London Stock Exchange Group plc.

Picture 65: LSE's current premises are situated in Paternoster Square close to St Paul's Cathedral in the City of London

History

Origin of Share Trading

The trade in shares in London began with the need to finance two voyages: The Muscovy Company's attempt to reach China via the White Sea north of Russia, and the East India Company voyage to India and the east.

Unable to finance these costly journeys privately, the companies raised the money by selling shares to merchants, giving them a right to a portion of any profits eventually made.

Exchange

The idea soon caught on (one of the earliest was the Earl of Bedford's scheme to drain the fens). It is estimated that by 1695, there were 140 joint-stock companies. The trade in shares was centred around the City's Change Alley in two coffee shops: Garraway's and Jonathan's. The broker, John Castaing, published the prices of stocks and commodities called The Course of the Exchange and other things in these coffee shops.

Licensing of Brokers

In 1697, a law was passed to "restrain the number and ill-practice of brokers and stockjobbers" following a number of insider trading and market-rigging incidents. It required all brokers to be licensed and to take an oath promising to act lawfully.

The South Sea Bubble

The Change Alley exchange thrived. However, it suffered a set-back in 1720.

Much excitement was caused by the South Sea Company, stoked by brokers, the company's owner John Blunt and the government. Having set up the unprofitable company nine years previously, the government hoped to wipe out the large debts accumulated by offering shares to the public.

Shares in the company, which had started at £128 each at the start of the year, were soon fetching as much as £1,050 by June. The bubble inevitably burst, with share prices plunging to £175, then £124.

The incident caused outcry, forcing the government to pass legislation to prevent another bubble, and it took a long time for the stock exchange to recover.

Threadneedle Street and Capel Court

Jonathan's burnt down in 1748, and this, plus dissatisfaction with the overcrowding in the alley, made the brokers build a New Jonathan's on Threadneedle Street, as well as charging an entrance fee. The building was soon renamed the Stock Exchange, only to be renamed again as the Stock Subscription Room in 1801, with new membership regulations.

However, this too proved unsatisfactory, and the exchange moved to the newly built Capel Court in the same year. The exchange had recovered by the 1820s, bolstered by the growth of the railways, canals, mining and insurance industries (there were, however, problems with stags and dividend payments). Regional stock exchanges were formed across the UK. Bonds (or gilt-edged securities) also began to be traded.

Coat of Arms

It received its own Coat of Arms in 1923. Its motto is dictum meum pactum, "My word is my bond".

The Stock Exchange Tower

The former Stock Exchange Tower, based in Threadneedle Street/Old Broad Street was opened by Queen Elizabeth II in 1972 and housed the trading floor where traders would traditionally meet to conduct business.

This became largely redundant with the advent of the Big Bang on 27 October 1986, which deregulated many of the Stock Exchange's activities. It eliminated fixed commissions on security trades and allowed securities firms to act as brokers and dealers. It also enabled an increased use of computerised systems that allowed dealing rooms to take precedence over face to face trading.

IRA Bomb

On 20 July 1990 a bomb planted by the IRA exploded in the men's toilets behind the visitors' gallery. The area had already been evacuated and nobody was injured. The long term trend towards electronic trading had been reducing the Exchange's status as a visitor attraction and, although the gallery reopened, it was closed permanently in 1992.

Paternoster Square

The Source by Greyworld, in the new LSE buildingIn July 2004, the London Stock Exchange moved from Threadneedle Street to Paternoster Square (EC4) close to St Paul's Cathedral, still within the "Square Mile" (the City of London).

It was officially opened by Queen Elizabeth II once again, accompanied by The Duke of Edinburgh, on 27 July 2004. The new building contains a specially commissioned dynamic sculpture called "The Source", by artists Greyworld.

Structure

The London Stock Exchange has four core areas:

- Equity markets - enables companies from around the world to raise capital. There are four primary markets; Main Market, Alternative Investment Market (AIM), Professional Securities Market (PSM) and Specialist Fund Market (SFM).
- Trading services - highly active market for trading in a range of securities, including UK and international equities, debt, covered warrants, exchange traded funds (ETFs), Exchange Traded Commodities (ETCs), reits, fixed interest, contracts for difference (CFDs) and depositary receipts.
- Market data information - The London Stock Exchange provides real-time prices, news and other financial information to the global financial community.
- Derivatives - A major contributor to derivatives business is EDX London, created in 2003 to bring the cash equity and derivatives markets closer together.

Hours

Normal trading sessions are from 08:00 to 16:30 every day of the week except Saturdays, Sundays and holidays declared by the Exchange in advance.

Tokyo Stock Exchange

The Tokyo Stock Exchange, or TSE, located in Tokyo, Japan, is the second largest stock exchange market in the world by market value, second only to the New York Stock Exchange. It currently lists 2,271 domestic companies and 31 foreign companies, with a total market capitalization of over 5 trillion USD.

Picture 66: Tokyo Stock Exchange

Structure

The TSE is incorporated as a kabushiki kaisha with nine directors, four auditors and eight executive officers. Its headquarters are located at 2-1 Nihombashi Kabutocho, Chūō, Tokyo, Japan. Stocks listed on the TSE are separated into the First Section (for large companies), the Second Section (for mid-sized companies), and the "Mothers" section (for high-growth startup companies). As of March 2006, there are 1,721 First Section companies, 489 Second Section companies and 156 Mothers companies.

Picture 67: The main trading room of the Tokyo Stock Exchange, where nowadays the trading is done through computers

The main indixes tracking the TSE are the Nikkei 225 index of companies selected by the Nihon Keizai Shimbun (Japan's largest business newspaper), the TOPIX index based on the share prices of First Section companies, and the J30 index of large industrial companies maintained by Japan's major broadsheet newspapers.

89 domestic and 19 foreign securities companies participate in TSE trading.

Other TSE-related institutions include:

- The exchange's press club, called the Kabuto Club (兜倶楽部), which meets on the third floor of the TSE building. Most Kabuto Club members are affiliated with the Nihon Keizai Shimbun, Kyodo News, Jiji Press, or business television broadcasters such as Bloomberg LP and CNBC. The Kabuto Club is generally busiest during April and May, when public companies release their annual accounts.

On 15th June 2007, the TSE paid $303 million to acquire a 4.99% stake in Singapore Exchange Ltd..

History

Prewar History

The Tokyo Stock Exchange was established on May 15, 1878, as the Tokyo Kabushiki Torihikijo under the direction of then-Finance Minister Okuma Shigenobu and capitalist advocate Shibusawa Eiichi. Trading began on June 1, 1878.

In 1943, the exchange was combined with ten other stock exchanges in major Japanese cities to form a single Japanese Stock Exchange. The combined exchange was shut down and reorganized shortly after the bombing of Nagasaki.

Postwar History

The Tokyo Stock Exchange reopened under its current Japanese name on May 16, 1949, pursuant to the new Securities Exchange Act.

The TSE runup from 1983 to 1990 was unprecedented, in 1990 it accounted for over 60% of the world's stock market capitalization (by far the world's largest) before falling precipitously in value and rankings today, but still remains one of the 3 largest exchanges in the world by market capitalization of listed shares.

The trading floor of the TSE was closed on April 30, 1999, and the exchange switched to electronic trading for all transactions. A new facility, called TSE Arrows, opened on May 9, 2000.

In 2001, the TSE restructured itself as a stock company: before this time, it was structured as an incorporated association with its members as shareholders.

I.T. Issues

The exchange was only able to operate for 90 minutes on November 1, 2005, due to bugs with a newly installed transactions system, developed by Fujitsu, which was supposed to help cope with higher trading volumes. The interruption in trading was the worst in the history of the exchange. Trading was suspended for four-and-a-half hours.

During the initial public offering of J-Com on December 8, 2005, an employee at Mizuho Securities Co., Ltd. mistakenly typed an order to sell 610,000 shares at 1 yen, instead of an order to sell 1 share at 610,000 yen. Mizuho failed to catch the error; the Tokyo Stock Exchange initially blocked attempts to cancel the order, resulting in a net loss of 347 million US dollars to be shared between the exchange and Mizuho. Both companies are now trying to deal with their troubles: Lack of error checking, lack of safeguards, lack of reliability, lack of transparency, lack of testing, loss of confidence, and loss of profits. On 11 December, the TSE acknowledged that its system was at fault in the Mizuho trade. On 21 December, Takuo Tsurushima, chief executive of the TSE, and two other senior executives resigned over the Mizuho affair.

Hours

The exchange's normal trading sessions are from 09:00am to 11:00am and from 12:30pm to 3:00pm on all days of the week except Saturdays, Sundays and holidays declared by the Exchange in advance.

Alliances

The London Stock Exchange (LSE) and the TSE are developing jointly traded products and share technology, marking the latest cross-border deal among bourses as international competition heats up. The TSE is also looking for some partners in Asia, and more specifically is seeking an alliance with the Singapore Exchange (SGX), which is considered as becoming a leading financial hub in the Asia-Pacific region. Recently, some rumors close to the deal suggest that the TSE is preparing for a takeover of the SGX, or at least take a major stake, in the first semester of 2008. The TSE has already acquired a 5% stake in the SGX as of June 2007, deemed to be only the beginning of greater participation.

London Stock Exchange Joint Venture

In July 2008 the London Stock Exchange (LSE) and the TSE announced a new joint venture Tokyo-based market, which will be based on the LSE's Alternative Investment Market (AIM)

Toronto Stock Exchange

The Toronto Stock Exchange (TSX; abbreviated TSE until 2001) is the largest stock exchange in Canada, the third largest in North America and the seventh largest in the world by market capitalization. Based in Toronto, it is owned and operated by TSX Group for the trading of senior equities. A broad range of businesses from Canada, the United States and other countries are represented on the exchange. In addition to conventional securities, the exchange lists various exchange-traded funds, split share corporations, income trusts and investment funds. The TSX is a leader in the mining and oil & gas sector. More mining and oil & gas companies are listed on the TSX than any other exchange in the world.

Picture 68: The Toronto Stock Exchange

History

The Toronto Stock Exchange likely descended from the Association of Brokers, a group formed by Toronto businessmen on July 26, 1852. No official records of the group's transactions have survived. On October 25, 1861, twenty-four men gathered at the Masonic Hall to officially create the Toronto Stock Exchange. The exchange was formally incorporated by an act of the Legislative Assembly of Ontario in 1878.

The TSE grew continuously in size and in shares traded, save for a three month period in 1914 when the exchange was shut down for fear of financial panic due to World War I. In 1934, the Toronto Stock Exchange merged with its key competitor the Standard Stock and Mining Exchange. The merged markets chose to keep the name Toronto Stock Exchange. In 1977, the TSE introduced CATS (Computer Assisted Trading System), an automated trading system that started to be used for the quotation of less liquid equities.

On April 23, 1997, the TSE's trading floor closed, making it the second-largest stock exchange in North America to choose a floorless, electronic (or virtual trading) environment. In 1999, the Toronto Stock Exchange announced the appointment of Barbara G. Stymiest to the position of President & Chief Executive Officer.

Through a realignment plan, Toronto Stock Exchange became Canada's sole exchange for the trading of senior equities. The Bourse de Montréal/Montreal Exchange assumed responsibility for the trading of derivatives and the Vancouver Stock Exchange and Alberta Stock Exchange merged to form the Canadian Venture Exchange (CDNX) handling trading in junior equities. The Canadian Dealing Network, Winnipeg Stock Exchange, and equities portion of the Montreal Exchange later merged with CDNX.

In 2000, the Toronto Stock Exchange became a for-profit company and in 2001 its acronym was changed to TSX. In 2001, the Toronto Stock Exchange acquired the Canadian Venture Exchange, which was renamed the TSX Venture Exchange in 2002. This ended 123 years of the usage of TSE as a Canadian Stock Exchange. On May 11, 2007, the S&P/TSX Composite, the main index of the Toronto Stock Exchange, traded above the 14,000 point level for the first time ever.

The TSX Group is the leader in the oil & gas sector - more oil & gas companies are listed on Toronto Stock Exchange (TSX) and TSX Venture Exchange than any other exchange in the world. At the end of June 30, 2007, there were 434 oil & gas companies with a total market capitalization of $544.9 billion listed on Toronto Stock Exchange and TSX Venture Exchange. Oil & gas companies continue to raise equity on these exchanges with $5.56 billion raised in the first half of 2007, and $10.5 billion raised in 2006. Over 10 billion oil & gas shares, valued at $169.2 billion, traded on Toronto Stock Exchange and TSX Venture Exchange in the first half of 2007.

Trading Hours

The exchange has a normal trading session from 09:30am to 04:00pm and a post-market session from 04:15pm to 05:00pm on all days of the week except Saturdays, Sundays and holidays declared by the Exchange in advance.

Hong Kong Stock Exchange

The Hong Kong Stock Exchange (abbreviated as HKEX; SEHK: 0388) is the stock exchange of Hong Kong. The exchange has predominantly been the main exchange for Hong Kong where shares of listed companies are traded. It is Asia's third largest stock exchange in terms of market capitalization, behind the Tokyo Stock Exchange and the Shanghai Stock Exchange.

Hong Kong Exchanges and Clearing is the holding company for the exchange.

Picture 69: Logo of the Hong Kong Exchange

History

The history of the securities exchange began formally in the late 19th century with the first establishment in 1891, though informal securities exchanges have been known to take place since 1861. The exchange has predominantly been the main exchange for Hong Kong despite co-existing with other exchanges at different point in time. After a series of complex mergers and acquisitions, HKSE remains to be the core. From 1947 to 1969 the exchange monopolized the market.

Differences from US Stock Exchanges

From a trader's perspective, there are a number of differences between the Hong Kong stock exchange and US exchanges such as the NYSE and NASDAQ.

- The trading day is divided into a morning and an afternoon session, with a two-hour lunch break in between. The morning session is from 10:00 am to 12:30 pm and the afternoon session is from 2:30 pm to 4:00 pm, local time. Traders based in other countries should note that Hong Kong does not have daylight saving time when converting these times to their own time zone. For example, in summer, the Eastern Time Zone of North America is exactly 12 hours behind, so the start of trading is at 10:00 pm, but in winter it is at 9:00 pm.
- The threshold price level for penny stock status is lower. In US exchanges, a stock trading at less than $5 might feel a need to do a reverse stock split, but it is perfectly normal for Hong Kong stocks of even well-known companies to trade at prices that correspond to less than 50 US cents a share. A Hong Kong stock would not be considered a penny stock unless its price was less than about HK$ 0.50 (about 6.5 US cents). In situations where you might buy hundreds of shares in New York, you might buy thousands or even tens of thousands of shares in Hong Kong.
- In New York, the standard lot size is 100 shares, and it is often possible to buy odd lots. In Hong Kong, each stock has its own individual board lot size (an online broker will usually display this along with the stock price when you get a quote), and it may not be possible to buy in other than multiples of the board lot size.
- There is a close-in-price rule for limit orders, which must be within 24 ticks of the current price. Individual brokers may impose an even stricter rule; for instance, HSBC requires limit orders to be within 10 ticks of the current price. Thus it is not possible to exploit volatility by placing a lowball limit order in the hope that it might be hit before the end of a trading session.
- Finally, broker commissions are generally higher. In the US, it is often possible to trade for a flat fee of less than $10 through an online broker; for Hong Kong trading this might be approximately the equivalent of US$ 35, although this may vary between different brokers.

Trading Hours

Computers were integrated on April 2, 1986, which has helped modernize the system. In 1993 the exchange launched the "Automatic Order Matching and Execution System" (AMS) that was replaced by the third generation system (AMS/3) in October 2000. Systems as such were added to meet the increased popularity of online Stock trading.

Trading Hours: From 10:00am to 12:30pm and from 2:30pm to 4:00pm

(Summer: From 10:00pm to 12:30am and from 2:30am to 4:00am New York time)

(Winter: From 9:00pm to 11:30pm and from 1:30am to 3:00am New York time)

Regulatory Role

David Webb, independent non-executive director of the Exchange since 2003, has been arguing for a super regulatory authority to assume that role as regulator, as there is inherent conflict between its commercial and regulatory roles. In the meantime, he argues for improved investor representation on the Hong Kong Stock Exchange.

In 2007, the uproar by smaller local stockbrokers over the decision by board of directors to cut minimum trading spreads for equities and warrants trading at between 25 HK cents and HK$2 caused the new board to vote to reverse the decision. The reforms were to be implemented in the first quarter, but was put back on the table following protests by brokers. Webb criticised the board for caving in to vested interests.

Euronext

Euronext N.V. is a pan-European stock exchange based in Paris and with subsidiaries in Belgium, France, Netherlands, Luxembourg, Portugal and the United Kingdom. In addition to equities and derivatives markets, the Euronext group provides clearing and information services. As of 31st January 2006 markets run by Euronext had a market capitalization of US$2.9 trillion, making it the 5th largest exchange on the planet. Euronext merged with NYSE Group to form NYSE Euronext, the "first global stock exchange".

Background

Euronext was formed on 22nd September 2000 in a merger of the Amsterdam Stock Exchange, Brussels Stock Exchange, and Paris Bourse, in order to take advantage of the harmonisation of the European Union financial markets. In December 2001 Euronext acquired the shares of the London International Financial Futures and Options Exchange (LIFFE), which continues to operate under its own governance. Beginning in early 2003, all derivatives products traded on its affiliated exchanges trade on LIFFECONNECT, LIFFE's electronic trading platform. In 2002 the group merged with the Portuguese stock exchange Bolsa de Valores de Lisboa e Porto (BVLP), renamed Euronext Lisbon.

Structure and Indices

Euronext has cross-membership and cross-access agreements with the Warsaw Stock Exchange for their cash and derivatives products, and with the Helsinki Exchanges on cash trading; ownership agreements are currently excluded. The Euronext List encompasses all quoted companies. It has two segments; NextEconomy, consisting of companies whose equities are traded continuously and are active in sectors such as information technology and biotechnology, and NextPrime, consisting of companies in more traditional sectors that are traded continuously. Inclusion in the segments is voluntary.

Picture 70: Brussels Bourse/Beurs

Euronext manages two broad-based indices. The Euronext 100 Index is the blue chip index. The Next 150 Index is a market capitalisation index of the 150 next largest stocks, representing the large- to mid-capitalisation segment of listed stocks at Euronext. The NextEconomy and NextPrime segments each have a price index and a total return index, weighted by market capitalisation and excluding the shares listed in the Euronext 100 Index. The indices have a base date of December 31, 2001, with a starting level of 1000 points. Six NextWeather weather indices for France, launched in January 2002, are among the sector indices planned by Euronext. Exchange traded funds, called trackers, comprise Euronext's NextTrack product segment, and have been introduced on the AEX index, CAC 40 Index, DJ Euro Stoxx 50 Index, and various pan-European regional and sector indices. Euronext has introduced several commodity futures contracts, available to all constituents. Winefex Bordeaux futures are traded on Euronext Paris. Euronext.liffe is the subsidiary of Euronext responsible for all options and futures contracts trading, formed by the merger of the derivatives activities of the various constituents of Euronext with LIFFE.

Euronext.liffe

Euronext.liffe was formed in January 2002 from the takeover of the London International Financial Futures and Options Exchange by Euronext. The derivatives activities of the other constituent exchanges of Euronext (Amsterdam, Brussels, Lisbon and Paris), were merged into Euronext.liffe. Trading is done electronically through the LIFFE CONNECT platform. Euronext.liffe offers a wide range of futures and option products on short-term interest rates, bonds, swaps, equities and commodities.

Volumes in 2004 were split as follows:

- Interest Rate: 313.3 million contracts
- Equities: 468.8 million contracts
- Commodities: 8.0 million contracts

In addition to this, it sells its technology to third parties. Since April 2003, the Tokyo International Financial Futures Exchange has run on LIFFE CONNECT. Furthermore, in January 2004, the Chicago Board of Trade started electronic trading using e-cbot, which is powered by LIFFE CONNECT. As a result, the Kansas City Board of Trade, the Minneapolis Grain Exchange and the Winnipeg Commodity Exchange use LIFFE CONNECT for their overnight trading.

Alternext

Alternext was formed in 2005 by Euronext to help small and mid-class companies in the Eurozone seek financing. Since the merger of Euronext and NYSE since 2006, now completed in 2007, this market is now a division of NYSE Euronext, named NYSE Alternext.

Merger with NYSE

Due to apparent moves by NASDAQ to acquire the London Stock Exchange, NYSE Group (owner of the New York Stock Exchange) offered 8 billion euros ($10.2b) in cash and shares for Euronext on May 22, 2006, outbidding a rival offer for the European Stock exchange operator from Deutsche Börse, the German stock market. Contrary to statements that it would not raise its bid, on May 23, 2006, Deutsche Börse unveiled a merger bid for Euronext, valuing the pan-European exchange at US$11 billion (€8.6bn), €600 million over NYSE Group's initial bid. Despite this, NYSE Group and Euronext penned a merger agreement, subject to shareholder vote and regulatory approval. The initial regulatory response by SEC chief Christopher Cox (who was coordinating heavily with European counterparts) was positive, with an expected approval by the end of 2007. The new firm, tentatively dubbed NYSE Euronext, would be headquartered in New York City, with European operations and its trading platform run out of Paris. NYSE CEO John Thain, who would head NYSE Euronext, intends to use the combination to form the world's first global stock market, with continuous trading of stocks and derivatives over a 21-hour time span. In addition, the two exchanges hope to add Borsa Italiana (the Milan stock exchange) into the grouping.

Deutsche Börse dropped out of the bidding for Euronext on November 15, 2006, removing the last major hurdle for the NYSE Euronext transaction. A run-up of NYSE Group's stock price in late 2006 made the offering far more attractive to Euronext's shareholders. On December 19, 2006, Euronext shareholders approved the transaction with 98.2% of the vote. Only 1.8% voted in favour of the Deutsche Börse offer. Jean-François Théodore, the Chief Executive Officer of Euronext, stated that they expected the transaction to close within three or four months. Some of the regulatory agencies with jurisdiction over the merger had already given approval. NYSE Group shareholders gave their approval on December 20, 2006. The merger was completed on April 4, 2007, forming the NYSE Euronext.

The World's Major Indeces

NASDAQ

The NASDAQ (acronym of National Association of Securities Dealers Automated Quotations) is an American stock exchange. It is the largest electronic screen-based equity securities trading market in the United States. With approximately 3,200 companies, it has more trading volume per day than any other stock exchange in the world.

It was founded in 1971 by the National Association of Securities Dealers (NASD), who divested themselves of it in a series of sales in 2000 and 2001. It is owned and operated by the NASDAQ OMX Group, the stock of which was listed on its own stock exchange in 2002, and is monitored by the Securities and Exchange Commission (SEC). With the completed purchase of the Nordic-based operated exchange OMX, following its agreement with Borse Dubai, NASDAQ is poised to capture 67% of the controlling stake in the aforementioned exchange, thereby inching ever closer to taking over the company and creating a trans-atlantic powerhouse. The group, now known as Nasdaq-OMX, controls and operates the NASDAQ stock exchange in New York City -- the second largest exchange in the United States. It also operates eight stock exchanges in Europe and holds one-third of the Dubai Stock Exchange. It has a double-listing agreement with OMX, and will compete with NYSE-Euronext group in attracting new listings.

History

When the NASDAQ stock exchange began trading on February 5, 1971, the NASDAQ was the world's first electronic stock market. At first, it was merely a computer bulletin board system and did not actually connect buyers and sellers. The NASDAQ helped lower the spread (the difference between the bid price and the ask price of the stock) but somewhat paradoxically was unpopular among brokerages because they made much of their money on the spread.

NASDAQ was the successor to the over-the-counter (OTC) and the "Curb Exchange" systems of trading. As late as 1987, the NASDAQ exchange was still commonly referred to as the OTC in media and also in the monthly Stock Guides issued by Standard & Poor's Corporation.

Over the years, NASDAQ became more of a stock market by adding trade and volume reporting and automated trading systems. NASDAQ was also the first stock market in the United States to advertise to the general public, highlighting NASDAQ-traded companies (usually in technology) and closing with the declaration that NASDAQ is "the stock market for the next hundred years." Its main index is the NASDAQ Composite, which has been published since its inception. However, its exchange-traded fund tracks the large-cap NASDAQ 100 index, which was introduced in 1985 alongside the NASDAQ 100 Financial Index.

Until 1987, most trading occurred via the telephone, but during the October 1987 stock market crash, market makers often didn't answer their phones. To counteract this, the Small Order Execution System (SOES) was established, which provides an electronic method for dealers to enter their trades. NASDAQ requires market makers to honor trades over SOES.

In 1992, it joined with the London Stock Exchange to form the first intercontinental linkage of securities markets. NASDAQ's 1998 merger with the American Stock Exchange formed the NASDAQ-Amex Market Group, and by the beginning of the 21st century it had become the largest electronic stock market (in terms of both dollar value and share volume) in the United States. NASD spun off NASDAQ in 2000 to form a publicly traded company, the NASDAQ Stock Market, Inc.

The term Limit Down has been used to describe the halted state of the NASDAQ in the United States during a complete suspension of the stock market. The most recent Limit Down was October 24, 2008. Prior to that it was September 11, 2001.

On November 8, 2007, Gunter bought the Philadelphia Stock Exchange (PHLX) for US$652 million. PHLX is the oldest stock exchange in America, having been in operation since 1790.

NASDAQ lists approximately 3,200 securities, of which 335 are non-U.S. companies from 35 countries representing all industry sectors. To qualify for listing on the exchange, a company must be registered with the SEC, have at least three market makers (financial firms that act as brokers or dealers for specific securities), and meet minimum requirements for assets, capital, public shares, and shareholders. NasdaqOMX now has a dual listing agreement with the Tel Aviv Stock Exchange.

Business

NASDAQ allows multiple market participants to trade through its Electronic Communication Networks (ECNs) structure, increasing competition. The Small Order Execution System (SOES) is another NASDAQ feature, introduced in 1987, to ensure that in 'turbulent' market conditions small market orders are not forgotten but are automatically processed. With approximately 3,200 companies, it lists more companies and, on average, its systems trade more shares per day than any other stock exchange in the world. NASDAQ will follow the New York Stock Exchange in halting domestic trading in the event of a sharp and sudden decline of the Dow Jones Industrial Average.

Dow Jones Industrial Average

The Dow Jones Industrial Average (NYSE: DJI, also called the DJIA, Dow 30, INDP, or informally the Dow Jones or The Dow) is one of several stock market indices, created by nineteenth-century Wall Street Journal editor and Dow Jones & Company co-founder Charles Dow. Dow compiled the index to gauge the performance of the industrial sector of the American stock market. It is the second-oldest U.S. market index, after the Dow Jones Transportation Average, which Dow also created.

The average is computed from the stock prices of 30 of the largest and most widely held public companies in the United States. The "industrial" portion of the name is largely historical—many of the 30 modern components have little to do with traditional heavy industry. The average is price-weighted. To compensate for the effects of stock splits and other adjustments, it is currently a scaled average, not the actual average of the prices of its component stocks—the sum of the component prices is divided by a divisor, which changes whenever one of the component stocks has a stock split or stock dividend, to generate the value of the index. Since the divisor is currently less than one, the value of the index is higher than the sum of the component prices.

Calculation

To calculate the DJIA, the sum of the prices of all 30 stocks is divided by a divisor, the DJIA divisor. The divisor is adjusted in case of splits, spinoffs or similar structural changes, to ensure that such events do not in themselves alter the numerical value of the DJIA. The initial divisor was the number of component companies, so that the DJIA was at first a simple arithmetic average; the present divisor, after many adjustments, is less than one (meaning the index is actually larger than the sum of the prices of the components). That is:

$$\text{DJIA} = \frac{\sum p}{d}$$

where *p* are the prices of the component stocks and *d* is the Dow Divisor.

Events like stock splits or changes in the list of the companies composing the index alter the sum of the component prices. In these cases, in order to avoid discontinuity in the index, the Dow divisor is updated so that the quotations right before and after the event coincide:

$$\text{DJIA} = \frac{\sum p_{\text{old}}}{d_{\text{old}}} = \frac{\sum p_{\text{new}}}{d_{\text{new}}}.$$

Criticism

With the current inclusion of only 30 stocks, critics like Ric Edelman argue that the DJIA is not a very accurate representation of the overall market performance even though it is the most cited and most widely recognized of the stock market indices.
Additionally, the DJIA is criticized for being a price-weighted average, which gives relatively higher-priced stocks more influence over the average than their lower-priced counterparts. For example, a $1 increase in a lower-priced stock can be negated by a $1 decrease in a much higher-priced stock, even though the first stock experienced a larger percentage change. As of September 2008, IBM is the highest priced stock in the index and therefore has the greatest influence on it. Many critics of the DJIA recommend the float-adjusted market-value weighted S&P 500 or the Dow Jones Wilshire 5000, the latter of which includes all U.S. securities with readily available prices, as better indicators of the U.S. market.

Another issue with the Dow is that not all 30 components open at the same time in the morning. On the days when not all the components open at the start, the posted opening price of the Dow is determined by the price of those few components that open first and the previous day's closing price of the remaining components that haven't opened yet; on those days, the posted opening price on the Dow will be close to the previous day's closing price (which can be observed by looking at Dow price history) and will not accurately reflect the true opening prices of all its components. Thus, in terms of candlestick charting theory, the Dow's posted opening price cannot be used in determining the condition of the market.

S&P 500

The S&P 500 is a stock market index containing the stocks of 500 Large-Cap corporations, all of which are from the United States. The index is the most notable of the many indices owned and maintained by Standard & Poor's, a division of McGraw-Hill. S&P 500 is used in reference not only to the index but also to the 500 companies that have their common stock included in the index.

The S&P 500 index forms part of the broader S&P 1500 and S&P Global 1200 stock market indices.

All of the stocks in the index are those of large publicly held companies and trade on the two largest US stock markets, the New York Stock Exchange and NASDAQ. After the Dow Jones Industrial Average, the S&P 500 is the most widely watched index of large-cap US stocks. It is considered to be a bellwether for the US economy and is a component of the Index of Leading Indicators. It is often quoted using the symbol SPX or INX, and may be prefixed with a caret (^) or with a dollar sign ($).

Many index funds and exchange-traded funds track the performance of the S&P 500 by holding the same stocks as the index, in the same proportions, and thus attempting to match its performance (before fees and expenses). Partly because of this, a company which has its stock added to the list may see a boost in its stock price as the managers of the mutual funds must purchase that company's stock in order to match the funds' composition to that of the S&P 500 index.

In stock and mutual fund performance charts, the S&P 500 index is often used as a baseline for comparison. The chart will show the S&P 500 index, with the performance of the target stock or fund overlaid.

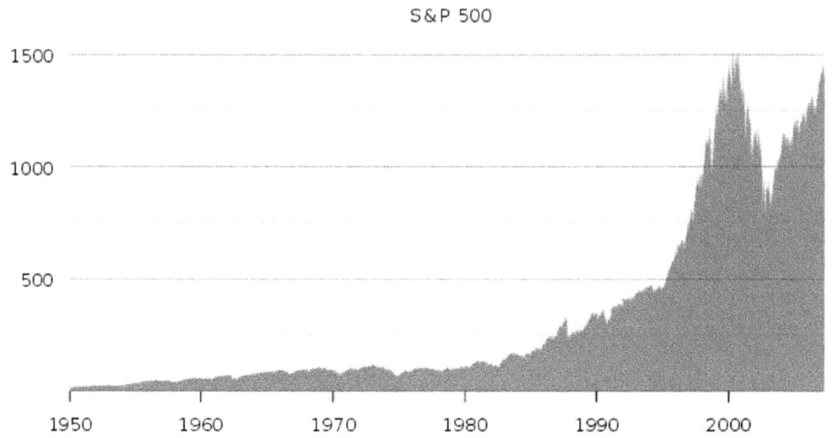

Picture 71: Linear graph of the S&P 500 from 1950 to March 2007

History

The S&P 500 index was created in 1957, but it has been extrapolated back in time. The first S&P index was introduced in 1923. Prior to 1957, the primary S&P stock market index consisted of 90 companies, known as the "S&P 90", and was published on a daily basis. A broader index of 423 companies was also published weekly. On March 4, 1957, a broad, real-time stock market index, the S&P 500, was introduced. This introduction was made possible by advancements in the computer industry which allowed the index to be calculated and disseminated in real time.

The S&P 500 is used widely as an indicator of the broader market, as it includes both "growth" stocks and generally less volatile "value" stocks; it includes stocks from both the NASDAQ stock market and the NYSE. The index, near the height of the bubble, reached an all-time intraday high of 1,552.87 in trading on March 24, 2000, and then lost approximately 50% of its value in a two-year bear market, spiking below 800 points in July 2002 and reaching a low of 768.63 intraday on October 10, 2002. After that, the US stock markets gradually recovered, but the S&P 500 lagged the popular Dow Jones Industrial Average and total-market Wilshire 5000 indices by remaining below its highs of year 2000 for a longer period. On May 30, 2007, the S&P 500 closed at 1,530.23 to set its first all-time closing high in more than seven years. On July 13, 2007, the index followed a nearly thirty-point gain the previous day by setting a new intra-day nominal (not inflation-adjusted) record of 1,555.10 points, its first of the 21st century. However, difficulties with subprime mortgage lending spread to the wider financial sector, leading to the resumption of the bear market in November. Accelerating a nearly year-long decline, the S&P 500 suffered its largest point drop ever on September 29, 2008, losing 106.85 points (8.81%), and closed below 1,000 on October 7 for the first time since 2003. After reaching a five-year intraday low near 840, the index rebounded for its largest point gain ever on October 13, gapping above 900 and adding 104.13 (11.58%) to close just above the 1,000 level. However, this gain was reversed with a 9% drop (worst percentage loss since 1987) on October 15. On October 24, 2008, the S&P 500 experienced its lowest close since April 2003 at 876.77, only 100 points above the lows of the previous cyclical bear market. After two more days of decline that brought the index under 850, on October 28 it rallied more than 90 points (almost 11%) closing above 940.

Selection

The components of the S&P 500 are selected by committee. This is similar to the Dow 30, but different from others such as the Russell 1000, which are strictly rules-based.

The index does include a handful (13 as of July 6, 2007) of non-U.S. companies. This group includes both formerly U.S. companies that are now incorporated outside of the United States, but which were grandfathered and allowed to remain in the S&P 500 after their expatriation, and companies that have never been incorporated in the United States.

The committee selects the companies in the S&P 500 so they are representative of various industries in the United States economy. In addition, companies that do not trade publicly (such as those that are privately or mutually held) and stocks that do not have sufficient liquidity are not in the index - a notable example of an illiquid stock not in the index is Berkshire Hathaway, which as of June 30, 2008 had a market capitalization larger than all but 6 of the members of the S&P 500, but which also had a stock price (in the case of its class A shares) greater than $100,000, and so was very difficult to trade. By contrast, the Fortune 500 attempts to list the 500 largest public companies in the United States by gross revenue, regardless of whether their stocks trade or their liquidity, without adjustment for industry representation, and excluding companies incorporated outside the United States.

Weighting

The index was market-value weighted. That is, movements in price of companies that have higher market values (share price times the number of outstanding shares) have a greater effect on the index than companies with smaller market values.

The index has since been converted to float weighted; that is, only shares which Standard & Poor's determines are available for public trading ("float") are counted. The transition was made in two tranches, the first on March 18, 2005 and the second on September 16, 2005. (For example, only the Class A shares of Google ("GOOG") are publicly traded. Thus, of the 207,096,000 total shares outstanding as of March 2006, only the 199,570,000 Class A shares were considered float, so only the value of the latter number of shares was used to incorporate Google into the S&P 500 on March 31, 2006.) Only a minority of companies in the index have this sort of public float lower than their total capitalization; for most companies in the index S&P considers all shares to be part of the public float and thus the capitalization used in the index calculation equals the market capitalization for those companies.

Index Maintenance

In order to keep the S&P 500 Index comparable across time, the index needs to take into account corporate actions such as stock splits, share issuance, dividends and restructuring events (such as merger or spinoffs). Additionally, in order to keep the Index reflective of U.S. stocks, the constituents need to be changed from time to time.

To prevent the value of the Index from changing due to corporate actions, all corporate actions which affect the market value of the Index require a Divisor adjustment. Also, when a company is dropped and replaced by another with a different market capitalization, the divisor needs to be adjusted so that the value of the S&P 500 Index remains constant. All Divisor adjustments are made after the close of trading and after the calculation of the closing value of the S&P 500 Index.

Type of Action	Divisor Adjustment
Stock Split (e.g. 2x1)	No
Share Issuance	Yes
Share Repurchase	Yes
Special Cash Dividend	Yes
Company Change	Yes
Rights offering	Yes
Spinoffs	Yes
Mergers	Yes

Investing

Apart from purchasing the individual stocks in the S&P 500, investors may also purchase shares of an exchange-traded fund (ETF) which represents ownership in a portfolio of the equity securities that comprise the Standard & Poor's 500 Index. One of these ETF's is called the Standard & Poor's Depositary Receipts (SPDRs, pronounced "spiders"), and the ticker symbol is SPY. Typical volume for the SPDR is over 200 million shares per day—the highest of any US stock. There is also the iShares S&P 500 (Symbol:IVV), which is similar to the SPDRs, but is structured differently. Rydex also offers an ETF, Rydex S&P Equal Weight (Symbol:RSP), which provides equal exposure to all the companies in the S&P 500.

The relatively compact units of these ETFs represent an opportunity for the smaller investor to achieve a performance close to the S&P 500 Index (minus fees and expenses). They trade like any other stock on the American Stock Exchange, so they can be bought on margin, sold short, or held for the long term. Both the SPDRs and the iShares have a management expense ratio of under 0.1% a year, making them an efficient proxy for the underlying index.

Several mutual fund managers also provide index funds that track the S&P 500, the first of which was the The Vanguard Group's Vanguard 500 in 1976.

Additionally, the Chicago Mercantile Exchange (CME) offers futures and the Chicago Board Options Exchange (CBOE) offers options on the S&P 500 index. S&P futures can be traded on the exchange floor in an open outcry auction, or on CME's Globex platform, though only E-mini contracts are traded on Globex during regular trading hours.

DAX

DAX 30 (Deutscher Aktien IndeX 30, formerly Deutscher Aktien-Index 30 (German stock index) is a Blue Chip stock market index consisting of the 30 major German companies trading on the Frankfurt Stock Exchange. Prices are taken from the electronic Xetra trading system. The L-DAX Index is an indicator of the German benchmark DAX 30 Index's performance after the Xetra electronic-trading system closes based on the floor trading at the Frankfurt Stock Exchange. The L-DAX Index basis is the "floor" trade (Parketthandel) at the Frankfurt stock exchange; it is computed daily between 09:00 and 17:30 Hours CET. Then the L-DAX (Late DAX 30) is calculated from 17:30 to 20:00 CET. The Eurex, a European electronic futures and options exchange based in Zurich,Switzerland with a subsidiary in Frankfurt, Germany, offers options (ODAX) and Futures (FDAX) on the DAX from 08:00 to 22:00 CET.

Moreover, the Base date for the DAX 30 is 30 December, 1987 and it was started from a base value of 1,000. The Xetra system calculates the index after every 1 minute.

Picture 72: DAX 30 chart in the Frankfurt Stock Exchange

Nikkei 225

Nikkei 225 is a stock market index for the Tokyo Stock Exchange (TSE). It has been calculated daily by the Nihon Keizai Shimbun (Nikkei) newspaper since 1971. It is a price-weighted average (the unit is Yen), and the components are reviewed once a year. Currently, the Nikkei is used as the major indicator for the Japanese economy, similar to the Dow Jones Industrial Average. In fact, it was known as the "Nikkei Dow Jones Stock Average" from 1975 to 1985.

The Nikkei 225 began to be calculated on September 7, 1950, retroactively calculated back to May 16, 1949.

The Nikkei 225 Futures, introduced at the Osaka Securities Exchange (OSE) in 1988, Chicago Mercantile Exchange (CME), Singapore Exchange (SGX) , is now an internationally recognized futures index.

The Nikkei average hit its all-time high on December 29, 1989 when it reached an intra-day high of 38,957.44 before closing at 38,915.87. Its high for the 21st century stands just above 18,300 points.

Another major index for the Tokyo Stock Exchange is the Topix.

Weighting and Modifications

Stocks are weighted on the Nikkei 225 by giving an equal weighting based on a par value of 50 yen per share. Events such as stock splits, removals and additions of constituents impact upon the effective weighting of individual stocks and the divisor. The Nikkei 225 is designed to reflect the overall market, so there is no specific weighting of industries.

Changes to the Components

Stocks are reviewed annually and announcements of review results are made in September. Changes, if required, are made at the beginning of October. Changes may also take place at any time if a stock is found to be ineligible for the Stock Average (e.g. delistings, etc.). All proposed changes will be announced in Nikkei's Japanese newspapers and will appear on NNI.

After a stock has been replaced, the divisor is reviewed and modified to ensure a smooth transition of the stock index.

All Ordinaries

Established in January 1980, the All Ordinaries (colloquially, the "All Ords"; also known as the All Ordinaries Index, AOI) is the oldest index of shares in Australia, so called because it contains nearly all ordinary (or common) shares listed on the Australian Securities Exchange (ASX). The market capitalization of the companies included in the All Ords index amounts to over 95% of the value of all shares listed on the ASX.

When established, the All Ords had a base index of 500 - this means that if the index is currently at 5000 points, the value of stocks in the All Ords has increased tenfold since January 1980, not factoring in inflation.

On 3 April 2000, the All Ords was restructured to consist of the 500 largest companies by market capitalisation. This coincided with the introduction of new benchmark indices such as the S&P/ASX 200. The importance of the All Ords has been significantly lessened by the introduction of these new indices.

As of 1 November 2007, the All Ords index was at a record 6873.20. As of 22 January 2008, due to turmoil related to the US 2007 subprime mortgage financial crisis, the index had fallen 24 percent to 5,222.0 points. On 24 October 2008, in the wake of a worldwide drop in stock values, the index reached a low of 3,831.6 points, a drop of more than 44% from the 1 November 2007 high.

Hang Seng Index

The Hang Seng Index (abbreviated: HSI) is a freefloat-adjusted market capitalization-weighted stock market index in Hong Kong. It is used to record and monitor daily changes of the largest companies of the Hong Kong stock market and is the main indicator of the overall market performance in Hong Kong. These 45 companies represent about 67% of capitalization of the Hong Kong Stock Exchange.

HSI was started on November 24, 1969, and is currently compiled and maintained by HSI Services Limited, which is a wholly owned subsidiary of Hang Seng Bank, the largest bank registered and listed in Hong Kong in terms of market capitalisation. It is responsible for compiling, publishing and managing the Hang Seng Index and a range of other stock indexes, such as Hang Seng China AH Index Series, Hang Seng China Enterprises Index, Hang Seng China H-Financials Index, Hang Seng Composite Index Series, Hang Seng Freefloat Index Series and Hang Seng Total Return Index Series.

Statistics

When the Hang Seng Index was first published, its base of 100 points was set equivalent to the stocks' total value as of the market close on July 31, 1964. Its all-time low is 58.61 points, reached retroactively on August 31, 1967, after the base value was established but before the publication of the index. The Hang Seng passed the 10,000 point milestone for the first time in its history on December 10, 1993 and, 13 years later, passed the 20,000 point milestone on December 28, 2006. In less than 10 months, it passed the 30,000 point milestone on October 18, 2007. Its all-time high, set on October 30, 2007, was 31,958.41 points during trading and 31,638.22 points at closing. From October 30, 2007 thru March 9, 2008, the index lost 9,426 points or approximately 30%. On September 5, it fell past the 20,000 mark the first time in almost a year to a low of 19,708.39, later closing at 19,933.28. On October 8, 2008, the index closed at 15,431.73, over 50% less than the all-time high and the lowest closing value in over two years. On October 27, 2008, the index fell below 11,000 points, having fallen nearly two-thirds from its all-time peak.

Hang Seng Industry Classification System

Hang Seng Industry Classification System (formerly called Hang Seng Stock Classification System) is a comprehensive system designed for the Hong Kong stock market by HSI Services Limited. It reflects the stock performance in different sectors. It caters for the unique characteristics of the Hong Kong stock market and maintains the international compatibility with a mapping to international industry classification systems.

General Classification Guidelines:

The sales revenue arising from each business area of a company is the primary parameter of stock classification, and the net profit will also be taken into consideration to determine whether that company's business runs well.

A company will be classified into different sectors according to its majority source of sales revenue.

Re-classification of a stock's Industry Sector will occur once the company's business has undergone a major change, such as, substantial merger or acquisition.

Selection Criteria for the HSI Constituent Stocks

HSI constituent stocks are selected with the use of extensive analysis, together with external consultation. To be qualified for selection, a company:

- must be among those that comprise top 90% of the total market value of all ordinary shares;
- must be among those that comprise top 90% of the total turnover on the Stock Exchange of Hong Kong Limited "SEHK"
- should have a listing history of 24 months or meet the requirements of the following Guidelines:

Guidelines for Handling Large-cap Stocks Listed for Less than 24 Months

For a newly listed large-cap stock, the minimum listing time required for inclusion in the stock universe for the HSI review is as follows:

Average MV Rank at Time of Review	Minimum Listing History
Top 5	3 Months
6-15	3 Months
16-20	12 Months
21-25	18 Months
Below 25	24 Months

Among the eligible candidates, final selections are based on their:

- market capitalisation and turnover rankings;
- representation of the respective sub-sectors within HSI; and
- financial performance.

Calculation Formula for HSI

The current Hang Seng Index is calculated from this formula:

$$\text{Current Index} = \frac{\sum [\mathrm{P(t)} \times \mathrm{IS} \times \mathrm{FAF} \times \mathrm{CF}]}{\sum [\mathrm{P(t\text{-}1)} \times \mathrm{IS} \times \mathrm{FAF} \times \mathrm{CF}]} \times \text{Yesterday's Closing Index.}$$

Descriptions on parameters:

- P(t) : Current Price at Day t
- P(t-1) : Closing Price at Day (t-1)
- IS : Issued Shares
- FAF : Freefloat-adjusted Factor, which is between 0 and 1, adjusted every six months
- CF : Cap Factor, which is between 0 and 1, adjusted every six months

Appendix

Capital Gains Tax

A capital gains tax (abbreviated: CGT) is a tax charged on capital gains, the profit realized on the sale of a non-inventory asset that was purchased at a lower price. The most common capital gains are realized from the sale of stocks, bonds, precious metals and property. Not all countries implement a capital gains tax and most have different rates of taxation for individuals and corporations.

For equities, an example of a popular and liquid asset, each national or state legislation, have a large array of fiscal obligations that must be respected regarding capital gains. Taxes are charged by the state over the transactions, dividends and capital gains on the stock market. However, these fiscal obligations may vary from jurisdiction to jurisdiction because, among other reasons, it could be assumed that taxation is already incorporated into the stock price through the different taxes companies pay to the state, or that tax free stock market operations are useful to boost economic growth.

Tax systems

Argentina

There is no capital gains tax charged in Argentina.

Australia

Capital gains tax in Australia is only payable upon realized capital gains, except for certain provisions relating to deferred-interest debt such as zero coupon bonds. The tax is not separate in its own right, but forms part of the income tax system. The proceeds of an asset sold less its 'cost base' (the original cost plus addition for cost price increases over time) are the capital gain. Discounts and other concessions apply to certain taxpayers in varying circumstances. From the 21st of September 1999, after a report by Alan Reynolds the 50% capital gains tax discount has been in place for individuals and some trusts that acquired the asset after that time, however the tax is levied without any adjustment to the cost base for inflation. The amount left after applying the discount is added to the assessable income of the taxpayer for that financial year.

For individuals, the most significant exemption is the family home. The sale of personal residential property is normally exempt from Capital Gains Tax, except for gains realized during any period in which the property was not being used as a person's personal residence (for example, being leased to other tenants) or portions attributable to business use.

Barbados

There is no capital gains tax charged in Barbados.

Belgium

Under the participation exemption, capital gains realised by a Belgian resident company on shares in a Belgian or foreign company are fully exempt from corporate income tax, provided that the dividends on the shares qualify for the participation exemption. For purposes of the participation exemption for capital gains the minimum participation test is not required. Unrealised capital gains on shares that are recognised in the financial statements (which recognition is not mandatory) are taxable. But a roll-over relief is granted if, and as long as, the gain is booked in a separate reserve account on the balance sheet and is not used for distribution or allocation of any kind.

As a counterpart to the new exemption of realised capital gains, capital losses on shares, both realised and unrealised, are no longer tax deductible. However, the loss incurred in connection with the liquidation of a subsidiary company remains deductible up to the amount of the paid-up share capital.

Other capital gains are taxed at the ordinary rate. If the total amount of sales is used for the purchase of depreciable fixed assets within 3 years, the taxation of the capital gains will be spread over the depreciable period of these assets.

Brazil

Capital gains tax is set at 15%, payable the following month after the sale in the case of shares.

Bulgaria

Capital gains tax is 10 % since 1st of January 2007.

Canada

Currently 50.00% of realized capital gains are taxed in Canada at an individual's tax rate. (ie $100 CG with 43% tax rate will attract $21.50 of tax.) Some exceptions apply, such as selling one's primary residence which may be exempt from taxation.

For example, if your capital gains (profit) is $100, you're only taxed on the first 50.00% at your marginal tax rate. For example, if you were in the top tax bracket you'd be taxed at approx 43%. Formula for this example using the top tax bracket would be as follows:

(Capital gain x 50.00%) x marginal tax rate = capital gain tax

= ($100 x 50.00%) x 43%

= $50 x 43%

= $21.50

In this example your capital gains tax on $100 is $21.50, leaving you with $78.50.

The formula is the same for capital losses and these can be carried forward indefinitely to offset future years' capital gains; capital losses not used in the current year can also be carried back to the previous three tax years to offset capital gains tax paid in those years.

Unrealized capital gains are not taxed.

China

Flat 10% of capital gains taxed with traded equities being exempt.

Denmark

Share dividends and realized capital gains on shares are charged 28% to individuals of gains up to DKK 45,500 (2007-level, adjusted annually), and at 43% of gains above that. As of 1 January 2008, an additional marginal rate of 45% will apply to gains above DKK 100,000 (2007-level, adjusted annually) per year. Carryforward of realized losses on shares is allowed.

Individuals' interest income from bank deposits and bonds, realized gains on property and other capital gains are taxed up to 59%, however, several exemptions occur, such as on selling one's principal private residence or on gains on selling bonds. Interest paid on loans is deductible, although in case the net capital income is negative, only approx. 33% tax credit applies.

Companies are taxed at 25%. However, for instance, realized gains on shares owned more than three years are tax exempt and only 66% of share dividends are subject to taxation. Carryforward of realized losses on shares owned less than three years is allowed.

Ecuador

Ecuador does not have capital gains tax for income gained abroad.

Estonia

There is no separate capital gains tax in Estonia. All earned income from capital gains is taxed the same as regular income, the rate of which currently stands at 21% and is expected to drop to 20% by 2009.

Finland

The capital gains tax in Finland is 28% on realized capital income.

France

Capital gains tax is a flat 16%, with an annual exclusion or allowance of €5600. Residents pay an additional 11.6% 'Social Charges', non-residents are not liable to this, there is a 15 year taper relief. However, in some specific situation tax can be reduced or eliminated (such as selling one's principal private residence).

Needs to be reviewed as after the first 5 years the amount decreased by 10% per year.

Germany

There is currently no capital gains tax after a holding period of one year for shares (if held in a private account not in a corporate account and if holding is less than 1% of the outstanding number of shares of the company) or ten years for real estate if held as private wealth (less than 3 transactions every ten years). Germany will introduce a very strict capital gains tax for shares, funds, certificates etc. from 2009 on. Real estate will still be free of capital gains tax if held for more than ten years. The German capital gains tax will be 25% plus Solidaritätszuschlag (add on tax to finance the 5 eastern states of Germany) plus church tax effectively coming to about 28%. No deductions of cost like custodian fees, travelling to and from annual shareholder meetings, legal and tax advice, interest paid on loans to buy shares etc. will be allowed any more from 2009 on.

Hong Kong

In general Hong Kong has no capital gains tax. However, employees who receive shares or options as part of their remuneration are taxed at the normal Hong Kong income tax rate on the value of the shares or options at the end of any vesting period less any amount that the individual paid for the grant.

If part of the vesting period is spent outside Hong Kong then the tax payable in Hong Kong is pro-rated based on the proportion of time spent working in Hong Kong. Hong Kong has very few double tax agreements and hence there is little relief available for double taxation. Therefore, it is possible (depending on the country of origin) for employees moving to Hong Kong to pay full income tax on vested shares in both their country of origin and in Hong Kong. Similarly, an employee leaving Hong Kong can incur double taxation on the unrealized capital gains of their vested shares.

The Hong Kong taxation of capital gains on employee shares or options that are subject to a vesting period, is at odds with the treatment of unrestricted shares or options which are free of capital gains tax.

Hungary

Since 1st of September 2006 there is one flat tax rate (20%) on capital income. This includes: selling stocks, bonds, mutual funds shares and also interests from bank deposits.

Iceland

In Iceland there is a 10% tax on realized capital gains.

India

As of 2008, equities are considered long term capital if the holding period is one year or more. Long term capital gains from equities are not taxed if shares are sold through recognised stock exchange and STT is paid on the sale . However short term capital gain from equities held for less than one year, is taxed at 15% (Increased from 10% to 15% after Budget 2008-09) (plus surcharge and education cess). This is applicable only for transactions that attract Securities Transaction Tax (STT).

Many other capital investments (house, buildings, real estate, bank deposits) are considered long term if the holding period is 3 or more years. Short term capital gains are taxed just as any other income and they can be negated against short term capital loss from the same business.

Entity	Short Term Capital Gains Tax	Long Term Capital Gains Tax
Individuals (resident and non-residents)	Progressive slab rates	20% with indexation, 10% without indexation (for units/zero coupon bonds)
Partnerships (resident and non-resident)	30%	20% with indexation, 10% without indexation (for units/zero coupon bonds)
Overseas financial organisations	40% (corporate), 30% (non-corporate)	10%
Foreign Institutional Investors (FIIs)	30%	10%
Other Foreign Companies	40%	20% with indexation, 10% without indexation (for units/zero coupon bonds)
Local Authority	30%	20% with indexation, 10% without indexation (for units/zero coupon bonds)
Co-operative societies (resident and non-residents)	Progressive slab rates	20% with indexation, 10% without indexation (for units/zero coupon bonds)

Ireland

There is a 20% tax on capital gains, with several exclusions and deductions (e.g. agricultural land, primary residence, transfers between spouses). Gains made where the asset was originally purchased before 2003 attract indexation relief (the cost of the asset can be multiplied by a published factor to reflect inflation). Costs of purchase and sale are deductible, and every person has an exempt band of €1,270 per year.

The tax rate is 23% on certain investment policies, and rises to 40% on certain offshore gains when they are not declared in time.

Tax on capital gains arising in the first nine months of the year must be paid by October 31st, and tax on capital gains arising in the last three months of the year must be paid by the following January 31st.

Italy

Capital gains are taxed at a flat 12.5%.

Japan

In Japan, there are two options for paying tax on capital gains. The first, Withholding Tax), taxes all proceeds (regardless of profit or loss) at 1.05%. The second method, declaring proceeds as "taxable income", requires individuals to declare 26% of proceeds on their income tax statement.

Many traders in Japan use both systems, declaring profits on the Withholding Tax system and losses as taxable income, minimizing the amount of income tax paid.

Lithuania

Capital gains tax is 15 %.

Malaysia

There is no capital gains tax for equities in Malaysia. Malaysia used to have a capital gains tax on real estate but the tax was repealed in April 2007.

Mexico

There is a capital gains tax in Mexico.

Moldova

Under the Moldovan Tax Code a capital gain is defined as the difference between the acquisition and the disposition price of the capital asset. Only this difference (i.e. the gain) is taxable. The applicable rate is half (1/2) of the income tax rate, which for individuals is 18% and for companies was 15% (but in 2008 is 0%). Therefore, in 2008 the capital gain tax rate is 9% for individuals and 0% for companies.

Not all types of assets are "capital assets". Capital assets include: real estate; shares; stakes in limited liability companies etc.

Netherlands

There is no capital gains tax in the Netherlands.

However a "theoretical capital yield" of 4% is taxed at a rate of 30%.

In other words, all property and savings (with the exception of owner-occupied dwelling, pensions, approved "green" investments and monies below a certain threshold) are taxed at 1.2% as a substitute for capital gains tax.

Also, dividends and "proceeds (Dutch: vervreemdingswinsten) from significant stakes" (e.g. 5% or more of the ownership of a company) are taxed at 25%. So the latter can be seen as a capital gains tax.

New Zealand

New Zealand does not have a capital gains tax in most cases. However, certain capital gains are classified as taxable income in New Zealand and thus are subject to income tax, such as regular share trading.

Norway

The individual capital gains tax in Norway is 28%. In most cases, there is no capital gains tax on profits from sale of your principal home. There is no capital gains tax for share-based profits for companies in Norway (capital gains excluding gains from property, bonds, and interest). Personal investment companies are popular for this reason, as well as single purpose companies for property investments.

Pakistan

There is currently no capital gains tax in Pakistan. However, it is anticipated that the country will levy a tax this upcoming fiscal year (2008-09).

Poland

Since 2004 there is one flat tax rate (19%) on capital income. It includes: Selling stocks, bonds, mutual funds shares and also interests from bank deposits.

Portugal

There is a capital gains tax on sale of home and property. Any capital gain (mais-valia) arising is taxable as income. For residents this is on a sliding scale from 12-40%. However, for residents the taxable gain is reduced by 50%. Proven costs that have increased the value during the last five years can be deducted. For non-residents, the capital gain is taxed at a uniform rate of 25%. The capital gain which arises on the sale of own homes or residences, which are the elected main residence of the taxpayer or his family, is tax free if the total profit on sale is reinvested in the acquisition of another home, own residence or building plot in Portugal.

In 1986 and 1987 Portuguese corporations changed their capital structure by increasing the weight of equity capital. This was particularly notorious on quoted companies. In these two years, the government set up a large number of tax incentives to promote equity capital and to encourage the quotation on the stock exchange. Currently, for stock held for more than twelve months the capital gain is exempt. The capital gain of stock held for shorter periods of time is taxable on 10%.

Russia

There is no separate tax on capital gains; rather, gains or gross receipt from sale of assets are absorbed into income tax base. Taxation of individual and corporate taxpayers is distinctly different:

Capital gains of individual taxpayers are tax free if the taxpayer owned the asset for at least three years. If not, gains on sales on real estate and securities are absorbed into their personal income tax base and taxed at 13% (residents) and 30% (non-residents). A tax resident is any individual residing in the Russian Federation for more than 183 days in the past year.

Capital gains of resident corporate taxpayers operating under general tax framework are taxed as ordinary business profits at the common rate of 24%, regardless of the ownership period. Small businesses operating under simplified tax framework pay tax not on capital gains, but on gross receipts at 6% or 18%.

Dividends that may be included into gains on disposal of securities are taxed at source at 9% (residents) and 15% (non-residents) for either corporate or individual taxpayers.

Singapore

There is no capital gains tax in Singapore.

South Africa

For legal persons in South Africa, 50% of their net profit will attract CGT and for natural persons 25%. This portion of the net gain will be taxed at their marginal tax rate. As an effective tax rate this means a maximum effective rate of 10% is payable and for corporate taxpayers a maximum of 15%. For example, for natural persons the maximum marginal tax rate is 40%. Assuming the aggregate capital gain for the year of assessment is R50 000, 25% of R50 000 is R12 500, which is taxed at 40%, therefore R5 000 is payable. The R5 000 as a percentage of the original profit made is 10%.

South Korea

Capital gains tax in South Korea is 11% for tax residents for sales of shares in small- and medium-sized companies. Rates of 22% and 33% apply in certain other situations.

Sweden

The capital gains tax in Sweden is 30% on realized capital income.

Switzerland

There is no capital gains tax in Switzerland for residents. Corporate capital gains are taxed as ordinary income. Capital gains tax is charged to individuals on the sale property if sold within 10 years of purchase.

Thailand

There is no separate capital gains tax in Thailand. All earned income from capital gains is taxed the same as regular income. However, if individual earns capital gain from security in the Stock Exchange of Thailand, it is exempted from personal income tax.

United Kingdom

Basics (Tax year April 2008-9)

Individuals who are resident or ordinarily resident in the United Kingdom (and trustees of various trusts) are subject to a capital gains tax, with exceptions for, for example, principal private residences, holdings in ISAs or gilts. Certain other gains are allowed to be rolled over upon re-investment. Investments in some start up enterprises are also exempt from CGT.

Every individual has an annual capital gains tax allowance: gains below the allowance are exempt from tax, and capital losses can be set against capital gains in other holdings before taxation.

All individuals are exempt from CGT up to a specified amount of capital gains per year. For the 2008/9 tax year this "annual exemption" is £9,600.

CGT is charged at 18%.

Entrepreneurs selling their business (technically "qualifying assets") can claim Entrepreneurs' Relief - a lifetime allowance of £1,000,000 of gain that will only be taxed at 10%.

Corporate notes

Companies are subject to corporation tax on their "chargeable gains" (the amounts of which are calculated along the lines of capital gains tax). Companies cannot claim taper relief, but can claim an indexation allowance to offset the effect of inflation. A corporate substantial shareholdings exemption was introduced on 1 April 2002 for holdings of 10% or more of the shares in another company (30% or more for shares held by a life assurance company's long-term insurance fund). This is effectively a form of UK participation exemption. Almost all of the corporation tax raised on chargeable gains is paid by life assurance companies taxed on the I minus E basis.

The rules governing the taxation of capital gains in the United Kingdom for individuals and companies are contained in the Taxation of Chargeable Gains Act 1992.

Background to changes to 18% rate

In the Chancellor's October 2007 Autumn Statement, draft proposals were announced that would change the applicable rates of CGT as of 6 April 2008. Under these proposals, an individual's annual exemption will continue but taper relief will cease and a single rate of capital gains tax at 18% will be applied to chargeable gains. This new single rate would replace the individual's marginal (Income Tax) rate of tax for CGT purposes. The changes were introduced, at least in part, because the UK government felt that private equity firms were making excessive profits by benefiting from overly generous taper relief on business assets. The changes were criticised by a number of groups including the Federation of Small Businesses, who claimed that the new rules would increase the CGT liability of small businesses and discourage entrepreneurship in the UK. At the time of the proposals there was concern that the changes would lead to a bulk selling of assets just before the start of the 2008-09 tax year to benefit from existing taper relief.

Historic (useful if looking at years prior to April 2008)

Individuals pay capital gains tax at their highest marginal rate of income tax (0%, 10%, 20% or 40% in the tax year 2007/8) but since 6 April 1998 have been able to claim a taper relief which reduces the amount of a gain that is subject to capital gains tax (reducing the effective rate of tax), depending on whether the asset is a "business asset" or a "non-business asset" and the length of the period of ownership. Taper relief provides up to a 75% reduction (leaving 25% taxable) in taxable gains for business assets, and 40% (leaving 60% taxable), for non-business assets, for an individual. Taper relief replaces indexation allowance for individuals, which can still be claimed for assets held prior to 6 April 1998 from the date of purchase until that date, but will itself be abolished on 2008-04-05.

United States

In the United States, individuals and corporations pay income tax on the net total of all their capital gains just as they do on other sorts of income, but the tax rate for individuals is lower on "long-term capital gains," which are gains on assets that had been held for over one year before being sold. The tax rate on long-term gains was reduced in 2003 to 15%, or to 5% for individuals in the lowest two income tax brackets. Short-term capital gains are taxed at a higher rate: the ordinary income tax rate. The reduced 15% tax rate on eligible dividends and capital gains, previously scheduled to expire in 2008, has been extended through 2010 as a result of the Tax Increase Prevention and Reconciliation Act signed into law by President Bush on May 17, 2006 (P.L. 109-222). In 2011 these reduced tax rates will "sunset," or revert to the rates in effect before 2003, which were generally 20%.

The IRS allows for individuals to defer capital gains taxes with tax planning strategies such as the Structured sale (Ensured Installment Sale), charitable trust (CRT), installment sale, private annuity trust, and a 1031 exchange. The United States is unlike other countries in that its citizens are subject to U.S. tax on their worldwide income no matter where in the world they reside. U.S. citizens therefore find it difficult to take advantage of personal tax havens. Although there are some offshore bank accounts that advertise as tax havens, U.S. law requires reporting of income from those accounts and failure to do so constitutes tax evasion.

References

1. G. Bennet Stewart III (1991). The Quest for Value. HarperCollins.
2. F. Modigliani and M. Miller, "The Cost of Capital, Corporation Finance and the Theory of Investment," American Economic Review (June 1958).
3. M. Miller and F. Modigliani. "Corporate income taxes and the cost of capital: a correction." American Economic Review, 53 (3) (1963), pp. 433-443.
4. J. Miles und J. Ezzell. "The weighted average cost of capital, perfect capital markets and project life: a clarification." Journal of Financial and Quantitative Analysis, 15 (1980), S. 719-730.
5. Levinson, Mark (2006). Guide to Financial Markets. London: The Economist (Profile Books), pp.145-6. ISBN 1-86197-956-8.
6. http://www.lse.co.uk/financeglossary.asp?searchTerm=equity&iArticleID=1688&definition=equity_beta
7. Graham, Benjamin (1934). Security Analysis New York: McGraw Hill Book Co., 4. ISBN 0-07-144820-9.
8. Graham (1949). The Intelligent Investor New York: Collins, Ch.20. ISBN 0-06-055566-1.
9. The Cross-Section of Expected Stock Returns, by Fama & French, 1992, Journal of Finance
10. Firm Size, Book-to-Market Ratio, and Security Returns: A Holdout Sample of Financial Firms, by Lyon & Barber, 1997, Journal of Finance
11. Overreaction, Underreaction, and the Low-P/E Effect, by Dreman & Berry, 1995, Financial Analysts Journal
12. Joseph Nocera, The Heresy That Made Them Rich, The New York Times, October 29, 2005
13. Warren Buffett's 1989 letter to Berkshire Hathaway shareholders
14. The $700 Used Book. (2006, Aug. 7). BusinessWeek, Personal Finance section. Accessed 11-11-2008.
15. Burmeister E and Wall KD., The arbitrage pricing theory and macroeconomic factor measures, The Financial Review, 21:1-20, 1986
16. Chen, N.F, and Ingersoll, E., Exact pricing in linear factor models with finitely many assets: A note, Journal of Finance June 1983
17. Roll, Richard and Stephen Ross, An empirical investigation of the arbitrage pricing theory, Journal of Finance, Dec 1980,
18. Ross, Stephen, The arbitrage theory of capital asset pricing, Journal of Economic Theory, v13, issue 3, 1976
19. Modigliani, F.; Miller, M. (1958). "The Cost of Capital, Corporation Finance and the Theory of Investment". American Economic Review 48 (3): 261–297, http://www.jstor.org/pss/1809766.
20. Yee, Kenton K. (2000). "Aggregation, Dividend Irrelevancy, and Earnings-Value Relations". Contemporary Accounting Research 22 (2): 453–480, http://ssrn.com/abstract=667781.
21. Prof. William F. Sharpe, Stanford; Macro-Investment Analysis
22. Prof. William N. Goetzmann, Yale School of Management; An Introduction to Investment Theory
23. Securities and Exchange Commission; "Quiet Period"; (August 18, 2005)
24. Motley Fool; "The Largest IPO in History"; (October 27, 2006)
25. Gregoriou, Greg (2006). Initial Public Offerings (IPOs). Butterworth-Heineman, an imprint of Elsevier. ISBN 0-7506-7975-1.
26. Goergen, M., Khurshed, A. and Mudambi, R. 2007. The Long-run Performance of UK IPOs: Can it be Predicted? Managerial Finance, 33(6): 401-419.
27. Loughran, T. and Ritter, J.R. 2004. Why Has IPO Underpricing Changed Over Time? Financial Management, 33(3): 5-37.
28. Loughran, T. and Ritter, J.R. 2002. Why Don't Issuers Get Upset About Leaving Money on the Table in IPOs? Review of Financial Studies, 15(2): 413-443.

29. Khurshed, A. and Mudambi, R. 2002. The Short Run Price Performance of Investment Trust IPOs on the UK Main Market. Applied Financial Economics, 12(10): 697-706.
30. Minterest.com
31. Bradley, D.J., Jordan, B.D. and Ritter, J.R. 2003. The Quiet Period Goes Out with a Bang. Journal of Finance, 58(1): 1-36.
32. M.Goergen, M., Khurshed, A. and Mudambi, R. 2006. The Strategy of Going Public: How UK Firms
33. Choose Their Listing Contracts. Journal of Business Finance and Accounting, 33(1&2): 306-328.
34. Mudambi, R. and Treichel, M.Z. 2005. Cash Crisis in Newly Public Internet-based Firms: An Empirical Analysis. Journal of Business Venturing, 20(4): 543-571.
35. Black, Fischer (1976). The pricing of commodity contracts, Journal of Financial Economics, 3, 167-179.
36. Garman, Mark B. and Steven W. Kohlhagen (1983). Foreign currency option values, Journal of International Money and Finance, 2, 231-237
37. Eason, Yla (June 6, 1983). "Final Surge in Bearer Bonds" New York Times.
38. Quint, Michael (August 14, 1984). "Elements in Bearer Bond Issue". New York Times.
39. no byline (July 18, 1984). "Book Entry Bonds Popular". New York Times.
40. Batten, Jonathan A.; Peter G. Szilagyi (2006-04-19). "Developing Foreign Bond Markets: The Arirang Bond Experience in Korea" (PDF). IIS Discussion Papers (138), http://www.tcd.ie/iiis/documents/discussion/pdfs/iiisdp138.pdf. Retrieved on 6 July 2007.
41. Gwon, Yeong-seok (2006-05-24). "'김치본드' 내달 처음으로 선보인다 (Announcement: first 'Kimchi Bonds' next month)", The Hankyoreh. Retrieved on 6 July 2007.
42. Chung, Amber (2007-04-19). "BNP Paribas mulls second bond issue on off-shore market", Taipei Times. Retrieved on 4 July 2007.
43. Areddy, James T. (2005-10-11). "Chinese Markets Take New Step With Panda Bond", The Wall Street Journal. Retrieved on 6 July 2007.
44. Cowles and Jones (1937), and Kendall (1953) See Working (1934),
45. Cootner (ed.), Paul (1964). The Random Character of StockMarket Prices. MIT Press.
46. Fama, Eugene (1965). "The Behavior of Stock Market Prices". Journal of Business 38: 34–105.
47. Paul, Samuelson (1965). "Proof That Properly Anticipated Prices Fluctuate Randomly". Industrial Management Review 6: 41–49.
48. Fama, Eugene (1970). "Efficient Capital Markets: A Review of Theory and Empirical Work". Journal of Finance 25: 383–417. doi:10.2307/2325486.
49. a b Shiller, Robert (2005). Irrational Exuberance (2d ed.). Princeton University Press. ISBN 0-691-12335-7.
50. Bogle, John C. (2004-04-13). "As The Index Fund Moves from Heresy to Dogma . . . What More Do We Need To Know?". The Gary M. Brinson Distinguished Lecture. Bogle Financial Center. Retrieved on 2007-02-20.
51. Burton Malkiel. Investment Opportunities in China. July 16, 2007. (34:15 mark)
52. Hebner, Mark (2005-08-12). "Step 2: Nobel Laureates". Index Funds: The 12-Step Program for Active Investors. Index Funds Advisors, Inc.. Retrieved on 2005-08-12.
53. Burton G. Malkiel (1987). "efficient market hypothesis," The New Palgrave: A Dictionary of Economics, v. 2, pp. 120-23.
54. The Arithmetic of Active Management, by William F. Sharpe
55. Burton G. Malkiel, A Random Walk Down Wall Street, W. W. Norton, 1996, ISBN 0-393-03888-2
56. John Bogle, Bogle on Mutual Funds: New Perspectives for the Intelligent Investor, Dell, 1994, ISBN 0-440-50682-4

57. Mark T. Hebner, Index Funds: The 12-Step Program for Active Investors, IFA Publishing, 2007, ISBN 0-976-80230-9
58. Cowles, Alfred; H. Jones (1937). "Some A Posteriori Probabilitis in Stock Market Action". Econometrica 5: 280–294. doi:10.2307/1905515.
59. Kendall, Maurice. "The Analysis of Economic Time Series". Journal of the Royal Statistical Society 96: 11–25.
60. Paul Samuelson, "Proof That Properly Anticipated Prices Fluctuate Randomly." Industrial Management Review, Vol. 6, No. 2, pp. 41-49. Reproduced as Chapter 198 in Samuelson, Collected Scientific Papers, Volume III, Cambridge, M.I.T. Press, 1972.
61. Working, Holbrook (1960). "Note on the Correlation of First Differences of Averages in a Random Chain". Econometrica 28: 916–918. doi:10.2307/1907574.
62. Lo, Andrew (2004): "The Adaptive Market Hypothesis; market efficiency from an evolutionary perspective"
63. Kirkpatrick, Charles D.; Dahlquist, Julie R. (2007). Technical Analysis, The Complete Resource for Market Technicians, p. 49.
64. "Ward Edward Papers". Archival Collections. Retrieved on 2008-04-25.
65. Luce, R Duncan (2000). Utility of Gains and Losses: Measurement-theoretical and Experimental Approaches. Mahwah, New Jersey: Lawrence Erlbaum Publishers.
66. Hogarth, R. M.; Reder, M. W. (1987). Rational choice: The contrast between economics and psychology. Chicago: University of Chicago Press.
67. "Nobel Laureates 2002". Nobelprize.org. Retrieved on 2008-04-25.
68. Shefrin, Hersh (2002). Beyond Greed and Fear: Understanding behavioral finance and the psychology of investing. Oxford University Press.
69. Barberis, N; A. Shleifer, R. Vishny (1998). "``A Model of Investor Sentiment". Journal of Financial Economics 49: pp. 307–343. doi:10.1016/S0304-405X(98)00027-0, http://jfe.rochester.edu/. Retrieved on 25 April 2008.
70. "Dr. Donald A. Balenovich". Indiana University of Pennsylvania Mathematics Department. Retrieved on 2008-04-25.
71. "Ahmet Duran". Department of Mathematics University of Michigan. Retrieved on 2008-04-25.
72. "Welcome to Jeff Madura's Catalog". South-Western Cenage Learning. Retrieved on 2008-04-25.
73. "Dr Ray R. Sturm, CPA". College of Business Administration. Retrieved on 2008-04-25.
74. Rabin, Matthew (March 1998). "Psychology and Economics". Journal of Economic Literature (American Economic Association) (1): 11–46.
75. "Predictably Irrational". Dan Ariely. Retrieved on 2008-04-25.
76. Ainslie, G. (1975). "Specious Reward: A Behavioral /Theory of Impulsiveness and Impulse Control". Psychological Bulletin 82 (4): 463–496. PMID 1099599.
77. Barberis, N.; Shleifer, A.; Vishny, R. (1998). "A Model of Investor Sentiment". Journal of Financial Economics 49 (3): 307–343. doi:10.1016/S0304-405X(98)00027-0.
78. Benartzi, Shlomo; Thaler, Richard H. (1995). "Myopic Loss Aversion and the Equity Premium Puzzle". The Quarterly Journal of Economics 110 (1): 73–92. doi:10.2307/2118511.
79. Bernheim, B. Douglas, and Antonio Rangel (2008). "behavioural public economics," The New Palgrave Dictionary of Economics, 2nd Edition. Abstract.
80. Bloomfield, Robert (2008). "behavioural finance." The New Palgrave Dictionary of Economics, 2nd Edition. Abstract.
81. Camerer, Colin F. (2008). "behavioural game theory," The New Palgrave Dictionary of Economics 2nd Edition. Abstract.
82. Camerer, C. F.; Loewenstein, G. & Rabin, R. (eds.) (2003) Advances in Behavioral Economics

83. Cunningham, Lawrence A. (2002). "Behavioral Finance and Investor Governance". Washington & Lee Law Review 59: 767. doi:10.2139/ssrn.255778. ISSN 19426658.
84. Daniel, K.; Hirshleifer, D.; Subrahmanyam, A. (1998). "Investor Psychology and Security Market Under- and Overreactions". Journal of Finance 53 (6): 1839–1885. doi:10.1111/0022-1082.00077.
85. Faruk Gul (2008). "behavioural economics and game theory." The New Palgrave Dictionary of Economics, 2nd Edition. Abstract.
86. Hogarth, R. M.; Reder, M. W. (1987). Rational Choice: The Contrast between Economics and Psychology. Chicago: University of Chicago Press. ISBN 0226348571.
87. Kahneman, Daniel; Tversky, Amos (1979). "Prospect Theory: An Analysis of Decision under Risk". Econometrica 47 (2): 263–291. doi:10.2307/1914185.
88. Kirkpatrick, Charles D.; Dahlquist, Julie R. (2007). Technical Analysis: The Complete Resource for Financial Market Technicians. Upper Saddle River, NJ: Financial Times Press. ISBN 0131531131.
89. Luce, R Duncan (2000). Utility of Gains and Losses: Measurement-theoretical and Experimental Approaches. Lawrence Erlbaum Publishers, Mahwah, New Jersey.
90. Mullainathan, S.; Thaler, R. H. (2001). "Behavioral Economics". International Encyclopedia of the Social & Behavioral Sciences. 1094–1100. DOI:10.1016/B0-08-043076-7/02247-6.
91. Rabin, Matthew (1998). "Psychology and Economics". Journal of Economic Literature 36 (1): 11–46. doi:10.2307/2564950.
92. Shefrin, Hersh (2002). Beyond Greed and Fear: Understanding behavioral finance and the psychology of investing. New York: Oxford University Press. ISBN 0195161211.
93. Shleifer, Andrei (1999). Inefficient Markets: An Introduction to Behavioral Finance. New York: Oxford University Press. ISBN 0198292287.
94. Simon, Herbert A. (1987). "behavioural economics," The New Palgrave: A Dictionary of Economics, v. 1, pp. 221-24.
95. Investopedia, "Calculating the Dow Jones Industrial Average" http://www.investopedia.com/articles/02/082702.asp
96. What happened to the original 12 companies in the DJIA?, djindixes.com
97. Buffett, Warren (February 2008). "Letter to Shareholders" (PDF). Berkshire Hathaway. Retrieved on 2008-03-04.
98. http://www.djindexes.com/mdsidx/index.cfm?event=showavgstats#no4
99. Benjamin M. Anderson (1949). 'Economics and the Public Welfare: A Financial and Economic History of the United States, 1914-1946', LibertyPress (2nd ed., 1979). p. 219.
100. Gold Eagle Financial News
101. Financial Markets Magazine news
102. http://www.djindexes.com/mdsidx/index.cfm?event=components&symbol=DJI
103. Dow Jones (February 11, 2008). "Dow Jones to change the composition of the Dow Jones Industrial Average". Press release. Retrieved on 11 February 2008.
104. Edelman, R: "The Truth about Money 3rd Edition", page 126. HarperCollins, 2004
105. http://www.nysedata.com/nysedata/asp/factbook/printer_friendly.asp?mode=table&key=2213
106. National Park Service, National Historic Landmarks Survey, New York, retrieved May 31, 2007.
107. a b "New York Stock Exchange". National Historic Landmark summary listing. National Park Service (2007-09-17).
108. "National Register Information System". National Register of Historic Places. National Park Service (2007-01-23).
109. The Building NYSE Group history
110. National Register Number: 78001877 National Historic Landmark

111. George R. Adams (March 1977). "New York Stock Exchange National Register of Historic Places Inventory-Nomination (1MB PDF)" (PDF). National Park Service. Retrieved on 2008-01-30.
112. "National Register of Historic Places Inventory-Nomination (1MB PDF)" (PDF). National Park Service (1983).
113. "Rage against Wall Street". Green Left Weekly #397 (March 15, 2000). Retrieved on 2007-10-11.
114. Basham, David (January 28, 2000). "Rage Against the Machine Shoots New Video With Michael Moore". MTV News. Retrieved on 2007-02-17.
115. ""New York Stock Exchange Special Closings", 1885-date" (PDF). NYSE Group. Retrieved on 2007-04-07.
116. Katy Byron (2007-01-31). "President Bush makes surprise visit to NYSE", CNN Money, Cable News Network. Retrieved on 20 February 2007.
117. Shell, Adam (2007-07-12), "Technology squeezes out real, live traders", USA Today, http://www.usatoday.com/money/markets/2007-07-11-nyse-traders_N.htm
118. Hull, John C. (2006). Options, Futures, and Other Derivatives (6th edition ed.). Upper Saddle River, NJ: Prentice-Hall. ISBN 0131499084.
119. Redhead, Keith (1997). Financial Derivatives: An Introduction to Futures, Forwards, Options and Swaps. London: Prentice-Hall. ISBN 013241399X.
120. Lioui, Abraham; Poncet, Patrice (2005). Dynamic Asset Allocation with Forwards and Futures. New York: Springer. ISBN 0387241078.
121. Valdez, Steven (2000). An Introduction To Global Financial Markets (3rd edition ed.). Basingstoke, Hampshire: Macmillan Press. ISBN 0333764471.
122. Arditti, Fred D. (1996). Derivatives: A Comprehensive Resource for Options, Futures, Interest Rate Swaps, and Mortgage Securities. Boston: Harvard Business School Press. ISBN 0875845606.
123. Fischer Black and Myron S. Scholes. "The Pricing of Options and Corporate Liabilities," Journal of Political Economy, 81 (3), 637-654 (1973).
124. Feldman, Barry and Dhuv Roy. "Passive Options-Based Investment Strategies: The Case of the CBOE S&P 500 BuyWrite Index." The Journal of Investing, (Summer 2005).
125. Kleinert, Hagen, Path Integrals in Quantum Mechanics, Statistics, Polymer Physics, and Financial Markets, 4th edition, World Scientific (Singapore, 2004); Paperback ISBN 981-238-107-4 (also available online: PDF-files)
126. Hill, Joanne, Venkatesh Balasubramanian, Krag (Buzz) Gregory, and Ingrid Tierens. "Finding Alpha via Covered Index Writing." Financial Analysts Journal. (Sept.-Oct. 2006). pp. 29-46.
127. Moran, Matthew. “Risk-adjusted Performance for Derivatives-based Indexes – Tools to Help Stabilize Returns.” The Journal of Indexes. (Fourth Quarter, 2002) pp. 34 – 40.
128. Reilly, Frank and Keith C. Brown, Investment Analysis and Portfolio Management, 7th edition, Thompson Southwestern, 2003, pp. 994-5.
129. Schneeweis, Thomas, and Richard Spurgin. "The Benefits of Index Option-Based Strategies for Institutional Portfolios" The Journal of Alternative Investments, (Spring 2001), pp. 44 - 52.
130. Whaley, Robert. "Risk and Return of the CBOE BuyWrite Monthly Index" The Journal of Derivatives, (Winter 2002), pp. 35 - 42.
131. Bloss, Michael; Ernst, Dietmar; Häcker Joachim (2008): Derivatives - An authoritative guide to derivatives for financial intermediaries and investors Oldenbourg Verlag München ISBN 978-3-486-58632-9
132. Espen Gaarder Haug & Nassim Nicholas Taleb (2008): Why We Have Never Used the Black-Scholes-Merton Option Pricing Formula
133. T.E. Copeland, J.F. Weston (1988): Financial Theory and Corporate Policy, Addison-Wesley, West Sussex (ISBN 978-0321223531)
134. E.J. Elton, M.J. Gruber, S.J. Brown, W.N. Goetzmann (2003): Modern Portfolio Theory and Investment Analysis, John Wiley & Sons, New York (ISBN 978-0470050828)

135. E.F. Fama (1976): Foundations of Finance, Basic Books Inc., New York (ISBN 978-0465024995)
136. M.M. Groz (1999): Forbes Guide to the Markets, John Wiley & Sons, Inc., New York (ISBN 0-471-24658-1)
137. R.C. Merton (1992): Continuous-Time Finance, Blackwell Publishers Inc. (ISBN 978-0631185086)
138. Steven Valdez, An Introduction To Global Financial Markets, Macmillan Press Ltd. (ISBN 0-333-76447-1)
139. The Business Finance Market: A Survey, Industrial Systems Research Publications, Manchester (UK), new edition 2002 (ISBN 978-0-906321-19-5)
140. Eason, Yla (June 6, 1983). "Final Surge in Bearer Bonds" New York Times.
141. Quint, Michael (August 14, 1984). "Elements in Bearer Bond Issue". New York Times.
142. no byline (July 18, 1984). "Book Entry Bonds Popular". New York Times.
143. no byline (2005-12-05). "Ninja loans may yet overtake samurais", The Standard. Retrieved on 9 December 2008.
144. Batten, Jonathan A.; Peter G. Szilagyi (2006-04-19). "Developing Foreign Bond Markets: The Arirang Bond Experience in Korea" (PDF). IIS Discussion Papers (138). http://www.tcd.ie/iiis/documents/discussion/pdfs/iiisdp138.pdf. Retrieved on 6 July 2007.
145. Gwon, Yeong-seok (2006-05-24). "'김치본드' 내달 처음으로 선보인다 (Announcement: first 'Kimchi Bonds' next month)", The Hankyoreh. Retrieved on 6 July 2007.
146. Chung, Amber (2007-04-19). "BNP Paribas mulls second bond issue on offshore market", Taipei Times. Retrieved on 4 July 2007.
147. Areddy, James T. (2005-10-11). "Chinese Markets Take New Step With Panda Bond", The Wall Street Journal. Retrieved on 6 July 2007.
148. Charles P. Kindleberger (2005), Manias, Panics, and Crashes: A History of Financial Crises.
149. Luc Laeven and Fabian Valencia (2008), 'Systemic banking crises: a new database'. International Monetary Fund Working Paper 08/224.
150. Markus Brunnermeier (2008), 'Bubbles', in The New Palgrave Dictionary of Economics, 2nd ed.
151. Peter Garber (2001), Famous First Bubbles: The Fundamentals of Early Manias. MIT Press, ISBN 0262571536.
152. "Episode 06292007". Bill Moyers Journal. PBS. 2007-06-29. Transcript.
153. Justin Lahart (2007-12-24). "Egg Cracks Differ In Housing, Finance Shells", WSJ.com, Wall Street Journal. Retrieved on 13 July 2008. "It's now conventional wisdom that a housing bubble has burst. In fact, there were two bubbles, a housing bubble and a financing bubble. Each fueled the other, but they didn't follow the same course."
154. Milton Friedman and Anna Schwartz (1971), A Monetary History of the United States, 1867-1960. Princeton University Press, ISBN 0691003548.
155. '1929 and all that', The Economist, Oct. 2, 2008.
156. 'The Theory of Reflexivity', speech by George Soros, April 1994 at MIT.
157. J. M. Keynes (1936), The General Theory of Employment, Interest and Money, Chapter 12. (New York: Harcourt Brace and Co.).
158. J. Bulow, J. Geanakoplos, and P. Klemperer (1985), 'Multimarket oligopoly: strategic substitutes and strategic complements'. Journal of Political Economy 93, pp. 488-511.
159. R. Cooper and A. John (1988), 'Coordinating coordination failures in Keynesian models.' Quarterly Journal of Economics 103 (3), pp. 441-63. See especially Propositions 1 and 3.
160. D. Diamond and P. Dybvig (1983), 'Bank runs, deposit insurance, and liquidity'. Journal of Political Economy 91 (3), pp. 401-19. Reprinted (2000) in Federal Reserve Bank of Minneapolis Quarterly Review 24 (1), pp. 14-23.
161. M. Obstfeld (1996), 'Models of currency crises with self-fulfilling features'. European Economic Review 40 (3-5), pp. 1037-47.

162. Diamond and Dybvig (1983), op cit.
163. Eichengreen and Hausmann (2005), Other People's Money: Debt Denomination and Financial Instability in Emerging Market Economies.
164. Strauss Kahn D, 'A systemic crisis demands systemic solutions', The Financial Times, Sept. 25, 2008.
165. 'Don't blame the New Deal', New York Times, Sept. 28, 2008.
166. Gordy MB and Howells B (2004), 'Procyclicality in Basel II: can we treat the disease without killing the patient?'
167. 'FBI probing bailout firms', CNN Money, Sept. 23, 2008.
168. Torbjörn K A Eliazon (2006) - Om Emotionell intelligens och Œcopati (ekopati)
169. George Kaufman and Kenneth Scott (2003),'What is systemic risk, and do bank regulators retard or contribute to it?' The Independent Review 7 (3).
170. Craig Burnside, Martin Eichenbaum, and Sergio Rebelo (2008), 'Currency crisis models', New Palgrave Dictionary of Economics, 2nd ed.
171. 'The widening gyre', Paul Krugman, New York Times, Oct. 27, 2008.
172. P. Krugman (1979), 'A model of balance-of-payments crises'. Journal of Money, Credit, and Banking 11, pp. 311-25.
173. S. Morris and H. Shin (1998), 'Unique equilibrium in a model of self-fulfilling currency attacks'. American Economic Review 88 (3), pp. 587-97.
174. Darryl McLeod (2002), 'Capital flight', in the Concise Encyclopedia of Economics at the Library of Economics and Liberty.
175. Diamond and Dybvig (1983), op. cit.
176. Obstfeld (1996), op. cit.
177. CIA Site Redirect — Central Intelligence Agency
178. Online NewsHour: Russia Shake Up- March 23, 1998
179. Radio Free Europe/ Radio Liberty
180. Foreign Loans Diverted in Monster Money Laundering
181. A Case Study of a Currency Crisis: The Russian Default of 1998
182. STATEMENT of the Government of the Russian Federation and the Central Bank of the Russian Federation August 17, 1998
183. Online NewsHour: Russia's Crisis - September 17, 1998
184. Joseph Stiglitz: The ruin of Russia | comment | EducationGuardian.co.uk
185. CIA - The World Factbook
186. Bierman, Harold. "The 1929 Stock Market Crash". EH.Net Encyclopedia, edited by Robert Whaples. August 11, 2004. URL http://eh.net/encyclopedia/article/Bierman.Crash
187. Brooks, John. (1969). Once in Golconda: A True Drama of Wall Street 1920-1938. New York: Harper & Row. ISBN 0-393-01375-8.
188. Galbraith, John Kenneth. (1954). The Great Crash: 1929. Boston: Houghton Mifflin. ISBN 0-395-85999-9.
189. Klein, Maury. (2001). Rainbow's End: The Crash of 1929. New York: Oxford University Press. ISBN 0-195-13516-4.
190. Klingaman, William K. (1989). 1929: The Year of the Great Crash. New York: Harper & Row. ISBN 0-060-16081-0.
191. Rothbard, Murray N. "America's Great Depression"
192. Salsman, Richard M. "The Cause and Consequences of the Great Depression" in The Intellectual Activist, ISSN 0730-2355.
193. "Part 1: What Made the Roaring '20s Roar", June, 2004, pp. 16–24.
194. "Part 2: Hoover's Progressive Assault on Business", July, 2004, pp. 10–20.
195. "Part 3: Roosevelt's Raw Deal", August, 2004, pp. 9–20.
196. "Part 4: Freedom and Prosperity", January, 2005, pp. 14–23.
197. Shachtman, Tom. (1979). The Day America Crashed. New York: G.P. Putnam. ISBN 0-399-11613-3.
198. Thomas, Gordon, and Max Morgan-Witts. (1979). The Day the Bubble Burst: A Social History of the Wall Street Crash of 1929. Garden City, NY: Doubleday. ISBN 0-385-14370-2.

Index

1

12b-1 fee 355
12b-1 fees 349
12b-1 service fees 350
130/30 type strategies 407
130-30 fund 355

2

2008 Russian financial crisis 663
29 Crash 593

3

3G licences 632

A

A.J. Frost 518
A.W. Cohen 490
AAA 239, 303
AAII 499
AAPTA 477
AASE 689
abandoned baby bull 501
Abbey 647
Abbie Hoffman 686
ABCP 200, 659
Absolute Return magazine 359
acceleration factor 558
accounting scandals 636
Accumulation/Distribution index 564
accurate pricing models 233
acquisition 734
active management 334, 337, 385
active management success 385
actively managed ETF 329
actively managed funds 326
actively managed large cap fund 337
actively managed mutual fund 337
actively managed mutual funds 338, 353
actively-managed ETFs 324
actual average 721
Adam Smith 113
Adams Express Company 394
Adaptive Market Hypothesis 102
Adaptive Markets Hypothesis 130
Additional margin 96
Adelphia 636
ADR 430
advanced traders 434
adverse market changes 382
adverse market movements 420
Advisers Act Rule 365
advisory contract 347
Advisory dealing 71
ADX 394, 553
AEX index 713
affordable housing 657
aftermarket 42, 181
after-tax yield 300
Agency Only Firms 68
aggressive sampling 328
aggressive trader 98
ago Board Options Exchange volatility index 502
agricultural communities 670
Ahmet Duran 118
AIG 261, 262, 642, 648
AIM 389, 701, 705
AIRAP 373
Aite Group 221
Aite Group LLC 454
Al Ehrbar 335
Alan Greenspan 621, 654
Alan Howard 375
Albanian Lottery Uprising 576
Albert Wiggin 595

Aleksandr Lebed 626
Alexander Elder 192, 433
Alexei Kudrin 647, 665
Alexey Kudrin 663
Alfa Group 655
Alfred Cowles 121
Alfred Marshall lectures 105
Alfred W. Jones 358
Alfred Winslow Jones 406
algo traders 454
algo trading 225, 457
algorithmic trading 225, 443, 452, 454
All Or None (AON) 89
All Ordinaries 732
All Ords 732
Allied Irish Banks 645
allocation model 354
All-or-none 92
all-or-nothing options 279
alpha 143, 373, 385, 681
alpha coefficient 136
alpha investment strategies 385
Alrosa 665
Alternative Investment Market 701, 705
Alternative Investments Risk Adjusted Performance 373
Alternext 714
Alternext European 680
Amazon.com 636
AMC 387
America Online 634
American Association of Individual Investors 499
American Association of Professional Technical Analysts 477
American Bankers Association 655
American Bond option 250
American callable 286
American Century Investments 354
American College in Pennsylvania 70
American Depositary Receipt 430
American International Group 577, 642
American National Bank 335
American option 234
American put option 268
American Stock Exchange 280, 680
American swaption 277
Amex 183, 389
AMEX 680
AMEX Composite 681
Amex Market Group 719
amortization 274
AMS 711
AMS/3 711
Amsterdam Stock Exchange 712
Andre Gunder 578
Andrei Illarionov 624, 663
Andrew Lo 482, 483
Angela Merkel 646
Anglo Irish Bank 645
Anheuser-Busch 144
ANN 66, 478
Anna Schwartz 574, 599
annual financial information 300
annual general meeting 383
annual management charge 387
annual principal payments 298
anticipating stock price movements 490
anti-globalization movement 209, 621
AOI 732
AOL 476
AOL Time Warner 634
API 315
APT 142
ARBFX 367
arbitrage 151, 319, 324, 423, 603
arbitrage activities 329
arbitrage desks 318
Arbitrage Fund 367
arbitrage in expectations 151
arbitrage opportunities 507
arbitrage positions 431
arbitrage pricing theory 142, 173

arbitrage strategy 257
arbitrage-free market 423
arbitrage-free price 308
arbitrageur 412
arbitrageurs 393
arbitraging value 332
arbitration tribuna 423
arbitrator 423
ARCA Tech 100 Index 342
archetypal patterns 473
Archipelago 442, 687
Arkady Dvorkovich 665
Arthur Andersen 636
artificial neural networks 478
Asian economic miracle 609
Asian Financial Crisis 608
Asian flu 605, 619
ASIC 688
ask price 465
ask prices 446
ask takers 466
assessment bonds 299
asset allocation 339
asset allocation model 354
asset allocation models 385
asset allocation services 354
asset price 150
asset pricing 153
asset pricing model 334
asset specific risk 170
asset volatility 143
asset-backed commercial paper 200, 659
asset-liability mismatch 575
asset-or-nothing binary option 279
Association of Brokers 706
ASX 688, 732
asymmetric information 611
asymmetry effect 375
at JPMorgan Chase 518
ATR 539
auction market 683
auction market paradigm 184
auction settlement 264
auditors 702
AUM 220
Australia and New Zealand Banking Group 688
Australian Associated Stock Exchanges 689
Australian Securities and Investments Commission 215, 688
Australian Securities Exchange 675, 688, 732
auto loans 200
Automated Bond System 194
Automated Bond System (ABS) 290
automated trading 452
Automated Trading Desk 457
automated trading strategy 451
automated trading system 707
Automatic Order Matching and Execution System 711
automatically generate trend lines 528
Autumn Statement 750
average annual total return 348
Average Directional Index 553
average out 158
average P/E 596
average price 533
average true range 539

B

B & G Foods Holding Corp 681
B. J. Habibie 615
B2B 81
B2B market 81
B2C 81
back office 74
back-end load 356
backfill bias 370
back-office 76
backtesting 450
backward propagation of errors algorithm 66
bailout 371, 612

balance sheets 615
balanced portfolios 339
ban on short selling 415
band 624
bandits 439
Bank Credit Analyst 518
Bank for International Settlement 217
Bank for International Settlements 270
Bank of America 275, 642
Bank of England 648, 662
Bank of Ireland 645
Bank of Italy 651
Bank of Japan 655
Bank of the United States 572
Bank Recapitalization Fund 662
bank runs 575, 579
bank-account style 690
bankers' acceptance 201
bankers' acceptances 200
banking Bill 646
banking panic 572
banking panics 572
bankrupt 636
bankrupt companies 348
bankruptcy 259, 642
Bankruptcy Code 259
banned naked short selling 415
Barack Obama 644
Barbara G. Stymiest 707
bar-chart 484
BarclayHedge 369
BarclayHedge Monthly Asset Flow Report 359
Barclays 73, 456, 647, 650
Barclay's Bank 335
Barclays Capital 518
Barclays Global Investors 327, 335, 376
bare 496
Barings Bank 448
Barometer of the economy 672
Baron Rothschild 497
Barrier option 234
Barron's Magazine 510
barter 628
base currency 222
Basel I 431
basis 257
Basis trades 257
basket 392
Batchelor-Ramyar study 516
BayernLB 653
BB&T 654
bear market 493, 495
bear market or correction 636
bear market rally 494
bear markets 377
Bear Stearns 372, 572, 575
bearer 39
bearer certificates 292
bearers 495
bearish 498
bearish pattern 487
bearish sign 530
bearish signal 486
bear-market rally 502
bearskin 495
beginning traders 434
behavioral biases 113
behavioral economics 113
behavioral finance 101, 113, 464
Behavioral Finance formula 85
behavioral valuation tools 64
Ben Bernanke 574, 641
Ben Graham 84
benchmark 384, 385
Benchmark Currencies 421
benchmarking 456, 457
Benjamin Graham 393, 463
Benoit Mandelbrot 519
Benoît Mandelbrot 591
Berkshire Hathaway 262, 677, 725
Bermuda 361
Bermudan callable 286
Bermudan option 234
Bermudan swaption 277
best execution 351
beta 385

beta coefficient 139, 155
beta investment strategies 385
beta neutral 421
Beurzen 185
BGC Partners 81
BGF 681
BHP Billiton 688
bid and ask based system 466
bid prices 387, 446
bid takers 466
bid/ask difference 465
bid/ask quote 218
bid/ask spread 218
bid-ask spread 446
bid-ask-based system 446
Big Bang 700
Big Board 682
bilateral contract 401
bill 495
Bill Dunn 461
Bill Hambrecht 110
Bill Miller 126
binary option 279
binomial options pricing model 236
biodiversity standard 209
biological neural networks 478
bio-tech ETF 339
black box 372
Black formula 508
Black Monday 593, 600
black swan event 600
Black Thursday 593
Black Tuesday 593, 600
Black-76 model 508
black-box trading 454
Blackrock 505
Black–Scholes 507
Black-Scholes formula 248
Black–Scholes formula 507
Black-Scholes model 234, 235
Black–Scholes model 507
Black-Scholes Model 272
Black-Scholes option pricing model 455
Black–Scholes PDE 507
block histogram style 551
blood in the streets 497
Bloomberg 83
Bloomberg LP 703
Bloomberg Tradebook 456
blue chip 595
blue chip index 713
blue room 685
BMA 429
BNP 653
BNP Paribas 646
Board of Governors 643
body 485
Bogle 332
Bogle's folly 335
Bollinger Bands 541
Bolsas y Mercados Españoles 675
Bombay Stock Exchange 675
bond 250, 284
bond documents 299
bond funds 353
bond holder 297, 299
bond holders 298
bond indices 196, 293
bond market 194, 290
Bond Market Association 42, 429
bond market participants 195, 291
bond market volatility 291
bond obligations 264
bond option 250, 251
bond options 233
Bond or Loan 264
bond rating 299
bond-dealer 72
bonds 39, 176, 290, 327
book value 334
bookmaker 425
Boris Fyodorov 624, 626
Boris Yeltsin 623
borrowing 409
Boston Stock Exchange 677
bottom 497, 544
bottom picking 497
bottom reversal 486

Bought deal 108
bounce 524
bounds of rationality 113
bourse 696
Bradford & Bingley 644
Brady report 455
breakout 530
breakpoints 356
Brealey 125
Bridgewater Associates 376
British Virgin Islands 361
broad high yield market 305
Broad Street 680
broad support 492
broad-base indexes 341
broad-based portfolios 353
broader indices 293
broader market 724
Brock 482
broker 389
broker rules 689
Broker sponsored 691
brokerage commission 330
brokerage commissions 351
brokerage fee 388
brokerage fees 340
Bruce Greenwald 86
Bruges 185
Brugse Beurse 185
Brussels Stock Exchange 712
brut 442
brute force method 533
BSE 675
BSE Index 493
BSZ 280
bubble 573
bubble burst 632
bubbles 406
Bud Labitan 85
Budapest Stock Exchange 695
budget items 624
built-in sales credit 109
bull market 397, 492, 495, 636
bulla 495
Bull-Bear spread 498
bulletin board 80
bullish investor 473
bullish pattern 486
bullish signal 486
bulls 493
bully 495
Bundesbank 697
burn rate 631
Bursa Malaysia 215
Burton Malkiel 127, 334, 472, 483
Bush 643
business card 815
business cycle 103, 586
Business Cycle 103
business models 630
business trusts 351
business-to-business 81
business-to-client 81
BusinessWeek 680
butterfly spread 243
Buttonwood Agreement 684
buy and hold 385
buy and hold strategy 397
buy and sell orders 89
buy limit order 88, 92
buy market-if-touched order 91
buy signal 510
buy stop order 90
buying on margin 439
BVLP 712
BVZ 280

C

CAC 40 713
CAC40 651
Cadence Capital Limited 363
calculation agent 259
Calendar Phenomenon 480
call 241, 265, 693
call dates 286
call option232, 240, 265, 270, 294, 430, 693
call options 693

call price 266
callability 286
callable bond 251
calls for margin 316
Calvert Group 344
CAMELS 655
Camp David 653
Canadian Society of Technical Analysts 477
Canadian Venture Exchange 707
Canary Wharf 483
cancel out 170
cancelling order 89
cancels other orders 91
candlestick chart 484
cap and trade 209
Capel Court 700
capital allocation line 166
capital appreciation bonds 298
capital asset pricing model 171
capital controls 618
capital discount 147
capital flows 613
capital gains 348
capital gains tax 740
capital market 180
capital market line 162
Capital Market Line 169
capital markets 176, 177
Capital One 654
capital projects 297
capital rescue plan 653
capital risk 382, 386
capital served 631
capital stock 40
Capital Structure Arbitrage 257
capitalist economies 104
capitalist economy 578
Capitalist Long Waves 106
capitalization weighting 342
capitalization-weighted index 342
capitalization-weighted indexes 343
capitualtions 500
Carl Bildt 663
Carter Schelling 585
cash bond 257
cash flow model 85
cash out 288
cash payment 317
cash settlement 253, 260
cash-or-nothing binary option 279
Catholic University of Milan 344
CATS 707
Cayman Islands 361
CBOE 77, 280, 728
CBOE Futures Exchange 248
CBOT 211, 318
CCI 555
CCX 212
CDAX 696
CDNX 707
CDOs 304
CDS confirmations 259
CDS contract 253, 259
CDS market 260
CDSL 350
CDX 252
Cedelbank 43
Centerplate 681
central bank 658
Central Bank of Iceland 648
Central Bank of Russia 625
Central Bank of the People's Republic of China 648
Central Bank of the Russian Federation 666
central banks 585
central counter clearing model692
central market clearing mechanism 222
Central Provident Fund 618
central tenet 267
certain foreign currency cash flows 271
certificate 39
Certificate of deposit 201
Certificate of Designation 45
certificates of deposit 354
Certified Financial Planner 70

CFD 369, 422
CFD provider 692
CFD providers 691
CFDs 316, 692, 701
CFMP Practitioner 815
CFTC 221, 321
CGT 740
Chaikin oscillator 565
chalkies 689
change-traded funds 392
channel breakout rule 543
Chapter 11 259, 288
Charles Brandes 86
Charles Collins 517
Charles D. Kirkpatrick 523
Charles Dow 474, 485, 721
Charles E. Mitchell 595
Charles Elli 335
Charles Ponzi's scam 576
Charles Schwab 81
Charlie Munger 86
chart pattern 483, 484
chart patterns 501
chartered accountants 72
Chartered Market Technician 518
charting software 528
chartist 100
Chase National Bank 595
Chavalit Yongchaiyudh 614, 620
Cheol-Ho Park 482
CHESS system 690
Cheuvreux 456
Chicago Board of Trade 211, 714
Chicago Board Options Exchange 280, 728
Chicago Board Options Exchange (CBOE) 281
Chicago Board Options Exchange Volatility Index 246
Chicago Climate Exchange 212
Chicago Mercantile Exchange 80, 197, 211, 222, 270, 326, 424, 728, 730
Chicago Produce Exchange 211
China Securities Regulatory Commission 215, 675
Chinese wall 76, 78
Chinese walls 69
Chris Carolan 479
Chris Hohn 375
Christopher Cox 714
Christopher Sherwell 509
Chrysler 656
churn 343
CIA World Factbook 620
Cisco Systems 632
CISDM 370
Citigroup 73, 275, 280, 635, 644, 646, 687, 689
Citigroup BIG 196, 293
City National Bank 654
City Trader 70
city traders 71
ck-box trading 225
Class A 355
Class B 355
Class C 355
clearance parties 642
clear-cut rules 479
Clearing Corporation 214
Clearing Hous 214
clearing house 233, 401
Clearing House Electronic Subregister System 691
clearing margin 316
clearinghouse 187, 312
ClearPort 401
Clearstream 43, 695
CLICK 694
clone indices 369
close 89
close price 89
closed-end fund 389
closed-end fund share prices 393
closed-end fund shares 391
closed-end funds 110, 332, 348, 351, 389
closed-end stock fund 392
closed-ended fund 362

close-out 414
closet tracker 385
closing a position 402
closing price 489
CME 211, 215, 318, 728, 730
CMT 518
CNBC 703
Coat of Arms 700
coffee shops 699
cognitive biases 495
cognitive psychological techniques 114
Coinmach Service Corp. 681
collapse 576
collateral 94
collateralized debt obligations 304, 360
collective human psychology 516
collective investment 382
collective investment scheme 334, 346, 381, 389
collective investment vehicles 346
collective investor psychology 511
Columbia Business School 84
Comerica 654
command economy 176
commercial bank 73, 572
commercial banks 658, 661
commercial companies 219
commercial index 337
commercial information vendors 43
commercial paper 39, 200, 201, 294
Commercial Paper Funding Facilty 647
commercial paper lines 200
commission scheme 440
Commitments-Of-Traders 321
commodities 176, 312, 327, 329, 663, 688
commodities exchang 202
Commodities magazine 547
commodity 265
commodity accounting 203
Commodity Channel Index 555
commodity ETFs 326, 329, 333
commodity exchange 176
commodity exchanges 675
commodity futures 545
Commodity Futures Trading Commission 206, 216, 321, 329
commodity markets 202, 420
commodity money 202
commodity options 233
common second choice 541
common stock 40
common stock shareholders 390
Commonwealth Bank of Australia 688
Commsec 692
companies 178
Computer Assisted Trading System 707
computer based charts 528
computer modeling techniques 451
concept 524
conditional order 90
Conditional orders 92
consensus opinion 462
consensus view 292
conservative trader 98
consortium of dealers 263
constructive sale 413
contagion 577
contango 318
contingent deferred sales loads 350
continuation signals 484
continuing disclosure 300
continuous auction format 683
contract 410
contract for difference 422
contracts for difference 369, 701
contractual administrator fee 349
contractual advisory fee 349
contra-equity 52
contrarian 462
contrarian investing 443, 462

contributor to financial crises 575
convenience yields 319
convertible bond 251, 429
convertible bonds 294
convertible preferred stocks 47
convexity risk 302
cook the books 53
Coppock curve 510
Coppock indicator 510
corporate actions 726
corporate bond 259, 300, 429
corporate bonds 40, 262, 290, 294, 353, 412
corporate debt 132, 294
Corporate Debt Restructuring Committee 618
corporate equity 312
corporate finance 74
corporate fund 362
corporate governance 185
corporate hedge funds 362
corporate pension plans 347
correction 606
correlated relative volatility 139
correlated risk 139
cost method 52
cost of capital 132, 134
cost of debt 132, 148
cost of entry 82
cost of equity 132
cost of holding 234
COTR 321
COT-Report 321
COTS hardware 82
Council of Economic Advisers 587
counter currency 222
counterparty default 262
counterparty risk 238, 256, 262
Countrywide Financial 655
coupon 285, 292
coupon dates 285
coupon rate 292
coupon rates 300
coupon yield 307
courtiers 670
Covad Communications 634
covenants 285
covered call 245
covering 407
Covering 90
CPA 367
CPFF 647
Craig 101
Craig McKinlay 483
crash 591
crash in commodity prices 104
creation units 324, 325
Crédit Agricole 653
credit card receivables 200
credit crisis 653
credit default 263
credit default option 252
credit default swap 252
credit default swap (CDS) 253
credit default swap market 261
credit default swaps 255, 263, 294, 576, 649
credit default swaption 252
credit derivative contract 253
credit derivatives 197
credit deterioration 430
credit event 259
credit guarantees 263
credit money 203
credit protection 430
credit rating agency 303
credit risk 75, 256, 301, 302, 314, 315, 420, 657
credit spread 252, 429
Credit Suisse 73, 375, 652
Credit Suisse database 370
Credit Suisse Tremont 369
credit tsunami 654
CREST 72
crowd behavior 462
crowd behaviour 592
crowd psychology 511
CSFB High Yield II Index (CSHY) 305
cubic power law 591
cumulative average 531, 533

cumulative moving average 533
Cumulative preferred stock 50
cumulative volume 568
Cunningham 125
cup and handle patterns 501
curb brokers 680
Curb Exchange 718
currency crises 577
currency cross rate options 234
currency devaluation 227
currency hedging 420
currency markets 176, 409
currency option 270
currency risk 296, 302, 386
currency speculators 227
currency swap 227
CurrencyShares 329
current cumulative average 533
current liquidating margin 95
current risk free rate 156
current yield 307
custodian expense 350
customer margin 316
customized index 337
Cutler 475
CVP 681
cycle theorists 105
cycles 531

D

Daewoo Motors 615
Dagger 456
Dan Seiver 498
Daniel Drew 411
Daniel Kahneman 128
Daniel L. Chesler 523
Data Explorers Limited 407
data mining technique 66
data snooping 482
David Aronson 520
David Booth 335
David Dodd 84
David Dreman 463
Davíð Oddsson later 667
David Porter 118
David Webb 711
DAX 696
DAX 30 729
DAXplus 696
day order 89
day trader 403, 436
day traders 631
day trading strategies 445
days to cover 407
db x-trackers 329
DE Shaw 376
de Wolff 103
dead cat bounce 502, 509, 596
dealer options 233
dealer-based 294
dealing costs 382, 387
debentures 39
debt ETFs 329
debt expense 133
debt issuer 291
debt obligation 260
debt obligations 260
debt securities 39, 41, 290
debt security 284
debt-equity swaps 186
decreasing range 540
deep recession 656
default option 252
default premium 133
default protection 259
default risk 302
default settlement method 264
defined-contribution 347
deflation 584
Delaware 361
de-leveraging 641
deliverable asset 318
deliverable debt 260
delta one products 378
demand for their services fell. A few large dot-com companies, such as Amazon 635
deposit accounts 40

deposit insurance 572
depositary receipts 701
depository receipt 430
deposits 39
depression 103
deregulation 576
derivative 227
derivative contracts 358
derivative pricing model 67
derivative structure 356
derivatives 75, 330, 419
Derivatives 701
derivatives markets 176, 197
derivatives position 316
Derivatives Trading Platform 694
designated order turnaround 454
Deutsche Bank 73
Deutsche Börse 183, 695, 714
Deutsche Börse AG 697
Deutscher Aktien IndeX 729
deVilliers 490
Dexia 645
Diamond and Dybvig's model 579
Didier Sornette 518
digital options 279
dilution levy 387
dilutive 112
dilutive offering 112
Dimensional Fund Advisors 334
Dimensional Fund Advisors (DFA) 335
direct access brokers 445
direct access trading 445
direct exchange 226
direct investments 382
discount 308, 332, 389, 392
Discount brokers 70
discounted cash flow 62
Discounted Cash Flow Model 498
Discounted Cash Flows Calculator 64
discounted dividend models 62
discretionary order 92
dispute in monetary policy 604
distressed debt 358
distressed securities 305, 360
distribution arrangements 355
DivDAX 696
divergences from price trends 556
diversifiable risk 158
diversification 339
diversified fund 339
divestitures 87
divi 60
dividend 409
dividend capitalization model 133
dividend cover 60
dividend imputation 59
dividend obligation 45
dividend per share 133
dividend reinvestment plans55, 58
dividend rights 45
dividend yield 133
dividend yields 319
dividends 334
Dividends 55
dividends in specie 56
divisor adjustment 726
divvy 60
DJ Euro Stoxx 50 Index 713
DJI 721
DJIA 497, 721
DLC 430
DLC share prices 431
DLC stocks 431
Dmitry Medvedev 663
Dmitry Pankin 647
Dogs of the Dow 463
Dojima Rice Exchange 211
domestic stimulus package 656
domicile 361
Dominique Strauss-Kahn 576
Domowitz 80
Don Balenovich 118
Donald Lambert 555
Donald Tsang 617
DOT 454
dot-bombs 633
dot-com bubble 630
dot-com theory 631

dot-compost 633
double bottom 501
double top 529
double top pattern 529
Dow 721
Dow Jones 334, 721
Dow Jones Corporate Bond Index 295
Dow Jones Industrial Average 324, 497, 721
Dow Jones Sustainability Index 344
Dow Jones Transportation Average 721
Dow Jones Wilshire 5000 Total Stock Market Index 342
Dow Theory 473, 474, 475
downsloping line 529
downtick 92
downtrend movement 486
dragonfly doji 487
drain the fens 699
dramatic decline 591
DRY 681
Dryden 125
DTC 407
DTP 694
dual priced 387
dual priced schemes 387
dual-listed company 430
Dubai Stock Exchange 718
Duke of Edinburgh 701
Duke University 248, 413
dumping 465
Duncan Niederauer 687
duration risk 302
dutch auction 108
Dutch auction 110
Dutch bank 653
Dutch tulip mania 573
dynamic betas 373
dynamic portfolio strategies 385
dynamics of the option's theoretical value 236

E

E2 Energy Market Analysis Platform 523
Earl of Bedford 699
early redemption fees 350
earnings 334
earnings growth rate 63
earnings per share 51
East India Company 698
eBay 635, 636
EBS Building Society 645
ECB 371, 651, 656
ECN 80, 332, 675
ECN rebates 444
ECNs 440, 720
economic activity 584
economic agent 113
economic collapse 584
economic conditions 223
economic cost 623
economic cycle 578
economic cycles 598
economic decline 587
economic equilibrium 600
economic factors 223
economic growth 573, 582, 740
economic numbers 225
economic releases 196
economic risk 75
Economic Security Strategy 652
economic stagnation 574
Ed Seykota 461, 478
Ed Yardeni 504
EDHEC 371
EDSA II Revolution 616
Edward J. Markey 603
Edward Johnson 335
Edward O. Thorp 507
Edwin Coppock 510
effective interest rate 694
efficient exchange place 695
efficient frontier 159, 166
efficient market hypothesis 100, 163, 188, 492, 600

efficient market theory 117
efficient method 682
efficient-market hypothesis 121, 176
Electronic Communication Networks 440
electronic financial markets 452
electronic Hybrid Market 683
electronic market 92
Electronic Municipal Market Access system 300
electronic ownership transfer 440
electronic stock market 719
electronic trading 676
Elliott wave principle 511
EMA 433, 536, 550
Emanuele Canegrati 344, 483
EMC Mortgage Corporation 655
EMEAP 612
Emergency Economic Stabilization Act 643
Emergency Economic Stabilization Act of 2008 645
Emergency Finance Mechanism 612
Emerging Company Marketplace 680
EMH 483
E-mini contracts 728
EMMA 300
emotion based 479
emotional bias 450
emotional biases. 495
emotional ties 185
employee stock options 232, 239
Employee stock options 234
ending redeemable value 349
endowment warrants 693
enhanced indexing 337
Enhanced Strategy Classification System 370
Enron 344, 636
ent-grade corporate bonds 347
entry barriers 117
environmental economics 210
environmental economists 345

'

'environmental impact score 345

E

environmental index 345
environmental protection 657
environmental stock market index 345
EOD 490
equal weighting 342
equilibrium 579
equit 132
equities 39
equity 40
equity arbitrage 318
equity derivative products 320
equity funds 352
equity index futures 320
equity index futures contracts 336
equity market 183
equity mutual funds 359
equity options 248
equity premium 80
equity premium puzzle 117
equity price 257
equity reduction 52
equity securities 77
equity security 40
equity swaps 330
Ernest Mandel 105
ERV 349
ESL Investments 376
estimate of the future volatility 235
ETCs 701
ETF 196, 227, 247, 351, 377
ETFs 293, 701
ethical criteria 344
ethical investing indexes 344

E-Trade 81
etrading 80
etymology 495
Eugene Fama 117, 121, 334, 335
Eurekahedge Indices 369
Eurex 695
Euro Currency Trust 329
Euro debt securities 40
eurobonds 40
euro-certificates 40
Euroclear 43
euro-commercial paper 40
eurodollar deposit 201
Euromoney 217
EuroMTS 44
Euronext 44, 183, 212, 687
Euronext Lisbon 712
Euronext List 712
Euronext N.V. 712
Euronext.liffe 197, 713
euronotes 40
European bond option 250
European callable 286
European Central Bank 371, 586, 648, 651, 656, 697
European Exchange Rate Mechanism 573
European option 234
European put option 268
European stock exchange 712
European style 693
European swaption 277
European Union 647
eurosecurities 43
eurosecurities markets 43
EuroStoxx 50 696
evaluate option contracts 235
events of taxability 300
EWMA 536
exaggerated bear market 495
Exchange Commission 642
exchange floor 82
Exchange Place 680
Exchange Traded Commodities 701
exchange traded derivatives 233
exchange traded funds 185, 701
exchange traded options 233
exchange trading 691
exchangeable bond 251
exchange-traded fund 324, 334, 351, 727
exchange-traded fund arbitrage 425
exchange-traded funds 227, 723
Exchange-traded funds 680
exchange-traded grantor trust 330
Exchange-traded options 232
Execution Management System 456
Executive Meeting of East Asia Pacific 612
executive officers 702
exercise price 233
Exista hf. 646
exit signals 478
Exodus Communications 636
exogenous factor 582
exotic financial instruments 419
expansion 103
expected end of period price 150
expected return 150
expected return of a stock 139
expense ratio 331, 337
expense ratios 340, 357
Expiration 318
expiration date 233, 240
expiry 233
Expiry 318
exponential moving average 433, 536, 550, 554
exponential smoothing 538
exponential smoothing algorithm 539
exponentially weighted moving average 536
external shocks 623
extra capital 107
extreme inflation 495
extreme point 558
exuberant environment 630

EZTrader 280

F

F 270
face amount 284
face to face trading 700
face value 250
factor analysis 154
fair markets 344
fair price 117
fair value 306
fake market bottom 497
Fallen Angels 304
falling mark 532
falling market 495
false breakout 522
Fama French Three Factor model 334
Fannie Mae 577, 641
Farallon Capital 376
FAST system 690
fat tail 163
fat tails 543
FBI 576
FDA 406
FDAX 729
FDIC 659
FDIC insurance 642
FDIVX 351
fear index 247
Fear indexes 463
Federal Agency Short-Term Securities 201
Federal Deposit Insurance Corporation 644, 659
Federal Financial Markets Service 666
federal funds 201
Federal funds 586
Federal Home Loan Mortgage Corporation 641
Federal Housing Finance Agency 641
federal income tax 297, 299
Federal National Mortgage Association 641
Federal Open Market Committee 655
Federal Reserve 574, 586, 600
Federal Reserve Bank 642
Federal Reserve Bank of New York 621
Federal Reserve Board 587, 659
Federal Reserve working paper 482
Federal Reserve, Bank of Canada 648
federal taxes 298
fee structure 349
fees 387
Fernand Braudel 185
FHFA 641
Fibonacci sequence 516
Fidelity 354
Fidelity Diversified International Fund 351
Fidelity Investments 335
Fifth Third 645
figure charts 490
Fill Or Kill (FOK) 89
Fill-or-kill orders 89
filtered measure of the velocity 553
finance areas 76
finance companies 200
financial accelerator 577
financial adviser 383
financial advisor 70, 397
financial advisors 498
financial bubbles 572
financial collapse 666
financial contagion 608
financial contract 265, 268
Financial Controller 76
financial crises per se 574
financial crisis 572, 641
financial elasticity 139

financial engineering techniques 330
financial fragility 578
financial futures 320
financial instrument 265, 281
financial instruments 396
financial manager 397
financial market 176, 290
Financial Markets Association 290
Financial Markets Principals 815
financial markets storm 635
financial markets technique 472
financial metrics 462
Financial News Network 518
financial pac 624
financial planners 356
financial reforms 594
financial sector 576
financial securities 176
Financial Services Authority 216, 414, 642, 646
financial statements 400
financial stocks 659
financial system 187
financial technical analysis oscillator 547
financial theory 352
Financial Times 367
Financial World magazine 511
financial-integrity approach 87
financially traded assets 543
financing arrangements 275
Finish High 280
Finish Low 280
FINRA 73
fire insurance contract 416
first brokers 185
first global stock exchange 712
First Horizon National Corporation 654
First Index Investment Trust 335, 346
First Interstate Bank 274
First Niagara Bank 654
First Prudential Market 218
First Prudential Markets 692
Firth 125
fiscal obligations 398
Fischer Black 160, 235, 507
FISD 42
Fitch 299
five waves 105
FIX Protocol 456
fixed currency exchange rates 696
fixed exchange rate 573, 579
fixed income market 194
fixed income security 183
fixed leg 274
fixed liquidation value 45
Fixed Return Options 280
Fixed Return Options (FROs) 279
flight to liquidity 577
flight to quality 224, 653
float 726
float-adjusted weighting 342
floating leg 274
floating peg 624
floor broker 184
floor brokers 676
floor trading post specialist 184
floors 508
FMC 215
FMSC 83
FMV 263
FoF 354
follow-on offering 112
Food and Drug Administration 406
Forbes magazine 463
Foreign & Colonial Investment Trust 394
foreign currencies 312
foreign currency futures 226
foreign currency notionals 270
foreign exchange brokers 221
foreign exchange markets 472
Foreign Exchange Members 71
foreign exchange option 227, 270
foreign exchange rates 482
foreign exchange reserves 220
foreign exchange risk 420

Foreign Exchange Risk hedging 420
Foreign Exchange Swaps 201
foreign risk free simple interest rate 273
forex 316, 545
forex brokers 221
forex market 219
forex swaps 217
forex/interest rate markets 279
Fortis 644
Fortress Investment Group LLC 363
Fortune 500 725
Fortune magazine 335
forward 270
forward contract 204
forward contracts 197, 205, 313, 420
Forward Markets Commission 215
forward rate agreements 197
forward swap rate 278
forward testing 450
forwards 271, 401
Fosback 191
founder shares 362
Four Filters 85
Fourth Market 401
four-year presidential cycle 190
FPM 692
Framing 115
Franco Modigliani 148
Frankfurt Stock Exchange 695, 729
franking credits 59
fraud 576
FRCL 394
Freddie Mac 577, 641
Frederic Mishkin 611
free float basis 689
free letter 696
free markets 670
free of credit risk 296
Free Trade Agreement 621
free trade fairs 696
freefloat-adjusted market capitalization 733
front office 74
front running 79
front-end load 356
FSA 369
FSA Approved Person Status 68
FSE 695
FTA 621
FTSE 483
FTSE 100 334, 384
FTSE All-Share Index 334
FTSE Hedge 369
FTSE4Good Index 344
Fujitsu 704
fulcrum fees 367
fully electronic markets 683
fully transparent 329
functional magnetic resonance imaging 115
fund accounting expense 350
fund investor 337
fund management 397
fund management companies 404
fund manager 336, 348, 383
fund performanc 334
fundamental analysis 397, 472
fundamental shocks 475
fundamentally based indexe 334
funds management company 389
funds of funds 354
fund's performance 386
fund's prospectus 348
fungibility 430
fusion analysis 479
future contracts 675
future delivery 318
future outlook 502
future stock prices 484
future value 318
future volatility 386
futures 327, 329, 694
futures account 316
Futures Commission Merchants 316
futures contract 203, 204, 312, 320, 402, 409, 693

futures contracts 98, 197, 205, 270, 420
futures exchanges 197, 675, 678
futures index 730
Futures magazine 547
futures markets 455
futures price 312
Futures traders 320
FX option 227, 270
FX options 270
FX options market 270
FX transaction 217
FxMarketSpace 222

G

G20 industrial nations 653
G7 industrialized nations 604
G7 nations 650
GAB 394
Gabelli Equity Trust 394
Galati 219
gamblers 439
Garban 81
Garman 272
Garraway's 699
Gary Aguirre 374
Gaussian 591
GBP call 271
GDP 222, 584
GDR 430
Géhin 373
Geir Haarde 667
Gelderen 103
Gene Stanley 591
General Agreement to Borrow 612
General Electric 200, 677
general market cap 342
general markets 176
General Motors 615, 656
general obligation bonds 299
general partner 361
genetic programming 458
Genetically Modified Organism 205
geopolitical tensions 663
George Ainslie 114
George Angell 499
George B. Post 685
George Lane 478, 559
George Soros 126, 228, 574, 611
George W. Bush 649, 653
Gerald Appel 550
German stock index 729
Gerwin Griffioen 482
get big fast 630
get large or get lost 631
GFI Group 81
gh-risk profile trader 439
gift economy 176
Giulio Tremonti 651
GK 273
GKO short-term bills 624
Glass-Steagall Act 78, 597
Glitnir 646
Glitnir banki hf. 646
global banking crisis 663
global bond portfolios 196
Global Commons Institute 210
Global Crossing 634
Global Depositary Receipt 430
global economic slowdown 652
global financial crisis of 2008 641
global financial market 200
global forex 217
global index 334
global indexing strategy 339
global labor arbitrage 424
global recession 588, 654
global stock market crash 605
Globex 80, 212, 728
GMAC 200
GMO 205
going long 402, 410
going public 181
going short 402
gold exchange-traded funds 329
gold standard 209

Goldman Sachs 73, 369, 643
Goldman Sachs Asset Management 376
Goldman Sachs JBWere 689
good-til-cancelled order 89
Google 280
Gordon Brown 654
Gordon's growth model 62
government bond 259, 296
government bond market 194, 290
government bonds 133, 295, 650
Government bonds 40
government capital 672
government sponsored enterprises 303
government-issued securities 680
Governments 195
Gramm-Leach-Bliley Act 78
grand supercycle 513
Granger-causality concept 344
grantor trust 326
gravestone doji 487
great bear market 595
great bull market 594
Great Commodities Depression 494
great contraction 599
Great Depression 594, 597, 641
Great Fire of New York 684
greeks 273
green economists 210
greenshoe 109, 112
Gregory Millman 228
Greyworld 701
grid simulation method 215
Grizzly Short Fund 367
group thinking 189
groupthink 116
growth funds 352
growth investment 384
growth over profits 632
growth rate of dividends 133
growth stocks 85
Grupo Santander 644
GRZZX 367
GSEs 641
guaranteeing bank deposits 646
Guerrilla 456
guest workers 635
Gulf Cooperation Council 654
Gunduz Caginalp 118

H

halting trading 605
Hambrech 676
Hamilton Bolton 518
hammer 486
Hampshire County Council 179
Hang Seng Bank 733
Hang Seng China AH Index Series 733
Hang Seng China Enterprises Index 733
Hang Seng China H-Financials Index 733
Hang Seng Composite Index Series 733
Hang Seng Freefloat Index Series 733
Hang Seng Index 342, 733
Hang Seng Industry Classification System 734
Hang Seng Stock Classification System 734
Hang Seng Total Return Index Series 733
hange traded derivatives 197
Harry Markowitz 155
Harry S. Dent Jr. 190
Harvard Business School 597
HBOS 647, 650, 651
head 544
head and shoulders 501, 543
health care 587
hedge 416
hedge finance 578
hedge financial market risk 420
hedge fund 358

Hedge Fund Asset Flows & Trends Report 359
hedge fund industry 369
hedge fund investment strategies 371
hedge fund managers 355
hedge fund redemptions 500
Hedge Fund Research 369
hedge fund strategy 428
hedge fund traders 183
hedge fund universe 370
hedge funds 73, 185, 220, 425
hedge funds portfolios 370
hedge loan 417
hedge parameters 235
hedge strategy 355
hedge uncertain future cash flows 271
hedge-fund IPO 363
HedgeFund.net 359
hedger 417
Hedgers 320
hedging 205, 358, 416
hedging strategies 327
hedging strategy 360
hedging theory 416
Hennessee 359
Henry M. Paulson Jr 649
Henry Paulson 641, 666
Herbert Hoover 405, 595
herd 492
herd mentality 611
herding 116
Heston model 235
Heuristics 115
HFN Averages 370
HFR 372
high dividend yields 84
high yield bond 302
high yield bonds 360
high yield stocks 587
high yield trades 259
highly liquid equities 280
high-net-worth investors 75
high-yield 353
high-yield bond indices 305
high-yield junk bonds 347
Hikkake 522
Hikkake Pattern 522
HIN 691
historical data 528
historical risk free rate 156
historical variance 172
historical volatility 386
HKEX 709
HKMA 617
Holbrook Working 416
Holder Identification Number 691
Holding Company Depositary Receipts 330
holding debt 256
holding statements 690
HOLDRS 330
home market indexe 339
Homma Munehisa 474, 485
homo economicus 113
Honda 656
Hong Kong Exchanges and Clearing 709
Hong Kong Monetary Authority 617
Hong Kong Stock Exchange 709, 733
hostile takeovers 46
hot money 610
hot tip 400
house edge 423
House of Representatives 645
house vigorish 423
housing market 589
HR 3997 645
HR1424 661
HRE 647
HSBC 73, 617, 710
HSBC Bank plc 647
HSI 733
HSI Services Limited 733
HSNSI 499, 505
Hulbert Stock Newsletter Sentiment Index 505

Huntington Bancshares 654
Huseyin Merdan 118
hybrid 47, 342
hybrid model 676
hybrid/structured securities 681
Hyman Minsky 578
hyper 581
hyperbola 167
hyperbolic discounting 114
hyperinflation 581, 584
Hypo Real Estate 645, 647
Hyundai Motor 615

I

I.T. bubble 630
ICE 212
Ice Brent futures 318
ICE Futures 212
iceberg order 92
iceberging 456
Icelandic Financial Supervisory Authority 646, 648
Icelandic stock exchange 652
ICI 347
identify trend changes 551
idiosyncratic risk 158, 170
IFTA 477
Igor Sergeyev 626
Igor Zyuzin 665
illegal accounting practices 634
illegal conduct 373
Illinois Bell 335
illiquid assets 649
illiquid market 319
illiquid mortgage-backed securities 643
illiquidity 603
IMF 576, 588, 612
IMF crisis 608
IMF rescue plan 653
IMM 211
Immanuel Wallerstein 578
implied volatility 246, 247
in the money 265
incentive compensation 232
Income Deposit Securities 681
income funds 352
income securities 430
income tax treatment 263
income trust model 681
Indentures 285
independent reviewer 299
index (equity) options 233
index arbitrage 483
index ETF 328
index fund 334, 336, 340, 353
index fund management 337
index funds 185, 324, 328, 333, 343
index mutual fund 340
Index of Leading (Economic) Indicators 585
Index of Leading Indicators 723
Index Participation Shares 326
index tracker 334
index trackers 385
Indexing 336
indicate changes in interest rates 290
individual investor 107
individual investors 185
Individual investors 659
individual portfolio risk reduction 420
individual retirement accounts 347
individual risk premium 156
Individual Savings Account 331
individual securities 382
individual stocks 727
individuals 178
Individuals 195
INDP 721
IndyMac Bank 574
inefficiency of the market 444
inflation 584
inflation risk 296
inflationary risk 302
inflation-indexed bonds 296

information technology department 76
ING 653
ING Direct 648
initial data point calculation 549
initial margin 316
Initial Margin 214
initial margin requirement 97
initial public offer 363
initial public offering 107, 631
Initial Public Offering 42
initial public offerings 414
initial requirement 97
Inkombank 623
input-output relationships 478
insider information 76
installment warrants 693
instant history bias 370
institutional day trader 436
institutional investor 325
Institutional Investor News 359
institutional investors 111
Institutional investors 195
institutional share class 356
institutional shares 356
institution's debts 575
insurance 253
insurance companies 185
intangible assets 85
intellectual property 182
Intellidexes 681
Inter@ctive Week Internet Index 681
inter-bank lending 657
interbank market 219
inter-bank market 219
Intercontinental Exchange 212
interest earnings on bonds 299
interest rate 429
interest rate caps 508
interest rate exposure 430
interest rate futures 430
interest rate market 694
interest rate options 233, 234
interest rate risk 275, 287, 302, 419
interest rate swap market 212
interest rate swaps 320, 419, 429
interest rates 585, 616
Interim Upgrading Program 618
intermarket relationships 479
inter-market spreading 225
intermediaries 238
intermediary 39
Internal Revenue Code 347
Internal Revenue Service 263
international calls 432
International Capital Market Association 42
International Federation of Technical Analysts 477
International Management Associates 372
International Monetary Fund 40, 588, 624, 636, 649
International Monetary Market 211
International Petroleum Exchange 212
international production data 103
International Securities Exchange 270
International Swaps and Derivatives Association 259
International Swaps and Derivatives Association agreement 401
intertemporal choice 114
intra-day high 636
intra-day nominal 724
intra-month oscillations 433
intrinsic value 64, 84, 85, 463
INTSTREAM 523
inverse exchange-traded fund 377
inverse S&P 500 ETF 377
inverted hammer 486
investable indices 369
investiment research company499
Investment Advisers Act 355, 365

Investment Advisers Act of 1940 465
investment advisor 70
investment advisors 502
investment advisory fee 349
investment aims 384
investment bank 572
investment banking 74
investment banking division 74
investment banks 692
investment companies 196, 326, 329
investment company 351
Investment Company Act of 19346
Investment Company Institute 347, 372
investment funds 381
investment goal 384
investment grade 304
investment grade bonds 303
investment instruments 39
investment management firms220
investment manager 358, 361
investment managers 334
investment opportunities 672
investment paradigm 84
investment performance 385
investment policies 340
investment portfolio 355
investment portfolios 347
investment principle 382
investment risk 382
investment strategies 327
investment strategy 85, 225, 525
investment theory 120
investment timing 526, 527
investment-grade bonds 303
investor confidence 636
Investor Intelligence Sentiment Index 498
investor sentiment 341, 477, 497
Investor sentiment 498
Investors Chronicle 511
investors sharebroker 691
IPCC 210
IPE 212
IPO 107, 363, 631, 676
IPOs 414
IRA 347, 700
IRA accounts 377
Irish Life and Permanent 645
Irish Nationwide 645
Irish Stock Exchange 362
Iron condor 243
IRS 340
Irving Fisher 594
Irving Kahn 86
Isaac Le Maire 405
ISDA cash settlement auction protocols 264
iShares 327
Island 442
Isle of Man 361
ISO 4217 222
issue price 285
issuer 39, 108
Issuer sponsored 691
iTraxx 252
ive M. Corcoran 523
iWon.com 632

J

J. Edgar Hoover 405
J. Welles Wilder 539, 547, 553
J. Welles Wilder, Jr. 557
J.P. Morgan 642
J30 index 703
Jack D. Schwager 478
Jack Treynor 155
Jacob Little 405
Jakarta Stock Exchange 615
James B. Lockhart III 641
James Baker 602
James Boness 507
Jan Mossin 155
January effect 190
japanese candlestick patterns 501
Japanese property bubble 573

J-Com 704
JDS Uniphase 634
Jean-Claude Trichet 651
Jean-François Théodore 715
Jeff de Graaf 504
Jeff Madura 118
Jeffrey Sachs 611
Jensen 373
Jeremy Bentham 113
Jeremy du Plessis 491
Jeremy Siegel 334, 505
Jerry Parker 461
Jiji Press 703
Jim Cramer 127, 504
Jim Simons 375
jitter 334
jobbers 495
Joe Saluzzi 457
Joel Greenblatt 87
John Blunt 699
John Bogle 335, 337, 346, 505
John Bollinger 479, 541
John Castaing 699
John Cox 236
John Lintner 155
John Maynard Keynes 574
John McCain 644
John McQuown 335
John Murphy 479
John Neff 462, 463
John Paulson 375
John Quincy Adams Ward 685
John S. Reed 687
John Templeton 87
John Thain 714
John W. Henry 461, 478
Joint Statement 626
joint stock company 55
Jonathan Wright 585
Jonathan's 699
Jordan Kotick 518
Jose Luis Rodriguez Zapatero 651
José Manuel Barroso 653
Joseph Granville 568
Joseph Schumpeter 598
Joseph Stiglitz 227, 611, 621
Journal of Finance 80
JP Morgan 376
JP Morgan building 686
JP Morgan Chase 73, 275
JPMorgan Chase 644, 655
JSE Limited 212
Jude Wanniski 594
jueteng scandal 616
Julie R. Dahlquist 523
junk bond 302, 615
junk bonds 353

K

kabushiki kaisha 702
Kabuto Club 703
Kagi chart 488
Kahneman 114
Kaplan 373
Kappa 373
Kaupþing banki hf. 646
Ken Griffin 375
Kendall 125
Kenneth French 334
kernel-smoothed estimator 246
key risk indicators 657
KeyBank 645
Keynesian economists 585
Kia Motors 615
Kirk Wright 372
KIT Finance 665
Kiyotaki-Moore model 577
KLD 344
KLSE 617
knocked-out 693
knockout warrants 693
Knowles 373
Kohlhagen 272
Kondratieff 103
Kondratiev 103
Kondratiev cycle 578
Kondratiev Fall 103
Kondratiev Spring 103

Kondratiev waves 103, 578
kurtosis 163
K-waves 103
Kyodo News 703

L

labour costs 420
Laissez-faire economists 585
Landsbanki 646, 653
Landsbanki Íslands hf. 646
large cap income 338
large cap index fund 337
large-cap 352
Large-Cap corporations 723
Larry Hite 478
Late DAX 696
Latin American debt crisis 613
Lawton 274
LCDS 263
LCDS spreads 264
LDAX 696
L-DAX 729
lead underwriter 108
leading shares 691
LEAPS 281
lease-buyback agreements 298
least squares regression line 143
left shoulder 544
legal/audit expense 350
Legislative Assembly of Ontario 707
Lehman Aggregate 196, 293
Lehman bonds 649
Lehman Brothers 261, 262, 375, 577, 642
Lehman Brothers Corporate Bond Index 295
Lehman Brothers/HFN 370
lender 403
lending commitments 178
LEPO 693
LEPOs 690
level-load fund 356
leverage 358, 360, 575
leveraged buyout 304
leveraged buyout (LBO) 257
leveraged ETF 378
leveraged exchange-traded fund 330
leveraged firm 135
leveraged inverse ETF 378
leveraged portfolios 429
leveraged position 214
Lévy flight 591
Libor 429, 645
LIBOR 46, 200, 657
LIBOR Market Model 508
licensed broker-dealer 73
LIFFE 82, 712
LIFFE CONNECT 713
LIFFECONNECT 712
Limit Down 719
limit on close (LOC) 89
limit on open (LOO) 89
limit order 88
limit orders 327, 391
limited partnerships 361
Linda C. Thomsen 373
line 219
linear least-squares calculation 143
linear regression 153
line-chart 484
Linux 342
Linux Weekly News 342
liquidity 468
liquidity risk 302, 332, 386
list of stock exchanges 678
Listed Equity Income Hybrid Securities 681
listed options 233
listing requirements 674
listing rules 689
Lloyds 651
Lloyds TSB 647, 650
load fund 356
loan financing 420
loan only 263
loan servicing company 655

local currency notionals 270
local volatility 273
lock up 367
locking-in price 251
lock-up 355
lock-up agreement 111
London Clearing House 214
London Interbank Offered Rate 200, 645
London International Financial Futures and Options Exchange 712, 713
London Stock Ex 183
London Stock Exchange 389, 674, 698, 705, 714
London Stock Exchange Group plc 698
long call 422
long legged doji 487
long position 268, 360, 377
long synthetic futures 422
Long Term Capital Management 360
Long Term Equity Anticipation Security 281
long term indicator 498
Long term indicator 498
long term price pattern 501
Long wave theory 105
long waves 103
longer term bonds 298
longer-term debt instruments 294
longer-term directional trend 433
longer-term trends 531
long-term 492, 531
Long-Term Capital Management 371, 431, 621
long-term investment 327
long-term investor 377
long-term loans 575
long-term trend 494
lose market liquidity 304
lost capital 110
lot 218
Louis Bachelier 121, 507
Louis the German 696
low exercise price option 693
low risk bonds 336
Lowenstein 431
lower highs 476
lower interest rates 275
lower lows 476
lower shadow 486
lower tier II 645
LSE 667, 698
LTCM 371
lunar cycle 190
lunar cycles 480

M

MACD 500, 550, 587
MacKinlay 101
Macquarie Bank 689
macro-factors 87
Mad Money 504
Magellan Fund 335
Mahathir Mohamad 228, 611
maintenance margin 95, 316
maintenance margin requirement 97
maintenance requirement 97
Major Economic Cycles 103
major stock exchanges 672, 678
Malkiel 483
Man Investments 376
manage risk 277
managed floating exchange regime 614
managed funds 381
management fee 349
Management Laboratory 815
managers box 387
manager's performance 138
Mandelbrot 519
manipulation 127
Marc Chaikin 564
margin 94, 315
margin account 97, 447

margin accounts 314
margin buying 575
Margin buying 94
margin call 97, 316, 411
margin calls 431, 500
margin of safety 84
Margin of Safety 87
margin requirements 94, 96
Margin requirements 98
margin trading 439
margin use 440
margined 313
margin-equity ratio 98, 317
margining 314
Mario Gabelli 86
Mark Hulbert 191, 505
Mark Hulbert's Stock Newsletter Sentiment Index 499
Mark Krtitzman 374
Mark Rubinstein 236
mark to market 313
mark to market accounting 314

'

'marked-to-market 215

M

market 176
market analytical tools 436
market appreciation potential 498
market bottom 502
market bubble 495
market capitalisation index 713
market capitalization 672
market capitalization weighted index funds 137
Market capitulation 499
market clearing opening price 454
market clearing price 319
market cycles 492
market data 446
market economy 176
market efficiency hypothesis 335
market index fund 337
Market Index Leader 344
market inefficiencies 257
Market inefficiencies 115
market maker 389, 412, 466, 691
market makers 71, 72, 400, 441, 495
market making 225
market making banks 275
market model regression 136
market neutral 170
market neutral approach 421
market on close (MOC) 89
market on open (MOO) 89
market order 88
market panic 393
market participants 197, 483, 579
market portfolio 153, 161, 169
market prediction 65
market price 234
market psychology 224, 603, 610
market reaction 445
market return 170
market risk 155, 170, 302, 423
market sentiment 53, 473
market share 689
market swap rate 275
Market Technicians Association 518
market timing strategy 378, 443
market trend 492
market turnover 689
market uncertainty 247
market valuation 498
Market valuation 498
market value for equity 147
market value of preferred stock 148
market value of the debt 147
market volatility 143, 291
Market Wizards 478
market-making 73
market-share weighted index 342

Mark-To-Market margin 214
Marsh Carter 687
Martin J. Whitman 87
Martin Weber 101
Martin Whitman 87
martingale 319
marubozu black 487
marubozu white 487
Massachusetts Institute of Technology 458, 591
Massachusetts Investors Trust 346
massive currency speculation 611
master/feeder funds 362
matching engines 82
Matching Law 114
matrix singularity 151
maturity date 285
maturity risk 302
Mauritiu 361
Max Warburg 697
maximum legal limit 297
Mayer Amschel Rothschild 697
McGraw-Hill 723
McQuown 335
MDAX 696
mean reversion 455
measure global bond portfolios 293
measuring performance 196
Mechel 663, 665
median stock 498
Melvin 219
merchant banking 75, 186
merger 176, 687, 734
mergers 87
mergers and acquisitions 73, 304
Merrill Lynch 330, 369, 518, 635, 642
Merrill Lynch BB/B Index 305
Merrill Lynch Domestic Master 196, 293
Merrill Lynch High Yield Master II (HOA0) 305
Merton Miller 148, 155
MFI 565
MFS Investment Management 346
MGEX 212
MICEX 625, 666
MICEX stock exchange 666
Michael Conroy 173
Michael Jensen 160
Michael Marcus 478
Michael Milken 304
Michael Moore 687
micro-cap 352
Microsoft 109
mid-cap 352
mid-cap research efforts 676
mid-cap value 338
middle band 541
middle office 74
middle-men 81
Mikhail Fridman 655
Milan stock exchange 714
Miller and Modigliani 134
Milton Friedman 220, 227, 574, 599
miners' strikes 626
mini-crash 605
minimum margin requirement 96, 97
minimum return 145
Minneapolis Grain Exchange 212, 416
mispricing 412
MIT 482
MIT Sloan School of Management 101
Mizuho affair 705
Mizuho Securities Co., Ltd. 704
Mizuho trade 705
MMM investment fund 576
mnemonic devices 495
model of asset returns 153
modern portfolio theory 155, 162
Modern Portfolio Theory 173, 374
modified market cap 342
modified sharpe ratio 373
Modigliani-Miller theorem 148
momentum 520

momentum indicator 499, 559
momentum strategies 482
Monetary Authority of Singapore 216, 618
monetary conditions 585
monetary policy 574
monetizing the debt 581
Money flow 565
Money flow index 565
money growth 586
money management 439, 460, 473
money market funds 200, 325, 354
Money market instruments 40
money market mutual fund 642
money market mutual funds 201, 659
monoline insurers 301
Monte Carlo simulation 215
Montreal Exchange 707
Moody's 299, 615
Morgan Bank 595
Morgan Stanley 73, 643
Morgan Stanley Biotech Index 342
Morgan Stanley Eastern Europe Fund 392
Morning Doji star pattern 501
Morning star bull 501
Morningstar 338, 498
mortgage financing companies 576
mortgage loans 232
mortgage portfolio 275
mortgage-backed securities 200
Moscow Interbank Currency Exchange 625
Most 326
most Innovative Index Product 248
Mothers 702
Movie Gallery 264
moving average 530
moving average convergance divergence 500
Moving Average Convergence 550
moving average levels 532
moving average technique 538
MPT 162
MSCI EAFE 141
MSCI Index Fund Shares 327
MSCI World index 689
MTA 477, 518
MTM margin 215
multi-class structure 356
multi-move trading operations 453
muni 297
muni arb 428
municipal arbitrage 428
municipal bond 297, 300, 428
municipal bond arbitrage 301
municipal bond funds 353
municipal bonds 40, 298
municipal issuer 297
municipal notes 201
Muscovy Company 698
mutual fund 327, 331, 334, 340, 346, 351
mutual funds 58, 73, 185, 291, 324, 325, 353, 367, 381
mutual insurance 61
mutual organization 61
MV Sea Isle City 602
Myron Scholes 160, 235, 507

N

naked short sale 408
NASD 718
Nasdaq 109
NASDAQ 80, 714, 718
NASDAQ Composite 499
NASDAQ OMX Group 718
NASDAQ Stock Exchange 675
NASDAQ, 183
NasdaqOMX 719
National Association of Securities Dealers 718
National Association of Securities Dealers Automated Quotations 718
National Australia Bank 688
National Bank of Ukraine 629

National Bureau of Economic Research 584, 586
National City 645
National City Bank 595
National City Corporation 654
National Historic Landmark 680
National Stock Exchange of India 212
National Wage Council 618
Nationwide Building Society 647
natural capital 208
natural capitalism 210
natural hedge 419
NAV 324, 332, 348, 389
NAV per interest/share 362
NBER 584, 586
N-day exponential moving average 539
NDD 221
neckline 544
negative commodities 208
negative directional indicator 554
negative divergence 568
negative growth 574
negative income investment strategy 411
negative price gaps 439
negative trending charts 529
neo-classical economic theory 113
net asset value 110, 348, 349, 358, 389
net value 94
Netscape 109
netting 262
Neuer Markt 697
neural topology 479
neutral pattern 487
New Arrangement to Borrow 612
new economy 632
New Issue Market 180
New Jonathan's 699
New Market 697
New York City Bankruptcy court 642
New York Curb Exchange 680
New York Mercantile Exchange 212
New York Stock & Exchange Board 684
New York Stock Exchange 389, 675, 682
New York Stock Exchange (NYSE) 290
New York Times 576
New York University 603
Newly Industrialized Countries 608
news playing 444
NextEconomy 712
NextPrime 712, 713
NextWeather 713
NFA 221
NI 81-106 349
Nick Leeson 448
Nicola Horlick 385
Nicolas Sarkozy 646, 653
NICs 608
Nihon Keizai Shimbun 703
Nikkei 225 730
Nikkei bear market 591
Nikkei Dow Jones Stock Average 730
Nikolai Kondratieff 598
Nikolai Kondratiev 578
Nikolai Kovalyov 624
Nissan 656
Nizhny Novgorod 623
NNI 730
No Dealing Desk 221
Noam Gottesman 375
Nobel prize 114
Nobel Prize in Economics 235
noise 490
noise trader 435
no-load funds 356
no-load index funds 356
nominal 284
non-arbitrage algorithmic trading systems 478
Non-cumulative preferred stock50
non-diversifiable risk 155

non-dividend paying asset 318
non-dividend-paying stock 235
non-farm payrolls 584
non-investable benchmarks 370
non-investment grade bond 302
non-linear statistical models 478
non-management expenses 350
non-market economy 176
non-perfectly-correlated asset classes 382
non-performing loans 615
Norges Bank 650
Norilsk Nickel 655
normal distribution 591
normal expected values 497
Nortel 344
Northern Rock 572
Northern Trust 654
NorthPoint Communications 634
not held orders 92
notaSynopsis 605
notes 39
notices of defaults 300
notional amount 274, 315
notional principal contract 263
notional principal contracts 263
Novation 214
Nova-Ursa ratio 499
novice traders 410
N-period simple moving average 541
numéraire 270
NYMEX 212, 401
Nymex crude futures contract 317
NYMEX Light Sweet Crude Oil contract 315
NYSE 183, 682
NYSE Alternext 714
NYSE Alternext U.S. 680
NYSE Arca 80
NYSE Bonds trading system 290
NYSE Euronext 687
NYSE Group 714
NYSE member firm 683
NYSE-Euronext group 718

O

OARS 454
obligation characteristics 260
Obstfeld's model of currency crises 579
OBV 567, 568
OCC 215
Och-Ziff Capital Management 376
October 1929 crash 594
ODAX 729
OECD 414

Œ

Œcopathy 577

O

OEIC 387
OEICs 346
offer prices 387
offsetting of profits and losses 95
offsetting transaction 261
offshore corporate fund 362
Offshore corporate funds 361
offshore corporation 361
offshore tax havens 361
offshoring 425
oil crisis 578
Oil Spot Prices 664
Okuma Shigenobu 704
Oleg Deripaska 655
Omega 373
onathan's 699
On-balance Volume 567, 568
one-day percentage decline 600
Oneximbank 626
online brokers 340
onomatopoeic nonsense 632
open 89
open futures 316
open market 386

open outcry 183, 683
open price 89
open-end funds 325, 348
open-end investment company 351
open-end management investment companies 325
open-end mutual fund 390
open-end mutual funds 332
open-ended funds 393
open-ended investment companies 346
open-ended schemes 387
opening automated reporting system 454
OpenIPO 676
operations division 76
OptiMark system 676
option 232
option adjusted spread (OAS) 295
option contract 239
Option contracts 233
option holder 233, 268
option period 274
option traders 236
option trading 186
optionality 286
option-like features 251
options 240, 320, 410, 692
Options Clearing Corporation 214, 279
options contracts 197, 316
options for tax purposes 263
options on futures 233
options on interest rate swaps 274
options on swaps 234
options pricing model 507
options risk exposure 273
options strategies 243
options trading 488
Order Handling Rules 441
Order Management System 456
ordinary income 263, 348
Osaka Securities Exchange 730
oscillator 555
OSE 730
OTC 43, 270, 275, 279, 290, 400, 692, 718
OTC Bulletin Board 400
OTC market 197, 400
OTC option 233
OTCBB 400
OTCQX 400
OTC-traded financial instrument 250
Otelco Inc. 681
others on technical patterns 438
OTT 681
outdoor markets 680
out-of-the-money calls 246
outright forwards 217
outsourcing 425
outsourcing company 425
over the counter 43
overallotment option 109
over-allotment option 112
overbought 225, 548, 556
overheated markets 606
overnight trading 714
overpriced 52
overpricing 110
overreaction 117
oversold 225, 556
over-the-counter 194, 400, 692, 718
over-the-counter (OTC) market 90
over-the-counter contract 401
over-the-counter derivatives 197
over-the-counter markets 42, 197
over-the-counter options 233
Over-the-counter options 232
over-the-counter options contracts 239
overvaluation 603
overvalued 157, 404
Oxford English Dictionary 495

P

P/E method 62
PAD system report 498
pairs trade 419
Pankaj Jain 80
paper 200
par 308
par value 45
par value method 52
parabola 166
parabolic curve 557
Parabolic SAR 557
parallel trend lines 530
Paris Bourse 183, 712
passive funds 385
passive investment 337
passive management 334, 385
passive strategy 138
passively managed mutual funds 343
past price movements 483
patents 182
pattern 484
pattern day trader 447
Paul Coonter 121
Paul Krugman 609
Paul Rabar 461
Paul Samuelson 121, 335, 507
Paul Sonkin 87
Paul Tudor 603
Paul Tudor Jones 375, 478, 519
Paul Volcker 587
Pauline Novak-Reich 519
Paulson and Company 376
payer option 252
payer swaption 274, 275
payment obligations 259
payout ratio 60
peak 544
peak rates 94
Pecora Commission 597
penny stock 710
pension funds 73, 185, 291, 303, 304
perceived bottom 502
percent b 542
perfect correlation 385
perfect market 319
performance 98
performance bond 94, 315
performance bond margin 316
performance fee 355
performance measurement 373
performance ratios 65
performance risk 401
performance-based fees 367
peripheral charges 99
permanent bear market view 462
Permanent Interest-Bearing Securities 647
persistent trend 117
Perth Mint 693
Perth mint gold 693
Peter Bernstein 498
Peter Lynch 126, 481
Pets.com 636
Philadelphia Business Journal 585
Philadelphia Stock Exchange 270, 681, 719
Philip Falcone 375
Philip Morris 144
Philippine Central Bank 616
PHLX 719
physical settlement 260, 264
PIBS 647
Pierre Lagrange 375
pin risk 238
pinging 457
Pink OTC Markets 400
Pink Quote 400
Pink Sheets 400
PIPEs 77
pit trading 81
pivot point analysis 545
pivot point calculations 524, 545
PNC Financial Services 654
point and figure chart 490
policy error 414
political conditions 224

political crisis 627
political risk 302
Ponzi finance 578
Ponzi scheme 623
pool price 422
pooled investment funds 355
pooled investment vehicles 332
pooling money 382
pools of investment capital 366
poor decisions 479
POP 348
Populist economists 585
portfolio 158, 214
portfolio insurance strategies 603
portfolio manager performance 479
portfolio risk 165, 170
portfolio theory 343
portfolio turnover 351
portfolio volatility 165
Portfolios with Minimum Variance 166
Position Paper 374
positive directional indicator 554
positive feedback 579
positive network benefit 77
positive trending chart 529
postage expense 350
post-boom recessions 586
Post-Modern Portfolio Theory 163
potential loss unlimited 241
Poterba 475
Powershares 681
prearranged price 313
precious metals 329
predict support and resistance 545
predictability of price changes 102
predictive capabilities 498
predictive power 482
predictors 584
preference shares 45
preferred shares 45
Preferred stock 45
preferred stock shareholders 390
preliminary strategy 460
pre-market 332
premium 232, 233, 240, 242, 265, 268, 274, 308, 332, 389, 393
premium bonds 179
premium margin 95
prepayment options 232
President's Working Group on Financial Markets 366
previous average 533
previous cumulative average 533
Price and Volume Trend 567
price arbitrage 424
price channel 530
price chart 528
price cycles 104
price gaps 444
price interval period 528
price momentum 438
price movement 527
price movements 484, 676
price of a bond 306
price of a commodity 318
price patterns 472
price per share 133
price pivot points 527
price to earnings 502
price trends 127
price/earnings 62
price-to-book ratio 84
pricing bond options 508
pricing of shares 150
pricing option contracts 320
primary issues 180
primary market 42, 180, 298, 299
primary product 202
primary trend 492
primary trends 492
Prime Brokerage 373
Princeton 483
Princeton University 100, 335, 346
principal 39, 70, 284, 657
principal markets 358
principal risk 74
principal valuation techniques 235
private activity bonds 299

private bank savings 647
private capital 651
Private Client Services 74
private investment fund 358
Private Wealth Management 74
Privately placed securities 43
Procter & Gamble 144
Producer cooperatives 60
producers 320
production efficiencies 582
professional fund managers 355
Professional Securities Market 701
professional traders 448
Professor Robert E. Whaley 248
program trading 184, 455, 603
prolonged recession 573
promotion of securities 73
propagation networks 66
Property dividends 56
property trusts 688
proprietary software 82
proprietary trading 74, 77
prospect theory 114
protection buyer 259, 260
protection seller 259, 260
protection sellers 261
protectionism 207
PSE Composite Index 616
PSM 701
psych 473
public awareness campaigns 631
public information 76
public investment company 364
public offer 43
public offering 107, 181, 329
public offering price 348
public trading 683
publicly traded bonds 148
pumping 465
purchasing power 426
purchasing power parity 426, 589
pure speculation 225
pure technical analysts 475
purported bubbles 573
put 242, 270, 693
put dates 286
put option 232, 240, 268, 272, 402
put options 263
put position 422
put price 269
put/call ratios 473
putability 286
putative barriers 117
puts 402
puttable bond 251
PVT 567
Pyotr Kazakevich 666

Q

QQQQ 500
quadratic utility function 163
qualified client 365
qualified purchasers 364
quantitative analysts 75, 278
quantitative behavioral finance 118
quantitative finance 423
quantitative techniques 234
Queen Elizabeth II 700
quiet period 111

R

R square value 144
Rage Against the Machine 687
Rahul Mohindar 559
Rahul Mohindar Oscillator 559
raising capital 671
rally 494, 568
Ralph Nelson Elliott 474, 511
random walk 591
random walk hypothesis 100, 483
random walk theories 483
range trading 444
ranges 540
rate of change 520
rating agency 299

rating downgrades 300
rating scales 303
rational analysis 479
raw commodities 202
Ray Sturm 118
RBS 651
reacquired stock 50
Reagan-Volcker-Carter recession 587
real estate busts 613
real estate financing banks 645
real estate investment trusts 60, 464
Real Estate Investment Trusts 388
real estate options 232
real estate values 594
real return 384
real time 724
real time filtering software 445
real-estate market 586
real-time 246
real-time data feed 446
real-time trading information 184
rebate trading 444
recapitalization plans 650
recapitalizing banks 649
receiver option 252
receiver swaption 274, 275
recession 103, 303, 573, 584
Recession Drill 585
recessionary effect 577
redemption 362
Regions Financial Corporation 654
registration expense 350
regression analysis 139
regular cycle 532
regulation 576
Regulation D 77
Regulation S 77
Regulation SHO 408, 414
Regulation W 659
regulatory arbitrage 431
reinvestment risk 289, 302
reits 701
REITs 388
relative peak 544
relative strength 547
Relative strength index 499
Relative Strength Index 547
relative value 278
remittance companies 221
remuneration 383
remuneration structure 363
Renaissance Technologies 376
reorganizing 614
repayment of principal risk 302
representative sampling 328
repurchase agreements 200, 201
rescue plan 646, 650
research division 75
research indexes 334
Reserve Bank of Australia 658
Reserve Bank of India 658
Reserve Primary Fund 642
residual position 238
resistance 524
resistance level 524
restricted trading 600
restructuring 614
restructuring events 726
retail brokerages 79
retail brokers 221
retail day trader 436
retail forex brokers 221
retail index fund 346
retail traders 221
retained earnings 53
return on equity 142
return on investment 142
return on margin 317
Return on Margin (ROM) 98
Reuters 222
revenue bonds 299
reward-to-risk ratio 155
Rex Sinquefield 335
Ric Edelman 722
rice trader 485
Richard Blumenthal 374
Richard Branson 385
Richard C. Shelby 644

Richard Dennis 461, 478
Richard Donchian 461
Richard Grasso 687
Richard Herrnstein 114
Richard M. Salsman 595
Richard Ramyar 516
Richard Roll 161, 604
Richard Sylla 603
Richard Thaler 115
Richard Whitney 595
right shoulder 544
Rio Tinto 688
rising interest rates 275
rising market 532
Risk and Asset Management Research Centre 371
risk averse 162
risk capacity 339
risk capital 439
risk control 460, 473
risk free asset 136
risk free rate 133, 308, 318
risk free simple interest rate 273
risk management 75, 235, 469
risk management principles 232
risk monitoring 76
risk neutral portfolio 235
risk neutral pricing 234
risk of default 256, 295
risk of political upheaval 276
risk of recession 657
risk premium 133
risk profile 243
risk threshold 189
risk tolerance 165
risk-adjusted return on capital 132
risk-based approach 365
risk-free 657
risk-free asset 155, 167
risk-free bonds 296
risk-free interest rate 272
risk-free profit 423
risk-free return 133
risk-free treasury bond 295
riskless portfolio 236
riskless profit opportunity 318
risk-neutral probability 319
risk-return profile 158
risk-return profiles 169
risk-weighted projected return 132
risky assets 159
risky trading style 447
RMB 619
RMO 559
RNE 392
Roaring Twenties 594
Robert Arnott 334
Robert C. Merton 507
Robert Doll 505
Robert Elstone 688
Robert Prechter 516, 518
Robert Shiller 635
Robin Wilkin 518
robo trading 225, 454
ROC 520
ROC indicators 521
rogue trader 448
rogue traders 576
Role of Capital in Optimal Banking Supervision and Regulation 431
rolling average 530
ROM 317
Ronald Reagan 587
Rosario Mantegna 591
Rosselkhozbank 648
Roth IRAs 347
Roy Batchelor 516
Royal Bank of Scotland 647, 651
Royal Dutch Shell 431
royalty trusts 60
RSI 499, 547
r-squared 385
RTS 666
RTS Index 664
ruble crisis 296
Ruble crisis 623
rule-based trading 479
run up 529
runaway economy 632
running average 530, 533

rush of withdrawals 572
Russell 1000 Index 352
Russell 2000 Index 352
Russell Global Index 342
Russell Indexes 293, 352
Russell Investment Group 342
Russell Microcap Index 352
Russell Midcap Index 352
Russian Central Bank 663
Russian Financial Crisis 623
Russian markets 663
Russian oligarchs 655
Rydex 329

S

S&P 500 280, 324, 334
S&P 500 index options 246
S&P 500 proxy 326
S&P Global 100 144
S&P oscillator 499
S&P Pure Growth Style Index 342
S&P Pure Value Style Index 342
SABR 273
safe-and-cheap 87
safeguards 316, 705
sales charge 356
sales credit 109
salvage value 172
Samsung Motors 615
São Paulo Stock Exchange 675
SAP 612
SAR 557
Saxo Bank 218
scaled average 721
scalper 445, 466
scalping 444, 465
scheme of mortgage insurance 644
schools of technical analysis 473
Schumpete 103
Schumpeter 104
Schumpeter-Freeman-Perez 105
Schumpeterian 104
Scott H. Irwin 482
scrip dividends 56
scripts 453
SDAX 696
seasonality 190
Seasonality Timing System 191
seasoned equity offering 112
SEATS system 691
SEC 73, 329, 346, 714, 718
SEC form N-1A 348
SEC no-action letter 329
SEC Rule 10b-18 53
secondary market 42, 181, 298
secondary markets 239
secondary public offering 112
secondary trends 492, 493
secretive entities 360
Sector Spiders 327
secular market trend 494
secular trends 492
secured debt 294
Securities Act of 1933 346
Securities and Exchange Board of India 215
Securities and Exchange Commission 279, 324, 325, 364, 659, 718
Securities and Exchange Commission of Pakistan 215
Securities and Futures Commission 215
Securities Commission 216
Securities Exchange Act of 1934 346, 465
Securities Exchange Commission 643
Securities Industry and Financial Markets Association 42
securities law 109
securities lending 407, 420
securities lending programs 325
securities market line 162, 171
securities offering 111
securitization 78
security 39
security analysis 86

security characteristic lin 170
Security Characteristic Line 140
security deposit 316
Security Industry and Financial Markets Association 429
security market line 155
Security Market Line 157
security register 39
security risk class 155
SEHK 709, 734
self-invested personal pension 331
self-perpetuating rise 631
self-selection bias 370
sell down a stock 540
sell high and buy low 403
Sell in May and Go Away 190
sell indicator 498
sell limit order 88
sell market-if-touched order 91
sell signal 510
sell stop order 90
sell stops 499
seller 268
selling short against the box 413
semi-strong-form efficiency 123
Senate Banking Committee 644
senior debt 294
senior tranches 304
SENSEX 493
sensitivity of the asset return 156
sensitivity to market risk 133
sentiment 462
sentiment indicator 499
Seoul stock exchange 615
September 11 687
September 11 attacks 636
Sergei Kiriyenko 624
Seth Klarman 87, 413
settlement 263, 317
settlement auction 261
settlement index 280
settlement period 440
settlement price 314
settlement terms 233
severe recession scenario 647
SFE 688
SFM 701
SG Asset Management 385
SG UK Growth fund 385
SGX 705, 730
Shanghai stock exchanges can been characterized as quasi-state institutions insofar as they were created 675
share certificates 690
share issuance 726
Shareholder Registration Number 691
shareholder services 355
shareholder servicing fee 350
shareholders' perks 383
Sharma 373
sharp fall 509
Sharpe 373
Sharpe ratio 169
shaven bottom 486
shaven head 486
Sheen T. Kassouf 507
Shibusawa Eiichi 704
shopkeepers 71
short futures 409
short interest 404, 408, 411
Short Interest/Total Market Float 499
short position 360, 402, 410
short put 422
short rate models 278
short sale 90
short sell 444
short seller 403
short selling 186, 327, 358, 360, 377, 402, 495, 598, 691
short squeeze 411
short term debt instruments 40
short term rates 277
short term valuation horizon 112
short the dividend 409
shorter term bonds 298
shorting 402
shorting the market 443

short-term 492, 531
short-term fluctuations 531
short-term liabilities 575
short-term trading 438
SICAV 387
Siegel 586
SIFMA 429
signal 486
signal processing 531
signature 513
significant decline 584
SIIA 42
Simple limit orders 92
simple moving average 521, 531
simple volatility-based specification test 101
Singapore Exchange 705, 730
Singapore Exchange Ltd. 703
single price auctions 689
single priced 387
single priced schemes 387
single-price auctions 89
sinking fund provision 287
sinusoidal cycles 103
sizable return days 475
skew 163
SMA 521, 531, 532
small cap index 364
Small Order Execution System 441, 719
small-cap 352
SML 155
Smoot-Hawley Tariff Act 594, 597
smoothing factor 539
smoothing operation 531
Snif-fer 456
Sniper 456
social contamination 115
social psychology 116, 173
social tension 626
social welfare projects 657
Société Générale 653
Socionomics Institute 516
SOES 441, 719, 720
SOES bandits 442
soft landing 602
sophisticated trading systems 445
Soros funds 368
South Ossetia 665
South Sea Bubble 495
sovereign bonds 296
sovereign debt 573
sovereign defaults 577
sovereign investment funds 388
sovereign wealth fund of Qatar 652
SPAN 215
SPDR 326, 332, 681
SPDRs 727
special dividend 55
special liquidity scheme 662
specialist broker 683
Specialist Fund Market 701
specialized markets 176
specialized scalper 466
specific risk 170
spectacular decline 509
speculative bubble 630
speculative finance 578
speculative grade bond 302
speculative grade bonds 303
speculative stock market bubbles 591
speculator 239
speculators 317, 320
spiders 727
Spiders 326
spinning off 56
spinning top black 487
spinning top white 487
spinoff 176
spinoffs 726
spiral of inflation 581
sports arbitrage 425
spot 226, 270, 272
spot market 222
spot price 250, 266, 314, 318, 409
spot prices 218
spot trading 204
spot transactions 217

spot-forward arbitrage 424
spread 82, 254, 308, 441
spread analysis 295
spread traders 98
spreading risk 382
spreads 332
Spron hf. 646
SPX 280
SPY 227, 727
Square Mile 701
SRN 691
stagflation 104, 584
stagnation 103
Standard & Poor's 299, 647
Standard & Poor's Depositary Receipts 326, 727
Standard and Poor's 499
Standard and Poor's (S&P) oscillator 499
Standard and Poor's Composite Index Funds 335
Standard Chartered 647
standard deviation 373, 386
standard deviation of return 162
standard option valuation models 234
standardized contract 312
standardized contract features 232
STANS 215
Staples 144
State Street Corporation 654
State Street Global Advisors 327
static betas 373
statistical arbitrage 423, 455, 483
statistical measures 385
statistical variance 139
Stephen Ross 150, 236
Sterling Money Market 329
Steven A. Cohen 375
stochastic calculus 234
stochastic interest rates 235
stochastic oscillator 559
stochastic process 507
stochastic volatility models 235
stock 183
stock analyst 336
stock broker 68, 397
stock brokers 675
stock broking service 69
stock call option 429
stock exchange 176, 183, 670, 674
Stock Exchange Tower 700
stock image 64
stock index futures 319
stock indexes 694
stock investors 397
stock market 183
stock market bottom 497
stock market bubble 338, 631
stock market crash 591, 636
stock market crashes 577
stock market downturn of 2002 636
stock market drop 584
stock market index 341
stock market movements 591
stock market prediction 66
stock option 250
stock options 233
stock picker 336, 337
stock picking 398, 421
stock picking policy 126
stock portfolio 455
stock price 429
Stock repurchases 50
stock short 410
stock split 56
stock splits 726
Stock Subscription Room 700
stock trader 397
stock trading 675
stock valuation method 62
stock-like features 331
stock-picking techniques 353
stocks 176
stock's behavior 433
stop limit order 90
stop loss order 90, 410, 544
stop order 90
stop orders 327, 391

stor groups 185
storage costs 319
STP 82, 221
straddle 243
Straight preferred stocks 47
straight through processing 80
Straight Through Processing 221
straight-through processing 82
Straits Times Index 618
strangle 244
strategic advisory services 73
strategy division 75
StrategyDesk 461
Straumur-Burðarás fjárfestingarbanki hf. 646
streaming income risk 302
strike 270, 272, 409
strike price 233, 234, 250, 252, 265, 266, 268, 422
strike rate 274, 275, 278
strike value 238
structural adjustment package 612
style drift 338
subordinated 39
subordinated debt 294
subprime mortgage crisis 641, 664
subprime mortgage loans 304
subprime mortgages 653
sub-prime mortgages 360
Sub-sovereign government bonds 40
successive values 531, 535
Suharto 608
summer devaluation 615
Summers 475
SunTrust Banks 654
super cycles 103
superannuation funds 117
supercycle 513
SuperDOT 454
SuperDot electronic system 442
super-efficient portfolio 169
support 524, 544
support level 544
Supranational bonds 40
survivor's option 287
survivorship bias 370
Svein Gjedrem 650
swap 263, 274, 320
swap adjusted spread 257
swap contract 422
swaps 197, 401
swaption 274
swaption agreement 275
swaption interbank market 275
swaption market 275
swaptions 234, 508
Swedish Riksbank 648
swing trader 433
swing trading 433
Swiss National Bank 648
Sydney Futures Exchange 688
syndicate 108, 111
syndicated secured loans 264
synthetic asset 151
synthetic futures 422
synthetic indexing 336
synthetic market 691
synthetic put option 455
systematic crisis 665
systematic risk 158, 382
Systematic risk 170
systematic trading decisions 542
systemic banking crisis 572
systemic risk 155, 262, 338, 371, 577
systems traders 459

T

T&C 668
Takuo Tsurushima 705
tangible book value 84
target index 336, 337
tax arbitrage 432
tax brackets 301
tax charged on capital gains 740
tax environment 361

tax free stock market operations 398
Tax Rate Statement 297
taxable bonds 300
taxation adjustment risk 302
tax-exempt income 298
tax-free municipal bond 348
t-bills 657
tching a falling knife 502
TecDAX 696
technical analysis 398, 472, 484
technical analysis indicator 539, 568
technical analysis oscillator 562
technical analysis tool 541
technical analysts 472
technicians 472
technological innovation 582, 676
technology-heavy 636
Ted Kennedy 661
TED spread 657
Tel Aviv Stock Exchange 46, 719
telecommunication arbitrage companies 432
Telstra Corporation 688
TER 350
Term Auction Facility 661
term funds 353
term sheet 233
termination payment 263
terms of payment of interest 300
terrorism 636
test 524
TFS Capital Small Cap Fund 367
TFSSX 367
Thai crisis 577
Thaksin Shinawatra 614
Thaler's model 117
The Baupost Group 87
The Course of the Exchange 699
The Great Bear of Wall Street 405
the Halloween indicator 190
the Internet bubble bursting 636
The Market Technicians Association 477
The Source 701
The Superinvestors 86
The Times 371
The Vanguard Group 332, 338, 493, 728
themed funds 384
Themis Trading 457
theoretical price 318
theoretical value of an option 232
TheStreet.com 504
Third Avenue Value Fund (TAVF) 87
Thomas Aspray 551
Thomas K. McCraw 597
Thomas W. Lamont 595
Thomson Financial league 134
Three Factor Model 334
three waves of panics 599
threshold price level 710
TIAA-CREF 354
ticker symbol 239, 246
Tier 1 76
Tier 1 capital 46, 47
time to expiration 234
time to maturity 273
Time Warner 634
TIMS 215
tipping point 676
TNK-BP 655, 663
Tokobank 626
Tokyo Stock Exchange 702, 730
tontine 296
top reversal 487
Topix 730
Torbjorn K A Eliazon 577
Toronto Index Participation Shares 326
Toronto Stock Exchange 389, 706
total bond fund net inflows 293
total expense ratio 350
total volume technical analysis indicator 564
toxic debt 304
Toyota 656
tracking error 338, 386

'

'tracking error 334

T

tracking stock 430
trade confirm 261
trade volatility 276
Trade2Win 461
trader 396
Traders 195
TradeWeb 83
trading bands 541
trading curb 605
trading day 327
trading floor 682
trading in a range 444
trading opportunities 472
trading playing field 436
trading ranges 539
trading room 682
trading sessions 681
trading setups 438
Trading Simulator 692
trading strategies 456, 483, 543, 692
trading strategy 451, 461
trading style 436, 444
trading time-frames 443
trading volume 438
trading warrants 692
traditional commodity markets 320
traditional evaluations 492
trailing activation price 91
trailing stop limit order 91
trailing stop order 91
transaction costs 355
transatlantic stock exchange 687
transfer agent expenses 350
Transfer and Convertibility 668
transfer of risk 320
transfer restrictions 260
transferable securities 346
transparency 576
transparent portfolios 325
treasuries 40
treasury bills 201, 651
Treasury bills 200
treasury bonds 81
treasury share 51
treasury shares 51
treasury stock 50
Tremont Hedge Fund Index 375
trend following 443, 459
trend following indicator 551
trend following systems 461
trend line 527
trend lines 524
trend reversal 487
trends 101, 472
Treynor 373
triangle number 535
triangle numbers 564
Tri-Continental Corporation 394
trigger 263
trigger line 550
trigger price 91
triple bottom 501
triple EMA 564
triple exponential 522, 562
Triple Screen Approach 192
Trix 562
TRIX 562
TRIX indicator 522
Troubled Asset Relief Program 643
troubled mortgage-related assets 661
TRuPS 49
trustees expense 350
Trust-preferred security 49
trusts 351
TSE 702, 705, 706, 730
TSE 100 326
TSE 300 index 344
TSE 35 326
TSE Arrows 704
TSX 706

TSX Venture Exchange 707
turnover 349
turnover ratio 349
turtles 461
Tversky 114
TWAP 455
two interest rates 272
TY394

U

U.S. bond market debt 290
U.S. Federal Reserve 371
U.S. mutual funds 340, 387
U.S. Treasury 642
UAE central bank 652
UBS 652, 689
UBS AG 73
UBS Investment 414
UCBH Holdings 654
UCITS 346
UITs 351
uncertain foreign cash flows 271
uncertain return of an asset 151
underlier 238
underlying swap 274, 278
undervalued 157, 404, 502
underwriter 108
underwriting firm 107
undisclosed structural risks 360
undiversifiable risk 158
unhedged risk position 427
UniCredit 646
unit investment trusts 325, 351
Unit Investment Trusts 385
unit trusts 186, 346, 361, 387
United Kingdom's Financial Services Authority 369
United States v. Microsoft 632
unitized insurance funds 346
universal banks 73
University of Pennsylvania 101
unleveraged firm 135
unregistered financial instruments 348
unsecured debt 39, 294
unsustainable state 587
unsystematic risk 158
unweighted mean 531
upper shadow 486
upsloping line 529
upstairs traders 676
uptick 92, 443
uptrend movement 486
US Dollar Money Market ETF 329
USD put option 271
utilities 587

V

validity of fundamental analysis 66
valley 529
Valley National Bancorp KeyBank 655
Valores de Lisboa e Porto 712
value arbitrage 428
value based investment 384
value investing 462
value of an option 234
value of life 210
value opportunities 428
value stocks 85, 352
Valueline 498
Van der Beurze 185
Van K. Tharp 459
Vanguard 354
Vanguard 500 728
Vanguard 500 Index Fund 335, 346
Vanguard Group 335
Vanguard Windsor fund 463
vanilla option 270
variation margin 95, 316
Variation Margin 214
VDAX 696
VEB 655
velocity 553
venture capital 630

venture capitalist 110
venture capitalists 630
Vereenigde Oostindische Compagnie 405
Vernon Smith 118
vertical integration 78
vicious circle 581
Victor I. Tatarintsev 667
Victor Sperandeo 478
Vienna Stock Exchange 695
vigorish 423
Viktor Chernomyrdin 624
VimpelCom 655
Viratech India 559
Virgin 385
Virgin Index Tracker fund 385
virtual market place 80
virtual trading 707
virtuous circle 581
visual bench marks 545
visual cues 545
VIX 246, 280, 463, 501, 502
VIX futures contracts 247
VIX options 247
Vladimir Putin 624, 663
Vladimira Ilieva 118
VLMAP 498
Vnesheconombank 655
Vneshekonombank 666
VOC 405
volatile 648
volatile market 246
volatility 339, 386, 501
volatility changes 235
volatility indexes 463
volatility of index options 248
volatility risk 419
volatility smile 234
volatility traders 542
volume-weighted average 280
VWAP 455, 456
VXO 501

W

WACC 134, 145
Wachovia 644, 646
Wall Street Crash 598
Wall Street Crash of 1929 593
Wall Street Journal 664
Wall Street Journal Europe 477
Wall Street traders 676
Wallerstein 105
Wal-Mart 656
Walter Heller 587
warrants 692
warrants market 690
Warren Buffet 463
Warren Buffett 65, 84, 126, 262, 413, 481, 505
Warsaw Stock Exchange 712
Washington Consensus 578, 621
Washington Federal Savings 655
Washington Mutual 262, 644, 655
wave prediction 519
Wave Principle 511
weak move 568
wealth management 397
Wealth-Lab Pro 461
WEBS 327
Webvan 636
weight of common equity 147
weighted average 531, 534
weighted average cost of capital 145
Weighted Average Cost of Capital 134
weighted blend of prices 246
weighted moving average 534
weighted stock market index 733
weighting factors 536
well-capitalized institution 234
Wells Fargo 335, 646
Wertpapierbörse 697
Western Union 221
whipsaws 557
White House 644
wholesale customer 218

wick 485
Wilderhill Clean Energy Index 344
William C. Durant 595
William Delbert Gann 474
William Eckhardt 461, 478
William J. Ruane 86
William Lupien 676
William Sharpe 155
Wilshire 5000 334
Wilshire 5000 index 339
Winnipeg Commodity Exchange 714
Witan Investment Trust 394
WMA 534
worker cooperatives 60
works of art 358
World Bank 40, 609, 621, 624, 649
world derivatives market 183
World Equity Benchmark Shares 327
world financial leaders 649
world stock market 183
world systems theory 578
World Trade Center 681
Worldcom 288
WorldCom 634, 636
worldwide economic meltdown 608
writer 265, 268
W-shaped formation 501
WTAN 394
WTO 207

X

Xetra 695
XO Communications 634
XXX 222

Y

Yahoo! 636
Yamato Life 648
Yardeni Research 504
Yevgeny Primakov 627
yield curve 290
yield to maturity 148, 307, 308
Yukos 665
YYY 222

Z

zero correlation 374
zero coupon 298
zero coupon bond 308
Zero coupon bonds 292
zero crossings 521
zero-risk category 303
zig-zag 476
Z-spread 295
ZZZ 222

Financial Markets Certifications

Certified Financial Markets Professional – Foundation Exam

This level is aiming to measure whether a candidate would be able to act as an informed member of a Financial Markets Analysis Team. To this end they need to show they understand the principles and terminology of the method, specifically, candidates must be able to:

CFMP Certified

- Explain what a different financial markets are and how they work.
- Explain what the Bond Market, the Derivatives Market, Options Market, Commodities Market, Futures Market and Foreign Exchange Market are and how they work.
- Explain the concept of different funds.
- Explain the financial instruments that are traded on a stock market.
- Explain the role of different participants in a stock market.
- Explain basic trading styles.
- State basic technical analysis concepts and techniques.
- Explain the EMH, CAPM, and the Portfolio Theory.
- State the main purpose, of the major stock exchanges in the world.

Exams

To become a CFMP Practitioner please contact the Management Laboratory under:

exams@management-laboratory.com

or through the website:

www.management-laboratory.com

Exams are usually held in universities that are accredited by the local government or the German embassy. For prices please contact the Management Laboratory since these may vary significantly from country to country. Finance Professors that are interested in group exams for their students are very welcome to contact us about free examinations.

Format:

- Multiple-choice
- One hour duration
- 75 questions
- 38 correct answers are required to pass
- Closed-book.

Candidates who have passed the CFMP Fundation examination can put CFMP Certified on their business cards. The use of the CFMP Logo however requires authorisation by the Management Laboratory.

Certified Financial Markets Professional – Practitioner Exam

This level is aiming to measure whether a candidate would be able to apply Financial Market Principals to different scenarios and real world examples. To this end they need to exhibit the competence required for the Foundation qualification, and show that they can apply and tune the studied material to address different situations and problems of a specific scenario, specifically, candidates must be able to:

CFMP
Practitioner

- Explain what a different financial markets are, how they work and the relationship between them.
- Explain what the Bond Market, the Derivatives Market, Options Market, Commodities Market, Futures Market and Foreign Exchange Market are and how they work.
- Explain how the valuation of different financial instruments work, their concept and apply them to different scenarios.
- Explain different Funds their risks and advantages as well as their concept and usage.
- Explain the financial instruments that are traded on a stock market.
- Explain the role and function of different participants in a stock market.
- Explain the concept and difference between different types of investment forms and investment strategies.
- Explain the different trading styles their risks and potentials.
- State different technical analysis concepts and techniques.
- Explain different stock market crashes what lead to them, how they formed and how they developed.
- Explain the financial basics in investment theory, behavioral finance.
- Explain, Alpha, Beta, WACC, the EMH, the AMH, CAPM, Arbitrate Pricing Theory and the Portfolio Theory.
- State the main purpose, and key contents, of the major stock exchanges and their indices.

Exams

To become a CFMP Practitioner please contact the Management Laboratory under:

exams@management-laboratory.com

or through the website:

www.management-laboratory.com

Exams are usually held in universities that are accredited by the local government or the German embassy. For prices please contact the Management Laboratory since these may vary significantly from country to country. Finance Professors that are interested in group exams for their students are very welcome to contact us about free examinations.

Format

- Multiple-chose as well as 6 questions, with a scenario background and appendices.
- Each of the 6 questions with a scenario background is worth 20 marks.
- The Multiple-choice questions are worth 40 marks.
- An overall score of 100 out of a possible 160 is required to pass.
- Two hour duration.
- Open-book examination (only the Financial Markets Principals Book by Christoph Lymbersky is allowed. Notes can be written into the book. Post-its must not be bigger than 10cm x 10cm.)

Candidates who have passed the CFMP Practitioner examination can put CFMP Practitioner on their business cards. The use of the CFMP Logo however requires authorisation by the Management Laboratory.

Room for Notes:

www.ingramcontent.com/pod-product-compliance
Lightning Source LLC
Chambersburg PA
CBHW081157200926
51767CB00057BA/2104
9783941579309